HISTORY OF
THE SECOND WORLD WAR
UNITED KINGDOM MILITARY SERIES
Edited by J. R. M. Butler

The authors of the Military Histories have been given full access to official documents. They and the editor are alone responsible for the statements made and the views expressed.

THE WAR
IN
FRANCE AND FLANDERS

BY

MAJOR L. F. ELLIS
C.V.O., C.B.E., D.S.O., M.C.

This edition of The War in France and Flanders
first published in 2004
by The Naval & Military Press Ltd

Published by
The Naval & Military Press Ltd
Unit 10 Ridgewood Industrial Park,
Uckfield, East Sussex,
TN22 5QE England
Tel: +44 (0) 1825 749494
Fax: +44 (0) 1825 765701
www.naval–military-press.com

Printed and bound by Antony Rowe Ltd, Eastbourne

CONTENTS

CONTENTS

MAPS

SITUATION MAPS

SKETCH MAPS INCLUDED IN TEXT

ILLUSTRATIONS

EDITOR'S PREFACE

THE military series of the United Kingdom history of the Second World War, of which Major Ellis's volume on the campaign in France and Flanders in 1939–40 is the second to appear, has been planned in accordance with a Government decision announced to the House of Commons on 25th November 1946. The purpose of the history, said the then Prime Minister, was 'to provide a broad survey of events from an inter-Service point of view rather than separate accounts of the parts played by each of the three Services'. The historians have thus felt themselves under no obligation to tell the story of operations in the same detail as was thought appropriate in the case of the war of 1914–18. For such detailed narratives the student must turn to the unit or formation histories, of which many have already appeared. We have set ourselves to present a single series of volumes in which the whole military story, and every part of it, is treated from an inter-Service aspect. Here and elsewhere throughout our work the word 'military' is used to cover the activities of all three fighting Services, as distinct from the other sides of the national war effort which are treated in the Civil Histories edited by Professor W. K. Hancock.

Even on the military side, however, it seemed that a 'broad survey' which confined itself to a description of campaigns and operations would fail to give a satisfactory account of how the war of 1939–45 was waged. The vast area over which operations were progressively extended, the number and the variety of the campaigns being fought simultaneously, the constant need of co-ordinating policy and strategy with governments overseas, together with the centralisation of command rendered possible by modern systems of communication— all these increased the range and importance of the part played by the supreme authority at home and seemed to demand that a fuller treatment of the higher direction of the war should be attempted than has been usual in military histories. It was accordingly decided to allot several volumes to Grand Strategy as devised in Whitehall and at Washington, including one volume on developments prior to the actual outbreak of war in September 1939.

For the rest, the history has been planned to cover the following themes or theatres: the defence of the United Kingdom, the maritime war viewed as a whole, the two campaigns of the early period in Norway and in north-west Europe, the strategic air offensive, and three epic series of military operations on the grand scale in the Mediterranean and Middle East, in the Far East, and again in the north-west of Europe in 1944 and 1945. Additional volumes have been allotted to the history of Civil Affairs or Military Government in view of the novelty and importance of the problems involved in this field of military responsibility.

In order to avoid undue detail, the standpoint from which campaigns have been viewed is that of the theatre commander. The intention has been to treat all the campaigns on the same scale; but it must be confessed that in some cases when the total forces involved were small, as in Norway in 1940 and in the Western Desert in the early phases, the narrative has descended to describe the operations of detached units in greater detail than their size would normally justify.

No doubt the proposed dual treatment of strategic problems, at the Whitehall level and at the level of theatre headquarters, involves a risk, indeed a certainty, of some overlapping. This would be the case even if it were not our aim, as it is, to make each group of volumes intelligible by itself and to that extent self-contained. We cannot unfortunately assume that the general reader, for whom as much as for military students our history is intended, will be prepared to buy or read the whole of our twenty or thirty volumes. We think that a moderate amount of overlapping is excusable and may even be welcomed if it avoids the necessity of constant reference to other volumes.

The description of a war waged by allies, in which 'integration' was successfully carried to lengths unattempted in previous campaigns, raises further problems. Granted that our commission is to write the history not of the Second World War as a whole but of the military effort of the United Kingdom, on what principle ought we to handle campaigns or actions in which men from the United Kingdom and from other nations fought side by side? Where United Kingdom forces served under foreign or Dominion command, or vice versa, it seems clear that decisions or actions of our fellow combatants must be described with sufficient fullness to preserve a proper balance in the story. On the other hand it is not desirable to duplicate the accounts given in the histories sponsored by our Allies and by other nations of the British Commonwealth, especially when the primary sources are under their control. Arrangements have indeed been made with them for mutual information on points of special interest and for an exchange of drafts; it is hoped that these arrangements will at least reduce the likelihood of controversy due to ignorance of another nation's point of view, though they will not, of course, eliminate differences of interpretation. It has not been possible to make such arrangements in the case of the U.S.S.R.

With regard to German military records, however, the Allied historians are fortunate, to an unprecedented degree, in having access to a mass of original documents, some of them of the highest importance, which were captured during the occupation of Germany and are now held under joint Anglo-American control. In the case of the other enemy Powers both the volume and the value of the documents captured are considerably less and details of their military plans and operations have of necessity been obtained from more conventional sources of information.

To the official United Kingdom records we have been allowed full access, and we have done our best to supplement them by reference to unofficial accounts, published and unpublished, written and oral. What we have written has, however, been subject to censorship from the aspect of military 'security', and in some cases cipher telegrams have been paraphrased, though not in such a way as to affect the sense. In accordance with the recognised British constitutional principle we have not held ourselves free to reveal individual differences of opinion within the War Cabinet nor, as a rule, to lift the veil of Civil Service anonymity.

We have taken it as our prime duty to present an accurate narrative of events. But events, properly speaking, include plans and intentions as well as actions, and it is the duty of a historian, as opposed to a mere annalist, to say why, as well as how, things happened as they did. He must interpret, not merely narrate, and interpretation implies a personal judgement. In any case the need to select from the vast mass of material implies a personal judgement of what is most relevant and important.

We all share the contemporary outlook, and some of us are laymen in military matters; it would be unbecoming in us to attempt to pronounce what a commander should have done or should not have done in a particular situation. Our ideal would be to let the facts speak for themselves, to point out how such a decision led to such a result, and to leave speculation and moralising to the strategists; but the facts can only speak to our readers as we have selected and presented them, and we have not shrunk from stating what seemed to us the lessons that emerged from a particular course of events.

Lord Tedder has remarked that as a nation 'we have a tendency to concentrate too much on our successes and our enemies' failures and consequently to draw our lessons too much from the final stages of war', when 'after some years of lavish expenditure' the Commander knows that he can more or less 'count on a blank cheque'. 'Surely', he says, 'it is the problems of the early stages of the war which we should study. Those are the difficult problems; those are the practical problems which we and every democratic nation have to solve. There were no big battalions or blank cheques then. Here is the real and vital test of our defence policies'.[1]

---

[1] Lord Tedder: *Air Power in War*, Hodder and Stoughton (1947), p. 25.

Lord Tedder's words apply with poignant relevance to the campaign described by Major Ellis. The conditions under which it was waged were determined by a Government policy improvised in the course of the six months preceding the outbreak of war, during which period not only the organisation of the Army as a whole but the composition of the Expeditionary Force itself was radically changed. But the predicament of the British land and air forces in France was due to a national defence policy extending much further back than the spring of 1939. To trace the development of this policy lies outside Major Ellis's task.

It is normally the duty and desire of a historian to support his assertions and arguments by detailed references to his authorities. Such references serve partly as an indication of his sources, partly as a challenge to his readers to verify his statements. Where, however, the main authorities are official documents which are not at present, and for some time are not likely to be, open to public inspection, published references have comparatively little point, since the challenge cannot be taken up. The nature of the material used can, we think, in most cases be sufficiently indicated in the prefaces or bibliographical notes to the several volumes. Accordingly our normal practice has been that explained by Professor Hancock in his introduction to the Civil Histories.[2] 'It has been decided not to clutter the published pages with references to official files which are not yet generally available to students. In the published series, footnotes have been confined to material that is already accessible. The completed documentation has been given in confidential print. There it will be immediately available to critical readers within the government service. No doubt it will become available in due time to the historians of a future generation. The official historians of this generation have consciously submitted their work to the professional verdict of the future.'

In the use of enemy documents the historians' labours have been immensely lightened by the help of their colleagues charged with the collection, collation and interpretation of this vast mass of material. Work on the German and Italian documents has been directed by Mr Brian Melland; Colonel G. T. Wards has advised with regard to the Japanese. Valuable assistance in this matter has also been rendered by Commander M. G. Saunders, R.N., of the Admiralty Historical Section, and by Squadron Leader L. A. Jackets, of the Air Historical Branch.

The maps have been prepared under the experienced direction of Colonel T. M. M. Penney, of the Cabinet Office Historical Section.

---

[2] *History of the Second World War: British War Economy*, by W. K. Hancock and M. M. Gowing, H.M. Stationery Office, 1949, p. xii.

The spelling of place-names follows in the main the system approved at an informal conference of British and American experts in October 1947, but current usage has been adhered to where not to do so would be pedantic. In the representation of Allied and enemy troops the conventional symbols and colours, where used, are those officially recognised during the war. Apart from the fact that work on some of our maps had begun before November 1950, when the British Army changed its system, it seemed natural to follow the convention used in contemporary maps.

The appointment of a civilian editor to be responsible for the production of the military histories made it desirable that on general questions as well as special points he should be able frequently to consult authorities whose opinions on Service matters would command respect; I am fortunate to have had so helpful a panel of advisers as Vice-Admiral Sir Geoffrey Blake, Lieutenant-General Sir Henry Pownall, Air Chief Marshals Sir Douglas Evill and Sir Guy Garrod, and Lieutenant-General Sir Ian Jacob. These distinguished officers not only have given me the benefit of their experience and judgement in the planning of the history and the selection of writers but have read and commented on the volumes in draft; in all these matters, however, responsibility rests with the Editor alone.

The history could not have been written without the constant assistance of the Service Historical Sections, and the historians would express their gratitude to Rear-Admiral R. M. Bellairs, Brigadier H. B. Latham and Mr J. C. Nerney, and also to Lieutenant-General Sir Desmond Anderson, of the War Office, and their staffs. The monographs, narratives and summaries produced by the Service Departments have greatly reduced the labours, though not the responsibilities, of the historians, and the staffs concerned have been lavish of their help in supplying information and comment. Similar acknowledgements are due to the authors of the Civil Histories, and we are grateful to Mr Yates Smith of the Imperial War Museum, and to other librarians for the loan of books.

Finally, the historians in general and the Editor in particular are deeply indebted to Mr A. B. Acheson, of the Cabinet Office. His advice and help have been of the greatest service to us in many ways; indeed, without the relief provided by Mr Acheson in administrative matters, a part-time editor could hardly have performed his task.

J. R. M. B.

AUTHOR'S PREFACE

THE story of this dramatic campaign, in which Germany conquered three countries in six weeks, contains within it the story of a small British force which though compelled to fall back with its Allies under the pressure of the enemy's stronger forces never lost its cohesion or ability to fight; when its final overthrow seemed certain it was withdrawn to England, there to lick its wounds and prepare to fight again.

It was too small a force to affect the final issue of a campaign in which Germany brought to battle 136 divisions, France over 100, Belgium 22 and the British Expeditionary Force only 14. Yet the part which it played in the northern phase of the campaign was an essential one, for it held a key position in the Allies' main front, and held it to the end. Its fighting withdrawal to the coast, while two groups of German armies attacked from east and west, was a notable military achievement. The following chapters tell how this was done, but there was one contributing factor which cannot easily be brought out in the telling and therefore should be mentioned here.

Before the war the Army had been so reduced in numbers that an unusually large proportion of its officers knew each other personally. The British Expeditionary Force was thus commanded and staffed for the most part by regular soldiers who had not only been trained for their work but had come to know and trust each other. They were not, therefore, greatly put out when, in the course of the withdrawal, normal procedure was interrupted by events and reliance on individuals took the place of orthodox administration. Amid confusion they were not confounded. A cement of mutual confidence strengthened the whole Expeditionary Force and helped it to withstand the appalling shocks it had to suffer.

In addition to the intrinsic interest of the story, the student of military history will find in it indications that new methods would distinguish the Second World War from the First. This campaign was the overture, in which were sounded themes to be developed throughout the war. The use of airborne troops to seize in advance positions of tactical importance; of massed formations of tanks rapidly to exploit a breach; of wireless to control a quickly moving battle; of air forces to assist ground troops in attack and for the transport of men and supplies; of mechanical transport and specially designed vehicles (the British Universal Carrier was an early example)—all these are illustrated, for the first time or on a new scale, in operations which involved British forces.

This volume deals only with the history of British operations in France and Flanders between the outbreak of war on September the

3rd, 1939, and the fall of France in June, 1940. It describes and discusses these as fully as is possible in a book of the size prescribed; it only describes those of Allied and enemy forces in so far as they affected the conduct of British operations. As, however, the British Expeditionary Force served under the orders of the French High Command, the bearing of the orders and actions of the High Command is considered more fully.

The amount of contemporary material available to a military historian is, to-day, truly appalling. Every unit and every formation keeps a day-to-day record of its doings and of all important telegrams, messages and orders received and issued. There are also innumerable returns and statistical records of each branch of the Services and many minutes of meetings and conferences on every level. Our Allies have a similar body of information in regard to their own operations, and for this campaign there is also a comprehensive collection of the enemy's contemporary records and documents. It would take a lifetime to study all this information; the historian can but select the more important, and since this history might be thought to mirror an official view it will be well to indicate the material on which this account is based and to state that I have had complete freedom in its use.

The Historical Sections of the three Services have all compiled detailed, factual and carefully checked narratives of day-to-day events from the War Diaries and other contemporary records. These have been used as the basis for the account of operations but I have gone behind them to the original records where this was necessary to reach a clear understanding of what happened or to appreciate what was of chief significance.

The principal commanders have all written dispatches, most of which have since been published. These have been studied as giving their authors' considered views of what happened, in so far as they knew the relevant facts.

A number of personal diaries and reports, written at the time, have been generously made available and, with many regimental histories, have been useful in showing how actions and events affected those engaged at various levels. In a book which is intended to give a broad survey of the campaign there is unfortunately little room for these detailed accounts, though they are rich in human interest; only one or two extracts have been quoted to serve as illustrations.

The minutes and papers of the Chiefs of Staffs Committee and its sub-committees and other high-level documents have been examined but only decisions and orders which were conveyed to commanders in the field and therefore directly affected operations have been specifically taken into account.

The most authoritative published accounts of our Allies' operations have been used, after consultation with the official Historical Sections of the French and Belgian Armies. Both have also most kindly supplied all additional information for which they have been asked.

German War Diaries and other contemporary documents captured from the enemy, including those subsequently produced at the Nuremberg trials, have been used, and enough are available to explain enemy operations. The post-war statements, published memoirs and studies of generals and others who occupied positions of responsibility at the time have also been carefully considered; but where there is a conflict of evidence between such post-war recollections and writings and contemporary records the evidence of the latter has been accepted. 'History, to be above evasion or dispute, must stand on documents, not on opinions.'[1] For the convenience of readers, quotations from French and German sources have been given in English, but since 'everything suffers from translation except a bishop'[2] the original texts are given in Appendix II.

All the ground in France and Belgium over which the British Expeditionary Force fought has been examined on the spot, in order to see how far physical conditions explain the course of operations; and a few photographs are reproduced to give the reader who does not know the country some conception of the waterways and coasts which figure prominently in the story. Similarly portraits of the principal commanders are included to supplement what is said of them in the text. Where the names of individuals are mentioned, orders and decorations have been omitted for the sake of brevity and the rank they held at the time is given; many subsequently rose to higher rank and greater fame.

The names of regiments, squadrons and ships have been given where this would not confuse the broad picture, but it is impossible to mention all in so small a book. Equally it is not possible to do full justice to the services which sustained the fighting forces. The forces in action were there only by virtue of work which cannot be brought within the focus of this volume. A list of the principal British forces employed with some notes on their organisation and equipment is given in Appendix I.

Many have helped me in the preparation of this book by information, advice or comment. I would first thank the Historical Sections of the three Services and in particular Rear-Admiral R. M. Bellairs and Commander Lloyd Owen; Brigadier H. B. Latham and Lieutenant-Colonel H. F. Joslen; and Mr J. C. Nerney. Mr Brian Melland, Mr R. R. A. Wheatley and Squadron Leader L. A. Jackets have given me invaluable help in the translation and study of enemy documents.

---

[1] Lord Acton: *Lectures on Modern History*, Macmillan, 1950, p. 17.
[2] Lord Chesterfield: *Letters to His Son*.

I must also thank the many officers of all three Services who have been kind enough to read and comment on the manuscript from their personal experience in the campaign. It is impossible here to mention all by name, but I am most grateful to them.

The Imperial War Museum kindly supplied many of the photographs reproduced. The portrait of Air Marshal Barratt was painted for the National Collection by the late T. C. Dugdale, R.A. The photograph of General Weygand is from the collection of the Press Portrait Bureau.

All the maps have been specially drawn under the direction of Colonel T. M. M. Penney, most of them by Mr D. K. Purle. General maps fold out to the left so that they may be referred to while several chapters are being read. Situation maps are usually at the end of the chapter in which the day's actions are described and fold out to the right. Places, roads and railways which are not mentioned in the text have for the most part been omitted. While this makes for clarity it is liable to give a false impression of the country. A full-scale map would show far more numerous villages and towns, linked in a network of communications by road, rail and waterways.

Finally, I would acknowledge with gratitude the continuous help I have had from Professor J. R. M. Butler. I am, of course, solely responsible for any mistake of fact or inference.

L. F. ELLIS

The War in France
and Flanders

CHAPTER I

PRE-WAR POLICIES AND PLANS

On the 3rd of September, 1939, at eleven o'clock in the morning, Great Britain was again at war with Germany. Only twenty years had passed since 'the war to end war' had finished in victory. At that time Germany had been beaten and disarmed; the Rhineland, giving access to the 'cock-pit of Europe', was occupied by Allied troops and was to be demilitarised for ever; and so that war might not recur, the League of Nations was being formed to settle international quarrels by more sensible means. For four years the achievement of peace had been men's chief desire, and an assumption that peace would continue was the background and basis of all their thinking. When the fighting ceased and the unity of a national purpose gave place to the clash of lesser interests, when economic and social pressures again produced divergent policies, the nation was still united in desiring above all else that the Government should 'seek peace and ensue it'.

It was in this mood that, while a general reduction of armaments was discussed with other nations, Britain herself disarmed. Successive British Governments assumed that at least there would be no major war for ten years, and from 1928 as each year passed the assumed decade of peace was moved forward with it. The Services were drastically reduced and for thirteen years deficiencies in equipment of the small forces retained were allowed to accumulate. It was not so with other countries. No general reduction of armaments followed from our lead, and in March, 1932, the danger of our position was at last admitted, the ten-year policy was abandoned and during the next two years the need for rearmament was discussed (there was little more than discussion) while economic, military and political policies contended for mastery.

> One would have lingering wars with little cost;
> Another would fly swift but wanteth wings;
> A third thinks, without expense at all,
> By guileful fair words peace may be obtained.[1]

A measure of rearmament was at last decided on in 1934, but by 1936, when Hitler's troops reoccupied the Rhineland in breach of the Locarno agreement, little progress had been made. By then Italy and Germany were openly creating huge armies and Japan was

---

[1] Shakespeare: *Henry VI, Part I.*

spending 46 per cent of the national income on armaments.[2] The League of Nations could not stop aggression in China or in Abyssinia and men perceived reluctantly that force, as the instrument of national ambition and the solvent of international quarrels, had not been superseded. Peace was not assured.

The First World War had come suddenly, without prelude, and the nation had embarked on it with a popular enthusiasm that was ignorant of what war means. The Second World War approached gradually, and the awfulness of war was understood. As the sky grew darker the nation watched and waited for the coming storm in a mood of sombre realism. Hitler's deeds and declarations made it daily seem more certain that he would pursue his way at whatever cost and day by day it became clearer to all that his way and ours must cross. Unless we or he altered course there must be a collision.

To the last minute the British people's desire to keep the peace and the Government's knowledge that we were in no condition for war were joined in a policy of appeasement to which the Government clung obstinately, hoping against hope to reach agreement with Hitler or, if that should prove impossible, to gain time for rearmament.

Months passed while the Government, swayed largely by economic considerations, debated what was to be the character and cost of their rearmament programme. By April, 1938, they had reached the conclusion that in a war with Germany the British contribution to Allied strength should consist mainly of naval and air forces. We should avoid sending a large army to the Continent; the role of the Army would be limited to home defence and the defence of British territories overseas. The rearmament programme, so far as the Army was concerned, accordingly provided for considerable increases of coastal and air defences, but for a field force of only five divisions, equipped for imperial defence rather than for continental warfare. No provision was made for the reinforcement of this field force and the Territorial Army was only to be supplied with training equipment.

The policy of limited liability did not apply to the other two Services, but the Government's conception of defensive war coloured the whole rearmament programme. Their decision as to what would be the role of the Royal Navy in a war with Germany (and possibly also with Italy and Japan) did not directly affect British operations in France and Flanders with which alone this volume is concerned; but their decision as to the role of the Royal Air Force profoundly affected the conduct of air operations and had considerable influence on the course of the campaign.

The Government's air policy was based on the principle that Britain should maintain a defensive air force strong enough to withstand any

---

[2] *Statement Relating to Defence* [Cmd. 5107], H.M.S.O. 1936.

likely attack, and an offensive striking force not inferior to any which Germany could bring against us. The first required fighter aircraft to destroy and drive away enemy air forces; the second required bombers to damage and destroy enemy targets on the ground. Apart from a small provision for army co-operation, the 1938 re-armament programme accordingly provided for a large expansion of the Royal Air Force so that it might be equipped and trained for the air defence of Great Britain and for counter-offensive operations against Germany. *Neither role required provision for air participation in large-scale land operations or for the dispatch of large mobile air forces over-seas*, though it was agreed with France that, in a war with Germany, until the number of our long-range bombers was increased we might station an advanced striking force of bombers on French airfields in order to bring them nearer to German targets. This was the Army and Air Force policy expressed in the Government's rearmament programme of 1938.

But after the Munich meeting in the autumn of 1938 the hope that we could avoid war evaporated quickly. By the spring of 1939 the mists of wishful thinking which had obscured facts and beclouded judgement were finally dispelled and the dangers of the situation were revealed in stark reality. Italy and Japan were alined with Germany, Austria had been absorbed, Abyssinia conquered, Czechoslovakia dismembered, and Albania invaded. In the Far East Japan was seeking to conquer China and in Europe Hitler was threatening Poland. Appeasement gave place to a more realistic policy and preparation for the war which now seemed unpreventable assumed new urgency. Radical changes in the rearmament policy which had taken years to arrive at were forced upon the Government in as many months by the swift movement of events.

It had always been clear that if war came Britain and France would fight together. It now became necessary to plan together for the con-flict that seemed imminent. A somewhat desultory exchange of technical information with the French General Staff had indeed been maintained since 1936, when Hitler first showed his hand by re-occupying the Rhineland, but full Staff conversations had been avoided. For such Staff conversations are apt to imply a military alliance and involve definite military commitments, and at that time the Government (and their military advisers) were unwilling to proceed so far while the policy of appeasement was being pursued. When, following the Munich agreement, it became clear that Hitler's word meant nothing and that in fact he was bent on the destruction of Czechoslovakia's independent existence, full Staff talks with France were authorised. The absorption of Austria had been a prelude to Germany's move on Czechoslovakia; the obvious intention to absorb Czechoslovakia presaged a move against Poland. German troops entered Prague on the 14th of March, 1939; on the 29th of March, six months before the Allies declared war on Germany, Anglo-French Staff conversations reopened. It is only necessary to refer here to discussions which were concerned with a war in North-West Europe, though the position which might arise in other theatres was also considered in the series of conversations which followed.

At the first meeting the French delegation stated that France's first objective, in a war with Germany, would be the defence of French territory. When this had been secured they intended to remain on the defensive, though maintaining an economic blockade of Germany, till sufficient resources for an offensive had been built up.

From this starting-point the Anglo-French Staffs found no difficulty in agreeing on a broad strategic policy for the Allies and an appreciation of probable German action. They concluded that we should be faced by enemies (assuming Italy to be involved) who would be more fully prepared than ourselves for war on a national scale, who would have superiority in land and air forces but would be inferior at sea and in general economic strength. In these circumstances we must be prepared to face a major offensive directed either against France, or Great Britain, or both. We should have to concentrate all our initial efforts on the defeat of such an offensive and our strategy during this phase must be defensive. Thus while we were building up our military resources our policy should be to hold Germany, and exercise rigorous economic pressure so as to reduce our enemies' power of resistance. The fact that these conclusions were the best which could be reached under the circumstances shows to what a precarious position pre-war policies had reduced the Allies. Because of their military weakness they had to base their strategic plan on an assumption that during the years needed to build up our military strength Allied armies could maintain the integrity of French soil against an enemy 'more fully prepared' and 'having superiority in land and air forces'. In other words they had to presume that the Allies could force Germany to accept a repetition of the static warfare of 1914–1918, in spite of the fact that mechanisation, tanks and air forces had made obsolete the pedestrian pattern of the First World War.

The precarious foundations of this intention are apparent when it is considered together with the appreciation of probable German action, on which the Anglo-French Staffs also agreed. 'In view of the defensive strength of the Maginot Line the Germans might, in the event of war with France, be impelled to seek success by turning the barrier through Belgium and Holland. By a sudden movement through the territory of these states they might hope rapidly to crush Belgian and Dutch resistance as it was being organised; further, they might hope that, by pushing boldly on until they gained contact with the French defences, they could find themselves well placed to attack those defences, whilst at the same time obtaining control of the North Sea coast and putting air forces within range of vital French and British objectives.' While the enemy covered their southern flank and immobilised the defences of the French fortified zone, their main attack, it was thought, would be directed towards Brussels and Cambrai with the object of reaching the French position from Hirson to the North Sea. It would be an *attaque brusquée*, followed by immediate and thorough exploitation of initial success.

It was agreed that the Allies would be unable to assist Holland to repel a sudden assault, but it was hoped that if a similar attack were made on Belgium it might be possible to collaborate in withstanding it. With this in mind alternative positions, on which such an attack could be held as far forward as possible, were examined. If time allowed it might be possible to reinforce the Belgians on their line of resistance on the Meuse-Albert Canal; as a minimum the line of the Scheldt (known to the French as the Escaut) might be held, connecting Maulde on the French frontier with the Belgian national redoubt above Ghent. Neither of these slender hopes was destined to be realised. Germany was held only when what remained of the Allied armies were behind the greater obstacle of the Channel and the North Sea. Then indeed the necessary time was secured to build up Allied strength till, in their turn, they had 'superiority in land and air forces'. But the integrity of French soil was not meanwhile preserved.

This, however, is looking ahead by the light of afterknowledge. In 1939 the Anglo-French Staffs still worked by the dim light of 1914–1918. And while they did not forget the desirability of passing to the offensive as soon as possible, the first object of the French was the defence of French territory and their chief hope the French Army and the Maginot Line. The British, for their part, knowing that it was proposed at this date to contribute so small a British force, could but accept the French soldiers' view as to the course which land operations on the Continent should take.

It is but fair to remember that when these talks began, in March 1939, no one then knew that war would begin in less than six months. Even so, the Government had failed till then, though known circumstances should have made it impossible, to recognise the extreme urgency of the situation. Thus while the French Government had been informed in the previous year that our initial contribution to the Allied forces could only be two Regular divisions, they were now told that it would be approximately eleven months before we could send out two more divisions. We had said that two armoured divisions would be sent as soon as possible; we now said that this part of the programme could not be fully realised before September 1940.

We could make no promise as to the use of our Territorial divisions (for which in any case there were neither reserves nor equipment) because they might be needed in some other theatre when they became available. Italy and Japan might have to be reckoned with as well as Germany—we might have to fight not on one front but on three. The French Staff, not unnaturally, 'viewed with dismay' such a minute and unpromising programme.

At the end of March the Government changed their policy. The belief that in a war with Germany the British contribution to Allied strength could be restricted in the main to naval and air forces and that we could avoid sending an army to the Continent was abandoned.

So far rearmament (with priority for the Navy and Air Force) had been proceeding on a non-emergency basis and a comparatively small scale. Only in the case of aircraft construction had provision been made for rapid expansion. But, however much the programme for producing trained men and equipment was enlarged and pressed forward, it was now too late to provide a large force at the outset. In Germany by contrast conscription had been proceeding at an accelerated pace since 1935 and a large proportion of German industrial organisation had been concentrated on war requirements. The mass production of war materials on a vast scale was already nearing the period of flood.

On March the 29th the Cabinet decided to increase British military strength by doubling the Territorial force and on the 27th of April to introduce conscription. A programme of expansion was adopted which would eventually provide Great Britain with an army of thirty-two divisions. By the end of April we had undertaken to double the size of our initial contingent. Two corps, each of two Regular divisions, and an air component of the Royal Air Force, were now promised for dispatch to France within thirty-three days of the date of mobilisation. We also gave the French Staff our latest forecast of future development, though nothing more definite could be promised about the dates on which further forces would become available.

The initial Expeditionary Force would consist of General Headquarters and two corps, comprising:

Two cavalry regiments (light tanks)
One army tank battalion
Twenty field regiments
Seven medium and one heavy regiment
Three anti-aircraft regiments } of artillery
Two light anti-aircraft batteries
Four light anti-aircraft regiments
Forty-three infantry battalions

Four machine-gun battalions
Four anti-tank regiments
Thirteen anti-tank companies
Engineers, signals and administrative units.

There would also be an air component of the Royal Air Force consisting at the outset of:

Two bomber reconnaissance squadrons
Six army co-operation squadrons
Four fighter squadrons
Two flights H.Q. Communications squadron.

As agreed in earlier conversations (page 3) an Advanced Air Striking Force of medium bombers (from the forces of Bomber Command) would, with French concurrence, be stationed in France, not to collaborate with land forces but to bring aircraft which at that time had a limited range nearer to military targets in Germany.

The first of the two armoured divisions which had been promised would now be available in approximately eight months' time; the second 'at a much later date'. With regard to the Territorial divisions, 'whose role has not been definitely settled', it was now expected that two would be available for dispatch to 'an overseas theatre' in four months' time; a further three, plus one motor division, in five months; and one horsed cavalry division in from four to six months. When the remaining divisions would become available could still not be forecast with any certainty for this did not only depend on the time required to train men. To produce the necessary equipment and weapons and the vast and varied quantities of ammunition on the scale required in modern warfare, mass-production methods must be employed; and since during these years of inaction the whole armament industry had been allowed to run down, considerable time must now elapse before production could be in full swing. Not even the fearful gaps in the Army's equipment could be filled quickly.

At this time it was understood that France would be able to mobilise seventy-two divisions in addition to fortress troops equivalent to another twelve or fourteen divisions. She would thus have approximately eighty-four to eighty-six divisions, of which twelve would be needed to guard the Italian frontier. Seventy-two to seventy-four would thus be available to garrison the Maginot forts and to operate against Germany. With the addition of the four British divisions, there would therefore be a total Allied force of, say, seventy-six divisions. Against this, it was estimated that Germany would be able to mobilise at least 116 divisions by the middle of September.

In the air Germany's numerical superiority was equally marked. The strength of an air force depends not only on the number but on the type and performance of aircraft and on reserves behind front-line formations. A note on British aircraft is included in Appendix I on the 'British Forces Engaged' in this campaign. An estimate was made of front-line air forces available for war in Europe (that is excluding units required to protect overseas possessions) in April 1939. At that date it was understood that the Allies had together 824 bombers, 856 fighters, and 954 army co-operation and reconnaissance aircraft, a total of 2,634 of all types. Germany was believed to have 1,900 bombers, 1,000 fighters, and 800 army co-operation and reconnaissance aircraft, a total of 3,700 aircraft. Moreover, Italy, if she joined in the war, could bring a further 1,400 aircraft to battle.

It was thought unlikely that France would be attacked till Poland was disposed of, but once that had been done Hitler would be able to employ something like a hundred divisions in an offensive against the Allies. Moreover, while the latter must extend their smaller forces so as to cover the 500-mile French frontier from Switzerland to the North Sea, Germany's larger forces could be concentrated against the selected point of attack. How soon Hitler would feel free to launch a western offensive, was, of course, not foreseeable. But it was with the sobering knowledge that when that time arrived he would have the double advantages of initiative and superior strength that we eventually declared war on Germany.

There were no similar Staff conversations with Belgium. The geographical position of Holland and Belgium made it highly probable that one or both would be involved in any war between Germany and a Franco-British alliance. Why, then, were they not joined in the Staff conversations of 1939? The answer is that both countries had announced that they would remain strictly neutral in such a war unless their own frontiers were attacked. When Hitler reoccupied the Rhineland in 1936, and before Belgium had declared her neutrality, she had asked for Staff conversations, but we had drawn back lest the fact that such conversations were being held should give Hitler an excuse for counter-measures. And when, later in that year, Belgium declared her neutrality, the British Chiefs of Staff argued that an effective Belgian neutrality would be greatly to our advantage and should not deliberately be rendered impossible, even though the chance of its being maintained throughout a West European war seemed remote. Yet when war became imminent three years later both Britain and France pressed Belgium to join in Staff conversations, urging that without preliminary planning they would be less able to assist her effectively if she were attacked. Belgium argued, as we had done earlier, that she could not engage herself to one set of neighbours while proclaiming her neutrality to another. So she now held back. The political implications of this decision must be sought in the volumes of this history which deal with grand strategy. Here, only the fact that there were no Staff conversations with Belgium needs to be recorded. When hostilities opened we were inevitably handicapped by the fact that there had been no full exchange of information and no concerting of plans, but such an abandonment of Belgian neutrality as would have been signified by Staff conversations might well have had other results which can now only be a subject of speculation. The course she took may even have been to our ultimate advantage, in that while we lost in efficiency through the absence of joint planning, we gained time, so long as Hitler respected Belgian neutrality, in which to strengthen our own forces and complete our own plans.

The case of Holland was different. Unlike Belgium she had remained neutral throughout the First World War, and it was recognised that in any event the Allies would not be able effectively to intervene if she were attacked by Germany.

Though there had so far been but inadequate preparation for a war with Germany, much was done in the last six months to remedy past neglect and to ensure that we should at least be ready to dispatch without delay the small force which was all we could contribute at the outset. The Services completed necessary arrangements. Plans were made ready. When war was declared they could be put into operation immediately. They provided for something that was new in military history, for this was the first occasion on which a wholly mechanised army was dispatched overseas. It was a considerable Staff achievement to complete plans in so short a time.

The Army plan—W4—was inevitably a complicated and highly technical document; here it is only necessary to note certain features.

(1) Because of the risk of air attack the main ports of disembarkation in France were to be on the western coast. This meant a longer sea passage, but was thought to be safer than the use of the Channel ports both for shipping and for the landing of troops, equipment, supplies and stores.

(2) There were to be two main bases—a northern base at Rennes and a southern base at St Nazaire–Nantes. There was also to be a medical base at Dieppe.

(3) The chief ports to be used were Cherbourg (for personnel, with motor transport and drivers); Brest (all stores for the northern base, with motor transport and drivers); St Nazaire (ammunition and frozen meat for the southern base, with motor transport and drivers); and Nantes (other stores for the southern base and, again, motor transport and drivers).

(4) After landing, troops not employed at the bases or on lines of communication would move at once to an assembly area south of Abbeville, and from there go to their allotted stations.

The Air Force plan—W.A.4—was complicated by the need to provide for two distinct formations, namely:

(1) the Air Component, intended to supply reconnaissance and protection for the Expeditionary Force, and

(2) the Advanced Air Striking Force of Bomber Command, stationed in France so as to be nearer to Germany and the probable scene of operations.

The movement of the former had only to keep pace with that of the Expeditionary Force: but bombing operations from French bases might be needed at once on the outbreak of war, so plans were completed by which the Advanced Air Striking Force could move to France immediately. To make this possible, arrangements had been made for part of the Royal Air Force to mobilise secretly in advance.

With the collaboration of the French Staff, necessary reconnaissance had been carried out before plans took final shape.

All these plans for the dispatch of land and air forces to France presupposed that the Royal Navy could ensure their safe passage and due arrival, and the naval plan for this operation had also been completed before war was declared. It was, of course, but part of the vastly greater operations in which the Navy was immediately to engage on the outbreak of war. Unless that is realised a delusive appearance of simplicity, arising from the Navy's skill in planning and performance, may give a misleading impression of their part in this campaign.

Apart from the obvious requirement that the Royal Navy and the Royal Air Force should protect our own shores from invasion by the enemy, the very life of this country and its ability to engage in war, whether in France or anywhere else in the world, depends on the Navy's ability to control sea communications—not, indeed, immediately to establish control of all seas, but so to employ our naval strength that zones of maritime control can be established wherever and whenever they are needed for the prosecution of war. One such zone of control, essential for the waging of war in France and Flanders, is, of course, the waters of the North Sea and English Channel—'the narrow seas'. As a part of the larger naval war plans concerted with the French Staff, the main tasks of the French Fleet were to be 'generally responsible' for the Western Mediterranean and to constitute a *force de raid* to operate in the Eastern Atlantic against enemy surface raiders. The control of the narrow seas was to be a responsibility of the Royal Navy, part of its wider responsibility for the control of our sea communications throughout the world. The success of that control alone made possible the Navy's use of the narrow seas for operations which formed an essential part of the campaign in France and Flanders. Its dependence on the success of wider operations must be borne in mind.

GENERAL THE VISCOUNT GORT

Commander-in-Chief of the British Expeditionary Force

GENERAL GEORGES

Commanding the French North-East Theatre
of Operations

Naval plans for the campaign provided, among other things:

(1) for the formation of a Channel Force whose primary purpose was to cover the passage of the British Expeditionary Force to France. (It was to be based at Portland and would consist of the battleships *Resolution* and *Revenge*, the aircraft carriers *Courageous* and *Hermes*, the cruisers *Ceres* and *Caradoc*, the anti-aircraft cruiser *Cairo*, and the 18th Destroyer Flotilla);

(2) for the shipping needed to bear to France our forces and the vast quantity of equipment, ammunition, stores, and supplies on which their maintenance depended;

(3) for the embarkation of troops and stores from Southampton, Avonmouth, Swansea, Barry, and Newport;

(4) for their escort in convoy and their local defence by flotillas of the Portsmouth and Western Approaches Commands; and

(5) for the co-operation of the Royal Air Force in reconnaissance and protection from air attack.

Two further decisions of major importance must be mentioned. On the 3rd of September the Cabinet decided to entrust the command of the British Expeditionary Force to General the Viscount Gort. Lord Gort was a Guardsman who had served with distinction through the First World War, first on the Staff and afterwards commanding in turn the 4th and 1st Battalions of the Grenadier Guards. (He was four times wounded, nine times mentioned in despatches, and was awarded the Military Cross, the Distinguished Service Order and two Bars, and the Victoria Cross.) Subsequently he held various Staff appointments including those of Director of Military Training in India, Commandant of the Staff College, and Military Secretary; he was Chief of the Imperial General Staff when he was selected to command the British Expeditionary Force. He was fifty-three years old and had no previous experience of a large command.

The second decision, which was largely to determine Lord Gort's conduct of British operations in France, was that he should serve under the French Commander-in-Chief, 'North-East Theatre of Operations'. The first two paragraphs of his Instructions read:

1. His Majesty's Government have decided to send a Field Force to France and to entrust its command to you.

The role of the force under your command is to co-operate with our Allies in the defeat of the common enemy.

2. You will be under the command of the French Commander-in-Chief 'North-East Theatre of Operations'. In the pursuit of the common object, the defeat of the enemy, you will carry out loyally any instructions issued by him. At the same time, if any order given by him appears to you to imperil the British Field Force, it is agreed between the British and French Governments that you should be at liberty to appeal to the British Government before executing that

order. Whilst it is hoped that the need for such an appeal will seldom, if ever, arise, you will not hesitate to avail yourself of your right to make it, if you think fit.

The following further paragraphs are also specially important as defining Lord Gort's position:

4. It is the desire of His Majesty's Government to keep the British Forces under your command, as far as possible, together. If at any time the French Commander-in-Chief 'North-East Theatre of Operations' finds it essential for any reason to transfer any portion of the British troops to an area other than that in which your main force is operating, it should be distinctly understood that this is only a temporary arrangement, and that as soon as practicable the troops thus detached should be re-united to the main body of the British Forces.

. . .

8. Whilst the Royal Air Force Component of the Field Force is included under your command, the Advanced Air Striking Force, which will also operate from French territory, is an independent force under the direct control of the Air Officer Commanding-in-Chief, Bomber Command, in the United Kingdom. The War Office has nevertheless undertaken the maintenance of this force from the common bases up to railhead and for this you, as Commander-in-Chief of the Field Force, will be responsible.

Finally the Commander-in-Chief was instructed to keep in constant communication with the War Office and report regularly on the situation; and he was to 'rely with absolute confidence on receiving the full and unqualified support of the Government, of the Army Council, and of the British people'.

Thus when war was declared the following preparations had been made:

(1) the general strategy which was to govern the Allies' conduct of operations had been agreed;

(2) the size and composition of the British Expeditionary Force and the date by which it would be assembled in France had been decided and naval plans had been made for its prompt dispatch and subsequent supply and maintenance;

(3) the Commander-in-Chief was selected (though only at the last minute) and the terms on which he would serve under the French Command had been defined;

(4) the size and composition of air forces to be employed in France had been decided, the necessary measures for their operation had been agreed, and plans had been made for their prompt dispatch and accommodation.

In all these matters there had been close and harmonious collaboration with France.

There was little of peace left in this last six months before war was declared. On the 15th of March Hitler announced that Bohemia and Moravia were taken under German 'protection'—Czechoslovakia ceased to exist as an independent state. In the two months which followed Germany seized Memel, the chief port of Lithuania, denounced her pact of non-aggression with Poland and her Naval Agreement with Great Britain, and signed a 'Pact of Steel' with Italy, who meanwhile had invaded Albania.

In Great Britain the growing menace of these events and of Hitler's warlike attitude to Poland led progressively to the adoption of conscription, the calling up of Army Reservists for training and the partial mobilisation of the Fleet and the Royal Air Force.

Germany's next move was to insure her eastern borders by concluding two treaties with Russia which included a secret agreement to divide Poland and left Russia free to rob Finland.[3] Two days later—on the 25th of August—the British Government signed an Anglo-Polish Defence Alliance, providing for mutual assistance in the event of aggression; but Hitler was not to be deterred. On the 1st of September Germany invaded Poland across every accessible frontier without any previous declaration of war and after heavily bombing Polish airfields without warning. Great Britain at once ordered full mobilisation and sent an ultimatum to Germany, timed to expire on the 3rd of September. To this there was no response and at eleven o'clock that morning the Second World War began.

---

[3] *Nazi-Soviet Relations, 1939–1941.* Edited by Sontag and Beddie. Department of State, Washington, 1948.

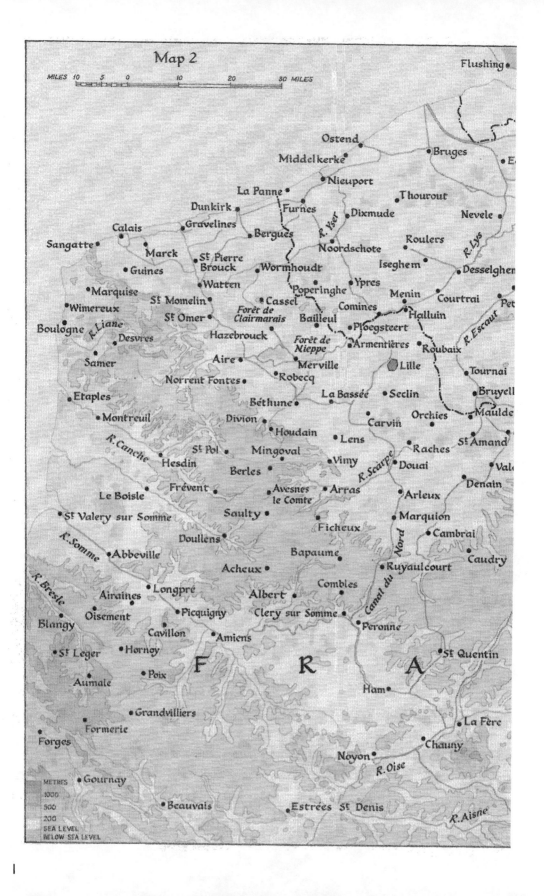

Map 2

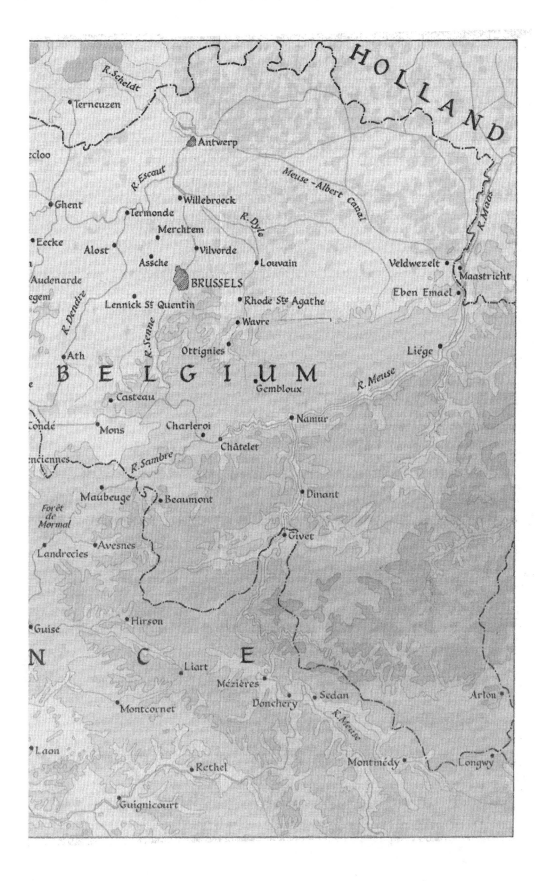

CHAPTER II

THE FIRST WINTER

3rd September, 1939, to 9th May, 1940

ON the day before war was declared the Royal Air Force flew to France a small advance party of eighteen officers and thirty-one other ranks. By the 27th of September the Royal Navy with shipping of the Mercantile Marine under their control had moved to France, without the loss of a single life,

152,031 army personnel
9,392 air force personnel
21,424 army vehicles
2,470 air force vehicles
36,000 tons of ammunition
25,000 tons of motor spirit
60,000 tons of frozen meat

in addition to other stores, equipment and supplies. Thereafter the build-up of our forces and of equipment, stores and supplies continued steadily.

Advance parties sailed from Portsmouth on the 4th of September, and the first convoy of troopships left Southampton and the Bristol Channel ports on the 9th. The first main landings took place at Cherbourg on the 10th and at Nantes and St Nazaire two days later. Thereafter convoys bearing men and material followed at frequent intervals. In their naval war plans, issued in May 1939, the Germans recognised that they would 'be excluded from the Channel in a very short time'. And during the first three weeks of September, when Hitler still hoped to avoid immediate war with the Western Powers, the action of German submarines was accordingly limited by his orders. After that date the restrictions were progressively removed.[1] Even then, their only attempt to interfere with our operations was by laying a few mines in the approaches to Dover and Weymouth, ports which they wrongly believed to be in use for embarkations. While foresight and careful planning had their reward in the smoothness with which the Royal Navy's plans worked, the effectiveness of security measures was thus proved by the enemy's mistaken action. All this, and all the going and coming which was to follow, was made possible by the completeness of the Navy's control of the narrow seas and of their approaches.

---

[1] Führer Naval Conferences, reproduced in *Brassey's Naval Annual*, 1948.

Almost from the start rolling-stock and loaded wagons had been sent by train ferry direct to Calais and Dunkirk, and Dieppe had been used as a medical base; but the carriage of all reinforcements and stores to the western ports of France placed a severe strain on shipping resources and on escort forces, and it quickly became apparent that for military as well as naval reasons it was desirable to make fuller use of the French Channel ports and so reduce both the sea passage and the overland carry. The French were anxious to avoid action which might invite air attacks on these ports and would not at first agree to their use, but in October they acquiesced; a start was made by sending cased petrol direct to Caen, and in the following month a base was opened at Havre. Eventually Rouen, Fécamp, St Malo, Dieppe, Boulogne, and Dunkirk were all used.

One further factor which certainly contributed to the continued safe passage to France of men and stores was the Navy's closing of the English Channel by a mine barrage across the Straits of Dover. This was carried out in three stages between the 11th of September and the end of October, and nearly 7,000 shallow and deep mines were used with other protective devices. It was a well-planned and carefully executed operation and it was completely successful. Before the first stage was completed one enemy submarine passed through to lay mines off Dover and Weymouth as mentioned above, but that was all. The U12 and the U40 were blown up in the minefield in October and a third U-boat, trying to avoid it, ran ashore on the Goodwins and was destroyed by surface vessels. Thereafter the enemy abandoned the attempt to penetrate to the western waters of the Channel, through which the British Expeditionary Force was being maintained, until he in turn occupied the French coasts.

The Army had now to provide in France for all the needs of a community of men which increased daily till in less than three weeks it was greater than the total population of either Brighton or Derby. This army had to be distributed, housed and fed, and vast stores for its immediate use and its future operations had also to be accumulated and conveniently disposed.

A 'Maintenance Project Plan' had been prepared ahead as a complement to 'Plan W.4'. In the application of both plans some unforeseen difficulties arose and minor miscalculations were discovered. For example, the railway journey from Cherbourg, where personnel were disembarked, to the ports at which their vehicles were landed was found to take about thirty hours, though the distance by rail was only about 150 miles, and in the more normal time-table should only take about seven hours. Some units, too, arrived in advance of their stores, and some fighting troops were shipped ahead of the supply and maintenance echelons on which they depended. Accommodation provided at the bases proved to be inadequate and a considerable building programme had to be set afoot as labour became available. But all difficulties were overcome. On the whole the plans which had been prepared ahead worked most successfully and the resource and initiative of Lord Gort's Quartermaster-General, Lieutenant-General W. G. Lindsell, his staff and services successfully solved unforeseen problems. The map overleaf shows diagrammatically the main routes of supply and the general lay-out of the lines of communication.

Our undertaking to have two corps assembled in France thirty-three days after mobilisation was fulfilled.

Commanded by Lieutenant-General Sir John Dill, I Corps (1st and 2nd Divisions) began taking over a sector of the frontier defences from French troops on the 3rd of October; II Corps (3rd and 4th Divisions), commanded by Lieutenant-General A. F. Brooke, moved into the line from its concentration area on the 12th of October. The sector for which British troops were eventually responsible lay east of Lille and stretched from Maulde to Halluin with a defensive flank along the River Lys from Halluin to Armentières. On their right was the French First Army; on their left the French Seventh Army.

General Headquarters was opened near Arras, with its various branches dispersed in neighbouring villages and in the town. For liaison with our Ally a military mission under Major-General Sir Richard Howard-Vyse was appointed to represent the Chief of the Imperial General Staff at the General Headquarters of the French Supreme Commander, General Gamelin. A second mission under Brigadier J. G. des R. Swayne was appointed to represent the British Commander-in-Chief at the Headquarters of General Georges, commanding the French North-East Theatre of Operations in which was included the British Expeditionary Force. Later, after Belgium was attacked, a mission to the Belgian Army Headquarters under Major-General H. Needham was appointed to keep the War Office informed of the Belgian situation and intentions and to repeat information acquired to the British Commander-in-Chief. As was the custom at the time, these missions will be referred to as 'the Howard-Vyse Mission', 'the Swayne Mission' and 'the Needham Mission'. Major-General H.R.H. The Duke of Gloucester was appointed Chief Liaison Officer on Lord Gort's Staff.

The six months which followed are unique in the history of modern warfare. Germany had attacked Poland, and because of this Britain and France had declared war on Germany. It was a brave act, for neither country was equipped for such a fight, and other free nations applauded as the Allies mobilised their forces and arranged them for battle on the French frontier. And then we waited. We waited while Germany conquered Poland and divided the spoil with Russia. We waited while Germany moved her armies to the west and disposed

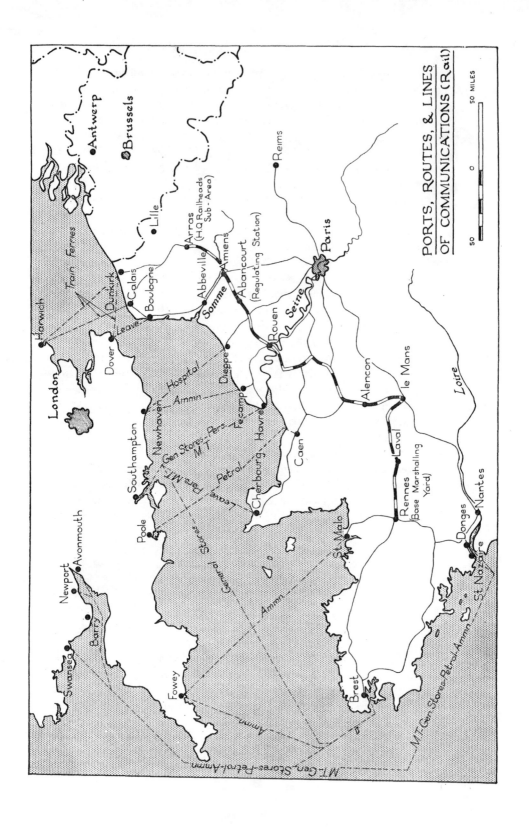

PORTS, ROUTES, & LINES OF COMMUNICATIONS (Rail)

50   0   50   MILES

them to attack us. We waited, then, for Hitler to choose the time and place for his assault. And while we waited, the applause of a world which could not know how ill-prepared we were changed into wonder, as Germany was allowed to mass her armies without interference on the western frontiers while the Allies prepared to defend themselves.

For six months after the British Expeditionary Force took its place in the Allies' line of battle it had neutral Belgium between it and the enemy. In those six months it had time to prepare for the coming battle, to build up its strength, to perfect its training, to strengthen the defences of the front it was to hold, and to develop rearward organisation for eventual expansion. And the time was put to good use.

The build-up of forces was, of course, dependent on the progress made at home in the training and equipment of additional units. By the end of 1939 it had proved possible to form another Regular division in France—the 5th Division. In January, 1940, the first Territorial division—the 48th (South Midland) Division arrived. In February came the 50th (Northumbrian) Division and the 51st (Highland) Division, and in April the 42nd (East Lancashire) and 44th (Home Counties) Divisions, all these high-numbered divisions being Territorial troops. By the 9th of April a third corps was operational, under the command of Lieutenant-General Sir Ronald F. Adam, and by the beginning of May 1940 the British Expeditionary Force had been increased from four Regular divisions in two corps to ten divisions (half Regular and half Territorial) in three corps and G.H.Q. reserve. As a measure of unification some Regular battalions were transferred to Territorial brigades and vice versa. As will be seen later three incomplete Territorial divisions were also sent out in April for labour duties and to complete their training. A list of the principal formations and their commanders is given in Appendix I. In April Sir John Dill handed over command of I Corps to Lieutenant-General M. G. H. Barker, on appointment as Vice-Chief of the Imperial General Staff.

By the end of April the strength of the British Army in France had increased to 394,165. Of this total, 237,319 were with G.H.Q. and in corps and divisions—that is the main fighting force; 18,347 were in the Territorial divisions sent out for labour duties and further training; 17,665 were reinforcements held at bases; 78,864 were on lines-of-communication duties; 23,545 were in headquarters of various services and missions, hospitals and miscellaneous employment; 9,051 were in drafts en route; 2,515 were not yet allocated and 6,859 were with the Advanced Air Striking Force.

Thus behind the main fighting force of nearly a quarter of a million there were over 150,000 men in the rearward areas. Large numbers of these men were preparing bases, depots and installations for the maintenance of the much larger fighting force which it was intended to build up as rapidly as possible. Many of them were skilled tradesmen with little or no military training.

It had been decided that as soon as the strength of the British Expeditionary Force was further increased to four corps these should be grouped in two armies each with its own army commander and staff, but this stage had not been reached when the battle began. Throughout the campaign Lord Gort acted both as Commander-in-Chief and as Army Commander with consequences which are discussed in a later chapter.

Training was vigorously pursued in so far as time could be spared from front-line duties and work on defences. It was some years since any considerable exercise with troops had been held in England, for before the war even the small Regular Army had been allowed to fall short of establishment by some 20,000 (including 5,000 officers) and many units on the home establishment were little more than cadres. They had been largely made up to strength by reservists but these and new recruits needed training in the use of new weapons and in modern methods. Weapon training, field exercises, practice in road movement and co-operation with the Royal Air Force were all included in the training programme. A number of schools of instruction were set up and many officers and non-commissioned officers were freed to attend courses in England. Finally training in day-to-day duties when in contact with the enemy was secured by co-operation with the French Army. As early as November the Commander-in-Chief arranged with the French High Command that British infantry brigades should in turn do a short spell of duty under the command of a French division on the Saar front. There they would hold forward positions in front of the Maginot forts; only no-man's-land would separate them from the forward posts of the enemy's Siegfried Line. Before hostilities began nine brigades had the advantage of this most valuable experience.

Towards the end of the winter it was decided to increase the Saar contingent to a whole division with attached troops including cavalry, machine guns and pioneers, and the 51st Division duly took over a divisional sector from the French by the 6th of May. What happened to it must be told separately for it was never able to rejoin the main British force under Lord Gort's command.

Work on the defences of the British sector of the front was set in hand as soon as the position was taken over. An anti-tank ditch covered by concrete pill-boxes had already been constructed by the French along much of the front, and while this provision for the close defence of the frontier was developed it was decided to organise the defences in depth by the eventual construction of three positions and a reserve position across the base of the salient made by the frontier east of

Lille. In November twelve field companies of Royal Engineers drawn from Territorial divisions at home, with companies of the Auxiliary Military Pioneer Corps and a special Excavation Company, reached France and were employed on digging anti-tank ditches, constructing breastworks, and other tasks. The majority of these men had had little or no military training and considerable numbers were not armed, facts which must be recalled later. The construction of successive positions and switch lines, strengthened by concrete pill-boxes, wire, and anti-tank obstacles, was pushed on, and before the offensive opened about forty miles of revetted anti-tank obstacle, covered by over 400 concrete pill-boxes, had been completed. Between 700 and 800 machines—bulldozers, angledozers, grabs and concrete-mixers—had been brought out to facilitate the work. When the time came to hold the frontier the value of this work was proved.

A system of inter-communications throughout our front was organised by the Royal Corps of Signals not only for the Army but for the whole of the British air forces in France, in the course of which many miles of armoured signal cable were buried.

Work at bases, in rearward areas and on lines of communication, in preparation for further expansion of British forces, had continued systematically so far as labour and materials allowed. Construction of fifty-nine new airfields and landing grounds for British air forces stationed in France employed upwards of 10,000 men, and other large units were engaged on railway and building construction, at bases and on the long lines of communication. Over a hundred miles of broad-gauge railway lines were laid and great quantities of barbed wire were put up.

It was to ease the problems of manpower for such duties that the three Territorial divisions already mentioned above—the 12th (Eastern), 23rd (Northumbrian) and 46th (North Midland and West Riding) Divisions—were brought out from England in April. They were neither fully trained nor equipped for fighting, and, while they were to be used largely for labour duties, a balanced programme of training was carried out so far as time permitted.

In December His Majesty King George VI spent three days with the British Expeditionary Force, inspecting both forward and rear-ward areas.

Heavy falls of snow, with intermittent spells of hard frost, thaw, and heavy rain, during much of the winter, delayed work on defences, handicapped training, and tried the health and temper of the troops. Both stood the test well. When so large a body of men must live in abnormal conditions among people whose language is strange to them and whose modes of thought and way of life differ from their own, there are bound to be some frictions and some misunderstandings. Yet in general the British soldiery lived happily with their neighbours through this trying winter and were chiefly impressed by the friendliness of the French people. The health of the troops remained good and there was almost complete freedom from epidemic disease, only influenza being troublesome. And when days grew longer and the sun shone more warmly the British Expeditionary Force was in good health and ready for the coming fight, fitter and better trained than it had been when it landed in France. Measures taken by the Royal Army Medical Corps to safeguard health, provision of welfare services on a generous scale, the efficiency of the Army Postal Service, and the opening of leave to England, all contributed to this result; but mainly it was due to the fact that the absence of hostilities had not been accepted as a justification for idleness. Most of the British troops had a very active winter.

Meanwhile the French High Command had decided on a project which was largely to shape the destiny of the British Expeditionary Force, if not also the destiny of France.

It was noted in the previous chapter that problems relating to the expected German offensive through Belgium and Holland were discussed in the pre-war Staff conversations with France and that alternative positions on which such an attack could be held as far forward as possible were considered.

The question was discussed throughout the autumn by the Allied Governments' Supreme War Council, at numerous conferences under General Gamelin, the French Supreme Commander, or General Georges, commanding North-East Theatre of Operations, in which Lord Gort or his Chief of the General Staff (Lieutenant-General H. R. Pownall) played their part, and in letters and meetings. It is unnecessary to trace in detail the evolution of plans which were shaped only gradually and were finally to be decided by General Gamelin. But it is worth noting that all discussions were based on an assumption that the main weight of the German attack would come through central Belgium and might involve Holland. No attempt seems to have been made to foresee what would result if the main attack fell elsewhere. And as no alternative plan of attack was envisaged, no alternative plans of defence were made by the Allies. There is no evidence in the records of these meetings or in orders and instructions which followed them that there was any study of the position which would arise if, while Allied armies moved eastward into Belgium, the enemy's main forces pierced the frontier farther south and advanced westward into France. In particular, the possibility of an attack through the Ardennes having once been ruled out by the French, no further thought seems to have been given to it or to its possible consequences.

By the middle of November the French High Command had decided that if Belgium were attacked only two courses could be

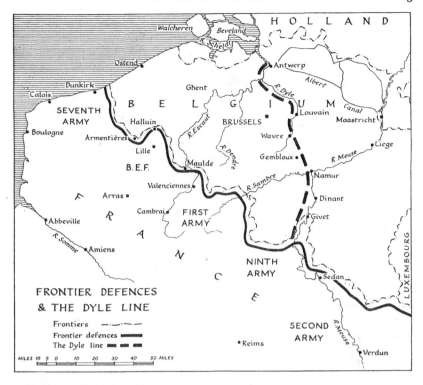

FRONTIER DEFENCES
& THE DYLE LINE

Frontiers —·—·—
Frontier defences ▬▬▬
The Dyle line ▬ ▬ ▬

MILES 10 5 0   10   20   30   40   50 MILES

regarded as practical for the Allies, namely, an advance to the River Scheldt—known to the British Expeditionary Force throughout the campaign by its French name Escaut—(Plan E) or an advance to the Dyle (known as Plan D). Which of these should be adopted would only be decided by the French High Command when the time came and when it was seen whether the Belgian Army was likely to hold the enemy's attack while the Allies moved forward. If Plan D were adopted the French Seventh Army would be given an independent role and would be placed behind and to the left of the Belgians at Antwerp in order to cover their left flank while if possible linking them to the Dutch. The Seventh Army consisted of six infantry divisions, two of them motorised, and a light mechanised division. General Georges had planned to hold it as a reserve behind the Allies' left: the decision to thrust it forward to the mouth of the Scheldt was taken by General Gamelin.

The Escaut plan was the simpler of the two, as the advance would involve only a day's march for the Allied left wing. The Dyle plan, on the other hand, would involve for the British Expeditionary Force an advance of some sixty miles, over roads not previously reconnoitred and likely to be crowded by refugees moving in the opposite direction to the Allied armies. The move would take several days to complete and it would only be practicable if a Belgian stand on their forward line of resistance held up the German advance while it was taking place. But if the Dyle line could be reached it had several advantages. It was a shorter line to hold. With the Dendre and Escaut rivers and the prepared defences of the French frontier lying behind it, the Dyle position could be organised in greater depth. And it would deny to the enemy a larger area of Belgian territory.

The position in regard to Belgium was inevitably difficult. The Belgian High Command sought to know the exact intentions of the Allies but were unwilling to supply information as to their own plan of defence. The only communications which passed were through the Allies' military attachés in Brussels and Paris, and the knowledge gained was indefinite and incomplete. The Belgian Command were informed by General Gamelin that the Allies were prepared to move immediately on a Belgian invitation and they were sent a series of papers prepared by the French Staff on such questions as the organisation of the Dyle position, defences to be constructed in the sector where there was no natural anti-tank obstacle, the safeguarding of Meuse bridges till Allied forces arrived, and the storage of engineer material in rear of the Dyle line so that Allied troops on arrival could at once proceed to strengthen the defences. On some of these they acted, but they would neither allow reconnaissance nor give detailed and exact information as to their own defence plans, though some British officers in plain clothes were allowed unofficially to visit the Dyle line.

At each stage reached in the evolution of the Allies' policy, British General Headquarters issued appropriate operation and administration instructions. When the German attack opened 'Operation Instruction No. 36' and 'Administration Instruction No. 10' were in force, providing together complete detail for an instant implementation of either Plan E or Plan D.

Meanwhile the long pause before active warfare began proved no less useful to our air forces in France whose problems were of a different order. With one modification the forces planned reached France by the due dates. Only the size of the Advanced Air Striking Force had to be reduced by half because the number of airfields which the French Air Force could then spare for their use could only accommodate ten squadrons without dangerous congestion. Even so, much work was needed to bring the allotted airfields up to the standard of equipment required for active operations.

Nevertheless, almost at once the French began to press for the supply of a larger fighter force and discussion on this question and on the use to be made of our bomber force continued throughout the period of passive warfare—and indeed throughout the campaign which followed. The issues raised involved political, strategical, and technical considerations which are outside the scope of this account of operations, but it is necessary to note their outlines in order to understand the action which was taken.

Stated shortly, the French view was that in order to defeat Germany the Allies' first task must be the defence of French territory; this task must have priority over all others and Allied forces must be devoted first to its assurance. The British view was that the immediate aim must be the defence of French *and British* territory and that while contributing as largely as possible to the defence of France, Great Britain must keep sufficient strength in hand for her own defence. Moreover, since our naval superiority made it certain that any German attack on Great Britain must come first from the air, it was essential to hold air forces ready to meet such an event. This fundamental difference of outlook explains both the French demands for greater air support and the British refusal to risk all in a battle for France.

The consequent difficulty in reaching agreement on air policy was further increased by contrasts in the circumstances of the two countries. France was vulnerable to attack by land, and for national defence relied mainly on her Army. Air defence had been regarded as of secondary importance, and when war was declared France was but poorly equipped to withstand an assault from the air. Three principal measures are necessary for effective air defence, namely— means to detect the approach of enemy aircraft and to follow their movements; anti-aircraft artillery to protect important localities; and, above all, fighter aircraft to destroy the enemy in the air. In all three respects the French air defence was weak. For detection they relied largely on personal observers reporting by the civil telephone; they were short of the anti-aircraft artillery needed to defend so large a country, and in France (in October 1939) they had a first-line strength of only 549 fighters (of which 131 were classed as '*anciens*'), only 186 bombers (of which all but 11 were '*anciens*') and only 377 reconnaissance and observation aircraft of which 316 were '*anciens*'. Consciousness of their own weakness not only inspired the French desire to obtain more fighter support from Britain but led them to advocate a policy for the use of bomber aircraft which was in sharp conflict with British proposals. The French argued that all bombers —heavy as well as medium—should collaborate with the Allied armies in opposing a German advance by bombing the enemy's military concentrations and forward communications. They were rigorously opposed to any bombing of targets in Germany for fear that this would provoke retaliatory attacks which France was ill-prepared to meet.

Great Britain, on the other hand, without land frontiers to defend and guarded from seaborne invasion by the Royal Navy, was only vulnerable to attack from the air. Air defence had accordingly been given priority in rearmament. When war was declared preparations for air defence were well advanced, with radar detection, anti-aircraft artillery, and modern fighters in numbers that would increase steadily. Fear of retaliation had little influence on British air policy. The British view was that if Germany started an offensive in the west the Allies should at once carry war into the enemy's country by attacking selected targets with heavy bombers. Not only would this be an effective way to damage the enemy but it would be the only proper way to use aircraft which had been designed for that purpose and which on technical grounds were ill suited to collaborate in a land battle.

A long series of discussions on air policy took place between Governments and Staffs and at the Supreme War Council. In the end, a measure of compromise was accepted though opposed views were never reconciled. The position reached by May 1940 was this. In the event of a German offensive the British Air Ministry could at once order bombing attacks by heavy bombers against communications and concentration areas in Germany west of the Rhine and against railway marshalling yards east of the Rhine. For air attacks against oil refineries in the Ruhr (which were thought to have special importance in the German war economy) Cabinet approval must first be obtained, and this was likely to be conditioned by the Allied Governments' agreement to avoid the risk of inflicting casualties on the civil population of Germany unless or until Germany started the bombing of other than strictly military targets.

There was no comparable difference of opinion as to how our medium bombers should be used. They too *might* be called on to help in the strategic bombing of targets in Germany, but their first and main task would be to collaborate with the Allied armies by bombing enemy columns, especially at road, rail, and river crossings and other traffic bottlenecks. This accorded well with French views but some British experts held that, having regard to their equipment and performance, even the medium bombers which we had at this date would be unwisely employed on such tasks.

The British decision as to what air forces should be sent to France was not only based on the general grounds outlined above but also on two practical considerations. An air force can only operate effectively if airfields and ground organisation are adequate; and it must be reasonably mobile. At this time, as already mentioned, France could not even provide enough airfields for all the squadrons which we were ready to send out as an advanced air striking force; and Britain could not provide all the vehicles needed to make those which were sent even partially mobile. Much time and effort, large quantities of materials, and a big force of army labour were expended

GENERAL GAMELIN

Commander-in-Chief of the French Army

Facing p. 26

AIR MARSHAL A. S. BARRATT

Air Officer Commanding-in-Chief,
British Air Forces in France

during the winter and spring on the acquisition, planning and construction of additional airfields; and something was done to increase the mobility of the squadrons in France. But when hostilities opened in May very few of the new airfields were yet usable and British squadrons still required over 600 vehicles to make them even semi-mobile. While such conditions existed, to have increased largely air forces which would have to operate with inadequate ground service and without ability to move with the tide of battle would have been to court avoidable losses of men and aircraft.

Some increase of our air strength in France was nevertheless effected during the winter, and much was done by regrouping and reorganisation to increase efficiency. The changes need not be traced in detail. Appendix I lists the principal units of the Royal Air Force which took part in the campaign, and shows how greatly the original forces were expanded. One major change had been made in organisation and command. As originally planned, the Air Component of the British Expeditionary Force was for operational purposes part of Lord Gort's command. The Advanced Air Striking Force on the other hand was under the orders of Bomber Command in England. In the autumn of 1939 there were thus three distinct air forces in France—the French Air Force, the Air Component of the British Expeditionary Force, and the Advanced Air Striking Force. Provision had been made for liaison and co-ordination of operations by the establishment of Air Missions at the headquarters of the principal commands, but air exercises, designed to test communications and the rapid passage of information and orders, showed that some more efficient arrangement was needed.

By the end of 1939 it had been decided to unify the command of the two British air forces in France and early in January 1940 Air Marshal A. S. Barratt was appointed to the new command. From that date the Air Component ceased to be part of Lord Gort's command (though it remained under his operational control) and the Advanced Air Striking Force ceased to be part of Bomber Command. Both came under Air Marshal Barratt as Air Officer Commanding-in-Chief, British Air Forces in France.

Air Marshal Barratt was made responsible for seeing that the Commander-in-Chief of the British Expeditionary Force had at all times 'full assurance' regarding air support and he was instructed to place at Lord Gort's disposal 'such bomber squadrons as the latter may, in consultation with him, consider necessary from time to time'. But the Air Ministry's directive also laid it down that as the British Expeditionary Force held only a fraction of the Allied front the British bombers in France should be required to operate 'in accordance with the day-to-day needs of the Allied situation on the western front as a whole'. In other words Air Marshal Barratt must do his

best to satisfy the demands of both Lord Gort and the French High
Command. It says much for the qualities of the two British Com-
manders-in-Chief that this somewhat ambiguous directive led to no
friction in battle, though at home the War Office and the Air Ministry
found it impossible to agree what air support was necessary for an
army in the field.

Before being appointed to the new command, Air Marshal Barratt
had been head of the British Air Mission at the headquarters in
Coulommiers of General Vuillemin, Commander-in-Chief of the
French Air Forces. Headquarters of the British Air Forces in France
were now established there so as to facilitate Anglo-French co-operation. At the same time Air Marshal Barratt decided that his advanced
headquarters in battle would be Chauny, where the French Air
Commander of the Northern Zone (General d'Astier) had his headquarters and where there had been constituted a British Air Intelligence Centre which developed into the Allied Central Air Bureau
—the nerve centre of air operations throughout the first critical
stages of the campaign. A further measure in which the Army and
Air Force combined was the constitution in November of a joint
mission to gather information of the progress of the battle if Germany
invaded the Low Countries. This Air Mission under Wing Commander J. M. Fairweather, 'No. 3 Air Mission', was to establish
itself alongside Belgian Army Headquarters where it would act in
air liaison matters and would sift information from this and other
sources before passing it on to Air Marshal Barratt and to Lord Gort's
Headquarters. The Military Mission under Lieutenant-Colonel G. F.
Hopkinson, 'the Hopkinson Mission', was a ground reconnaissance
force in armoured cars, trucks and motor cycles whose task was to
gather information from formation headquarters and supply this to
the Air Mission and to General Headquarters. Both missions were
fully mobile and both were supplied with high-power wireless sets
and mobile wireless stations. They were thus well equipped for their
task, and when the time came the work they did was of great value
to the British Expeditionary Force and to Air Marshal Barratt.

On taking up his Command the latter at once raised with the Air
Ministry the question of mobility. The Air Component had been
equipped with transport which would enable its squadrons to move
forward quickly if the advance to the Dyle were ordered but it was
held that 'owing to the strategic position of the Advanced Air
Striking Force behind a strong fortified line the degree of mobility
required by units is small'. Air Marshal Barratt did not share this
confidence in the strength of the French front and, after a committee
had been sent out to investigate, a new establishment was approved
which would make the Advanced Air Striking Force 'semi-mobile'.
Unfortunately it did not prove possible to implement this new policy

promptly owing to failure of contractors, shortage of materials and other urgent demands. Eventually it will be seen that for self-preservation French lorries had to be borrowed and the time taken to move squadrons' equipment, ammunition and stores proved a serious handicap to operations.

During the autumn the necessity to be ready for immediate operations restricted opportunities for air training, except on squadron level, and severe weather made it impossible in mid-winter. It was limited, too, by shortage of some training equipment and, more seriously, by French flying regulations. But after the turn of the year facilities were improved and much useful training was then carried out, including a number of tactical exercises (some in co-operation with the Army) and practice in night flying, some of which was done over Germany. And although divergencies of policy or opinion might disturb relations in high places, and some difficulties be found in reconciling differences in the organisation and procedures of British and French air forces, personal relations in the field were uniformly happy. Contemporary records constantly refer to the helpfulness of the French Air Force and to the great kindness received by the Royal Air Force in France during the winter and spring.

From the outset air training was intermixed with operations which, if limited in character and in results, were fruitful in experience. There were no bombing raids on Germany, for the Allies had decided to refrain from this form of attack until Germany began it and the enemy dropped no bombs on France till the offensive opened. But both bombers and fighters were engaged in strategic and tactical reconnaissance and the fighters were in fairly frequent combat with reconnaissance aircraft of the enemy engaged on similar missions. The measure of success achieved in these operations is difficult to gauge. Some of our pilots had had insufficient training and experience when they went into action for the first time, and many forms of equipment which subsequently came to be regarded as essential had not yet been evolved.

A number of enemy planes were destroyed, but our own losses were considerable. Experience proved that none of our bomber reconnaissance aircraft of that date—Battles and Blenheims—had adequate defence against enemy fighters and showed that they were not well adapted for reconnaissance except perhaps at night. On the other hand it proved that the eight-gun Hurricane fighters of the latest pattern could deal effectively with the latest German Messerschmitt. And it proved the *élan* and skill of our pilots and their readiness to attack the enemy even when he was encountered in greater strength. It is well to realise at the outset and to bear in mind continuously the comparatively primitive equipment with which our pilots flew and fought in 1940. They were not yet provided with scientific aids to navigation and had to find their way and their target by map and compass and by what they could see. Accurate map reading while moving at speed is always difficult and sometimes impossible, especially at night or when inherent difficulties are increased by an enemy's ground defence or aircraft. Moreover at this time medium bombers had to attack stone and concrete bridges with bombs which were not big enough to do any vital damage. They had only 250-pound bombs and usually carried four. It was proved in 1944 that from 100–200 *tons* of bombs were required to guarantee the destruction of a substantially built river bridge.

By that date the medium bombers of 1940 (Battle and Blenheim) were no longer used, while those classed as heavy bombers in 1940 were regarded as medium bombers in 1944 though their capabilities had by then been much improved. Whereas in the 1940 campaign an average bomb load of one ton was carried by the heavy bombers they carried up to ten times as much in 1944. The Battle and Blenheim had for protection only two light machine guns ($\cdot$303); the medium bombers of 1944 had nine. The heavies of 1940 were armed with five light machine guns; in 1944 they had up to ten guns of larger calibre ($\cdot$5) with far higher powers of penetration.

These facts illustrate some of the difficulties under which our air forces operated in 1940.

At intervals throughout the autumn and winter leaflets addressed to the German people were dropped from bombers of Bomber Command over industrial towns in the Ruhr, Hamburg and other heavily populated areas including Berlin and later Vienna. It was hoped that such raids might impress the German Government and people by the evidence of Germany's vulnerability to air attack and lead to the adoption of defence measures which might interrupt work in factories. Such raids gave our pilots valuable experience of night flying and reconnaissance over Germany and led to important improvements in equipment for high-altitude flying and in aids to navigation. With the equipment then available they sometimes needed to show great endurance. A raid on the night of the 27th of October involved four aircraft of No. 51 Squadron. The first dropped leaflets over Frankfurt, the second over Munich, the third over Stuttgart and the fourth also over Munich. All encountered thick cloud: all crews suffered greatly from intense cold and all aircraft were partly disabled by heavy icing, yet all carried out their tasks. The conclusion of their journeys may be told:

> *No. 1.* The instrument glasses were thick with ice . . . two members of the crew were unconscious . . . both engines had stopped and four inches of ice protruded from the engine's cowling . . . The wireless transmitter was frozen . . . the rudder and elevator were immovable . . . The aircraft brushed through the tops of trees, dropped flatly into

a field, travelled through a wire fence, skidded broadside and came to rest against a tree . . . The crew climbed out and with difficulty put out a fire in one engine. Then they returned to the fuselage and went to sleep. Fortunately they had landed in France.

No. 2. The navigator and operator had to lie down and rest every few minutes . . . everyone was frozen . . . continuous movement of the controls was needed to prevent them freezing up . . . when the air-craft homed the crew were incapable of coherent thought or action.

No. 3. Ice rapidly formed on all the control surfaces, building up to about six inches . . . the front gunner in his turret was completely covered in snow and ice.

No. 4. The air-speed indicator froze up . . . snow lay on the floor of the front turret and ice covered the cabin windows . . . the centre turret froze and remained immovable. A cylinder blew off and one engine failed . . . Finally the Captain gave the crew orders to jump and followed them. He did not realise that intercommunication had failed and that the tail gunner had not received the order and was still on board when the plane hit the ground. The gunner escaped through the tail door as the aircraft blazed up. Convinced that his companions were in the fire he searched the debris vainly and then walked to a village—where he found them in a café.

There was, however, some evidence that the leaflets were being read and were having some effect, and from the training point of view these raids were valuable: so they were continued until active operations began and then as subsidiary to bombing raids on Germany.

One fact stands out clearly. Although a winter's air reconnaissance provided the Allies with much useful information, it discovered nothing which led to any fresh appreciation of what was likely to be the German plan of attack, nothing which led the Allies to make any change in their own dispositions, which are shown on the situation map at the end of this chapter.

To this general account of how the British Expeditionary Force and the British Air Forces in France spent the winter of 1939 and the first four months of 1940 must be added a note of relevant events elsewhere.

Poland was defeated by Germany by the end of September, after putting up a brave fight against unequal odds. The campaign had shown conclusively that armoured forces, well handled and supported by a strong air force, could quickly overwhelm an army which was weak in both those respects. It had shown too the ruthless methods which Germany would employ (and especially her disregard for civilian life) when these would assist military convenience. The murderous bombing of Warsaw, defenceless against air attack, was the culmination of that campaign. As it closed, Russia invaded Poland from the east and reaped the fruits of her bargain with Hitler by occupying half of the conquered territory.

Two months later Russia invaded Finland having previously obtained without fighting the mastery of Estonia, Latvia, and Lithuania. Throughout the winter Finland held the enemy at bay, but on the 1st of February Russia opened a new offensive with overwhelmingly greater forces, backed by artillery and aircraft which Finland could not match. The battle raged furiously for six weeks, when shortage of ammunition and the exhaustion of her troops compelled Finland to seek an armistice. Thus Russia's position had been trebly strengthened by the virtual acquisition of the Baltic States, half of Poland, and a slice of Finland.

Germany, in the meantime, began transferring her armies to the west as soon as Poland was conquered. By the end of November Allied intelligence estimated that between ninety-seven and ninety-nine divisions were already concentrated on the western front, facing Holland, Belgium, Luxembourg, and France. In November there were indications that Germany would attack, and various moves took place to bring our forces to their battle stations. But the expected attack did not come and the *alerte* was called off. Allied intelligence had, however, been good. On the 5th of November Hitler issued orders for an offensive but on the 7th postponed the attack.

On the 10th of January a German aircraft made a forced landing in Belgium and although one of the two officers on board tried to burn orders which he was carrying, these were retrieved while much of them was still readable. They consisted of instructions to units subordinated to No. 2 Air Fleet about the offensive which the German Western Army was to carry out across Belgium from the Moselle to the North Sea.[2]

Other Allied intelligence pointed to an early attack, and again there was an *alerte* with consequent movements. And, again, intelligence was good, for on January the 10th Hitler issued fresh orders for the offensive to open on the 17th of January, only to postpone it on the 13th. It is moreover significant that at this date plans for the German offensive followed closely the pattern forecast by the Allies. The main thrust was to be made by their Northern Group of Armies through the Belgian plain.

After the *alerte* was cancelled comparative quiet again descended on the western front, though it was known that German forces were moving there in increasing numbers and sorties by their reconnaissance planes grew in strength and frequency.

On the 9th of April Germany seized Denmark and started an invasion of Norway. The story of the British part in the campaign which followed is told in another volume.[3] It is only necessary to note here

---

[2] *Belgium: The Official* (Belgian) *Account of what happened 1939–40*, Evans Brothers, 1941, p. 14.

[3] T. K. Derry: *The Campaign in Norway*, H.M.S.O. 1952.

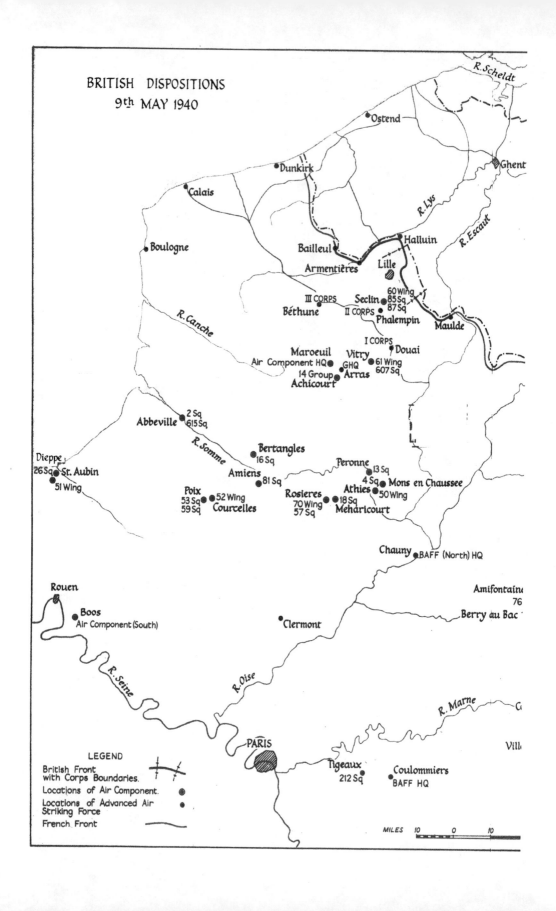

BRITISH DISPOSITIONS
9th MAY 1940

R. Scheldt

Ostend

Dunkirk

Ghent

Calais

R. Lys

R. Escaut

Boulogne

Halluin

Bailleul

Armentières

Lille

III CORPS

Seclin

60 Wing
85 Sq
87 Sq

Béthune

II CORPS

Phalempin

Maulde

R. Canche

I CORPS

Douai

Maroeuil

Vitry

Air Component HQ

GHQ

61 Wing

14 Group

Arras

607 Sq

Achicourt

2 Sq
615 Sq

Abbeville

R. Somme

Bertangles

16 Sq

Peronne

13 Sq

Dieppe

26 Sq

St. Aubin

Amiens

81 Sq

4 Sq

Mons en Chaussee

51 Wing

Athies

50 Wing

Poix

Rosieres

53 Sq

52 Wing

70 Wing

18 Sq

59 Sq

Courcelles

57 Sq

Meharicourt

Chauny

BAFF (North) HQ

Rouen

Amifontaine
76

Boos

Air Component (South)

Clermont

Berry au Bac

R. Seine

R. Oise

R. Marne

PARIS

Vill

LEGEND

British Front
with Corps Boundaries.

Tigeaux

Coulommiers

212 Sq

BAFF HQ

Locations of Air Component.

Locations of Advanced Air
Striking Force

French Front

MILES   10   0   10

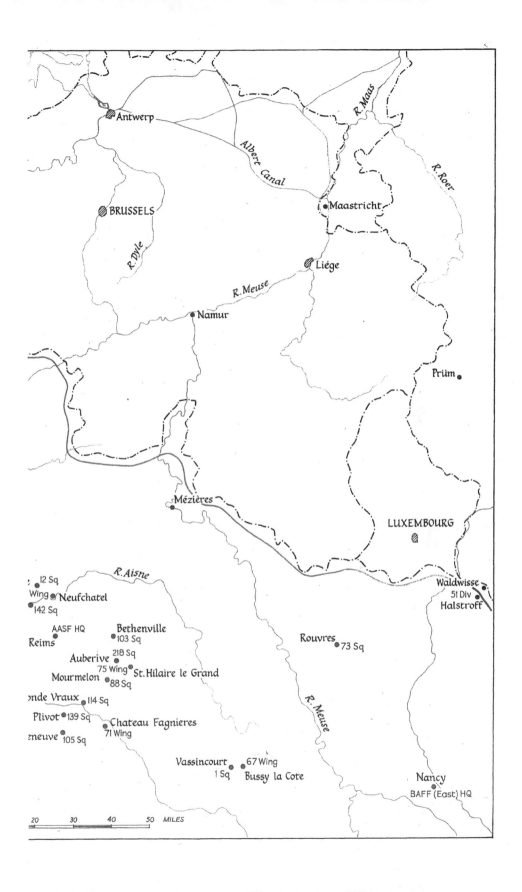

Antwerp

Albert Canal

R. Maas

R. Roer

BRUSSELS

R. Dyle

Maastricht

Liége

R. Meuse

Namur

Prüm

Méezières

LUXEMBOURG

R. Aisne

12 Sq

Wing Neufchatel

142 Sq

Waldwisse

51 Div

Halstroff

AASF HQ

Bethenville

103 Sq

Reims

Auberive

218 Sq

75 Wing St. Hilaire le Grand

Mourmelon

88 Sq

Rouvres

73 Sq

onde Vraux

114 Sq

Plivot

139 Sq

Chateau Fagnieres

71 Wing

neuve

105 Sq

R. Meuse

Vassincourt

67 Wing

1 Sq

Bussy la Cote

Nancy

BAFF (East) HQ

20   30   40   50   MILES

that operations in Norway made rival claims on our naval, military and air forces and equipment which were to be sorely needed for the campaign in France and Flanders. The 15th Brigade of the 5th Division was ordered home for dispatch to Norway and left Lord Gort's Command on the 15th of April. The struggle in Norway continued during April and into May and tension increased in Holland and Belgium as more and more enemy troops gathered beyond their frontiers. But while anxiety deepened in high places, for the Army in France the quiet which had been maintained so long was still undisturbed.

A lovely spring had succeeded the bitter winter, leave was open in the British Expeditionary Force, and the troops were in good heart.

D

CHAPTER III

ADVANCE INTO BELGIUM

10th May to 15th May, 1940

AT General Headquarters in Arras the stillness of a spring night was rudely broken just before daybreak on the morning of the 10th of May, when German aircraft roared over the city and bombed the neighbouring airfields. The raid was part of a general and widespread attack by the *Luftwaffe* on the Allies' airfields, railways, headquarters and key supply points in an effort to cripple air forces and disrupt communications as the opening move of the German western campaign. Except in one or two places it did comparatively little military damage to British installations on the first day, and nothing that affected our plans, but it sounded noisily the call to battle.

Shortly afterwards, at about a quarter to six, a message from French Headquarters was received ordering a complete *alerte*, and about half an hour later came a further message through the Swayne Mission at General Georges' headquarters to say that orders had been issued by the Supreme Command for the immediate execution of Plan D—that is, for the projected move forward to the River Dyle in Belgium (see Map 2). British General Headquarters accordingly sent out the following order:

> Plan D. J.1. today. Zero hour 1300 hours. 12.L may cross before zero. Wireless silence cancelled after crossing frontier. Command Post opens 1300 hours. Air recces may commence forthwith.

In untechnical language this meant that 'Plan D comes into operation today at 1 p.m. 12th Lancers may cross the Franco-Belgian frontier before then. Wireless silence is cancelled after entering Belgium. The Commander-in-Chief's Command Post will open at Wahagnies at 1 p.m. Air reconnaissance may commence forthwith'. The rest of the morning was busy with preparations for the move forward and at one o'clock, punctually to time, the armoured cars of the 12th Royal Lancers crossed the western frontier of Belgium. In the early morning the leading German troops had crossed the eastern frontiers of Belgium, Holland, and Luxembourg. Without provocation, without warning, without regard for her own honour, Germany's pledge to respect the neutrality of her neighbours was again treated as but 'a scrap of paper', though it had been renewed, unsolicited, only a few months before. Unlike Britain and France who were at

35

war with Germany, Holland and Belgium had trusted the German promise and were at peace when far more violent air raids than had disturbed Arras shattered alike the stillness of the night and Belgian and Dutch dreams of undisturbed neutrality.

News of German movements towards the frontier had reached the Belgian Government during the night and at four o'clock in the morning their Foreign Minister, M. Spaak, called on the British Ambassador in Brussels, Sir Lancelot Oliphant, and appealed for British help in resisting the German invasion.

The German zero hour was fixed for 5.35 that morning and troops began the invasion of France, Luxembourg, Belgium and Holland punctually; but a sabotage unit of sixty-four men, organised in five parties, crossed the frontier between Roermond and Maastricht two to three hours before. Three parties wore Dutch steel helmets and great-coats over their German uniforms; the other two wore fitters' and mechanics' overalls. Their aim was to capture various bridges but the bridge guards succeeded in blowing most of those attacked. The German XI Corps War Diary contains a report from one of these parties which states that it captured seven Dutch soldiers who, 'were taken along, some in front and some flanking the detachment, to provide cover against enemy fire'.[1]

For months the British Expeditionary Force had been deployed along the Franco-Belgian frontier between Halluin and Maulde. A rapid advance across strange country to a position which had indeed been photographed from the air but had not been reconnoitred, involved complex movements and required careful planning if it were to be carried out smoothly and without congestion of traffic on the roads; and the move must take some days to complete. But British plans for an advance to the Dyle had been carefully prepared and rehearsed and as a result all went well. The 12th Lancers arrived first, and the armoured reconnaissance units allocated by General Headquarters to I and II Corps reached the Dyle that night and were eventually deployed across the whole front. These were the 4th/7th Royal Dragoon Guards, the 13th/18th Royal Hussars, the 15th/19th King's Royal Hussars and the 5th Royal Inniskilling Dragoon Guards—all now mechanised but still fulfilling the old role of a cavalry screen moving ahead of the main force. They and the troops who followed them were greeted warmly by the Belgian people and saw nothing as yet of the fear and confusion which was soon to choke the roads with refugees. One unit of the 3rd Division had a frontier barrier closed against them because they could not show the faithful but ill-informed official in charge 'a permit to enter Belgium'. But they charged the barrier with a 15-cwt truck and the advance of the division proceeded.

---

[1] For all original texts see Appendix II, p. 375 et seq.

The German Air Force made no serious attempt to interfere, though as Lord Gort had decided to risk moving in daylight as well as by night, the long columns should have been very obvious to the enemy's reconnaissance aircraft (in spite of good march discipline which maintained wide intervals between vehicles), if they had been able closely to observe the area. As it was, the welcome immunity from the attentions of the German aircraft was doubtless due partly to the protection given by the Royal Air Force Air Component, who flew 161 sorties that day. But two other considerations help to explain the German conduct. In the first place, their air force in this phase of the battle was used mainly against pre-arranged targets or took the place of artillery in support of German ground forces. The opening raids on Belgian airfields had destroyed half the Belgian aircraft before ever they could leave the ground, and key positions in Holland had been seized by airborne troops following hard on heavy raids. Some of the French airfields and communications had also suffered severely, but only in one instance did the enemy have any considerable success over airfields in British use. At Condé Vraux, the field of No. 114 Squadron, they destroyed completely six of the eighteen Blenheims and rendered unserviceable the remaining twelve, the airfield and offices were severely damaged, and the nearby petrol dump was fired. Thus the whole squadron and the airfield were virtually put out of operation at the start of the battle. The fact that our ground defence brought down more than half the attacking aircraft was poor compensation for such a loss. Elsewhere, however, our defence was more successful and damage not serious. In the second place, the German High Command expected that for both political and military reasons the Allies would advance into Belgium and this being so they were prepared to fight the Allied armies in the north as far forward as possible from the fortified French frontier. It was not, therefore, the aim of the German Air Force to interfere with our advance at this stage.

The new front to which the French and British armies were moving runs from Sedan in the south to Antwerp in the north. Except in one twenty-mile sector it is covered throughout by watercourses which serve as ready-made tank obstacles. From Sedan the front follows the Meuse through Givet and Dinant to the fortress of Namur. From there to the River Dyle at Wavre is the one unprotected sector, known as the Gembloux gap. There an incomplete obstacle had been put by the Belgians. The front is thereafter covered by the Dyle from Wavre to Louvain and from there runs behind canalised rivers to Antwerp and the sea.

The French High Command expected the main German effort in the Belgian plain between Namur and Antwerp, so they had concentrated strong forces there. On the right the French First Army in the Gembloux gap held a front of approximately twenty-five miles with eight infantry divisions and two light armoured divisions of the Cavalry Corps operating out in front. In the centre, the British force holding approximately seventeen miles of the Dyle, from Wavre to Louvain, had nine divisions deployed in depth with three in the front line and with the cavalry mentioned above out ahead of them. On the British left the Belgian Army was falling back to continue the Allied line of defence to the sea. The French Seventh Army advancing to the mouth of the Scheldt had six infantry divisions with a light mechanised division operating out in front. A French military historian, Commandant Pierre Lyet, states that the First and Seventh Armies were made up for the most part of Active and Series A Units—Active units being Regular troops of high fighting quality and Series A not much inferior though unequal in quality. Five motorised infantry divisions formed part of them, 'as well as almost the whole of our resources in motor transport, anti-aircraft groups, regiments of tractor-drawn artillery, and battalions of modern tanks. In front of them were the three light armoured divisions, whose armour was the most powerful of the French Army's mobile formations'.[2]

On the other hand, in the sector farther south between Longwy, Sedan, and Namur, where the Ardennes and the River Meuse were thought by the French Command to make an armoured attack impracticable—where, therefore, they did not expect the main German effort—'the Ninth and Second Armies were made up chiefly of Series A and Series B divisions. Reinforcements from units of general reserve were on a smaller scale and those units were equipped with less modern material'. . . . Elsewhere Lyet writes: 'The resources at the disposal of the two Series B divisions who were to bear the brunt of the attack were weak. They had almost no Regular officers. They had not been broken in to war conditions by being in contact with the enemy on the Lorraine front'.[3] The Second Army holding about *forty miles* had five infantry divisions between Longwy and Sedan with two cavalry divisions and a cavalry brigade in front; the Ninth Army held a front of *over fifty miles* with seven infantry divisions, two light cavalry divisions composed largely of horsed units with a few light tanks, and a brigade of Spahis out in front.

The French Second, Ninth and First Armies were comprised in the First Group of Armies under command of General Billotte. To the left of this group, sandwiched between the French First Army and the Belgian Army, was the British Expeditionary Force under the direct command of General Georges, commanding the

---

[2] Commandant Pierre Lyet: *La Bataille De France, Mai–Juin 1940*, Payot, Paris, 1947 (hereafter referred to as Lyet), p. 39. See Appendix II, p. 375.

[3] Ibid, pp. 39 and 47. See Appendix II, p. 375.

whole of the French north-east theatre of operations, including also the French Seventh Army with its independent role (page 23). His Second Group of Armies lay to the right of the First Group on the Maginot Line. The general reserve which General Georges had at his disposal was weak, namely thirteen divisions. It was much spread out and unable to act quickly in a counter-stroke. In addition there were four divisions (one Polish) in course of formation. Moreover 'it must be noted too that the "centre of gravity" of these reserves was in Army Group 2, whereas this army group had no part in the advance into Belgium'.[4] Thus the reserve was not placed so as to be easily available where the main German effort was expected.

In the plans of the French High Command there was another miscalculation which contributed to the disaster which followed. It was assumed that the Belgians' defence of their frontier and the delaying action of the French and British cavalry screen would be enough to prevent the German forces reaching the new main line of resistance in the north (the Dyle line) before the Allies' move forward was completed. This assumption proved to be at fault in so far as the French Ninth Army was concerned. When battle was joined some of the French Ninth Army were engaged before they were established on the new line; and the small general reserve was so situated that it could not effectively intervene.

During the first phase of the battle, however, the British Expeditionary Force suffered directly from none of these disadvantages. The main German effort was not directed on its front through the Belgian plain, and though the Belgian Army defending the eastern frontier was forced backwards more quickly than was expected the British defence was adequately organised when the enemy eventually reached our sector on the Dyle. Though the actual front line was held by only three divisions (2nd, 1st and 3rd) two were in support (48th and 4th), two were to be in reserve (5th and 50th), and two more were back on the Escaut (42nd and 44th). Lord Gort's disposition of his divisions in depth was soon proved to be wise (see pages 47 and 48).

The Dyle position in the British sector was a fairly strong one, though three divisions on a front of 30,000 yards meant that the river-line itself would be somewhat thinly guarded. The river is little more than a wide stream. The fact that its banks are extensively wooded made infiltration of infantry a continuing risk, but the river and the railway, which for most of the way follows the eastern or enemy bank, are together fairly effective protection against tanks, and near Louvain the Belgians had built a few pill-boxes to strengthen the defence of the town. The low-lying vale through which the Dyle

---

[4] Lyet, p. 42. See Appendix II, p. 375.

flows quietly is from 500 to 1,500 yards wide and was in places flooded; the high ground which flanks the valley rises more steeply on the enemy side and from the hill ridge there a wide stretch of country to the west is overlooked. Some of our gunners found it difficult to choose sites which were hidden from German observation, but the artillery was deployed to give the maximum cover and an enemy would have found it expensive to attack successfully between Wavre and Louvain. It was in these two flanking towns, each on important roads and with important bridges, that the chief danger lay. A typical stretch of the Dyle is shown opposite page 68.

Our leading infantry brigades took up their positions on the river on May the 11th, and by the 15th the front was held as shown on page 47 and in the sketch map on page 48. East of the Dyle the cavalry had made touch with the enemy for the first time on the 13th.

While the British troops had thus been able to occupy their new front without interference, the Dutch, Belgian, and French troops had met the first onslaught of the German armies farther to the east. In Holland the use of airborne troops covered by heavy bombing and followed up by tanks had enabled the Germans to get behind defences which had been planned to resist frontal attack. Already by the 13th coherent defence of the country was becoming impossible and it was clear that Holland could not hold out for long.

The Belgian plan was to fight a delaying action on the Albert Canal from Antwerp to the Meuse and thence along the Meuse from Liége to Namur, till the Allied forces could reach the Dyle. The Belgian Army was then to withdraw to the left sector of that line, between Louvain and the sea. But early on the opening morning of the campaign, before the German forces reached Maastricht (which is in the tongue of Holland, stretching south towards Liége), the Belgian defence of the Albert Canal front had been gravely prejudiced by the loss of the bridges at Briedgen, Veldwezelt and Vroenhoven, immediately west of Maastricht, and of the nearby frontier fortress of Eben Emael which was designed to protect them. For airborne forces, landed in rear of the bridges and on top of the fort, had seized the former and put the latter out of action almost before the defenders realised that the battle had begun, and although the Belgians won back and destroyed the bridge at Briedgen, the others remained firmly in German hands.[5] By the 13th of May the Belgian Army was conducting a fighting withdrawal towards the northern sector of the Allied front.

Further south the position was graver. The Ardennes country was not after all proving to be an effective obstacle to the advance of German armoured divisions. The French outpost screen of horsed

---

[5] *Belgium: The Official* (Belgian) *Account of what happened 1939-40.*

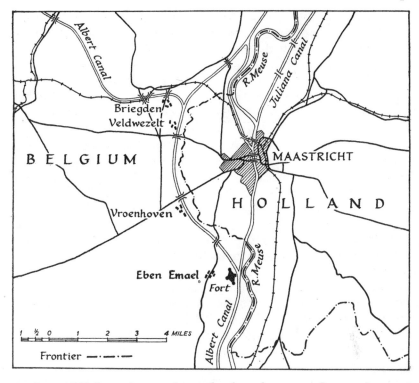

cavalry and light tanks was drawn back as the enemy forces advanced there, and by the night of the 12th all the outposts of the French Ninth Army had retired to the west of the Meuse. On that night advanced German troops crossed the Meuse in rubber dinghies at a number of points and by the 13th of May they had formed small bridgeheads on the western bank near Sedan and Dinant. The 'strong forces' which had been stationed by the French High Command where the main attack was expected were already in danger of having their position turned three days after the opening of the battle. For though the bridgeheads over the Meuse were as yet only small, the advanced German armoured divisions had reached the eastern bank and were ready to cross, while further west the French Ninth Army's move forward was not yet completed. 'In view of the imminence of attack the density achieved on the 13th of May in the defensive positions where battle was likely to take place, and the general organisation of resources, were far from satisfactory.[6]

On May the 13th, while our 48th and 4th Divisions moved eastward to support the divisions of I and II Corps on the Dyle, German armoured divisions away to the south began moving westward over the Meuse.

[6] Lyet, p. 46. See Appendix II, p. 375.

On May the 12th a momentous meeting had been held at the Chateau Casteau, five miles north-east of Mons. His Majesty the King of the Belgians, who had assumed command of the Belgian Army, and his aide-de-camp and chief military adviser, General Van Overstraeten, represented Belgium. M. Daladier and Generals Georges, Billotte, and Champon—the last-named was head of the French Military Mission at the Belgian Army Headquarters—represented France. General Pownall, representing Lord Gort, and Brigadier Swayne, head of the British Military Mission at General Georges' headquarters, attended from the British Expeditionary Force. The main purpose of the meeting was to secure co-ordination in the northern theatre of war. The Belgian Army was falling back to a position on the left of the British Expeditionary Force, acting under the independent command of the King. The French First Army, lying on the right of the British Expeditionary Force, was in the French First Group of Armies under General Billotte. The British Expeditionary Force, though under General Georges' command, was not under General Billotte. It was clearly desirable that the operations of all these forces should be interlocked, and when General Georges asked if the King of the Belgians and Lord Gort would be willing to accept co-ordination by General Billotte as his representative, the King, and General Pownall speaking for Lord Gort, readily agreed.

From now on therefore Lord Gort must look to General Billotte for orders of the French High Command; after this meeting he would no longer expect to receive direct orders from General Georges. For such an arrangement to be fully effective, the 'co-ordinator' must be able to appreciate the position of the commanders who look to him, and to translate directives from the High Command into practical orders which they can carry out. On the other hand the commanders whose actions he is to co-ordinate must have confidence in his judgement and be willing to act on his orders. In this instance the arrangement worked but haltingly, for neither of these conditions was ever wholly fulfilled.

The German break-through on the Meuse determined the whole course of the campaign and in particular the operations of the British Expeditionary Force. It will be well therefore to see how it came about that what was regarded by the French Command as a strong natural position fell so quickly, to understand why the defence failed and the attack succeeded almost without pause.

In the first place the French theory that the Ardennes country was 'impracticable for tanks and unsuitable for the deployment of any considerable armoured forces'[7] was proved to be mistaken. Provided

---

[7] Lyet, p. 46. See Appendix II, p. 375.

that there was careful planning and good organisation, the ground offered no serious hindrance to the rapid advance of considerable forces including numerous armoured divisions. Having regard to this fact and to the further fact that a thin screen, largely consisting of horsed cavalry and light tanks, was all the opposition to the enemy's advance, it is easy to understand how German mechanised forces reached the river so unexpectedly early.

They found there, as has been explained, only weak opposition. Even if the French Ninth Army had had time to complete its move forward it would still have been far weaker than the forces which the enemy could quickly bring against it. But in fact even its leading units were hardly in position when the Germans reached the river. 'On the left wing of the Ninth Army the manner of occupying the position was changed several times in two days by the arrival of divisions in echelon and by the juxtaposition of infantry and the cavalry that had withdrawn from the Ardennes. The result was bad liaison, an embryonic state of organisation of the ground, and defective subordination of command.'[8]

In the Second Army sector the new front was not yet fully organised when the enemy attacked west of Sedan. '. . . unfortunately the movement to establish the position still went on, and the battle was to start before staff and troops were familiar with their new tasks.'[9] As the Series B divisions involved had 'almost no Regular officers' and had no previous contact with the enemy, it is not difficult to understand the failure of the defence.

But the speed and success with which the enemy exploited this weakness are also noteworthy. Vigorous action brought them to the Meuse on the night of the 12th/13th. Infantry using rubber dinghies to cross the river established small bridgeheads in the night, but the first attempt to get armour across was frustrated by the defenders. A full attack was therefore ordered for the following afternoon, the preliminary bombardment being undertaken not by artillery but from the air. It was a new experience for the Allies, and in this case it was completely effective. The defending troops, their artillery positions, and their headquarters were subjected to heavy dive-bombing and its effect on some of the troops was, in the delicate phrase of the French historian, 'to weaken those reactions necessary for battle'.[10] Following quickly, German infantry enlarged the bridgeheads on the western bank and pushed on rapidly the construction of bridges for the armour to cross.

For the main German effort was not being directed through the

---

[8] Lyet, p. 47. See Appendix II, p. 375.
[9] Ibid. See Appendix II, p. 376.
[10] Ibid.

Belgian plain, where the strongest Allied forces in the north had been stationed to meet it, but through the Ardennes, where the weaker Ninth Army was to defend the Meuse. In fact, the German plan had been radically changed after the postponement of the attack originally ordered in January. Up to that date the French appreciation of German intentions had been correct. Now it was completely at fault. German security measures had successfully hidden their changed intentions. The strength of their total forces had been fairly accurately estimated by the Allies, but their new grouping and the changed plan for their deployment had not been discovered. It had not been realised that the main thrust was to be further south. As the adjoining sketch map shows, the German Army Group B (Colonel-General von Bock) facing Holland and the Belgian plain north of Liége had been given only twenty-eight divisions, three of them armoured. But south of Liége Army Group A (Colonel-General von Rundstedt) facing Luxembourg and the Ardennes had forty-four divisions, including seven armoured. Army Group C (Colonel-General Ritter von Leeb) facing the Maginot line from Longwy to Switzerland had only seventeen divisions and no armour. Behind the attacking army groups, well placed for use where needed, was a reserve of forty-five divisions, three times the size of the ill-placed French reserve. Moreover, co-operating with the two attacking army groups—A and B— were two 'Fleets' of the German Air Force, which together had about 3,700 aircraft when the offensive began. The German command as developed during early operations is shown in Appendix III.

 The evolution of the new German plan is discussed in a supplement on 'The Planning and Conduct of the German Campaign'. But neither the change of plan nor the consequential dispositions were known at this time. All that was known was that four days after the battle had been joined a German advance through the Ardennes had so far succeeded that leading units were already across the Meuse. If they were not stopped the Allied position on the Dyle would soon be outflanked, and, while the British forward divisions concentrated their attention on their immediate front, Lord Gort was already having to look over his right shoulder at what was happening in the south. The news from there went from bad to worse. On the 14th of May, in the words of Commandant Lyet, 'The Meuse position was forced on a front of about twenty kilometres. To restore the position we worked all day to mount a counter-attack towards Dinant but ... the counter-attack could not be launched.'[11] 'The situation was very serious, since the complete disorganisation of our routed divisions seemed to offer no hope of their rehabilitation. Facing the breach, into which about 500 German tanks were pouring, the imme-

---

[11] Lyet, p. 52. See Appendix II, p. 376.

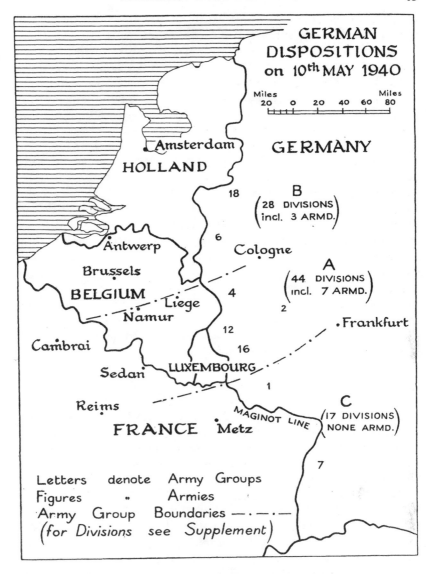

GERMAN
DISPOSITIONS
on 10th MAY 1940

Miles   Miles
20   0   20   40   60   80

GERMANY

Amsterdam

HOLLAND

18

B
(28 DIVISIONS
incl. 3 ARMD.)

6

Cologne

Antwerp

A
(44 DIVISIONS
incl. 7 ARMD.)

Brussels

BELGIUM

4

Liege

2

Namur

Frankfurt

12

Cambrai

16

Sedan   LUXEMBOURG

1

Reims

C
(17 DIVISIONS
NONE ARMD.)

MAGINOT LINE

FRANCE   Metz

7

Letters   denote   Army   Groups
Figures   "   Armies
Army   Group   Boundaries —.—.—
(for Divisions   see   Supplement)

diate reserves were infinitesimal . . . as to the reserves which General
Georges was sending to the nerve centre, they would not be in a
position to intervene for several days.'[12]

For, as the German attacks on airfields declined, their attacks on
the communications behind the Allied front increased in intensity and
with significant results. Most of the French Army's mechanical road
transport had been allocated to their First and Seventh Armies; to
move reserves which were stationed south of the Aisne they relied

[12] Lyet, p. 53. See Appendix II, p. 376.

mainly on slow horse-drawn transport or on the railway system. During these first few days the latter had been interrupted at so many crucial points that repairs could not keep pace with damage, and the movement of troops to the battle-zone or for the purpose of counter-attack became a slow, roundabout and precarious business. The Ninth Army and the Second Army sought to maintain touch but 'this stop-gap front had no cohesion on the morning of the 14th. The units of two armies were intermingled, liaison was bad. No commander co-ordinated the whole'. And 'On the south bank of the Meuse the battalions of the Ninth Army's extreme right were successively "rolled up" from their right.'[13]

Meanwhile the French Cavalry Corps, out in front of the French First Army astride the Gembloux gap, were heavily engaged and gradually forced back, fighting hard, till the main position held by the infantry was reached. At one point this was indeed penetrated by the enemy, but a counter-attack restored the position. The 12th Lancers and the other cavalry units in front of the British sector withdrew in conformity with the French on their right and during the 14th crossed the Dyle. The infantry outposts on the east bank of the river were at the same time withdrawn and bridges destroyed as the enemy approached our main position. By the afternoon of the 14th we were in contact along our whole front.

The War Diary of Bock's Army Group B records that the Sixth Army had been told that it was of the greatest importance 'to break through the enemy position between Louvain and Namur in order to prevent the French and Belgian forces establishing themselves in this position'.[14] They lost no time in trying but our artillery (which played a large part throughout the campaign) was already disposed in depth and the concentration which they put down in the late afternoon caused the enemy to draw back; at about seven o'clock in the evening, however, they made the first of a series of attempts to capture Louvain where Major-General B. L. Montgomery's 3rd Division held the front. The 2nd Royal Ulster Rifles beat them off, but the 1st Grenadier Guards' forward posts on the east bank were forced to draw back to the line of the river.

Throughout the next day, May the 15th, attacks were resumed along the whole British front, the German IV Corps attacking in the 2nd Division's sector near Wavre and their XI Corps the 3rd Division in action at Louvain. Fighting began on the front of the 2nd Division during the morning, where elements of the German 31st Division made a small penetration across the Dyle in the sector held by the 6th Brigade. This was cleared up in the afternoon by counter-

---

[13] Lyet, pp. 53, 54. See Appendix II, p. 376.
[14] See Appendix II, p. 376.

DYLE FRONT
British Dispositions 15th May 1940

(a) Infantry

	Divisional Reserve	Front
II CORPS — 4 Div 3 Division	8 Bde { 2nd E. Yorkshire 4th R. Berkshire 1st Suffolk	7 Gds Bde { 1st Coldstream Gds 2nd Grenadier Gds 1st Grenadier Gds 9 Bde { 2nd R. Ulster Rifles 2nd Lincolnshire 1st K.O.S.B
I CORPS — 1 Division	1 Gds Bde { 2nd Coldstream Gds 2nd Hampshire 3rd Grenadier Gds	2 Bde { 2nd N. Staffordshire 6th Gordons 1st Loyal Regt 3 Bde { 1st Duke of Wellington's 2nd Foresters 1st K. Shropshire L.I.
2 Division 48 Div	5 Bde { 1st Camerons 7th Worcestershire 2nd Dorsetshire	6 Bde { 1st R. Welch Fusiliers 1st R. Berkshire 2nd Durham L.I. 4 Bde { 1st/8th Lancs Fusiliers 2nd R. Norfolk 1st R. Scots

(b) Royal Armoured Corps, Artillery, & Machine Guns.

	GHQ & Corps Troops	Divisional Artillery & Attached Machine Guns
II CORPS	5th R. Inniskilling Dragoon Gds 15th/19th King's R. Hussars 2nd R. Horse Artillery 2nd Medium Regt 53rd Medium Regt 88th Army Field Regt 59th Medium Regt 53rd Lt. Anti-Aircraft Regt 8th Middlesex (MG) 4th Gordons (MG)	3 Division { 33rd Field Regt 7th Field Regt 76th Field Regt 20th Anti-Tank Regt 1st/7th Middlesex (MG) 2nd Middlesex (MG)
I CORPS	12th R. Lancers 13th/18th R. Hussars 4th/7th R. Dragoon Gds 1st Army Tank Bde 1st Medium Regt 140th Army Field Regt 3rd Medium Regt 1st Heavy Regt 98th Army Field Regt 5th Medium Regt 61st Medium Regt 63rd Medium Regt 52nd Lt. Anti-Aircraft Regt 4th Cheshire (MG) 6th Argyll & Sutherland (MG)	1 Division { 67th Field Regt 2nd Field Regt 19th Field Regt 21st Anti-Tank Regt 2nd Cheshire (MG) 2 Division { 99th Field Regt 16th Field Regt 10th Field Regt 13th Anti-Tank Regt 2nd Manchester (MG)

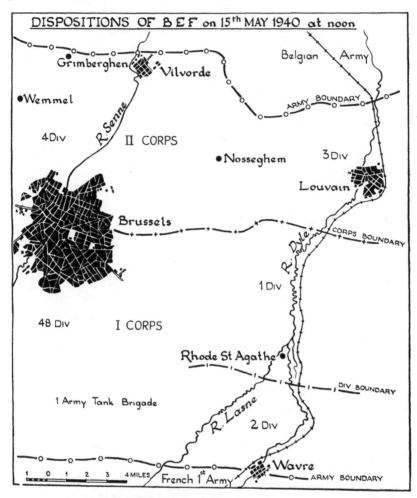

attack, the 1st Royal Welch Fusiliers and the 2nd Durham Light
Infantry being chiefly involved in fighting which continued throughout the day. Second-Lieutenant R. W. Annand of the Durham Light
Infantry was awarded the Victoria Cross for his gallantry in this
action. A renewed attempt to take Louvain from the 3rd Division
had started earlier, prefaced by a two-hour bombardment of the area
north of the city held by the 9th Brigade and the 7th Guards Brigade.
Here a tangle of railway lines and sidings, goods yards, sheds and
warehouses made it a difficult area to preserve inviolate. Units of two
German divisions succeeded for a time in pressing back some posts of
the 2nd Royal Ulster Rifles, but a counter-attack by the 1st King's
Own Scottish Borderers restored the position and drove the enemy
out of the railway yards. North of Louvain the 1st Coldstream Guards
were heavily attacked and their right company was for a time forced

back. But here too a counter-attack in which light tanks of the 5th Royal Inniskilling Dragoon Guards took part drove the enemy out and completely re-established the front. All other assaults were successfully driven off. The German Sixth Army reported to Army Group B that they had not succeeded in penetrating the Dyle defences at any point.

In the afternoon it was learned that the French First Army on our immediate right had been heavily engaged and that a 5,000-yard breach had been made in their front where there was no river protection. Lord Gort, who had established his Command Post at Lenneck St Quentin, to the west of Brussels, offered to lend General Billotte a brigade of the 48th Division, then in I Corps reserve, to help in restoring the situation. But the French Commander decided to withdraw the First Army to a line between Châtelet and Ottignies, and the British I Corps had to conform by swinging back its right from Rhode St Agathe along the line of the River Lasne to link up with the French in their new position. The Wavre sector of the Dyle was evacuated on the night of the 15th/16th under cover of remorseless artillery fire on the enemy's advancing troops.

While this adjustment was taking place in the right or southern sector of our front, II Corps stationed the 4th Division in a defensive position behind our left flank, with two brigades on the road between Nosseghem and Grimberghen and the third in a middle position behind them near Wemmel. The 5th Division in G.H.Q. reserve was moving up to the Senne, having now to stem an almost overwhelming stream of refugees flooding westwards. The 50th Division was on the Dendre: the 42nd and 44th were working on the defences of the Escaut.

In the north, catastrophe had overtaken Holland. The troops which had pierced her frontiers or landed from the skies were not, in truth, numerically greater than those of Holland, but the enemy had two decisive advantages. While the Dutch Army had extensive positions to defend and was to a large extent rendered immobile by the very nature of its task, the enemy was free to concentrate his force at points of his own selection; and he had an air force and armour against which Holland had no effective defence. One position after another was turned and the enemy decided to end the campaign by an overwhelming demonstration of German air power. Rotterdam was accordingly bombed till most of the business heart of the city lay in ruins. The French Seventh Army had carried out the role allotted to it. It had moved with all speed across Belgium in an endeavour to support Belgian and Dutch forces at the mouth of the Scheldt. But there it had suffered severe losses, had run short of ammunition and had not succeeded (how could it?) in materially affecting the issue of the fighting in Holland. On the 14th of May the

E

Commander of the Dutch Army gave orders to cease fire. In five days Holland had been conquered.[15]

Three days before, a composite battalion, hastily formed from the 2nd Irish Guards and a company of the 2nd Welsh Guards, engaged on training near Camberley, had been sent to The Hook to co-operate with the local commander in operations designed to safe-guard the Netherlands Government and restore the position at The Hague; but in the event of the Government evacuating The Hague, the battalion was to withdraw to The Hook for re-embarkation. They found on arrival that no local operations were in progress and that the position at The Hague was obscure. Until the situation be-came clearer they took up a defensive position round The Hook. There they were bombed repeatedly and saw parachute troops being landed in the distance but there were no enemy troops in the vicinity. On the 14th of May, when it became clear that Dutch resistance was almost at an end, the battalion was re-embarked on the orders of the Cabinet. The British Military Mission to the Dutch Army Head-quarters returned with them.

It would only be necessary to mention thus briefly an episode which had little military significance and no direct influence on the course of the land campaign, if it were not for the fact that its setting was in a series of naval operations of larger purpose, longer duration, and more lasting importance. As early as October 1939, when an attack on the Low Countries was first threatened, the Admiralty had pre-pared plans for operations off the coasts of Holland and Belgium. Their aim in such an event would be to clear Allied shipping from the threatened ports; to bring home diplomatic staffs and other important personages; to prevent Dutch or Belgian harbours from capture by the enemy with their installations and oil stores intact; and finally to lay a defensive minefield off the Dutch shores in order to hamper coastal movements by enemy surface vessels. Admiral the Hon. Sir Reginald A. R. Plunkett-Ernle-Erle-Drax, Commander-in-Chief The Nore, was to be in charge of all these operations excepting only port demolitions, which would be the responsibility of Vice-Admiral Sir Bertram H. Ramsay, Flag Officer Commanding Dover. The opera-tions would involve a considerable number of warships and, although by the time the enemy's invasion of the Low Countries actually began loss and damage inflicted on the German fleet in the Norwegian campaign had made it unlikely that our ships would be engaged by surface vessels, they were liable to be attacked by U-boats and certain to be attacked from the air. When, therefore, in the first week of May, intelligence pointed to an early offensive in the west, the Nore Command was reinforced by the *Galatea* and the *Arethusa* of the

---

[15] Lt.-Colonel P. L. G. Doorman: *Military Operations in the Netherlands from 10th–17th May, 1940.* Allen & Unwin, 1944.

2nd Cruiser Squadron, by the cruiser *Birmingham* and by eight destroyers of the 2nd and 5th Flotillas. All these were from the Home Fleet and were stationed at Harwich. As it was feared that Holland would not for long be able to withstand a German assault, all was in readiness when the campaign opened on the 10th of May. On that day the minelayer *Princess Victoria* and the 20th (minelaying) Flotilla sailed to lay the defensive minefield off the Dutch coast; cruisers went to Ijmuiden to bring off (by previous arrangement) the Dutch gold reserves and diamond stocks and to clear the port of merchant shipping; and four destroyers sailed for Ijmuiden, Flushing, The Hook, and Antwerp with demolition parties which included military elements to assist in the destruction of large oil stocks in or near those ports. Reinforcements of flotilla vessels were ordered by the Admiralty to the Nore Command and Dover. The British Military Mission to Dutch Army Headquarters was also landed at Flushing.

On the 11th of May the *Arethusa* and two destroyers escorted to England two merchantmen carrying gold and diamonds. By then it was already clear that the situation on land was rapidly getting worse and a Royal Marine guard was hastily sent across in two destroyers to ensure the safety of demolition parties, followed shortly after by the composite Guards battalion whose short stay at The Hook has been recorded above. On the 12th the destroyer leader *Codrington* fetched the Crown Princess and her family from Ijmuiden and on the 13th the *Hereward* brought to England Her Majesty Queen Wilhelmina and her suite and Sir Nevile Bland, British Minister to the Netherlands. Later in the day members of the Netherlands Government and of Allied Legation staffs sailed in the destroyer *Windsor*. On the 14th destroyers brought the Guards battalion back.

During these hectic four days, when rumour was rife and news uncertain, the demolition parties which had been landed had a difficult time, for the Dutch authorities on the spot were not at first convinced that the drastic measures we proposed were immediately necessary. Eventually those at Amsterdam, Flushing, Rotterdam and The Hook agreed that the time for the destruction of oil stocks had come and large quantities were destroyed or rendered useless at all four centres. Some demolitions were also effected in the ports, but only Ijmuiden, with the effective co-operation of the Dutch fortress Commandant, was blocked effectively. At other places delays imposed on the starting of preparations prevented the completion of the work, though some ships and shore parties stayed till the 17th—two days after the Dutch cease-fire.

All this time enemy aircraft were busy bombing and sowing mines, and our destroyers and minesweepers carried out their arduous duties in mine-infested waters under almost continuous air attack. Some air cover was afforded by Blenheims and Hurricanes of the .

Royal Air Force flown from England, but the former had not speed enough to intercept the enemy dive bombers and the latter could not remain in the air long enough to give protection for more than short periods. The destroyers were almost incessantly in action and as long as they had sea room in which to manœuvre losses were avoided, but in the narrow approaches and confined waters of the ports self-defence was inevitably handicapped. The destroyers *Winchester* and *Westminster* were seriously damaged and the *Valentine* was lost. When these operations off the Dutch coast were completed, however, it was clear that achievement had well outweighed the cost. Allied shipping which was of great value had been secured; the Dutch Royal Family and Government had been transferred to England; gold reserves and diamonds had been placed beyond the enemy's reach; large stocks of oil had been denied him; and something had been done to delay his immediate full use of Dutch ports and harbour installations. The only ships of the Royal Netherlands Navy which were stationed in home ports at this time—a cruiser, a destroyer, and two submarines —had also moved safely to English harbours.

Although it was hoped that the enemy's assault on Belgium could be held, it seemed only prudent to prepare for the possible loss of Antwerp. As soon as the German offensive opened on May the 10th, accordingly, the destroyer *Brilliant* had sailed for Antwerp with naval and military parties to clear Allied shipping and prepare for demolitions and the destruction of oil. By noon on the 14th twenty-six Allied merchantmen, fifty tugs and six hundred barges, dredgers and floating cranes had been cleared for England. Some demolitions were prepared, but King Leopold forbade execution of the more important until the threatening situation on May the 17th brought his consent. Then 150,000 tons of oil were rendered unusable and the entrances to the docks and basins were blocked. But much that would have discomfited the enemy (and was therefore desirable from the British point of view) had to be left undone. Naval operations off the more westerly Belgian coast reached their climax later; it will be better to describe them in their due order as the story of the campaign unfolds.

One unusual form of operation, operation 'Royal Marine', had been prepared during the winter. It was designed to damage the heavy traffic of barges and other water transport using some of the main German rivers. Floating mines were to be launched into these rivers (1) from tributaries and (2) from the air. The first was a naval operation, carried out by Royal Marines under command of Commander G. R. S. Wellby, R.N. It started as soon as the German attack began and by May the 24th over 2,300 floating mines had been streamed into the Rhine, Moselle and Meuse. The second method was only used by the Royal Air Force in the closing days of the campaign and then on a small scale. There is evidence that damage was inflicted on the enemy but its extent could not be ascertained with accuracy in the circumstances which then existed. Later in the war similar methods were used with great effect.

Meanwhile what of the position in the air? The fact that our fighters played an important part in keeping the enemy air forces clear of the area through which the British Expeditionary Force was advancing has been noted already. The fighters of the Air Component, reinforced by two additional squadrons on the first day of the battle and by thirty-two more aircraft and their pilots three days later, flew without resting, as did the three fighter squadrons with the Advanced Air Striking Force. For the latter the first task was to protect airfields we were using and the fact that only one airfield sustained any serious damage (page 37) is evidence of their success in this duty. Their second task was to give fighter cover over targets attacked by our bombers. It will be seen presently what that involved and will be realised how greatly the odds were against them. They had not the requisite strength to be fully successful, yet, undaunted by the enemy's superior numbers, undeterred by their own fatigue, the fighters of both forces went up again and again to contest for air mastery over the zones they were committed to defend. They lost heavily—the three Air Striking Force squadrons lost twenty aircraft and the Air Component forty-one in the first six days—but they brought down a large number of the enemy. Our fighter pilots proved to themselves that in skill and in the qualities of the aircraft they flew they were more than a match for the German Air Force. Unfortunately many of the detailed records of their deeds were lost during subsequent moves.

Bombers of the Air Component and of the Advanced Air Striking Force had in the same time sustained without hesitation even heavier losses. The detailed account of their actions makes splendid but sad reading. It is only possible to describe them in broad outline, to illustrate them by a few examples, and to estimate their results. In conformity with prearranged plans, these medium bombers were mainly engaged in attacks against enemy columns, concentrations, and communications behind the enemy front. They soon found that such targets were strongly guarded at high level by large numbers of fighters and at low level by quick-firing anti-aircraft artillery and machine guns. Our fighter forces were not strong enough to contest successfully the enemy's air mastery over his own positions, so our bombers mostly went in to attack at low level, trusting to speed and surprise to save them from ground defence. But their speed was not great enough and the enemy's defence was too strong to give them more than an outside chance to return unscathed, if at all, from such sorties.

Thus on May the 10th four waves, each of eight Battles, attacked successively German columns advancing through Luxembourg into France under cover of large fighter forces. Six of our fighters went up in an effort to clear the way while thirty-two Battles of Nos. 12, 103, 105, 142, 150, 218 and 226 Squadrons attacked at low level in spite of heavy fire from the ground. Thirteen were shot down and all the remaining nineteen were damaged. On May the 11th eight Battles of No. 218 Squadron went up to attack an enemy column on the borders of Germany. One returned, badly damaged. He reported that one of his comrades had made a forced landing in France; he knew that two others had been shot down; of the remaining four there was no news at all. On May the 12th one outstanding action was the attack on the bridges near Maastricht, over which the enemy was pressing forward into Belgium. The bridges and the advancing columns had been attacked the day before by both British and French bombers, apparently with little success. It was, of course, an area of prime importance to the enemy, for it was his main gateway to central Belgium; as such, it was strongly protected by his fighters and ground defence. Knowing this, Air Marshal Barratt ordered that the crews of the attacking planes should be volunteers. Volunteers were asked for from No. 12 Squadron—and the whole squadron volunteered. So six crews were chosen by lot, though in the end only five were actually employed; for cover they were given two squadrons of fighters from the Air Component and ten Hurricanes from the Advanced Air Striking Force. But these were, of course, no protection from ground defences. The five Battles duly attacked. One returned so badly damaged that the pilot ordered the crew to bale out over Belgium; he alone brought it home. Of the rest nothing more was learned—or has been learned since. The evidence of the surviving pilot and other contemporary records are somewhat vague and a little contradictory. But there is no doubt that these five crews drove knowingly into an inferno of enemy fire and pressed home their suicidal attack to its inevitable end. The pilot and navigator of the aircraft which led the attack, Flying Officer D. E. Garland and Sergeant T. Gray, were each posthumously awarded the Victoria Cross—the first to be awarded in the campaign. The German War Diary of XVI Corps records that on May the 11th the Maastricht bridges and the marching columns of the 4th Armoured Division 'are separately attacked by enemy bombers. Considerable delays result from this.'[16] General Guderian's XIX Corps War Diary notes on the 13th that 'Enemy fighter activity is exceptionally vigorous; in the evening the enemy carried out repeated air attacks against the crossing-points and in doing so sustains heavy casualties' and adds

---

[16] See Appendix II, p. 376.

'Repeated requests for increased fighter protection are without apparent success'.[17]

On the first day of hostilities French General Headquarters expressed appreciation of our bombers' attacks on German forces in the Bouillon area and considered that these 'had checked the German advance and saved a serious situation'. But it was soon clear that, taking our air operations as a whole, this was an over-generous estimate. Their effects cannot be measured accurately. Certainly they caused some delay in the early passage of the Meuse, both at Maastricht and further south, but it was insufficient to affect significantly the course of the battle. And whatever value is attached to air operations in the opening days of the campaign, the figures given above show that the cost was prohibitive. If the same rate of loss continued there would soon be no bombers left. But there was to be one more expensive day of desperate effort to stop the German advance in the neighbourhood of Sedan before bomber policy was modified.

In operations on May the 14th, in which the French Air Force also took part, six Blenheims bombed road and rail communications and two enemy columns near Breda in Holland to relieve pressure on the French Seventh Army, fought off an enemy fighter, eluded heavy ground fire, and returned without loss. It seemed at first that luck had turned, for by nine o'clock in the morning ten sorties had also been carried out by bombers of the Advanced Air Striking Force against the enemy's pontoon bridges near Sedan and all had returned. But by mid-day there was grave news from the same area, where the enemy had greatly enlarged his bridgehead. General Gamelin and General Georges both asked Air Marshal Barratt for the maximum support, and this was promptly given. The Battles and Blenheims of Nos. 71, 75, and 76 Wings attacked in successive waves in spite of strong opposition from the enemy's fighters and ground defence. The cost of this concentrated effort can best be shown in bald figures:

No. 76 Wing
No. 12 Squadron. Of five Battles sent against enemy columns four were lost.
No. 142 Squadron. Of eight Battles ordered to attack bridges four were lost.
No. 226 Squadron. Of six Battles also attacking bridges three were lost.

No. 71 Wing
No. 105 Squadron. Of eleven Battles which attacked bridges six were lost.

[17] See Appendix II, p. 375.

No. 150 Squadron. Of four Battles also attacking bridges four were lost.

No. 114 Squadron. Of two Blenheims which attacked columns one was lost.

No. 139 Squadron. Of six Blenheims (flown by No. 114 Squadron crews) against enemy columns four were lost.

No. 75 Wing

No. 88 Squadron. Of ten Battles which attacked bridges and columns one was lost.

No. 103 Squadron. Of eight Battles sent against bridges three were lost.

No. 218 Squadron. Of eleven Battles attacking bridges and columns ten were lost.

Fifty-six per cent of the seventy-one bombers employed were lost in action that afternoon. In such circumstances results are hard to determine. Photographic evidence was not obtainable. But the German XIX Corps War Diary's situation summary at 8 p.m. notes that 'The completion of the military bridge at Donchery had not yet been carried out owing to heavy flanking artillery fire and long bombing attacks on the bridging point . . . Throughout the day all three divisions have had to endure constant air attack—especially at the crossings and bridging points. Our fighter cover is inadequate. Requests [for increased fighter protection] are still unsuccessful.'[18] And the summary of the *Luftwaffe*'s operations includes a note of 'vigorous enemy fighter activity through which our close reconnaissance in particular is severely impeded'.[19] It is clear from what meagre records remain that such fighter protection as was available was given to our bombers but that this was inadequate to cover seventy-one bombers against the strength of German opposition over the target area. Later in the evening twenty-eight bombers, Blenheims of Bomber Command, attacked again with stronger fighter protection. Five were lost and two more made forced landings in France. In all, out of 109 Battles and Blenheims which had attacked enemy columns and communications in the Sedan area, forty-five had been lost, and the impossibility of continuing such attacks by day seemed proved. On May the 15th daylight bombing was cut down. Only twenty-eight aircraft were employed and only four failed to return. But the German XIX Corps War Diary says 'Corps no longer has at its disposal its own long-range reconnaissance . . . [Reconnaissance squadrons] are no longer in a position to carry out vigorous, extensive reconnaissance, as, owing to casualties, more than half of their aircraft are not now available'.[20]

The Lysanders and Blenheims of the Air Component and the

---

[18] See Appendix II, p. 376.
[19] Ibid., p. 377.
[20] Ibid.

squadron (No. 212) of Spitfires specially equipped for photographic reconnaissance were continuously engaged on both tactical and strategic observation. By May the 15th the density of refugee traffic flooding steadily westwards was a theme which recurred frequently in their reports of enemy movements. At one time, enemy transport on roads twenty to thirty miles east of Louvain and Wavre appeared to be virtually held up by the dense civilian procession.

In view of the heavy daytime losses the Battles of the Advanced Air Striking Force were on May the 15th switched to night bombing in the Sedan area and, although results could be neither so effective nor so well observed, the change-over was justified by the fact that all returned safely.

But the night of May the 15th/16th is chiefly memorable in Air Force history as the first on which the Royal Air Force attacked German industrial objectives in the Ruhr. Till then the heavy bombers were held back from such targets in Germany by the British Government, partly to conform with French policy but also because they were themselves determined not to risk the infliction of civilian casualties so long as Germany observed similar restraint. The ruthless bombing of Rotterdam on May the 14th showed, however, that no regard for humanitarian principle influenced German policy. Their action was dictated solely by military convenience, and if this was to be the criterion it was now imperative to divert the *Luftwaffe*, if possible, from its concentration on France and Belgium. Even though civilian casualties might result, it was calculated that a British attack on vital objectives in the Ruhr would provoke the enemy to transfer some of his attention to this country and so weaken his attack on France and Belgium.

On this first night seventy-eight heavy bombers were directed from England against oil targets, nine against blast furnaces and steel works, and nine against railway marshalling yards; all were given as secondary objectives self-illuminating targets such as coke ovens and blast furnaces and, as a last resort, marshalling yards. Sixteen failed to locate any targets and brought their bombs home again; only twenty-four found oil plants, some of which were reported to have blown up and some to have been left burning fiercely. The remainder had to be content with marshalling yards. But all returned safely, which augured well for the future and for the vital conservation of British air power.

On May the 14th M. Paul Reynaud appealed for stronger fighter forces, urging that 'if we are to win this battle, which might be decisive for the whole war, it is necessary to send at once, if possible today, ten more squadrons'. Lord Gort and Air Marshal Barratt made equally urgent appeals for additional squadrons to protect our own bombers, airfields and troops. But in England the expectation that the German air attacks would shortly be directed against this country reinforced the unshakable opposition of Air Chief Marshal Sir Hugh Dowding (Air Officer Commanding-in-Chief, Fighter Command) to the dispatch of further fighter squadrons to France. Already, in his view, so many had been sent that home defence was endangered, and after hearing his argument the War Cabinet decided not to send out additional squadrons at the moment, though they ordered preparatory steps for the early despatch of ten squadrons in case it should be decided to send them later.

Meanwhile the toll of fighters in France continued. In the battle zone our small patrols were contending with enemy forces of twenty to thirty bombers protected by large numbers of fighters, and the Air Component and the Advanced Air Striking Force on May the 15th lost twenty fighters in the forward areas and on the constantly compelling task of guarding their own airfields, some of which were now threatened by the enemy's advancing army.

It is not possible to state with certainty the number of enemy aircraft destroyed by the Royal Air Force in these six days. A daily return was issued by the Quartermaster-General of the German Air Ministry. It does not show whether aircraft were lost through the action of the British or French aircraft or from the fire of ground defences, but its totals are likely to be accurate, for it was on the basis of this return that replacements were claimable. The total German air losses on operations, as shown in the return for these first six days of the campaign, were 539 aircraft destroyed and 137 damaged in operations over France and the Low Countries.

British losses in the same days were 248, including all aircraft which failed to return from operations or were destroyed on the ground, and those damaged and irrecoverable in the circumstances of the campaign.

Just before midnight on May the 15th the most northerly units of the Advanced Air Striking Force were ordered to move to airfields further south, and an hour and a half later Air Marshal Barratt closed his Advanced Headquarters at Chauny and moved back to Main Headquarters at Coulommiers.

On May the 10th Mr Chamberlain's Government had resigned and a National Government had been formed by Mr Winston Churchill. The Conservative, Liberal and Labour parties were all represented, differences of opinion and conflicting loyalties being, in Mr Churchill's phrase, 'all drowned by the cannonade'. In the new Government Mr Churchill was not only Prime Minister and First Lord of the Treasury, but also Minister of Defence. Mr A. V. Alexander became First Lord of the Admiralty, Mr Anthony Eden Secretary of State for War, and Sir Archibald Sinclair Secretary of State for Air.

CHAPTER IV

WITHDRAWAL TO THE ESCAUT

16th May to 19th May, 1940

NEWS from the French front continued to grow hourly more disquieting. If the penetration of the Meuse front led to further withdrawal of the French First Army our troops on the Dyle would be left in a dangerous salient on either side of Louvain. At five o'clock on the morning of the 16th Lord Gort therefore sent Major-General T. R. Eastwood to Caudry to learn General Billotte's intentions. There he was shown orders which the French commander was preparing to issue that day directing the withdrawal of the First Army, the British Expeditionary Force, and the Belgian Army, to the line of the Escaut. The movement was to be so carried out that on successive nights the following lines would be held:

Night of 16th/17th   Charleroi–Brussels–Willebroeck Canal (known to the British Army as the line of the *Senne*).

Night of 17th/18th   Maubeuge–Mons–Ath–River Dendre to Termonde—thence the line of River Escaut to Antwerp and the sea (known to the British Army as the *Dendre* line).

Night of 18th/19th   The frontier defences to Maulde—the line of River Escaut to Ghent—thence the canal to Terneuzen (known to the British Army as the *Escaut* line).

The major portion of the French Seventh Army (on the British left) was to be moved south. General Eastwood further ascertained from General Billotte that the brigade of the 48th Division on loan to the French First Army was to be returned at once; that it was the intention to fight during the day on the 'lines' laid down and retire at night; that there was no present intention of retiring beyond the line of the Escaut; and that General Billotte's headquarters would move to Douai that afternoon.

General Eastwood lost no time in informing Lord Gort and the latter proceeded at once to issue a warning order: the British Expeditionary Force would retire that night to the line Charleroi–Brussels–Willebroeck Canal, i.e. the Senne line. At eleven o'clock that morning he held a conference at I Corps Headquarters at which he described the situation and the plan of retirement. Major-General Needham, head of the British Military Mission at Belgian Army

Headquarters, attended the conference and left to report the decisions taken to the Belgian Command. On his way he was seriously hurt in a car accident and some time elapsed before either British or Belgian Headquarters was informed of the accident. Only then did Belgian Headquarters learn of the steps being taken by the British Expeditionary Force that night in compliance with General Billotte's order to withdraw.

When shortly afterwards orders to retire became known at the British front, the soldiery were puzzled and disappointed. Less than a week before they had advanced sixty miles to meet the enemy. They had met him on the Dyle and had so far defeated his attempts to break their line. They were in great heart and full of confidence. And now they were to retire! To tell them that miles away to the south the French front had broken did not seem to them a sufficient explanation. John Buchan's description of the men of the old Army was still largely true of British soldiers and its truth was to become more and more apparent in the days which followed. 'They generally took a dark view of the immediate prospect; therefore they were never seriously depressed. They had an unshakable confidence in the ultimate issue; therefore they never thought it worth mentioning. They were always slightly puzzled; therefore they could never be completely at a loss; for the man who insists on having the next steps neatly outlined before he starts will be unnerved if he cannot see his way; whereas others will drive on cheerfully into the mist, because they have been there before, and know that on the further side there is clear sky.'[1]

If the infantry facing the enemy across the Dyle could hardly be expected to appreciate the significance of what was happening on the Meuse, the gravity of the situation there was obvious enough to the higher command. Early on the 15th General Billotte had informed General Gamelin that 'the Ninth Army is in a critical situation: all its front is pushed back'[2] and had suggested that General Giraud was the man best fitted to 'revive this failing army'.[3] Now that retirement to the Escaut was ordered, all but two divisions of General Giraud's French Seventh Army were being moved in rear of the British Expeditionary Force towards the gap in the south.

On this day (May the 16th) the French High Command made further urgent requests for additional air protection and both Lord Gort and Air Marshal Barratt strongly endorsed the demand for additional fighter squadrons. The War Cabinet decided that the equivalent of four further squadrons should be sent immediately, and

---

[1] Buchan: *The King's Grace*. Hodder and Stoughton, 1935, p. 146.
[2] Général G. Roton: *Années Cruciales*. Charles-Lavauzelle, Paris, 1947 (hereafter referred to as Roton), p. 174. See Appendix II, p. 377.
[3] Ibid.

eight flights left for France during that afternoon and the following morning. This decision had hardly been taken when the Prime Minister, on a visit to France, telegraphed urging that six more fighter squadrons should be sent. At this point the Air Staff advised that the limited number of airfields and servicing units in France made it undesirable to base further squadrons there, so it was agreed that six squadrons of Hurricanes should be concentrated in the south of England and should fly to France daily for operations over the battlefield. Thus the equivalent of ten extra squadrons for which the French had asked was operating from French or English bases by the 17th.

Meanwhile the pace at which the advanced units of the German Army Group A were advancing brought its own embarrassments to the German Command. On May the 15th the Army Group A War Diary notes the growing vulnerability of their southern flank: '. . . the question has arisen for the first time as to whether it may not become necessary temporarily to halt the motorised forces on the Oise . . . the enemy is in no circumstances to be allowed to achieve any kind of success, even if it be only a local success, on the Aisne or later in the Laon region. This would have a more detrimental effect on operations as a whole than would a temporary slowing-down of our motorised forces'.[4] And early on the 16th, after learning that troops of the 6th Armoured Division had by then reached Liart and Montcornet, Rundstedt issued orders by telephone that only advanced units of the Fourth and Twelfth Armies were to pass the line Beaumont–Hirson–Montcornet–Guignicourt, though bridgeheads over the Oise were to be seized between Guise and La Fère. The Aisne flank was to be covered as the armies closed up; and the Second Army was to be brought forward with all speed so that when it had made the southern flank more secure from French attack the front of the advance could be broadened.

Thus while General Billotte was ordering a retreat from the Dyle to the Escaut the German armies were closing up in preparation for a fresh advance. The bulk of the motorised units of the German Fourth Army and some of the infantry divisions reached the French frontier fortifications south-east of Maubeuge during the day, while the Twelfth Army, too, closed up to the line laid down for them. 'Army Group Headquarters had no doubt', says the Army Group A War Diary, 'that if motorised formations were to continue their push in advance of the Twelfth Army they would probably be able to cross the Oise between Guise and La Fère without difficulty. Their commanding officers are convinced of this and would like to act accordingly, especially Generals Guderian and von Kleist. But look-

---

[4] See Appendix II, p. 377.

ing at operations as a whole the risk involved does not seem to be justified. The extended flank between La Fère and Rethel is too sensitive, especially in the Laon area. This southern flank is just an invitation for an enemy attack. . . . If the spearheads of the attack are temporarily halted it will be possible to effect a certain stiffening of the threatened flank within twenty-four hours.'[5]

For the time being, therefore, Rundstedt ordered that the Sambre and the Oise should not be passed without his authorisation and when the Commander-in-Chief (Colonel-General von Brauchitsch) visited his headquarters during the day he endorsed Rundstedt's decision.

Only at Louvain, which the enemy made further and equally unsuccessful attempts to capture, was the British front seriously tested on the 16th. Again the 3rd Division's Louvain sector was heavily and continuously shelled. Again it was on the 2nd Royal Ulster Rifles and the 1st Coldstream Guards that the main attack fell, though this time the Belgian troops on our left were also involved and were forced back. But again the British position was held intact till withdrawal to the Senne line began that night.

The somewhat complicated movements of the following days, in which the Allied front was withdrawn successively to the Senne, the Dendre, and the Escaut, were a testing time for the troops. Frequent changes and the organisation of each new position gave them little opportunity for sleep or relaxation. Fortunately the enemy did not at first follow up very vigorously. Having failed to penetrate the Dyle front on May the 15th, Bock had ordered a 'prepared attack' for the 17th, designed to break through between Wavre and Louvain. By then however the British front had been withdrawn to the Senne, and for the most part without enemy interference, although Army Group B had given emphatic directions that the attacking forces were 'to follow up their thrust forthwith' if the enemy attempted to escape. The Royal Engineers had a busy time and the effectiveness of their demolitions of bridges and river crossings as each line was evacuated helped considerably to delay the enemy's advance.

The general plan of withdrawal was for the two front-line brigades of each division to thin out and finally retire through the reserve line held by the third brigade. This rearguard withdrew later through a screen of cavalry, machine guns, anti-tank guns and sappers who in their turn fell back when the new position was firmly occupied. With a few minor exceptions all went according to plan. In one or two instances river bridges were destroyed before the last troops had crossed and some equipment could not be got away. There were some failures in transport arrangements which involved the infantry

---

[5] See Appendix II, p. 377.

in long marches. The 6th Brigade (2nd Division), who had been holding the Lasne position, marched forty miles in twenty-seven hours after having been in close contact with the enemy for thirty-six hours. The Gunners too had a gruelling time, deploying their guns to cover one line after another, siting new positions, getting in and getting out again when the next move required it, and handicapped in all their moves by refugees fleeing to the west.

In accordance with General Billotte's order the line of the Charleroi–Willebroeck Canal (the Senne line) was held throughout the 17th and the only anxiety was caused by the position of the right and left wings of the British front. The French First Army on the right were being heavily attacked towards the southern wing of their frontage which ran back to the Sambre. The frontier defences south of Maubeuge were lost, while remnants of the Ninth Army tried, without much success, to reconstitute a line on the Sambre from Landrecies southwards. South of the gap made by the German break-through other French divisions were moving up to establish a defensive line on the Aisne–Somme, and it became evident to the enemy that defence rather than attack was the immediate French aim on their flank. Rundstedt decided that, this being so, it would be safe to make a further advance and he ordered Kleist to push forward 'strong advanced units' next day (the 18th) to the zone Cambrai–St Quentin while he closed his main force up to the Oise. Brauchitsch, still anxious about the Aisne flank, rang up Rundstedt urging that the infantry defence of the Aisne flank should be strengthened. And Hitler, who visited Rundstedt's headquarters, is reported in the Army Group War Diary as saying 'At the moment decision depends not so much on a rapid thrust to the Channel, as on the ability to secure as quickly as possible an absolutely sound *defence* on the Aisne in the Laon area, and, later, on the Somme; the motorised forces at present employed there [*i.e.* on flank protection] will thus be made available for such a thrust. All measures taken must be based on this, even if it involves temporary delay of the advance to the west.'[6] But he approved the arrangements which Rundstedt had already made to this end, and gave no fresh instructions. The order that Kleist should push forward to Cambrai and St Quentin on the 18th remained unmodified.

British General Headquarters did not of course know of these German moves, indeed they knew very little about what was happening on the French front. Throughout the campaign, information of what was happening to the French was scanty, vague, and often inaccurate. All that was known at this date was that the gap in the French front was growing bigger and the German penetration

---

[6] See Appendix II, p. 377.

deeper. General Headquarters had no information that any effective steps were being taken by the French to close the gap. The area in which the break occurred was quite outside the area of Lord Gort's responsibility, which was defined anew in an order issued on this day by General Georges. This order described the southern boundary of the territory to be held by the British Expeditionary Force as running back from Maulde on the Escaut through Orchies, Raches and Henin-Lietard (five miles east of Lens). Arras, with British Headquarters still there, was thus outside the zone of British responsibility —a fact which did not deter Lord Gort from continuing to hold it.

I Corps, under the command of Lieutenant-General M. G. H. Barker, on the British right was in touch with the French First Army's III Corps and knew the position they held; all beyond that was confusion and uncertainty. It was clear, however, that the French First Army was involved in severe fighting with the northern wing of the German armoured advance and as this fighting progressed westwards the danger to the British right flank increased. To meet this, a scratch force was formed under Major-General F. N. Mason MacFarlane, Director of Military Intelligence at General Headquarters. It consisted of a brigade of infantry (127th) from the 42nd Division; two field regiments of artillery and an anti-tank battery; the Hopkinson Mission; with engineers, signals and elements of the Royal Army Medical Corps and the Royal Army Service Corps. The 1st Army Tank Brigade was to join the force later. This mixed force was 'to protect the right rear of the B.E.F.' In particular it was to deny the crossings of the Scarpe from Raches to St Amand, a distance of some fifteen miles. It was known as 'Macforce'.

The necessity for this step may perhaps be questioned and in the progress of events it proved to be a measure of insurance against a risk which did not materialise. At the time Lord Gort feared that the French First Army might fail to prevent the German armour from curling round his right flank, but as things turned out the First Army never gave way and they were always between Macforce and the enemy. It might have been better if the 42nd Division had not been weakened; almost certainly it would have been wiser not to take General Mason MacFarlane and a senior staff officer from the work of intelligence at Command Post. Had he remained in charge, Lord Gort might not so often have been without adequate information.

In parenthesis it may be stated that the poverty of intelligence, which was a persistent handicap at a time when it was important for commanders to be well informed, was largely due to a faulty organisation of Lord Gort's Headquarters' Staff when he formed his Command Post. This is too technical a subject to be discussed fully here and though it affected other branches this one example is enough to illustrate its impact on operational efficiency. When Lord Gort formed his Command Post and moved forward into Belgium he took with him General Mason MacFarlane and two staff officers from the Intelligence Branch at General Headquarters, which was left behind in Arras. Thereafter information received direct at General Head-quarters often failed to pass from the Intelligence staff at the Command Post to formations at the front in time to be of use to them, while much of the information which divisions at the front sent into the Command Post was never passed back to General Headquarters at Arras. Depletion of the Intelligence Staff at the Command Post when Macforce was formed aggravated the difficulty (which had already been experienced) of co-ordinating information received there with that received by the Intelligence Staff at General Head-quarters. It was the same in varying degree with other branches. The distribution of responsibility between General Headquarters and the Command Post was not well planned, and the difficulty of maintaining an adequate system of communications when the Command Post was compelled by the course of events to make frequent moves, accentuated errors of organisation.

Two further steps were taken on May the 17th in consequence of the threat to British communications and rearward areas. First, General Headquarters at Arras organised a garrison for the defence of the city under the command of Lieutenant-Colonel F. A. V. Copland-Griffiths, Welsh Guards. This garrison consisted at first of the 1st Welsh Guards (less one company which was on duty at Lord Gort's Command Post); troops from the Royal Artillery Base Depot, manning eighteen field guns; searchlight and Royal Engineer units in the area; and personnel from the 2nd Light Armoured Recon-naissance Brigade Headquarters, who formed a squadron of armoured fighting vehicles drawn from an ordnance depot which were fami-liarly known as 'Cook's Light Tanks'.

Secondly, orders were issued for the employment of three Terri-torial divisions which had been working on lines of communication —the 12th, 23rd, and 46th. The 12th was to concentrate in the neighbourhood of Amiens; the 23rd was to move to the Canal du Nord (on an order from General Georges); and the 46th was to move to Seclin. On the 18th the troops in the Arras area, namely the Arras garrison, the 23rd Division and one brigade (the 36th) of the 12th Division were grouped under the command of Major-General R. L. Petre and became known as 'Petreforce'.

At the same time the Chief Engineer, Major-General R. P. Pakenham-Walsh, was ordered to organise in battalions all available engineers employed at General Headquarters and on the lines of com-munication, while the Provost-Marshal, Colonel S. V. Kennedy, was to withdraw all available provost personnel and to concentrate them as a further reserve. Finally all units of General Headquarters and

F

'X' Lines of Communication Sub-area (formed to deal with units left in rearward areas when the Allies advanced into Belgium) were to move north of the Orchies boundary line, and all branches of General Headquarters at Arras which could be spared were to move back to Boulogne. What remained of General Headquarters at Arras moved back to Hazebrouck on the following day—*i.e.* the 19th.

During the morning a suggestion had been made that the move back to the Dendre, which according to General Billotte's plan was due to take place in the coming night, 17th/18th, should be postponed for twenty-four hours. It reached Lord Gort's Command Post in a message brought by a liaison officer from General Georges; it reached Belgian Headquarters as an order from General Billotte. Both British and Belgian Commands regarded such a last-minute modification of the original plan as impracticable. Major-General Eastwood saw General Billotte on Lord Gort's behalf and the latter agreed that the original plan should be adhered to and the move to the Dendre take place in the coming night. Belgian Headquarters meanwhile informed Lord Gort that they also intended to adhere to the original programme.

During the late afternoon a message was received from the British Mission at Belgian Headquarters saying that as the latter had only received late in the afternoon General Billotte's confirmatory order to move that night, there might now be some delay in completing their move. They asked therefore that their flank might be protected while the move was in progress. This was promised and an order to provide flank protection was presumably issued to II Corps. But there is no note of its issue in Command Post records and no note of its receipt in II Corps records and at one point or another a costly mistake seems to have been made. A report sent from General Head-quarters to the War Office that night says that both the British and the Belgian armies *are* withdrawing to the Dendre on the night of the 17th/18th and that a flank guard will be maintained for the Belgians as far forward as Assche *until eight o'clock in the morning* of the 18th. But the II Corps order for the formation of the flank guard says that the Belgians *are not* retiring from the Senne line till the night of the 18th/19th and that their open flank between the Senne and the Dendre will be guarded *throughout the 18th*. No record exists to prove whether the Command Post or II Corps was initially responsible for this mis-statement of Belgian intentions, and the question is un-important now. What is important is that the misrepresentation of fact contained in the II Corps order led to unfortunate consequences. For the Belgians did retire during the night, and by nine o'clock in the morning they were back at the Dendre–Escaut line on the British left. But the flank guard (acting on the information in II Corps order) believed the Belgians to be remaining all day on the Senne line, to be on their left front when in fact they were in their rear; they tried (in accordance with the II Corps order) to maintain their position instead of falling back at eight o'clock in the morning as the General Headquarters Report to the War Office had foreshadowed. They failed, naturally enough, to make contact with the Belgians (who were already behind them on the Dendre); and they were soon engulfed by the enemy forces who were pressing forward in pursuit with nothing to oppose their approach to the Dendre except the misinformed flank guard, now out in the blue.

The withdrawal during the night had not been easy, for north of Brussels the enemy were attacking at nightfall in an effort to capture the crossing at Vilvorde and other crossings in the Belgian sector. The 10th and 11th Brigades (4th Division) had to fight hard to hold them off and only got away with difficulty in the early hours of the morning. The flank guard meanwhile had taken up a position a few miles back from the Senne, and when 4th Division troops were clear they moved to the country between Assche and Merchtem. The force consisted of the 2nd Light Armoured Reconnaissance Brigade, now comprising the 5th Inniskilling Dragoon Guards and the 15th/19th Hussars; the 32nd Army Field Regiment and the 14th Anti-tank Regiment of the Royal Artillery; and a machine-gun battalion (the 4th Gordon Highlanders) with the 4th Division. At six o'clock in the morning, patrols sent to gain touch with the Belgians, who were wrongly expected to be on their left front, ran instead into German armoured cars moving west. Soon they found that the enemy were round and between them and their supporting artillery and machine guns. Fighting went on all morning and when orders to withdraw were issued at noon they failed to reach some units for several hours. By then these units were surrounded. When those who were able to extricate themselves reached the Dendre they found the enemy already there and some of the bridges they had relied on already blown and under attack. The 4th Gordons' casualties amounted to about the strength of a company. The 14th Anti-Tank Regiment lost seven guns. But the 15th/19th Hussars were reduced to one squadron, two tank troops, and two carrier troops—only about a fifth of their strength remained.

Though the enemy had followed up closely to the new river-line, he made no serious attempt to cross it during the 18th. Our front was held by the following divisions from the right: 48th, 2nd, 1st and 3rd. The 4th and 5th were already moving to the Escaut; the divisions on the Dendre were due to move there in the coming night (*i.e.* the night of the 18th/19th) but as there was insufficient transport to move the whole force simultaneously and as the marching brigades, who had already covered long distances, might be late, it was decided to leave strong rearguards on the Dendre till the morning of the 19th.

The 5th Division was to go into G.H.Q. reserve near Seclin.

About midnight General Billotte visited Lord Gort's headquarters and gave him an account of the overall situation as he saw it.

> He also told me of the measures which were being taken to restore the situation on the front of the French 9th Army, though clearly he had little hope that they would be effective. Reports from the liaison officers with French formations were likewise not encouraging; in particular I was unable to verify that the French had enough reserves at their disposal south of the gap to enable them to stage counter-attacks sufficiently strong to warrant the expectation that the gap would be closed.[7]

What if the gap could not be closed?

Looking ahead Lord Gort saw only two alternatives. Unless the gap could be closed the Allied forces in the north must either withdraw to the line of the Somme or to the coast. With ten armoured divisions operating on their flank they clearly could not maintain their present position. General Billotte had given him no reason to hope that the gap could be closed. It remained, then, to consider the alternatives of withdrawal to the Somme or to the sea. The former had the obvious advantage that the British Expeditionary Force would be falling back on their lines of communication and would keep touch with the French; it would have the disadvantage that the Belgian Army would have to abandon either Belgian soil or its association with the Allies. On the other hand withdrawal to the sea followed by evacuation meant, if it succeeded, withdrawal from the scene of operations at a time when France would be in dire need of all possible support. In either case valuable stores would be lost, and in the case of evacuation much of our armament and equipment must be lost too.

General Billotte had shown a situation map on which nine, or probably ten, German armoured divisions were marked as operating in the gap to the south. Leading elements had that day approached Cambrai and reached Peronne, and there were now no French troops between them and the sea. They were but twenty miles from Arras and only thirty from Amiens. If it seemed unlikely that the gap could be closed, it seemed equally improbable that the British Expeditionary Force could now retire to the Somme with this strong armoured force on its flank. Thus, of the alternatives, withdrawal northwards to the sea alone seemed feasible. 'It was therefore only prudent to consider what the adoption of such a plan might entail.'

---

[7] Lord Gort's Despatches. Supplement to *The London Gazette*, 17th October, 1941, p. 5915.

(*Right*)
River Dyle,
about five miles
south of Louvain,
looking north-east
towards high
ground occupied
by the enemy

(*Below*)
The Dendre,
about two miles
north of Ath,
looking south

The Escaut, between Bruyelle and Tournai, looking north

The Canal Line near Givenchy, looking east

On the 19th therefore, Lord Gort's Chief of Staff telephoned to the Director of Military Operations and Plans at the War Office and discussed the situation with him.

Meanwhile the withdrawal to the Escaut had begun during the 18th and continued during the early hours of the 19th while the rearguards were falling back in daylight. The move was not effected without difficulties, for the enemy were now pressing forward more vigorously. Some of the retiring columns were repeatedly bombed from the air, but casualties were not serious. Some, notably the 48th Division, had had much marching and counter-marching in the past few days and were badly in need of rest. But on this occasion the enemy followed them up so quickly that by four o'clock in the afternoon German troops not only reached but got across the Escaut at one point of the divisional front and the 1st Buckinghamshire had to counter-attack to drive them back over the river. The rearguard of the 1st Division (the 3rd Brigade) was attacked and nearly surrounded on its way back, but got away in time with the assistance of the 13th/18th Hussars and guns of the 19th Field Regiment. During the day the enemy made contact along the whole front, and in the northern sector German artillery began quickly to register our positions. Audenarde was also heavily bombed and it looked as though a serious attack was impending there.

By midnight on the 19th/20th the withdrawal was completed and various adjustments ordered so that finally by the early morning of May the 21st the front would be held as shown on the adjoining diagrams. Seven divisions would be holding a thirty-mile front. On an average each battalion in a forward position was to be responsible for something like a mile of winding river-bank. The artillery dispositions are also shown diagrammatically. (See also sketch map on page 122.)

Company and platoon positions were so sited as to give mutual support and were organised for all-round defence, but it was impossible to keep every yard of the river under constant observation and there were inevitably places where an enterprising enemy could cross and penetrate undetected for some little distance without great difficulty, especially in darkness or in early-morning mist.

The Escaut is a considerable military obstacle, as can be seen from the picture facing this page. As a stop to infantry its value was at the time reduced by a fall of several feet in the water level owing partly to a long spell of dry weather (it had not rained since the fighting started) and partly to the closing of the sluices farther south. Except where the river runs through towns it is bordered by low-lying meadow land, intersected by tree-lined boundaries and starred with woods and coppices. On the west or British side there is some slightly higher ground in the northern sector—a low ridge that runs

ESCAUT FRONT
British Artillery Dispositions 21st May 1940

GHQ & Corps Troops

Divisional Artillery &
Attached Machine Guns

III CORPS

56th Medium Regt
139th Army Field Regt
4th Medium Regt
58th Medium Regt
69th Medium Regt
32nd Army Field Regt
54th Lt. Anti-Aircraft Regt

44 Division
- 58th Field Regt
- 65th Field Regt
- 57th Field Regt
- 57th Anti-Tank Regt
- 8th Middlesex (MG)

4 Division
- 30th Field Regt
- 77th Field Regt
- 22nd Field Regt
- 14th Anti-Tank Regt
- 2nd R. Northumberland Fus (MG)

II CORPS

2nd R. Horse Artillery
53rd Medium Regt
88th Army Field Regt
59th Medium Regt
2nd Medium Regt
53rd Lt. Anti-Aircraft Regt

3 Division
- 33rd Field Regt
- 76th Field Regt
- 7th Field Regt
- 20th Anti-Tank Regt
- 1st/7th Middlesex (MG)
- 2nd Middlesex (MG)

1 Division
- 2nd Field Regt
- 67th Field Regt
- 19th Field Regt
- 21st Anti-Tank Regt
- 4th Gordons (MG)
- 2nd Cheshire (MG)

I CORPS

3rd Medium Regt
98th Army Field Regt
61st Medium Regt
140th Army Field Regt
115th Army Field Regt
5th Medium Regt
63rd Medium Regt
1st Medium Regt
1st Heavy Regt
52nd Lt. Anti-Aircraft Regt

42 Division
- 53rd Field Regt
- 27th Army Field Regt
- 56th Anti-Tank Regt
- 7th Cheshire (MG)

2 Division
- 16th Field Regt
- 99th Field Regt
- 10th Field Regt
- 13th Anti-Tank Regt
- 2nd Manchester (MG)
- 6th Argyll & Sutherland (MG)

48 Division
- 18th Field Regt
- 68th Field Regt
- 24th Field Regt
- 53rd Anti-Tank Regt
- 4th Cheshire (MG)

ESCAUT FRONT
British Infantry Dispositions 21st May 1940

	Divisional Reserve		Front	
III CORPS	44 Division	133 Bde { 4th R. Sussex / 2nd R. Sussex / 5th R. Sussex	132 Bde	{ 5th R. West Kent / 1st R. West Kent / 4th R. West Kent
			131 Bde	{ 2nd Buffs / 1st/5th Queen's / 1st/6th Queen's
	4 Division	12 Bde { 6th Black Watch / 1st S. Lancashire / 2nd R. Fusiliers	11 Bde	{ 5th Northamptons / 1st E. Surrey / 2nd Lancs Fusiliers
			10 Bde	{ 2nd D.C.L.I / 6th E. Surrey / 2nd Beds & Herts
II CORPS	3 Division		9 Bde	{ 1st K.O.S.B. / 2nd R. Ulster Rifles / 2nd Lincolnshire
			7 Gds Bde	{ 2nd Grenadier Gds / 1st Coldstream Gds / 1st Grenadier Gds
			8 Bde	{ 4th R. Berkshire / 2nd E. Yorkshire / 1st Suffolk
	1 Division		1 Gds Bde	{ 2nd Hampshire / 2nd Coldstream Gds / 3rd Grenadier Gds
			2 Bde	{ 2nd N. Staffordshire / 6th Gordons / 1st Loyal Regt
			3 Bde	{ 1st Duke of Wellington's / 2nd Foresters / 1st K. Shropshire L.I.
I CORPS	42 Division	[Note:– / 127 Bde / was with / MacForce]	125 Bde	{ 1st Border Regt / 1st/5th Lancs Fusiliers / 1st/6th Lancs Fusiliers
			126 Bde	{ 1st E. Lancashire / 5th Border Regt / 5th King's Own
	2 Division	6 Bde { 2nd Durham L.I. / 1st R. Berkshire / 1st R. Welch Fus.	4 Bde	{ 2nd R. Norfolk / 1st/8th Lancs Fusiliers / 1st R. Scots
			5 Bde	{ 1st Camerons / 2nd Dorsetshire / 7th Worcestershire
	48 Division	143 Bde { 1st/7th Warwickshire / 1st Oxford & Bucks L.I. / 8th Warwickshire *	144 Bde	{ 5th Gloucestershire / 8th Worcestershire / 2nd Warwickshire
			145 Bde	{ 2nd Gloucestershire / 1st Buckinghamshire Bn / 4th Oxford & Bucks L.I.

*Temporarily under command of 2 Division on the left front of the 5th Brigade.

roughly parallel to the river—but apart from this the level, cultivated plains stretch westwards into France. To the east of the river
two steep tree-clad hills rise suddenly from the plain—Mont St Aubert
in the south and Bois de l'Enclus in the north. They enabled the
enemy to overlook not only our forward position but all the ground
behind it as far as the French frontier. Later in the war, from the
woods which crown their summits, V-weapons were discharged on
England.

During the first three days of the British withdrawal towards the
Escaut—that is, on May the 16th, 17th and 18th—the bombers of the
Advanced Air Striking Force were virtually out of action. The movement of squadrons from the more northerly airfields which were
threatened by the enemy's advance demonstrated very clearly how
dangerous was the absence of adequate transport, for there were some
confusion and delays which might have had disastrous consequences
had the German armoured columns struck southwards across the
Aisne. As it was, the moves were accomplished only by the help of
200 vehicles borrowed from the French Air Force; and the trans-
ference of accumulated bomb-stocks, ammunition and other stores
and equipment was not completed until the end of the month, as
the available transport had to make repeated journeys to get these
away.

While the moves were in progress it was decided to reorganise the
Advanced Air Striking Force. Casualties had greatly reduced its
effective strength, for two squadrons had each only two serviceable
aircraft left, a third had but seven, and a fourth nine. The original
ten squadrons were therefore now reduced to six. Two Blenheim
squadrons went home to refit; nine serviceable aircraft were sent to
reinforce the depleted Blenheim squadrons of the Air Component;
and No. 71 Wing as an operational formation was eliminated. The
smaller force as reorganised was at least fully mobile.

Reconnaissance by day and the night bombing of targets in
Germany by heavy bombers from England were continued; and the
fighters were as busy as ever, though the loss of Air Component
records of these days makes it impossible to note their actions in
detail. On the whole losses were rather less serious.

The progress of the enemy towards Cambrai and Arras led to
further moves. On May the 19th the Air Component moved back its
Advanced Headquarters to Hazebrouck; Rear Headquarters had
already gone to Boulogne. A number of its squadrons also moved
away from the path of the German advance. These various moves,
and the fact that communications were beginning to fail, greatly
increased the difficulty of operational control. Organised reconnaissance was hard to arrange and reports difficult to co-ordinate; and
pilots were often puzzled to determine whether the moving columns

observed were retiring French or advancing Germans. Thus for one reason or another 'collaboration bombing' over the battlefield was much reduced on these most critical days. On May the 19th, for instance, early reconnaissance revealed a large armoured force moving towards Arras, but there were no bombers available at the time and the enemy moved on unmolested. And during that afternoon a considerable part of the Air Component was withdrawn to operate in future from English bases. The remaining squadrons were concentrated on two airfields at Merville and Norrent Fontes, where they were safer and easier to operate, though they were there divorced from their normal sources of information. In fact if not in name the Air Component ceased to be under Air Marshal Barratt's effective command. From now on it came progressively under the general control of the Air Ministry.

Ten days' experience had finally convinced the Air Staff at home that, even if all our air forces were concentrated on collaboration with the Allied armies, the effect on land operations could only be limited, local, and temporary, and that only if we could incite the German Air Force to turn their attack on Great Britain could we fight them effectively and relieve pressure on the armies in the field. Accordingly they decided, firstly, that in view of the prohibitive wastage rates by day and the consequent diversion of fighters for escort duty, medium bombers should only be used for 'collaboration' tasks at night, and then only during favourable moon conditions; after agreement with the Admiralty they would be strengthened by aircraft from Coastal Command. Secondly, that during favourable moon conditions heavies should concentrate on attacking oil plants and railways; and thirdly, that both medium and heavy bombers should operate at maximum intensity during moonlight, and thereafter be conserved till the next moonlight phase. But it was also agreed that this policy must be 'subject to collaboration requirements of the Commander-in-Chief of the British Air Forces in France, as agreed with the French High Command, being met in full'.

However well grounded these decisions may appear, collaboration requirements of the French, urgent demands by Air Marshal Barratt, and the even more potent pressure of events quickly combined to negative their application. So far from all the weight of the heavies being used against German oil targets, they were henceforth to make a greater effort than ever to disrupt communications in rear of the German Army. So far from medium bombers being employed only at night, a proportion continued to operate by day and with the close escort which the Air Staff regarded as a wasteful misuse of our fighter strength.

That night (the 19th) the 50th Division—less one brigade group— was ordered to concentrate on the Vimy Ridge north of Arras and to prepare for offensive action. The 5th Division had already moved to Seclin in G.H.Q. reserve.

For in the south the leading German armour had by now reached the Canal du Nord. They were only fifteen miles from Arras and only fifty from Abbeville and the sea. The British Expeditionary Force was outflanked and the sensitive lines of communication on which its life depended stretched out, practically undefended, across the path of the German armour.

CHAPTER V

ISOLATION OF THE NORTHERN ARMIES

20th May, 1940

ONDAY, May the 20th, was for Lord Gort a day of manifold anxieties. Enemy pressure on the main Escaut front increased throughout the day and his corps commanders warned him that they could not hold the position for long. He had done all he could to cover his lines of communication from the German advance through the gap farther south by measures about to be described. These were soon to be tested, for the enemy's armoured divisions began crossing the Canal du Nord very early in the morning. To add to his troubles the Chief of the Imperial General Staff arrived from England early that day with Cabinet instructions which Lord Gort felt to be impracticable. It will be convenient to consider these three reasons for his anxiety in turn.

The troops had had an anxious and exhausting four days by the time they reached the Escaut and they had no respite there. The enemy was not yet in a position to launch a serious attack, but he was in close contact everywhere and at both extremities of our front began to probe our defence. On the I Corps front, in the south, he found a thinly held sector near Bruyelle and at the end of the day's fighting had a small post on our side of the river, though counter-attacks had driven back other parties which succeeded in crossing. Company Sergeant-Major G. G. Gristock of the 2nd Royal Norfolk Regiment was awarded the Victoria Cross for his gallant part in this fighting. As reliefs were taking place that night, the further counter-attack needed to dislodge the enemy was delayed and as a result there was hard fighting in the area during the day which followed. The centre of our front was comparatively quiet, though enemy guns and mortars were active and their reconnaissance planes flew unmolested overhead. Our own artillery dispersed a number of concentrations preparing to attack, but artillery ammunition was running short and II Corps orders were issued restricting its use to five rounds per gun per day. The most dangerous point, as it turned out, was at the northern sector, held by the 44th Division. There as elsewhere our forward defence line was meant to cover the river. But the positions actually taken up by the right of the division lay on rising ground 800 to 1,000 yards from the river banks and insufficient care was taken to cover the banks at night. The enemy established himself on our side of the river during hours of darkness and was well placed for a further advance next day. Counter-attacks failed to dislodge him. It was already clear that it would be difficult to prevent further penetrations on a thirty-mile front without larger reserves for counter-attack than were then available.

But it was to the south of our main front, in the gap beyond the French First Army (which was on our immediate right), that the greatest danger threatened. The French line ran from Maulde to Valenciennes but was then folded back to Douai and Arras. This withdrawn flank faced south and between it and the Somme the French now offered no organised resistance. On the 17th of May, while the withdrawal to the Escaut was in progress, General Georges had ordered the British 23rd Division to occupy sixteen miles of the Canal du Nord, which runs from Douai to Péronne across the path of the oncoming enemy. The southern fourteen miles was to be held by French troops but they in fact never arrived, for the power, and above all the speed, of the German advance defeated all the French Command's efforts to reconstruct the front and close the gap. Commandant Pierre Lyet, whose account has already been quoted, says that 'surprised by an audacious attack on the centre . . . when they were expecting an operation on the outer flank as in 1914, our High Command had also to face new methods, the efficacy of which they had under-estimated and so they were unable to foresee the result. They failed to realise the *tempo* of the rhythm of battle dictated by the enemy. Every manœuvre, conceived on too short-term a basis, was already outstripped by events at the very moment of its translation into orders. For eight days the Command lacked either the power or the understanding to adjust its own conceptions effectively'.[1] Thus it was that, after their initial breakthrough, the German armoured divisions of Rundstedt's Army Group A met only piecemeal opposition from the battered elements of the French armies in unco-ordinated positions. Fighting at some points was bitter and prolonged: at others resistance was weak and in wide stretches of territory it was non-existent.

Lord Gort's task was to hold the thirty-mile sector of the Escaut position. In face of the growing threat to that line from the German Army Group B, this alone was a big responsibility, for not only were the fortunes of his own army at stake, but the fate of the Belgian Army on his left and of the French First Army on his right depended on his ability to maintain unbroken his central, key position in the Allied front. It was a task which demanded his whole mind, but he knew now that the French Command had been unable to close the

---

[1] Lyet, pp. 71–74. See Appendix II, p. 378.

gap in their front and the growing threat to his communications and the danger of encirclement competed for his attention. He knew that when the German armoured divisions reached the Canal du Nord the 23rd Division could do little to stop them. He realised that his lines of communications with the distant supply bases in Normandy were in imminent peril. The danger lay in territory for which he was not responsible, but as the French Command appeared unable to avert it he had done the only thing in his power to delay a calamity which he had no means to prevent. The 12th Division had been ordered to cover Albert, Doullens, Amiens and Abbeville, all considerable towns and important traffic centres. Thus the 12th and 23rd Divisions were alone interposed between the oncoming German armies and the sea.

To appreciate the significance of this fact and of the events which followed, it is necessary to know the respective strengths and characteristics of the forces now to be opposed in the thirty-mile-wide belt of rolling country which lies between the Scarpe and the Somme.

The leading German forces which approached the Canal du Nord —the eastern boundary of this belt of country—were the 1st, 2nd, 6th, 7th and 8th Armoured Divisions. They were part of the forces grouped under Generals Kleist and Hoth, and formed the spearhead of Rundstedt's Army Group A; close behind them were the 5th and 10th Armoured Divisions. They had had casualties both in men and machines before they reached the Canal Du Nord and their exact strength at this date cannot now be determined. But on May the 10th, according to a German return, the five armoured divisions which were to lead the advance on this day had then comprised seventeen tank battalions in all, armed with over 900 guns (2·0, 3·7 and 7·5 cm) and over 2,000 machine guns. Apart from other units they also included some fifteen battalions of motorised infantry and five motor-cycle battalions: and twelve batteries of field and medium guns in addition to anti-tank and anti-aircraft artillery.

The two British infantry divisions which alone stood between this force and the English.Channel were less formidable. The 12th and the 23rd Divisions were two of the three Territorial divisions (the other was the 46th) which had been sent out from England during the spring for labour duties and to continue training. Most of their time in France had been spent on various works of construction in rearward areas. Their training was far from complete and they were not equipped as fighting divisions. Armament and transport were on a much reduced scale; they had divisional engineers but no artillery; signals and administrative units were only in skeleton form. The total strength of each was little more than half that of a normal division. The 23rd Division had only two instead of the usual three brigades. The 12th Division, which was to be distributed in four widely-separated towns, was now provided with the artillery protection of an improvised troop of four field guns manned by personnel from a Royal Artillery school of instruction. The 23rd Division fared somewhat better; they were found eleven field guns from the same source, and two 4·5-inch howitzers. But they had no artillery instruments; eleven of the guns could only fire over open sights—the others had no sights at all.

The seven German armoured divisions consisted largely of experienced and seasoned troops; many had fought victoriously through the Polish campaign, and they had so far overcome all Belgian and French opposition and had already penetrated about 100 miles into enemy country since they crossed the Meuse. The two British Territorial divisions 'had never heard a shot fired in anger'.

By the evening of the 18th, the few British pawns were being set out on the board. The 23rd Division was on the Canal du Nord—the 69th Brigade with its left in touch with the French First Army at Arleux; the 70th with its right (in the air) at Ruyaulcourt, half-way between Douai and Péronne. The 12th Division was moving into the positions ordered. Its 36th Brigade had put two battalions at Doullens and sent one—the 7th Royal West Kent—to Clery sur Somme to cover the western exits from Péronne with the help of the four field guns which constituted the whole of the division's artillery. The 37th Brigade—less the 2nd/6th East Surrey—was caught entrained at Amiens in a heavy bombing attack by the German Air Force, and one of the trains was wrecked. But the troops were extricated and its two battalions moved out to the south of Amiens. The 35th Brigade arrived somewhat later at Abbeville and occupied positions on the north-east and south-east of the town.

On the evening of the 18th, advanced troops of the German 1st Armoured Division reached the Canal du Nord and occupied Péronne. Some tanks and infantry then pushed out from the western exits but they were met by the fire of the Royal West Kent battalion and of the four field guns. Fighting continued till darkness fell, when the enemy, having made no headway, drew back into Péronne. The Royal West Kent and the troop of field guns now received orders to retire to Albert and moved in the night without interference, first to Acheux on the north-west, and later to the town itself.

On the 19th the Germans reached the Canal du Nord in force. The 7th Armoured Division surrounded Cambrai and approached Marquion where the Arras road crosses the canal. On its left, advanced troops of the 8th and 6th Armoured Divisions crossed the canal and formed bridgeheads at Inchy en Artois and east of Beaumetz les Cambrai without meeting opposition. The 2nd Armoured Division got nearly as far west as Combles, and the 1st began to form a bridgehead over the canal to the west of Péronne and also south of the Somme. Immediately behind the two flank divisions were the 5th Armoured Division (on the north) and the 10th (on the south). The positions are shown on the situation map facing page 86. Meanwhile the line of the canal having been outflanked in the Péronne sector which was to have been held by French troops, the 23rd Division were ordered to fall back. The 69th Brigade were to withdraw to the Scarpe on the east of Arras, and did so during the night without enemy interference; the 70th Brigade were to move to the west of Arras and cover the Arras–Doullens road as far south as Saulty.

The infantry of the 70th Brigade had had much marching and little rest in the past two days, and Brigadier Kirkup decided to ferry as many as possible in the scratch collection of transport which the brigade had accumulated. The troops marched to Neuville Vitasse during the night of the 19th/20th and rested there till daybreak. Then in the early hours Brigade Headquarters and advance parties from the battalions moved by motor transport. Brigade Headquarters were opened at Gouy by 4 a.m. and the advance parties were taken to Saulty and Beaumetz les Loges on the Arras–Doullens road. The transport then went back to begin ferrying the battalions, which were to march meanwhile and be picked up by the transport *en route*. Enemy aircraft were already active, so the infantry marched in open formation with wide intervals. The transport duly met their leading units on the road which runs through Mercatel, Ficheux and Blairville, and picked up a battalion headquarters and a considerable body of Royal Army Ordnance Corps men and some Auxiliary Military Pioneers, mostly unarmed, who had joined up with the brigade. They had hardly re-started westwards when they ran into the enemy. At the same time, tanks of the German 8th Armoured Division who, also, had moved at daybreak, attacked the marching companies. The latter, as explained above, were widely dispersed and though they fought stoutly they were no match for the tanks. Comparatively few got back; those who managed to break away made for Brigade Headquarters. But the enemy tanks also pressed westwards and Brigade Headquarters was itself compelled to fall back, first to Berles, then to Mingoval, and finally to Houdain. There remnants of the battalions were eventually collected. That night Brigade Headquarters and the survivors of three infantry battalions and some Engineers who had joined them numbered in all 14 officers and 219 other ranks.

The German 7th Armoured Division had been attacking Arras all day without success for the garrison prevented all attempts to enter the town. Major-General Rommel, who commanded this division, went forward with his advanced armour. They reached Beaurains, but the rest of the division were slow in following up so he turned back with his signal detachment 'to re-establish communications'. Protected only by one tank and an armoured car he returned down the Arras–Cambrai road. In Vis en Artois he encountered 'heavy enemy tanks' which were in fact French cavalry patrolling to the south of the Scarpe. His War Diary says that these 'put his own tanks out of action and he was surrounded here for several hours with his Signal Staff'.[2] If only the French had realised this and collected their prisoners, much subsequent trouble might have been avoided.

During the evening a motorised division—the S.S. *Totenkopf* [Death's Head] Division began to come up on the left of the 7th Armoured Division carrying the encirclement of Arras a stage further.

On the left of this S.S. division, the 8th Armoured Division, after its encounter with the 70th Brigade near Ficheux and Blairville, went on through Saulty and Avesnes le Comte, and by nightfall not only reached its objective at Hesdin but had advanced units at Montreuil. The 6th Armoured Division meanwhile reached Doullens. There they met the battalions of the 36th Brigade, who fought so gamely, though hopelessly outnumbered, that the town was in enemy hands only just before nightfall. The German War Diary says they met for the first time 'English troops who fought tenaciously (a battalion of the Buffs). . . . The battle for Doullens claimed the whole attention of the troops. In spite of the use of numerous tanks it was only possible to break down their resistance after about two and a half hours.'[3] But other advanced formations had meanwhile pressed on and reached Le Boisle.

The German 2nd Armoured Division went straight to Abbeville. There the tanks broke in between the positions held by the battalions of the 35th Brigade. There was another unequal fight but the Territorials were gradually overcome and only remnants managed to get back across the Somme. The enemy occupied the town that night. On the way they had overrun the troop of field guns behind Albert. It had exhausted its ammunition and the German War Diary speaks of it as 'a troop of English artillery without ammunition on a field exercise'.[4]

The German 1st Armoured Division had an equally successful day. The Royal West Kent battalion at Albert fought hard to stop them but were overwhelmed, and the tanks went on to take Amiens and to establish a considerable bridgehead south of the Somme. In doing so they destroyed the 7th Royal Sussex (37th Brigade) which stood and fought to a finish.

At the end of this momentous Monday the enemy were masters of

---

[2] See Appendix II, p. 378.
[3] Ibid.
[4] Ibid.

Albert, Doullens, Amiens, and Abbeville—with Montreuil thrown in for good measure. The whole tract of country between the Scarpe and the Somme was in their hands; the British lines of communication were finally cut; and the way to the Channel ports was open. The 12th and 23rd Divisions, as divisions, had practically ceased to exist.

Was their sacrifice on that day justified? The War Diary of the German XXXXI Corps says of the 6th and 8th Armoured Divisions that 'from about 1300 hours onwards they were only able to gain ground slowly and with continual fighting against an enemy who defended himself stubbornly'.[5] This is notable praise of the fighting quality of Territorial infantry who in widely dispersed units fought armoured divisions far stronger numerically and incomparably better armed.

One of the Territorial battalions which indeed fought courageously and suffered heavily claimed afterwards with pride that they had delayed the German advance for five hours. It is a modest estimate of what these two Territorial divisions did to damage and delay the enemy's forces. But it may perhaps be accepted, with this important rider—at this time every single hour's delay was of incalculable service to the rest of the British forces in France.

The battalions principally involved in this day's unequal fighting were:

Of the 23rd Division:
   1st Tyneside Scottish (Black Watch) and the 10th and 11th Durham Light Infantry, who fought on the Mercatel, Ficheux, Blairville road.

Of the 12th Division:
   7th Royal West Kent who fought near Péronne and in Albert; 6th Royal West Kent and 5th Buffs at Doullens; 7th Royal Sussex south of Amiens; and the 2nd/5th, 2nd/6th and 2nd/7th The Queen's Regiment at Abbeville.

It remains to examine why our air force played so comparatively small a part in these critical hours.

At half past eight in the morning Hurricanes of the Air Component on reconnaissance reported a continuous column with its head halted at the Marquion crossing of the Canal du Nord and others on the canal further south. Extensive fires were also seen in Cambrai, Douai, and Arras, which the German Air Force had been bombing heavily earlier in the morning. The Director of Plans from the Air Ministry (Air Commodore J. C. Slessor) was that morning at General Headquarters, having come from England to arrange for the withdrawal

---

[5] See Appendix II, p. 378.

G

of the Air Component to an English base. In his own words 'the news from Arras became more and more menacing and all available bombers in the Component were told off to go and try to delay the tank columns converging on Arras. . . .' But just as the bombers of the Advanced Air Striking Force had been moving to safer bases during the three days in which the Allied retreat to the Escaut was taking place, so now most of the Air Component was busy completing the move to its new base in England. The conditions necessary to collect and summarise quickly information received by the Advanced Air Striking Force in the south, by the Air Component remaining with the British Expeditionary Force in the north and by the Air Ministry at home no longer obtained. It was difficult to co-ordinate the operations of two air forces in France and a third in England, especially when squadrons in France were constantly having to move with inadequate transport and many were operating now from partly prepared airfields lacking adequate telephone arrangements. These and other factors all combined to make impossible an immediate response to requests that fleeting targets should be attacked.

It is difficult to see how conditions could have been improved. The Advanced Air Striking Force was virtually cut off from effective communication with the British Expeditionary Force by the German forces which separated them. Similarly the Air Ministry and the squadrons now stationed in England were too far away for close co-operation with the Army in France. But the progress of the German advance through the gap in the French front made it impossible to retain larger air forces behind the British Expeditionary Force in the shrinking country north of the gap.

From England two squadrons of bombers with fighter protection were ordered to attack the columns which had been reported at 8.30 in the morning. The first was over the target area at 11.30 and bombed a closely packed column moving west across the Bapaume road; the second, arriving shortly after, saw only a few enemy troops. In such quick-moving warfare both were, of course, too late for the original targets. Targets reported at 8.30 were 'cold' three hours later. Long before 11.30 the leading units of six armoured divisions had advanced across the Canal du Nord, as has already been told. By noon the divisions were widely dispersed in the country between Arras and the Somme.

Soon after noon General Georges renewed his request that all available bomber forces should be directed to attack the enemy columns in the triangle Cambrai–Arras–Péronne. It was then agreed between Air Marshal Barratt and the Air Ministry that, notwithstanding the conclusion reached on the day before (as recorded in the previous chapter), the maximum Blenheim effort should be exerted by day so long as fighter cover could be provided. Yet only one further attack was ordered on this day, and that was neither very strong nor very effective. Again two squadrons were directed to attack columns approaching Arras from Bapaume which had been reported by French aircraft at two o'clock in the afternoon. The first Blenheim squadron arrived over the area only at half past six, and attacked columns near Albert and Doullens to the west of Arras. The second found only small enemy concentrations and bombed a village on the Bapaume–Arras road 'to create a block'. To state it bluntly the Air Force took no effective part in the fighting on this most critical day. And though 130 bombers of Bomber Command and the Advanced Air Striking Force attacked a wide variety of 'collaboration' targets during the night, it is impossible to conclude that their action had any very significant effect on the course of the battle. Fortunately all but five returned safely.

But in spite of all these adverse happenings Arras still held out though more than half surrounded, and in order to be ready to check the enemy pressure at this important point, the 1st Army Tank Brigade and the 5th Division had been ordered to join the 50th Division in the Vimy area to the north of the town in preparation for offensive action. This force was to be known as 'Frankforce'.

The third matter to claim Lord Gort's attention on this critical day was of another kind. At eight o'clock in the morning General Sir Edmund Ironside, Chief of the Imperial General Staff, arrived at the Command Post, having flown from England. He brought with him an Instruction from the War Cabinet, which became known as Order A and which read:

> 1. The Cabinet decided that the C.I.G.S. was to direct the C.-in-C. B.E.F. to move southwards upon Amiens attacking all enemy forces encountered and to take station on the left of the French Army.
>
> 2. The C.I.G.S. will inform General Billotte and the Belgian Command making it clear to the Belgians that their best chance is to move tonight between the B.E.F. and the coast.
>
> 3. The War Office will inform General Georges in this sense.

The genesis of this intervention by the British War Cabinet was the conversation which Lord Gort's Chief of Staff had had with the War Office on the 19th (page 69). General Pownall had then told the War Office that, as the French appeared unable to take effective action to close the gap in their front, Lord Gort was being forced to consider the possibility that he might have to withdraw towards the coast. This conversation had one good result. It led the War Office that day to initiate discussions with the Admiralty on the practicability of evacuation from Dunkirk and was thus the first step towards an operation which had such far-reaching consequences. But its other immediate effects were less happy.

On Sunday, the 19th of May, at a meeting held at half past four in the afternoon, the Chief of the Imperial General Staff told the War Cabinet of the telephone conversation between General Pownall and the War Office, at which the possibility that the British Expeditionary Force might be compelled to withdraw to the coast had been mentioned. General Ironside went on to say that this course could not be accepted: instead, the British Expeditionary Force should move south-west through the Béthune–Arras area in order to get back on the lines of communication and fight it out alongside the French. The latest information he had was in a note reviewing the position as it was known to the War Office that morning. This argued:

> Unless, therefore, the French are in a position to launch an organised counter-offensive on a large scale, the chances of preventing the German thrust reaching the sea are receding . . .
> . . . If a counter-offensive is considered impossible the only alternative would be to endeavour to hold the general line Ham–Péronne–Douai for sufficient time to enable the Allied left wing to withdraw to the line Péronne–Amiens–the sea . . .
> . . . The Germans cannot yet be in any great strength and must be considerably disorganised by demolitions, the distance they have marched, and above all by air action . . . The present appears a favourable moment, with the German mechanised forces tired and main bodies strung out.

But while this reasoning convinced General Ironside and the War Cabinet, Lord Gort on the spot knew that if the Germans were 'tired' the French were certainly more tired. There was no indication that they could stage 'an organised counter-offensive on a large scale', and what appeared to the War Office as the 'only alternative' was in his view impracticable. 'The general line Ham–Péronne–Douai' had already been broken on the 19th when the Germans reached the Canal du Nord and took Péronne; and by the morning of the 20th, when General Ironside reached Lord Gort's headquarters, the enemy were crossing the canal in force. The right flank of the British Expeditionary Force was already turned; it seemed to Lord Gort that at all costs he must prevent the left flank from also being turned, as it must be if its junction with the Belgians were severed. If the French could not close the gap the only practical course, as Lord Gort saw it, was to withdraw northwards. He explained this to General Ironside and, in the absence of any fresh orders from the French commander under whom he served, he proceeded with arrangements for the limited offensive action south of Arras for which he had already ordered the 5th and 50th Divisions to prepare.

It will be easier to appreciate what else happened at this higher level of command if it is deferred to another chapter. But it must be said here that Lord Gort had a high sense of the soldier's duty of obedience, and throughout this critical day and those which followed he was troubled by the fact that he felt unable to implement the order of the Cabinet.

The last entry in Army Group A War Diary for May the 20th includes the following reflections: 'Now that we have reached the coast at Abbeville the first stage of the offensive has been achieved... The possibility of an encirclement of the Allied armies' northern group is beginning to take shape.'[6] As it turned out, Lord Gort's adherence to the course he knew to be right prevented 'the possibility of encirclement' from being fully realised and kept the way to the coast open till the British Expeditionary Force in the north and part of the French First Army had been evacuated.

---

[6] See Appendix II, p. 378.

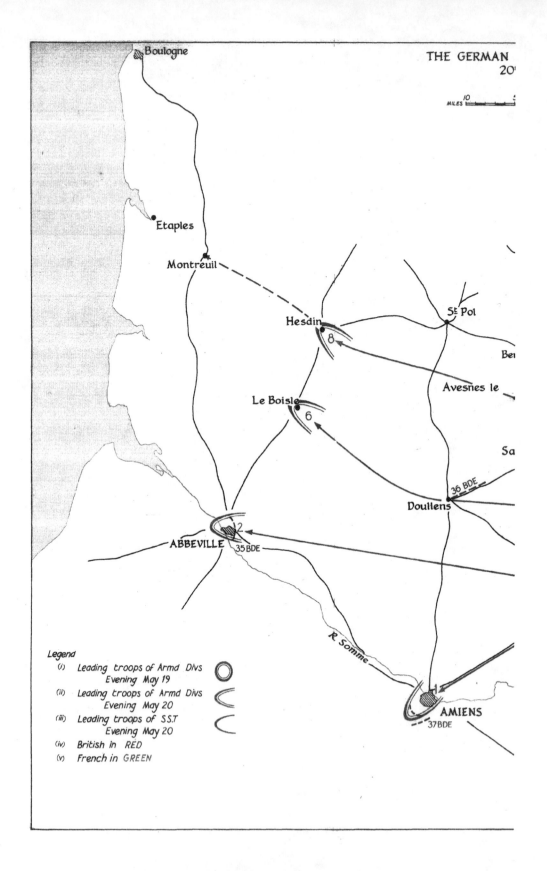

MILES 10

Boulogne

Etaples

Montreuil

Hesdin
8

St Pol

Ber

Avesnes le

Le Boisle
6

Sa

36 BDE

Doullens

2
ABBEVILLE
35 BDE

R Somme

AMIENS
37 BDE

Legend
(i)   Leading troops of Armd Divs
       Evening May 19
(ii) Leading troops of Armd Divs
       Evening May 20
(iii) Leading troops of S.S.T
       Evening May 20
(iv) British in RED
(v)   French in GREEN

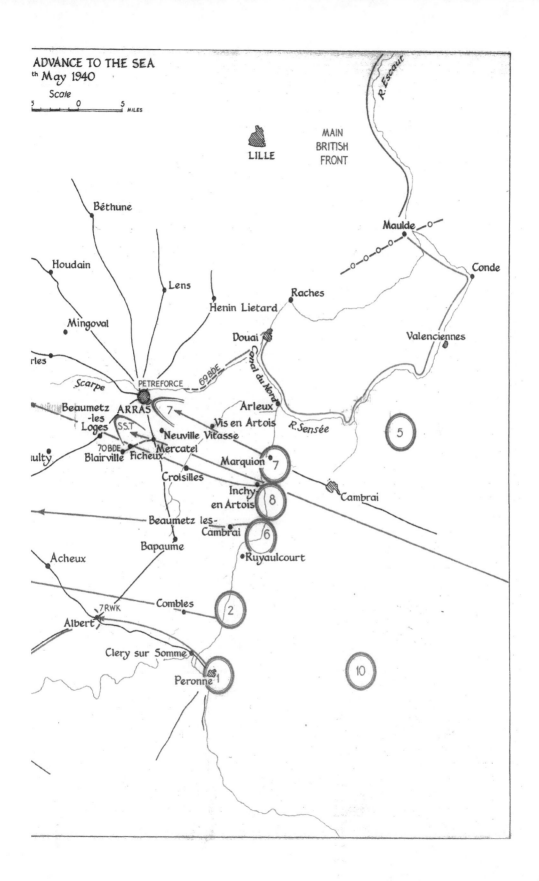

ADVANCE TO THE SEA
th May 1940

Scale

5   0   5
MILES

MAIN
BRITISH
FRONT

R. Escaut

LILLE

Béthune

Maulde

Conde

Houdain

Lens

Raches

Valenciennes

Mingoval

Henin Lietard

Douai

Canal du Nord

Scarpe

PETREFORCE

69 BDE

Arleux

R. Sensée

5

rles

Beaumetz
-les
Loges

ARRAS

7

Vis en Artois

S.S.T

Neuville Vitasse

70 BDE

Mercatel

Marquion

7

ulty

Blairville

Ficheux

Croisilles

Cambrai

Inchy
en Artois

8

Beaumetz les-
Cambrai

6

Acheux

Bapaume

Ruyaulcourt

Combles

2

7RWK

Albert

Clery sur Somme

Peronne

1

10

CHAPTER VI

THE COUNTER-ATTACK AT ARRAS

21st May, 1940

BEFORE completing the story of what was happening at the higher level it will be best to record the fighting which took place on May the 21st.

There was at the time, and there still is, some confusion of ideas about what is commonly known as the British 'counter-attack' at Arras.

Lord Gort's original intention, the role of Frankforce as set out in an order given to General Franklyn early on May the 20th, was to 'support the garrison in Arras and to block the roads south of Arras, thus cutting off the German communications [via Arras] from the east'. He was 'to occupy the line of the Scarpe on the east of Arras' and establish touch 'by patrols' with the French. Nothing was said about a counter-attack or any larger objective, nor was there any suggestion that the French would be associated in the operation.

After this order had been issued Sir Edmund Ironside arrived at Lord Gort's Command Post with the Cabinet's Order A (page 83). Lord Gort explained the situation and convinced the C.I.G.S. that while it was clear that the gap must be closed if disaster were to be avoided this must depend chiefly on the French. Already his only two available divisions had been ordered to operate south of Arras on the following day; all other divisions were already committed on the main front.

Sir Edmund Ironside and General Pownall then went to see General Billotte at his headquarters in Lens. They urged the importance of an immediate attempt to close the gap and told him of the action being taken by the two British divisions on the 21st. General Billotte agreed that the French would attack with two divisions towards Cambrai on the same day: they would concert plans with General Franklyn.

Imperceptibly General Franklyn's operation now began to be thought of at Lord Gort's Command Post as a preliminary move in the projected attempt to close the gap, but no fresh orders were issued to General Franklyn, who was not told that his operation was now regarded as related to a bigger counter-attack in which the French were involved.

87

Meanwhile, General Franklyn visited General Prioux, commanding the French Cavalry Corps, whose patrols were on the Scarpe. He found the General in conference with General Blanchard (First Army), General Altmayer (V Corps); while he was there General Billotte came in for a time. The French generals were discussing the 'project' of a counter-attack southwards, directed in the first phase towards Bapaume and Cambrai; they asked if General Franklyn could co-operate by attacking towards Bapaume on the following day (21st). General Franklyn explained that he could not undertake more than the operation which he had already been ordered to carry out. For this operation he proposed to General Prioux that Frankforce should 'occupy the line of the Scarpe on the east of Arras' and be responsible for its defence between Arras and Biache, and that the French cavalry, on being relieved, should move to the west of Arras and watch that flank. General Prioux offered to do more; he would arrange for part of a mechanised cavalry division to operate on the outer flank of the British force in their action on the 21st. This promise of French co-operation was duly honoured when the time came.

Later in the day the French found that they could not launch their attack towards Cambrai before the 22nd, and they informed General Franklyn of their decision during the night. When this was learned at Lord Gort's headquarters, where by now the separate British and French operations were thought of as related parts in the first stage of a bigger counter-attack southwards, it was felt that a French undertaking to co-operate with Frankforce on the 21st had been unfulfilled. But General Franklyn had no such feeling. His plans were unaffected, for the operation he had been ordered to carry out did not depend on any further French collaboration than he was being given by General Prioux.

The fact that 'the British counter-attack at Arras' was not planned as a 'counter-attack' but as a large-scale mopping-up operation designed to support the garrison of Arras in blocking German communications from the east, explains why the major part of the two divisions was used to strengthen the defence of Arras on the Scarpe and only a minor part was directly employed to clear the surrounding country to the south. What is less clear is why the German forces in the area were so badly under-estimated. In two Frankforce orders which General Franklyn issued on the morning of the 21st it was said that an enemy column of light and heavy tanks had attacked Arras on the 20th; enemy tanks had been seen west of Arras between the Arras–Doullens road and the Arras–St Pol road (that is between our troops and the 'start-line' set for the operation on the 21st); tanks had also been seen passing through Avesnes and approaching St Pol; and 'strong columns of infantry with tanks' had been seen *leaving*

Cambrai by the road to Arras on the evening of the 20th—that is, moving towards the area into which the operation on the 21st was directed. A later Frankforce order said that at 10.20 on that morning (the 21st) concentrations of enemy lorries and tanks were reported on the Arras–St Pol road (which is well to the north of the ordered start-line); a column of enemy motor transport was also reported moving north-west from Doullens. Notwithstanding the fact that all this information was given in Frankforce operation orders, the operation order of the 151st Brigade, which with the 1st Army Tank Brigade was to carry out the mopping-up operations, says only that infantry and tanks were 'known to be operating south and south-west of Arras', but 'in numbers not believed to be great'.

The British 'counter-attack' at Arras is frequently referred to as having been made by the 1st Army Tank Brigade and two infantry divisions, but a much smaller force was actually engaged in the opening fighting on May the 21st. In the first place, the selected divisions—the 5th and the 50th—had each at this time only two infantry brigades instead of the usual three. Of these, the 5th Division sent one brigade (the 13th) to relieve the 23rd Division and the French cavalry on the Scarpe in order that the latter might be freed to take part in the action. Its other brigade (the 17th) was to be held in reserve till the first phase of the operation had been completed. Only the 50th Division was to be used in the opening phase. Of this division one brigade (the 150th) was sent to strengthen the Arras garrison and to hold the Scarpe immediately to the east of the town. Thus at the beginning of the operation only the 50th Division's second brigade (the 151st) was employed in the clearing-up action, and of this brigade's three infantry battalions one was kept back in support of the attacking troops. The attacking infantry on May the 21st were thus not two *divisions* but two *battalions*. In the second place, the 1st Army Tank Brigade had covered very long distances by road with few opportunities for maintenance and it was by now much reduced in strength through mechanical breakdown. Fifty-eight Mark I and sixteen Mark II tanks were all it could muster that day, and many of them were in urgent need of thorough overhaul. (The Mark I tank was the first infantry tank—very slow and, though protected by heavy armour, equipped with only one 7·9-mm machine gun. The Mark II was a much bigger heavy infantry tank with one 2-pounder gun and one 7·9-mm machine gun.) To the attacking force was added artillery and a motor-cycle battalion.

It will be remembered that on the night of the 19th the 70th Brigade of the 23rd Division had been ordered to occupy the line of the Arras–Doullens road to Saulty. General Franklyn may have had this in mind when he fixed that road as the start-line for the planned operation. News of the calamity which overtook the 70th Brigade *en route* may not have reached him, and though the 12th Lancers, scouting on the west of Arras, reported the approach of the enemy, it may not have been realised that the latter were already far beyond the Doullens road. Be that as it may, the fact remains that the right flank of the forces engaged in the operation fought its way forward for several miles and yet the infantry never reached the 'start-line'.

It seems clear that the enemy forces in the area were much under-estimated, for Major-General G. le Q. Martel, who had been given command of the attacking troops, was issued more detailed orders for the first phase of the operation requiring him to 'clear and capture the area south of the River Scarpe from inclusive southern outskirts of Arras including Pelves and Monchy (about five miles to the west), thence line of Cojeul river as far as road Arras–Bapaume'. It would have needed a much bigger force to clear and capture and to mop up any enemy met in an area which covered over forty square miles.

In the first phase a composite force starting from the west of the town was to sweep round to the Cojeul river. In the second phase the 13th Brigade of the 5th Division was to follow this up by advancing south from its river-front position on the east of Arras to join up with troops of the 151st Brigade employed in the first phase.

General Martel planned the opening operation as an advance by two mobile columns, each to consist of a tank battalion, an infantry battalion from the 151st Brigade, a battery of field artillery, a battery of anti-tank guns, with a company of motor-cyclists for reconnaissance. The following troops were detailed:

> *Right Column*
>   7th Royal Tank Regiment
>   8th Durham Light Infantry
>   365th Battery, 92nd Field Regiment, R.A.
>   260th Battery, 65th Anti-Tank Regiment, R.A.
>   One platoon 151st Brigade Anti-Tank Company
>   One scout platoon 4th Royal Northumberland Fusiliers
>   (Motor-cycle)

> *Left Column*
>   4th Royal Tank Regiment
>   6th Durham Light Infantry
>   368th Battery, 92nd Field Regiment, R.A.
>   206th Battery, 52nd Anti-Tank Regiment, R.A.
>   One platoon, 151st Brigade Anti-Tank Company
>   One company and one scout platoon, 4th Royal Northum-
>   berland Fusiliers (Motor-cycle)

They were to cross the Arras–Doullens road at two o'clock in the afternoon. The infantry had an eight-mile march to reach their forming-up places; there was much congestion and refugee traffic on the roads leading north from Arras and some of the troops were late in arriving. There was little time to study orders and none for reconnaissance.

Marœuil was being shelled when the right-hand column moved off at half past two, and rifle fire was coming from a nearby wood. They had to fight to take Duisans, and French tanks moving forward on the right reported enemy tanks advancing further west—these were part of the German 7th Armoured Division (25th Armoured Regiment). Two companies of the 8th Durham Light Infantry and two troops of the 260th Anti-Tank Battery were left to hold Duisans and to deal with the prisoners captured, and the column pushed on towards Warlus. Here again the enemy was found in possession, but the village was cleared and some more prisoners taken. Berneville was then captured and an advanced guard of the 8th Durham Light Infantry with some of the 7th Royal Tank Regiment pushed on towards the Doullens road. But here they met the leading units of the German 7th Infantry Regiment and troops of their S.S. 'T' (*Totenkopf*) Division which had been concentrating in the area on the previous night and were now resuming their advance. They were pinned down by heavy machine-gun and mortar fire, while enemy aircraft made a twenty-minute attack on the main body. Having lost heavily, the advanced guard withdrew to Warlus. Enemy tanks then attacked both Warlus and Duisans, and though they were held off they established themselves astride the road between the two villages. Our right column could do no more.

The left column had also had fighting all the way, with both tanks and infantry. They had occupied in turn Dainville, Achicourt, Agny and Beaurains, and a small advanced party had reached Wancourt. But they were too weak a force to hold all the ground they had covered against the far larger forces which the enemy had in the area. The infantry held Agny and Beaurains while the 4th Royal Tank Regiment fought off the German armour and occupied ground south of Beaurains. They had fought the German 6th Infantry Regiment (the right flank of the 7th Armoured Division) all afternoon, and they had heavy losses in both men and tanks. Like the right column the left had shot its bolt, and there were no fresh troops to follow up their success, or even to make good the ground won. As the evening closed, both columns were ordered to withdraw. Some elements of the French cavalry, acting under French orders, remained in the positions they had reached in the Warlus area, but in the night they were surrounded and only a few tanks succeeded in breaking out.

The infantry of the right column who held Warlus were only extricated with the help of six French tanks which arrived in the nick of time with two armoured troop-carriers. In these they broke through the German hold on the Warlus–Duisans road, while the troops who had held Duisans withdrew after darkness had fallen, with the help of the carriers of the 9th Durham Light Infantry and anti-tank guns of the brigade reserve at Marœuil. The infantry of the left column were heavily bombed from the air in Beaurains and Agny, and were attacked by German tanks when they moved out. Most of them got away, but one party missed their road and eventually reached Boulogne!

In so short an account of a day's confused fighting, it is impossible to conjure up the picture of what it meant to the men of the Royal Tank Regiment and the infantry and gunners who attacked together for the first time in the war. All fought with courage and enterprise, and in such open and dispersed actions there was abundant need of personal initiative and self-reliance. Among the reports made subsequently by those who took part is one from a sergeant of the Royal Tank Regiment which lifts a corner of the veil of anonymity which must cover actions described so briefly.

Secret   24.5.40.

Report on engagement with German forces west and south-west of Arras on 21st May 1940.

To: Officer Commanding,
        7th Royal Tank Regiment.

Sir,—Concerning the above engagement I have the honour to make the following report.

On 21st May, at approx. 1145 hours, I left Petit Vimy in B Coy light tank 'Guinivere', TB476, as reconnaissance element of B Coy Mk I force under Captain M. W. Fisher.

While proceeding along the road Neuville–Marœuil, anti-tank shells from our left struck the road about ten to twenty yards ahead. It was impossible to discover the guns, so I went on to a position of shelter and reported by radio. No reply was obtained.

About twenty or thirty minutes later I observed a force, about a company strong, of tanks to the west of Dainville, about one mile away. These machines may have been French, but retired when we turned to approach them.

The level-crossing near Dainville was closed, so I was compelled to break through it, and proceeded about half a mile at high speed. Seeing two men attempting to hide in a cornfield I pursued them and opened fire with the ·303 Vickers. One man—an N.C.O. in German uniform—surrendered and the other was apparently killed. I put the prisoner in the rear of the tank, covering him with my revolver while we went down the road. Three wrecked motor-cars were passed and one dead civilian. A mile further on we ran into a village occupied by German forces who opened fire with rifles. I turned round and came back to report to Captain Fisher. I continued into Dainville and handed over the prisoner to a captain of the Durham Light Infantry for conveyance to Provost personnel . . .

I then followed two Mk II tanks of 6 sec. B Coy intending to pass them and catch up with the Mk I vehicles. Odd groups of the enemy were seen and engaged, but near a main road west of Achicourt ($\frac{1}{2}$–1 mile) we came under anti-tank fire and sustained three direct hits. The effect was that of hitting a large stone at speed, and the track on the right-hand side was seen a yard or two in front of the tank. Two more shots followed, and then the guns were silenced by our fire, and that of the I tanks, which went on without seeing us.

We were subjected to intense rifle fire for some minutes, and then left alone, apparently in the belief that we were all killed. After five or ten minutes about thirty to fifty Germans were congregated in groups on the road and to the right of us. We estimated the range of each group, and then opened fire. Many of the enemy fell, but some doubtless were unhurt. Later an abandoned anti-tank gun, about 800 yards to our right front, was re-manned, but was seen to be deserted after we fired upon it.

In the intervals of firing we attempted to report by radio, but could obtain no reply, although the receiver was working and radiation was shown on the ammeter. The aerial had been damaged by rifle bullets.

Soon afterwards more tanks appeared, both Mk I and Mk II, and the firing died down. Infantry also appeared.

I then got out to inspect the damage. About five track plates and pins were damaged, there was a hole about two inches in diameter in the right-hand sprocket which had two teeth missing, and the radiator, which could not be opened, was leaking. The engine would run, but smelt strongly of burning. I made several attempts to get more track plates while my crew, Troopers Tansley and Mackay M., worked at the tank often under fairly heavy shell fire. At times this was so severe that work had to be suspended. Enemy aircraft also caused interference.

During this time it was reported to me that Sgt Temple's tank (Mk II) was out of action in front of us and the sergeant was believed killed. As soon as the shelling and rifle fire permitted I went out with an R.A.M.C. officer, and found the tank with its right track off and Sgt Temple and another man, who was unrecognisable by me, dead outside the tank. The tank was abandoned with a bomb inside it, which duly exploded.

At dusk most of the infantry had withdrawn and since it was obvious that a counter-attack was coming and that in the dark I could do no useful work against it I prepared to abandon the tank. I set fire to three German motor-cycles (one a combination from which I removed a map, later given to Captain Holden) and the three anti-tank guns. These were nearly all metal so did not burn well. They appeared similar to a very large Boys rifle in mechanism, firing a shell of about $\frac{3}{4}$ to 1 lb. judging from the empty cases.

All movable kit, including guns, wireless, pyrenes, etc., was piled on an abandoned Bren carrier which we managed to start, and when it was obvious no help was coming, the tank was fired. It was soon blazing fiercely.

Being informed that Neuville-Vitasse was in enemy hands I rallied with Major Fernie of the 4th Bn outside Achicourt.

The German counter-attack was launched as soon as darkness was complete. Hot machine-gun fire was opened and a heavy tank (possibly a captured one of French design) came down the road from Neuville, firing its gun at random . . . I followed in the carrier, which however broke down and had to be abandoned. This too was set on fire, but I have reason to believe did not burn.

I had now with me Trooper Nichol, driver of Lieut. Nugent's tank. His tank, like another Mk II I saw, had caught fire and the crew had separated.

An infantry straggler made up my party to five, so securing two Bren guns, and a water bottle and rations each, we made our way into the country, halting at a ruined aerodrome about 0230 hours on the 22nd.

On the following morning I led my party into Arras. We reported to Area Headquarters and were later sent back to Vimy.

I have the honour to be, sir,

Your obedient servant,

T. HEPPLE

It is but one sergeant's account of how he did his duty on this one day. As such it must stand for the many others who made no report.

The general aim of this action was to ease the enemy's pressure on Arras and to delay his encircling movement round the rear of the British Expeditionary Force; the immediate objective of its first phase was to clear of enemy forces the ground between Arras and the Cojeul river. In its general purpose the action had a considerable measure of success. Busy defending himself, the enemy could make no concerted attack on Arras that day, and so vigorous was the British action that Rommel's situation maps show our attack as coming from *five* British divisions round Arras! Moreover, as will be seen, it delayed the advance of all the leading German divisions.

On the other hand, its immediate object was bound to fail unless the initial penetrations of the attacking columns could be followed up by a force that was strong enough to occupy and hold so wide a stretch of country. Yet even in its immediate purpose it may be counted at least a limited success. For it destroyed many of the enemy's men and vehicles and took many prisoners of war. The day's entry in the War Diary of the German 7th Armoured Division admits to having lost, that day, nine medium and several light tanks; and in personnel, 378 killed, wounded and missing. Either the diary understated the missing, which are given as 173, or a considerable number of our prisoners must have come from other German divisions which were involved, for nearly 400 prisoners were taken during the attack. If the German killed and wounded are similarly understated in Rommel's War Diary, the true sum of the damage inflicted on the enemy was substantial.

That night the tanks of the German 7th Armoured Division harboured to the south of Dainville. Some of their infantry were near the south bank of the Scarpe, but none were across the river, and the remainder spent the night in the Berneville area. The plan of the German Army Group Commander had been seriously interfered with. Originally he had intended to give the armoured divisions a day's rest after their spectacular advance on May the 20th, and early in the day the forward divisions did not know whether, having reached the coast, they were to turn north towards the Channel ports or south towards Paris and the heart of France. But by the middle of the morning Rundstedt ordered them to swing to the north for the encirclement of the Allied northern armies. With this in view, the 5th and 7th Armoured Divisions, trying to take Arras, were to be relieved of that task by the 20th Motorised Division and the 11th Motorised Brigade with the 12th Infantry Division supporting them. The 5th and 7th Armoured Divisions were to move round to the west of Arras and cross to the north of the Scarpe. The S.S. *Totenkopf* Division was to follow suit on the left of the 7th and the German line of battle was to be continued westwards by the 6th and 8th Armoured Divisions who were to take station along the road to St Pol and farther westwards.

Then came news of the British 'counter-attack'. To Rommel it seemed an attack by 'very strong enemy tank forces', a 'very heavy battle against hundreds of enemy tanks and following infantry'. 'The 1st Battalion of the 6th Infantry Regiment', he says in the War Diary, 'suffered particularly heavy casualties . . . Our own anti-tank guns were not effective enough even at close range against the heavy British tanks. The defensive front they [that is, the 6th Infantry Regiment] had formed was penetrated by the enemy, the guns destroyed by fire or over-run and their crews mostly annihilated.' He claims that the attack was finally wrecked by 'defensive fire, particularly of all troops of the 78th Artillery Regiment, the 86th Light Anti-Aircraft Battery . . . the 3rd Troop of the 59th Anti-Aircraft Regiment . . . an 8·8-cm troop of the 23rd Anti-Aircraft Regiment and parts of the 42nd Anti-Tank Battalion'.[1] Indeed, nothing is more striking in his situation maps for that day than the artillery shown in position, deployed well up with advance formations. Our troops met a gun-line which stretched to the west from Wailly, and there was much in Rommel's claim that this was a decisive factor in

---

[1] See Appendix II, p. 379.

the battle. No comparable support could be provided by the artillery with our own attacking formations.

If our offensive made such an impression on Rommel's mind, it is not surprising that its results were felt farther afield. The original orders of the 6th Armoured Division to move into position for the resumption of the advance to the north were superseded. Instead, they were ordered to take up defensive positions west of Arras, which can be identified on the situation map following page 101. Only after the day's operations were broken off were the majority of their units regrouped on the St Pol road ready to start northwards on the 22nd, and even then a strong column was retained on the Arras–Doullens road as a flank guard against the renewal of our attack. There were other modifications of the orders to the 8th, 1st and 2nd Armoured Divisions, and when XIX Corps started advancing north-wards 'strong elements [which included the 1st and 2nd Armoured Divisions] had to be left in the bridgeheads and the need for these was felt very much, during the later attack on Boulogne'.[2] And the XIX Corps Diary records that the British counter-attack had 'appar-ently created nervousness throughout the entire [Kleist] Group area'.

Our own casualties were heavy, as casualties are bound to be when a small force attacks a stronger. Inexperience in the joint use of tanks and infantry no doubt increased them, for there had been no oppor-tunity for careful preparation, and there were times during the action when tanks and infantry were out of touch. The enemy's smaller guns were ineffective against our tanks but lighter vehicles and infantry suffered much from the forward deployment of their artillery. Both commanding officers of our tank battalions were killed because the light tanks they used were vulnerable to German anti-tank guns. The Northumberland Fusiliers record that their wireless communications worked perfectly all day, but the tank battalions, who had had insufficient time for recharging and 'netting', found theirs 'practically useless' and had to rely on liaison officers to convey orders, an expensive and inadequate substitute for the con-tinuous contact which wireless makes possible.

During the day the 150th Brigade made a raid across the Scarpe and discomfited the enemy they encountered: and the 13th Brigade of the 5th Division established a bridgehead further east in prepara-tion for the second phase of the operation. But when General Franklyn realised that the ground taken on the first day could not be held and that the enemy was continuing to work round his right flank in considerable strength, he decided that the operation must be abandoned in order to stave off the threatened envelopment of Arras and his whole force.

On the other hand the German High Command issued an order

---

[2] See Appendix II, p. 379.

to Army Group B stating that 'the question of an attack by Army Group A in a northerly direction will only arise when the infantry divisions have gained possession of the high ground north-west of Arras'[3] and stressing the importance of an attack by Army Group B against the southern wing of our main Escaut front, the other jaw of a pincer movement.

The close and effective collaboration between German land and air forces which marked the whole campaign was very clearly exemplified on this day. As noted above, when the former found our attacking troops difficult to hold at Berneville, Beaurains, and Agny they called on the *Luftwaffe* for help, and bombing attacks on these places were delivered just where and when they were needed.

It was very different on the British side. There was no air formation in France on which General Franklyn could call for help at short notice in support of our troops in action. Targets for the Blenheim attacks in this area during the day were selected, not in France but by the Air Ministry in consultation with the War Office, for by now rapid communication with commanders in the field was impossible. Fifty-seven Blenheims of No. 2 Group, stationed in England, were employed in four separate attacks based on the results of reconnaissance sorties also flown from England. The targets reported (mostly between Arras and the coast) could seldom be identified by the time the Blenheims reached the area, but enemy columns were bombed—when they could be distinguished from refugee traffic crawling away before the German advance. And even in the matter of reconnaissance the limited value of intermittent reports to the Air Ministry was clearly shown on this day by the fact that General Franklyn received no indication of the fact that six armoured divisions were moving that morning through the country south of Arras where the British force was directed to operate. From 7.30 in the morning a number of reconnaissance sorties had been flown over the area, yet an early report that infantry in open order were moving across the Arras–Cambrai road seems to have been the only air report of enemy movement in the counter-attack zone.

A new 'Back Component' was forming in Kent from the returned squadrons of the Air Component and the organisation of air reconnaissance was being made their task.

Air Vice-Marshal C. H. B. Blount, commanding the Air Component of the British Expeditionary Force, had now only one squadron and one flight of Lysanders left in France; the rest of the Air Component was in England. Moreover, he was now effectively cut off from the commander of the British Air Forces in France though nominally still under his command.

Air Marshal Barratt's only effective control was now over the

---

[3] See Appendix II, p. 379.

H

Advanced Air Striking Force of three fighter squadrons and six bomber squadrons, stationed well south of the German break-through. Control of the bomber squadrons stationed in England was being exercised by the Air Ministry without reference to him, as was mentioned above in describing the day's bombing operations. For the rest, Bomber, Fighter and Coastal Commands all operated under the Air Ministry in England. When by May the 24th these moves were completed the locations of the Back Component and the Advanced Air Striking Force would be as shown on the adjoining sketch map.

As the fighting drew daily nearer to the coast, there were obvious advantages in thus concentrating our air forces in England, where their bases were in less immediate danger and provision for servicing was far better than it could now be in France. Damaged machines which would have become useless there could be repaired and made serviceable again. This alone was an important consideration, as one example will show. The Hurricanes of the Air Component when ordered home (including sixty-nine replacements) had mustered in all 261 aircraft. Seventy-four of these were recorded as shot down in combat; of the rest a considerable number would normally have been repairable, but in the circumstances prevailing in France 121 damaged in battle became complete losses. Only sixty-six flew back to England.

But there were counterbalancing disadvantages at a time when it was urgently desirable to make the power of the air arm felt on the field of battle. The Allied armies in the north were almost surrounded and in dire peril. Attacked on all sides and from the air, they asked that the Royal Air Force should devote all its strength in an effort to hold the enemy.

Belgium also appealed for help in the north. Lord Gort seconded her requests and Air Marshal Barratt supported with all his power appeals from the French which grew daily more urgent. But the close collaboration which all commanders in France sought to obtain was hardly possible under existing arrangements. The Air Ministry in England could not possibly satisfy all or deliver attacks 'just where and when they were needed'. With all, or nearly all, of the Royal Air Force now based in England, they could indeed only plan operations with a broad overall view of reported needs. To that end they could maintain long-distance touch with Lord Gort in the north and Air Marshal Barratt in the south, and, through the missions at French and Belgian Headquarters, with Allied Commands. They could combine their intelligence with that of the War Office and agree on a general plan of operations. But they could not do all this so quickly that operations could be related to the swift movements of the enemy, they could not ensure a sensitive reaction to increased danger at a threatened point. The Royal Air Force at this date was neither

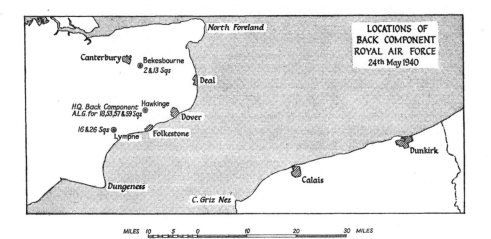

LOCATIONS OF
BACK COMPONENT
ROYAL AIR FORCE
24th May 1940

North Foreland

Canterbury

Bekesbourne
2 & 13 Sqs

Deal

H.Q. Back Component
A.L.G. for 18,53,57 & 59 Sqs

Hawkinge

Dover

16 & 26 Sqs

Lympne

Folkestone

Dunkirk

Dungeness

Calais

C. Griz Nez

MILES 10   5   0   10   20   30   MILES

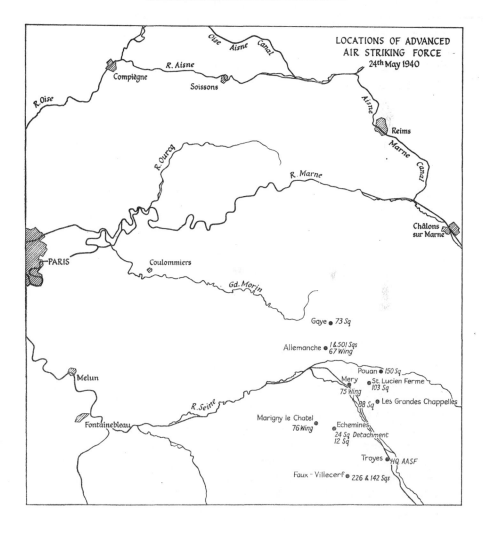

LOCATIONS OF ADVANCED
AIR STRIKING FORCE
24th May 1940

Oise Aisne Canal

R. Aisne

Compiègne

Soissons

R. Oise

Aisne

Reims

R. Ourcq

R. Marne

Marne Canal

Châlons
sur Marne

PARIS

Coulommiers

Gd. Morin

Gaye • 73 Sq

Allemanche • 1 & 501 Sqs
67 Wing

Melun

Pouan • 150 Sq

Mery • St. Lucien Ferme
103 Sq

75 Wing

R. Seine

88 Sq • Les Grandes Chappelles

Marigny le Chatel
76 Wing

Echemines
24 Sq Detachment
12 Sq

Fontainebleau

Troyes • HQ AASF

Faux - Villecerf • 226 & 142 Sqs

organised nor equipped, nor indeed was it trained, except in some small 'army co-operation' elements, for close collaboration in a moving battle. But, even if it had been, such collaboration in a battle in France could hardly be controlled effectively from the Air Ministry in England.

On the other hand, night attacks on the enemy's concentrations and communications were more easily conducted from England. One hundred and thirty-seven sorties were made on a wide range of targets on the night of the 21st/22nd, including twelve by the Advanced Air Striking Force, and only six aircraft failed to return.

The British 'counter-attack' at Arras had started in the afternoon, but units of Army Group B began their attacks on our main Escaut front early in the morning and these were maintained throughout the day. In the south the 48th Division had to meet several attempts to break their line, and the 2nd Royal Warwickshire, 8th Worcestershire and 5th Gloucestershire were all heavily involved. The 1st Oxfordshire and Buckinghamshire Light Infantry were brought forward and successfully counter-attacked to regain positions temporarily lost. On the 2nd Division's front the 8th Royal Warwickshire (temporarily under command and in the front line) also withstood a heavy attack which drove in their forward positions, and followed up with a counter-attack in which the commanding officer and second in command were both killed, without the position being retaken. At this point the enemy established a small bridgehead about three miles south of Tournai. The 1st Royal Scots, whose flank was threatened by this penetration, counter-attacked twice yet failed to dislodge the enemy. Meanwhile, on their left, the 2nd Royal Norfolk successfully repulsed an attack. (For dispositions see pages 71 and 122.)

The 42nd Division covering Tournai were attacked in the morning. Forward companies of the 1st Border Regiment were cut off, but the 1st/6th Lancashire Fusiliers counter-attacked and drove the enemy back across the river. In the 1st Division's sector the Germans, preceded by soldiers disguised as civilians or as British officers, penetrated at a number of points on a 2,000-yard front after strong artillery preparation. The 1st King's Shropshire Light Infantry counter-attacked successfully at one point, and the 2nd North Staffordshire stopped another advance. The 3rd Grenadiers made two determined counter-attacks against a strong position which the enemy had won, losing so heavily that they could only form two companies at the end of the day. But the enemy, too, had suffered heavily from these counter-attacks, and when Grenadier patrols went forward again they found that he had retired across the river and our position was restored. There was some activity on the 3rd Division's front, but pressure was less severe and all attempts to cross the river there were frustrated.

On the 4th Division's front the enemy got over the river early in the morning, but were driven back again by the 2nd Bedfordshire and Hertfordshire, while the 2nd Duke of Cornwall's Light Infantry successfully prevented an attempted crossing after a heavy artillery bombardment. On most of the front the troops had to endure severe and accurate artillery fire. The enemy's observation planes flew unhindered that day and the German gunners must have been kept well informed of our positions.

But the only material foothold gained by the Germans on the west bank of the Escaut was in the north, where the line held lay back from the river and the enemy were established already on the west bank. Starting from this vantage point they penetrated the front of the 44th Division for some distance in the early morning mist before their presence was detected. Bock's War Diary shows that this, in his view, was the key point in the Escaut front. Here, at the junction of the British and Belgian Armies, he determined to concentrate on an effort to break through to the sea-coast. The High Command's intention on the other hand was that he should force the southern flank in support of the break-through by Army Group A, but Bock maintained that the general aim to cut off and annihilate the Allied armies in the north would be realised by 'a break-through in the direction of Courtrai, rather than by running up against the Lille fortifications'.[4]

The German penetration of the 44th Division's front reached Petegem (two miles south-west of Audenarde and a mile from the river), which was the centre of severe and confused fighting. German troops got there during the night of the 20th/21st. The 2nd Buffs counter-attacked at three o'clock in the morning, but failed to eject them. The 1st/5th Queen's were more successful, and by half-past seven Petegem was clear again. But in the afternoon the enemy returned to the attack. Two companies of the 1st/6th Queen's were isolated, and Battalion Headquarters and a third company held a nearby chateau grounds; what remained of the 2nd Buffs, the 1st/5th and 1st/6th Queen's withdrew to positions in the rear. The Queen's could only muster one composite company, and they were attached to the 5th Royal Sussex to stop further penetration. In the adjoining sector the enemy's advance had isolated a company of the 1st Royal West Kent, but they were freed in a counter-attack by other companies of the battalion which then went on finally to recapture Petegem and to clear it of the enemy. Only between Petegem and the Escaut did the Germans still retain a bridgehead on the western bank as the result of this long day's fighting. They had neither broken our main front nor captured Arras.

---

[4] See Appendix II, p. 379.

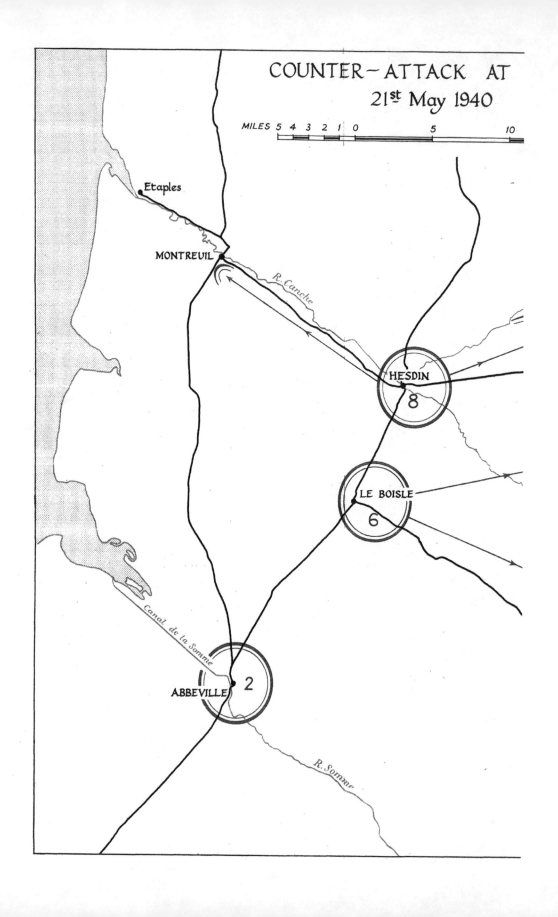

COUNTER—ATTACK AT
21st May 1940

MILES 5 4 3 2 1 0   5   10

Etaples

MONTREUIL

R. Canche

HESDIN
8

LE BOISLE
6

Canal de la Somme

ABBEVILLE
2

R. Somme

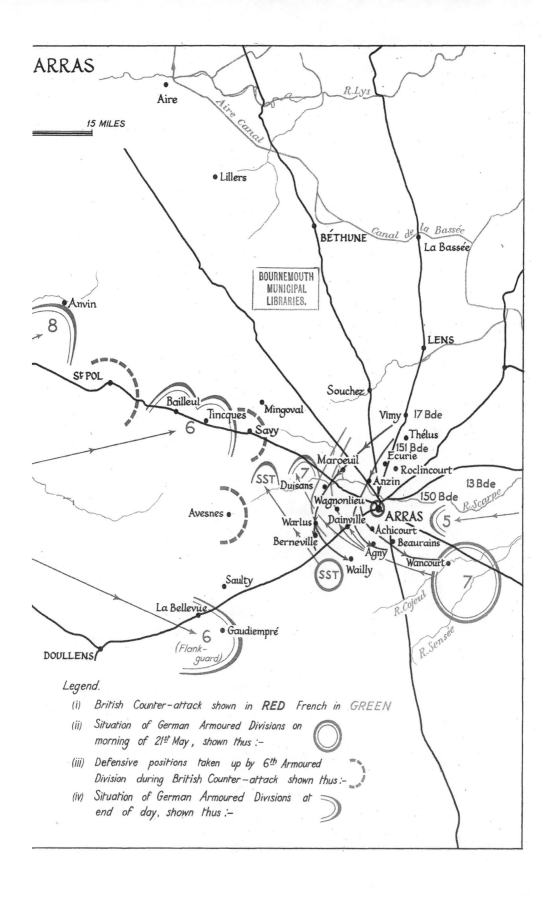

ARRAS

15 MILES

Aire

R. Lys

Aire Canal

Lillers

BÉTHUNE

Canal de la Bassée

La Bassée

BOURNEMOUTH
MUNICIPAL
LIBRARIES.

Anvin

8

St POL

LENS

Bailleul

Mingoval

Souchez

Tincques

Savy

Vimy

17 Bde

6

Thélus

Maroeuil

151 Bde

Ecurie

SST

7

Duisans

Roclincourt

Anzin

Avesnes

Wagnonlieu

13 Bde

150 Bde

R. Scarpe

Warlus

Dainville

ARRAS

5

Berneville

Achicourt

Beaurains

Agny

SST

Wailly

Wancourt

7

Saulty

La Bellevue

R. Cojeul

Gaudiempré

6

R. Sensée

DOULLENS

(Flank-
guard)

Legend.

(i)   British Counter-attack shown in **RED** French in GREEN

(ii) Situation of German Armoured Divisions on
      morning of 21st May, shown thus :-

(iii) Defensive positions taken up by 6th Armoured
      Division during British Counter-attack shown thus :-

(iv) Situation of German Armoured Divisions at
      end of day, shown thus :-

CHAPTER VII

HIGH-LEVEL MOVES

20th May to 22nd May, 1940

WHILE the Arras counter-attack was in progress, events of great significance were taking place at a higher level. Something of what happened on May the 20th has already been told, but it remains to complete the account of high-level moves on that day and on the two which followed.

It will be remembered that on May the 20th the last attempt to stem the flood which broke the Meuse barrage had failed. The enemy had reached the sea and the Allied armies were finally cut in two; the crucial testing time for Allied generalship had been reached. The last and indeed the only definite order which Lord Gort had received from the French Commander under whom he served was to withdraw to the Escaut and hold that line. This he had carried out; his troops stood where they had been ordered to stand, between the French First Army and the Belgians. Early on May the 20th he had received the War Cabinet's Order A (page 83) but orders necessary to implement the policy it embodied had not been issued by his French superiors, and only they could translate policy into action. At this most critical juncture the French High Command proved unable to exercise effective control.

The normal order of things was in fact reversed, and while Cabinets, Councils, Conferences and High Commanders decided what must be done to meet the overall situation as they saw it, subordinate commanders in the field decided what *could* be done, and countered each order of the High Command with reasons why it could not be carried out. And always in the end it was the subordinate commanders' views which prevailed.

Vigorous splashing at the centre produced only feeble ripples at the circumference. Orders grew ever weaker as they passed each link in the chain of command. Large-scale plans and high-sounding exhortations to 'fight like tigers' or 'like dogs' were, alas, to prove no substitute for definite and practical orders.

There was much coming and going, much writing and telegraphing and telephoning, conference succeeded conference, and many people were involved. On the French side, the Government was reconstructed, and M. Paul Reynaud, the Prime Minister, became Minister for National Defence and War, while General Weygand succeeded General Gamelin in Supreme Command of the Allied

Forces. They were involved. So, too, were General Georges as Commander of the Armies of the North-East, and General Billotte as Commander of the First Group of Armies, with which was now included the British Expeditionary Force. On the British side, General Sir Edmund Ironside, Chief of the Imperial General Staff, and General Sir John Dill, his deputy, both came over to France to take a hand. The British Prime Minister intervened vigorously, and flew to Paris during the week to press his views in person. Finally there was the King of the Belgians, with Admiral of the Fleet Sir Roger Keyes at his side. All these were involved in the making and modifying of plans—which in the end came to nothing.

The War Cabinet's opening move has already been told. After General Ironside had handed their 'Order A' to Lord Gort early on May the 20th he was convinced by the latter that any large-scale operation of the kind envisaged by the Cabinet must be mainly dependent on the action of the French. He sent a telegram to General Georges urging immediate action by the French Army, but informed the Secretary of State for War by telephone that the 'difficulty of disengaging completely on the Scheldt [or Escaut] is that the enemy now approaching in considerable strength will certainly slip through any gap round the B.E.F.'s left'. He then went to meet Sir Roger Keyes and explained to him the Cabinet's instruction. Afterwards with General Pownall he visited General Billotte at Lens to urge French co-operation in the limited counter-attack south of Arras which Lord Gort had ordered for the 21st. He was no longer advocating that the British Expeditionary Force should 'move south-west' to rejoin the French armies south of the Somme. He realised how difficult was the prevailing mood of the French Command, for he telegraphed the Secretary of State for War that 'any brusque order such as was sent last night might upset things' and added 'can't do anything in a hurry'.

From French Headquarters Sir John Dill, who had not seen Lord Gort and who had therefore an imperfect knowledge of the situation in the north, sent an account of his discussion with General Weygand and General Georges to the Prime Minister:

> I said that the British Government were most anxious that the B.E.F. should continue to act in the closest co-operation with the French Army under General Georges. I was, however, confident that, unless the most energetic measures were taken the communications of the B.E.F. would be cut and we should then have to take what steps we could independently for the security of our forces and this might involve withdrawing to cover the Channel ports. I explained that in your view and, indeed, in the view of all of us, a move southwards by the armies acting under General Billotte was the only means

GENERAL MAXIME WEYGAND

Succeeded General Gamelin as Commander-in-Chief
of the French Army on the 20th of May, 1940

of restoring the situation. I added that the B.E.F. were fully prepared to play their part in this operation.

I then asked General Georges if I could assure my Government that a bold stroke southwards would be made. His reply was that General Billotte's first preoccupation was to block the holes and that the movements of his First Army were made to that effect and indeed that was at the moment all that Billotte was planning to do.

At this moment a call came through from General Billotte and General Weygand asked to speak to him. General Weygand spoke in the most energetic terms. He said that the decisive moment of the battle had arrived and it was essential that he, Billotte, should thrust southward in the direction of Cambrai with all his strength. This attack must be made regardless of loss. Infantry must attack tanks and artillery be pushed forward to meet them . . . .

This brought a characteristic rejoinder from the Prime Minister. He was horrified, he said, to learn that General Billotte's main preoccupation had been to stop holes. We had to punch holes, not to stop them. This was to be pointed out to General Georges in Mr Churchill's name.

Lord Gort learned during the day what were the Belgian King's reactions on being told of the Cabinet's policy. Sir Roger Keyes reported:

The King pointed out that the Belgian Army existed solely for defence, it had neither tanks nor aircraft and was not trained or equipped for offensive warfare. He also told me that in the small part of Belgium left there was only sufficient food for fourteen days, possibly less, owing to the influx of refugees.

He did not feel that he had any right to expect the British Government to consider jeopardising perhaps the very existence of our ten divisions in order to keep contact with the Belgian Army. He wished to make it clear that he does not want to do anything to interfere with any action which may be considered desirable for the B.E.F. to undertake towards the south, if the circumstances make it necessary.

He realises, of course, that such action would finally lead to the capitulation of the Belgian Army.

The King asked me to try to ascertain the intentions of the British Government, if the German thrust towards the sea succeeds in separating us from the main French forces in the south . . . .

It was a pertinent question, for this was the day on which the German 'thrust towards the sea' did in fact succeed in 'separating us from the main French forces in the south'.

Last thing on the night of the 20th the Prime Minister sent the following telegram to Sir Roger Keyes with a copy to Lord Gort:

Weygand is coming up your way tomorrow to concert action of all forces. Essential to secure our communications southward and to strike at small bodies intruding upon them. Use all your influence to persuade your friends to conform to our movements. We must preserve power to advance southwards and make effort to regain local initiative. Belgian Army should keep hold of our seaward flank. No question of capitulation for anyone. We greatly admire the King's attitude. German thrusts towards coast must not succeed in separating us from main French forces. Have complete confidence in Gort and Weygand who embody offensive spirit vital to success.

This was the only information of General Weygand's visit to the north which reached Lord Gort; it gave no indication of where or when the meeting would take place and by the time it reached him should have read 'today' rather than 'tomorrow' for it was not dispatched till the early hours of the 21st.

That morning, the 20th, Lord Gort informed the Secretary of State for War that he could not immediately carry out the War Cabinet's 'Order A':

Am at present in close contact along my front and subject to attack. I hold Arras and Allied counter-attack going in this morning general direction Cambrai. My only reserve at present is one light reconnaissance brigade but hoping to get one division relieved by Belgians tonight. Reliable report received enemy mechanised column approaching Abbeville early this morning. Until situation on First Army front and to south of me is fully re-established my withdrawal south-west is in my opinion entirely impossible.

To this Mr Eden answered:

All your immediate proposals approved, and we have full confidence in your discretion. Naturally Weygand will today concert the action of the three Allied Armies concerned. Dominating object must remain to ensure your power to retreat down your communications through Amiens, should this be enforced upon you. Pray keep us informed.

During the morning General Sir John Dill again saw General Georges and gave him the Prime Minister's declaration that this was not a time to plug holes but to punch them. He was told that General Billotte was 'said to be regrouping for strong offensive southwards but not yet ready to strike', and General Georges 'could not give time or details'. In reporting this General Dill added his personal impression that although it was intended to use French divisions coming up to the Somme for a simultaneous attack northwards 'I feel that any such action early improbable'. He too seems to have sensed the enfeebling atmosphere at the high level.

On May the 20th the Howard-Vyse Mission had sent Lord Gort a telegram to say that General Weygand would arrive at Norrent Fontes aerodrome at nine o'clock on the morning of May the 21st, but the message miscarried; there is no record of its receipt at Lord Gort's Command Post or at advanced General Headquarters, and neither he nor General Pownall knew more than that Sir Roger Keyes had been told the Supreme Commander was 'coming up your way tomorrow'. In any case General Weygand's plans had to be changed. His plane landed near Calais on the morning of the 21st and he then arranged to meet the King of the Belgians and General Billotte at Ypres in the early afternoon; but he took no direct steps to inform Lord Gort of these arrangements or to invite him to Ypres.

There were three meetings that day at Ypres. At the first, General Weygand met the King of the Belgians and General van Overstraeten, his A.D.C. and Chief Military Adviser. At the second, General Billotte and General Fagalde were added. General Weygand then left. At the third meeting Lord Gort and General Pownall joined the French and Belgian members who had waited for their arrival. With the Belgian King were also General Champon, head of the French Mission at Belgian Headquarters, and Sir Roger Keyes. Two members of the Belgian Government, M. Pierlot, Prime Minister, and M. Spaak, Foreign Minister, also attended and though they took no part in the military conferences they had discussions in turn with the King and General van Overstraeten, General Weygand and General Billotte.

Most of those who were present at Ypres have recorded their personal recollections of what took place. Naturally the picture varies with the point of view but these differences do but make what is common to all stand out more solidly.

The heart of the matters discussed was General Weygand's plan for an offensive designed to close the gap in the south through which the German armoured divisions had advanced to the sea. His plan required a dual attack. Divisions of the French First Army and of the British Expeditionary Force would disengage and strike southwards while other French forces, assembling south of the Somme, would strike northwards to meet them. Until General Billotte arrived at the meeting, and in the absence of Lord Gort, the parts to be played by the French and British could not be decided, but General Weygand explained that the Belgian role would be to safeguard the Allies' left and rear. To do this they should withdraw to the Yser; there the Allied front would be consolidated and shortened and British divisions could be freed for the offensive southwards. General van Overstraeten replied that it had been 'absolutely necessary to suspend withdrawal because the divisions were beginning to disintegrate under a succession of night retreats—the bane of discipline'.[1]

Then General Billotte arrived. According to a report of General van Overstraeten, after hearing General Weygand's plan General Billotte explained that the French First Army was in a very confused situa-

---

[1] Général van Overstraeten: *Albert I.-Léopold III. Vingt Ans de Politique Militaire Belge 1920–1940*. Desclée de Brouwer, Brussels, p. 649. See Appendix II, p. 379.

tion, tired and severely tested, incapable of launching an attack, barely capable of defending itself. In his view the British Army alone still constituted a powerful offensive element. As a result of these Franco-Belgian discussions General Weygand proposed that, if General van Overstraeten's statement that the Belgian Army could not withdraw to the Yser were maintained, it should extend its present front and so relieve part of the British Army for offensive action.

Meanwhile the King and General van Overstraeten had urged that an effort should be made to bring Lord Gort to the meeting since nothing could be settled without his views being known. General van Overstraeten tried to reach him on the telephone and, failing in this, motored with Sir Roger Keyes to Hazebrouck where Lord Gort was thought to be. There they traced him to the Command Post at Premesques (he had waited all day for news of General Weygand's visit), told him of the meeting which was then taking place, and arranged that he and General Pownall should go at once to Ypres. When they arrived they found that General Weygand had already gone.

The third meeting then began. General Billotte reported what had taken place and Lord Gort in turn explained the British situation. The counter-attack at Arras was in progress. All his available reserves were committed, and he could only join with the French in a further offensive if some of his divisions now in the line could be relieved to form a reserve; moreover his rear was now seriously threatened, and he could not continue to hold the Escaut line. It was eventually agreed that the Belgian Army would withdraw to the Lys and the British Army to their old position on the French frontier between Maulde and Halluin; and in order to free British divisions the Belgian Army would relieve one and the French First Army two. Neither could do this however till the night of the 23rd/24th. The relieved divisions could not therefore be ready to attack before the 26th at the earliest. It was evident to Lord Gort, as to the French, that sooner or later the Belgian Army would have to swing back to the Yser but when the matter was raised again all that the King would agree was that if he were forced to withdraw from the Lys no alternative to the Yser existed. Beyond this he would not commit himself.

The significance of this question can best be appreciated by reference to the adjoined sketch map.

It will be seen that on the line of the Yser and the frontier the Allies would stand shoulder to shoulder, facing the enemy on a short and compact front. On the other hand withdrawal to the Lys would do nothing to strengthen the Allied position—would in fact make it more dangerous. For the Belgian line on the Lys and the British line on the frontier would lie at right angles, inviting an enemy to attack where the two fronts hinged. If then the Belgian Army were forced

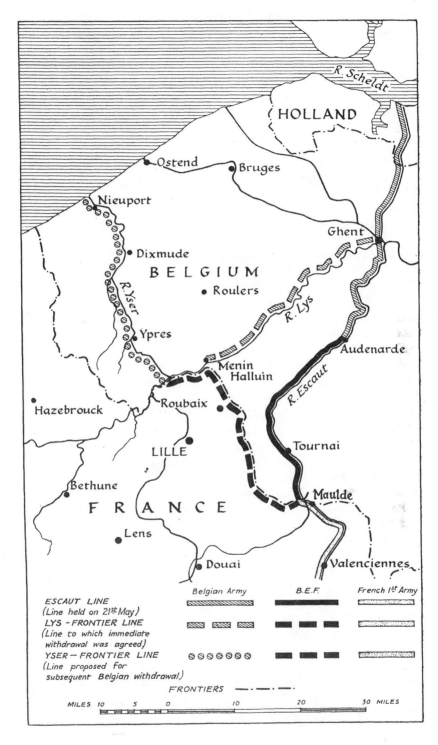

ESCAUT LINE
(Line held on 21st May)
LYS – FRONTIER LINE
(Line to which immediate
withdrawal was agreed.)
YSER – FRONTIER LINE
(Line proposed for
subsequent Belgian withdrawal.)

Belgian Army   B.E.F.   French 1st Army

FRONTIERS —·—·—·—·—

MILES 10   5   0   10   20   30 MILES

back at this point they must inevitably go northwards; the Belgian Army would thus be separated from the Allies and could not for long avoid surrender. No one present can have failed to appreciate what was involved in this question. In maintaining that the Belgian Army could not withdraw to the Yser, the King and General van Overstraeten were in effect accepting defeat. Indeed M. Pierlot, who met the King after seeing General Weygand, says: 'The King considered the position of the armies in Flanders almost if not quite hopeless'. He also says that when asked if the French Supreme Commander had not 'a right to give orders for a counter-attack, the King replied in the negative, emphasising the fact that in reality unity of command did not exist'.[2]

These Ypres meetings are significant not for what little was decided but for the absence of decision as to the proposed offensive; and above all for the appalling absence of confidence which was revealed. General Weygand had no confidence that he could order withdrawal to the Yser for he has written since of 'the orders I had given, or rather, tried to get others to accept'.[3] The King (and his military adviser) had no confidence in the Belgian Army's ability to withdraw and, as he told his Prime Minister, considered the Allied position almost, if not quite, hopeless. General Billotte had no confidence that the French First Army could do more than hold on, for they were 'barely capable of defending themselves'. And Lord Gort? British divisions were that day counter-attacking at Arras, and, if other British divisions were relieved, he was ready to join with the French in a further offensive. But after what General Billotte had said he could have little confidence that the First Army could join effectively in an attack. And after hearing the views of the Belgian King and General van Overstraeten he could no longer have any confidence in the safety of his left flank.

General Weygand had flown north to give a new and more vigorous lead to Allied commanders on the spot. The meetings at Ypres had settled little and finally broke up, according to General van Overstraeten, in a very depressed atmosphere.

Then tragedy intervened. General Billotte was seriously injured in a motor accident on his way back to his headquarters and died in hospital two days later. There was now no French commander with the northern armies who knew at first hand either General Weygand's plan for a counter-offensive or General Billotte's arrangement with the Belgian King and Lord Gort for withdrawal to the Lys and the frontier and the relief of British divisions. There was now no one to

---

[2] M. Hubert Pierlot: '*La Conférence d'Ypres*', article published in *Le Soir*, 12th July, 1947. See Appendix II, p. 379.

[3] Commandant J. Weygand: *The Role of General Weygand*. Eyre and Spottiswoode, 1948 (hereafter referred to as Weygand), p. 59.

co-ordinate French, British and Belgian actions. General Blanchard, commanding the hard-pressed French First Army, did his best to act in General Billotte's stead, but he had neither the overall knowledge, the personal authority, nor the power of decision that were needed at this desperate juncture, and in any case three days elapsed before General Weygand confirmed his appointment to General Billotte's Command. What had been largely true from the beginning of the offensive now became patently true. The conduct of Allied operations was not determined by the Supreme Command but by commanders on the spot.

By nightfall on this 21st of May the British counter-attack at Arras had been concluded, and although it had checked the enemy's advance and Arras was still held, some German forces were now facing north, their leading divisions ranged between Arras and St Pol and others farther west were ready to start next day for the Channel ports. They were well behind the British Expeditionary Force and firmly astride its lines of communication.

On May the 22nd the Prime Minister flew to Paris, where he met M. Reynaud, the French Prime Minister, and General Weygand at a meeting of the Supreme War Council. Later he sent a message to Lord Gort which read:

I flew to Paris this morning with Dill and others. The conclusions which were reached between Reynaud, Weygand and ourselves are summarised below. They accord exactly with general directions you have received from War Office. You have our best wishes in the vital battle now opening towards Bapaume and Cambrai. It was agreed:

1. That the Belgian Army should withdraw to the line of the Yser and stand there the sluices being opened.

2. That the British Army and the French First Army should attack south-west towards Bapaume and Cambrai at the earliest moment—certainly tomorrow with about eight divisions—and with the Belgian Cavalry Corps on the right of the British.

3. That as this battle is vital to both Armies and the British communications depend upon freeing Amiens, the British Air Force should give the utmost possible help both by day and by night while it is going on.

4. That the new French Army Group which is advancing upon Amiens, and forming a line along the Somme should strike northwards and join hands with the British divisions who are attacking southwards in the general direction of Bapaume.

These decisions embodied the plan put forward by General Weygand at the Ypres meeting, though they took little account of what had been said there. Moreover paragraph two, as worded, was quite unpractical. In 1711 Marlborough's army, assembled for battle before the French host on the west of Arras, could march off the field at a few hours' notice and deliver a decisive blow many miles away to the east.[4] But at no time in history could eight divisions—100,000 men—facing east and already engaged with the enemy, march away and attack south-west with so little preparation.

However, after the Paris meeting on the 22nd, General Weygand issued an Operation Order 'No. 1' which was far less specific. It read as follows:

I. The group of forces for whose co-ordination the General Commanding the First Group of Armies is responsible under the Commander-in-Chief North-Eastern Front (the Belgian Army, the British Army and the First French Army) has the imperative task of preventing the German attack from making its way to the sea, in order to maintain contact between its armies, to restore contact with the main body of the French forces, and to regain control of the British lines of communication through Amiens.

II. The only way to hold, and beat, the Germans is by counter-attack.

III. The forces necessary for such counter-attack are already in being within the group, which is moreover much too thick on the ground, namely:

certain divisions of the First Army and the French Cavalry Corps; the British Army which could with advantage be moved in its entirety to the right of the disposition by accentuating the movements already begun, and by extending the Belgian Army's front.

Finally, every effort must be made to obtain from the Belgian High Command the use of the Belgian Cavalry Corps.

These counter-attacks will be supported by the entire strength of British air forces based in Great Britain.

IV. This offensive movement in a southerly direction should be protected on the east, by the Belgian forces retiring in successive bounds on to the line of the Yser.

V. This covering disposition must be completed by the occupation and, if necessary, the recapture of the Somme crossings and the reinforcement of port defences from the frontier to the lower Seine.

Enemy mobile detachments which, supported by the bombing of aerodromes and ports, are trying to spread confusion and panic in our rear between the frontier and the Somme have taken a chance, and should be wiped out locally.

On the whole the greatest mistake made up to now is leaving the road system entire and intact at the enemy's disposal. Every formation commander must therefore seize all communications in his zone by the establishment of a complete network of strong-points, and should not hesitate even to exaggerate the depth of his zone.

---

[4] Winston Churchill: *Marlborough*. Harrap, 1947. II, p. 842 et seq.

The German Panzer Divisions must be hemmed in within the arena into which they have so rashly advanced.

They must not get out again.

Signed: WEYGAND.[5]

This was much less definite than 'certainly tomorrow with about eight divisions'. Indeed the order is so indefinite as to be puzzling, and the final sentences show little appreciation of the true strength of German forces operating in the breach. Where is 'the way to the sea' which the enemy must be prevented from taking? They had reached the sea two days before the Paris meeting. In which sector of the long front were the Allied forces 'much too thick on the ground'? How was the British Army, with difficulty holding off the enemy on the Escaut, to 'be moved in its entirety to the right of the disposition'? How could 'an offensive movement in a southerly direction' be 'protected on the east by the Belgian forces retiring in successive bounds on to the line of the Yser'? Finally where are the troops to be found with which to 'seize all communications . . . by the establishment of a complete network of strong points'? In any case, the British, Belgian and French First Army Commanders could not act on the order until General Georges or his deputy (if a successor to General Billotte were appointed) gave them more direct and co-ordinated instructions for the parts they were to play. Instead they received on the same day an order (Operation Order No. 17) from General Georges which stated that:

> . . . The task of the Armies remains unaltered, especially the offensive role allotted to the Seventh Army [which had been reformed south of the Somme]. Foreseeing a German movement by way of the Oise valley, the General Officer Commanding-in-Chief attaches the greatest importance to the constitution of our covering force on the Somme from Péronne to Amiens . . . as quickly as possible.[6]

The order goes on to detail various moves and groupings of French troops which were to form a defensive flank on the south side of the German break-through. Except for the one reference to the French Seventh Army in the south it says nothing of the offensive action indicated by General Weygand, and indeed gives no directions to the armies in the north.

All that has been related above was within Lord Gort's knowledge, but it is relevant here to mention something that he did not know at the time. On the 18th of May (that is while the German armour was moving up to the Canal du Nord) General Georges issued orders for a movement of French formations designed to close the gap in their front. For various reasons these were not carried out and on the 19th

---

[5] See Appendix II, p. 380.
[6] Ibid., p. 381.

I

General Gamelin handed General Georges a directive (No. 12) in somewhat the same sense though very timidly expressed. It reads:

> Without wishing to interfere in the conduct of the battle at present taking place, which is the responsibility of the Commander-in-Chief of the North-East Front, and while approving all the decisions he has made, I now consider that:
>
> 1. It would be well to continue to extend westwards the front of our eastern armies for the protection of Paris and to maintain close contact with the First Army Group.
>
> 2. Rather than allow the First Army Group to be encircled the boldest action should be taken, on the one hand by opening up if necessary the way to the Somme and on the other by launching specially mobile forces against the rear of the German armoured divisions followed by divisions of motorised infantry. It seems that at present there is a gap behind their first wave.
>
> 3. An offensive in the direction of the Mezières bridges should be prepared with all means available.
>
> 4. All French and British air forces should take active part in the battle. . . .

After suggesting action to be taken by the air forces it concludes;

> It is all a question of hours.[7]

No fresh action was taken on General Gamelin's directive. General Weygand proceeded to acquaint himself with the situation and his first order was issued on the 22nd. The general policy initiated by General Georges and confirmed by General Gamelin was not materially changed, but in the three days which had elapsed the situation had changed radically and for the worse.

By the evening of the 22nd of May the danger of the Allies' situation was indeed greatly aggravated. It was to be the last day on the Escaut and in the southern and central sectors it passed comparatively quietly. Enemy concentrations in preparation for attacks in those sectors were at several points broken up by our artillery fire, and all attempts to cross the river were repulsed. At night, withdrawal to the old frontier positions which had been ordered was carried out, carrier platoons and machine-gun battalions playing a useful role as rearguards.

But in the northern sector Bock's attempt to break through towards Courtrai was renewed in a series of determined attacks, which began at seven o'clock in the morning on the front of the 44th Division, and by the afternoon extended to the 4th Division on their right. Starting from the position on the west bank which they had won the previous day, the enemy made a number of penetrations and overran several posts. Bitter and confused fighting went on all day and continued far

---

[7] See Appendix II, p. 381.

into the night, and withdrawal to the frontier position when the time came was a difficult and hazardous operation. A company of the 1st Royal West Kent had to counter-attack at ten o'clock at night in order to free the rest of the battalion, and there were others which had to fight their way out. During the day and in the course of disengaging, some battalions had suffered severely, the 1st/6th Queens in particular having had 400 casualties in two days. The field guns of the division had been ordered on the 21st to remain in position and fight it out. On the 22nd when divisional orders reached them to withdraw the enemy were only a few hundred yards away. The quads (gun tractors) were some distance back, the road was choked by terrified refugees, and there was some confusion and misunderstanding of orders. As a result thirty-four field guns were lost or destroyed.

But there had been no break-through. Of the day's fighting on this front the German Army Group B situation report says that 'the enemy is offering stubborn resistance, supported by strong artillery'.[8] During the night our withdrawal was completed and on the 23rd the British Expeditionary Force was again holding the frontier between Maulde and Halluin. The defence works so laboriously constructed during the winter were now valuable.

To their right rear the small Arras garrison still held off all the enemy's attacks, as they had done now for four days. The town had been heavily and repeatedly bombed and almost all civilians had gone. And to the west of the town the weight of the enemy divisions was beginning to press back the battalions from the line of the Scarpe. But the Allied forces north of the Somme were now being threatened on three sides. The Belgians, the main British Expeditionary Force and the French First Army held the eastern front. Arras still held, and from behind this strong-point a thin semblance of protection stretched out northwards along the line of canals towards Gravelines and the sea. Boulogne and Calais were still held, but both were threatened and between them and the British Expeditionary Force were the advancing divisions of the German Army. The account of what was happening at this time to the south of the Somme—beyond the gap in which the German armoured divisions were now operating—must be told in a later chapter.

Both the Belgian and French Armies had had much hard fighting, with many difficult withdrawals and anxious rearguard actions. Their casualties had been heavy; their soldiery got little rest in this first fortnight and were very tired. And both armies had had the agonising duty of leaving home and kinsfolk behind them to the tender mercies of the enemy. Moreover, up to the 20th the French alone of the Allies had contended with the main weight of the enemy's armoured

---

[8] See Appendix II, p. 381.

divisions. These things must be remembered in any attempt to realise the conditions under which our Allies fought. Doubtless many of the German troops were also tired. They too, the infantry at least, had marched long distances and had little rest. The divisions which formed the attacking forces had also had heavy casualties; but the enemy's troops were sustained by a sense of success, by the knowledge that each day they were moving forward, deeper and deeper into enemy territory. All that they had been taught about the invincibility of German arms was proving to be true, all that they had been promised was being fulfilled.

The British troops were in a different situation from either of the other contestants. They had made the long advance to the Dyle and the fighting withdrawal to the Escaut. They also had had some hard fighting, much marching and little rest. They too were physically tired. And now they were back where they started—only this time the enemy was behind them as well as in front. They had not the same reasons for depression as the French and Belgian soldiers, or the same grounds for elation as the Germans, for notwithstanding the calamities which had overtaken their allies, their front was unbroken. Yet their situation was most dangerous. They were cut off from their bases and their supplies must soon run out; they were separated from the main seaports and it was unlikely that stocks could be replenished from England; they were nearly surrounded by a numerically superior foe, and they could hardly hope to escape. The airfields on which so much labour had been expended had fallen into enemy hands, and the Air Component of the Royal Air Force was now largely based in England, with all the handicaps to co-operation with an army overseas which must follow such a separation.

Thus on the 22nd, when only one flight of Air Component's No. 4 Squadron was left in France to carry out close reconnaissance for the Army, Advanced Headquarters of the Air Component still with the British Expeditionary Force signalled home that it was virtually impossible to continue tactical and artillery reconnaissance unless a fighter flight could be attached for duty with the remaining flight of Lysanders and unless fighter patrols in strength were flown over the battle area at agreed times and places. The enemy, it was said, was constantly operating flights of nine fighters over our entire front, and severe Lysander losses were being sustained to no purpose. 'Failing direct support must discontinue tactical and artillery reconnaissance except for attempts in extreme urgency. Enemy air supremacy naturally has moral effect on troops.'

The Air Mission at Belgian Headquarters also signalled that they were getting no information from British air reconnaissance and added: 'As Belgian Air Force now virtually non-existent must seriously urge undesirability leaving them blind on their front.' It is not clear that anything did, or could result from these appeals. Long-distance reconnaissance could not effectively take the place of the close observation of army co-operation squadrons within easy reach of Corps Headquarters.

The question of fighter protection over the front was also now more difficult. Twenty-six fighter patrols were flown that day from England, involving 198 sorties, mainly over Boulogne and Calais (where, as told later, garrisons were being strengthened) and in the country through which the German armour was seeking to surround the Allied armies in the north. It is not evident from the records preserved that any were flown over the main battlefront. Air Component head-quarters with the British Expeditionary Force reported that 'enemy aircraft reconnoitre our position, registering batteries unimpeded and enjoying complete freedom of action' against the British Expeditionary Force and the French and Belgian armies. They also complained of the absence of fighter cover over Arras for the past two days. The explanation appears to have been, not that offensive fighter patrols were not flown, but that at this date fighter patrols flown from England were almost bound to encounter the enemy air force before they got as far east as Arras and the eastern battlefront. And also that, as always in this campaign, they could not fight everywhere against enemy air forces in greatly superior numbers. Eighty-one medium bombers attacked enemy columns observed in the western area during the day, and in the country south of Boulogne had some success in slowing enemy movements as told later in the account of the defence of the channel ports in Chapter X. And at night fifty-three heavy bombers attacked targets at the Meuse crossings, hindered badly, for the first time, by rain, low cloud and ground mist. On this day, also for the first time, rations were flown to Merville for the British Expeditionary Force where the feeding problem was beginning to look threatening.

Bad as was the situation of the British Expeditionary Force, it would have been worse had not Lord Gort foreseen early that, if the French were unable to close the breach in their line, he might be forced to retreat towards the coast. As early as the 17th he had begun to build up some protection for his southern flank by the formation of Macforce (page 64). Measures to defend Arras itself have been described. Further west—behind the British front a flank guard was formed from such troops as could be found. Everyone capable of firing a rifle and not required for other duties was pressed into service. The Royal Engineers worked untiringly, first to destroy bridges and disrupt the enemy's lines of advance, and then to hold positions as infantry. And almost every type of unit to be found in the rear of a fighting force added some men to this rearward flank guard. Only a few infantry battalions could be spared to reinforce these heterogeneous forces, and though with their help a line gradually took shape, it was held only in skeleton, and many of those who helped to hold it were neither trained nor equipped for such a task. Thus on the right of Macforce came 'Polforce', which was put under the command of Major-General H. O. Curtis, commanding the 46th Division, on the 20th of May. The order appointing him is illuminating:

(*a*) You will take over command of Polforce. This force consists of:

One 25-pdr bty, detailed by I Corps, and Bde H.Q. and units of 46 Division at present en route by rail to the Seclin area.

[137th Brigade Headquarters and the 2nd/5th West Yorkshire Regiment were all that arrived.]

These units detrain this afternoon at St Pol where you will meet them and give them orders . . . .

Your role is to establish localities in St Pol–Frévent . . . and Divion . . . ensuring that all roads entering into the position are blocked and that a 'keep' is established at which posts on the roads can rally if necessary.

(*b*) You will also command the La-Bassée Canal defences between Aire and exclusive Carvin. On your left you will be in touch with Macforce whose H.Q. are in Orchies.

Forces under your command [for the Canal defences] will consist of 25 Inf. Bde of 50 Div. and certain R.E. units, the details of which you will obtain direct from the E.-in-C.

In the event there was not time to carry out more than (*b*) above. How inadequate was the available force for the task needs no emphasis, for the frontage to be covered—the distance between Aire and Carvin—is approximately twenty-eight miles, nearly as long as the whole of the main Escaut front held by the British Expeditionary Force. Nevertheless, as other units were added the front was gradually extended through St Omer to St Momelin, a further seventeen miles. In practice, all that could be hoped in such circumstances was to guard the principal canal crossings—for between St Momelin and Carvin there were forty-four crossings where bridges had to be prepared for demolition and the crossing held. Similarly in Macforce, battalion frontages were from three to seven miles wide. A single battalion cannot defend seven miles.

By the night of the 22nd, this rearward defence line was thinly occupied and from then on, as will be seen later, it was mended and patched, when the shortening of our main eastern front freed troops for the purpose.

The supply position, though inevitably bad, was not as bad as it might have been. Lieutenant-General W. G. Lindsell, Lord Gort's Quartermaster-General, had taken the precaution to accumulate twelve days' requirements of supplies and ammunition in the forward areas, and so far as possible these were kept on wheels. Enemy bombing seriously interfered with rail-head arrangements and 'we were forced to use rail-heads which were by no means ideal and would have gained no marks if used during an exercise'. Nevertheless, although the bombing caused some disorganisation, supplies themselves were undamaged. With Amiens and Abbeville in enemy hands, the British Expeditionary Force were now dependent on the ammunition and supplies entrained in forward areas. As the days passed, there were times when particular formations went short of ammunition, yet there was no general or really serious shortage. The position in regard to rations was less good, and next day—May the 23rd—the British Expeditionary Force was put on half rations. But here again local purchases often made it possible to supplement official supplies, and where the local population had fled troops could augment rations without much difficulty or any expense 'off the country'. In any case, these difficulties had not yet begun to be acute on May the 22nd though they were in Lord Gort's mind when the possibilities of the operation ordered by General Weygand were under discussion. He pointed out that 'the administrative situation made it unlikely that sustained offensive operations could be undertaken. . . . The mobile echelons of gun and small arms ammunition were full, but once they were exhausted I could not safely reckon on being able to replenish them.'[9]

On this day (May the 22nd) Colonel Schmundt, Wehrmacht Adjutant to Hitler, telephoned Rundstedt's Headquarters saying that the Führer wished for information concerning the situation at Arras. He was told of the 'strong' enemy forces which had attempted to break through to the south by way of Arras—for so the Arras counter-attack appeared to the Germans. These forces, he was told, had succeeded in pushing back the 7th Armoured Division in a few places; later the attack was held. 'The Führer requires that all mobile troops in any way available be used in the area on either side of Arras and *westward* from there to the sea. . . . Further, all other infantry divisions of the Twelfth, Second and Sixteenth Armies are to be rapidly brought up westward. These instructions are *in accordance with the arrangements already made by Army Group Headquarters.*'[10]

In view of all that the German generals have said and written since the war on the subject of Hitler's responsibility for orders which now seem to them open to criticism in the light of later knowledge, and of the readiness with which their afterthoughts and recollections have been accepted as evidence of what really happened, the sentence italicised here, though not underlined in the original, is of importance;

[9] Lord Gort's Despatches, p. 5916.
[10] See Appendix II, p. 381.

for it is contemporary evidence of a procedure which the War Diaries show to have been frequently followed. The War Diaries were written up day by day. They note the chief events and add the comments—often very outspoken comments—of the formation commander. They record what he thought and did at the time and thus make it clear when Hitler did not originate orders but confirmed or modified orders which the Army Group commander had already initiated.

The Army Group A War Diary shows that for some time Rundstedt had been nervous about his long, exposed southern flank; it shows, too, that on the 20th and the 21st he expected an attempt by the Allies to break through towards the Somme while, south of the Somme, the French Army appeared to be moving up for an offensive northwards. Although he had still to reckon with the possibility of concerted action by the Allied forces in the north and the French forces south of the Somme he was now less anxious than he had been about the probable result of either of such moves. The Somme flank was more firmly held by advanced mobile units of Kleist Group with bridgeheads at key points, and, as shown above, the infantry divisions of three armies were moving up to reinforce this flank. The arrest of the Arras counter-attack and the steady improvement of the German position lessened his fear of an Allied attempt to break through from the north.

On the other hand, the High Command and the Army Group commanders (especially Rundstedt) were beginning to think about the operations which would follow after the Allied armies in the north had been successfully rounded up—a task which now seemed to Rundstedt merely a matter of days. For these forthcoming operations —for the attack southwards across the Somme to be known as Operation 'Red'—he had little time in which to prepare and he wanted to husband and recondition his battered armour. From now on, this need was continuously in his mind. And when the Commander-in-Chief (Brauchitsch) visited his headquarters on the 21st the forthcoming Operation 'Red' was the main subject of discussion. The details of the discussion were not recorded 'owing to considerations of security'. The importance of bridgeheads at Abbeville, Amiens, Péronne and towards Noyon was however noted.[11] This growing preoccupation with plans for Operation 'Red' which was to follow the completion of 'Yellow' is the key to much that would otherwise be unexplainable in the German conduct of their campaign in the north from now onwards.

---

[11] See Appendix II, p. 382.

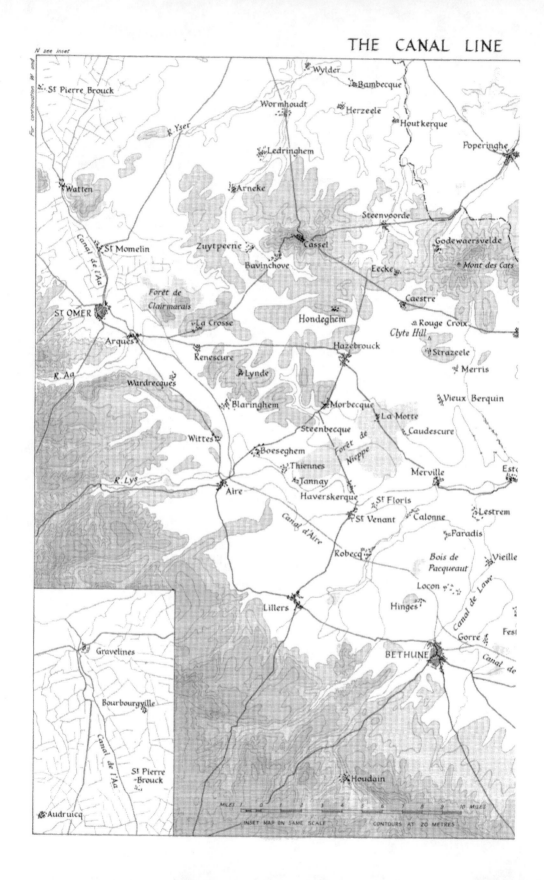

THE CANAL LINE

St Pierre Brouck

Wylder
Bambecque
Wormhoudt
Herzeele
Houtkerque
R. Yser
Poperinghe
Ledringhem
Watten
Arneke
Steenvoorde
Godewaersvelde
St Momelin
Zuytpeene
Cassel
Mont des Cats
Canal de l'Aa
Bavinchove
Eecke
Caestre
Forêt de
Clairmarais
La Crosse
Hondeghem
Rouge Croix
ST OMER
Clyte Hill
Strazeele
Arques
Hazebrouck
Renescure
Merris
R. Aa
Lynde
Wardrecques
Vieux Berquin
Blaringhem
Morbecque
Wittes
La Motte
Steenbecque
Caudescure
Forêt de
Nieppe
Boeseghem
R. Lys
Thiennes
Merville
Este
Aire
Tannay
Haverskerque
St Floris
Canal d'Aire
St Venant
Calonne
Lestrem
Robecq
Paradis
Bois de
Pacqueaut
Vieille
Locon
Lillers
Hinges
Canal de Lawe
Gorre
Fes
BETHUNE
Canal de

INSET

Gravelines

Bourbourgville

Canal de l'Aa

St Pierre
Brouck

Audruicq

Houdain

MILES 1 0 1 2 3 4   5   6   7   8 9 10 MILES

INSET MAP ON SAME SCALE   CONTOURS AT 20 METRES

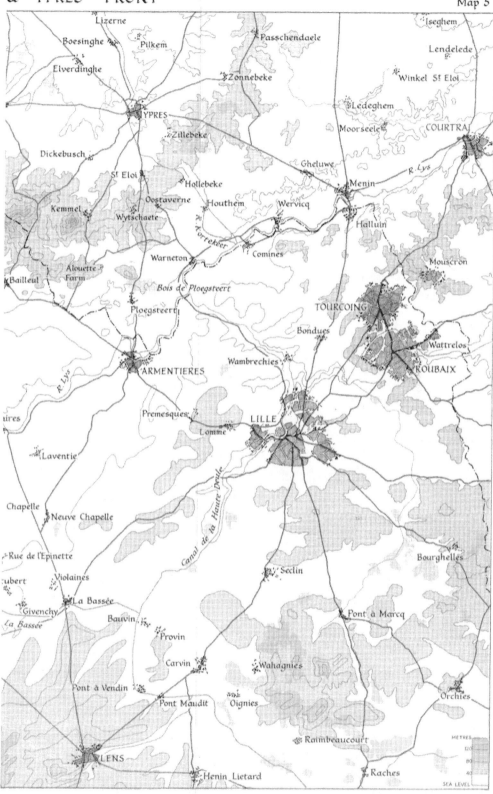

Iseghem
Lizerne
Boesinghe
Pilkem
Lendelede
Elverdinghe
Passchendaele
Winkel St Eloi
Zonnebeke
YPRES
Ledeghem
Zillebeke
Moorseele
COURTRAI
Dickebusch
Gheluwe
R. Lys
St Eloi
Hollebeke
Menin
Kemmel
Oostaverne
Houthem
Wervicq
Wytschaete
Halluin
Warneton
Comines
Mouscron
Bailleul
Alouette
Farm
Bois de Ploegsteert
TOURCOING
Ploegsteert
Bondues
Wattrelos
R. Lys
Wambrechies
ROUBAIX
ARMENTIÈRES
ires
Premesques
LILLE
Lomme
Laventie
Chapelle
Neuve Chapelle
Bourghelles
Rue de l'Epinette
Seclin
ubert
Violaines
La Bassée
Pont à Marcq
Givenchy
Bauvin
La Bassée
Provin
Carvin
Wahagnies
Pont à Vendin
Orchies
Pont Maudit
Oignies
Raimbeaucourt
METRES
LENS
120
80
Henin Lietard
Raches
40
SEA LEVEL

CHAPTER VIII

THE CANAL LINE

23rd May, 1940

D URING the 23rd the moves necessary to effect the new disposition of the British Expeditionary Force continued. On their completion the shortened front, which followed the frontier defences from Bourghelles to Halluin on the Lys, would be held by four divisions—on the right I Corps with the 42nd and 1st Divisions; on the left II Corps with the 3rd and 4th Divisions. The new dispositions are shown on the sketch map overleaf. Of the divisions thus freed, the 2nd and 48th were to assemble in the area south-west of Lille for employment in defence of the Canal Line on the west; the 44th Division was for the moment to be held in General Headquarters reserve; the 5th and 50th were still, as Frankforce, holding the Arras salient. Some of the consequent reliefs and movements could not be carried out till the night of the 23rd/24th. So, as the enemy pressure round Arras and the threat to the Canal Line near Béthune and La Bassée increased, the 2nd and 48th Divisions were each ordered to find a small force to move in advance of the divisions to the threatened sector. These advanced forces, consisting of artillery, machine guns and infantry, were 'X' Force under Brigadier the Hon. E. F. Lawson, Commanding Royal Artillery, the 48th Division, and 'Y' Force under Brigadier C. B. Findlay, Commanding Royal Artillery, the 2nd Division.

The full significance of the Canal Line stretching from Gravelines on the coast through St Omer, Béthune and La Bassée, can be clearly seen on the adjoining map and on the German situation map for May the 24th, which is enclosed at the end of this book. It followed approximately the old line of fortified towns which played so important a role in French military history. Gravelines, Aire, St Venant, and Béthune were among the key places selected by Vauban for the exercise of his genius; Aire, St Venant, and Béthune were among the towns which Marlborough found it necessary to take in 1710 as a preliminary to his campaign in the following year. These places stood then on important rivers—today they are linked together by an unbroken line of canalised rivers or canals, and this Canal Line was the only natural barrier that could hinder the armoured divisions of the German Army Group A from driving into the rear of the British Expeditionary Force as the latter faced the pressure of Army Group B from the east. Lord Gort had taken the first steps towards the

BRITISH DISPOSITIONS ON THE ESCAUT
AND FRONTIER LINES

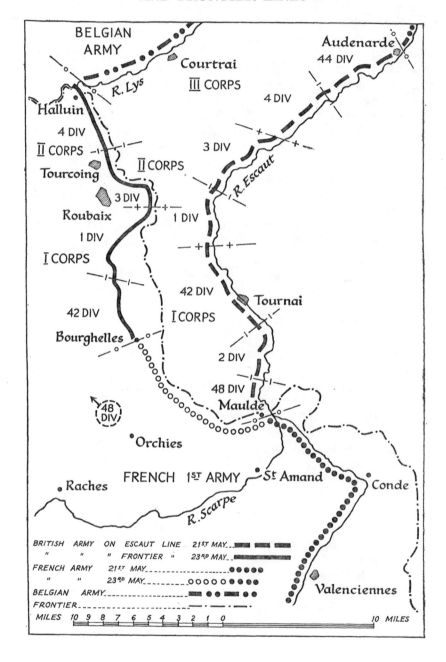

BELGIAN ARMY

Audenarde

44 DIV

Courtrai

III CORPS

4 DIV

R. Lys

Halluin

4 DIV

3 DIV

II CORPS

II CORPS

R. Escaut

Tourcoing

3 DIV

Roubaix

1 DIV

1 DIV

I CORPS

42 DIV

Tournai

42 DIV

I CORPS

Bourghelles

2 DIV

48 DIV

48 DIV

Maulde

Orchies

FRENCH 1ST ARMY

St Amand

Conde

Raches

R. Scarpe

BRITISH ARMY ON ESCAUT LINE 21ST MAY

"   "   " FRONTIER " 23RD MAY

FRENCH ARMY   21ST MAY

"   "   23RD MAY

BELGIAN ARMY

FRONTIER

MILES 10 9 8 7 6 5 4 3 2 1 0   10 MILES

Valenciennes

defence of this line on the 20th, when Polforce had been constituted to defend it from Aire to Pont Maudit. On that date the line was continued by Macforce, but by the 23rd the concentration of the French First Army had made the defence of this southern sector by British troops unnecessary, and most of Macforce was ordered to move to a more northerly sector of the Canal Line in the Nieppe Forest area. Only the 139th Brigade of the 46th Division (now in Macforce) was left in position between Carvin and Raches, where it joined up with the French when Macforce moved north. The 139th Brigade then came under the command of Polforce, whose responsibility was temporarily increased by this extension of its left flank and also by an extension of its right from Aire to St Momelin. Between St Momelin and Gravelines, where there were also elements of a French division, miscellaneous British troops in the area were now grouped under the command of Colonel C. M. Usher and were known as 'Usherforce'. On the 20th Colonel J. M. D. Wood had begun to organise a garrison for Hazebrouck—'Woodforce'. By the 23rd, therefore, starting at the northern extremity the troops were disposed along the Canal Line with Usherforce on the right and Polforce on the left. Macforce was moving up towards the Forest of Nieppe and the advanced forces of the 2nd and 48th Divisions were moving to the Aire–La Bassée front. The positions of British forces by the evening of the following day (the 24th) have been super-imposed on the German situation map for the 24th, inside the back cover. How thin were the defences, how great was the need for the stiffening which the 2nd, 44th and 48th Divisions could give now that they were freed from the main front, can be judged from the fact that although French troops had by then taken over the northern sector Polforce was still spread out over 40 odd miles.

The formation of these improvised 'forces' is a feature of Lord Gort's conduct of the campaign which has sometimes been criticised. Such 'forces,' hastily organised from miscellaneous and sometimes ill-equipped units, could have little time or opportunity to make sound administrative arrangements, or to ensure an effective system of communications. There were obvious disadvantages inherent in their constitution. On the other hand what was the alternative? Till the main British Expeditionary Force retired from the Escaut to the frontier the regularly organised and equipped infantry divisions were fully committed: none, till then, could be freed for the protection of the flank and rear. But behind the main front, organising for a sustained campaign as the British Expeditionary Force had been doing, until the German break-through at Sedan, were considerable numbers of men who in the present predicament must be used if possible to make up the deficiency in fighting divisions. 'Don Details' in Polforce, for instance, were officers and men of the 2nd Division who had been on leave when the fighting began and were waiting in an assembly camp to rejoin their units when they were formed into this six-company battalion which helped to hold the Canal Line during critical days. There were, too, considerable numbers of Royal Engineers who had been engaged on work behind the front —construction companies, tunnelling companies, chemical warfare companies. There were the staffs of training and supply depots and men of the Royal Army Service Corps and Royal Army Ordnance Corps from various establishments. What Lord Gort did was to en-sure that these scattered groups should as far as possible be gathered into 'forces'; and to each he added as much artillery as could be spared and such infantry as could be found without weakening seriously the divisions fighting on the main front. The only infantry available at first were the 25th Brigade, which had been an in-dependent formation under G.H.Q. orders before it joined the 50th Division; the 46th Division, the third of the partially equipped Territorial divisions which had been brought to France for labour duties and to continue their training; and what remained of the 23rd Division, whose fight near Arras on the 20th has been described. The 'forces' were thus, in the main, supplementary to the regularly constituted divisions, whose composition was not seriously affected. Their formation, under commanders who could act on their own initiative once they had been given a general directive, secured a measure of organisation and of fighting value where otherwise these rearward units would have been unco-ordinated and wholly in-effective for defence purposes. It is difficult to see what better arrange-ment could have been made for their use at this time. The defence which they put up was at least sufficient to persuade Rundstedt that the Canal Line was being held and to make him hesitate to use his armour against it. It will be seen later that in the time thus gained Lord Gort was able to bring stronger forces up for its defence.

On the morning of the 23rd no orders or instructions for the pro-jected Anglo-French counter-attack having reached him, Lord Gort sent a telegram to the Secretary of State urging that 'co-ordination on this front is essential with the armies of three different nations'; later in the morning General Blanchard arrived at the Command Post. A discussion followed as to the part which British troops could play in the implementation of the Weygand plan. Knowing what a com-paratively small force he could make available and what General Billotte had said of the condition of the French First Army, Lord Gort made it clear that in his view the attack from the north could not be more than a strong sortie; if the gap was to be closed the main effort must come from the south. Accordingly he proposed that the northern attack should be made by two British divisions, one French division, and what remained of the French Cavalry Corps, and that it should take place on the 26th *if this would fit in with plans for the complementary attack from the south.* Of the latter, Lord Gort had no information; he had received no details or timings for it, nor, indeed, had he any knowledge of the strength or situation of the French forces south of the Somme. He suggested May the 26th because he knew that reliefs then in progress made any earlier date impossible. General Blanchard concurred in these proposals and undertook to submit them to the High Command. It is noteworthy that he did not feel able to decide without reference to French Headquarters.

In a message to the Secretary of State for War Lord Gort had also expressed his view that only a limited part could be played by the northern armies:

> My view is that any advance by us will be in the nature of a sortie and relief must come from the south as we have not, repeat not, ammunition for serious attack.

It is clear now that General Weygand held an opposite view:

> To ease the task allotted to the Northern Group of Armies I had decided that the forces in position on the Somme should attack simultaneously in order to join up with them. I was too well aware of the weakness of the numbers at my disposal . . . to allow myself to indulge in any illusions regarding the strength of this thrust from the south—that is, from the neighbourhood of Amiens. But I calculated that however feeble it might be, it would at least create an additional threat to the German flank and thus increase the chances of success for the northern offensive.[1]

Explanation of these divergent views may perhaps be found in their authors' differing appreciations of the strength and situation of the French First Army. General Weygand says that when he took over on the 20th May there were, to the north of the breach and in the 1st Army Group, forty-five divisions, consisting of the Belgian Army of twenty divisions, nine divisions of the British Army (already heavily engaged) and sixteen French divisions which included their best motorised units.[2] He must have been counting largely on the French divisions when he attended the Paris meeting on the 22nd which decided that eight of the Allied divisions should attack southwards on the 23rd (page 111) for he seems to have expected that the French First Army could contribute five or six divisions to the attacking force. Lord Gort, on the other hand, realised that the French First Army was in no condition to do anything of the kind. In addition to what was left of the Cavalry Corps, it had but eight divisions. Many of these had had desperate fighting before they reached the salient they now held, and although this was small in area, the front running through Condé, Valenciennes, and Douai measured over forty miles.

---

[1] Weygand, p. 65.

[2] Ibid., p. 48.

The depleted and battle-weary French troops were only with difficulty holding this salient (had not General Billotte said at the Ypres meeting that the First Army was barely capable of defending itself?) and since it held the bottom of the pocket in which the northern armies were now being contained, the position of the Allies would have been desperate indeed had the French troops failed to hold it intact. Too little credit has been given to the unspectacular but vitally important role which was played successfully by the French First Army in this phase of the campaign.

On the morning of the 23rd General Georges issued Special Order 105 which read:

I. It has been decided:
1. That the joining-up operation in progress between the right of the First Army Group and the Third Army Group shall continue so as to close the return route of the German armoured divisions which have ventured towards the west.
2. That the enemy shall be hemmed in by the simultaneous construction of defences on the Somme from Amiens to the sea, on the sea-coast and on the southern flank of First Army Group.
II. For the Third Army Group this will entail closing up of the Somme from Péronne to Amiens, and fighting back towards the north-east in the general direction of Albert–Bapaume.
III. Pending the completion of the formation of the Altmayer Cavalry Group to the left of the Seventh Army, it is vital that the Evans armoured Division with the forces it has available at present should immediately undertake a mopping-up operation directed at all speed towards Abbeville. Later this operation should be directed towards St Pol so as to cover the right of the British Corps in action from the Arras area towards the south.[3]

It may be well to explain that General Robert Altmayer commanded a cavalry group of three divisions, now with the Seventh Army south of the Somme. It was his brother, General René Altmayer, who commanded V Corps with the French First Army Group in the north. The 'Evans armoured Division' meant the British 1st Armoured Division, recently landed at Cherbourg, whose movements are described in later chapters dealing with the fighting south of the Somme. It was never able to join the British Expeditionary Force or take part in the fighting north of the Somme. It will be realised that while General Georges's order notes the importance of constructing defences on the Somme, on the coast, and on the southern flank of the First Army Group, the importance of the Canal Line, of a defence line between the German armoured divisions and the rear of the Allied armies which faced eastwards, does not seem to be recognised. General Georges's reference to the

---

[3] See Appendix II, p. 382.

southern flank may have been meant to include this or he may not have known how far north the German armour had already penetrated.

Copies of two further orders were received by Lord Gort during the afternoon. The first, No. 18, was from General Weygand:

> I. The German armoured divisions have ventured towards the sea in rear of our lines. It is to be expected that they will try to reopen their path eastwards by attacking on the right flank of the First Army Group while the latter is fighting on its left.
>
> II. It is of primary importance to continue the manœuvre which is in progress, to join up the First and Third Army Groups and to form a solid barrier which will prevent the withdrawal of the armoured divisions to their rear.
>
> III. Simultaneously with the joining up of our forces facing east, every means must be used to block the enemy and paralyse the action of the armoured divisions on the flanks and in the rear.
>
> Defence zones must be organised immediately and simultaneously on the Somme (Altmayer Detachment), on the right flank of the First Army Group (area of Boulogne, Béthune, and further south) and on the coast (naval action).
>
> IV. The armoured divisions which have ventured thus far must perish there. Signed: WEYGAND.[4]

This recognised the need 'to block the enemy' on the flanks and in the rear of the main front, though the fact that Boulogne was now closely invested and German armoured divisions were between it and Béthune does not appear to be appreciated.

The second order was received by telegram (No. 1698):

> General Weygand thus lays down the imperative task of General Blanchard. Shut off the route to the sea from German attack; re-establish touch with the main body of the French forces, so as to regain control of the British lines of communication through Amiens; hold, and then beat, the German Army by counter-attacks. To this end, secure the necessary means from First Army and by moving the British Army to the right after the Belgian Army has been extended southwards. Seventh Army is responsible for the retaking of the Somme crossings. Signed: GEORGES.[5]

General Blanchard, seeking approval for the proposed Anglo-French attack on the 26th, can hardly have been enlightened by any of this and especially by being told that he should 'hold and then beat the German army by counter-attacks'.

In a personal telegram to Lord Gort, General Weygand expressed his regret that they had not met, said that the attack from the south in the direction of Albert 'is in very good shape' and asked Lord Gort

---

[4] See Appendix II, p. 382.
[5] Ibid., p. 383.

to continue the move in which he was combining with General Blanchard 'with confidence and with the energy of a tiger'.

General Weygand's mistaken belief that a manœuvre to join up the First and Third Army Groups was 'in progress' and that the attack from the south was 'in very good shape', was further underlined when the Prime Minister spoke to him and M. Reynaud on the telephone. General Weygand then told Mr Churchill that the French Seventh Army (which was south of the Somme) was advancing successfully northwards and had already recaptured Péronne, Albert and Amiens. This was mistaken information; in reality they had not even succeeded in reaching the Somme, where the enemy now held the river line firmly, with infantry divisions in position and with a number of well-established bridgeheads. Further messages which the Prime Minister addressed to Lord Gort were doubtless based on General Weygand's mistaken report, but the Secretary of State's faith in the Weygand Plan showed signs of wavering. A message from Mr. Eden concluded by assuring Lord Gort that:

> Should, however, situation on your communications make this at any time impossible you should inform us so that we can inform French and make naval and air arrangements to assist you should you have to withdraw on the northern coast.

Later in the day he sent Lord Gort a message on behalf of the Cabinet:

> Need not assure you that we are all following your action with utmost sympathy for your almost overwhelming difficulties and with complete confidence in your fortitude and resource.

While these affairs were occupying part of the attention of the Commander-in-Chief he was also concerned by what was happening on the Canal Line and at Arras. The first German armour and infantry had reached the Canal Line opposite St Omer during the night of the 22nd/23rd. A party of the 58th Chemical Warfare Company, Royal Engineers, sent to demolish the main bridge found the enemy clearing a road block at its western approach. They pushed a truck-load of explosives on to the middle of the bridge under fire and there blew it up, but the bridge was not wholly destroyed. A platoon of 'Don Details' and some gunners defending it were gradually driven back and eventually withdrew to fresh positions at Hazebrouck, while German troops occupied St Omer (which lies on the enemy side of the canal) and began to form a bridgehead. At other crossings in this sector, detachments of 392nd Battery, 98th Field Regiment, Royal Artillery, fought gamely with single guns.

A brief account of what they did may be given, simply as an illustration of the part played by such small detachments of artillery, infantry, sappers and men of the Royal Army Ordnance Corps at this time, when the enemy sought to enlarge their bridgehead east of the canal and no British divisions were yet in position to oppose them.

On the 22nd two troops from the 392nd Battery of the 98th Field Regiment Royal Artillery were hastily sent up to form part of the defence between St Momelin and Wittes. They had only seven guns, for one was being repaired in workshops. One gun with its detachment was therefore sent to cover each of the bridges at St Momelin, St Omer, Arques, Renescure, Wardrecques, Blaringhem and Wittes. This, briefly, is what happened when the Germans attacked.

The gun at St Momelin. Enemy-occupied houses and mortar positions across the bridge were destroyed by gunfire and the gun and detachment, being well dug in, survived retaliation and repulsed attempts to cross till they were relieved by French troops on the 25th.

The gun at Hazebrouck. On its way to St Omer (which was already in enemy hands) the gun detachment was ordered to defend Hazebrouck. It was sited to cover the road from St Omer and fifteen minutes after digging in it stopped an enemy column advancing down the road, the leading vehicles being knocked out. Eleven enemy tanks then attacked the gun. One (probably two) tanks were put out of action. Then four shells from the enemy tanks brought disaster. The first disabled the layer and Sergeant Mordin took over. The second wounded Sergeant Mordin in the eye but although in great pain he carried on. The third killed Lance-Sergeant Woolven, the gun's No. 1, and badly wounded the remaining member of the detachment. The fourth hit and exploded the gun's ammunition trailer. The gun, being now useless, was somehow withdrawn with its wounded detachment.

The gun at Arques. Sappers were blowing the bridge when the gun arrived. A position was taken up about a mile to the east. Advancing enemy troops were fired on but were nearing the gun position when the 12th Lancers arrived (page 130) and, under cover of their fire, the gun was withdrawn.

The gun at Renescure. Enemy-held houses across the bridge were destroyed by gunfire, and though two of the detachment were wounded the gun remained in action till the late afternoon. An enemy attack then developed from the flank. One enemy tank was knocked out but accurate mortar fire was put down on the gun position and under cover of this the enemy closed in. It was decided that the gun must be saved, but as it was limbering up the tractor was put out of action. Before anything could be done the position was over-run.

The gun at Wardrecques. The gun was placed under the command of an officer with a party of French infantry. Houses opposite were destroyed and an enemy machine gun silenced, but heavy retaliation killed the French officer and caused a temporary withdrawal of his men. The gun remained in action, but was destroyed by a direct hit shortly afterwards.

K

The gun at Blaringhem. This gun also covered parties of French and British troops. An attack at half past eight in the morning was repulsed and an enemy tank and two armoured troop carriers were hit. A second attack came in two hours later and the troops were forced back, but the gun remained in action and had fired 130 rounds when the enemy closed in. It was then limbered up and was being withdrawn when a shell from a German tank broke the connection and the gun had to be abandoned.

The gun at Wittes. This gun was got into position during the night of the 22nd/23rd. Nothing further was heard of it, though later it became known that the detachment was captured.

Thus at seven crossings detachments with single guns played a part in delaying the enemy advance for longer or shorter times. Clearly they could have done no more.

Early in the morning of the 23rd A Squadron, 12th Lancers—by now only five armoured cars—was sent forward to reconnoitre the St Omer area. They arrived in time to cover the 392nd Battery's withdrawal of their gun from Arques to Morbecque, extricated a party of Royal Engineers under fire of enemy tanks, engaged with good effect enemy infantry on the ridge near Lynde, and had an encounter with enemy tanks astride the road from St Omer to Cassel, near La Crosse. But they found no British troops in the area St Omer–Renescure–Lynde or between Renescure and Hazebrouck.

By the end of this day's fighting the enemy had a fair-sized bridge-head here, and the units of Polforce in this sector had taken up fresh covering positions at Morbecque, Steenbecque and Boeseghem. Some detachments on the Canal Line were, however, overrun and failed to get away. During the day the 5th Inniskilling Dragoon Guards, with a squadron of the 15th/19th Hussars (from G.H.Q. Troops) under their command, were sent to strengthen the position; and at Morbecque, Blaringhem and Boeseghem they were in action with enemy forces in some strength. From St Omer through Aire to Robecq the Germans had now won the canal crossings, our small detachments being either driven back or overcome by the enemy. From Robecq to Hinges, and south of Hinges, through Béthune and La Bassée, the Canal Line was unbroken.

Fifteen miles away to the south of the Canal Line, Arras still held out. When the morning of the 23rd dawned, the advanced elements of the German 5th and 7th Armoured Divisions had crossed the Scarpe to the west of the town but the 17th Brigade (5th Division) still held Marœuil and tanks of the French Cavalry Corps were still at Mont St Eloy. Bitter fighting ensued, and both places were lost and retaken during the day. Gradually, however, weight of numbers told and our troops were forced back. By nightfall the French cavalry had withdrawn north of Souchez while the 17th Brigade held precariously a line from Berthonval Farm to Ste Catherine, with the 151st Brigade (50th Division) in a defensive position behind their right rear between Souchez and Vimy. Tanks of the 1st Army Tank Brigade in action with the enemy's armoured divisions had covered first Carency and then Souchez and had fought advanced units which reached the high ground above Carency: but when night fell they were ordered to rally behind the Canal Line and they withdrew to the neighbourhood of Carvin.

Meanwhile to the east of Arras the enemy attacked persistently and after two hours preparation with artillery and mortar fire succeeded in getting across the river at the junction of the 150th and 13th Brigades. The left battalion of the former—the 4th Green Howards—lost heavily and finally stopped the enemy only a little short of Brigade headquarters at Bailleul. Of the 13th Brigade the 2nd Wiltshire fought off a number of desperate attempts by the enemy to cross the river Scarpe in assault boats. The German infantry advanced to the river in waves and suffered extremely heavy casualties and a bridging team moving up was destroyed by our artillery. But the attack persisted and about eight o'clock in the evening a crossing was effected at Roeux and the 2nd Wiltshire with part of the 9th Manchester's machine guns were withdrawn to hold a defensive flank between Bailleul, Gavrelle and Plouvain. From there the 13th Brigade front still followed the line of the Scarpe to Biache. The position at the end of the fighting is shown on the accompanying map from which the desperate situation of the troops in the Arras salient is apparent.

In Arras itself the garrison had a hard day. The 11th German Motorised Brigade tried on three sides to penetrate the town, roadblocks and barriers at the exits being subjected to heavy dive-bombing before their attacks began. But everywhere the garrison held them at bay, and when night fell the enemy had made no gains here.

At about seven o'clock in the evening, Major-General Franklyn received Lord Gort's order that the town was to be held 'to the last man and the last round.' The map shows clearly how hopeless its position had become. The troops of the 5th and 50th Divisions were being pressed back by the weight and numbers of the enemy—three divisions and a motorised brigade. The town was closely invested on three sides and less than five miles now separated the enemy's forces on the north-east and north-west of the town. The 17th Brigade and the 150th Brigade could not hope to maintain their positions for long with the German armour working round their right flank and already before Béthune. That evening the Arras garrison barricaded the northern exits in preparation for a final siege. But later in the evening Lord Gort decided that as it was now impossible to hold the high ground to the north of Arras, the Béthune–La Bassée Canal Line must be his southern line of defence; no good purpose would therefore be served by leaving to their fate the Arras garrison and the forces covering the town. Major-General Franklyn was ordered to withdraw his whole force (including the garrison) behind the Canal Line. Orders reached units a little before midnight, and most of the covering forces managed to withdraw during darkness without serious interference. But the garrison and units of the 150th Brigade could not all get clear before daybreak. They had been ordered to retire via Douai, but the enemy were actually astride of the main road leading there from Arras through Gavrelle and some units had to fight their way out. Lieutenant The Hon. Christopher Furness, of the 1st Welsh Guards who formed the rearguard, was awarded a posthumous Victoria Cross for his gallantry in this fighting.

In the words of Lord Gort's despatch the defence of Arras 'had been carried out by a small garrison, hastily assembled but well commanded, and determined to fight. It had imposed a valuable delay on a greatly superior enemy force against which it had blocked a vital road centre'.[6]

From the 19th to midnight of the 23rd/24th Arras had indeed troubled the enemy. Rommel had been ordered to take it on the 20th, but failed to do so. Our counter-attack on the 21st upset German plans still further and delayed the enemy's advance northwards. On the 22nd the German Fourth Army commander reported to Army Group A that Arras would be attacked that afternoon from three sides. He asked whether Kleist Group should push on to Boulogne and Calais as ordered, or await clarification of the situation at Arras. Rundstedt decided '*first* to clear up the situation at Arras and only *then* to push on to Calais and Boulogne'.[7]

When darkness fell on the 23rd it was still not cleared up but, as will be seen later, Kleist had been allowed to move against the Channel ports. If the holding of Arras was of such importance, its evacuation had corresponding significance. It left the French First Army deployed in the quadrilateral Maulde, Condé, Valenciennes, Douai in an uncomfortably narrow salient. None the less, the evacuation of the Arras salient is not open to criticism. With the enemy pressing in on both flanks it could not have served as a jumping-off ground for an attack. It could not have been held much longer unless altogether stronger forces could have been spared for the purpose. And in fact there were none to spare—either French or British—at this time, though this was the day on which, according to the decisions of the Paris meeting on the 22nd, the British Army and the French First Army should attack south-west with eight divisions.

---

[6] Lord Gort's Despatches, p. 5917.
[7] See Appendix II, p. 383.

Air reconnaissance from England penetrated, for the first time in two days, to the main British front, the reconnoitring planes being given fighter support. Doubtless their information was useful to the Air Ministry, but the divorce of the Air Component from the British Expeditionary Force and the growing difficulty of communications greatly limited any value it might have had to those engaged in the battle. The one slender wireless link between England and Lord Gort's headquarters was overloaded with traffic and there seems to have been little or no interchange of information regarding air operations except in daily situation reports. Day bombing was confined to the Boulogne area, for the one attack ordered in the Arras area was unable to locate the target owing to low cloud. Fighters were again active, providing cover for reconnaissance planes, escorting transport aircraft, and conducting offensive patrols over Arras, Cambrai, Lille, St Omer, and the Channel ports and coastal area. In all, 250 fighter sorties were flown and a number of enemy aircraft were destroyed. And at night 161 bombers attacked the enemy's communications in France and Belgium.

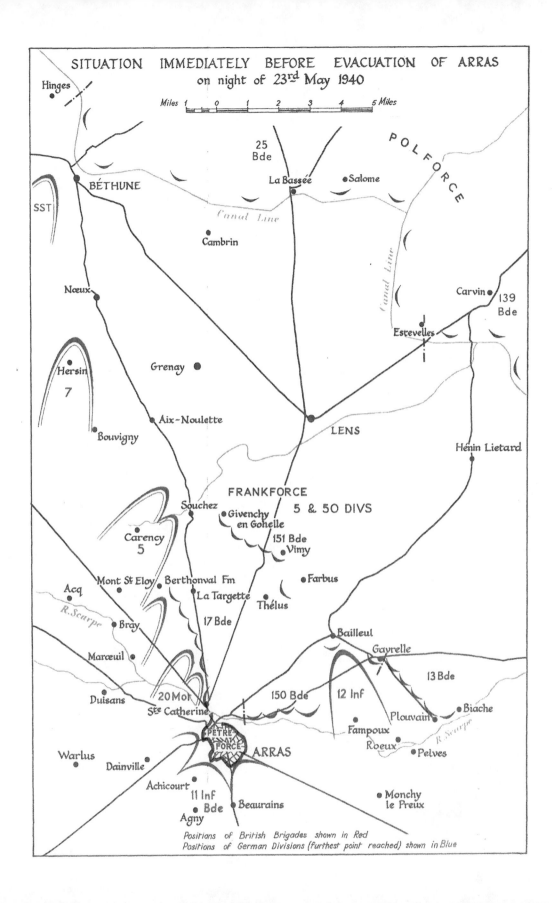

SITUATION IMMEDIATELY BEFORE EVACUATION OF ARRAS
on night of 23rd May 1940

Miles 1   0   1   2   3   4   5 Miles

Hinges

POLFORCE

25 Bde

La Bassée   Salome

BÉTHUNE

SST

Canal Line

Canal Line

Cambrin

Nœux   Carvin   139 Bde

Estevelles

Hersin   Grenay
7

Aix-Noulette   LENS   Hénin Lietard

Bouvigny

FRANKFORCE

Souchez   5 & 50 DIVS

Givenchy en Gohelle

151 Bde
Carency   Vimy
5

Farbus

Mont St Eloy   Berthonval Fm

Acq   La Targette
Thélus

R. Scarpe   Bray

17 Bde

Marœuil   Bailleul

Gavrelle

13 Bde

20 Mot   150 Bde   12 Inf

Duisans   Plouvain   Biache

Ste Catherine   Fampoux
R. Scarpe

PETRE FORCE   ARRAS   Roeux   Pelves

Warlus   Dainville

Achicourt   Monchy le Preux

11 Inf   Beaurains
Bde

Agny

Positions of British Brigades shown in Red
Positions of German Divisions (furthest point reached) shown in Blue

CHAPTER IX

FIGHTING ON TWO FRONTS

24th May and 25th May, 1940

ON the 24th of May there seemed at first to be a lull in the gathering storm. The enemy, following up our retirement from the Escaut to the French frontier, made contact along the whole position but was not yet in the necessary strength for a serious attack. The four British divisions on what has up to now been regarded as our main front were chiefly occupied in strengthening defences and in active patrolling. Enemy bombers were indeed busy behind the line and Armentières and Kemmel suffered heavy and repeated attacks. British artillery, in turn, put down harassing fire to interrupt German movements, but ammunition was running short and restrictive orders were issued, though later in the day two trains loaded with ammunition and engineer stores were found near Lille. Enemy patrols, captured dead or alive, provided identifications of a number of German units, but on the British side only the 3rd Division engaged in any offensive action. This took the form of a reconnaissance in force by the 8th Brigade. It was ordered to start at seven o'clock in the evening and was to be completed by nine-thirty. Each of the three battalions of the brigade, 1st Suffolk, 4th Royal Berkshire, and 2nd East Yorkshire was to find two companies. They were to advance north-east of Wattrelos to a railway line about 1,000 yards in front of our forward positions, to clean up any enemy in the intervening area, and to return. Machine guns of the 2nd Middlesex were to give flank protection. The right battalion found the enemy established in some strength, were unable to get far forward, and suffered considerable casualties; the centre battalion got further and suffered less; the left battalion reached their objective with little opposition. One enemy unit was identified and the troops withdrew to the original brigade position. Nine officers had been wounded, of whom three were missing. Of other ranks four were killed, four missing and ninety-seven were wounded; five carriers were lost. It is not clear that any good purpose was served by this somewhat expensive sortie.

The 4th Division, holding the left or northernmost sector of the British front, had a more anxious day. Mobile troops were seen to be moving in some strength, but their objective proved to be the Belgian front on our left flank. A four-division attack on the Courtrai sector of the Belgian-held Lys which Bock had ordered had in fact begun. By four o'clock in the afternoon the enemy had crossed the Lys between Wijk and Courtrai, and by nightfall the Belgians had been forced back to the line Menin–Moorseele–Winkel St Eloi. The German attack did not extend as far south as the 4th Division's left, but this flank was becoming dangerously exposed and would be completely uncovered if the Belgians retired further. Steps were accordingly taken to strengthen the flank by moving up a machine-gun battalion (the 1st/7th Middlesex) and an anti-tank battery (99th Battery, 20th Anti-Tank Regiment) from the 3rd Division. The rest of the eastern front had an uneventful day.

Meanwhile our second front, the Canal Line facing west and south, had now assumed equal importance. Boulogne was on the point of falling and Calais was closely invested. The enemy now had four armoured divisions, two motorised S.S. divisions and an armoured reconnaissance unit deployed on the canal front and between St Omer and Robecq he had a fair-sized bridgehead on the eastern bank.

It would hardly be possible to give a comprehensible picture of the British defences if all the troops which composed its improvised forces and all their frequent changes and movements were shown in detail. But a broad outline can be drawn with a few details added to illustrate and explain the course of events.

In Usherforce sector, in the north, the 6th Green Howards and detachments of the 3rd Searchlight Regiment, who guarded the bridges at Gravelines and for three miles to the south, held off all attempts by the German 1st Armoured Division to seize the bridges, till they were relieved during the day by French infantry and artillery. At St Pierre Brouck a detachment of the 1st Super-Heavy Battery, fighting as infantry, held off for several hours other troops of the German 1st Armoured Division which began their attacks on the bridge at dawn; but the gunners were forced back late in the morning. Another party of gunners—of the 3rd Super-Heavy Battery—held the crossing at Watten against a German armoured reconnaissance battalion till they were relieved late in the day by French infantry. The 52nd Heavy Regiment similarly fought as infantry at St Momelin until French troops relieved them on the night of the 25th. Usherforce then withdrew to Bergues to strengthen the French garrison there. From St Omer southwards to Raches Polforce was in command, with Woodforce holding Haze-brouck. Macforce was already moving up to strengthen the defence where the enemy were across the canal between St Omer and the Forest of Nieppe. The divisions now being freed from the main eastern front (2nd, 44th and 48th) were to take over the defence of the Canal Line as soon as possible.

It was where the Germans had got across the Canal Line on the previous day, from St Omer to the south of Aire, that the most dangerous position developed. Here, though there was to be no general advance, the leading troops of the two German armoured divisions and a motorised S.S. division sought to expand and con-solidate the foothold they had gained on the east of the canal, while our skeleton forces did their best to hold them back. At daybreak patrols of the 5th Inniskilling Dragoon Guards were at Blaringhem, Boeseghem and Thiennes with a detachment covering Morbecque in rear. About eleven o'clock in the morning thirty enemy tanks moved round their flank from the direction of Lynde. Tanks had been seen near Hazebrouck at about seven o'clock and later in the morning a mixed column advanced from St Omer towards the town. A counter-attack by the Inniskilling Dragoon Guards brought a vigorous reply from the enemy's stronger forces and our cavalry were forced back to Morbecque. Later in the day the defence there was reinforced by the 4th/7th Dragoon Guards and a squadron of the 13th/18th Hussars and with the help of machine guns of the 9th Royal Northumberland Fusiliers and infantry of Don Details (page 123) the enemy were stopped. But there were as yet no troops who could drive back the units of the enemy's armoured and motorised divisions, and these were now in possession of the ground between the forests of Clairmarais and Nieppe and had strong parties in both. Hazebrouck and Cassel were in great peril.

Macforce, covered by the 1st Light Armoured Reconnaissance Brigade, arrived in the area during the morning and formed a close perimeter defence of Cassel, while 137th Brigade headquarters took up positions between Hazebrouck and Morbecque. In the Polforce sector between Thiennes and Robecq a French unit which had been holding the canal was withdrawn, leaving a gap in the defence which there were then no troops to fill. Here elements of a German motorised division—the S.S. *Verfügungs* (or general service) Divi-sion—had crossed unopposed and had advanced to St Venant, and the 2nd/5th West Yorkshire on the canal from Robecq to Hinges had moved companies back to Calonne and St Floris, to hold the flank of this enemy salient.

South of Hinges, through Béthune and La Bassée to Raches, all the enemy's efforts to cross the canal were repelled. In particular he made determined and costly attempts to cross in the sector held by the 25th Brigade, but the 1st Royal Irish Fusiliers defeated the most serious attack and elsewhere the enemy was no more successful.

South-west of Raches the French First Army blocked every attempt by the enemy to advance between the two British fronts.

Twice during the morning and again in the afternoon and early evening Blenheims of No. 2 Group attacked enemy columns, our reconnaissance aircraft having noted long columns of his vehicles moving towards the canal in the St Omer area. Just before dark twenty-four Blenheims made a further attack. The rest of the day's reconnaissance and bomber operations, which involved 105 sorties by aircraft of No. 2 Group and Swordfish of Coastal Command, were in the Calais–Boulogne area and the country inland through which the German divisions were advancing northwards and against the Canal Line. Fighter Command again made a big effort in the same area; about twenty offensive fighter patrols, mostly of squadron strength, had some stiff fighting and shot down a number of enemy aircraft.

While the German troops under Rundstedt thus sought to consolidate and enlarge their bridgehead south of St Omer and, if possible, to win bridgeheads at other points on the Canal Line, there was no major attack nor any large-scale effort to break through our defence on this flank. Why was this? Partly it was due to the fact that though Arras had been evacuated the 5th Division fought a rearguard action back to the Canal Line; the high ground north of Arras to which the German Command attached such importance was not wholly and finally occupied till late in the day. But Rundstedt's hesitation is more fully explained by other considerations.

A study of the War Diaries shows that the situation as Rundstedt saw it on the evening of the 23rd may be summarised as follows:

(*a*) The possibility of concerted action by Allied forces in the north and French forces south of the Somme had to be reckoned with.

(*b*) It was of vital importance to close up the mobile formations as well as to consolidate the German northern flank. British and French attacks about Arras and Cambrai had underlined this need.

(*c*) The XIX Corps having so far failed to take Boulogne and Calais, and the defence of the Somme flank not yet being secure, the advanced units of Kleist and Hoth Groups should deny the Canal Line to the enemy but should not cross it.

About six o'clock on the evening of the 23rd a directive in this sense was given by Army Group A to the Fourth Army, who in turn ordered that 'in the main Hoth Group will halt tomorrow; Kleist Group will also halt, thereby clarifying the situation and closing up'.[1]

About eighteen hours after Rundstedt had given Kluge his directive—that is at about 11.30 on the morning of the 24th—Hitler visited Rundstedt at his headquarters. 'He agreed entirely with the view that east of Arras an attack had to be made with *infantry*, while the *mobile forces* could be halted on the line reached—Lens–Béthune–Aire–St Omer–Gravelines—in order to intercept the enemy under pressure from Army Group B. He emphasised this view by *insisting* that

---

[1] See Appendix II, p. 383.

it was in any case necessary to conserve the armoured forces for future operations and that any further compression of the ring encircling the enemy could only have the highly undesirable result of restricting the activities of the *Luftwaffe*.'[2] Thus it is clear that the decision to halt the armour on the Canal Line on the 24th (taken on the day before Hitler arrived and endorsed it) was originally Rundstedt's decision. But after Hitler had left, Rundstedt issued a directive which read: 'By the Führer's orders . . . the general line Lens–Béthune–Aire–St Omer–Gravelines (Canal Line) will *not* be passed.'[3] The armoured divisions were to close up to the canal and use the day as far as practicable for repairs and maintenance. This hold-up puzzled divisional commanders straining to get forward, and their war diaries show how disappointed they were by 'the Führer's orders' to halt. They were to quote this years later, as an instance of Hitler's interference with the conduct of the campaign—for so it must have appeared to them at the time. 'By the Führer's orders' was all they could know of the origin of this decision; but Rundstedt and Hitler knew the true facts, and, while Hitler was only too anxious to appear as the director of operations, Rundstedt saw that if he was to get his own way when it differed from the intentions of O.K.H. he must make it appear that what he did was 'by the Führer's orders'. This and cognate questions are more fully discussed in the Supplement on the 'Planning and Conduct of the German Campaign'.

The absence of any major attack on the 24th enabled progress to be made in the adjustment of our forces which recent operations—and especially the development of a western front—had made urgently necessary. During the day General Headquarters issued an 'Operation Instruction' defining the changes to be made. This provided for the abolition of improvised forces, which could now be replaced by divisions freed from the eastern front. From three o'clock in the morning of the 25th (when the Instruction was to take effect) Frankforce, Petreforce, Polforce and Macforce were abolished.

Some of the moves involved could not be completed till the following day (the 25th) but thereafter, whilst I and II Corps would still hold the British sector of the frontier line facing east, III Corps would be responsible for the defence of the Canal Line. But before the Instruction could be wholly carried out it was modified. Now III Corps, comprising the 5th and 50th Divisions and the 1st Army Tank Brigade, was relieved of responsibility for the Canal Line and ordered to concentrate on preparation for the Anglo-French counter-attack planned to begin on the 26th. Defence of the canal front by 2nd, 44th and 46th Divisions was put under command of

---

[2] See Appendix II, p. 383.
[3] Ibid.

Major-General T. R. Eastwood, who at this time was on General Headquarters Staff.

Moreover, later in the day 48th Division, less one brigade, was ordered first to send a brigade to take over the defence of Cassel and then to move to the Dunkirk area with responsibility for strengthening the defence of Bergues, Wormhoudt, Cassel and Hazebrouck. For the enemy held a small bridgehead across the canal at St Pierre Brouck, now in the French sector, and in their other bridgehead on our front advanced elements had penetrated to Cassel, Hazebrouck, Nieppe Forest, St Venant and Robecq. Only from Robecq, by Béthune and La Bassée to Raches, was the Canal Line still in our hands in spite of enemy pressure against it. Thus when these moves were completed responsibility would be distributed as follows:

The main frontier line facing east:
I Corps (1st and 42nd Divisions) and II Corps (3rd and 4th Divisions).

The Bergues–Cassel–Hazebrouck Area:
The 48th Division (less the 143rd Brigade).

The Area South of Hazebrouck:
The 44th Division (with troops in the area taken over from Polforce).

St Venant–Robecq–La Bassée front:
The 2nd Division (with the 25th Brigade from Polforce).

The Canal Line from La Bassée to Raches:
The 46th Division (now only 139th Brigade and troops attached from other formations).

For the Anglo-French attack southwards on May the 26th:
III Corps (5th and 50th Divisions and 1st Army Tank Brigade which was now reduced to a composite 4th/7th Royal Tank Regiment).

The French First Army still held its position between Raches and the British sector of the frontier line. Other French troops now held the northern sector of the Canal Line from the sea at Gravelines to St Momelin.

There were other consequential changes to complete this tidying-up process. The allotment of artillery was adjusted, and, of the armoured formations, the 1st Light Armoured Reconnaissance Brigade (East Riding Yeomanry and the Fife and Forfar Yeomanry) was to join the 44th Division; the remaining units of the 2nd Light Armoured Reconnaissance Brigade (now a composite regiment of the 5th Inniskilling Dragoon Guards, the 15th/19th Hussars and the 4th/7th Dragoon Guards) would go to the 2nd Division. The 13th/18th Hussars, the 12th Lancers, and the 1st Welsh Guards were to be held in G.H.Q. reserve.

This inevitably complex account of the main regrouping ordered may nevertheless convey an over-simplified impression of what was involved. The British Expeditionary Force and the French First Army were now confined to a long promontory stretching southwards from the coast for some seventy miles, at the widest point only twenty-five miles across and at the narrowest only thirteen. Against it flooded a rising tide of German forces. Within its cramped area large bodies of troops were required to move for longer or shorter distances, often by roads already filled by pitiful streams of refugees trudging hopelessly northwards, unshepherded and unregarded, hungry, hampered by their belongings, harried by those who sought to clear the way for troops, bombed at intervals by enemy aircraft; by parties of men who had been separated from their units in the stress of fighting and were now seeking to rejoin formations which were themselves on the move and hard to trace; by French troops going south to join the First Army or north towards the coast mostly with horse-drawn transport; and by supply columns of both armies on their several fronts. The planned system of communications was disordered. Supplies were hard to come by and harder to distribute when there was no time to organise the normal means of distribution. The wonder is not that some things went wrong, but that so much went comparatively well.

During the 24th copies of various telegrams from General Weygand to General Blanchard were received at Lord Gort's Command Post. These urged the 'continuance' of the offensive movement southwards to effect a junction with the French forces there and reported preliminary moves for a complementary attack northwards by French forces south of the Somme. Early on the 25th, Lieutenant-General Sir Ronald Adam (commanding III Corps) and General René Altmayer (commanding V Corps of the French First Army) completed their plan for the attack southwards and some preliminary reconnaissance was carried out:

> The final plan was for a counter-attack with three French and two British divisions under the command of General Altmayer. As a first stage, on the evening of 26th May, bridgeheads were to be established south of the Scarpe, and the main attack was to start the following morning, with the objective Plouvain–Marquion–Cambrai. Sir Ronald Adam with three divisions (two British and one French) was to advance east of the Canal du Nord and General Altmayer with two French divisions to the west of the Canal du Nord, his right being covered by the French Cavalry Corps.[4]

But while these preparations were being pushed forward Lord Gort received copies of telegrams which had been passing at the higher level on the 24th:

Monsieur Reynaud to Prime Minister begins: You telegraphed me

---

[4] Lord Gort's Despatches, p. 5922.

this morning that you had given orders to Gort to persevere in execution of Weygand's plan. General Weygand, however, informs me, according to a telegram from General Blanchard and contrary to formal orders confirmed this morning by General Weygand that the British Army has decided and carried out a withdrawal forty kilometres in the direction of the ports at a moment when our forces from the south were gaining ground towards the north to join up with the Allied Armies of the North. This withdrawal has naturally obliged General Weygand to modify his whole plan. He is now compelled to give up his attempt to close the breach and establish a continuous front.

It is unnecessary to emphasise the gravity of the consequences which may result.

On this it may be remarked that the British Army had not 'carried out a withdrawal forty kilometres in the direction of the ports'; only two divisions had withdrawn from the Arras salient to the Canal Line, twenty-five kilometres away. And the withdrawal was not 'contrary to formal orders', for the British commander had never had any orders to hold the Arras salient. It was also incorrect to say that 'our forces from the south were gaining ground towards the north'. They had made no real progress, and the enemy held the Somme line in force and had strong bridgeheads across the river. To this inaccurate telegram the Prime Minister replied:

We have every reason to believe that Gort is still persevering in southward move. All we know is that he has been forced by the pressure on his western flank, and to keep communication with Dunkirk for indispensable supplies, to place parts of two divisions between himself and the increasing pressure of the German armoured forces, which in apparently irresistible strength have successfully captured Abbeville and Boulogne, are menacing Calais and Dunkirk, and which have taken St Omer. How can he move southward and disengage his northern front unless he throws out this shield on his right hand. Nothing in the movements of the B.E.F. of which we are aware can be any excuse for the abandonment of the strong pressure of your northward move across the Somme, which we trust will develop . . .

Should I become aware that extreme pressure of events has compelled any departure from the plan agreed, I shall immediately inform you . . . You must understand that having waited for the southward move for a week after it became obvious, we find ourselves now ripped from the coast, by the mass of the enemy's armoured vehicles. We therefore have no choice but to continue the southward move, using such flank guard protection to the westward as is necessary . . .

But General Weygand had other information. He knew from General Blanchard's liaison officer the state and situation of the French First

Army and he knew (as Lord Gort did not know) that the complementary attack from the south would not now materialise. For General Besson, who was to command it, had seen in the withdrawal from Arras cover for his own inability to mount the necessary forces and had telephoned to General Weygand: 'The First Group of Armies has had to withdraw to the north and the enemy is being reinforced in front of us. The offensive operation cannot therefore be considered for the time being.'[5] The First Group of Armies had not in fact withdrawn at this time; the French front between Douai and Valenciennes had not moved; the distance between French forces north and south of the gap was unchanged; only the British Frankforce had been withdrawn from the Arras salient and was now preparing, in agreement with General René Altmayer, to attack southwards on the 26th.

Commandant Pierre Lyet sums up what happened in the French Command on this day: 'While General Blanchard reported the *difficulties* of the proposed operation, General Weygand saw it as *impossible*, and General Besson ordered its *abandonment*.'[6]

But though M. Reynaud's telegram to the Prime Minister had said that General Weygand was 'compelled to give up his attempt to close the breach', the latter's reply to General Blanchard had been less definite. 'You are the sole judge of what decisions are to be taken in order to save what is possible and before all the honour of the colours of which you are the guardian'[7] and, earlier, 'if the withdrawal on the Haute Deule [from Arras] makes the operation [that is, the Franco-British attack southwards] impossible, try to set up a bridgehead as wide as possible covering Dunkirk'.[8] On this General Blanchard did not at once decide that the Franco-British operation *was* impossible; on the contrary he left III Corps and the French V Corps to continue preparations for it.

It is well to avoid the needless reopening of old sores or exposure of forgotten disagreements between allies, but this account of the campaign would be incomplete if it took no cognisance of the relations between commanders, for these bore directly on the conduct of operations. Full allowance must be made for differences in language, training, and technique of French and British staffs. But the very existence of such differences lent special importance to the co-ordination of orders. Lord Gort was in an extremely difficult position. It must be remembered that he was responsible to his own Government for the troops committed to his command, but he served under the orders, first, of the French Supreme Commander;

[5] Lyet, p. 98. See Appendix II, p. 383.
[6] Ibid.
[7] Ibid., p. 99. See Appendix II, p. 384.
[8] Ibid., p. 97. See Appendix II, p. 384.

second, of the Commander-in-Chief of the Armies of the North-East, General Georges; and third, in the First Group of Armies, under the command of General Billotte (later, General Blanchard). The manner in which the co-ordinating function entrusted to General Billotte was exercised necessarily determined the effectiveness of the High Command's orders. So far as the British Expeditionary Force was concerned, all depended on the third link in the rather cumbrous chain of command.

General Billotte moved slowly and gave few orders. There were days on end when Lord Gort heard nothing from him; more than once in a critical situation he had to be asked for instructions or for the endorsement of a course of action proposed. Knowing little of his intentions, Lord Gort lost confidence in the French general's ability to grasp quickly the significance of a situation, to forecast the enemy's next move, and above all, to issue prompt and practical orders to counter it. After General Billotte's accident, three most critical days were allowed to pass before (on May the 24th) General Blanchard was officially put in command of the French First Group of Armies and General Prioux succeeded him in command of the French First Army. And when on that day Lord Gort conferred with General Blanchard the latter had to send an officer to Paris for directions. It never occurred to Lord Gort to question the intentions or good faith of the French commanders, but by now he had been led seriously to distrust their capacity to control a swiftly changing situation or make effective riposte to the enemy's thrusts.

On the other hand, the French High Command did not appear to question Lord Gort's capacity. General Weygand said of him after the war 'one thing is certain: whatever he may have personally thought of our plan, he was the first who was ready to take the offensive, and from the very beginning proved himself to be a most energetic leader.'[9] He was indeed left to carry on from day to day without fresh instructions though the situation changed almost from hour to hour. But the French Command seems to have distrusted alike his intentions and his good faith. Thus, speaking of the Ypres meeting, General Weygand says that the fact that there were subsequent differences of opinion between Lord Gort and the French generals 'inclined us to draw what seemed to be the only possible conclusion—namely that the former had purposely abstained from coming to the Ypres conference'.[10] Had General Weygand not distrusted the intentions of the British Commander-in-Chief, such an imputation would never have occurred to him; on the contrary he would have assumed that there must be some good reason for Lord Gort's non-appearance. He might even have drawn the obvious and

[9] Weygand, p. 66.
[10] Ibid., p. 58.

true conclusion that his own staff had omitted to notify Lord Gort of the time and place of meeting and that the preliminary warning sent through the Howard-Vyse Mission had failed to reach him. For at that time General Weygand himself says that he could not communicate with his own commander, General Billotte, except through Belgian Headquarters; and though he flew north for the meeting he could only get back by travelling round the coast in a destroyer. When communications were so difficult, the failure of a message to reach Lord Gort was at least a possible explanation.

One other instance must be quoted, for it shows how French distrust of Lord Gort's good faith bore on operations. When, on May the 19th the Arras counter-attack was first proposed by Lord Gort, he told General Billotte that the moment seemed ripe for a constructive offensive plan and *in order to form a reserve for this purpose* asked that fresh British divisions on the Escaut should be relieved by tired French divisions. General Georges' Chief of Staff says that this made the Staff of the French First Group of Armies (that is General Billotte's Staff) think that the request was a cover for plans to evacuate.[11] This state of distrust may explain why the French High Command would never disclose any detailed information in regard to French forces and their dispositions. At no time either before or during active operations could Lord Gort or the British Government get such information except in general terms. In the field British and French officers worked in happy accord; but on the high level absence of mutual trust weakened Allied collaboration when every ounce of strength was needed and increased the unhappiness of those unhappy days.

The changes in the over-all command of the British divisions moving up to defend the western or canal front had no immediate effect on the operations of May the 25th—or indeed subsequently. The situation there was becoming so fluid, so many formations were on the move, and administration had become so largely a matter of divisional initiative and unit enterprise, that from now on divisional commanders had largely to exercise their own initiative, basing decisions on their knowledge of the Commander-in-Chief's intentions rather than on any specific instructions. Thus, on his arrival at Dunkirk on the 25th, Major-General A. F. A. N. Thorne (48th Division) found that the French general in command of the local defences of Dunkirk felt that the port and its immediate neighbourhood were adequately protected by French troops. Accordingly General Thorne placed the 144th Brigade at Wormhoudt and the 145th at Cassel and Hazebrouck. The 44th Division was moving up on his left and the 2nd Division with the 25th Brigade and the 46th Division (less the

---

[11] Roton, p. 207.

L

137th and 138th Brigades) would complete the front to Raches where the French First Army extended the front to the east.

For the most part the enemy remained comparatively quiet during the 25th on this front. German tanks in the neighbourhood of Aire penetrated at one time to within a few miles of Merville, but these were knocked out by artillery fire, and when the 2nd Division arrived, the 5th Brigade established our positions between Tannay and Robecq, turning the enemy out of St Venant and rebuilding the bridge there which had been destroyed. Small bodies of German infantry managed to cross the canal on either side of Béthune, but there was no serious attack and by nightfall the defence of this front was considerably stronger.

On the eastern front, too, there was no serious attack during the 25th against the British sector. Considerable shelling and aerial bombardment of the rearward areas of both fronts were maintained all day, doubtless as a softening-up process before resumption of the general attack.

But throughout the day messages in regard to the Belgian front grew more and more disquieting. The first was sent by the Needham Mission at Belgian Headquarters half an hour after midnight of the 24th and reached General Headquarters early in the morning. It read:

> Position serious Belgian front between Menin and canal junction N.W. of Desselghem . . . Enemy penetration on this front everywhere exceeds one mile. Belgians are NOT repeat NOT counter-attacking this morning but may later in day. . . .

At half past six the 12th Lancers were ordered to watch the left flank of II Corps north of the River Lys and to get into touch with the Belgian forces in the Halluin–Ypres area. By nine-forty that morning (25th) the Lancers made contact with the enemy near Lendelede, and touch was established with II Corps south of the Lys Canal and with the Belgians near Iseghem. They found that Courtrai was still held, but the enemy had crossed the canal near Harlebeke and were advancing westwards on the north bank; enemy infantry were also met in Moorseele.

Meanwhile a further report had come in from the Needham Mission:

> Heavy German attack developing against Belgian 4 Corps front east and west Courtrai. Enemy reported captured Lendelede . . .

A liaison officer sent from Lord Gort's Command Post to Belgian Headquarters confirmed the seriousness of the situation and reported urgent appeals from Belgian Headquarters for British air cover.

The records of fighter action on this day are somewhat meagre.

Some patrols were flown over 'the Lille–Ypres area' from the 151 sorties that day, but our fighters working from England could not maintain a sufficiently consistent cover to prevent the Germans bombing practically at will. And although a bombing attack was made (by twenty-four Blenheims of No. 2 Group with fighter protection) against pontoon bridges over the Lys in the Courtrai area, the attack was not delivered till about five o'clock in the afternoon. The bombing programme of the night before (24th) had been arranged in response to French requests that enemy communications at various distances from the battlefield should be attacked. Forty-one Battles of the Advanced Air Striking Force attacked the Meuse crossings; aircraft went for road communications in advance of the main British front and in the 'gap' to the south, and attacked a number of important railways. Coastal Command aircraft also made a number of attacks. In all 108 bombers were employed and none was lost.

About seven o'clock in the morning of the 25th General Sir John Dill had arrived at Advanced General Headquarters from England to discuss the situation with Lord Gort. Shortly afterwards General Blanchard and his Chief of Staff also arrived, and there was a full discussion of plans for the forthcoming Franco-British attack southwards. General Blanchard confirmed the arrangement that two or three French divisions, supported by 200 tanks, would co-operate with General Sir Ronald Adam's 5th and 50th Divisions. Thus at this point General Blanchard did not regard the withdrawal from Arras as having made the proposed operation impossible or the 'difficulties' which he had reported to General Weygand as insuperable.

Sir John Dill reported these discussions to the Prime Minister:

> Have just seen Gort. There is NO blinking the seriousness of situation in northern area. B.E.F. is now holding front of eighty-seven (87) miles with seven divs. in line exclusive of remnants three T.A. labour divs. which are being used as stops on bridges. Line runs Dunkirk St Omer Aire Bethune Carvin Raches then French First Army holds Denain–St Amand–Bourghelles here B.E.F. takes up line of original frontier defences to Halluin where Belgians continue line along Lys to Ghent, two B.E.F. divs. in reserve preparing attack in conjunction French for evening 26. Germans in contact along whole front and are reported to have penetrated Belgian line north-east Courtrai yesterday evening. In above circumstances attack referred to above cannot be important affair . . . General Blanchard just arrived . . .

And later:

> Since seeing Blanchard I understand attack being planned on wider front. Preliminary operations only on date in my last telegram

main attack next day. Blanchard realises fully how much depends
on operation but regards attack from south as principal offensive . . .

The fact that, according to M. Reynaud's telegram of the day
before, General Weygand then felt compelled to give up his attempt
to close the breach does not seem to have been made known, yet, to
General Blanchard.

Throughout the day Lieut.-General A. F. Brooke, commanding
the British II Corps, urged the importance of strengthening our left
flank to cover the gap that was opening towards Ypres, for German
plans captured by the 3rd Division confirmed the seriousness of the
attack that was beginning.

An enterprising patrol had attacked and set fire to a German staff
car adventuring too near the divisional front. The driver was killed
but the passenger ran off and escaped. He was Lieutenant-General
Kinzel, the German Commander-in-Chief's liaison officer with Army
Group B, and he left behind him in his haste to escape two most
valuable papers. The first bore the very highest classification for
military security—only four copies had been issued to be taken forward. It contained the German 'Order of Battle and Commands' on
May the 1st, 1940, and gave particulars of army groups, armies, corps
and divisions, with their commanders and chiefs of staff. A few pages
were missing; apart from these it gave the War Office for the first
time an authoritative picture of the German Army, a grasp of its
composition which was never subsequently lost.

The second of the captured documents was of even more immediate importance to Lord Gort and General Brooke. It was the
German Sixth Army's orders for the attack which had begun that
morning. It showed in particular that the IX Corps had been
ordered to attack towards Ypres and the VI Corps towards
Wytschaete five miles further south. General Brooke's anxiety to
cover the gap which the Belgian retirement had opened was indeed
justified for he knew now that the enemy were attacking there with
two corps to his one.

At about half past six in the evening the Needham Mission at
Belgian Headquarters reported:

> German attack 1700 hrs today drove back Belgian right to
> Gheluwe. Gap exists between Gheluwe and Lys which Belgians
> cannot close. Last reserves used already . . .

Quarter of an hour later came another message:

> Belgians now taking inclusive Gheluwe and Zonnebeke as right
> boundary with British. They have no troops west of this line . . .
> Belgians especially anxious about gap between Gheluwe and Lys.

But at six o'clock Lord Gort had already taken what was perhaps
his most fateful action during the whole campaign. Without waiting

to ask authority from the French commander he ordered the 5th and 50th Divisions to abandon preparations for the attack southwards on the 26th and to move at once to the threatening gap between the British and Belgian armies.

By doing so he saved the British Expeditionary Force. For the gap developing between Menin and Ypres was closed only in the nick of time; had the 5th and 50th Divisions arrived but a few hours later they would have been too late. Bock would have secured his breakthrough and the British Army would have been separated from the sea and surrounded. The reasoning by which Lord Gort explained his action subsequently is set out in his despatch:

> By 6 p.m. that night (25th May) I was convinced that the steps I had taken to secure my left flank would prove insufficient to meet the growing danger in the north.
>
> The pattern of the enemy pincer attack was becoming clearer. One movement from the south-west on Dunkirk had already developed and was being held; the counterpart was now developing on the Belgian front.
>
> The gap between the British left and the Belgian right, which had been threatening the whole day, might at any time become impossible to close: were this to happen, my last hope of reaching the coast would be gone. At this time, it will be recalled, I had no reserves beyond a single cavalry regiment, and the two divisions (5th and 50th) already earmarked for the attack southwards.
>
> The French First Army, which was not affected in the same way as the B.E.F. by the situation which was developing on the Belgian front, had, it will be remembered, agreed to provide three divisions and the Cavalry Corps for this attack. Therefore, even if no British divisions could be made available, the possibility of carrying out the operation would not be entirely precluded. I did realise however that the French were unlikely to take the offensive unless British support was forthcoming.
>
> Even so, however, the situation on my northern flank was deteriorating so rapidly that I was convinced that there was no alternative but to occupy, as quickly as troops could be made available the line of the Ypres–Comines canal and the positions covering Ypres.[12] . . .

These considerations were in Lord Gort's mind, but when giving his decision to his Chief of Staff he did not stop to express them; he said, simply, he had a 'hunch' that calamity threatened in the north-east and only instant action could avert it. Then, having given his orders, he communicated his decision to the Headquarters of the French First Group of Armies.

The War Diary of the German Army Group B records that where the Belgian hold on the Lys had been broken the attack was to be

---

[12] Lord Gort's Despatches, p. 5923.

continued in the general direction of Ypres. As a preparation the heavy artillery was ordered to put down 'vigorous harassing fire' during the night on the roads and exits of Lille, Armentières, Warneton and Ypres. The army involved (the Sixth) was strengthened by the addition of a new corps (X); and one of the attacking corps (IV) by the addition of another division, the 61st.

On the other hand, war diaries of formations engaged on the canal front again illustrate Rundstedt's desire to husband his armoured divisions for the second phase of the campaign (Operation Red), with the preparation for which he was now largely preoccupied. Very early on the 25th he received a new O.K.H. instruction from the Operations Branch of the General Staff authorising the resumption of the attack on the canal front. Across this order was written and initialled by Blumentritt, Rundstedt's Operations Officer: '*By order* of the C.-in-C. [Rundstedt] and the Chief of Staff, *not* passed on to Fourth Army, as the Führer has delegated control to the C.-in-C. of the Army Group.'[13] This disregard of the O.K.H. authority is recorded in Army Group A War Diary with the added comment: 'The C.-in-C. [of the Army Group] . . . considers that, even if their further advance is extremely desirable, it is in any case urgently necessary for the motorised groups to close up'.[14] It may perhaps be assumed that Rundstedt's decision not at once to renew the attack was notified to O.K.H., who may in turn have reported it to Hitler. The diary does not say, but records that during the morning of the 25th 'the Führer's orders' of the day before, confirming Rundstedt's decision to hold his armour on the Canal Line, were repeated by telephone, and these *were* passed on to the German Fourth Army.

> By the Führer's orders . . . the north-western wing (Hoth and Kleist Groups) will hold the favourable defensive line Lens–Béthune–Aire–St Omer–Gravelines, and allow the enemy to attack it. This line may only be crossed on express instructions from Army Group headquarters. The principal thing now is to husband the armoured formations for later and more important tasks.[15]

In the course of that afternoon the German Fourth Army reported that the attack of their right wing against the French First Army 'had failed to make ground against very tenacious enemy resistance',[16] and by the evening:

> The attack of the Fourth Army, its eastern flank still held facing Valenciennes, Denain, and the river line to the south-west, had

---

[13] See Appendix II, p. 384.
[14] Ibid.
[15] Ibid.
[16] Ibid.

advanced in the centre to the line Henin-Lietard–Lens [that is to say, the Arras withdrawal had been followed up]. The motorised groups remained—as ordered—along the canal and had closed up.[17]

The day's entry concludes with the remark: 'The task of Army Group A can be considered to have been completed in the main',[18] a view which further explains Rundstedt's reluctance to employ his armoured divisions in the final clearing-up stage of this first phase of the campaign. Their losses had already been heavy. The Kleist Group reported on the 23rd that their tank casualties amounted to over fifty per cent. The War Diary of the XXXIX Corps in the Hoth Group, which then comprised the 5th and 7th Armoured and the 20th Motorised Divisions, notes on May the 24th: 'Casualties for each armoured division, approximately 50 officers and 1,500 N.C.O.s and men, killed or wounded; armour, approximately 30 per cent. Owing to frequent encounters with enemy tanks, weapon losses are heavy—particularly machine guns in the infantry regiments'.[19] If other armoured divisions had suffered comparable losses there was therefore good reason to save them now for Operation Red. On May the 25th, while advanced units of the 1st, 3rd, 4th, 6th, 7th and 8th Armoured Divisions were facing the Canal Line defences, the 2nd was still occupied at Boulogne and the 10th was engaged in trying to take Calais. It will be well to see what was happening at these Channel ports before continuing the main story.

As noted in the previous chapter a reproduction of a German situation map for the evening of May the 24th will be found inside the back cover.

---

[17] See Appendix II, p. 384.
[18] Ibid.
[19] Ibid.

CHAPTER X

DEFENCE OF THE CHANNEL PORTS

22nd May to 26th May, 1940

WHEN the German armour broke through to the coast at Abbeville on May the 20th, Boulogne and Calais acquired a new importance for, apart from Dunkirk, they were then the only ports through which the British Army could be supplied. Lord Gort had no troops which could be spared for their defence. Accordingly the War Office ordered the 20th Guards Brigade to Boulogne, and from the 1st Armoured Division (which was on the point of leaving for Cherbourg) they deflected to Calais the 3rd Royal Tank Regiment and the newly created 30th Brigade, formed from the infantry of the division's Support Group. As these forces set out from England the German armoured divisions began their advance northwards from the Somme.

The subsequent actions at Boulogne and Calais went on simultaneously, but once begun there was no communication between the two: they are therefore described separately.

BOULOGNE

Boulogne had been used only as a port: no British garrison had been stationed there. On the 20th of May anti-aircraft defences had been provided: eight 3·7-inch guns of the 2nd Heavy Anti-Aircraft Regiment and eight machine guns of the 58th Light Anti-Aircraft Regiment, with one battery of the 2nd Searchlight Regiment, made up its total British armament. The French had 'two salvaged 75-mm. guns; two 25-mm. anti-tank guns; and two tanks, one of which was broken down and only usable on the spot'.[1]

But Boulogne was not empty of troops. There were considerable numbers of young French and Belgian recruits not yet trained for fighting; about 1,500 British of the Auxiliary Military Pioneer Corps, most of whom had had no military training and none of whom were equipped as fighting soldiers; and finally, smaller groups of men, mostly French, who had made their way back from the south— 'fractions of infantry and artillery lacking uniformity . . . officers, non-commissioned officers and men driven back to Boulogne by the

---

[1] Général J. Armengaud: *Le Drame de Dunkerque*. Plon, Paris, 1948 (hereafter referred to as Armengaud), p. 105. See Appendix II, p. 385.

rapid advance of the enemy, various isolated detachments on the
move, troops on leave and men recently out of hospital'.[2] There were
also large numbers of French refugees crowding into the town from
the surrounding country.

The 20th Guards Brigade was training at Camberley on the
morning of May the 21st when orders were received from the War
Office to proceed immediately to Dover for service overseas. Less
than twenty-four hours later it arrived at Boulogne (having been
escorted across by the destroyers *Whitshed* and *Vimiera*) and began to
disembark. Only two of its battalions had been ordered out, the 2nd
Irish Guards and the 2nd Welsh Guards, with the Brigade Anti-Tank
Company and the 275th Battery (less one troop) of the 69th Anti-
Tank Regiment. Brigadier W. A. F. L. Fox-Pitt commanded the
brigade.

Rear General Headquarters of the British Expeditionary Force
had moved back by now to Wimereux, three miles up the coast,
and Brigadier Fox-Pitt reported there at seven o'clock in the morning
of the 22nd. He saw the Adjutant-General, Lieutenant-General
Sir Douglas Brownrigg, who had been given instructions from the
Commander-in-Chief to get rid of all 'useless mouths' from the ports
of Dunkirk, Calais and Boulogne as soon as possible, and to go on
evacuating personnel arriving at these ports who were not of military
value. Brigadier Fox-Pitt was told that enemy transport had been
reported at Etaples, sixteen miles south-east of Boulogne, and that
German armoured forces were said to be in the Forest of Crécy area.
The French 21st Infantry Division was coming up to hold a line
between Samer and Desvres about ten miles south of Boulogne; it
had already about three battalions deployed and the rest of the
division was being moved from the east by train. Brigadier Fox-Pitt's
orders were to hold Boulogne and for this task a regiment of tanks
(the 3rd Royal Tank Regiment) and another infantry battalion
(the 1st Queen Victoria's Rifles) should join him from Calais on the
following day.

With this information in mind the Brigadier disposed his force for the
defence of the town. The positions taken up are most easily realised
by reference to the map facing page 158. They were largely determined by the situation of the town and the nature of the surrounding
country. Boulogne lies at the mouth of the River Liane, which winds
its way to the sea through a valley in the surrounding hills. The comparatively level ground near the harbour is small in area and congested by building; almost at once the town begins to climb the hill,
and the roads up to the old walled town—known as the Haute Ville
or 'the Citadel'—are steep. The river and the harbour basins cut the
lower town in half, as the map shows. The Irish Guards held the south-

---

[2] Armengaud, p. 104. See Appendix II, p. 385.

western ground between the river west of St Léonard and the sea north of Le Portel; while the Welsh Guards covered the part of the town which lies north-east of the river, holding the western slopes of the Mont Lambert ridge and the high ground through St Martin Boulogne. Together they were extended over a six-mile perimeter; inevitably, therefore, they were thin on the ground. A much more considerable force would be needed to defend the position successfully, for the ground round Boulogne is high, rolling, open country, providing by its undulations both hidden approaches and commanding heights well suited to the manœuvring of armoured troops. It must be defended on these surrounding hills, for once an enemy wins these, Boulogne lies at his mercy. Mont Lambert ridge in particular commands most of the town and harbour.

About fifty men of the 7th Royal West Kent who had made their way north after the fight at Albert, described on page 80, and about a hundred Royal Engineers of the 262nd Field Company had reached Boulogne, and they occupied positions on the right of the Welsh Guards after destroying a road bridge across the river. Brigadier Fox-Pitt reported the dispositions of the British battalions to General Lanquetot, commander of the French 21st Division, who had arrived with some of his staff and was organising the defence of the town with the various French elements available.

The German armoured divisions whose advance had been slowed down by the British counter-attack at Arras on the 21st had now been ordered to resume the advance northwards. The War Diary of Guderian's XIX Corps (1st, 2nd and 10th Armoured Divisions) has two entries on the 22nd May which are relevant to the action at Boulogne. The first is timed 1240: '2nd Armoured Division will advance direct to Boulogne via the line Baincthun–Samer; 1st Armoured Division via Desvres to Marquise, in order to protect, on this line, 2nd Armoured Division's flank against attack from Calais.'[3] And at the end of the day's entries, recognising the need for quick action, 'the corps commander sent 2nd Armoured Division towards Boulogne at noon without waiting for orders from [Kleist] Group. In consequence the division succeeded in penetrating to the town.'[4] This division had had some difficulty in overcoming French resistance at Samer (where the French forces consisted mainly of troops from a French divisional instruction centre) but reached the outskirts of Boulogne and made first contact with the Irish Guards in the middle of the afternoon. Soon after five o'clock they attacked with tanks and artillery, but the Irish Guards held them off and the attack died away after about an hour. The enemy had lost a tank and made no gain. They attacked the Welsh Guards with tanks at about eight

---

[3] See Appendix II, p. 385.
[4] Ibid.

o'clock and again when darkness was falling, but each time they were driven off. At about ten o'clock they had their one minor success, when in a renewed attack on the Irish Guards a post was cut off, though some men got away.

Reports were received that enemy armoured columns were moving on the town from the north-east and north, but Major-General H. C. Loyd, from Rear General Headquarters, who visited the Brigadier during the night, assured him again that the 3rd Royal Tank Regiment and the 1st Queen Victoria's Rifles would probably arrive from Calais early in the morning. It will be found when the account of what happened at Calais is given, that in fact no move to Boulogne was attempted, and this was not the only hope to be disappointed. Of the troops already deployed by the French 21st Division, those near Desvres succeeded in holding up the advance of the German 1st Armoured Division, who, according to their War Diary, fought vainly to overcome the French resistance on the 22nd and were still held up at midday on the 23rd. But the bulk of the 21st Division was attacked while still entrained and dispersed by enemy tanks. It could not now form a line south of Boulogne. There would now be nothing but the 20th Guards Brigade and the improvised French forces in the town to resist Guderian's attack on Boulogne.

The Royal Air Force did their utmost to hamper the German movement towards Boulogne. Our fighters were in action in the coastal area and twelve Battles, eleven Lysanders, and fifty-eight Blenheim bombers operated; four were lost, but the losses of aircraft which the enemy returned on this day totalled twenty-four destroyed and six damaged.

At daybreak on the 23rd the German attack was resumed. Fort de la Crèche on the hill to the north was captured from the French, and a troop of the 2nd Anti-Aircraft Regiment in the vicinity had their guns knocked out after they had destroyed two of the enemy's tanks. About half past seven in the morning attacks on the 20th Guards Brigade frontage came in from all sides. Tanks and infantry supported by artillery and mortar fire inflicted considerable casualties on our infantry and anti-tank gunners, and some companies were forced to give ground. By the end of a long morning's fighting it was clear that the original perimeter could not be held, and the battalions were drawn back to the outskirts of the town.

Throughout the morning destroyers of the Royal Navy were coming and going in spite of the fact that the enemy now had the harbour under close-range artillery, mortar and machine-gun fire. In addition to those already mentioned the destroyers *Vimy*, *Venomous*, *Wild Swan* and *Keith* were all employed. French destroyers were also in action against shore targets and one (*L'Orage*) was sunk. The commander of the *Keith* was killed on his bridge and the commander of the *Vimy* was mortally wounded. But in harbour and off the coast the ships shelled enemy gun-sites and machine-gun nests with conspicuous success and were of great help to defending troops, while non-combatant and wounded men were being steadily evacuated under the direction of a contingent of Royal Marines brought out to deal with the large number of unorganised men reaching the port. Meanwhile preparations to destroy port installations were being carried out by a naval demolition party. The 20th Guards Brigade were, however, ordered to remain and fight it out.

In the afternoon there was a lull in the fighting, which is explained in an entry in the German XIX Corps War Diary: '1445. At about this time Corps Headquarters has the impression that in and around Boulogne the enemy is fighting tenaciously for every inch of ground in order to prevent the important harbour falling into German hands. *Luftwaffe* attacks on warships and transports lying off Boulogne are inadequate: it is not clear whether the latter are engaged in embarkation or disembarkation. 2nd Armoured Division's attack therefore only progresses slowly.'[5] The German commander had asked for an air attack on the harbour which was eventually delivered two hours later by forty to fifty aircraft, but was partly frustrated by the Royal Air Force. Three of our aircraft were lost but eight of the enemy were brought down and others damaged. The German War Diary notes: '1930 hrs. The long-awaited air attack on the sea off Boulogne temporarily relieves pressure on 2nd Armoured Division,'[6] and for a short time the evacuation of non-combatant troops was interrupted.

At about half past six that evening fresh orders were received from the War Office. The 20th Guards Brigade were to be evacuated immediately.

By now the enemy had closed in; the whole harbour was under fire and entry was extremely hazardous. The *Whitshed* and *Vimiera* went in first and engaged enemy batteries in a fierce gun-fire duel as they berthed. Embarkation of the Irish and Welsh Guards and Royal Marines began, about 1,000 leaving in each destroyer. Then the *Wild Swan*, *Venomous* and *Venetia* took their places, again under a murderous fire. The *Venetia* was damaged and had to back out of the harbour; and all three ships engaged in a most unusual naval action, firing over open sights at enemy tanks, guns and machine guns only a few hundred yards away while they took the troops on board. They bore away about 900 men each and later the *Windsor* arrived and took off a further 600, including many wounded and the demolition party. The last ship to reach the stricken port was the *Vimiera*, making her second trip; she entered the harbour at about 1.40 on the morning of the 24th in an eerie silence. She remained at her

---

[5] See Appendix II, p. 385.
[6] Ibid.

berth over an hour and took on board 1,400 men. In this dangerously overloaded state she reached England in safety.

The *Wessex* had also been ordered to Boulogne, and had she arrived a further 300 Welsh Guards who remained might have been brought back. But the *Wessex* seems to have been diverted to Calais (see below) and no further ships went to Boulogne. Some of the Welsh Guards who were left behind were captured in the town next day and some later while trying to break out. Under the leadership of Major J. C. Windsor Lewis, the remnant of his company and details of other regiments, including a party of French infantry, were established on the seaward end of the mole and held out for a further thirty-six hours, with the enemy surrounding the basins on either side and under heavy fire from tanks, artillery and mortars. Only when it was clear that no more ships could get in and when food and ammunition were giving out, did they capitulate. The French garrison of the Citadel capitulated about the same time, after making a sortie which was unsuccessful. On May the 25th the enemy could report that Boulogne was captured.

An entry in the War Diary of Guderian's Corps for May the 24th reads 'As Boulogne will be threatened from the sea by English forces especially after its capture, 2nd Armoured Division is ordered at 1400 hrs to begin preparations for the repair and re-use of the fortifications of Boulogne, employing for this purpose prisoners of war'.[7] The use of prisoners of war on such tasks is forbidden by international agreement to which Germany was a party.

Further entries in the XIX Corps War Diary show that Guderian was not pleased. The essential thing seemed to him to be 'the push to *Dunkirk*' but this had been 'strangled at the outset' by orders from Kleist Group. The causes of the comparatively slow advance of the attack in the north-west of France he attributes in the first place to the fact that 'for reasons unknown to the Corps Command the attack on Boulogne was only authorised by [Kleist] Group at 12.40 hrs on the 22nd. For about five hours 1st and 2nd Armoured Divisions were standing inactive on the Canche.' He complains that for the heavy attack on the two strongly defended sea harbours of Boulogne and Calais he could only at first use the 1st and 2nd Armoured Divisions as the 10th Armoured Division was then in Group reserve; and he winds up his 'Conclusion' on the 23rd of May: 'Corps' view is that it would have been opportune and possible to carry out its *three tasks* (Aa Canal, Calais, Boulogne) quickly and decisively, if, on the 22nd, its *total forces*, i.e. all three divisions, had advanced northward from the Somme area in one united surprise stroke.'[8] (It will be seen that later, when he had been able to look at the ground, he con-

---

[7] See Appendix II, p. 385.

[8] Ibid., p. 386.

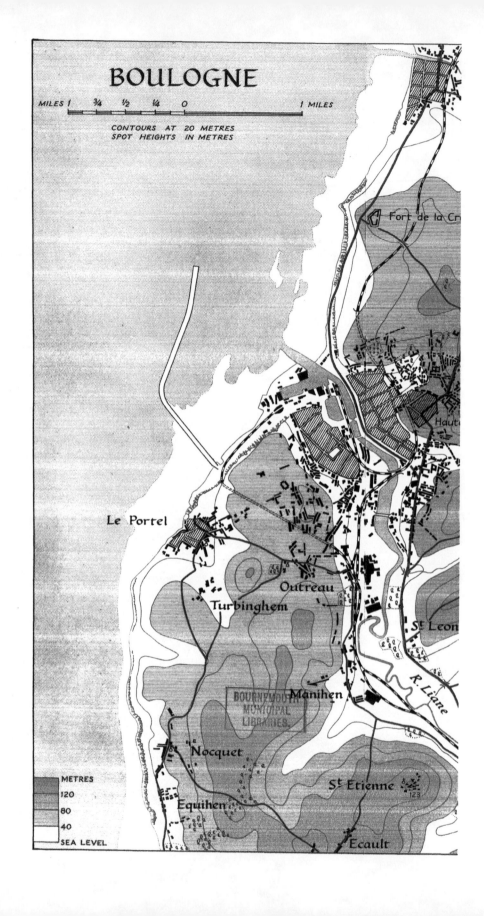

BOULOGNE

MILES 1   ¾   ½   ¼   0   1 MILES

CONTOURS AT 20 METRES
SPOT HEIGHTS IN METRES

Fort de la Cr

Haut

Le Portel

Outreau

Turbinghem

St Leon

R. Liane

Manihen

BOURNEMOUTH
MUNICIPAL
LIBRARIES.

Nocquet

St Etienne
123

METRES
120
80
40
SEA LEVEL

Equihen

Ecault

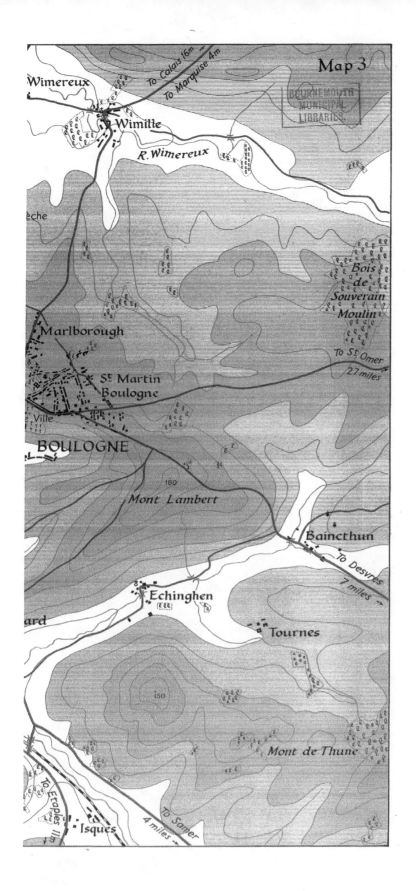

Map 3

sidered that the use of tanks to attack Dunkirk would entail needless sacrifice—see page 208.)

It would indeed have been awkward for the 20th Guards Brigade if the 2nd Armoured Division had reached Boulogne five hours earlier, but to Rundstedt, commanding a group of armies with a long exposed flank, with neither Amiens nor Abbeville yet securely held, and with Arras still unconquered, the position did not look quite so simple on May the 22nd. A delay of five hours till it was seen whether the Arras counter-attack was to be renewed was hardly unreasonable.

There is one other aspect of British action at Boulogne which must be noted—the aspect seen by the French—for it shows how easily misunderstanding may arise between allies in such a confused situation. The 20th Guards Brigade acted under orders of the British Government. They were ordered out at short notice to defend Boulogne, and when after fighting off the first attacks it was clear that two battalions could not hold the town they were ordered home again at even shorter notice. Both orders seemed reasonable to British eyes.

But when Brigadier Fox-Pitt received the order to re-embark he was unable to communicate with General Lanquetot before leaving, for the General's headquarters were away up in the Citadel and the enemy were already between it and the lower town where the Guards battalions were fighting. It will be remembered that General Lanquetot had also had orders to hold Boulogne with his 21st Division; that having got there ahead of his troops, he learned that these had been intercepted and would not join him; and that he had therefore organised what defence he could, taking into account the dispositions of the British battalions which were only a part, though much the most substantial part, of the town's defences. When, therefore, he learned on the morning of May the 24th that the whole British force had gone home to England during the night, without warning him that they were doing so, it is easy to realise that in his eyes British action appeared to be less reasonable. And since French troops in the Citadel and only Major Windsor Lewis's contingent in the harbour held out for a further twenty-four hours it is easy to see why the British part in the action at Boulogne appears as a sub-ordinate one to French eyes. The truth is that the German armoured division was held at Boulogne till May the 25th by the joint action of British and French troops.

CALAIS

The troops who held Calais fought against overwhelming odds with a cheerful courage and unquestioning devotion to duty which match the finest traditions of the British Army. Unfortunately the conditions under which they were required to fight show some of the failings which have been matched too often in the conduct of our military excursions.

Infantry were sent out short of their full complement of arms and equipment. Of the single battery of anti-tank artillery, only eight guns reached France; the rest were left at Dover because there was no room for them in the ship provided for their transport. And some ships were ordered home before they had completed the unloading of personnel, weapons and stores which they had just ferried across. But the handicaps under which the troops fought were not confined to such matters as these. Within a period of forty-eight hours contradictory orders were given to the force by General Headquarters in France, Lord Gort's Adjutant-General, then in Dover, and the War Office in London. It is hardly surprising that the French commander in Calais (who came under the British Command by order of General Fagalde) found the British intentions 'nebulous'.[9] The troops employed at Calais could not have fought more bravely than they did, had they had all their arms and equipment; and they could not have held Calais indefinitely had that been their single task, for the forces against them were overwhelmingly stronger. But they would not have fought under so great a handicap if they had been fully equipped and if their commander had been free to concentrate on the sufficiently arduous duty of defending the town.

Calais lies in flat country flanked by low sand dunes. Much of Vauban's fortifications still enclose it, interrupted only in the southwest by railway construction and industrial buildings. The Citadel still guards the inner, water-ringed 'old town' and eight of the eleven bastions still stand in the angles of the outer ramparts. On the east face the moat still holds water and in other places the ditch is traceable, though it is dry. Uncle Toby and Corporal Trim would find much to interest them even now, though the 'ravelins, bastions, curtains and hornworks' with other refinements of the fortified towns which they laboured untiringly to reproduce in Uncle Toby's garden are blurred and buried by neglect.[10] It is nevertheless a comparatively strong defensive position, granted an adequate force to hold the eight-mile perimeter. The criss-cross ditches in the low ground to the east and south confine attacking vehicles narrowly to the built-up roads which lead into the town; only on the west and south-west does the nature of the surrounding country change as the ridge of high ground which sprawls diagonally across northern France reaches out to the sea between Calais and Boulogne. On that flank Calais is overlooked from nearby hills and is an easy target for artillery situated on the higher ground, as the map facing page 170 shows.

---

[9] Armengaud, p. 121. See Appendix II, p. 386.
[10] Laurence Sterne: *Tristram Shandy*.

On May the 19th Colonel R. T. Holland had been appointed to command British troops in Calais, consisting then of a single platoon of infantry and some anti-aircraft defences. Base details of the Argyll and Sutherland Highlanders who formed the infantry platoon were sent to guard a block on the road to Dunkirk; two batteries of the 1st Searchlight Regiment were disposed in Forts Risban and Vert and in a series of outlying posts outside the town; a battery of the 2nd Anti-Aircraft Regiment had four guns near Sangatte on the west and three near Fort Vert on the east; and part of a battery of the 58th Light Anti-Aircraft Regiment sited their two guns to cover lock gates in the harbour. French troops in Calais consisting of naval personnel manning some coast-defence guns, and various 'small fragments of units driven back by the German advance',[11] including infantry and about a company of machine guns, were distributed in old forts outside the town, in the citadel, and in two of the bastions on the north-west. A large and daily-growing number of stragglers and refugees poured into the town, greatly hampering the construction and control of road blocks and the movement of troops when they arrived.

On May the 22nd, when the German 2nd Armoured Division was already closing in on Boulogne and the 1st Armoured Division was moving north from the Somme, the first of the British troops now sent to Calais began to land.

The 1st Queen Victoria's Rifles, a first-line Territorial battalion, arrived first. They were a motor-cycle battalion, but came without their machines, without transport, without 3-inch mortars, and with only smoke bombs for their 2-inch mortars; many were armed only with pistols. On disembarking they were ordered to move out at once to block the principal roads into Calais, to guard the cable-entry at Sangatte and to patrol the beaches on either side of the harbour entrance so as to prevent enemy landings there. As they had no transport, they had to man-handle stores and ammunition. Hard behind came the 3rd Royal Tank Regiment and two hours later their vehicles arrived. Unloading began at once, but proceeded slowly and under great difficulties. Only the ships' derricks were workable as electricity had been cut off from dockside cranes. Moreover, 7,000 gallons of petrol in tins, stacked on deck, had to be landed before the tanks and vehicles in the holds below could be unloaded and refuelled. The stevedores had been working without rest for many hours unloading rations for the British Expeditionary Force and they were nearing the point of exhaustion. Although the work went on nearly all night, unloading was not completed till well on in the following day.

---

[11] Armengaud, p. 118. See Appendix II, p. 386.

M

At five o'clock in the afternoon of the 22nd General Sir Douglas Brownrigg, passing through Calais on his way from Wimereux to Dover, ordered the 3rd Royal Tank Regiment to proceed *south-westwards*, as soon as landing was completed, in order to join the 20th Guards Brigade in the defence of Boulogne (page 154). The tanks were accordingly ordered to assemble in the area of Coquelles on the road which runs from Calais to Boulogne. They consisted of twenty-one light tanks and twenty-seven cruisers.

Six hours later a liaison officer brought other orders from General Headquarters. The tank regiment was to proceed as soon as possible *south-eastwards* to St Omer and Hazebrouck, where contact was to be made with General Headquarters. As the regiment could not be ready to move for some time, a patrol of light tanks was sent to reconnoitre the road to St Omer. It found the town unoccupied but under enemy shell-fire and lit by the flames of burning houses; it rejoined the regiment near Coquelles, without having encountered enemy troops, about eight o'clock on the morning of the 23rd. It had been very fortunate, for leading units of the German 6th Armoured Division (of Reinhardt's XXXXI Corps) had lain that night round Guines, only a few miles west of the St Omer road. The division had been advancing northwards but had been ordered to turn east to St Omer while the 1st Armoured Division moved on Gravelines and the 10th Armoured Division came up to take Calais.

As already mentioned, the 3rd Royal Tank Regiment had been detached from the British 1st Armoured Division which was on the point of being sent to Cherbourg. The 30th Brigade was ordered to Calais at the same time. It left Southampton on the 22nd, arrived at Dover early on the 23rd, and sailed again for Calais during the morning. At Southampton Brigadier C. N. Nicholson, commanding the brigade, was informed by the War Office that some German tanks with artillery were moving in the direction of Boulogne, but the general situation was obscure; the 30th Infantry Brigade would land either at Calais or Dunkirk and would then be used offensively against the German columns. At Dover Brigadier Nicholson saw Lord Gort's Adjutant-General newly back from Calais. Sir Douglas Brownrigg did not know that the orders which he had there given to the 3rd Royal Tank Regiment before leaving France had since been superseded by different orders from General Headquarters, and he instructed Brigadier Nicholson that the 30th Brigade was to proceed with the 3rd Royal Tank Regiment to the relief of Boulogne as soon as possible. With this order Brigadier Nicholson sailed for France.

Meanwhile the 3rd Royal Tank Regiment at Calais, having received their patrol's report on St Omer, sent an escort of light tanks to protect the liaison officer returning to General Headquarters. But by then the German 6th Armoured Division was again on the move going eastward towards St Omer; the road from Calais to St Omer was no longer clear. Our light tanks quickly ran into advanced elements of the enemy armoured division and all were lost in the ensuing fight. Only the liaison officer's faster car got back to Calais with its occupant wounded. The remainder of the Tank Regiment had begun to follow the advance party from their assembly area near Coquelles. But the German 1st Armoured Division were also moving and had deployed tanks and anti-tank guns on the high ground covering Guines as they turned north-eastwards towards Gravelines. The British tanks soon met these on their way to the St Omer road and, though they drove off the light tanks which were first met, the heavier tanks and anti-tank guns were too strong for them to master. After knocking out some of the enemy's tanks but losing twelve of their own it became clear that they could not break through the German division to St Omer. Accordingly they fell back on Calais.

Meanwhile other units of the German 1st Armoured Division on their way to Gravelines encountered at Les Attaques a detachment of the 1st Searchlight Regiment, which after putting up a stout defence was surrounded and overwhelmed. The enemy's tanks and infantry then attacked a post at Le Colombier, but with the help of fire from other posts and from guns of the 58th Light Anti-Aircraft Regiment on the rising ground near Boulogne these were driven off.

Thus when the 30th Brigade convoy docked at Calais on the afternoon of May the 23rd Brigadier Nicholson found that the 3rd Royal Tank Regiment had already had considerable losses, that the enemy were closing in on the town, and that it was not possible to move either south-east to St Omer or south-west to Boulogne. It was indeed clear to him that the one urgent task was to organise the defence of Calais itself. Accordingly he ordered the infantry battalions of the 30th Brigade—the 1st Rifle Brigade (on the east) and the 2nd King's Royal Rifle Corps (on the west)—to hold the outer ramparts behind the advanced posts of the Queen Victoria's Rifles and the outlying anti-aircraft units.

But he had hardly made these dispositions when, shortly after four o'clock in the afternoon, he received yet another order, this time from the War Office. He was now instructed to convey 350,000 rations for the British Expeditionary Force *north-eastwards* to Dunkirk and he was told to regard this duty 'as over-riding all other considerations'. So he recalled part of the infantry from the perimeter defence and sent them to picket the first stretch of the road to Dunkirk while the convoy was formed. By now yet another German armoured division—the 10th—had come up from the south and was shelling Calais from the high ground which overlooks it.

An hour before midnight the 3rd Royal Tank Regiment sent a

squadron of tanks to reconnoitre the road to Dunkirk which the convoy must take. They soon ran into troops with which the German 1st Armoured Division was blocking the road from Calais to protect its own rear as it advanced on Gravelines. Three of our tanks broke through and went on to join the British troops at Gravelines; the rest were lost. But this was not known in Calais and in the morning when nothing was heard from the squadron another squadron went forward with a company of the 1st Rifle Brigade to contact the advance party and to clear the road for the convoy. Infantry and tanks fought hard to dislodge the enemy rearguard which they found astride the road but the latter had deployed field artillery and anti-tank guns, and when losses mounted and no progress was made the attack was called off by Brigadier Nicholson and the troops were ordered back to Calais. The 3rd Royal Tank Regiment was by now reduced to nine cruiser and twelve light tanks. Between our remaining twenty-one tanks and Gravelines was a German armoured division and it was clearly impossible to get the convoy through.

Calais was by then under heavy shell-fire. The artillery and mortar bombardment had started at dawn on the 24th in preparation for an attack by the 10th Armoured Division which was launched by tanks and infantry against the western and south-western sectors. On the west Sangatte was abandoned, and everywhere the outlying search-light, anti-aircraft, and infantry detachments were withdrawn to join the infantry holding the ramparts. The first heavy attacks that morning were all stopped, except at one point in the south where the enemy made some headway and the defence was penetrated. But there a prompt counter-attack by the King's Royal Rifle Corps supported by tanks of the Royal Tank Regiment drove the enemy back and restored the original position.

Shells were now reaching the harbour area, where a hospital train full of wounded men waited for a ship; and in a laudable desire to get these away the Control Staff ordered them to be put aboard ships which had not yet completed the unloading of vehicles, weapons and equipment of the infantry battalions, and supply personnel of the tank regiment which had landed in Calais the day before. The stevedores and other non-fighting troops were embarked at the same time and returned to England. It may be that further unloading was considered unnecessary, for early that morning Brigadier Nicholson was informed by the War Office that evacuation had been decided on 'in principle' and that, while fighting personnel must stay to cover the final evacuation, non-fighting personnel should begin embarking at once. But it was unfortunate that the fighting troops were thus deprived of weapons and equipment which they sorely needed.

In the afternoon the enemy launched further heavy attacks on all three sides using infantry and tanks. On the west Fort Nieulay was surrendered by the French commander of the garrison (which included a small detachment of the Queen Victoria Rifles) after very heavy shelling, and French marines in Fort Lapin and manning coastal defence guns disabled their guns and got away. In the south the British defence was pierced, and the enemy gained a foothold in the town from which he could not be dislodged. The defenders of the ramparts had been troubled all day by fifth-column sniping from buildings in their rear; they were now enfiladed by fire from the houses held by the enemy.

Ammunition on the ramparts was beginning to run short. All but two of the 229th Battery's anti-tank guns had been put out of action. The German 10th Armoured Division War Diary's entry at four o'clock that afternoon reads 'Enemy resistance from scarcely perceptible positions was however so strong that it was only possible to achieve quite slight local success', and three hours later Corps Headquarters were told that a third of the German equipment, vehicles and personnel and 'a good half of the tanks' were casualties; the troops were 'tired out'.[12]

Yet Brigadier Nicholson realised that he could not hold the outer perimeter much longer, for he had no reserve with which to counter any penetration. A further message from the War Office confirmed the decision to evacuate, but final evacuation of the fighting troops would not take place until seven o'clock next morning. On this information Brigadier Nicholson shortened his front by withdrawing the infantry to the line of the Marck Canal and the Boulevard Léon Gambetta. There was further fighting there and after dark the defenders were withdrawn to the old town and the quadrangle to the east, which is enclosed by the outer ramparts and the Marck and Calais canals. The chief danger-points in this new defence line were, of course, the bridges. It had been understood that the French would prepare these for demolition, but this had not been done and the British force had neither explosives nor equipment for the task.

While the troops were withdrawing through the town that afternoon, Brigadier Nicholson received a message from the C.I.G.S. in London informing him that the French commander in the north 'forbids evacuation'. This was expanded by a message sent just before midnight: 'In spite of policy of evacuation given you this morning, fact that British forces in your area now under Fagalde who has ordered no, repeat no, evacuation, means that you must comply for sake of allied solidarity. . .' Brigadier Nicholson's role now, he was told, was to hold on, and as the harbour 'was now of no importance to the B.E.F.' he was to select the best position in which to fight to the end. Ammunition was being sent but no reinforcements. But the

---

[12] See Appendix II, p. 386.

48th Division 'started marching to your assistance this morning'. Unfortunately this last information was mistaken; the 48th Division was required for the defence of Cassel and Hazebrouck, and was never ordered to march on Calais.

Brigadier Nicholson's only recorded comment on this order to fight it out 'for the sake of allied solidarity' was recorded by Admiral Sir James Somerville who crossed the Channel that night to confer with him: 'Given more guns which were urgently needed, he was confident he could hold on for a time.' He agreed with the Admiral that ships in the port could now serve no useful purpose by remaining.

There are two other laconic entries in the records of those who fought at Calais which illustrate the spirit of the defence.

After noting that in the early evening of May the 24th an enemy aircraft dropped leaflets stating that Boulogne had fallen and calling on the Calais garrison to surrender—they were to lay down their arms and march out on the Coquelles road, otherwise the bombardment, which would cease for an hour, would be renewed and intensified—the writer merely adds: 'The company took advantage of the lull to improve its position to give better all-round protection.'

During the morning of May the 25th the Mayor of Calais (who was captured when our troops withdrew to the old town) was brought under enemy escort to where the 2nd King's Royal Rifle Corps held the front, with a proposal for Brigadier Nicholson to surrender. 'The Mayor was detained under guard and his escort returned to the enemy' is the only comment.

At daybreak on the 25th the enemy resumed his bombardment, concentrating now on the heart of the old town. Collapsed buildings blocked the streets, fire fanned by a high wind raged unchecked on every hand; the smoke of explosions and burning houses be-clouded the scene of destruction and obscured the movements of troops. As the day wore on the dust and choking smoke made the garrison's task more and more difficult. The troops had been fighting for three days and were much reduced by casualties, the last remaining guns of the 229th Anti-Tank Battery were knocked out, and only three tanks of the 3rd Royal Tank Regiment remained in action. Food and ammunition were difficult to distribute and some went short, and water was scarce as the mains had burst and the little that could be got came from half-ruined wells. The German artillery and mortar fire grew in intensity as the day wore on, and the defence had no artillery with which to reply, though the Royal Navy did their best to help by shelling enemy gun positions.

On the east side, where the 1st Rifle Brigade and detachments of the Queen Victoria's Rifles held the outer ramparts and the Marck and Calais canals, the enemy fought hard to break through. An attempt was made by the defence to organise a sortie in order to relieve pressure, but the carriers which were to attack from the north and take the enemy in the flank got bogged down in sandhills and the attempt had to be abandoned. In the end the enemy succeeded in breaking across the canals at a number of places. The positions of the defenders being thus turned, they fell back fighting to the area of the Bassin des Chasses, the dock railway-station and the quays.

Meanwhile the King's Royal Rifle Corps, and other detachments of the Queen Victoria's Rifles in the old town, fought grimly to hold the three main bridges into the town from the south. Two were held, but the enemy won the third with the help of tanks and established himself in houses north of the bridge, where he was pinned down. A mixed British and French force held a key bastion and the French garrison in the Citadel fought off all attacks upon it though sustaining heavy casualties. Brigadier Nicholson established there a joint headquarters with the French commander.

During the afternoon a flag of truce was brought in by a German officer, accompanied by a captured French captain and a Belgian soldier, to demand surrender. Brigadier Nicholson's reply as recorded, in *English*, in the German War Diary was:

1. The answer is no as it is the British Army's duty to fight as well as it is the German's.
2. The French captain and the Belgian soldier having not been blindfolded cannot be sent back. The Allied commander gives his words that they will be put under guard and will not be allowed to fight against the Germans.

Thereafter the attack was renewed and only broken off finally, says the German 10th Armoured Division War Diary, because 'the Infantry Brigade Commander considers further attack pointless, as the enemy resistance is not yet crushed and as there is not enough time before the fall of darkness'.[13]

About two o'clock in the afternoon the Secretary of State for War (Mr Eden) had sent Brigadier Nicholson a message which read:

Defence of Calais to the utmost is of highest importance to our country as symbolising our continued co-operation with France. The eyes of the Empire are upon the defence of Calais, and H.M. Government are confident you and your gallant regiments will perform an exploit worthy of the British name.

Shortly before midnight the War Office sent a further exhortation which read:

Every hour you continue to exist is of greatest help to the B.E.F. Government has therefore decided you must continue to fight. Have greatest admiration for your splendid stand.

[13] See Appendix II, p. 386.

This was intercepted, read with great interest and recorded in the War Diary of the German XIX Corps.

Early in the morning of May the 26th the German bombardment was resumed with greater violence, additional artillery having been brought up from Boulogne. In the words of the Corps War Diary: '0900 hrs. The combined bombing attack and artillery bombardment on Calais Citadel and on the suburb of Les Baraques are carried out between 0900 and 1000 hrs. No visible result is achieved; the fighting continues and the English defend themselves tenaciously.'[14] Les Baraques is between the Citadel and Fort Lapin.

There was also much heavy dive-bombing, and though one aircraft was shot down and the tanks and infantry which followed up each air attack were repeatedly driven off, the defenders were gradually forced back into the northern half of the old town. The Citadel, after renewed assaults, was surrounded and isolated from the town—and in the town itself and in the bastions most of the defenders, by the afternoon, fought in parties which were separated from each other alike by the course of the battle and by piles of broken masonry. In the late afternoon the enemy broke into and captured the Citadel with Brigadier Nicholson and his headquarters; and as evening came one group after another of those who fought on in the town were surrounded and overwhelmed. Gradually the fighting ceased and the noise of battle died away as darkness shrouded the scene of devastation and death.

The reader who has already followed the fortunes of the British Expeditionary Force may perhaps doubt the value at this date of the contribution to 'allied solidarity', but will have no doubt about the service rendered by the little garrisons of Boulogne and Calais to the British Expeditionary Force and the French First Army. They engaged two of Guderian's three armoured divisions and held them during most critical days. By the time the Germans had taken Calais and Boulogne and had 'sorted themselves out', the divisions of the British III Corps had been moved west to face them, covering the rear of the British Expeditionary Force and guarding the routes for the final withdrawal to Dunkirk.

The 20th Guards Brigade at Boulogne were fortunate in that, having proved their mettle, they were withdrawn to fight another day. The 30th Brigade and the rest of the Calais garrison were less fortunate in that regard, but they gained the distinction of having fought to the end, at a high cost of life and liberty, because this was required of them. They helped to make it possible for the British Expeditionary Force to reach Dunkirk and by their disciplined courage and stout-hearted endurance they enriched the history of the British Army.

---

[14] See Appendix II, p. 386.

Officers and men, many of them wounded, who fell into the enemy's hands that Sunday evening and went with Brigadier Nicholson into captivity which was to last for years, compiled a number of records of what happened in Calais. Brigadier Nicholson had not finished writing his own version when he died in a German prisoner-of-war camp. But other versions were completed and they give a détailed and vivid picture of the fighting till, in the end, its coherence dissolved as dwindling groups fought unco-ordinated actions in the rubble. Any student of these accounts must be struck by the high spirit with which their tale is told, by the unquestioning loyalty which all-unconsciously they reveal. Nowhere is there any sign of the bitterness of defeat, any hint of complaint, any suggestion that they were hardly used. There is only a plain account of the fight they fought, and a sober satisfaction in what they did. One regimental record, written by an infantryman during the years of his imprisonment, concludes with a sentence which typifies the spirit of them all: 'It would not be easy to find any who regret the days of Calais.'

They were picturesquely, if inaccurately, described in the War Diary of the German 10th Division, as belonging, for the most part to 'the Queen Viktoria Brigade, a formation well known in English military and colonial history'.[15]

In order that the military action at Calais could be read as an uninterrupted story the Royal Navy's part in the operations has been left to the end. It began with the transhipment of the troops and the sending over of the usual demolition party. It continued at intervals with the landing of rations and ammunition, the embarkation of wounded and the bombardment of shore targets. It ceased only when the Government ordered that no further evacuation would take place. The ships employed included the destroyers *Grafton*, *Greyhound*, *Wessex*, *Wolfhound* and *Verity* and the Polish ship *Burza*. Of these the *Wessex* was sunk by enemy bombers and the *Burza* was damaged. And when evacuation of the fighting troops was stopped Sir Bertram Ramsay, the Vice-Admiral, Dover, sent over a number of small craft in the hope that more of the men not required for the garrison might still be got away. The launch *Samois* made four trips into the beleagured port and each time brought away casualties, and the echosounding yacht *Conidaw* berthed early on the 26th, grounded on a falling tide and remained there under fire till the tide rose again in the afternoon, and then sailed with 165 men including a remnant of the Royal Marine harbour-guard whose officers had all been killed or captured. Others similarly brought away many of the casualties. Only after the fighting ceased and Calais was in enemy hands did the Navy's efforts also come to an end.

---

15 See Appendix II, p. 387.

The Royal Air Force put forth a big effort to cover our troops in the coastal area during these days. Their intervention in the *Luftwaffe's* attack on Boulogne on the 23rd has already been mentioned (page 156). On the 24th twenty fighter patrols at squadron strength were flown and there were some hard combats with much larger German formations. Ten of our aircraft failed to return; but the enemy lost in all twenty-four aircraft and had twelve seriously damaged. On the 25th there were twenty-one bomber sorties by day (on which two Blenheims were lost) and 151 fighter sorties when, again, two aircraft were lost. But the enemy return of daily losses shows twenty-five lost and nine damaged. Finally on the 26th a similar programme was carried out. No bombers and only six out of 200 fighters employed were lost. The German Air Situation Reports complain of strong fighter opposition in the coastal areas, the enemy aircraft 'operating from bases in southern England'. According to their return of daily losses over France and Belgium 160 of their aircraft were destroyed or damaged in the five days of 22nd to 26th May. In the same period our corresponding total was 112.

There is a footnote to this story. At first light on May the 27th, in response to a request from the War Office received on the evening of May the 26th, twelve Lysanders dropped supplies of water in Calais and at ten o'clock in the morning seventeen Lysanders dropped supplies of ammunition in the Citadel while nine Fleet Air Arm Swordfish bombed enemy gun posts near the town. Three Lysanders failed to return and one of the Hectors which accompanied the Swordfish crashed at Dover. But unknown to Whitehall the Citadel had fallen before the War Office request was made to the Air Ministry; Calais was in enemy hands on the evening before the Lysanders set out on their costly mission.

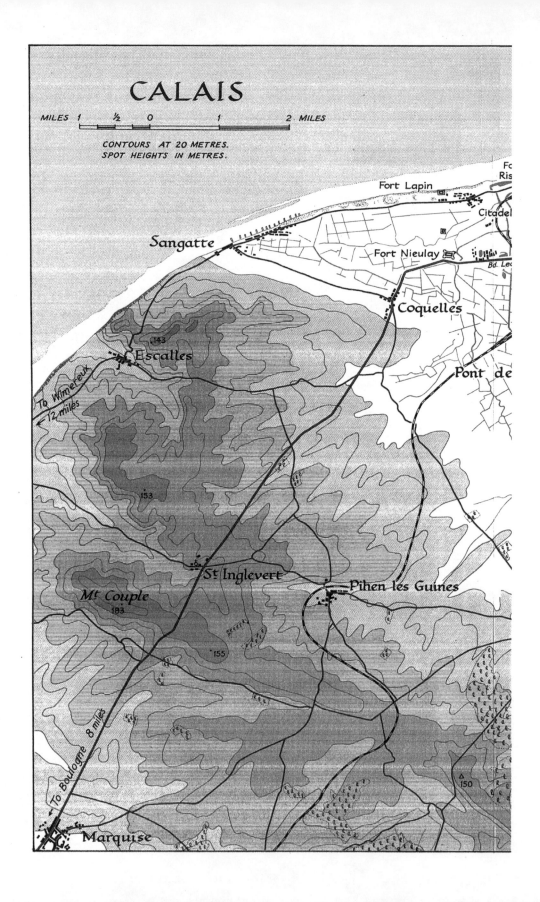

CALAIS

MILES 1   ½   0   1   2 MILES

CONTOURS AT 20 METRES.
SPOT HEIGHTS IN METRES.

Fo
Ris

Fort Lapin

Citadel

Sangatte

Fort Nieulay

Bd. Leo

Coquelles

·143

Escalles

Pont de

To Wimereux
12 miles

·153

St Inglevert

Pihen les Guines

Mt Couple
·183

·155

To Boulogne 8 miles

△
150

Marquise

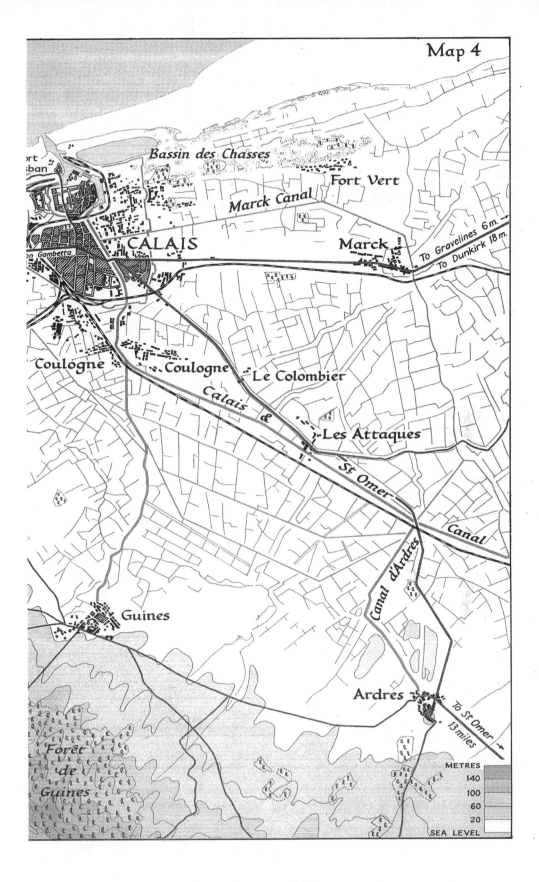

Map 4

Bassin des Chasses

Fort Vert

Marck Canal

CALAIS

Marck

To Gravelines 6 m.
To Dunkirk 18 m.

Coulogne

Coulogne

Le Colombier

Calais

Les Attaques

St Omer

Canal

Canal d'Ardres

Guines

Ardres

To St Omer 13 miles

METRES
140
100
60
20
SEA LEVEL

Forêt
de
Guines

CHAPTER XI

THE DECISION TO EVACUATE

26th May, 1940

BEFORE resuming the account of British operations which was interrupted to describe the happenings at Boulogne and Calais, it may be well to take stock of the situation on the morning of May the 26th as it appeared at the time to the Commander-in-Chief.

He knew that the British and French forces were enclosed by two German Army Groups in a pocket which with its open mouth at the Dunkirk coast hung down to the River Sensée. He knew that the forces which held its margins were stretched out on a front of 128 miles and that though in some sections the front was held by French troops and in some was held jointly, yet his own troops were extended over 97 miles. He knew now that the 1st Armoured Division, description of whose movements must be postponed to later chapters, would now never reach him, for elements were at Calais and the rest away south of the German-held breach in the French front. He knew that no reinforcements were being sent out and that ammunition and supplies were running short, though as many as possible of the non-fighting troops were being evacuated. Finally he knew that the Belgian Army on his northern flank was in danger of being isolated and was nearing the point of collapse. To prevent the enemy from sweeping round his left flank between the British Expeditionary Force and the sea he had sent the 5th and 50th Divisions to the danger spot. They could not now join General Altmayer's forces in a counter-attack southwards; whether or not the French would attack without British support he did not yet know. Nor did he know any details of the complementary attack from the south which was an essential part (in his view the major part) of the Weygand Plan, much less did he know that the attack from the south had in fact been cancelled.

The British Expeditionary Force was indeed in a desperate situation, more desperate even than bare facts revealed. For the forces holding the long front were greatly outnumbered by those opposed to them. In the north-east where the 5th and 50th Divisions were moving into the gap between Comines and Ypres three German divisions of Army Group B were seeking to break through. In the west, apart from improvised detachments, there were one Regular division (the 2nd) and three Territorial divisions (the 48th, 44th and 46th). Of the latter, the 48th and 44th had at this time only two brigades each on this front, and the 46th, though fighting stoutly, was the third of the divisions which had been sent out originally to continue training and for labour duties. There were also some of the mechanised cavalry and the 1st Light Armoured Reconnaissance Brigade. Ranged against this slender array the German Army Group A had six armoured and four motorised divisions, with more in rear. These details of the enemy forces were not fully known to Lord Gort but he knew that nine or ten armoured divisions and many others were operating on this flank and that if they were to be held off, the total frontage which he had to defend must be shortened.

Early on this Sunday morning Lord Gort informed the Secretary of State for War that he had dispatched the 5th and 50th Divisions to fill the gap which the Belgian withdrawal northwards was creating. He and General Pownall then went to General Blanchard's headquarters where they learned that the French general had already decided to cancel the planned attack southwards: orders to that effect had been issued just before midnight but had not reached Lord Gort's Command Post before he left. General Blanchard's operation order No. 30 was as follows:

I. The enemy has crossed the Lys on both sides of Courtrai and has reached Menin, Iseghem, Ingelmunster.

The British divisions which were to have attacked towards Marchiennes-Péronne are no longer available for this purpose.

II. In consequence, the attack envisaged in the Marchiennes-Péronne direction will not take place.

The First Army, the B.E.F. and the Belgian Army will regroup progressively behind the water-line demarcated by the Aa Canal, the Lys, and the 'Canal de dérivation' so as to form a bridgehead covering Dunkirk in breadth.

This bridgehead will be held with no thought of retreat.

III. The First Army will start its withdrawal on the 26th May, bringing its reserves back to the north of the Scarpe.

The withdrawal from the Sensée–Escaut line is intended to take place during the night of the 26th/27th.

The First Army will put one light mechanised division in the area east of Ypres, to go into action towards Courtrai (special order).

IV. The Belgian Army will make every effort to reduce the pocket achieved by the enemy north of the Lys at Courtrai.

The light mechanised division put in east of Ypres can act on its own behalf on the orders of the commander of the group of armies.

V. The forces at the disposal of Admiral Nord will throw back the enemy to the west of the Aa, where the enemy has crossed the river, and will afterwards be responsible for the defence of the river.

Signed: BLANCHARD.[1]

Thus the northern thrust envisaged in the Weygand Plan was now

---

[1] See Appendix II, p. 387.

finally abandoned, and since, as we have seen, the southern thrust had been abandoned too, the Weygand Plan was dead.

Detailed plans to implement the above order for withdrawal northwards were agreed in the following terms, 'subject to no deterioration on Belgian front'. British orders were issued accordingly.

1. *Night of 26th/27th May*

    The French: Rearguards on the Scarpe; main body on the line Pont à Vendin–Thumeries–Pont à Marcq–Bourgh-elles.

    The British: Rearguards *on the frontier* position; main body on the line Sainghin–Annappes–Marcq–Warneton.

2. *Night of 27th/28th May*

    The French: Rearguards on the Deule; main body on the Lys.

    The British: Departure of rearguards from the frontier position at midnight on 27th to occupy the line Warneton–Wambrechies–the Deule at Lille; main body on the Lys.

    The forces holding the La Bassée Canal to Robecq remain in position during these two nights.

3. *Night 28th/29th May*

    French and British: Withdrawal of rearguards on to the Lys and of the forces holding the La Bassée Canal to Robecq.

It should be observed that both in General Blanchard's order and in the agreement implementing it, only withdrawal to the Lys was provided for. There was no discussion of any further withdrawal, and General Blanchard's report to General Weygand read:

. . . British Expeditionary Force, First Army and Belgians will withdraw to line Aa–Lys–Canal de Dérivation from which there will be no further retirement. First Army will withdraw to line Scarpe night 26th. Belgians supported by French mechanised division will reduce pocket at Courtrai. Admiral Nord will act against enemy west of Aa.

On returning to his Command Post Lord Gort found a personal message from Mr Eden:

I have had information all of which goes to show that French offensive from Somme cannot be made in sufficient strength to hold any prospect of junction with your armies in the north. Should this prove to be the case you will be faced with a situation in which safety of B.E.F. will be predominant consideration. In such conditions only course open to you may be to fight your way back to west where all beaches and ports east of Gravelines will be used for embarkation. Navy would provide fleet of ships and small boats and R.A.F. would give full support. As withdrawal may have to begin very early preliminary plans should be urgently prepared. You should also consider urgently security of Ostend and Dunkirk to which latter port Canadian Bde group is being sent night 26th/27th. Prime Minister is seeing M. Reynaud tomorrow afternoon when whole situation will be clarified . . .

This was followed by another message to say that the Canadian Brigade would *not* be sent.

Lord Gort reported in turn to the Secretary of State that plans for a withdrawal northwards had that morning been agreed with the French, but that news from the Belgian front was disquieting. He concluded 'I must not conceal from you that a great part of the B.E.F. and its equipment will inevitably be lost.'

Another message came from Mr Eden:

Prime Minister has had conversation with M. Reynaud this afternoon. Latter fully explained to him the situation and resources French Army. It is clear from this that it will not be possible for French to deliver attack in the south in sufficient strength to enable them to effect junction with northern armies. In these circumstances no course open to you but to fall back upon the coast in accordance terms my telegram . . . M. Reynaud communicating General Weygand and latter will no doubt issue orders in this sense forthwith. You are now authorised to operate towards coast forthwith in conjunction with French and Belgian Armies.

The policy of evacuation seemed thus to have been accepted on the highest political level. Moreover, the Howard-Vyse Mission at French Headquarters informed the War Office that after receiving a copy of General Blanchard's order for withdrawal, quoted above, General Weygand had 'consequently sent for Admiral Darlan to study re-embarkation'. Unfortunately, inability to take a prompt decision and to give clear orders again resulted in misunderstanding, for neither General Blanchard nor the Admiral in charge of the Dunkirk area was told by the French High Command that evacuation was intended. General Blanchard was left to believe that a final stand was to be made on the Lys and so he failed to realise the need, much less the urgency, to plan any further withdrawal.

Lord Gort suffered from no such handicap. A week before, he had been clear in his own mind that if the French failed to close the gap in their front he might be forced to retreat to the coast. The War Office and the Admiralty had been led to realise this too, and had been preparing for such a possible contingency. And now that the attempt to close the gap was abandoned the Government saw that the contingency had become a reality. At once, they told Lord Gort: 'You are now authorised to operate towards coast forthwith' and at the same time they told the French Government that the policy must therefore be to evacuate and orders to this effect had been given to

Lord Gort. There was no ambiguity here, nor any room for misunderstanding of British intentions. Had the French High Command made known the decision to French commanders in the field with equal promptitude and clarity, much subsequent trouble would have been avoided.

With the cancellation of the Weygand Plan, III Corps were free to resume command of the forces on the western front. General Adam was however appointed to organise the Dunkirk bridgehead, and Major-General S. R. Wason (who had been Major-General Royal Artillery at General Headquarters) was appointed to command III Corps. He spent much of the next two days trying to co-ordinate plans for the withdrawal with the French commander on his left. In this he had great difficulty owing to the breakdown of communications, the frequent moves of headquarters and the growing congestion of the roads; he did not in fact succeed in gaining personal touch with his own divisions till the latter finally reached the Dunkirk bridgehead shortly before they were evacuated.

Meanwhile the divisions which were to come under his command had had an anxious day, for the German order forbidding resumption of the advance had not prevented the enemy from continuing his efforts to enlarge bridgeheads across the Canal Line.

The northern sector, now thinly held by French troops, was still on the Canal Line from Gravelines to St Momelin, though the enemy had a bridgehead over the canal near St Pierre Brouck. The main British defence on this flank was now forming farther east on a front reaching from Bergues through Soex, Wormhoudt, Cassel and Hazebrouck. Here the 48th, 44th and part of the 46th Divisions were now in position, and though Cassel and other places were shelled and bombed they were not attacked on this 26th of May. On the front of the 2nd Division, however, where the enemy already had a bridgehead east of Aire, the 2nd Division had to fight their way forward in an effort to reoccupy the Canal Line. They advanced to within a mile of the canal but they were then held up. Fighting went on here all day, and the left flank battalion of the 6th Brigade—the 1st Royal Welch Fusiliers—was gradually forced to fall back on the 2nd Durham Light Infantry in St Venant with heavy loss, leaving one company in Robecq, surrounded and reduced by casualties to a small party. Meanwhile enemy tanks and infantry passed between Robecq and St Venant to attack Merville. They made repeated attempts to capture the southern bridge leading into the town, but the 6th King's Own (a pioneer battalion) with the help of a single field gun defeated all their efforts, captured twenty prisoners, and destroyed two armoured cars and three tanks. During the night the garrison was reinforced by a troop of the 10th Field Regiment and two guns of the 115th Army Field Regiment.

On the rest of the 2nd Division's front there were strong attacks through Bois de Pacqueaut and in the Béthune salient. The 4th Brigade finally held the enemy at the northern edge of the Bois de Pacqueaut and the 5th Brigade stopped his advance towards Estaires. But here, behind Béthune, he won a small bridgehead, and there were signs that he was massing for a more formidable effort to break through. It was in fact the opening of a battle in which the 2nd Division was to fight to a finish while the first moves in the general withdrawal took place behind them.

On the left of the 2nd Division, about four miles east of La Bassée, the enemy attacked near Bauvin, where the La Bassée Canal joins the Haute Deule Canal before the latter makes a right-angle bend through Pont à Vendin to Oignies. At Oignies too the enemy attacked. The 139th Brigade of the 46th Division held the salient, interspersed with troops of two French divisions who, as withdrawal progressed, were to take over the line to La Bassée. By ten-thirty in the morning forward posts had been overrun and the enemy had reached a line facing Provin, Carvin, and Oignies. The 151st Brigade of the 50th Division, which had been withdrawn to the area south of Lille when Arras was given up and had not been moved to the Ypres front, came to the assistance of the troops attacked, and a line across the salient was established. Carvin was in enemy hands at one time but was re-taken by counter-attack.

In this southern sector the enemy were trying to link up with units of Army Group B attacking towards Seclin from the east. The embargo which kept the German divisions facing the canal line further north did not apply here, or where the French First Army stood between the two British fronts. The French were heavily attacked during the day but held out, and the enemy's efforts to break through both British and French sectors were defeated.

British divisions in the old Frontier Line were not seriously attacked though they were subjected to heavy shelling. From our forward positions considerable bodies of enemy troops were seen in the distance moving northwards across our front, but by now it was essential to husband carefully the very meagre supplies of ammunition which remained and the artillery were forced to let them pass unmolested. Yet the position on our left grew hourly more threatening as Belgian withdrawals under heavy attack widened the gap between our left and their right. It was now known that they would not withdraw westwards to continue the Allied front, for Lord Gort had received through the Belgian Mission at his Headquarters a note from General Michiels, the Belgian Chief of Staff, containing the following passage:

> Today, 26th May, the Belgian Army is being attacked with extreme violence on the front Menin–Nevele, and since the battle is now

spreading to the whole of the area of Eecloo, the lack of Belgian reserves makes it impossible to extend our boundaries, which were notified yesterday, further to the right.

We must therefore, with regret, say that we have no longer any forces available to fill the gap in the direction of Ypres.

As regards the withdrawal to the Yser the idea must be ruled out since it would destroy our fighting units more quickly than the battle now in progress, and this without loss to the enemy.

Lord Gort also received a number of messages from the British Mission at Belgian Headquarters and from Sir Roger Keyes in the same sense but also appealing urgently, on the Belgian behalf, for additional air cover and a British counter-attack at this threatened point of the Belgian front. 'If enemy is not driven back in Courtrai salient the whole front may collapse.' But a British counter-attack here was out of the question, for the only British units not already engaged were being hurried northwards to close the gap. The 5th Division found the position they were to occupy south of Ypres already under German shell-fire when they arrived and, indeed, they only just managed to be there before the enemy. General Brooke spent a hectic day collecting troops and artillery with which to extend his front northwards and had certainly neither troops nor ammunition for counter-attack elsewhere. The 12th Lancers operating on the flank had found Ypres undefended with its bridges unblown; and the nearest Belgian troops they could locate were at Zonnebeke eight miles away to the east.

The situation on this evening is shown on the situation map at the end of this chapter.

The Royal Air Force too could do but little for the Belgians in view of their other commitments. During the morning three reconnaissance sorties were sent to the area of German pressure on the Belgian front and all failed to return. But at eight o'clock in the morning, on reports received from the Air Mission at Belgian Headquarters, eighteen bombers under fighter protection attacked enemy troops and transports approaching the Lys crossings on either side of Courtrai as well as bridges and roads. They also bombed a number of airfields about St Pol which the enemy was reported to be using.

On this evening the opening moves were made in the withdrawal of the British Expeditionary Force to the Lys. Eventually they were to lead to Dunkirk.

Dunkirk is an ancient seaport which has figured many times in military history. The remains of Vauban's fortifications are still traceable, though less well preserved than those of Gravelines on the west. East of the town the coast which was to be included in the

N

Allies' bridgehead stretches away to Belgium, eight miles off, and from there to Nieuport, nine and a half miles farther still. For the whole seventeen and a half miles the shore is a wide belt of shelving sand. At Malo les Bains, Bray Dunes and La Panne there are long sea-walls or parades of brick for the convenience of their summer visitors. Behind, between and beyond these resorts, lie undulating sand dunes—mile after mile of them—half clothed with long sharp grass and patches of sea thistle. To landward of the dunes is, first, a mile-wide strip of common and scrub, and thereafter meadow land intersected by a number of canals (chief of which is a broad canal running direct from Dunkirk to Furnes not far behind the sand dunes) and by numberless smaller waterways for the drainage of this low-lying flood-threatened land. (See map facing page 238.)

Six miles south-east of Dunkirk stands the old fortified town of Bergues. The Bergues Canal, which joins the two, formed a western boundary to the British sector of the perimeter, for the French were to hold the sector west of this line. From Bergues, the Bergues–Furnes Canal winds its way first to Furnes, yet another of the towns which Vauban fortified, fourteen and a half miles from Bergues and four from the sea coast at La Panne; and then to Nieuport, six and a half miles further east and only two miles from the coast. This canal line formed a southern boundary to the bridge-head; the whole perimeter to be held extended for about thirty miles. It is a fairly strong defensive position. Much of the land inside the canal-marked boundary is easily flooded, and outside it, for many miles, the ground is of the same low-lying, much-beditched sort; it is almost impassable by tanks or guns except on built-up conspicuous roads, with ditches either side, which a few well-sited guns could make unusable. (Four years later we were to find that very similar country in 'the Island' between Nijmegen and Arnhem was impass-able by our armoured divisions so long as the enemy's guns covered the causeway roads.)

It may be well to review what had happened in the Dunkirk bridgehead before the Government's decision to attempt full evacua-tion was reached. As already told, it was as far back as May the 19th when Lord Gort first reported to the War Office that retreat to Dunkirk might become inevitable. Inter-departmental consultations which eventually resulted in the Admiralty plan 'Dynamo' began next day. At the same time Lord Gort's Adjutant-General was instructed to get rid of all 'useless mouths', an uncomplimentary but expressive term for those whose service would no longer be needed by the constricted fighting forces in France. On the following day Colonel G. H. P. Whitfield, Assistant Adjutant-General, was ordered to take command of British non-fighting troops in the Dunkirk area and to start evacuating those no longer required, at his discretion and as the situation permitted. There were many who could be spared from the floating population of men who when hostilities began had been going on leave or returning, who had been attending a course of training, had been out of the line for rest or convalescence or, for one reason or another, were in the back area temporarily; and from those who had been permanently employed there as the staffs of training establishments, reinforcement centres, or supply depots, or in a variety of duties on the long lines of communication. Finally there were the further large numbers who had been engaged on the making of airfields or on other constructional tasks. All this activity would inevitably be found behind an army in the field for which a large expansion was being prepared. A considerable proportion of these men had been specially enlisted for the work they were engaged on: they were neither trained as soldiers nor equipped for fighting. They were now not an asset but a liability and the sooner they were got away the better. In addition many of the fighting units, when ordered at short notice to advance to the Dyle, had left behind dumps of their surplus stores in charge of small rear parties who still further swelled the total number in rearward areas. When the German armoured divisions broke through the French front to our right, cut British communications at Amiens and Abbeville and swirled northwards, all these men, dispersed throughout the back areas, were caught between our retiring army and the tide of enemy forces pressing northwards to the coast. There was neither time nor the necessary transport to collect and move them all on any carefully worked out plan. All that could be done in such an emergency was to order them to make their way north, first to the line Orchies–Lens–Frévent (and this order was given on the 17th) and later to the Dunkirk bridgehead. Some, as has been told, were organised as fighting units in one or other of the special 'forces' or formations (Macforce, Polforce, Don Details, etc.). Some were evacuated from Boulogne or Calais before those places were lost; but most of them eventually found their way to the Dunkirk bridgehead in larger or smaller parties. Following the general order to withdraw, many had made their way through enemy-infested country without trained officers or detailed orders to guide them, and if the unsoldierly appearance of some parties shocked better-trained soldiers who witnessed their arrival, the fact that they arrived at all was, in reality, more remarkable evidence of untutored initiative and a dogged determination to avoid capture—which is at least one mark of a good soldier.

On May the 23rd Colonel C. M. Usher had been ordered to take charge of this movement and in particular to sort out fighting troops who could be used for the defence of the Canal Line and the Dunkirk bridgehead till the divisions from the east arrived to take it over.

From some of these he had formed 'Usherforce' (page 123), which, with the French troops there, held Bergues and screened Dunkirk until more solid defence could be organised.

An order from the War Office had been received on May the 24th laying down the policy of partial evacuation as they envisaged it at that date. They then held it to be essential to retain in France (*a*) all personnel who might possibly be of value for working the port, unloading supplies, and getting them forward, and (*b*) all fighting personnel. But on the same day more heavy German bombing badly damaged the dock area of Dunkirk and caused much ruin in the town. The main water supply was cut and never functioned again. It looked as though evacuation from Dunkirk might soon become impracticable, and other possibilities were studied. Meanwhile the anti-aircraft defence was strengthened. Major-General H. G. Martin, Major-General Anti-Aircraft Artillery on General Headquarters Staff, assumed command; the 2nd Anti-Aircraft Brigade took command of all anti-aircraft artillery in the area, and the 5th Searchlight Brigade of all searchlight units.

By May the 25th the 48th Division had arrived on the western flank and Usherforce, in Bergues, came under General Thorne's command. And when on the 26th the policy of complete evacuation (in so far as that was possible) had been accepted by the Government and Lord Gort had been informed, Lieutenant-General Sir Ronald Adam was appointed to take command of British troops in the Dunkirk bridge-head and to arrange in conjunction with the naval authorities for the evacuation of troops to England. Sir Ronald Adam was to have had with him Lord Gort's Adjutant-General, but the latter had moved to Dover with Rear General Headquarters which left *via* Boulogne on May the 23rd. Instead he was assisted by Lieutenant-General Lindsell, Quartermaster-General, Major-General R. P. Pakenham-Walsh, Chief Engineer, with Lieutenant-Colonel the Viscount Bridgeman as General Staff Officer.

The first task was to organise the defence of the perimeter. For this, General Thorne lent Brigadier the Hon. E. F. Lawson, commanding Royal Artillery, 48th Division, who proceeded to assemble and post the troops already available or arriving in the bridgehead. The second task was to organise the bridgehead for the reception, and later the evacuation, of the retiring divisions. It was divided into three Corps Areas, each with a collecting area outside the perimeter, a sector of the perimeter to defend, and a sector of the beach for evacuation. II Corps was allotted the eastern sector, I Corps the central sector, and III Corps the western sector nearest to Dunkirk. In each sector dumps of rations and ammunition were established.

The third problem was traffic. As troops and their transport began to arrive in increasing numbers from all three corps it became apparent that the order to disable and abandon their vehicles outside the perimeter had not always reached them. For this reason, and because the number of men available for traffic control was not at first adequate, large numbers of vehicles were entering Dunkirk and the bridgehead at this time. In the congested state of roads, vehicles were liable to be separated from their units during the withdrawal and units from their formations. Such detachments, arriving without clear orders, were sorted out and sent to reinforce the defence or to the coast for evacuation as seemed best to those in control. Thus by the 26th the organisation and defence of the bridgehead was already taking shape when an instruction that, 'as withdrawal may have to begin very early preliminary plans should be urgently prepared' was received from the Secretary of State for War.

From now on all three Services faced their most difficult and dangerous tasks. The Army still had to fight its way back to the coast, facing both ways as the enemy attacked from the east and from the west, and with the knowledge that Belgian resistance was nearing its breaking point. The Royal Navy had to conduct a most complicated and hazardous operation in which they must contend not only with inevitable risks of wind, weather and navigation in crowded and constricted waters, but must do so in the teeth of violent opposition, working always against time. And the Royal Air Force had to frustrate the *Luftwaffe's* declared intention to make evacuation impossible.

In the evacuation of non-fighting troops already in progress the Navy had begun by using Boulogne, Calais, Dunkirk and Ostend, and by midnight on the 26th of May they had brought to England 27,936 men who were no longer needed in France. At first it was hoped that if general evacuation became necessary the same ports could be used, but by May the 26th Boulogne and Calais were in enemy hands and, with Belgium likely to collapse, Ostend was no longer available. Dunkirk and the eastward beaches alone remained and enemy bombing threatened to make the continued use of Dunkirk harbour impracticable.

Almost continuous cover was provided by the Royal Air Force during the greater part of this day, patrols at squadron strength taking off from British airfields at approximately fifty-minute intervals from half past four in the morning till half past seven at night and intermittently till nearly dark. They had four contests with the enemy before nine o'clock in the morning and, shortly after, they fought a force estimated to consist of twenty-one bombers protected by thirty fighters which was attacking Dunkirk and the shipping off the coast. There were further combats in the afternoon, but in the evening fewer enemy aircraft were met. In all, about 200 sorties were flown. Six of our aircraft were lost, but the enemy's air return for the day shows that thirty-seven of their own machines were destroyed and seven damaged, most of them in the Dunkirk area. The *Luftwaffe* reported strong anti-aircraft defence behind the front and over the ports and fighter defence considerably stronger than on the previous day particularly near the coast. It was observed that fighter formations were exclusively British, operating from the other side of the channel.

Yet while many of the enemy's aircraft were thus engaged in battle with our fighters, others bombed and machine-gunned the port and shipping. The non-fighting troops evacuated during the week had been brought home by a few ships sailing at intervals. These had managed to ward off or evade the *Luftwaffe's* attacks, but full evacuation would require an offshore concentration of shipping which would be far more vulnerable. Vice-Admiral Sir Bertram H. Ramsay, Flag Officer Commanding Dover, had been appointed to plan and control evacuation if it should be ordered. On Thursday the 23rd he had informed all concerned that, if ordered, the operation would be known as 'Dynamo'. His initial plans were well advanced when, on this Sunday evening, May the 26th, shortly before seven o'clock the Admiralty sent the signal which would influence the whole course of the war:

'Operation Dynamo is to commence'.

SITUATION ON THE EVENING OF 26TH MAY

MILES 10 — 5 — 0 — 10 MILES

LEGEND

British troops are shown in Red, French in
Green, Belgian in Brown and German in Blue.

British & French

Corps.. III

Divisions.. (48

Divisions in reserve or moving........... (23)

Army Boundary................................... —o—o—

Divisional " .... —I—I—

German

Armoured Divisions..................... 8 (10)

Motorised " .... 20Mot (2 Mot)

Infantry " 18 (35)

Armoured Group Boundary............... —"—"—

Dunk...

Gravelines

Calais

10

Sangatte

Coquelles

Cap Gris Nez

St Pierre Brouck

1

SFF

W...

Ledi...

Watten

Ar...

Wimereux

K L E I S T   G R O U P

20 Mot

St Mor...

Boulogne
2

St Omer

29 Mot

Foi...
C...

R. Liane

6

R. Aa

Blaringl...

Desvres

Samer

R. Lys

Etaples

ARMY
GROUP
'A'

Montreuil

R. Canche

Hesdin

St F...

FOURTH A...

R. Authie

Frévent

St Valery sur Somme

13 Mot

9

CHAPTER XII

DUNKIRK, BETHUNE AND YPRES

27th May, 1940

THE fear of impending disaster haunted the minds of all who knew what was happening in France at this time. In the week which had just closed one shock had followed another with appalling rapidity. On the Monday morning (May the 20th) Admiral Ramsay had held his first meeting at Dover to consider the possibility of large-scale evacuation if, 'as then seemed *unlikely*', the need should arise. On that morning our main front was on the Escaut, our lines of communication were intact, north-western France was still inviolate and the Channel ports were in the Allies' hands. By the following Sunday evening, when Operation Dynamo was ordered, all France north of the Somme was in enemy hands except the narrowing strip through which the British Expeditionary Force now sought to reach the coast. Dunkirk was the only northern port left to the Allies and it was threatened.

The inside of a week would be a very short time in which to plan and prepare so difficult a feat as the evacuation of a large beleaguered force, even if military requirements were precisely known from the outset; but Operation Dynamo could be planned with no such certainty for the military situation was changing hourly. No one could say how many of our fighting troops would reach the coast or under what conditions they would arrive. When Dynamo began it was thought in London that the enemy could be held at bay for, perhaps, two days and if so that about 45,000 men might be brought home. Naval arrangements were being shaped accordingly, and though the manning and assembly of all the ships and boats that would be needed was not yet complete, the first vessel sailed for Dunkirk two hours after the Admiralty made the signal to begin.

The decision to withdraw British forces in the north, not only to the coast of France but if possible to England, brought the intervening sea into the field of active operations. Control of the Army's movements till the coast was reached remained with Lord Gort in France, but their final movement to England would be controlled from Admiral Ramsay's headquarters at Dover. It was from England too that the vital battle of the Royal Air Force off, over, and behind Dunkirk would be ordered and controlled. Kent was the base from which the fighters of No. 11 Group fought their fight with the *Luftwaffe*. Operations of the three Services during the next nine days were thus determined partly in France and partly in England, and it would simplify the account of their actions to describe each in turn. But such a simplification would be quite unreal. It did not happen that way. The Services played their parts in the drama together, and in each day's scene all three were on the stage at the same time. If the story of events seems complicated, so, too, were operations, which now stretched out from where the Army fought in France to the coast of Kent.

The first ship which left Dover on Sunday evening (26th) was the armed boarding-vessel *Mona's Isle*. Her experience on that first trip foreshadowed things to come. She berthed in Dunkirk harbour during an enemy air attack but took on board 1,420 troops. After leaving harbour to return she was straddled by enemy guns on shore between Gravelines and Les Hemmes and shortly after she was heavily machine-gunned from the air. Twenty-three of the men on board had been killed and sixty wounded when she reached Dover at noon on Monday morning, May the 27th. Meanwhile five transports which had sailed earlier that morning were shelled so heavily off the French coast that they could not reach Dunkirk and returned to Dover empty.

Reference to the adjoining sketch chart makes it easy to realise that the loss of Calais on Sunday evening had given the enemy possession of a coast from which artillery could command the last reach of the short sea route from Dover. Ships sailing by this western route (route Z) must approach to within a few miles of Calais and then sail eastwards past the shore where enemy batteries were now sited. An alternative northerly route (route Y) was now swept for mines and adopted, but the diversion more than doubled the length of passage. Route Z covers thirty-nine sea miles, route Y eighty-seven. Moreover, although this diversion reduced the difficulty of reaching Dunkirk by avoiding the fire of land-based artillery, the longer passage increased the danger of attack both by enemy surface vessels and aircraft.

The Royal Air Force began a supreme effort to ward off the *Luftwaffe* attacks, an effort which was to last as long as evacuation went on. Fighter Command ordered sixteen squadrons to cover the area as continuously as possible from five o'clock in the morning till nightfall and most of them on this day carried out two or even three patrols, which varied in size from twenty aircraft to only nine. They nearly always met the enemy in far greater strength. Often they were themselves beset by enemy formations called up to rescue those they were attacking. Eleven aircraft of No. 74 Squadron fought ten bombers and twenty fighters of the enemy; five of No. 145 Squadron fought twelve bombers and a large formation of fighters; nine of No. 601 Squadron engaged ten bombers and twenty fighters; and about seven o'clock in the evening twenty aircraft of Nos. 56 and 610

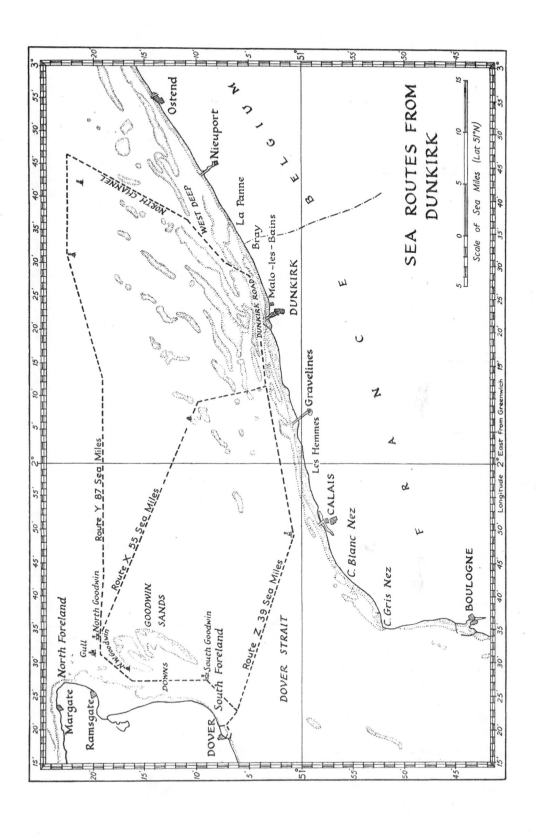

SEA ROUTES FROM DUNKIRK

Scale of Sea Miles (Lat 51°N)

Route Y 87 Sea Miles
Route X 55 Sea Miles
Route Z 39 Sea Miles

NORTH CHANNEL
WEST DEEP

DUNKIRK ROAD
DUNKIRK

Ostend
Nieuport
La Panne
Bray
Malo-les-Bains
Gravelines
Les Hemmes
CALAIS
C. Blanc Nez
C. Gris Nez
BOULOGNE

BELGIUM

FRANCE

Longitude 2° East from Greenwich

North Foreland
Margate
Ramsgate
DOVER
South Foreland
GOODWIN SANDS
North Goodwin
Mid Goodwin
South Goodwin
Gull
DOWNS
DOVER STRAIT

Squadrons did battle with an enemy fighter force of nearly twice their number. Fourteen of our Spitfires and Hurricanes failed to return from this brave effort to cover the evacuation. The German returns show that in all they lost on this day thirty-eight aircraft; our own total losses in night and day fighting were twenty.

But, while the air battles went on and while aircraft of the *Luftwaffe* concentrated largely on attacking Belgium, they also bombed Dunkirk heavily that day on twelve separate occasions. They destroyed a large part of the town and made the docks and harbour so dangerous that Captain W. G. Tennant, Senior Naval Officer at Dunkirk, decided that for the time at least they could not be used. He reported to Dover that only the outer mole and beaches could be used and asked for every available craft to be sent there immediately, since 'evacuation tomorrow night problematical'. This was a severe blow to naval hopes for experience taught that evacuation from an open beach is a comparatively slow process. In the shallow waters off Dunkirk beaches no ship of any size could come close inshore, and though the base establishments of the Nore Command at Sheerness, Chatham and Ramsgate were working night and day to collect, condition, equip and man a fleet of small craft for off-shore work these were not yet available at Dunkirk.

The anti-aircraft cruiser *Calcutta*, two transports, nine destroyers, four minesweepers, seventeen drifters and a few Dutch schuyts (motor coastal vessels escaped from Holland), were ordered to the beaches, where they were to use their own boats to ferry men from the shore to the ships. Unfortunately news that the use of the port had been stopped led to a false rumour that Dunkirk was in enemy hands and to the passing from ship to ship of a warning not only to avoid Dunkirk but to return to England. By midnight only 7,669 men had been landed and of these about two-thirds came on ships which had entered Dunkirk harbour before its use was suspended. Operation Dynamo thus made an inauspicious beginning. At the end of the day there was little to encourage hope that a large proportion of the Army could be saved.

It was not even certain that our main forces would be able to fight their way to the coast. For as the Allied armies started to move northwards the German order which had held the divisions of Army Group A to the Canal Line was superseded by another; their advance was now authorised and fighting broke out all along the western front. In the east too, the German attack on the Ypres front was continued with mounting violence; in the south the French First Army was attacked from both sides of the narrow pocket which they still held.

The enemy's double purpose is clear. The Kleist Group of Army Group A sought in the north-west to get within artillery range of Dunkirk but their main attack was further south from St Omer to

Robecq. There they sought to break through to the Poperinghe–Kemmel line where they should meet the divisions of Army Group B, now seeking to breach the Ypres sector with the same objective. If Dunkirk and Ostend were made unusable, all evacuation would be stopped; if the attacks converging on Kemmel succeeded, a large part of the Allied armies would be surrounded and cut off from the sea. To carry out Allied plans both of the enemy's aims must be frustrated.

At the same time Hoth Group, starting from the Béthune–La Bassée area, also struck north-east towards Armentières–Lille, where a considerable part of the French First Army might be cut off. Bridgeheads had been won over the Canal Line in the previous days: the main attack was timed to begin at eight o'clock on the morning of the 27th.

In the attack aiming at Dunkirk in the north-west the enemy made some progress. The French were heavily engaged to the south of Gravelines and by the end of the day had been forced back with heavy losses. During the night they withdrew from Gravelines and the Aa and occupied a line which followed canals from Mardick through Spycker to Bergues. The German hold on the Channel coast was thus brought to within four miles of Dunkirk. The port and its approaches were now within artillery range.

The object of the British 48th Division, deployed south of Bergues, was now to hold the road which runs southward from Bergues through Wormhoudt, Cassel and Hazebrouck. Between Wormhoudt and Cassel, forward positions were occupied at Arneke and Ledringhem. The former was strongly attacked, and in fierce fighting both sides had heavy casualties; and the garrison of the 2nd Warwickshire, now greatly reduced, was withdrawn during the coming night. When night fell on the 27th Ledringhem was still held by the 5th Gloucestershire, though a German column had penetrated for some distance between it and Cassel; another column was moving round the north of Wormhoudt. Covering Cassel itself, the 48th Division's forward positions were at Zuytpeene and Bavinchove and, after very heavy bombardment of both places and of Cassel, the enemy attacked with tanks and infantry. A company of the 2nd Gloucestershire fought valiantly to hold Zuytpeene, and were reduced to a handful before the place was captured at seven o'clock in the evening. Bavinchove too was eventually lost, and the enemy reached the western foot of the sugar-loaf hill on which Cassel is built. From there German mortars could range freely on the town, while they were themselves masked from our artillery fire by the steep contour of the hill. The enemy's main attack on Cassel itself began about ten o'clock in the morning of the 27th, coming in from the south and south-east, and it was maintained throughout the day. German forces tried, too, to work round the northern outskirts but were driven back by the 2nd

Gloucestershire, and on the south-east they attacked Hondeghem. There K Battery of the 5th Royal Horse Artillery and a troop of the 2nd Searchlight Regiment fought back all day, but they suffered heavy casualties and by the evening were almost out of ammunition, when a squadron of the 1st Fife and Forfar Yeomanry arrived and relieved the pressure. These were part of Brigadier C. W. Norman's 1st Light Armoured Reconnaissance Brigade, which had come under the command of the 48th Division and was to play a notable part in the fighting of the next few days.

Late in the evening the enemy's attack on Cassel died away. They had failed to take the town and had suffered heavily in men and armour. Further south they strove all day to take Hazebrouck with tanks and infantry, and although the companies of the 1st Buckingham-shire who held the outskirts were gradually overcome or driven out of their positions, battalion headquarters and headquarters company held out in a 'keep' in the centre of the town, isolated and surrounded, but unsubdued.

The 44th Division was on the flank immediately south of Haze-brouck. At the beginning of the day (27th) they held Morbecque, and behind it a line running south-east to La Motte, south-west along the Nieppe Canal and again south-east on the road through the Forest of Nieppe towards St Venant. There was heavy fighting, and though Morbecque was lost, the enemy's attacks made no headway against this zigzag line. But armoured columns pushed through the gap between Cassel and Hazebrouck and attacked our positions on a road (not shown on the situation map) which runs south-east from Eecke through Caestre, Strazeele, Vieux Berquin, and so to Estaires on the Lys. They attacked Eecke but were held off. They attacked Caestre and were driven back by the 4th Royal Sussex, who knocked out six tanks and captured their crews. They attacked the 5th Royal Sussex who were holding Strazeele and the road towards Estaires, and again were unsuccessful. And in the afternoon they withdrew after an expensive and unprofitable day. Then the 131st Brigade (only arrived that morning from the eastern front) came in to strengthen this line, occupying Strazeele with a flank guard at Merris and the nearby Clyte Hill. What remained of the 23rd Division was behind them but by now incapable of further fighting. The rest of the 46th Division was also now in the rearward area of the 48th Division.

From the Lys Canal at St Venant to La Bassée is a distance of about fifteen miles. To guard this, so that the main French and British forces could be withdrawn to the Lys during the coming night, was the 2nd Division's responsibility. For them the battle reached its crisis on this day. Their 6th Brigade was on the right, responsible for the St Venant–Robecq sector; the 4th Brigade was in the centre, responsible to beyond Béthune; the 5th held from there to La Bassée. Further east the French First Army held the front.

No one visiting the quiet little town of St Venant for the first time would consider that it had military importance. Yet the contrast between its past and the peaceful history of any comparable town in England could hardly be greater. St Venant has seen many actions and suffered many sieges. Sir Thomas Morgan, one of Cromwell's commanders, took it from the Spaniards in 1657; Marlborough took it from the French in 1710; in 1940 it had been taken by the Germans on May the 24th and recaptured by the British 2nd Division on May the 25th (page 146). It was held on the morning of the 27th by the 6th Brigade's right flank battalion, the 1st Royal Welch Fusiliers, and part of the 2nd Durham Light Infantry. It will be remembered that the Welch Fusiliers had a detached company holding Robecq, but between St Venant and Robecq the enemy had penetrated. On the morning of the 27th composite forces of tanks and infantry attacked both places. The troops holding St Venant had heavy casualties and were gradually borne back and enclosed. As evening drew on, the enemy had tanks beyond the canal bridge behind St Venant. When at last the order to withdraw north of the Lys reached the reduced garrison they had to fight their way out and but a fraction of the battalions got through. The detached company of Welch Fusiliers holding Robecq, which had been isolated and completely surrounded the day before, also tried to fight its way back to the Lys, but few avoided capture.

Through the gap east of St Venant the enemy's armoured columns had advanced on Merville and Lestrem. Merville was practically surrounded. A machine-gun company of the 6th Argyll and Sutherland Highlanders sent to assist the 6th King's Own came under heavy fire as they approached, and could not get into the town. The enemy was reinforced by troops landed by aircraft on the nearby airfield (which our gunners shelled) but the garrison held out till night-time when, on orders to withdraw, those who were left managed very skilfully to get away. The third battalion of the 6th Brigade—the 1st Royal Berkshire—also suffered heavily before they too were drawn back to the north.

Meanwhile the 4th Brigade had met an armoured attack, preceded by artillery fire and dive-bombing, and had been gradually forced to fall back on Paradis and Locon. The 1st Royal Scots, the 2nd Royal Norfolk and the 1st/8th Lancashire Fusiliers fought there to a finish and were gradually overwhelmed. Their last signals were received late in the afternoon. The 25th Brigade, which was being held as a reserve north of the Lys, sent the 1st Royal Irish Fusiliers and a battery of the 65th Anti-Tank Regiment to form a defensive line on the Canal de Lawe from Lestrem to Vieille Chapelle, and the

5th Dragoon Guards continued this rearguard position from there to Neuve Chapelle.

On the 5th Brigade front between Béthune and La Bassée the enemy established posts across the canal at dawn, on the left of the 7th Worcestershire. At five-thirty in the morning, the reserve company of the 1st Camerons—now only forty-five strong—supported by six French tanks and artillery fire, counter-attacked and drove the enemy back across the canal. But in doing so thirty-nine of the forty-five were killed or wounded, and though the gap between the Camerons and the Worcestershire was cleared, numbers were so reduced that it could not be reoccupied. In the meantime the enemy had advanced from Gorre northwards and the 2nd Dorsetshire faced west to form a defensive flank. The 1st Camerons similarly formed a defensive flank covering the gap between the battalion and the 7th Worcestershire.

By ten o'clock in the morning the enemy again succeeded in crossing the canal in the 7th Worcestershire sector, and throughout the morning the enemy's tanks were massing north of the canal between Givenchy and La Bassée; opposite the 1st Camerons, seven were put out of action. Festubert, Givenchy, and Violaines, north of La Bassée, were now being held, and in the early afternoon the enemy's armoured attack reopened. La Bassée and Violaines were attacked from the west and a column of tanks moved round the north of Violaines and attacked La Bassée from the east. The 1st Camerons were almost surrounded but the 5th Brigade Anti-Tank Company helped them to claim twenty-one tanks! About three o'clock Brigadier G. I. Gartlan ordered a withdrawal when opportunity offered. Shortly after, ten tanks of the Royal Tank Regiment counter-attacked the German armour at Violaines, and though they lost all but three of their tanks their action helped the remnant of the Camerons and Worcestershire to get away. About one hundred, all that were left of the two battalions, reached Laventie by early evening. The 2nd Dorsetshire and a company of the 7th Worcestershire remained holding a defensive position at Festubert. The enemy attacked with tanks from half past five in the evening till seven o'clock; and though they came in from three sides they were held off. Remnants of the two battalions began to fall back at half past nine and, moving across country, got through the enemy and reached Estaires soon after midnight.

The fight of the 2nd Division has been described in some detail in an attempt to convey an idea of what lay behind the sentence in Lord Gort's despatch: '2nd Division, now reduced to less than the strength of an infantry brigade, had fought hard and had sustained a strong enemy tank attack.' It had indeed sacrificed itself to keep open the line of retirement to the Lys and delay the junction of the two German army groups which would have cut off all the French First Army. The outline that has been drawn would need to be filled in to give an adequate picture of the steadfast courage of the troops in the division. It would not be enough to tell the deeds of the infantry, for they were supported with equal stout-heartedness by all available artillery and machine guns and by what few tanks remained of the 4th/7th Royal Tank Regiment. The artillery comprised the 10th, 74th and 99th Field Regiments, 139th Army Field Regiment, 61st Medium Regiment and 13th Anti-Tank Regiment; and the machine-gun battalions were the 6th Argyll and Sutherland and the 2nd Manchester. All lost heavily.

While the main British forces were on this night behind the Lys according to plan, only part of the French First Army managed to get there. Many of their units had had to come from much farther south and were still in the Lille area. Before they could get back to the Lys, German attacks from the east and from the west met behind them and a considerable part of the French First Army was enclosed.

The German forces which had been attacking the 2nd Division were the 3rd, 4th and 7th Armoured Divisions and the motorised S.S.T. (*Totenkopf*) Division: the 44th Division had opposed the 8th and part of the 6th Armoured Divisions and the motorised S.S.V. (*Verfügungs*) Division. All these were in the Kleist and Hoth Groups in the Fourth Army of Army Group A. In the War Diary of the Sixth Army (Army Group B) it is recorded that Group Kleist wire-lessed that their objective on the 27th was Kemmel and Poperinghe and that the Kleist Group were informed that the objective of the Sixth Army (which was attacking our 5th Division between Ypres and Comines) was also Kemmel. This pincer movement on Kemmel had been ordered by the German Army High Command on the 26th; as has been shown the southern claw had made little progress. The German accounts of the British interference with Kleist's arm of this dual attack tell how the fighting during the afternoon appeared to the XXXXI Corps of the Group:

> . . . At every position heavy fighting has developed—especially at every village and indeed in every house. In consequence the corps has not been able to make any notable headway to the east or north-east. Casualties in personnel and equipment are grievous. The enemy are fighting tenaciously and, to the last man, remain at their posts: if they are shelled out of one position, they shortly reappear in another to carry on the fight. The enemy appear to have very good observation for their artillery fire. . . .[1]

Army Group B were constantly lamenting the absence of armour,

---

[1] See Appendix II, p. 387.

but the XXXXI Corps Diary contains a note here on the unsuit-
ability of tanks against well-defended positions:

> As already stressed above the actions fought on this day have exac-
> ted severe losses in personnel and equipment, and from them it is
> clearly possible to draw the following brief conclusion: when engaged
> against enemy troops stubbornly defending a partly fortified field
> position, and particularly barricaded villages, the armoured division
> is not so suitable because it does not command sufficient infantry
> forces and because tanks make good targets for numbers of emplaced
> anti-tank weapons.[2]

And the following conclusion is recorded by XXXIX Corps in
Hoth Group:

> As foreseen, the enforced two-day halt on the southern bank of
> the canal produced two results on 27th May:
>
> 1. The troops suffered considerable casualties when attacking
> across the La Bassée Canal, now stubbornly defended by the enemy.
>
> 2. There was no longer time to intercept effectively the stream
> of French and English troops escaping westward from the Lille area
> towards the Channel.[3]

The German conduct of the day's fighting was stained by the
shameful misconduct of one of the formations engaged. A hundred
men of the 2nd Royal Norfolk were taken prisoner when the house in
which they were surrounded was finally overrun by troops of the S.S.
Totenkopf Division. They had fought hard and many were wounded.
After being disarmed and searched they were ordered to march in
single file past a large barn wall. As they did so two machine guns
which had been set up 300 yards away mowed them down. Between
them and the barn wall there was a large declivity into which they
fell and there any who still showed signs of life were shot or bayoneted.
Two, who were badly wounded but were hidden by bodies which fell
across them, managed to crawl away when the Germans had left the
scene of butchery. They were subsequently taken prisoner by another
unit who knew how to behave and were sent to hospital and well
cared for, and eventually they were repatriated. The German officer
who gave the order for this mass-murder was himself captured later
in the war, convicted by a British court martial and sentenced to be
hanged. It is but fair to the German Army to note that these S.S.
units were formed by the Nazi Party and were not part of the Regular
Army, though many of their officers had been Regular soldiers. But it
is also noteworthy that the Army authorities left the crime un-
punished, though it was fully reported to them at the time.

The Royal Air Force had done their best to interfere with the

---

[2] See Appendix II, p. 388.
[3] Ibid.

enemy's progress on this day. Reconnaissance had noted the increased movement during the morning, and in the afternoon successive attacks were made by Blenheims at half past two, four, just before seven, and again half an hour later. Their targets were moving columns, tanks, anti-aircraft batteries, troop concentrations, a troop train, and motor transport. Thirty-six bombers were employed; two were lost. Six Swordfish of the Fleet Air Arm, under the orders of Coastal Command, also bombed enemy batteries near Mardick, the western limit of the Dunkirk bridgehead after the French had withdrawn from Gravelines.

An even larger bombing programme, which had been arranged with the French Command, was carried on through the night by Bomber Command and the Advanced Air Striking Force. Thirty-six Battles bombed enemy airfields, dumps, and railways, and ten Hampdens bombed enemy communications in the Meuse area. Thirty-five Wellingtons bombed communications near Courtrai, Tournai, Aire, and St Omer. Thirteen Hampdens bombed railways in Germany. Thirty-eight Whitleys bombed marshalling yards. Eighteen Hampdens bombed oil refineries in Germany. The great effort made by Fighter Command to cover the Dunkirk area has already been told.

On the eastern front the divisions still holding the old frontier position—the 42nd, 1st, 3rd, and 4th Divisions—were to withdraw during the night to the Lys, with the French First Army conforming. The 42nd Division was to keep a rearguard (125th Brigade) on the Deule Canal between Lille and Marquette, while the 126th and 127th Brigades moved back to the Lys. The 1st Division was to send three battalions to help the 5th Division to fill the gap which had opened between the British left and the Belgian Army, and for the rest the division was to move back to hold the Dunkirk perimeter. The 4th Division was to move one brigade (the 12th) to the Lys, while the 10th and 11th went to strengthen the 5th Division on the front between Ypres and Comines. The 3rd Division was to sidestep in order to prolong the front on the Ypres–Comines Canal from Boesinghe northwards. The result of these moves is seen in the map facing page 202, which shows where the divisions were on the morning of the 28th.

The moves were successfully carried out. The 42nd Division encountered some enemy tanks in the Lille area but drove them off, and an enemy attack on the 2nd Bedfordshire and Hertfordshire in the 4th Division was driven back by the 1st Coldstream Guards, who covered the final withdrawal of the 10th Brigade. The 2nd Royal Fusiliers of the 12th Brigade also held off a determined attack which was maintained all day, and then managed to withdraw during the night.

Withdrawal routes had been agreed with the French First Army,

o

but throughout the withdrawal to the coast French troops with horse-drawn transport cutting in to the roads allotted to the British Expeditionary Force made movement difficult and at times almost impossible. As already told only a part of the French First Army withdrew to the Lys on this day; a large force remained in the Lille area, where they were surrounded and surrendered only after holding out for four more days. During that time, as the situation maps show, considerable enemy forces were occupied in attacking these stubbornly resisting divisions of the French First Army—forces which would otherwise have been able to intensify the attack on Allied divisions withdrawing to the coast.

While these moves were in progress a furious battle was developing on the II Corps front south of Ypres which had been exposed by the Belgian withdrawal. There, three enemy divisions—the northern claw of the German pincer movement, sought to break through to Kemmel. The 2nd Division had, as already told, held off the attack of the southern claw and their task was completed at the end of the day (27th) when our main forces were behind the Lys. On the Ypres front it was General Franklyn's 5th Division which bore the weight of the enemy's attack, and on this front the battle was to rage for three days till our main forces were inside the Dunkirk bridgehead. It will be seen later that as it grew in intensity the corps commander (General Brooke) strengthened the 5th Division progressively by additional artillery and infantry, until by the evening of the 27th General Franklyn had under his command in addition to the artillery and infantry of his own division (the 5th) the corps artillery of I Corps; 13th/18th Hussars; a brigade group (143rd) from the 48th Division; two brigades (10th and 11th) and the Royal Engineers from the 4th Division; three battalions from the 1st Division; and two battalions of machine guns. The presence of these additional units must be remembered when the 5th Division is mentioned in the story of their fight. As the battle progressed the 3rd and 50th Divisions also played important parts, but it was the augmented 5th Division with which General Franklyn fought off the main attack at this most critical stage.

On the 26th, the 143rd Brigade from the 48th Division had arrived first of the troops being sent to extend the II Corps' front to the north of Comines. Between Comines and Ypres they put their three battalions over the whole stretch of the canal between those places until the 5th Division's arrival in the area. Then the 143rd (who then came under the command of the 5th Division) closed up in the sector immediately north of Comines and the 5th Division's own 13th and 17th Brigades occupied the remainder of the Canal Line to the right-angle bend north of Hollebeke and from there continued on the railway line to Zillebeke, three miles south-east of Ypres.

The 12th Lancers, holding Ypres till infantry arrived, had found there only a few Belgian engineers preparing bridges on the *west* of the town for demolition, for on this front Belgium had signified her neutrality by preparing defences which faced France. The town was not attacked on the 27th, but the canal and railway line from Comines to Ypres, which was held when morning broke by three brigades (the 143rd, the 13th and the 17th), was attacked violently by three German divisions after a heavy bombardment by artillery, mortars and dive-bombers. In the 143rd Brigade sector immediately north of Comines, the battalions on the front fought till they were being borne down by numbers, before they were ordered to retire. On their left the 13th Brigade had the 2nd Cameronians and the 2nd Royal Inniskilling Fusiliers on the canal, and the 2nd Wiltshire in reserve on high ground 500 to 1,000 yards to the east of the Warneton–St Eloi road. The main weight of the enemy's thrusts penetrated at Houthem and Hollebeke (on the flanks, that is, of the brigade frontage) and also between the Cameronians and the Inniskillings. With each forward battalion doubly outflanked, they were ordered to fall back, and the 2nd Wiltshire reserve position then became the front.

Meanwhile a counter-attack was made in the southern sector of the 143rd Brigade front, between the Warneton–Comines Canal and the road between those places. It was a spirited affair, planned by the commanding officer of the 6th Black Watch, who, with his headquarters and one weak platoon, was in Warneton. Royal Engineers of the 4th Division, acting as infantry, had taken up a defensive line screening Warneton on the east. The Black Watch platoon and these sappers constituted the infantry for the counter-attack: the latter were the 7th, 59th, and 225th Field Companies. They were to support two squadrons of the 13th/18th Hussars. The counter-attack went in at seven o'clock in the evening and succeeded in driving the enemy back and in consolidating the line of the Kortekeer river. The 13th/18th Hussars in fact reached the Ypres–Comines Canal, but suffered heavy casualties in doing so and had to be drawn back. Earlier in the day General Brooke, impressed by the threatening position in the gap caused by the Belgian withdrawal, ordered the 1st Division to reinforce General Franklyn with three infantry battalions, and the 3rd Grenadier Guards, the 2nd North Staffordshire, and the 2nd Sherwood Foresters were moved north. Late in the evening they too counter-attacked on the left of the 143rd Brigade, supported by the guns of the 97th Army Field Regiment, four Medium regiments and one Heavy battery of I Corps artillery. The attacking infantry, the 3rd Grenadier Guards and 2nd North Staffordshire, started shortly after eight o'clock and came under heavy artillery and mortar fire from the enemy; but they continued to advance in spite of casualties till, an hour before midnight, they reached the line of the Kortekeer river and gained touch with the sappers who had counter-attacked earlier on the right. When the day ended, our front here had been pressed back to a line which ran from the junction of the Kortekeer river with the canal, west of Comines, to St Eloi on the Warneton–Ypres road. Farther north the 17th Brigade's forward battalions, the 2nd Royal Scots Fusiliers and the 6th Seaforth Highlanders, had also been withdrawn, after hard fighting, from the railway line south of Zillebeke to the west bank of the Ypres–Comines Canal, where the 2nd Northamptonshire had a small reserve. At about eight in the evening the enemy attacked them again, and the 17th Brigade were gradually forced back to the Warneton–St Eloi road. The 10th Brigade from the 4th Division was meanwhile brought up and the 2nd Bedfordshire and Hertfordshire and the 2nd Duke of Cornwall's Light Infantry were put in to hold a two-mile stretch of the road north of Oostaverne.

By now the 50th Division had arrived, and the 150th and 151st Brigades prolonged the line through Ypres northwards while the 12th Lancers made touch with the Belgian Army near Roulers. The Belgians were found to be swinging back in a north-easterly direction so that the gap between them and the 50th Division was widening. For the time being it was covered by the 12th Lancers with a detachment of the 101st Army Field Company of the Royal Engineers, but the 3rd Division was side-stepping and, before the night was over, they were in position on the left of the 50th Division. So far the enemy had achieved nothing of importance. His plan to break through had failed and the gap created by the Belgian withdrawal had been nearly closed. Yet the situation was critical and the danger increased as the hours wore on.

At Lord Gort's Command Post the day had opened with the receipt of a personal message from the Prime Minister to the Commander-in-Chief:

> At this solemn moment I cannot help sending you my good wishes. No one can tell how it will go. But anything is better than being cooped up and starved out . . . I feel very anxious about Ostend till it is occupied by a brigade with artillery . . . A column directed upon Calais while it is still holding out might have a good chance . . . We shall give you all that the Navy and Air Force can do . . .

Mr Churchill realised that Lord Gort's main purpose must now be withdrawal to the coast for evacuation, but the suggestion that he should send a column to relieve Calais and put a brigade group into Ostend also shows that the Prime Minister did not, at that time, appreciate fully either the strength of the surrounding German forces, the weakness of the Belgian position, or the danger in which these involved the British Expeditionary Force. Nor did he know, apparently, that Calais had been in enemy hands since the previous evening.

The Secretary of State for War sent a message to Sir Richard Howard-Vyse, head of the British Military Mission at French General Headquarters, instructing him to consult General Weygand as to the eventual destination of the British Expeditionary Force and any French force that it might prove possible to evacuate 'especially in respect destination in France to which they wish these units transferred in due course. . . .' He was to 'make plain that we have every intention continue struggle side by side with our Allies'. The Prime Minister had already sent a message on this subject to Sir Roger Keyes for transmission to the King of the Belgians. '. . . What can we do for him? Certainly we cannot serve Belgium's cause by being hemmed in and starved out. Only hope is victory and England will never quit the war whatever happens till Hitler is beat or we cease to be a State. . . . Should our operations prosper and we establish effective bridgehead we would try if desired to carry some Belgian divisions to France by sea.'

It is clear, therefore, that at this date evacuation was seen as a way to reunite the severed forces of the Allies by use of the sea. The Weygand Plan had sought to do so on land, but transfer by sea via England was now the only route open and the Secretary of State 'in case smallest doubt' informed Lord Gort that 'your sole task now is to evacuate to England maximum of your forces possible'.

French policy was less clear-cut. At seven-thirty in the morning (27th) General Sir Ronald Adam attended a conference in Cassel at which there were also present Admiral Abrial (the French commander at Dunkirk), General Fagalde (commanding the French XVI Corps—two French divisions of the original Seventh Army, which remained in the coastal sector)—General Blanchard (commanding the First Group of Armies) and General Koeltz, representing General Weygand. Before the conference began, Sir Ronald Adam and General Fagalde drew up a plan for the defence of the Dunkirk perimeter from Gravelines to Nieuport. The French were to be responsible for the sector west of Dunkirk; the British for the area from Dunkirk to Nieuport. 'The possibility of the Belgian Army being included was not discussed as its situation was obscure . . .' These matters were reopened at the full conference and the plans agreed were not questioned, and various consequential decisions in regard to transport and the organisation of troops retiring within the Dunkirk perimeter were considered. Yet early in the afternoon General Prioux, commanding the French First Army, issued a General Order to his corps commanders that 'The battle will be fought without thought of retreat on the Lys position'.

Thus, while the Cassel conference agreed how the *Dunkirk bridge-*

head was to be organised for the reception of retiring forces, the whole
of the French effectives which were not already in the coastal sector
were ordered to stand finally *on the Lys*. This was not all. The commander of the French XVI Corps had agreed with Sir Ronald Adam
to be responsible for defending the western half of the bridgehead.
But General Koeltz speaking for General Weygand urged the French
XVI Corps to recapture Calais, and neither General Blanchard nor
General Fagalde pointed out that the proposal was incompatible
with what had been agreed and was quite impracticable: for even
while it was being urged French troops were preparing to withdraw
from Gravelines under pressure of enemy divisions which they would
have to defeat if Calais were to be recaptured.

Meanwhile on the Belgian front affairs went from bad to worse.
By midday, the line held by Belgian forces came to an end at
Zonnebeke. From there to Ypres there was a gap which the Belgians
could not fill though General van Overstraeten stated in a message
that 'the Belgians believe that the protection of the British left is
assured in the most effective way by the dispositions of the Belgian
Army and by the fight which they have been waging for four days on
a 50-kilometre front forward of the Yser'.

With the end of Belgian resistance in sight Lord Gort received the
following message from Sir Roger Keyes who was with the Belgian
King:

> . . . He wishes you to know that his army is greatly disheartened.
> It has been incessantly engaged for four days and subjected to intense
> air bombardment which the R.A.F. have been unable to prevent.
> The knowledge that the allied armies in this sector have been
> encircled and that the Germans have great superiority in the air has
> led his troops to believe that the position is almost hopeless. He fears
> a moment is rapidly approaching when he can no longer rely upon
> his troops to fight or be of any further use to the B.E.F. He wishes
> you to realise that he will be obliged to surrender before a debâcle.
> The King fully appreciates that the B.E.F. has done everything in its
> power to help Belgium and he asks you to believe that he has done
> everything in his power to avert this catastrophe.

While the Commander-in-Chief now realised that the Belgian front
was collapsing and might shortly expose his left flank, while all the
British forces were fully engaged in a final effort to hold the German
attack and to fight its way back to the coast—while his mind was
concentrated on these grim and urgent tasks, Lord Gort received
one more message from General Weygand:

> General Weygand makes a personal appeal to General Gort. The
> British Army must participate strongly in the necessary joint
> counter-attacks. Situation demands hard hitting.[4]

---

[4] See Appendix II, p. 388.

What were the counter-attacks in which the British Army was to participate strongly is not clear.

Sir Roger Keyes' message that the Belgian King 'wishes you to realise that he will be obliged to surrender before a debâcle' had been received by Lord Gort late in the morning. During the afternoon the Needham Mission at Belgian General Headquarters sent a telegram giving the position at three o'clock that afternoon and adding: 'Situation still very confused but indications are that the Belgian front may be crumbling.' Just before six o'clock they sent a further message. 'Belgian front has broken under ceaseless bombing. King asking for an armistice now.' This message seems to have gone astray. The War Diary makes no mention of its receipt and certainly it did not reach either Lord Gort or his Chief of Staff. Although therefore the earlier messages had prepared Lord Gort for what was likely to happen, it came to him as a shock when, at eleven o'clock that night, he learnt from the French admiral's headquarters at Dunkirk that the Belgian surrender was timed for midnight. In fact the Belgian emissary had arrived in the German lines at seven-thirty in the evening to ask the terms on which an armistice would be granted. The German reply was 'unconditional surrender', terms which in later years were imposed by the Allies on the German Army.

By midnight on May the 27th the King of the Belgians had accepted defeat and the Belgian Army had been ordered to cease fire.

On the eastern front there was now a twenty-mile open gap between the left of II Corps and the coast near Nieuport. The position is shown on the adjoining situation map.

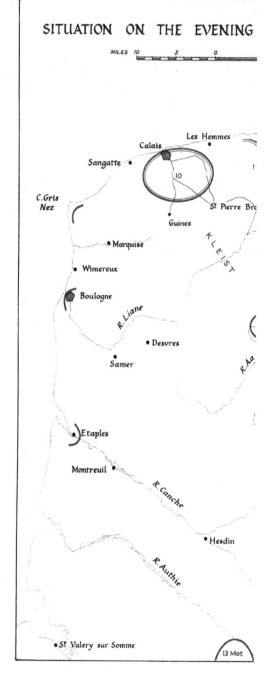

SITUATION ON THE EVENING

MILES 10 5 0

LEGEND

British troops are shown in Red, French in Green, Belgian in Brown and German in Blue.

British & French

Corps	III
Divisions	(48
Divisions in reserve or moving	(23)
Army Boundary	—o—o—
Divisional "	—I—I—

German

Armoured Divisions	8 10
Motorised "	20 Mot 2 Mot
Infantry "	18 35
Armoured Group Boundary	—II—II—

Les Hemmes

Calais

Sangatte

10

St Pierre Br

C.Gris
Nez

Guines

KLEIST

Marquise

Wimereux

Boulogne

R. Liane

Desvres

Samer

R. Aa

Etaples

Montreuil

R. Canche

Hesdin

R. Authie

St Valery sur Somme

13 Mot

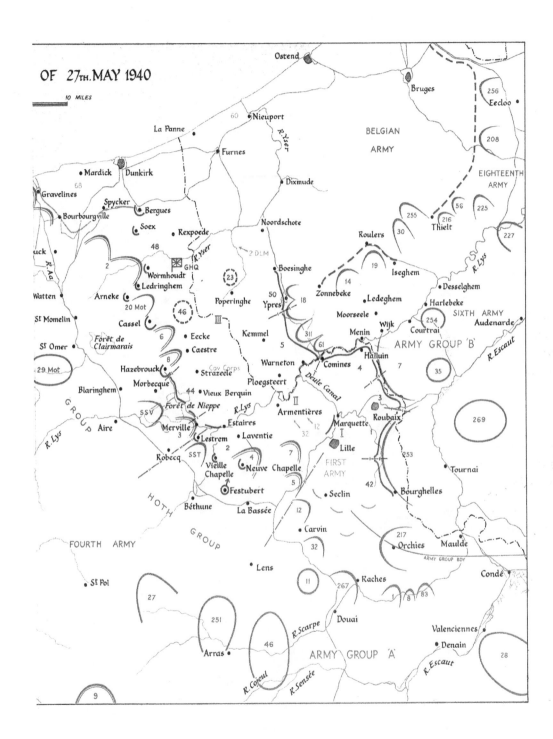

10 MILES

Ostend

Bruges

256
Eecloo

BELGIAN
ARMY

60 Nieuport

La Panne

Furnes

208

EIGHTEENTH
ARMY

R. Yser

Mardick   Dunkirk

Gravelines

68

Spycker

Bourbourgville

Bergues

Soex

Rexpoede

Dixmude

Noordschote

Roulers

225

56

255   216
       Thielt

30   227

uck

R. Aa

48

2

Wormhoudt

Ledringhem

GHQ

R. Yser

23

2 DLM

Boesinghe

19   Iseghem

Desselghem

14

Zonnebeke

Ledeghem   Harlebeke

Moorseele

SIXTH ARMY

254   Audenarde

Watten

Arneke

20 Mot

46

Poperinghe

50
Ypres   18

Menin   Wijk   Courtrai

Kemmel

St Momelin

Cassel

Forêt de
Clairmarais

III

6

Eecke

Caestre

5

31   61

Halluin

ARMY GROUP 'B'

R. Escaut

St Omer

29 Mot

8

Hazebrouck

Morbecque

Strazeele

Cav. Corps.

Ploegsteert

Warneton   Comines

4

7

35

Blaringhem

44   Vieux Berquin

Forêt de Nieppe

R. Lys

II

Armentières

3

Roubaix

GROUP

SSV

Aire

Merville

3

Lestrem

Estaires

Laventie

32   12

Marquette

I

Lille

269

Robecq

SST

2

Vieille
Chapelle

4

Neuve Chapelle

7

5

253

FIRST
ARMY

Tournai

42

Bourghelles

Festubert

Béthune

La Bassée

12

Seclin

HOTH

GROUP

Carvin

32

217

Orchies   Maulde

FOURTH   ARMY

Lens

11

267

Raches

ARMY GROUP BDY

Condé

St Pol

27

251

R. Scarpe

Douai

1   8   83

Valenciennes

Denain

Arras

46

ARMY GROUP 'A'

R. Escaut

28

9

R. Cojeul   R. Sensée

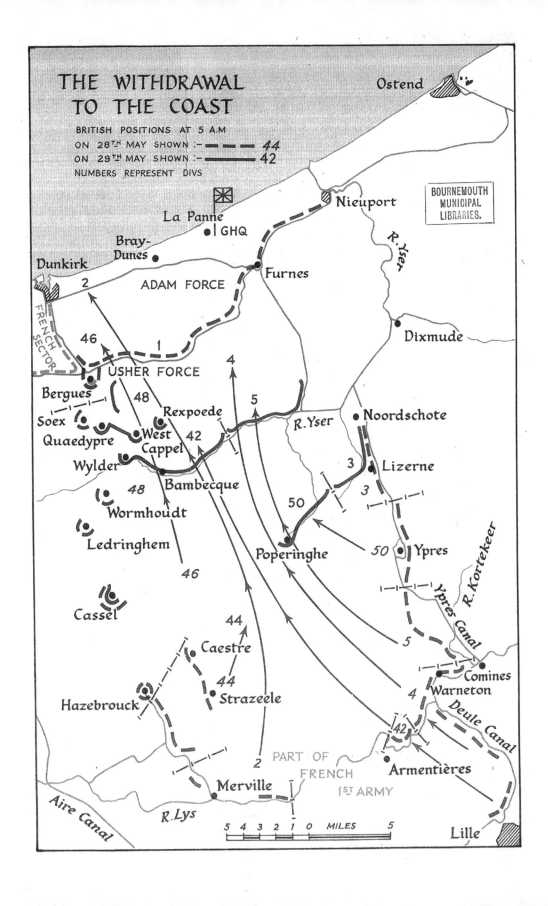

THE WITHDRAWAL
TO THE COAST

BRITISH POSITIONS AT 5 A.M
ON 28TH MAY SHOWN :— ▬ ▬ *44*
ON 29TH MAY SHOWN :— ▬▬ 42
NUMBERS REPRESENT DIVS

Ostend

Nieuport

BOURNEMOUTH
MUNICIPAL
LIBRARIES.

R. Yser

La Panne
● GHQ

Bray-
Dunes ●

Dunkirk

Furnes

2

Dixmude

ADAM FORCE

FRENCH SECTOR

46

1

USHER FORCE

4

Bergues

48

5

Soex

Rexpoede

R. Yser

Noordschote

Quaedypre

West
Cappel

42

3

Lizerne

Wylder

Bambecque

3

48

50

50

Wormhoudt

Poperinghe

50 ● Ypres

Ledringhem

46

5

Cassel

44

Ypres Canal

R. Kortekeer

Caestre

Comines

44

Warneton

Hazebrouck

Strazeele

4

42

Deule Canal

Armentières

2

PART OF
FRENCH
1ST ARMY

Merville

Aire Canal

R. Lys

5 4 3 2 1 0   MILES   5

Lille

CHAPTER XIII

AFTER THE BELGIAN SURRENDER

28th May, 1940

THE movements of the British Expeditionary Force in the withdrawal to the Dunkirk bridgehead will be most easily understood by reference to the situation map facing page 202. The positions held by the British Army at five o'clock in the morning of the 28th are shown first. It will be seen from these that the retreat *to the Lys* had been practically completed during the night. By five o'clock in the morning of the 28th only the 42nd Division still had a rearguard of one brigade (the 125th) on the bend of the Deule Canal running northwards from Lille; while the 4th Division's 12th Brigade had also a small rearguard on the canal bend. On the main eastern front, facing the German Army Group B, the augmented 5th Division and the 50th and 3rd Divisions still held the line from Warneton through Ypres to near Noordschote. In the twenty-mile gap between Noordschote and the coast beyond Nieuport, there were as yet no British divisions; only some cavalry of the French 2nd Light Mechanised Division (which had been placed by General Blanchard under General Brooke's command) and the 12th Lancers watched this open left flank, while a detachment of sappers from the 101st Army Field Company, Royal Engineers, worked energetically to destroy the bridges between Dixmude and Nieuport. The surrender of the Belgian Army left the way clear for a rapid German advance at this point of supreme danger to the army retiring to the coast, and throughout the day German divisions which were no longer required to overcome Belgian resistance were being moved towards it. Meanwhile their attack on our positions between Warneton and Ypres was renewed with increased violence.

As already pointed out this battle, which had begun on the 25th and was to continue until all our forces were within the Dunkirk bridgehead, was of crucial importance to the British Expeditionary Force. Just as the 2nd Division fought the south-western battle to keep the way open for the first stages of the British retreat, so the divisions of II Corps fought this longer, fiercer battle of the north-east to keep open the way for the last stages. General Brooke directed operations with great skill on a plan which the enemy was not allowed seriously to upset. And it succeeded because the troops under his command fought with a steadfast courage which matched his leadership.

The augmented 5th Division, under General Franklyn, again endured violent and sustained attacks on this day. The sappers who on the previous day had held the line of the Kortekeer river immediately north of the Comines–Warneton Canal were withdrawn in the night of the 27th/28th, and there the full weight of the renewed attack on the morning of the 28th fell on the 3rd Grenadiers and the 2nd North Staffordshire. Well supported by artillery and machine guns, they fought all day and yielded no ground although they suffered heavy losses. On their left—all under command of the 5th Division—were the 2nd battalions of the Sherwood Foresters (1st Division), Wiltshire, Cameronians, Royal Inniskilling Fusiliers (5th Division), Bedfordshire and Hertfordshire, Duke of Cornwall's Light Infantry (4th Division), Royal Scots Fusiliers and Northamptonshire, with the 6th Seaforth Highlanders (5th Division) continuing the defence northwards. The attacks began at four o'clock in the morning under cover of heavy artillery, mortar and machine-gun fire. In attack and counter-attack all the battalions had severe casualties, but the line of the Warneton–St Eloi road was held. At one critical point carriers of The Duke of Cornwall's Light Infantry counterattacked and restored the situation, though they lost more than half their strength in doing so. When the battle died down at the end of a long day's fighting the strength of the 5th Division's two brigades was reduced in each case to about 600. The artillery deserve a large share of the credit for holding the German attack. Not only the field regiments but I Corps artillery fired almost continuously till their ammunition was in the end exhausted.

But the German divisions had been held off for another day, and the 5th Division, in accordance with plans for the withdrawal to the Dunkirk bridgehead, moved in the night to the line of the Yser where they were joined by the 42nd Division.

The 50th and 3rd Divisions on their left, heavily shelled and subjected to some attacks from the air, were in contact with the enemy all day, but, except for one assault on the centre of the 50th Division which was beaten back, the enemy was not yet up to our line in strength for a serious effort to advance. During the night the 50th Division moved as planned to a line running north-east from Poperinghe, and the right of the 3rd Division swung back to conform. The French 2nd Light Mechanised Division had moved behind the Loo Canal, and the French 60th Infantry Division which had come from near Bruges 'had been overwhelmed in the loop of the Yser; its survivors were gathered up by the 2nd Light Mechanised Division . . . and by the British who held the Furnes–Nieuport Canal'.[1]

Thus, in spite of all the enemy's efforts to break through, in spite

---

[1] Armengaud, p. 58. See Appendix II, p. 388.

of the Belgian surrender, and in spite of heavy losses in General Franklyn's 5th Division, II Corps, holding the eastern flank of the corridor to the coast, completed the penultimate stage of the withdrawal. The positions held by five o'clock next morning (the 29th) are shown on the situation map facing page 202.

The 5th Division's staunch defence of the Ypres–Comines front had defeated the assault of three German divisions, had certainly saved II Corps, and equally certainly the British Expeditionary Force. What these two days' fighting meant to the troops involved has been indicated. What they meant to the corps commander can be seen in an extract from General Brooke's diary for two critical days:

26th May. LOMME

Left early to visit 5 Div. in Plugstreet Wood: found them busy getting in. Motored to left of 5 Div. on canal to find them just debussing. On to country east of Ypres to look for Belgians. Not a sign of them anywhere.

In Zillebeke found Postal Services of 1st French Motorised Div., but no fighting troops.

Proceeded south along canal and railway on east side of it. Half mile north of Houthem crossed under railway bridge to west side, I was barely across when bridge was blown up; and on proceeding into Houthem, found German shells bursting which I mistook for bombs to start with. Situation was very serious: Germans had started attack on canal at Houthem and 4,000 yards further north the flank was entirely open.

Dashed back to G.H.Q. where I secured 1 Brigade of 50th Div. and directed it on Ypres in M.T. [motor transport]. Informed that G.H.Q. had received instructions for evacuation of B.E.F.

Later secured second Brigade of 50th Div. and instructed it to follow on to Ypres to extend line northwards.

Very heavy bombing of Armentières and surrounding country.

27th May: L'ALOUETTE FERME

A very heavy day.

Held conference of 3 and 4 Divs. at Bondues at 8 a.m. Called on 1 Div. H.Q. Wambrechies to stop them using 3 Div. road for retirement.

Proceeded to 5 Div. H.Q. Plugstreet where I discovered that his front was being very heavily shelled. On to Ypres to see Martel, found Haydon's Brigade holding Ypres but out of touch with 5 Div. Other Brigade coming up. Some of 2 D.L.M. on canal north of Ypres.

Back to 5 Div. to organise steps to establish touch with 50 Div.

On to G.H.Q. to report situation.

Back to my H.Q. in Lomme where I ordered 3 Div. to relieve 1 Bde. of 4 Div., latter to proceed at once to assistance of 5 Div.

On to I Corps where I raised 3 Bns. of 1 Div. which had already been withdrawn and were behind Plugstreet.

Placed them also under 5 Div.

Back to G.H.Q. where I raised 7 Infantry Tanks [from what remained of the 1st Army Tank Brigade now in G.H.Q. reserve] which were also directed to 5 Div. Then back to Lomme against treble stream of French Army retiring. Orders for further Bde. from 4 Div. to proceed to 5 Div. on withdrawal and to be established on Wytschaete.

Back to Bondues to 3 Div. H.Q. to explain situation and final dispositions for withdrawal of 3 Div.

Returned to Lomme and on to G.H.Q. to find they had gone without any orders as to where they were going.

8 p.m. closed down Lomme and moved to L'Alouette just north of Plugstreet. From there back to 5 Div. to discover situation and discuss results of fighting and plans for next day's retirement. Then called on 4 Div. H.Q. Rossignol on way back to Command Post.

3 Div. commenced retirement and rumbled past all night within a few thousand yards of front on which 5 Div. supported by 3 Bds. and all Corps Heavy Artillery had been fighting a life and death struggle all day.

Belgians seemed to have vanished off the map.

Lord Gort's Headquarters had left Premesques that afternoon, spent the night at Houtkerque and on the 28th were established at La Panne in the Dunkirk bridgehead. The 3rd Division was side-stepping to the left of the British front (page 196) at the time of the above entry.

On the long western flank of the corridor, where British troops faced the armoured and infantry divisions of Army Group A, the position was less satisfactory. General Wason's III Corps was far weaker. The 48th Division had only two brigades, for it will be remembered that the 143rd had gone to strengthen the 5th Division on the Ypres front. The only other division 'in the line' was the hard-fought 44th, for what little remained of the 46th was held back in reserve behind Cassel. And not only were much smaller forces available in these two divisions; they were extended over more than twenty miles, so that there must be many gaps through which German armour could penetrate unhindered. It will be seen from the map facing page 202 that, at the beginning of the 28th, the 48th Division held a series of strongpoints—Soex, Wormhoudt, Ledringhem, Cassel and Hazebrouck. The 144th Brigade held the Soex–Ledringhem sector; the 145th Cassel and Hazebrouck.

An order issued from General Headquarters at about two o'clock in the afternoon of the 28th set Poperinghe as the pivot of the line to which withdrawal would take place in the night, but 'within the outline of these orders' corps commanders were to use their full discretion and to move as many men as possible into the Dunkirk bridgehead. II Corps needed no fresh instructions and was given freedom to hold a line from Poperinghe to Ypres and on to some point north of Ypres. In fact, they held from Poperinghe to near Noordschote. I Corps, now only the 1st Division (less the three battalions which had gone to strengthen the 5th Division) and the 42nd Division, were to retire to a position between Poperinghe and Proven, but in fact the 42nd Division went further north to the Yser and the 1st Division reached the perimeter of the Dunkirk bridgehead. Instructions to III Corps were less clear. The 48th Division was given no orders but was told that these would be issued when French dispositions had been ascertained; the 44th Division was ordered to retire 'to the frontier defences' but no area was specified; the 2nd Division was to move back to Beveren on the Yser (the sector to which the 42nd actually retired). The 44th and 2nd Divisions could not carry out these instructions, and clearly they were based on insufficient information in regard to conditions on the corps front.

The wide dispersal of the 48th and 44th Divisions and the fact that the enemy's advanced columns had already penetrated between the positions they held had made the maintenance of communications very difficult, and General Wason was not yet able to get into personal touch with his divisional commanders.

Use of wireless was very limited and uncertain. Much had to depend on liaison officers and dispatch riders, and as the principal roads were often choked with traffic or cut by the enemy, the delivery of messages was a slow and precarious business. Moreover, Advanced General Headquarters was moving on both the 27th and the 28th and had been forced off the line of the buried cable which ran through Cassel. Only meagre and uncertain information was available to senior commanders and they could only communicate infrequently and with difficulty with units who were fighting or on the move. The divisional commanders who controlled this fighting knew that they were acting as flank guard during the withdrawal to the coast. Troops in their commands were largely ignorant of what was happening outside their own observation, and to many of them all seemed confusion. They encountered the enemy in unlikely places, they moved often in seemingly purposeless ways, and, contrary to all their training, they were ordered to dump unessential kit and stores, to destroy guns that could not be moved and vehicles no longer required. The over-all control by III Corps was in fact largely ineffective at this date. But the divisional commanders knew what it was they must do and their action ensured that the general plan of withdrawal was carried out. Many men of the units who fought to the end to hold back the enemy were inevitably killed, wounded, or finally captured—but practically no one else was left behind. Below the surface confusion the tide ran strongly northwards, and parties which had been separated from their units in the course of fighting or by the congestion of traffic, and refugees on the line of march, were caught up by the stream setting towards the coast. When they arrived there they were reorganised to hold the perimeter or were sent to the beach for evacuation to England if they could now be spared.

In default of orders, General Thorne could not know how long the 48th Division was expected to maintain its extended position. Even if the garrisons of Soex, Wormhoudt, Cassel and Hazebrouck could hold out, enemy penetration between those places might seriously interfere with withdrawals taking place farther east. He appealed to General Headquarters for reinforcements, and Brigadier Norman's 1st Light Armoured Reconnaissance Brigade and the 1st Welsh Guards (both of whom had been sent the day before to strengthen the defences of Cassel) were put under his command, as were also the 6th Green Howards from Usherforce. Part of Brigadier Norman's brigade—the 1st East Riding Yeomanry—was left to help the 145th Brigade group at Cassel, but the rest, with the Welsh Guards, were moved north to hold the area Quaedypre, Vyfweg, West Cappel.

The enemy attacked all the 48th Division's strongholds during the day, and by six in the evening the road between Bergues and Cassel could no longer be used, Soex had been lost, Wormhoudt had become untenable, and all communications with Cassel and Hazebrouck had been cut. General Thorne ordered the 144th Brigade to retire during the night to the line of the Yser from Wylder to Bambecque and the move was duly carried out. But his messsage to the 145th Brigade at Cassel did not get through to them till six o'clock next morning, owing to the ditching of the armoured car which carried it.

The 144th Brigade had heavy fighting before the time for their retirement. At Wormhoudt the 2nd Warwickshire were first attacked by tanks and infantry at eight o'clock in the morning, after heavy bombing followed by artillery and mortar fire. The attack was driven off, but later was renewed. Much of the town was on fire when enemy tanks and infantry broke in from two sides and there was fierce fighting amid the burning ruins. When the time for withdrawal arrived, the battalion was reduced to about a hundred of all ranks. But the War Diary of the attacking German XIX Corps has an entry timed 1430 hours on this day which reads: 'The Corps Commander is not counting on any success from this attack and is of the opinion that further useless sacrifice must be avoided after the severe casualties which the 3rd Armoured Regiment has suffered during the counter-attack.'[2]

Meanwhile the 5th Gloucestershire in Ledringhem were sur-

---

[2] See Appendix II, p. 388.

rounded, and they were unable to disengage when the order to withdraw reached them. The enemy maintained his attack till after midnight, but failed to take the village. A little later, the fighting having died down, the Gloucestershire, much reduced in strength and with their commanding officer wounded, made their way across country through the enemy lines and rejoined their brigade on the Yser in accordance with their orders. The 8th Worcestershire had already arrived there.

The 145th Brigade at Cassel were under continuous artillery and mortar fire all day, and the 2nd Gloucestershire fought off an attack on their position north of the town. But apart from this Cassel was not seriously attacked on the 28th.

In Hazebrouck, however, where the battalion headquarters and headquarters company of the 1st Buckinghamshire still had their 'keep' in the middle of the town, the enemy tried all day to overcome them. They shot the men of a German battery which sought to bring guns to bear at close range, and thereafter the Germans relied on mortars and sniping. The Buckinghamshires' commanding officer was killed and the garrison steadily wasted through casualties. Ammunition began to run out, for the reserve supply in trucks blew up. A report adds laconically 'The survivors were now definitely tired'. At about half past six in the evening, the building which formed the keep collapsed under continuous shelling and mortar fire, and the enemy's tanks and infantry, pushing in from all sides, at last overcame this stout-hearted garrison. Of the 48th Division, only the 145th Brigade group at Cassel remained south of the Yser that night, for the 46th Division, which had been held under command in reserve behind Cassel, moved during the night to Teteghem in the Dunkirk bridgehead.

The 44th Division, in position on the canal running south-east from Hazebrouck and on the Caestre–Strazeele line, were subjected to heavy and continuous shelling and mortar fire all day, and were repeatedly attacked by infantry and tanks. Rouge Croix, between Caestre and Strazeele, was lost and retaken. Further south the road was crossed by the enemy, who took Clyte Hill, but that too was retaken. On the canal sector, La Motte was entered, recaptured, and lost again in a prolonged struggle; but though the Canal Line was eventually secured by the enemy, they made no substantial progress beyond it, and in the evening they abandoned the attack. Round both flanks of the divisional position, however, where there were no troops to oppose him, the enemy penetrated to Godewaersvelde on the north and Caudescure on the south. The 2nd, 4th and 5th Royal Sussex, 1st/5th and 1st/6th Queen's, 1st, 4th and 5th Royal West Kent, a company of the 2nd Buffs and a detachment of Don Details suffered heavily in this day's fighting, and some battalions were reduced to the strength of weak companies before they were ordered to move north.

During the day the German XIX Corps commander (Guderian) made a tour of his forward positions. The Diary records his opinion that further tank attacks would involve 'useless sacrifice of our best troops': in his view the wise course is 'to hold positions reached and to let 18 Army's attack from the east take effect'.[3]

The Diary adds that after returning from his tour of the front Guderian advised the Chief of Staff to Kleist Group as follows:

> (1) After the Belgian capitulation continuation of operations here is not desirable as it is costing unnecessary sacrifices. The armoured divisions have only 50% of their armoured strength left and their equipment is in urgent need of repair if the Corps is to be ready again in a short time for other operations.
>
> (2) A tank attack is pointless in the marshy country which has been completely soaked by the rain. [It had rained heavily in the past twenty-four hours.] The troops are in possession of the high ground south of Dunkirk; they hold the important Cassel–Dunkirk road; and they have favourable artillery positions . . . from which they can fire on Dunkirk.
>
> Furthermore 18 Army [of Army Group B] is approaching [Kleist] Group from the east. The infantry forces of this army are more suitable than tanks for fighting in this kind of country, and the task of closing the gap on the coast can therefore be left to them.[4]

The Diary adds that Kleist Group agreed: all three armoured divisions were to be withdrawn.

Between the British 44th Division and the divisions of II Corps on the eastern front lay the French First Army. By the morning of the 28th only its III Corps and the Cavalry Corps had got back to the Lys; the rest were still in the Lille area nearly surrounded by German divisions. Decision as to the French Army's further movements had become a matter of urgency, for unless the French also moved promptly to the coast they would be left isolated when the British withdrawal from the Lys took place in the coming night. General Blanchard visited the Command Post at about eleven o'clock in the morning of the 28th and conferred with Lord Gort and General Pownall. It was quickly apparent that although he had been present at the discussion of the defence of a Dunkirk bridgehead which had taken place at Cassel on the day before (page 197) he regarded retirement to *the Lys* as the final move; apparently the British decision to retire to the coast and evacuate to England, which had been notified to M. Reynaud and General Weygand on the 26th, had not been made known to him. When the British Government's telegram

---

[3] See Appendix II, p. 388.
[4] Ibid.

to Lord Gort was read to him, he was horrified. It is unnecessary to add anything to the account of this conference which is given in Lord Gort's despatch, for the facts are not in dispute:

Next morning (28th May) General Blanchard arrived at my headquarters at Houtkerque at about 11 a.m., and I read him the telegram which I had received the previous day from the Secretary of State. It was then clear to me that whereas we had both received similar instructions from our own Government for the establishment of a bridgehead, he had, as yet, received no instructions to correspond with those I had received to evacuate my troops. General Blanchard therefore could not see his way to contemplate evacuation.

I then expressed the opinion that now the Belgian Army had ceased to exist, the only alternatives could be evacuation or surrender. The enemy threat to the north-eastern flank appeared certain to develop during the next forty-eight hours. The long south-western flank was being subjected to constant and increasing pressure, especially at Cassel and Wormhoudt, and the arrival of the enemy heavy columns could not be long delayed. These considerations could not be lightly dismissed. While this discussion was taking place a liaison officer arrived from General Prioux, now in command of the French 1st Army, to say that the latter did not consider his troops were fit to make any further move and that he therefore intended to remain in the area between Béthune and Lille, protected by the quadrangle of canals.

I then begged General Blanchard for the sake of France, the French Army and the Allied Cause to order General Prioux back. Surely I said, his troops were not all so tired as to be incapable of moving. The French Government would be able to provide ships at least for some of his troops and the chance of saving a part of his trained soldiers was preferable to the certainty of losing them all. I could not move him. Finally he asked me formally whether it was my intention to withdraw that night to the line Cassel–Poperinghe–Ypres.

I replied in the affirmative and informed him that I now had formal orders from His Majesty's Government to withdraw the B.E.F. and that if I was to have any hope of carrying them out I must continue my move that night. General Blanchard's parting was not unfriendly, and when he left I issued my orders for withdrawal to provide for that change of mind on the part of the French High Command for which I so sincerely hoped and which in fact took place later.[5]

The subsequent decisions of General Prioux, commanding the French First Army, were doubtless influenced by his knowledge of General Blanchard's intention to stand on the Lys and by the absence of any orders to the contrary from General Georges or General Weygand. A liaison officer from Lord Gort's headquarters who visited him during the morning understood him to say that he had

---

[5] Lord Gort's Despatches, p. 5927.

P

asked for permission to abandon all material (except a few guns for anti-tank protection) and withdraw across country through the area between lines drawn from Estaires to Bergues and from Armentières to Furnes (see situation map for 27th May). He had lost touch, then, with General Blanchard, and if the British withdrew from the Lys he too would withdraw on his own responsibility, starting before daylight on the 29th. He regarded his V Corps, still in the Lille area, as lost. This was in the morning.

At half past three in the afternoon, Major-General Osborne (whose 44th Division was immediately on the right of the French and who was therefore directly concerned to know when and by what routes the French intended to move) went to see General Prioux. There he learnt that General Prioux had now decided not to withdraw but to remain with his IV Corps on the Lys: only his III Corps and what remained of the Cavalry Corps would withdraw, starting at midday on the 29th. General Osborne tried hard to shake his decision and offered to stay and protect his flank if the whole French force would retire. But General Prioux held to his decision and General Osborne went to visit General de la Laurencie, commanding the French III Corps, which had been ordered to withdraw at noon on the 29th. General de la Laurencie told him the III Corps would withdraw at *eleven o'clock that night* (the 28th), that is in two hours' time; after that time there would be no protection for the 44th Division's flank.

General Osborne decided that instead of trying to make a long march immediately following such a hard day's fighting, he would move only to the Mont des Cats, a naturally strong position six miles in rear, and from there continue the withdrawal on the following night. But moving cross-country in darkness units lost touch, and by dawn only the divisional headquarters and some elements of the division reached the Mont des Cats. Till then the Mont had been held by a party of Royal Engineers, acting as infantry, with the 2nd Royal Horse Artillery, the 52nd and 65th Field Regiments and the 1st/8th Middlesex machine-gun battalion. The Horse Artillery had but two guns left and the Middlesex only twelve; and the gunners, who had done much to save the infantry and to damage the enemy, were now few in numbers and short of ammunition. The 44th Division was hardly capable of further operations, but it had fulfilled its task.

During the night the fragment that remained of the 2nd Division, no longer operational, withdrew to the Dunkirk bridgehead, moving with difficulty on the congested roads.

The roads to the coast presented an astonishing spectacle in those days when motor and horse-drawn transport of two armies, refugees on foot, stragglers and the fragments of units, and the withdrawing divisions all sought to find a way northwards. In the roadside fields burning equipment and abandoned stores heightened the appearance of disintegration. But through the formless texture of the scene the British divisions which had been fighting by day and retiring at night wove a firmer thread; marching doggedly, tired and often hungry, shocked by all the crowding and confusion but too preoccupied to bother much, they moved imperturbably through a crumbling world, upheld by discipline and the traditions of their Service.

The enemy sought in vain to stem the flow, and at intervals German bombing added to the confusion. Indeed, every circumstance seemed designed to upset calculations and interfere with plans, but Sir Ronald Adam's arrangements for the organisation of the Dunkirk bridgehead worked, and with increasing efficiency, as the days wore on and the fighting divisions came in. The traffic problem had been largely solved by good organisation, when on this day (the 28th) it was again immensely complicated as elements of the French 6oth Division and later of their III Corps began to arrive. Some of their transport was mechanised but much of it horse-drawn, and none of the French troops appeared to have received orders to leave their vehicles outside the perimeter. Seldom would they do so unless compelled by British control posts, and some of the roads inside the perimeter became choked and impassable.

British III Corps headquarters had taken over responsibility for the western sector of the bridgehead and for the defence of its perimeter from Dunkirk through Bergues to Warhem. Similarly, I Corps were now responsible for the central sector. For the eastern sector, Brigadier Lawson was still responsible until the arrival of the II Corps. This was at the moment the most dangerously exposed part of the bridgehead.

At eleven o'clock on the morning of the 28th when only a few hours had passed since the Belgian surrender, advanced troops of the enemy reached the perimeter between Nieuport and the sea coast. The 12th Lancers, guarding the exposed flank, drove off the first German patrols with considerable loss, but later in the day more of the enemy's troops reached the perimeter defences. The divisions of II Corps had not yet arrived and, interspersed with some French detachments, the defending troops consisted mainly of detachments of the 53rd Medium and 2nd Medium Regiments, the 1st Heavy Anti-Aircraft Regiment of the Royal Artillery, and of the 7th Field Company, Royal Engineers, all fighting as infantry. Heavy mortar and machine-gun fire was put down on their positions, and the enemy succeeded in capturing and holding an undestroyed bridge and a small bridgehead in the town of Nieuport. But all subsequent attacks that day were successfully repulsed. The enemy's possession of the Belgian coast, now that Belgium had surrendered, meant that La Panne beach could soon be brought under enemy fire. Realising the danger here General Brooke, who was to be responsible for the eastern sector of the bridgehead, ordered all that was available of the 4th Division to move into the bridgehead as quickly as possible. Only the 12th Brigade was free to do so immediately, as the 10th and 11th were under command of the now much depleted 5th Division; and even the 12th Brigade could not arrive till the morning of the 29th. Nor could they then take over till evening, for the flat open country adjoining the canal made it impossible to carry out reliefs in daylight. The 4th Division took over the same night the front from Wulpen to Nieuport Bains.

But while the eastern sector of the bridgehead was thus threatened, the situation in Dunkirk harbour on the 28th had improved, and early in the morning Captain Tennant asked for ships to be sent in to the mole, which had been found on the night before to be a practical substitute for the harbour quays. The destroyers *Mackay*, *Montrose*, *Vimy*, *Worcester*, *Sabre* and *Anthony* all entered and embarked large numbers, while others lifted men from the beaches. There were still not enough small boats to ferry men from the shore and not enough skilled control of their use; and their handling was made harder by a swell at sea which raised a surf on the beaches and led to the swamping of a good many boats in the hands of inexperienced soldiers. In the afternoon Lord Gort informed the War Office that some 20,000 men were waiting in the dunes and that the situation was critical. But the Admiralty had already ordered 'every available destroyer' of the Portsmouth and Western Approaches Commands to be sailed for Dover and vigorous steps were being taken to collect still more small boats from rivers and estuaries of southern England. The Dutch schuyts, now mostly manned by naval crews, were starting to run a continuous service to Dunkirk from Margate and Ramsgate and a greatly increased and still increasing fleet was now at Admiral Ramsay's disposal.

Another good omen was that there was less interference from the air on this day for 'the greater part of German bomber formations was employed in attacking the retreating enemy'.[6] The Chief of Air Staff at home had called on the heads of all operational commands 'to make their greatest effort today to assist their comrades of the Army and Navy' and Fighter Command were ordered 'to ensure the protection of Dunkirk beaches (three miles on either side) from first light until darkness by continuous fighter patrols in strength'. To fly continuously and in strength was beyond the power of the forces available, but they flew patrols at two-squadron strength with slightly longer intervals than the day before, when only single squadrons had patrolled. Three hundred and twenty-one sorties were flown, a record to that date. Four squadrons (Nos. 213, 229, 242 and 616) went out three times and most of the others employed

---

[6] See Appendix II, p. 389.

VICE-ADMIRAL SIR BERTRAM H. RAMSAY

Flag Officer Commanding, Dover

destroyers to embark men from the east mole of Dunkirk harbour with some twenty destroyers, nineteen mine-sweepers, seventeen drifters, over twenty schuyts, five coastal steamers and many motor boats, tugs, lifeboats and ships' boats to work off the beaches. Provided the passage between Dunkirk and the buoy off Calais could be made in darkness the short route Z was to be used.

German troops knew that the British were embarking along the coast, and the Kleist Group had reported on the 27th, 'it is very bitter for our men to see this'.[7] When Fourth Army (of which the Group were a part) were told that on Goering's order Dunkirk was being attacked by the *Luftwaffe* 'in such a manner that further embarkations are reported to be impossible' the Fourth Army Chief of Staff retorted, 'the picture in the Channel ports is as follows: big ships come alongside the quays, planks are run up, and the men hurry aboard. All material is left behind. But we do not want to find these men, newly equipped, up against us again later.'[8] He might well protest, for notwithstanding Goering's boast, the Royal Navy had in fact landed 25,473 men in England in two days.

The picture which the German War Diary of the Fourth Army draws of the fighting on 28th May is extremely confused. Army Group A issued no fresh directive, and the battle was fought by the various commanders on what knowledge they had. Confusion was increased by absence of co-ordination between the two Army Groups A and B. A lack of grip is evident from the German records at this time. Slowly various corps halted and reorganised while others struggled forward. In the Lille area there was chaos, troops of the Fourth Army (Army Group A) becoming entangled with those of the Sixth Army (Army Group B). In the War Diary of Army Group A the statement that its main task had been completed had appeared more than once. On this day (the 28th) two corps consisting of six divisions were pulled out, and although the Hoth and Kleist Groups continued their attacks (to join up with Army Group B), the main preoccupation of Army Group A Headquarters was now the forthcoming offensive southwards from the Somme–Aisne line. Halder, Chief of Staff of the Army High Command, had come to a conference, which Staff officers from all the army groups attended, when the matter for discussion was *future* operations. After this the Army Group Staff began discussions with the armies in its command concerning regrouping, assembly and boundaries for the operation which had been explained by Halder—to be known as Operation 'Red'.

The position on the evening of the 28th is shown on the adjoining situation map.

---

[7] See Appendix II, p. 389.
[8] Ibid.

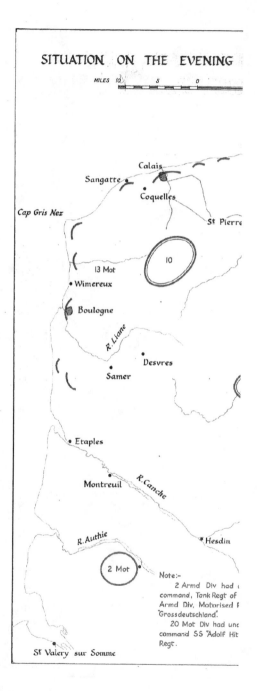

SITUATION ON THE EVENING

MILES 10   5   0

LEGEND

British troops are shown in Red, French in
Green, Belgian in Brown and German in Blue.

British & French

Corps... Ⅲ

Divisions... ⟨48

Divisions in reserve or moving.......... ⟨23⟩

Army Boundary..................................... —o—o—

Divisional " .... —ı—ı—

German

Armoured Divisions.................. 8 ⟨10⟩

Motorised " .... 20Mot ⟨2Mot⟩

Infantry " .... 18 ⟨35⟩

Armoured Group Boundary................ —ıı—ıı—

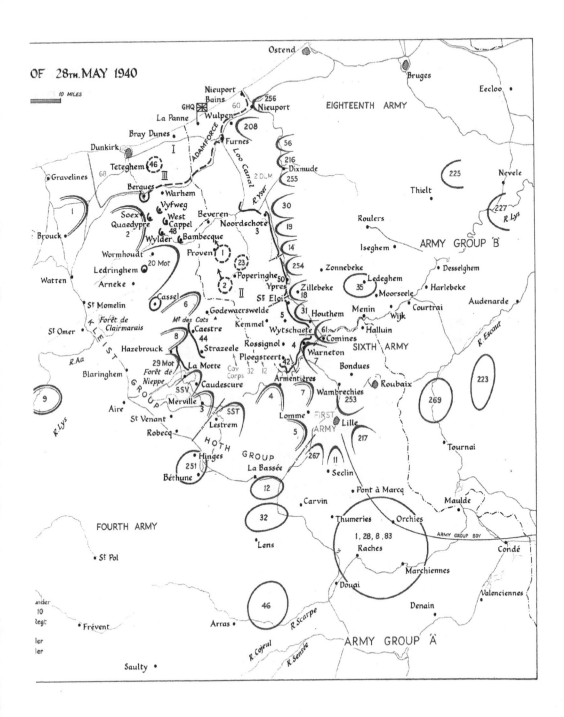

10 MILES

Ostend

Bruges

Eecloo

Nieuport
Bains
GHQ
60
Nieuport
256

EIGHTEENTH ARMY

Wulpen
La Panne

208

Bray Dunes

Furnes

56

Dunkirk

I

216
Dixmude
255

225

Nevele

Teteghem
46
68

III

2 D.L.M.

Thielt

227
R. Lys

Gravelines

Berques
Warhem
Vyfweg

Soex

West
Cappel

Beveren

Noordschote
3

30

19

Roulers

Iseghem

ARMY GROUP 'B'

Brouck

Quaedypre
2

Wylder
Bambecque

14

Desselghem

Wormhoudt

Proven
I

254

Zonnebeke

Ledringhem
20 Mot

23

Poperinghe
50

Ledeghem
35

Moorseele

Harlebeke

Watten

Arneke

2

II

Ypres
St Eloi

Zillebeke
18

Menin
Wijk

Courtrai

Audenarde

St Momelin

Cassel
6

Godewaerswelde

31

Houthem

Forêt de
Clairmarais

Mt des Cats

Caestre
44

Kemmel

Wytschaete

61
Comines

Halluin

SIXTH ARMY

R. Escaut

St Omer

8

Strazeele

Rossignol

4

Warneton
7

Hazebrouck

Ploegsteerts
32 12

42

Bondues

Roubaix

223

R. Aa

29 Mot
Forêt de
Nieppe

La Motte

Cav
Corps

Armentières

Blaringhem

SSV

Caudescure

4

7

Wambrechies
253

269

9

Merville

3

SST

Lomme

FIRST

Lille

Tournai

R. Lys

Aire

St Venant

Lestrem

5

ARMY

217

Robecq

HOTH

Hinges

GROUP

267

11

Maulde

251

La Bassée

Seclin

Béthune

12

Pont à Marcq

Condé

Carvin

Thumeries

Orchies

ARMY GROUP BDY

FOURTH ARMY

32

Lens

1, 28, 8, 83
Raches

Marchiennes

Valenciennes

St Pol

Denain

under
10
Regt

46

Arras

R. Scarpe

Douai

ler
ler

Frévent

R. Cojeul

ARMY GROUP 'A'

Saulty

R. Sensée

CHAPTER XIV

THE FINAL WITHDRAWAL

29th May, 1940

B Y the early morning of the 29th German forces were closing up to the Poperinghe–Noordschote line where rearguards of the 50th and 3rd Divisions covered the eastern flank of the retiring army. To the south of that line the depleted 44th Division were in the Mont des Cats position and the 48th Division's 145th Brigade in Cassel still held their isolated post.

Early in the morning the 44th Division were subjected to heavy mortar fire and this was followed later by intense dive-bombing, and enemy tanks and lorried infantry were seen apparently preparing for an attack. Shortly before ten o'clock in the morning the troops moved out in two columns, and though the enemy shelled them they were not molested. Greatly reduced in strength, the remnants of the division reached the beaches for embarkation next day.

Orders to retire on the night of the 28th did not reach the commander of the Cassel garrison till six in the morning of the 29th. By then the town was surrounded and German forces had penetrated deeply on either flank. It was impossible to move out in daylight, and when a little later wireless communication with 48th Divisional Headquarters was re-established, orders were received to hold Cassel till nightfall and then to withdraw. All through the day Cassel was heavily bombarded and at intervals attacks by tanks and infantry were repulsed. In adjacent country patrols sent out by the 1st East Riding Yeomanry met the enemy at a number of points and suffered considerable loss in men and vehicles. From the hill-top on which Cassel stands strong German forces of all arms could be seen moving north-east behind the town, and when night fell and the garrison set out, the enemy was across their line of march. The 4th Oxfordshire and Buckinghamshire Light Infantry formed the advanced guard; then came brigade headquarters, artillery and engineers; next the 2nd Gloucestershire; and finally the combined carrier platoons of the two infantry battalions and what was left of the 1st East Riding Yeomanry formed the rearguard. The move started at nine-thirty and leading troops soon encountered the enemy. When daylight came a series of fights led to a separation of units and as the day wore on many were killed, wounded or surrounded and captured piecemeal. Only a few got through to reach Dunkirk. So ended a stand of great value to the British Expeditionary Force. Cassel occupies a key position at the junction of five important roads, including the main route, on this flank, to Dunkirk. Its use by the enemy had been blocked throughout these most critical days, and considerable forces had been compelled to concentrate on a fruitless effort to take the town. By occupying substantial numbers of the enemy throughout the 29th the Cassel garrison helped to weaken his attack on the flank of the army moving back to the coast.

For the planned movements were duly carried out, though other units which constituted the rearguard also had a hard day's fighting to make this possible. The elements of the 50th and 3rd Divisions on the Poperinghe–Lizerne line suffered heavily from bombardment throughout the day. The enemy regained contact with the 50th Division rearguard by midday, and when later the time for withdrawal came, one company of the 8th Durham Light Infantry was cut off. The 3rd Division's rearguard on their left (the 8th and 9th Brigades) was vigorously attacked and some units were forced to yield ground. But the enemy made no substantial progress, though fighting continued till the time for further withdrawal, and then the 2nd Lincolnshire carriers had to counter-attack in order to free the battalion. All units suffered severely in the day's fighting, but their front was unbroken.

Meanwhile the western flankguard was also hard pressed. Troops of the 48th and 42nd Divisions in the area Bergues, Quaedypre, Wylder, Bambecque, were attacked by tanks and by infantry of the 20th Motorised Division, the motorised *Grossdeutschland* Regiment and the S.S. Adolf Hitler Regiment. There were inevitably considerable gaps between the places occupied, and although the latter were held till the time ordered for withdrawal, the enemy made deep penetrations between them and there was much confused fighting. Brigadier Norman's force of the 1st Light Armoured Reconnaissance Brigade and the 1st Welsh Guards held off a sustained attack till ordered to withdraw. The 8th Worcestershire on the Yser between Wylder and Bambecque also had a perilous day. Deep penetrations had been made on both flanks of the position they held, and after losing heavily they were forced to give some ground. But the enemy was unable to break their resistance and at night they succeeded in withdrawing in accordance with their orders.

Behind the western sector of the upper Yser advanced elements of the German forces reached positions held by the 42nd Division at Rexpoede and Oost Cappel towards evening, but withdrawal, when the time came, was achieved successfully; and on the rest of the Yser line what remained of the 5th Division was not seriously attacked and withdrew to the perimeter in the night. The fighting of the last few days had sadly exhausted its strength. Many of its battalions, and those of the 143rd Brigade which had fought with it, were reduced by now to the strength of one or two companies. Of the carriers of the 17th Brigade, only six were left. In the 13th Brigade, the 2nd Sherwood Foresters mustered only 156 of all ranks. Battle casualties accounted for most of the losses, but the difficulties of the withdrawal added something to the total. The inevitable difficulties had been immensely increased by the fact that the French Command had been unwilling to co-ordinate road movements in the final stages or to collaborate in maintaining road discipline. The roads became choked by French and British troops moving on the same routes under differing orders, in motorised and horse-drawn transport and on foot—the British aiming at the eastern and the French at the western sector of the bridgehead, so that their paths crossed. Units were all too easily separated in the turgid stream of traffic, moving often in darkness and sometimes under shellfire. And, though many of these detached parties eventually reached the beaches, their absence while the rearguard fighting lasted increased the difficulties of those who fought.

The situation maps for these days show how greatly superior in numbers were the German forces which sought to defeat the retiring army. Yet nowhere during the whole withdrawal were they able to make a clean break in our defence; nowhere could they overcome the resistance of rearguards which stood their ground till they were either destroyed by weight of numbers or ordered to retire. The line of defence had been perilously weak, but the fighting spirit had been too strong for the enemy to break, and now his opportunity was lost.

Many of the British Expeditionary Force had already sailed for England and during the coming night and the following morning the remainder entered the Dunkirk bridgehead; there the journeying of the divisions which had marched so often and so far was practically completed.

The stubbornness of the British resistance by day and the speed of their withdrawal by night had combined to frustrate German plans. On this 29th of May Army Group B War Diary states that three divisions were being moved rapidly westward to join forces with Kleist's armour at Poperinghe, and from there to wheel against the British flank on the Poperinghe–Lizerne line. During the afternoon the German Sixth Army reported that this wheeling movement had begun 'in order to cut off the enemy from Poperinghe' but, as already told, the troops on the Poperinghe–Lizerne line withdrew before the enemy could intercept them. The pincers closed not round the British Expeditionary Force but behind it. Yet the German Diary also states that 'the attack designed to annihilate the enemy forces still encircled in the area south and south-east of Dunkirk will be continued with the greatest vigour. An order to this effect is again issued by the Army Group Command.'[1]

During the morning the enemy had indeed reached the canal on the eastern outskirts of Furnes and the town itself was heavily bombed and mortared. The Germans were in close contact now on the west near Bergues and on the east from Nieuport to the sea, but all their attempts to cross the canal at Bergues were frustrated and they were prevented from enlarging their small hold in Nieuport. With the relief of the improvised defence that night by the 4th Division and with the arrival of II Corps, Sir Ronald Adam's task was completed and he sailed for home next morning.

Lord Gort's headquarters had arrived at La Panne on the afternoon of the 28th and an order was issued laying down the order of evacuation. III Corps were to go first; II Corps second. I Corps was to have the honour of acting as rearguard. For belief that perhaps 45,000 troops might be got away had given place to a growing hope that the greater part of the British Expeditionary Force could be evacuated. And in consequence the Navy's task expanded from the swift evacuation of a part to a sustained attempt to bring the whole force home.

A heartening message was received by Lord Gort from His Majesty the King:

> All your countrymen have been following with pride and admiration the courageous resistance of the British Expeditionary Force during the continuous fighting of the last fortnight. Placed by circumstances outside their control in a position of extreme difficulty, they are displaying a gallantry that has never been surpassed in the annals of the British Army. The hearts of every one of us at home are with you and your magnificent troops in this hour of peril.

The message was at once issued to the troops, and Lord Gort replied:

> The Commander-in-Chief with humble duty begs leave on behalf of all ranks of the B.E.F. to thank Your Majesty for your message. May I assure Your Majesty that the Army is doing all in its power to live up to its proud tradition and is immensely encouraged at this critical moment by the words of Your Majesty's telegram.

Late in the evening the Commander-in-Chief received the following personal message from the Prime Minister:

> . . . If you are cut from all communication from us and all evacuation from Dunkirk and beaches had in your judgement been finally prevented after every attempt to re-open it had failed, you would become the sole judge of when it was impossible to inflict further damage upon the enemy. H.M.G. are sure that the repute of the British Army is safe in your hands.

---

[1] See Appendix II, p. 389.

On this afternoon, three days after the British Government's decision to evacuate as many as possible of the British Expeditionary Force had been notified to the French High Command, General Weygand authorised the evacuation of as many as possible of the French First Army. 'Operation Dynamo' had been in progress since the 26th, and over 70,000 British troops had been embarked before the French commander's decision was taken. Large numbers of French troops were by then reaching the coast. Four French torpedo boats and two of their mine-sweepers arrived to help with the embarkation of French troops and more of their ships followed in succeeding days.

Organisation on the beaches was being strengthened and improved and the concentration of warships and other vessels was nearing its peak. Their very names conjure up a vision of the assembling fleet of warships, merchantmen, liners and fishing craft, of tugs and lifeboats, barges, sailing yachts and launches. The great and the small were joined in common effort. The *Royal Sovereign* was there and the *Emperor of India* and there were several *Queens*; the *Princess Elizabeth* and the *Princess Maud* were there, with the *Duchess of Fife*, *Lord Howard* and *Lord Howe*, the famous *Gracie Fields* and obscure *Polly Johnson*. *Our Bairns* and *The Boys* were there with *Girl Pamela* and a *Yorkshire Lass*. Many towns took part from *Canterbury* to *Bideford*, from *Worcester* to *Dundalk*, and footballers were represented by *Blackburn Rovers* and the *Spurs*. *Wakeful*, *Gallant* and *Intrepid* were there to typify the spirit of them all and, as emblems of the freedom they toiled for and the hope that inspired them, there was a *Golden Gift* and a *Silver Dawn*.

But the enemy's attempt to disrupt operations also increased and the Navy only carried on by facing graver risks and by paying a high price for their achievement. The ships had already braved the fire of land-based guns, bombing and machine-gunning from the air and the hidden menace of magnetic mines. This day began with the revelation of further dangers on the passage to and from the French coast.

A little before midnight the destroyer *Wakeful*, carrying 650 troops embarked from the beach at Bray, sailed for Dover by the northerly route Y. She had just cleared the North Channel and turned sharply to westward when two torpedo tracks were seen. One torpedo was avoided but the other hit amidships. The *Wakeful* was broken in half by the explosion; the two halves sank in a few seconds, settling with their midships sections on the shallow bottom while bow and stern projected high above the surface. The troops on board, asleep below, went down with the ship and only a few and the crew on deck floated clear.

Soon after, the drifters *Comfort* and *Nautilus*, *en route* for La Panne, reached the scene of disaster and started to pick up survivors; later the mine-sweeper *Gossamer*, bringing 420 troops from Dunkirk, joined in the rescue. Then the destroyer *Grafton* arrived with 800 troops on board and the drifter *Lydd* came with 300 on their way to England. They too lowered boats to look for survivors from the *Wakeful*. Two hours had elapsed since the torpedo attack but it was still very dark. A small unlighted vessel was thought by the *Grafton* to be another drifter and she was signalled to join the search. Within a few seconds the *Grafton* was torpedoed.

The *Comfort*, lying nearby, was almost swamped by the force of this explosion and the Captain of the *Wakeful*, whom she had rescued from the sea, was again washed overboard. Although sinking, the *Grafton* opened fire on a vessel which in the darkness she took to be an enemy torpedo boat and following the *Grafton's* example the *Lydd* rammed and sank this dimly seen vessel. But in fact it was the *Comfort* moving in the darkness; only one of her crew and four of the men she had rescued from the *Wakeful* were saved. It became known later that the *Grafton* was sunk by the enemy's submarine U.69.

The 800 troops on board the *Grafton*, some seriously wounded, were taken off by the passenger ship *Malines* returning from Dunkirk, and before the *Grafton* went down she sighted an enemy vessel and sank her by gunfire. The Captain of the *Wakeful*, for the second time, was picked up, swimming, five hours after his own ship had been hit. By then it was at last light.

There were other misfortunes on this day. The destroyers *Montrose* and *Mackay* were damaged by collision and grounding and the passenger ship *Mona's Queen* blew up on one of the magnetic mines which enemy aircraft were now sowing in the approaches to Dover and Dunkirk. Only one other ship was destroyed by this means during the evacuation.

But it was the enemy's bombing that caused the heaviest damage. The scale on which evacuation was proceeding had been reported by their air reconnaissance formations and 'the bulk of the German bomber forces were employed to prevent the enemy achieving this and to annihilate him in his present state of collapse' (*sic*). In the afternoon 'the full force of the air attacks was directed against the numerous merchant vessels in the adjacent sea area and the warships escorting them'.[2] The German air fleets co-operating with Army Group A and Army Group B were both employed. Between midday and eight o'clock at night there was hardly a break in the attack and five times it reached major proportions with large concentrations of both bombers and fighters. On two of these occasions our fighter patrols were not at the time over the area: on the

---

[2] German Air Ministry Situation Report. See Appendix II, p. 390.

remaining three the enemy were intercepted—once before, once during, and once after their main attack. Our patrols had been doubled in size since their unequal battles of the day before, but intervals between patrols were correspondingly longer and they found that with patrols numbering from twenty-five to forty-four aircraft they were still often outnumbered. On more than one occasion they were wholly engaged with enemy fighters and could not reach the bombers. Sixteen squadrons fought this day. Nineteen fighters were lost and though the squadrons claimed to have brought down a larger number of enemy aircraft the *Luftwaffe's* report that day only admitted the loss of eighteen; on the other hand it claimed (mistakenly) to have shot down sixty-eight of our aircraft!

It must always be difficult if not impossible to assess and apportion an enemy's air losses accurately. More than one aircraft engaged may with good reason claim credit for a kill, and throughout Operation Dynamo anti-aircraft artillery on land and fire from ships in harbour and at sea accounted for some of the enemy destroyed. But losses are not the true criteria by which achievement in action should be measured. The enemy's attacks this day could not be prevented, for he had far larger forces than the squadrons who fought him. But his attacks were so far interfered with and broken up that he failed in his intention. He could neither weaken the Army's defences nor stop the Navy's operations. The fact that he was prevented from realising his aim is the best proof of what the Royal Air Force achieved.

While some who suffered from the enemy bombing complained that our air cover was inadequate, both the Army and the Navy acknowledged gratefully the help they had received. The Army fighting its way to the coast was largely freed from air attack and reported 'little bombing today'; and the Vice-Admiral Dover signalled Fighter Command: 'Reports from Senior Naval Officer state your assistance has been invaluable. I am most grateful for your splendid co-operation. It alone has given us a chance of success . . .' This generous message showed an appreciation of the part played by the Royal Air Force which might well have been warped by the day's happenings.

For the Navy had endured great losses with a fortitude which the enemy's fury could not shake. The early-morning misfortune has been told to illustrate the dangers faced in darkness and at sea. The even greater danger which ships faced in harbour and in daylight may be illustrated by what happened on this afternoon.

Men who came home from Dunkirk remember most vividly the beaches (if they embarked there), or, if they came from the harbour, the long, narrow, eastern mole, jutting out for 1,600 yards, naked of all defence. It was built as a breakwater, not to provide berthing for ships, but it was the easiest place for ships to reach and leave and, in order to speed up the pace of evacuation, the Navy continued to use it throughout these operations though it was cruelly exposed. It was often hit but gaps in its planked footway were soon repaired and tens of thousands came home that way.

On this afternoon two destroyers, the *Grenade* and the *Jaguar*, were lying against the inner side of the mole. Six trawlers were berthed behind them, and the passenger ship *Canterbury*. Against the outer side of the mole at the same time were the passenger ships *Fenella* and the *Crested Eagle*. Their positions are shown on the adjoining sketch.

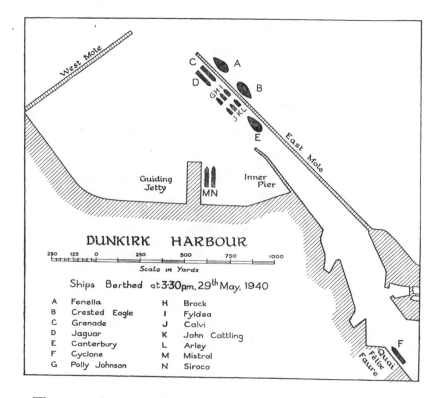

West Mole

East Mole

Guiding Jetty

Inner Pier

Quai Félix Faure

DUNKIRK HARBOUR

280 125 0 250 500 750 1000

Scale in Yards

Ships Berthed at 3·30pm, 29th May, 1940

A	Fenella	H	Brock
B	Crested Eagle	I	Fyldea
C	Grenade	J	Calvi
D	Jaguar	K	John Cattling
E	Canterbury	L	Arley
F	Cyclone	M	Mistral
G	Polly Johnson	N	Siroco

The enemy's onslaught from the air began at about half past three in the afternoon and continued till about eight o'clock, rising in a crescendo four times. Of the eleven British ships against the mole the *Grenade*, *Fenella*, *Crested Eagle*, *Polly Johnson* and *Calvi* were so damaged that they sank at once or shortly afterwards; the *Jaguar* and *Canterbury*, though they reached home, could take no more part in Dynamo. At six o'clock that night the harbour was only occupied by burning and sinking ships. A report reached Admiral Ramsay that the entrance was blocked and for a time all ships were directed to the beaches. But it was a mistaken report, for by strenuous effort all sinking ships had been moved from the fairway.

Meanwhile, equally sustained attacks had been made on the shipping off the beaches and, as evacuation continued in spite of it, losses were heavy. The destroyers *Gallant*, *Greyhound*, *Intrepid* and *Saladin* and the sloop *Bideford* were all badly damaged. The passenger ships *Normania* and *Lorina* were sunk. The merchantman *Clan Macalister*, which had carried across from England eight assault landing craft, and the armed boarding vessel *King Orry* were sunk and many smaller vessels were sunk or damaged. The story of one must serve to illustrate the off-shore conditions under which they worked.

The paddle-minesweeper *Gracie Fields*, carrying about 750 troops from La Panne beach, was hit amidships by a bomb soon after starting home. Her upper deck was enveloped in clouds of steam; her engine could not be stopped and as her rudder was jammed at an angle she continued to circle at about six knots. Two schuyts nevertheless made fast alongside and took off as many troops as they could carry. Then the minesweeper *Pangbourne* arrived. While embarking troops off Bray beach she had already been holed on both sides by near misses and thirteen men had been killed and eleven wounded: and her compass had been put out of action. But she went alongside the *Gracie Fields* and took off a further eighty troops. Then led by another returning vessel, she took the *Gracie Fields* in tow and started again for England. In the darkness of early morning the *Gracie Fields* began to sink, so the *Pangbourne* slipped the tow and took off her crew. There she was abandoned, but her crew and the troops they had brought from the beaches reached England safely in the ships that had gone to her aid.

If the records of this day be compared with those of the previous days, three facts stand out clearly. More ships and small craft were in action; they were exposed to heavier bombing attacks and they suffered greater losses: yet they brought away a much larger number of men. This is the measure of the day's achievement —47,310 men were landed in England by midnight and many more were on their way across the sea.

MILES 10   5   0

LEGEND

British troops are shown in Red, French in Green, Belgian in Brown and German in Blue.

British & French

Corps	III
Divisions	(48
Divisions in reserve or moving	(23)
Army Boundary	—o—o—
Divisional "	—·—·—

German

Armoured Divisions	8	(10)
Motorised "	20 Mot	(2 Mot)
Infantry "	18	(35)
Armoured Group Boundary	—"—"—	

Calais
Sangatte
Coquelles
Cap Gris Nez
St Pierre Br
10
Wimereux
Boulogne
13 Mot
R. Liane
2
Desvres
Samer
Etaples
Montreuil
R. Canche
R. Authie
Hesdin
2 Mot
St Valery sur Somme

Note :-
    9 Armd Div & 20 Mot
had under command :-
SS "Adolf Hitler" Regt,
Mot Regt "Grossdeutschlan
11 Mot Bde.

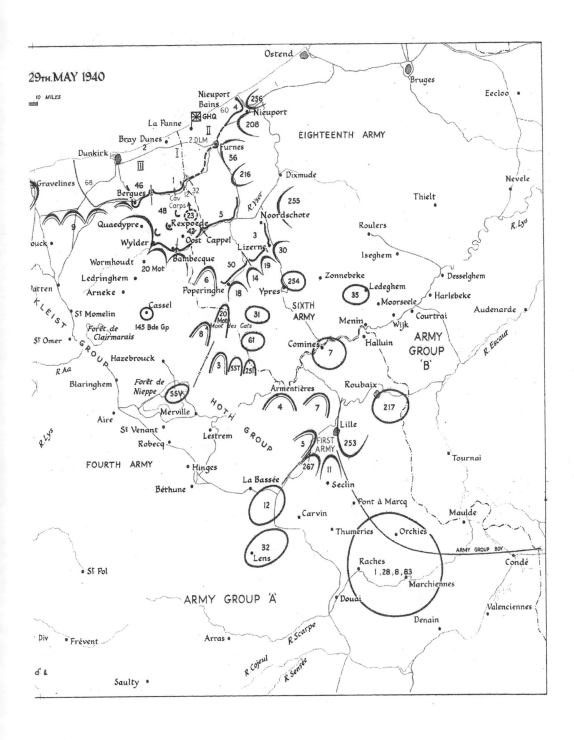

29TH. MAY 1940

10 MILES

CHAPTER XV

THE DEFENCE OF THE BRIDGEHEAD

30th May and 31st May, 1940

BY midday on the 30th practically all our retiring forces were within the perimeter with the enemy pressing round them. From now on all interest is focused on the Dunkirk bridgehead, and to form a true picture of the operations their double aspect must be kept in mind. First, as being fundamental to all else, is the Army's fight to hold back the German forces while evacuation takes place. Only as that succeeds can the scene be enacted on the quays and beaches and at sea.

The map facing page 238 shows who they were that held the bridgehead on this day. I Corps were now responsible for the western half of the British sector, from Dunkirk to the French frontier; II Corps for the eastern half from the frontier to the sea at Nieuport. III Corps was moving to the beaches for evacuation or had already gone home. But the map cannot expose the fact that none of the divisions marked on it were complete, that all were greatly reduced in strength. Of I Corps the 1st Division was short of three battalions which had been taken to help II Corps in the battle of the Ypres front (page 194). In the 42nd Division only the 126th Brigade was still capable of operations and only six battalions of the 46th Division had ever come effectively under Lord Gort's command during the battle. Of the 2nd Division only a composite *company* formed from men of the 5th Brigade was now left. In II Corps the 5th and 23rd Divisions were no longer capable of further fighting and some battalions had now little more than the strength of a normal company.

As the last of the divisions entered the bridgehead the enemy followed up quickly and before the day was over they were in close contact with our defences and were shelling and mortaring them with mounting-violence. They reported that 'the bridgehead is held by British troops who are fighting back very stubbornly'.[1] In many places the waterlogged state of the ground made it impossible for the defending troops to dig in, and as a consequence some units had heavy casualties from the bombardment. But the enemy were only ready to make one serious attempt to break our front on this day.

---

[1] German Air Ministry Situation Report. See Appendix II, p. 390.

After artillery preparation they tried to cross the canal just north of Furnes, where the front of the 3rd Division was held by the 7th Guards Brigade and the 8th Brigade. The attack was beaten off, but the 4th Royal Berkshire (now about the strength of one company) suffered heavily and a company of the 1st Coldstream Guards was sent to take over part of their position. About ten o'clock at night the attack was renewed and the enemy succeeded in breaking across the canal. But the Coldstreamers counter-attacked, drove them back across the water and restored the front.

The confusion and loss of grip on the German side which is noticeable at this time (page 214) had not been resolved. On the 29th of May Army Group A War Diary had noted that their Fourth Army could make little headway 'owing to very stubborn enemy resistance'. They now asked the Fourth Army whether Dunkirk could not be attacked through Bergues by mobile forces, but fear of a possible heavy loss led to this proposal being dropped. Instead the Fourth Army directed Kleist Group to close in, so as to be able to shell Dunkirk with 10-cm guns. It is recorded in Fourth Army War Diary that the operations officer at Army Headquarters complained to the Kleist Group: 'there is an impression here that nothing is happening today, that no one is any longer interested in Dunkirk. Town and harbour must be bombarded, embarkation prevented, panic caused'.[2] About three o'clock in the afternoon, Army Group A informed Fourth Army that O.K.H. had sanctioned an attack on Dunkirk; to which the officer receiving the message replied that the Fourth Army was ready to attack but Army Group B's Sixth Army must also take part, and the Sixth Army had apparently pulled out to rest! Rundstedt's Chief of Staff then asked whether Fourth Army knew that Kleist Group had informed Richthofen's VIII Air Corps that they intended to attack Dunkirk that afternoon. He was told that this was not known; on the contrary, Kleist Group had asked for Dunkirk to be bombed. However, the Fourth Army ordered Kleist Group to 'attack Dunkirk on both flanks, penetrate right up to the coast, and then continue the pursuit eastwards'.[3] Kleist Group Chief of Staff replied that their formations were unsuitable, since tanks could not be used there. He was told that 'By higher orders an end must finally be made of the embarkation at Dunkirk. . . .' And the Fourth Army commander intervened personally to order: 'All forces to the coast east of Dunkirk immediately. . . . The Divisional Commander is to be told that he is to reach the coast without fail today.'[4] Later Kleist Group reported that their 20th Motorised Division was 'advancing towards Bray Dunes. . . . The left wing is in

---

[2] See Appendix II, p. 390.
[3] Ibid.
[4] Ibid.

front of Bergues and in Gravelines, on the Canal and is unable to get on. The fortified bridgehead of Dunkirk lies in front of them'.[5] Attempts would now be made to fire on Dunkirk with light artillery, for the medium artillery had run out of ammunition the day before.

At this point the whole of the operations against Dunkirk were put under the command of Army Group B's Eighteenth Army. It had been engaged in Holland and against the Belgian Army; it was now made responsible for the destruction or capture of the Allied troops in the bridgehead. The forces which came under its command were the IX, X, XIV and XXVI Corps, comprising the 14th, 18th, 56th, 216th, 254th, 256th Infantry Divisions plus the 61st which was moving up; and also the 9th and 11th Motorised Brigades, the motorised Regiment *Grossdeutschland*, with the 20th Motorised Division and the S.S. Adolf Hitler Regiment in reserve. The change-over was to take effect at 2 a.m. on the 31st.

Army Group A ceased from now on to have any responsibility for the attack on Dunkirk; Rundstedt had got his wish. He had regarded his real task as accomplished when his forces reached the coast, cut British communications and seized the channel ports. Thereafter it was his policy (confirmed by Hitler though disliked both by the Commander-in-Chief, Brauchitsch, and at first by his own subordinate commanders) to husband his armoured formations for the coming offensive southwards. And though it is clear that he missed an opportunity by not attacking the Canal Line in rear of the British Expeditionary Force before Lord Gort could move back divisions for its defence, it was a sound and soldierly policy not to use his armour afterwards for an attack on Dunkirk. As already pointed out (page 178) the beditched ground is unsuited to the use of armour. In less than a week, moreover, Rundstedt had to be ready to attack southwards over the Somme–Aisne line. There, as he believed, a major part of the French Army had still to be brought to battle. The German forces must break and defeat this army if they were to conquer France. They had proved that for such a task the quick-thrusting armoured divisions were the most effective weapon, and already Rundstedt had lost nearly fifty per cent of his armoured strength (page 151). To waste more in attacks on Dunkirk would have shown bad judgement.

The entry on the 31st of May in the War Diary of Army Group A concludes with a long post-mortem in which Rundstedt's success is attributed:

(1) to initial surprise and speed of operations which 'led the enemy to take steps which only appear comprehensible if one assumes that the decisive point of German operations—lying with Army Group A—was not realised or was realised too late';

---

[5] See Appendix II, p. 390.

(2) to the work of the air force whose co-operation was 'ideal';

(3) to all the army formations on the ground 'where alone the annihilation of the enemy's fighting power can be achieved';

(4) to the fact that mobile formations 'overwhelmed the enemy at a tempo to which neither his leaders nor the training of his troops were equal'.[6]

Few will question this assessment of the factors which contributed to Army Group A's 'success'. But that success was hardly as complete as Rundstedt imagined and his complacency was not altogether justified by facts. For what is open to criticism is his own conduct of the latter part of this northern battle. Success is a relative term. The measure of success gained by Army Group A up to the 19th of May was gained by fighting the French Army on a front for which the British Expeditionary Force was not responsible and with which this history is therefore not directly concerned. The detail of that fighting has not been studied and it cannot therefore be appraised here. But after the 19th the British Expeditionary Force was involved, with results which have been described. On that day five of Rundstedt's armoured divisions reached the Canal du Nord; two more were just behind them; and other armoured, motorised and infantry divisions were moving up. And in front of them there was virtually no opposition. In these circumstances the leading divisions reached the coast next day and cut our communications in doing so. The mere threat of our small counter-attack at Arras was enough to slow down their progress on the 21st, but by the 22nd that threat had been mitigated and Rundstedt had by then seven armoured divisions, six motorised divisions and four infantry divisions in the rear of the British Expeditionary Force. At that time Lord Gort had only the 5th and 50th Divisions to guard his right rear at Arras, and some scratch formations scattered thinly along the Canal Line. Yet in the days which followed, all that Rundstedt did with his greatly superior force was to take the lightly garrisoned ports of Boulogne and Calais, to harry our divisions in their retreat to the coast, and then to stand by, preparing for the next offensive, while they embarked to refit in England. Was his success so complete after all? After the 19th of May he advanced quickly through country in which there was no one to oppose him, but after hesitating to strike eastwards at our rear while it was virtually undefended, he thereafter advanced only as fast as our retiring army allowed, in spite of the fact that without the help of Army Group B he had stronger forces at his disposal than the whole of the British Expeditionary Force. It is arguable that after the 19th of May his part in the northern battle should be regarded as a very qualified success if not actually a failure, in that having won a

---

[6] See Appendix II, p. 390.

good opening he was unable to exploit it. The extent to which Hitler was responsible is discussed in the Supplement on the 'Planning and Conduct of the German Campaign'; but it may be said here that there is no contemporary evidence to indicate that Rundstedt was conscious of any interference or that he was ever persuaded from following the course which he wished to adopt.

Meanwhile, Army Group B, whose Eighteenth Army had now taken over responsibility for the final capture of Dunkirk, recorded the following telephone message from the German High Command.

> The Commander-in-Chief, Army [Brauchitsch], would like to make some personal suggestions for overpowering the enemy around Dunkirk.
>
> For instance, the following points have been considered:
>
> (a) The landing of units from the sea in rear of the British forces.
>
> (b) The withdrawal of advanced infantry units from the bank of the [perimeter] canal in order to allow unobstructed and effective air support.
>
> (c) The use of anti-aircraft shells with time fuses for fighting in the dunes in order to compensate for reduced effectiveness of artillery.
>
> (Suggestion made by the Führer and Supreme Commander.)[7]

So much for the story, propounded later, that Hitler wished to let the British Expeditionary Force escape.

At British General Headquarters in La Panne there was an almost continuous exchange of messages with England. Someone was almost always on the telephone to the War Office, explaining the situation in France or receiving information or instructions from England. A few minutes after midnight on the 29th/30th May, the War Office were told that the perimeter could not be held for long and asked that as many boats as possible should be sent over quickly, for enemy action had died away with nightfall and was not causing trouble during hours of darkness. And more ammunition for Bofors guns to deal with aircraft by day was needed urgently.

Four hours later the War Office replied that the Vice-Admiral Dover would get as many small craft as possible across and that an ammunition barge was ready to sail and would be directed to La Panne. It would be followed the next day by other barges containing approximately 75 tons each in the proportion of one-third food, one-third water and one-third ammunition in each barge.

Once in the bridgehead Lord Gort came under the immediate command of Admiral Abrial, the French commander of the Dunkirk area. On May the 29th General Weygand had ordered General Blanchard to 'establish with all available forces a bridgehead south of Dunkirk–Nieuport . . . to provide for progressive evacuation

---

[7] See Appendix II, p. 391.

by sea',[8] but there was still ambiguity about how the policy was to be carried out. In a long conversation with the War Office Lord Gort asked that the position might be made clear both to him and to the French High Command. Did the British Government wish him to make good the escape of the British Expeditionary Force or was he to hold the Dunkirk perimeter so long as the French Admiral wished him to do so. 'He thinks that we can hold on indefinitely, but I believe that as soon as we are encircled and the full force of artillery and other arms is brought to bear the position will become untenable.' If his object was to extricate the British Expeditionary Force it was important that this should be made clear to the French.

Subsequently he received from the War Office the final instructions of the Government: they had been dictated by the Prime Minister.

> Continue to defend the present perimeter to the utmost in order to cover maximum evacuation now proceeding well. Report every three hours through La Panne. If we can still communicate we shall send you an order to return to England with such officers as you may choose at the moment when we deem your command so reduced that it can be handed over to a Corps Commander. You should now nominate this Commander. If communications are broken you are to hand over and return as specified when your effective fighting force does not exceed the equivalent of three divisions. This is in accordance with correct military procedure and no personal discretion is left you in the matter. On political grounds it would be a needless triumph to the enemy to capture you when only a small force remained under your orders. The Corps Commander chosen by you should be ordered to carry on the defence in conjunction with the French and evacuation whether from Dunkirk or the beaches, but when in his judgement no further organised evacuation is possible and no further proportionate damage can be inflicted on the enemy he is authorised in consultation with the senior French Commander to capitulate formally to avoid useless slaughter.

Various estimates of the number and timings of withdrawal were given to the War Office. The British troops remaining were about 60,000; the rearguard should leave in the early morning of June the 2nd and might number 15,000. About 45,000 should therefore be lifted on the night of the 30th and on the night of 31st May/1st June. But the position was complicated by the question of French evacuation. French troops in large numbers were now in the bridgehead and 'evacuation in equal numbers' was laid down as the British Government policy. Comparatively few French ships had arrived, and though Lord Gort had arranged for two ships to be put at their disposal, only a few thousand French soldiers had so far sailed. How-

---

[8] Lyet, p. 111, footnote. See Appendix II, p. 391.

ever the Prime Minister spoke to him at midnight, emphasising the importance of evacuating French troops and asking him to see that General Blanchard and General Fagalde were enabled to sail.

It was decided that II Corps (except for the 50th Division) should withdraw for evacuation on the night of 31st May/1st June. At that point the Belgian sector of the bridgehead would be abandoned and only the sector stretching from Dunkirk to the French frontier would then be held. The 50th Division would withdraw behind the frontier (where the remains of the French 12th Division were deployed) and come under the command of I Corps. General Brooke, with most of his staff and other personnel of II Corps who could be spared, embarked for England that afternoon, and the corps, which was to follow next night, was put under the command of Major-General B. L. Montgomery, whose division (3rd) was in turn taken over by Brigadier K. A. N. Anderson.

Meanwhile evacuation proceeded in face of great difficulties. Rear-Admiral W. F. Wake-Walker arrived early in the morning to take charge of all evacuation from a succession of ships off the coast, and the shore staff under his direction was strengthened. When the Admiral first saw the scene by daylight, long dark lines of men stretched to the water's edge and larger groups of men were gathered on the sands. Off Bray the *Bideford* was aground with her stern blown off. The *Crested Eagle* was high and dry—burnt out. Lying off the beaches were destroyers and other vessels to which men were making their way in small craft. A light swell made beach work difficult and many boats lay stranded by the tide. The troops, orderly and under control, continued to file down from the dunes and 'at the back of our minds all this time', he says, 'was the question of how long the defence line could hold and the weather remain fair'. The need, still, was for boats and more boats. Small craft were hastening from Portsmouth, Newhaven and Sheerness. Six tugs were plugging along from Tilbury towing twenty-three motor and forty-six rowing lifeboats; five others were coming from Gravesend towing barges; car ferries, coasters and cockle boats, speed-boats and picket boats, seaplane tenders, pleasure craft, private yachts and a Thames fire-float were heading for the coast in increasing numbers, all desperately anxious to help. But they had not yet arrived off the beaches.

There was a time in the morning when troops were crowding down to the water's edge but could not yet be taken off, though the build-up of shipping continued and thirty-one miscellaneous vessels arrived with a most valuable dozen of the long-awaited motor boats to ply between them and the shore.

One weakness in the organisation of Dynamo was the failure to establish any effective system of communications between the various beaches, reliance being placed on messages carried by car or motor-cycle. Until the afternoon of the 30th there was no communication between the beach controls at La Panne and Bray, and in the morning an absence of sufficient shipping off the former had seriously held up work there.

During the morning sappers and troops of the 1st Division built a long pier of lorries stretching into the sea at Bray and decked it with planks. It was not strong enough to be used by heavy craft but it proved invaluable later for embarking men into boats and a similar pier was built at La Panne. At Bray evacuation went better as more shipping arrived there and divisions who had waited patiently for many hours were taken off. In Dunkirk, seven destroyers, a passenger ship and three drifters arrived in the morning and four more drifters and a yacht in the evening, but the harassed naval staff in their dug-out at the shore end of the east mole felt that 'a great opportunity was missed that morning, for mist and low visibility restricted enemy activity'.

More shipping came in the evening and even quicker loading did something to compensate for the time lost. A naval officer rigged up a loudspeaker and appealed to the troops moving slowly up the mole: 'Remember your pals, boys, the quicker you get on board the more of them will be saved!' On this the troops broke into a double and kept it up along the whole length of the eastern arm for more than two hours, and over 15,000 were embarked in that time. It was, however, the only day on which more men were lifted from the beaches (29,512) than from the harbour (24,311), and in spite of all difficulties and disappointments the day's total was the largest yet reached. By midnight 53,823 had been landed safely in England. Shipping losses, on the other hand, were much smaller, only two destroyers being damaged.

Fifteen French vessels also arrived and entered Dunkirk—two destroyers, three torpedo boats, two minesweepers, four trawlers, a tug and three fishing vessels.

In spite of the fact that cloud and poor visibility made air operations very difficult, Fighter Command patrols at three- or four-squadron strength operated at frequent intervals throughout the day and the only enemy bombers they met were driven off. South of Dunkirk our Blenheims bombed enemy troops and at night Wellingtons endeavoured to interfere with enemy movements towards Dunkirk, but their efforts were limited by adverse weather conditions.

During the day Lord Gort sent two telegrams to the Secretary of State expressing the Army's thanks for the work of the Royal Navy and the Royal Air Force. He had already asked the War Office over the telephone to pass on to the naval authorities 'our unbounded admiration' of the magnificent way they carried out the evacuation on the previous day, when conditions could not have been more difficult. Operation Dynamo had now been in progress for four days. In that time—that is by midnight of May the 30th—a total of 126,606 had been borne to England. Of these 77,412 had come from the harbour and 49,194 from the beaches.

A few hours later, on the morning of May the 31st, a message from General Weygand was received by the War Office through the Howard-Vyse Mission. It asked for the co-operation of four or five British divisions in defence of Dunkirk. It was not clear whether the divisions were to cover evacuation or to hold out indefinitely, but after consultation with General Georges it was learned that only the former was intended, and as Lord Gort had already been instructed 'continue to defend the present perimeter to the utmost in order to cover maximum evacuation' (page 230) General Weygand's request did not involve any change of policy and it was not necessary to vary the orders given on the day before.

During the morning Lord Gort visited Admiral Abrial at his headquarters in the Bastion at Dunkirk to co-ordinate plans for the evacuation of British and French forces. Among other French Service representatives at the meeting were General Fagalde and General de la Laurencie, and after other details had been agreed Lord Gort invited the two generals to accompany him when he left for England. To his regret they declined, though it was arranged that some of the French III Corps Staff should sail with the remaining officers of the British General Headquarters Staff.

Having tried vainly to get permission to remain to the last, Lord Gort now issued his final operation order, of which the following are the most important paragraphs:

Withdrawal

1. . . . .

2. It is intended, after consultation with French authorities at Dunkirk, that both Corps and Dunkirk base should continue the withdrawal of troops, maintaining the defence of Dunkirk in co-operation with our French allies, in accordance with orders already issued. It is further intended that the final withdrawal of II Corps shall be completed during the night 31st May/1st June. Shipping resources will be allotted accordingly, and action taken as in following paras. II Corps will not finally abandon the perimeter before 2300 hrs., 31 May.

3. I Corps will assume command of 5 and 50 Divs. from 1800 hrs. 31st May. I Corps will use these divisions to man the frontier defences and will issue orders, after consultation with II Corps, for their withdrawal to the frontier defences. 5 and 50 Divs. reps. report H.Q. I Corps forthwith. An outpost line will be maintained, to be selected by I Corps.

4. II Corps will be responsible for the evacuation of the beaches at La Panne.

Command

5. When the withdrawal of II Corps is completed G.H.Q. will be withdrawn and command will pass to Command I Corps. In default of further instructions command will pass at 1800 hrs. 31 May.

Lord Gort had decided that Major-General Alexander (1st Division) should take command of I Corps for the final phase, and he now sent for him and handed him his instructions:

1. You have been selected to command the I Corps of the British Expeditionary Force and to assist our French allies in the defence of Dunkirk.

2. The responsibility for the defence of Dunkirk rests with the French Admiral Commanding-in-Chief, the Naval Forces of the North; you will act under his orders, but should any orders which he may issue to you be likely, in your opinion, to imperil the safety of the Force under your command you should make an immediate appeal to His Majesty's Government, through the Secretary of State for War, at the same time notifying the Admiral du Nord that you are doing so.

3. In addition to any sector of the defence of Dunkirk for which you may assume responsibility you will also occupy yourself with arrangements for the evacuation of the Force under your command. This you will do in collaboration with the Admiral du Nord and also in accordance with the policy which may be laid down from time to time by H.M. Government.

It is important that the troops of the French Army should share in such facilities for evacuation as may be provided by H.M. Government. The allotment of facilities for evacuation in accordance with this policy will be made by the authorities at Home; if at any time you consider that the allotment is unreasonable, you should represent the matter to the Senior Naval Officer, Dunkirk, without delay.

4. If at any time in your judgement no further organised evacuation is possible, and no further proportionate damage can be inflicted on the enemy you are authorised in consultation with the Admiral du Nord to capitulate formally to avoid useless slaughter.

There is a revealing description of the preparation of these instructions in the personal record of a staff officer who took part in it:

The Chief said that he had placed General Alexander in command of I Corps and was going to give him his instructions. I took them down. They were a replica of his own...He then told me to go through them and see if there were any corrections to be made . . . This was a little embarrassing because he had left out the words of the [Government's] telegram making him the judge of the necessity for surrender. I did not like to mention the word, so I asked if I could compare it with the telegram which I went downstairs to fetch. Then I showed him the telegram and asked if he wanted those particular words reflected in the instruction. He said he did, so I added them to the draft, which I had typed, and the Chief signed it.

He adds 'I have a recollection of him sitting in his room and cutting ribbons off a jacket which he would have to leave behind, for he took no more kit home than any private soldier'.

Though there was fighting all along the southern front and especially near Bergues, the enemy's attack on this day (31st May) was concentrated mainly on the Belgian half of the bridgehead, which was to be evacuated in the coming night but must be held till the time to leave arrived. On the 50th Division front between the frontier and Bulscamp, on the 3rd Division front near Furnes, and in the 4th Division sector at Nieuport, the enemy attacked heavily. Ground was lost and recovered by counter-attack and only small local gains remained to the enemy at the end of the day. And in the night II Corps withdrew to the beaches, leaving only the 50th Division in reserve behind the French troops holding the frontier. All the bridgehead was now within reach of the German artillery and though our own artillery retaliated, shortage of ammunition severely limited what they could do.

One of the really successful examples of close co-operation with the Royal Air Force took place late in the evening. There had been fighting all day at Nieuport and while attack and counter-attack had led to no great change, the enemy were moving up additional troops and the threat of a real break-through was serious. In the early evening six Albacores of the Fleet Air Arm and eighteen Blenheims bombed the enemy in Nieuport and troops behind the town massing for a further attack. The enemy's concentration there was broken up and no further attack was made before the 4th Division retired to the beaches. There were other successful sweeps by bombers of Bomber Command which attacked enemy columns moving towards the bridgehead from east and south and both Bomber Command and the Advanced Air Striking Force continued all night to attack enemy supply lines and communications. The German situation report notes that fighter and anti-aircraft defences were strong over the battle area and that one of their attacks was stopped by fifteen Spitfires 'which approached at a great height from the south-east'.[9] In addition to the patrols of Fighter Command, Hudsons, Blenheim fighters, Skuas and Rocs of Coastal Command and the Fleet Air Arm patrolled the sea routes between Dover and the French coast. The enemy's return to the Quartermaster-General admits to the loss of seventeen aircraft destroyed and damaged during the day. The *Luftwaffe* reports that one Spitfire was shot down, but twenty-eight of our aircraft of all types (including bombers) were in fact lost that day.

And in spite of all this air protection, the enemy delivered three

---

[9] See Appendix II, p. 391.

major attacks on our shipping in the afternoon and early evening and small sporadic attacks throughout the day. In the morning there was an onshore wind with an unpleasant sea breaking. Reports reached Admiral Ramsay that beach embarkation was practically impossible and that enemy artillery fire made it dangerous for ships to remain offshore or at loading berths beside the harbour mole for any length of time. The dispatch of passenger ships was therefore suspended till darkness but as compensation for this the small boats were now arriving in hundreds and in spite of less favourable weather and enemy action evacuation proceeded steadily. One or two examples of the experiences of larger ships have been given. It will be well to illustrate the experiences of the small craft.

There were six bawleys, which normally fish for shrimps or cockles off the Essex coast. 'The conduct of the crews of these cockle boats was exemplary. They were all volunteers who were rushed over to Dunkirk in one day, probably none of them had been under gun fire before and certainly none of them had ever been under naval discipline. These boats were Thames Estuary fishing boats which never left the estuary and only one of their crews had been further afield than Ramsgate before. In spite of this fact, perfect formation was maintained throughout the day and night under the control of a Sub-Lieutenant, R.N.V.R., in command of the Unit and all orders were carried out with great diligence even under actual shell fire and aircraft attack.'[10] One, the *Renown*, was disabled by a mine on the way home and her skipper was killed. She was taken in tow by the drifter *Ben and Lucy*, who was already towing a disabled drifter, three lifeboats and the bawley *Letitia*. An hour later the *Renown* was blown to pieces and a hail of wood and splinters fell on the *Letitia*, whose skipper says: 'in pitch darkness we could see nothing, and after the explosion we heard nothing and we could do nothing except pull in the tow rope . . .'

The motor-boat *Triton* reached La Panne at about five o'clock on the morning of the 30th and from then until two o'clock on the following morning she towed boat-load after boat-load of soldiers to the destroyers lying offshore. Then she grounded but refloated at about four o'clock and carried on rescuing a number of men who were in danger of drowning. During the night the eastern sector of the bridgehead was abandoned, but Lieutenant R. H. Irving, R.N.R., in command, did not know this. All he knew was that enemy shelling grew increasingly heavy and because of this the destroyers moved west to Dunkirk. He followed them and in harbour took a boat-load in tow. A heavy air attack was in progress and bombs and shells were falling thickly. He saw a ship hit, closed her and took off two officers

---

[10] Vice-Admiral Sir Bertram Ramsay's Despatch. Supplement to *The London Gazette*, 15th July, 1947, p. 3312.

and two ratings who had all been wounded. 'I now had a full load of soldiers, a full boat-load in tow and soldiers clinging to the stern.' Bombs were still dropping and at this point a rope got round the propeller of the *Triton* so she closed a yacht and was herself taken in tow for England. When his activities ceased Lieutenant Irving had been on his feet for nearly thirty-six hours. He says in his report that he had eaten a tin of bully beef, some tinned herring and bread, 'also four cups of tea, each without sugar'. He adds 'the crew sent with me knew nothing of making fast ropes or steering but under fire were A.1 and exhibited, on and off, great interest in all that was happening'.

Before the eastern sector of the bridgehead was abandoned the situation at La Panne had become serious. Far more men were there than ships to take them off and the enemy's artillery fire on the beach and on the ships at sea steadily increased. It was therefore agreed with Major-General Johnson, commanding the 4th Division, that about 6,000 men remaining at La Panne should march to Dunkirk. The men of that division will not forget their ten-mile tramp along the loose sands though they remember thankfully the ships they reached when it ended at last on the mole at Dunkirk. Towards evening the weather had improved and, though a number of boats were lost or damaged during the day from one cause or another, naval casualties were not so heavy as on some other days and a further 68,014 men were landed in England by midnight—the largest number for a single day during the whole operation.

There was of course an element of good luck in these grim days— 'We had a bit of luck over a steamer which had been bombed and sunk on the way into Dunkirk, but as she was in very shallow water she only settled a few feet and kindly remained on an even keel. On one of the worst days, when there were very numerous dive-bombing attacks on the mole and the ships approaching it, no less than twenty-four of these attacks were made on this derelict ship, sitting on the sand bank. We reckoned she was worth about a million pounds to the country in shipping saved.'

There was the further good fortune that throughout the evacuation the weather was fine and the sea calm; only on three days did a little swell at sea raise surf on the shore which made boat work difficult and for a time impossible. Had the weather been stormy and the sea rough 'Dunkirk' might well have been remembered as a great tragedy.

Lord Gort had had one further conversation with the War Office during the afternoon in which he reported that pressure along the whole front had increased. He told of his decision (noted above) to shorten the front by withdrawing from the Belgian portion of the bridgehead so that the line held would swing northwards to the coast, marching with the French frontier. Then his headquarters closed down and Lord Gort and the staff who had remained with him left for England.

By midnight 194,620 of the men he had commanded and of their Allies had already landed there.

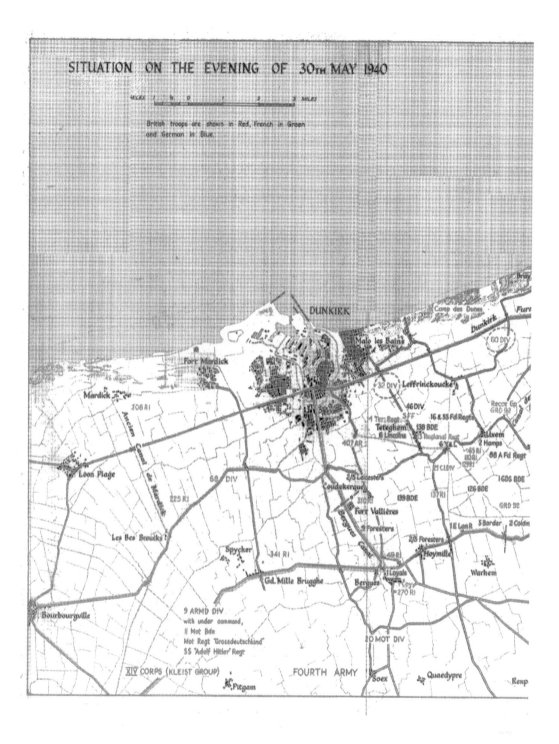

SITUATION ON THE EVENING OF 30TH MAY 1940

MILES 1   ½   0   1   2   3 MILES

British troops are shown in Red, French in Green
and German in Blue.

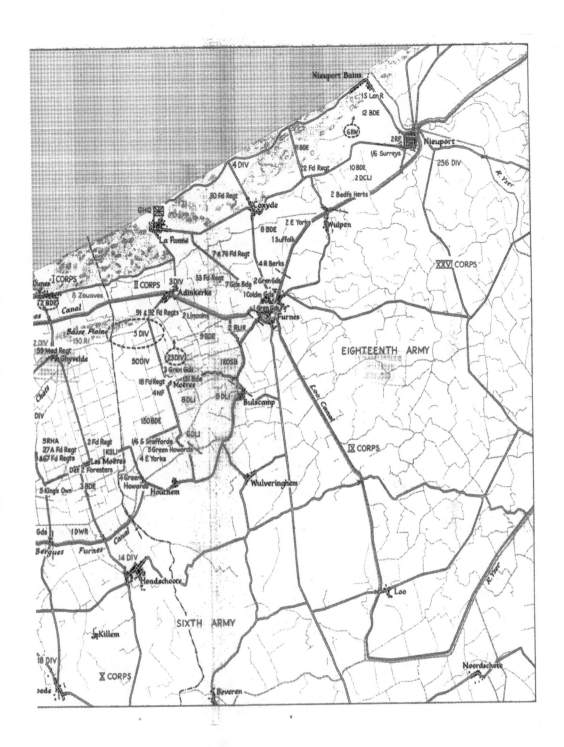

Nieuport Bains

1 S Lan R

12 BDE

6 BW

2 RF   Nieuport

11 BDE

22 Fd Regt   10 BDE

1/6 Surreys

2 DCLI

256 DIV

R. Yser

4 DIV

30 Fd Regt

Coxyde

2 Bedfs Herts

2 E Yorks   Wulpen

8 BDE

GHQ

La Panne

7 & 76 Fd Regt

1 Suffolk

4 R Berks

XXVI CORPS

I CORPS

II CORPS   3 DIV

53 Fd Regt   7 Gds Bde

2 Gren Gds

Dunes

Adinkerke

1 Coldm Gds

8 Zouaves   Canal

12 BDE

91 & 92 Fd Regts   2 Lincolns

1 Gren Gds   Furnes

2 RUR

EIGHTEENTH ARMY

5 DIV

9 BDE

Basse Plaine

150 R!

2 DIV

50 DIV   23 DIV

3 Gren Gds

100 SB

59 Med Regt

A Ghyvelde

18 Fd Regt   151 Bde

4 NF   Moëres

8 DLI   9 DLI   Bulscamp

Chats

150 BDE

DIV

6 DLI

5 RHA

2 Fd Regt

1/6 S Staffords

27 A Fd Regt

1 KSLI   5 Green Howards

IX CORPS

3 & 67 Fd Regts

4 E Yorks

Les Moëres

Def 2 Foresters

3 King's Own   3 BDE

7 Green

Howards   Houthem

Wulveringhem

Gds   1 DWR

Canal

Furnes

Bergues

14 DIV

Hondschoote

Loo

SIXTH ARMY

Killem

18 DIV

X CORPS

Noordschote

oods

Beveren

CHAPTER XVI

LAST DAYS AT DUNKIRK

1st June to 4th June, 1940

THE most critical phase of the operations at Dunkirk, both for the Army and for the Navy, had now been reached. The withdrawal of II Corps for evacuation left few British troops for the defence of the bridgehead sector for which they were responsible. Though the reduction of the front was of advantage to the Army, it made the Navy's task more difficult, for it allowed the enemy to move his artillery to positions from which the harbour, the beaches, and the sea approaches could all be covered by fire from the east.

On the morning of June the 1st about 39,000 of the British Expeditionary Force remained in the contracted British sector. The French held a reduced sector to the west, their forces joining up with the British on the Bergues Canal. From there the British held the southern face of the bridgehead while the east face, following the French frontier to the sea, was now held by the French 12th Division with the British 50th Division in support. Other French troops were in position on the intermediate line behind the British defence of the Bergues–Furnes Canal. There were on this date about 50,000 French troops in defensive positions. In addition 80,000 had been assembled for evacuation in the dunes, of whom 30,000 had already sailed. It has been calculated since that there were also about 20,000 in detached small groups not included in the French reckoning.[1]

After Lord Gort had handed over command on the previous day General Alexander had conferred with Admiral Abrial. The latter thought it possible to contract the bridgehead still further and to hold a front (on the east of Dunkirk) running roughly from Bergues, through Uxem and Ghyvelde to Basse Plaine and from there by the French frontier to the sea—what is called above the intermediate line.

General Alexander thought that this proposal was impracticable. The danger of the naval and military situation was increasing hourly; in his view if the bridgehead were thus further contracted the line held would be so near to Dunkirk and the beaches that the enemy's close-range artillery-fire would make continued evacuation impossible. On the other hand he thought that the British rearguard

---

[1] Armengaud, pp. 216, 217.

could hold their present position for another twenty-four hours (but no more) and he proposed that the evacuation of all remaining troops should therefore be completed in the coming night of 1st/2nd June. Admiral Abrial reported these opposed views to General Weygand, and General Alexander to the British Secretary of State for War. The latter replied 'You should withdraw your forces as rapidly as possible on a 50–50 basis with the French Army, aiming at completion by night of 1st/2nd June. You should inform French of this definite instruction.'

When shown this message Admiral Abrial agreed that the existing British front should be held till midnight of the 1st and that the troops should then be withdrawn to the beaches under cover of darkness. In the meantime while French evacuation would also continue French troops would man the intermediate position which he had named (Uxem–Ghyvelde–Basse Plaine) through which the British could retire, leaving only anti-aircraft and anti-tank guns and any troops who could not be got away.

General Alexander's view that the intermediate line could not be held was based on his knowledge that few British troops were left to hold it and on his ignorance of the number of French troops still available for defence. In the event, as will be seen, French troops fought for two days and held off the German attacks while about 10,000 British and some 70,000 French troops were evacuated to England. General Alexander, therefore, underestimated the time for which the intermediate position could be held, but he delayed the enemy's attack on that line by holding the forward position on the Bergues–Furnes Canal for twenty-four hours after Admiral Abrial had proposed its abandonment.

Much has been written of the scene at Dunkirk during the evacuation of the British Expeditionary Force, and much that has been written is almost inevitably out of true perspective. To the un-informed observer, especially in the early days, it seemed that ships came and went at unexplained intervals, boats struggled between ship and shore apparently without order and often with little skill, and on shore the apparent confusion suggested that the troops acted mainly on their own initiative. The ultimate success of the operation appeared to these observers as a triumph of improvisation. Such a reading of the scene is largely mistaken. It had been foreseen on May the 19th that evacuation might become necessary. When Operation Dynamo began on the 26th the Royal Navy had had six days in which to frame preliminary plans and, as already told, Sir Ronald Adam's organisation of the bridgehead had been well worked out. In the first few days before the fighting troops arrived, lack of military training, the absence of adequate direction, insufficient naval beach parties and shortage of small boats led to scenes of confusion among the men from rearward areas and the confusion was increased by French troops unwilling to conform to British orders. The ineptitude of men with no experience of boats, and shortage of skilled seamen, at times led to a wasteful loss of small craft, and there were mistakes and setbacks in plenty. But all were overcome. In general ships sailed on Admiral Ramsay's orders, though especially in the early days much was left to local initiative and personal enterprise, both in England and on the scene of operations. On shore the troops moved as they were ordered and embarked where and when they were directed. To the very end General Headquarters and corps and divisional commanders issued detailed and written orders. The Army Postal Service even delivered letters and parcels to some units waiting on the shore. In the execution of orders much depended of course on individual enterprise, and unforeseen circumstances combined with enemy action to upset plans on occasion. But the apparent absence of plan was deceptive, the visible confusion was but skin-deep. Beneath the surface operations both on land and sea were astonishingly well controlled. Only thus could so many have been brought away. The triumph of Dunkirk was not the element of improvisation but the display of discipline and good organisation.

Without full knowledge of all the back-stage planning the drama on the stage itself might well mislead observers, for the scenes enacted were so deeply moving that they were apt to absorb all attention. Many thousands of men had reached painfully the goal they had been set to reach. Their fight was finished. Of those who were to leave from the beaches, some stood in long queues which wound across the sands to the water's edge, moving slowly into the sea to be ferried to the waiting ships; others whose turn to leave had not yet come slept the sleep of exhaustion in the sand-hills. Units who had orders to embark from the harbour trudged wearily through the loose sand towards Dunkirk, where smoke from shell-bursts and exploding bombs mingled with the black and billowing pall that rose and spread from burning oil tanks. The wide sea-washed shore was in places dirtied and disfigured by the inevitable litter of a large crowd, by abandoned equipment and broken-down lorries and by personal belongings which had been carried doggedly for many miles but now must be cast away. And among the groups of the living, blanket-covered bodies of men killed on the beach showed darkly against a background of pale sand.

A large part of Operation Dynamo was conducted in darkness. Some dangers from enemy action were then reduced but all other difficulties and dangers were enhanced. It was hard enough in daylight to manœuvre ships in a crowded seaway and a cramped port; it was infinitely harder and more dangerous to do so in the night. It was harder to load boats in darkness and to ferry the troops to ships but dimly seen. And it was harder in darkness to find units and to keep them together, to lead them to the appointed place and ensure that none was left behind.

There were times when many ships lay off the land and boats plied tirelessly between them and the beach; when the harbour was busy, with ships entering to fetch men gathered on the mole and quays or leaving to bear them home to England. There were times when bombs were falling, when the sky was smudged by the trails of weaving aircraft and the bursts of anti-aircraft shells, when the air was filled with clamour as the guns on ship and shore roared at low-flying bombers and a more distant crackle of machine-guns told of the Royal Air Force fighters fighting up above.

There were other times when the sea was a cheerless blank and there were intervals of strange quiet. Then the sound of distant firing was a reminder that behind the scenes there were divisions which still fought, without rest or respite, to hold the enemy at bay while their comrades sailed for home, divisions which still turned their backs on the sea in order to confront the enemy—the soldiers of the Allied armies who made evacuation possible.

The British troops had bitter fighting during this, their final day on the canal. Shelling and mortaring continued without pause and all units had heavy casualties. The enemy's main attacks were at Bergues and Hoymille on the sector held by the 46th Division; and on the 1st Division front in the sectors held by the 1st East Lancashire, the 2nd Coldstream Guards, and the 1st Duke of Wellington's Regiment. At Hoymille the attack penetrated the front held by a company of the 2nd Warwickshire and, by brigade orders, the 1st Loyals on their right withdrew from Bergues itself to the canal on the northern outskirts of the town. From there in the afternoon they counter-attacked the enemy who had crossed the canal in the Warwickshire position. The ground was waterlogged through flooding and only slow movement was possible. Enemy machine-gun fire was severe. The counter-attack failed and the companies were back on their start-line by five o'clock. But the commanding officer of the Loyals was not satisfied. He ordered a further attack 'with more vigorous action'. At five-thirty the companies advanced again and this time they drove back the enemy and re-established the line on the canal bank.

Further east the 1st East Lancashire Regiment could not prevent some of the enemy from crossing the canal, but they were stopped from making progress till the East Lancashire had retired to the Canal des Chats. Captain H. M. Ervine-Andrews of the East Lancashire Regiment was awarded the Victoria Cross for his action on this occasion. The Coldstream were not attacked, and held the original front on the canal with both flanks refused, i.e. drawn back. For on their right the 5th Border Regiment were also withdrawn to the Canal des Chats and on their left the 1st Duke of Wellington's Regiment were forced to fall back behind the nearby dyke as a result of heavy fighting. So the day passed, and after dark the British troops were all withdrawn behind the intermediate line held by the French. By the morning of June the 2nd they were all on the coast ready for evacuation.

The Royal Navy, meanwhile, had had one of the most dangerous and yet one of the most successful days since Operation Dynamo began. From dawn and all day long heavy gunfire was brought to bear on the harbour, on the only beach (Malo les Bains) which now remained in our hands, and on the shipping off shore. The German Air Ministry situation report says that 'Throughout the day waves of aircraft attacked troops assembled for embarkation, the harbour of Dunkirk and warships and merchant vessels off the coast and in the sea area between Dunkirk and England'.[2] Both German air fleets were employed in these attacks.

The Royal Air Force flew eight fighter sweeps at a strength of three to four squadrons and Coastal Command flew patrols over the route between the North Goodwins and the French coast, but no one could foresee the timing of the enemy's attacks and there were inevitably spells when none of our aircraft could be over the area. The enemy's air attacks began soon after four o'clock in the morning—they had, indeed, endeavoured to bomb ships using the harbour during the night.

Our first patrol had been ordered to be over the area soon after five, and they were heavily engaged on arrival. Others followed shortly after six, nine, ten and eleven o'clock and all were involved in fighting. There was then a lull in air activity by both sides during the middle of the day, but soon after three o'clock in the afternoon our patrol was again in action and Coastal Command's patrol intervened to help. At four o'clock our aircraft found the enemy engaged in a renewed attack and again Coastal Command's patrol joined in the fight. The light was beginning to fail but further sweeps soon after five, six and eight o'clock all engaged the enemy after which failing visibility led to a decline of air operations. It was the heaviest day's air fighting, and though our fighters could not keep the *Luftwaffe* away they did much to scatter and destroy attacking aircraft and to disrupt the enemy's plans. The Royal Air Force lost thirty-one aircraft on this day, but the German return admits that ten of their fighters and nineteen bombers were lost and thirteen aircraft seriously damaged, making a total of forty-two enemy aircraft destroyed or put out of action in this day's operations.

Throughout the day the Royal Navy pressed on with evacuation

---

[2] See Appendix II, p. 391.

under cruel conditions and in spite of heavy losses from bombing and gunfire, E-boats and mines. The destroyer-leader *Keith*, flying Rear-Admiral Wake-Walker's flag, the destroyers *Basilisk* and *Havant*, the minesweeper *Skipjack* with many troops on board, the French *Foudroyant*, the passenger ships *Brighton Queen* and *Scotia*, both heavily laden with French soldiers, were all sunk; the *Prague*, with 3,000 troops on board, and many others were seriously damaged. Yet the work went on without pause, and on June the 1st 64,429 men were landed in England, 47,081 from the harbour, 17,348 from the shore. In spite of all the enemy could do it was the second largest number transported on a single day during the whole operation.

Inevitably shipping losses involved also some loss of life, but this was not so heavy as might be expected. As soon as a ship was hit or in trouble others promptly—almost instinctively—went to her rescue. There could be no roll of the men who had been crowded on board from the long queues on the harbour mole or the beaches, and it is not possible to know the number of those who were lost. But a few of the reports by ships mentioned above lift for a moment the veil which shrouds this unmeasurable drama. There were about 700 French and Moroccan troops on the *Brighton Queen* when she was sunk. The minesweeper *Saltash* picked up about 400 survivors and reported that: 'The French troops behaved steadily and intelligently though nearly half of them were killed by the explosion.' The *Scotia* had about 2,000 French troops on board when she was hit by at least four bombs. The destroyer *Esk* came out from Dunkirk and took off nearly 1,000 and the *Worcester* and small craft rescued many others. But twenty-eight of the crew and between two and three hundred of the troops were lost. Thus of the 2,700 men on these two ships something like 2,100 were saved. But sometimes the proportion of loss was greater. The *Skipjack* had been embarking troops from the Malo beach for over three hours when she was sunk; she had been continuously bombed and machine-gunned and nearly all the 275 men on board were under cover below decks. They had no chance to escape when the ship sank and only a few survivors were rescued by two nearby ships. So the story goes on, but from it comes the conviction that a large proportion of the men on ships which were sunk were saved by others and brought to England.

Throughout the early hours of June the 2nd the night's evacuation continued and many of I Corps who had reached the beach during the night were got away. But Admiral Ramsay stopped daylight evacuation in order to avoid a repetition of the previous day's losses.

French troops holding what has been called the intermediate position had been attacked at a number of points, and although the right of their line had been forced back, counter-attacks had stopped the enemy's advance for the time being.

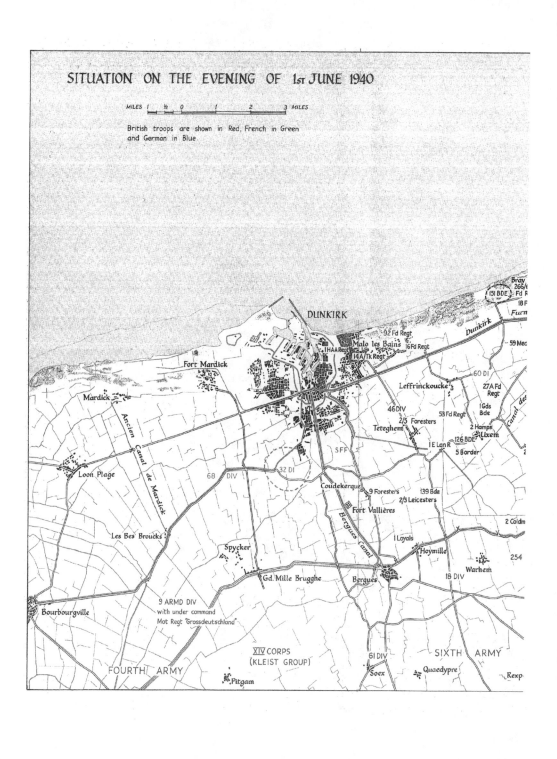

SITUATION ON THE EVENING OF 1st JUNE 1940

MILES | ½ | 0 | 1 | 2 | 3 MILES

British troops are shown in Red, French in Green
and German in Blue.

DUNKIRK

Malo les Bains

92 Fd Regt
1 HAA Regt   6 Fd Regt
14 A/Tk Regt

Fort Mardick

Mardick

Leffrinckoucke

60 DI

59 Med

27 A Fd
Regt

46 DIV

2/5 Foresters
Teteghem

53 Fd Regt   1 Gds
Bde

2 Hamps
Uxem
126 BDE

1 E Lan R   5 Border

SFF

Loon Plage

68   DIV

32 DI

Coudekerque   9 Foresters   139 Bde
2/5 Leicesters

Fort Vallières

2 Coldm

Les Bes Broucks

Spycker

1 Loyals

Hoymille

254

Warhem

18 DIV

Gd. Mille Brugghe   Bergues

Bourbourgville

9 ARMD DIV
with under command
Mot Regt "Grossdeutschland"

XIV CORPS
(KLEIST GROUP)

SIXTH ARMY

61 DIV

Quaedypre

Rexp

FOURTH ARMY

Pitgam

Soex

Bray
266/6
151 BDE   Fd R

18 F
Furn

Canal de

Ancien Canal de Mardick

Bergues Canal

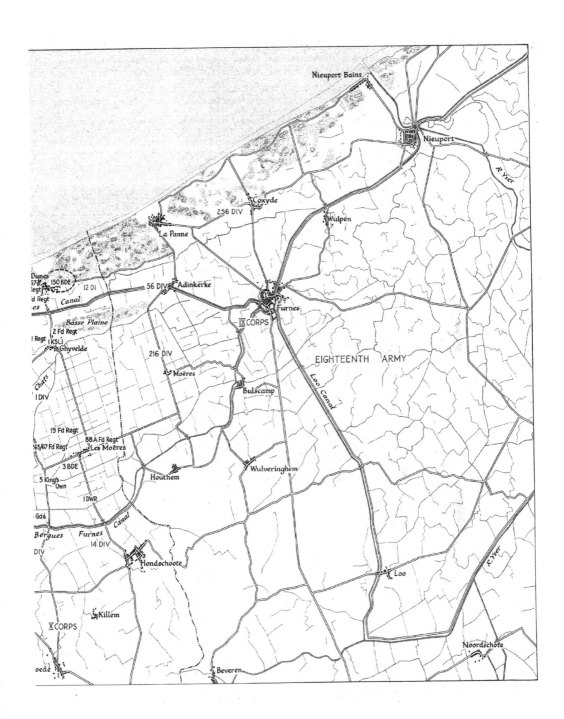

During the day a naval demolition party carried out its work on the port equipment and arrangements were made to block the harbour entrance after the last evacuation. The coming night's work (which was expected to be the last) was planned with great care. Movement across the Channel began about five o'clock in the evening, and eleven destroyers, thirteen passenger ships with minesweepers, drifters, schuyts and a host of small craft were sent over with French and Belgian contingents added.

Rear-Admiral Wake-Walker now controlled the ships from a motor boat in the harbour, while Captain W. G. Tennant, who had acted as Senior Naval Officer in Dunkirk through all these gruelling days, directed operations on the shore. The ships as they arrived loaded quickly and took off all the men who reached the harbour or the beach during the night; but fewer French troops came than had been provided for and many of the ships that had been sent to fetch them returned empty.

Evacuation went on during the early hours of June the 3rd and when daylight put an end to the night's operations at about three o'clock there were no more British troops to be brought away. In the early hours of the 3rd General Alexander and Captain Tennant themselves sailed for England.

There was more fighting during the day that followed. The situation report of Army Group B records that the French troops were fighting for every house and for every foot of ground, but in spite of counter-attacks their defence was forced back to the line of the Dunkirk–Furnes Canal. There the enemy were less than two miles from the beach and that afternoon Admiral Abrial, in a conference with General Fagalde, General de la Laurencie and others, decided that the coming night must see the final French evacuations.

Naval operations duly restarted with the fall of darkness, fifty vessels being used. The harbour was very congested but order was achieved and every effort was made to embark the remaining French troops quickly. Some arrived late at the jetty and owing to the general confusion were unable to make contact with the control.[3] Up to midnight, however, 26,746 were embarked, and a further 26,175 in the early hours of the 4th when daylight put an end to operations. The fine discipline of the French troops left behind when the last ship sailed was noted by Commander H. R. Troup who had been directing evacuation from the centre pier:

> About 1,000 men stood to attention four deep about half-way along the pier, the General and his staff about thirty feet away; and after having faced the troops, whose faces were indiscernible in the dawn light, the flames behind them showing up their steel helmets, the

[3] Armengaud, Chap. 5.

officers clicked their heels, saluted and then turned about and came down to the boat with me and we left at 0320.

Admiral Abrial, General Fagalde, General de la Laurencie and General Barthélemy had crossed to England during the night, and at Dover Admiral Ramsay discussed with Admiral Abrial the possibility of continuing evacuation during yet one more night, notwithstanding that the strain of the past nine days was telling severely on men and ships. The French Admiral held, however, that further evacuation was impossible, for the enemy were now closing in on every side. In fact the remaining French troops surrendered at nine o'clock that morning, June the 4th. No authoritative record of their number is available. The most detailed estimate is that there were approximately 40,000.[4]

During the night three blockships had been led to Dunkirk by the destroyer *Shikari*. One was mined outside Dunkirk, the others sank themselves in the channel near predecessors sunk during the previous night. The *Shikari*, after embarking 383 French troops, was the last ship to leave Dunkirk.

At ten-thirty in the morning of June the 4th the fleet of rescue ships was ordered to disperse and Operation Dynamo was officially ended by an Admiralty message timed 2.23 p.m. on that day.

It marked the failure of Allied operations in the north, yet it also marked a triumph for all three Services. While Dynamo was in progress the Allied armies had fought off the enemy not for two days but for nine: the Royal Navy had brought home not 45,000 troops but more than a third of a million: and the Royal Air Force had defeated the *Luftwaffe's* intention to make evacuation impossible. But all had paid a heavy price. In the land fighting of those last nine days and in the passage home the Army had heavy casualties, and lost all except their personal equipment. In the naval operations many seamen lost their lives and 228 ships were lost and 45 badly damaged in addition to a considerable number of smaller vessels and boats. And the Royal Air Force lost 177 aircraft destroyed and damaged during the nine days from May the 26th to June the 3rd. Since the enemy attempted only minor interference at sea, there is no comparable enemy figure to set beside the price paid by the Navy; but German air losses in operations over France and Belgium, from all causes and in the same period, amounted to 240 aircraft destroyed and damaged. A fuller analysis of the costs of the campaign is given in the final chapter of this volume.

In Operation Dynamo 58,583 British troops and 814 of our Allies had already been brought back when, three days after it had started, General Weygand authorised the general evacuation of French

---

[4] Armengaud, pp. 360–362.

troops and the British Government ordered facilities to be shared equally. Thereafter a further 139,732 British troops and 139,097 of our Allies were brought away. When the operation ended 338,226 had been evacuated—308,888 of them in the ships under Admiral Ramsay's orders. Nearly 100,000 had been lifted from the beaches. Of the British 8,061 were casualties; of our Allies 1,230.

National pride in this remarkable feat and abiding thankfulness for the British foresight, skill and courage which delivered so many men from death or captivity and brought them home in safety must not lead us to forget or undervalue the part played by France. Once the bridgehead was surrounded French troops held the smaller western part from Dunkirk to Mardick almost to the end; and although British divisions were chiefly responsible for defence of the larger eastern sector, which enclosed the precious beaches, until June the 1st they were French troops who covered evacuation during the two succeeding days. The Royal Navy was responsible for the planning, organisation and conduct of Operation Dynamo with the essential aid of the Royal Air Force, but French ships and French sailors also played a part. It was a very much smaller part, but in playing it the French Marine paid its inevitable cost.

Throughout the operation British staffs who directed operations and all men who toiled and fought afloat, on shore and in the sky were uplifted by the thought that British soldiers were coming home. But to Frenchmen Dunkirk meant something different. The French soldiers who were borne to England did avoid the major calamity of surrender to the enemy, but in order to do so they left home and France behind them to face, as they thought, indefinite exile in a strange if friendly land. One Frenchman who sailed from Dunkirk expressed the thoughts of many when he wrote: .

> La France sous nos pieds, comme une étoffe usée,
> C'est petit à petit à nos pas refusée.
>
> . . .
>
> Les parfums du printemps le sable les ignore :
> Voici mourir le mai dans les dunes du Nord.[5] .

The Dynamo figures alone do not give the whole picture of what had so far been achieved. It will be recalled that on May the 20th Lord Gort had ordered the evacuation of non-fighting troops and men of services no longer needed when the British Expeditionary Force was finally separated from its bases south of the Somme. Five days later General Weygand had issued a similar order that the French First Army were to embark in returning supply ships 'all superfluous Staff elements'.[6] As a result of these orders 26,402

---

[5] Louis Aragon: *Les Yeux d'Elsa* (La Nuit de Dunkerque).
[6] Armengaud, p. 40. See Appendix II, p. 391.

British troops (including 4,992 casualties) and 1,534 of our Allies were evacuated in British ships before Operation Dynamo started. To the Dynamo total of 338,226 there must therefore be added 27,936 making the grand total of those evacuated by this date 366,162. Included in this number are 224,320 men of the British Expeditionary Force. The military significance of this achievement is discussed in the final chapter of this history, for the campaign did not end with Dunkirk and the full story is not yet told. A new German offensive opened on the following day and the British part in the fighting south of the Somme has still to be described. But first there is yet something to be said about the operations of the past nine days.

'Dunkirk' is a classic example of co-operation by three Services. The Army's fight to hold off the enemy and the desperate battle of the Royal Air Force with the *Luftwaffe* were the culmination of continuous fighting which had started on the Dyle. But for the Royal Navy 'Dynamo' was a distinct operation; as such it holds a unique place in naval history. There have been considerable evacuations before and since. There has never been any other like this when, from a half-destroyed harbour and few miles of open beach, a third of a million men were brought away in spite of all that the strongest army and air force in the world at that date could do to stop it.

As a feat of naval organisation, evolved under the stress of emergency, it has no parallel. At a few days' notice 765 British ships of all sorts and sizes were assembled from diverse sources and devoted to a single end. About a third were warships or craft in regular naval employ. The rest came from the merchant marine and the fishing fleets and from other callings of the sea and inland waterways. Naval skill brought these heterogeneous vessels under effective control and ordered their movements but for the most part they were worked by their own civilian crews. It was a naval affair—destroyers brought home more men than even the passenger ships—but a naval affair in which civilians played so large a part that the people of England felt it to be also a family affair in which they were involved. Because of this, and not only because so many men of the Army were brought home, 'Dunkirk' holds a unique place in the hearts of British people.

CHAPTER XVII

FROM THE SAAR TO THE SOMME

10th May to 25th May, 1940

WHILE operations in the north were engaging the main British Expeditionary Force, the few British units which were south of the Somme, separated by the German advance from Lord Gort's control, were linked with the French Army in other operations which continued till France capitulated. It is an unhappy story, relieved only by the loyalty of our intention to fight with all we had till larger forces could rejoin the battle, by the bravery of the few troops engaged and by the fact that a large proportion of the men and some equipment were eventually saved for future fighting.

It will be remembered that during the winter British brigades had been sent in turn for a tour of duty in the Maginot Line, in order to give them experience of conditions in close contact with the enemy (page 20). For the first time a whole division (the 51st) had taken over an extended sector on the Saar between April the 30th and May the 6th. The composition of the division, a Territorial division of Highlanders which had made a famous name in the 1914–18 War, is given in the list of troops in Appendix I. The frontage which they occupied on the Saar at the time lay roughly between Colmen in the south and Launstroff in the north (see adjoining map).

They held it in three brigade sectors, each with one battalion in the *ligne de contact*, one in the *ligne de recueil*, and one in reserve, the latter prepared in emergency to man various infantry positions in the neighbourhood of the Maginot forts and in the intervals between them. The central sector was the position which had been held by the British brigades during the preceding months.

The divisional command was larger than usual. Besides the units which normally formed the division, a mechanised cavalry regiment and additional artillery, machine-gun battalions and other units were attached. The detail of these is shown under the 51st Division in Appendix I. In addition a number of French troops were put under General Fortune's command, which also included a composite squadron of the Royal Air Force consisting of one army co-operation flight and one flight of fighters.

The comparative quiet which had persisted all through the winter

249

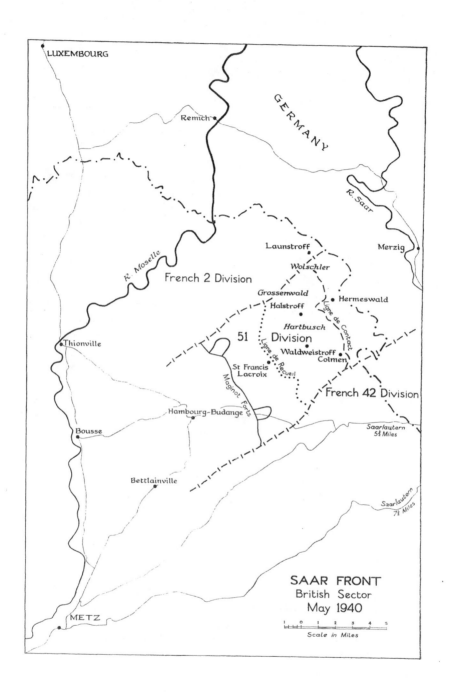

SAAR FRONT
British Sector
May 1940

Scale in Miles

continued during the early days of the 51st Division's occupation of the line, though the enemy's patrols were increasingly active and there was some larger-scale skirmishing near Hartbusch in which the artillery of both sides was employed. From the beginning of May this activity died down and an uncanny quiet persisted in the central sector. In the flanking sectors occupied by British troops for the first time the enemy was more inquisitive, patrolling actively and on several nights attempting, though unsuccessfully, to raid British posts. From May the 6th onwards the enemy's artillery was busy registering.

On the night of the 9th/10th an exceptional number of enemy aircraft passed over the divisional positions to targets elsewhere and in the early hours of the 10th came news that Germany had invaded Belgium and Holland. A general 'stand-to' was ordered but the day passed quietly and enemy patrols which attacked several of our posts during the night were all driven off.

On the afternoon of the 11th further small attacks on posts of the 4th Black Watch were all beaten off. On the 12th complete calm rested on the whole front. Next day the expected attack began in earnest.

At four o'clock in the morning of May the 13th a heavy barrage opened on the central and northern sectors and extended to the southern end of the Hartbusch. It lasted for half an hour and was answered by British artillery, firing its defensive fire-tasks. As soon as the German barrage lifted the enemy attacked Wolschler wood and the Grossenwald and various posts between the two. But the 2nd Seaforth Highlanders and the 4th Black Watch held their ground. North of the Grossenwald the enemy made other attacks but these too were defeated. The rest of the front was shelled and the French sectors on either flank were both attacked strongly.

At seven o'clock in the morning heavy shelling preceded renewed attacks on the British front and close-quarter fighting lasted for several hours, especially in the Grossenwald and Wolschler. All attacks were defeated except a small lodgement in the north of the Grossenwald. Two hours later a third barrage was laid down by the enemy and a third attack followed. This also was frustrated, though two posts which had been flattened by shell-fire had to be evacuated. Meanwhile our artillery broke up enemy concentrating in Hermeswald orchards and pursued the retreating formation. 'The rest of the day was comparatively quiet.'

There was renewed shelling and machine-gun fire on the 14th, but such attacks as were made were half-hearted, and were driven off. In and around the Grossenwald the 7th Argyll and Sutherland Highlanders spent the afternoon burying the enemy dead.

On May the 15th the whole of the divisional front was quiet except in the extreme north where a heavy attack on the neighbouring

French sector spilled over on to a post held by the 5th Gordon High-landers, who drove off the first assault but were eventually overrun.

Later in the afternoon French orders were received for the withdrawal of the whole division to the *ligne de recueil* in conformity with adjustments on the division's flanks. Subsequently the line held by the division was extended southwards, but no further attack was made on it and early on the 20th a warning order was received from the French that the division was to be relieved. Relief began that night and was finally completed on the night of the 22nd/23rd when the division was concentrated in the Etain area twenty-five miles west of Metz. It was the night on which German armoured divisions reached Boulogne and St Omer, having by then established their hold on the Somme and so cut the lines of communication between the British Expeditionary Force and its main base ports at Cherbourg and Nantes in Brittany. The 51st Division, unable to rejoin Lord Gort's command, waited further orders at Etain. It was destined to fight south of the Somme.

The country lying immediately south of the Somme constituted the Northern District of our lines of communication; it contained two sub-areas—the Dieppe and Rouen Sub-areas—which were of prime importance to the British Expeditionary Force. For Dieppe was the chief medical base, with valuable medical stores; Havre was a supply base, with large supply and ordnance stores; and in the St Saens–Buchy area, north-east of Rouen, was a large and well-dispersed ammunition depot; there were also infantry, machine-gun and general base depots at Rouen, Evreux (thirty miles to the south) and L'Epinay near Forges. The main railway connections with all these places, and between the bases behind them in Normandy and the B.E.F. in front of them in the north, passed through Rouen, Abbeville and Amiens. The commander of this Northern District, Brigadier A. B. Beauman, was responsible on the operational side for the protection of all depots and installations in the District from sabotage, ground attack, or attack by parachute or airborne troops; in addition, he had to find guards for thirteen unfinished airfields. The troops employed on these duties came, for the most part, either from specialist corps such as the Royal Engineers, the Royal Army Ordnance Corps, and the Royal Corps of Signals, or from formations of older men, fit only for garrison duties. When hostilities began, there were employed farther back in the Southern District three Territorial divisions—the 12th, 23rd and 46th Divisions, part of whose story has already been told. There were also three Territorial battalions—the 4th Border Regiment, 4th Buffs, and 1st/5th Sherwood Foresters—which were lines of communication troops (see

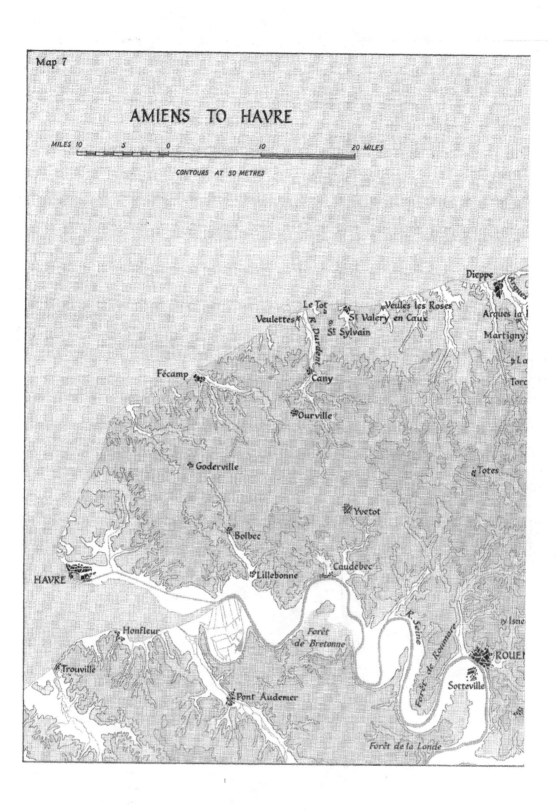

Map 7

AMIENS TO HAVRE

MILES 10   5   0   10   20 MILES

CONTOURS AT 50 METRES

Dieppe

Le Tot   Veules les Roses

Veulettes   St Valéry en Caux   Arques la
St Sylvain   Martigny

La

Fécamp   Durdent   Cany   Torc

Ourville

Goderville   Totes

Yvetot

Bolbec

Caudebec

HAVRE   Lillebonne

Honfleur   Forêt   R. Seine   Isne
de Bretonne   Forêt de Roumare   ROUEN

Trouville   Sotteville

Pont Audemer

Forêt de la Londe

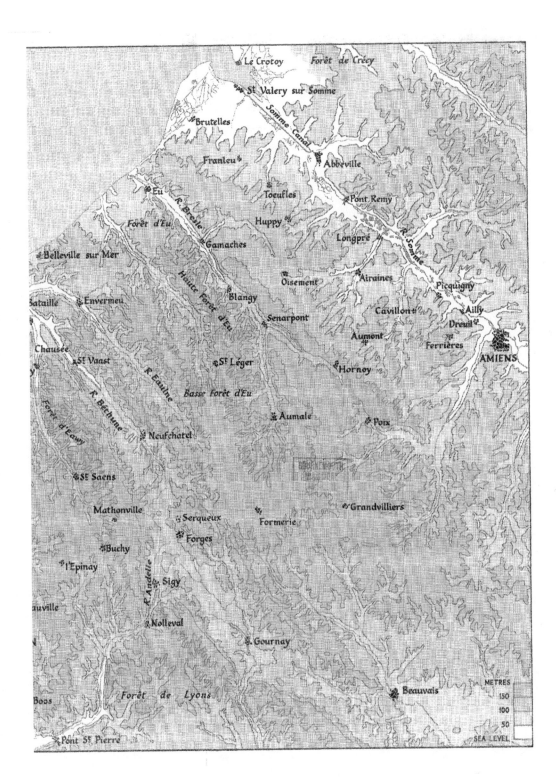

Appendix I). These were moved forward to the Northern District on May the 17th when it first became evident that the German break-through on the French front threatened to disrupt British com-munications.

By May the 20th the transport situation between the Somme and our bases was becoming increasingly confused. Movement by rail or road was only possible under stress and difficulty owing to the great congestion of traffic and interference by enemy bombing, and such trains as got through from the north were largely filled with French and Belgian troops. The roads were thronged with civilian refugees and a varied crowd of troops and transport moving away from the battle area. Brigadier Beauman was unable to communicate direct with General Headquarters or to discover whether any attempt was being made by French or British troops to establish a line of resistance on the Somme or south of it. And when, after taking Amiens on the 20th, the Germans pushed out armoured reconnaissance units south of the Somme as a preparation for the seizure of bridgeheads, the appearance of their patrols was enough to cause the wildest rumours to circulate and to spread alarm, for there was no one who could give exact information.

On May the 18th, acting under orders of Major-General P. de Fonblanque, commanding lines of communication, Brigadier Beauman took two steps to strengthen the defences of the District for which he was responsible. A small mobile force, 'Beauforce', was formed consisting of the 2nd/6th East Surrey from the 12th Division, which had been under orders to join the 51st Division on the Saar, the 4th Buffs, four machine-gun platoons and the 212th Army Troops Company, Royal Engineers. Secondly 'Vicforce' was formed under the command of Colonel C. E. Vicary. This consisted of five pro-visional battalions (Perowne's, Wait's, Ray's, Davie's and Meredith's) raised from reinforcements in the infantry and general base depots, where considerable numbers of officers and men were available, though shortage of arms and equipment severely limited their em-ployment as a fighting force. The former of these forces was ordered to move to Boulogne by road on May the 20th to help in the defence of that place, but it could not get through, reverted to 12th Division, and was involved in the fighting round Abbeville on the 20th which has already been described in the account of what happened that day (page 80).

In the absence of other orders, Brigadier Beauman decided to use what troops remained in organising a defensive position along the rivers Andelle and Béthune, covering Dieppe and Rouen from the east. Neither is an important river, but together they provide the most effective tank obstacle available after the Bresle has been crossed. Orders were given to prepare the bridges for demolition and to erect obstacles where most needed. This was on May the 20th.

Meanwhile the 1st Armoured Division, for which Lord Gort had been pressing, had begun to arrive in France. Initial elements had landed at Havre on the 15th and small advance parties had reached the neighbourhood of Arras where it was originally intended to concentrate the division, when the approach of the German armoured divisions made it clear that this would be impossible; moreover, Havre was rapidly being rendered unusable by enemy bombing and mining. Accordingly Major-General R. Evans arranged with the War Office on May the 19th that the remainder of the division should be landed back at Cherbourg and make the training area at Pacy-sur-Eure, thirty-five miles south of Rouen, the assembly area for the division. The first flight landed at Cherbourg that day. This was the first armoured division ever to be formed in the British Army. Its intended composition, as laid down, is given in Appendix I (page 367). But it arrived in France without artillery and short of one regiment of tanks and all of its infantry which had been sent to Calais (page 162). It was deficient of some wireless equipment; and it had only a small supply of spare parts, no reserve of tanks and no bridging material. It comprised 114 light tanks and 143 cruisers.

During the evening of May the 21st General Evans received a message from General Headquarters which instructed him:

(*a*) to seize and hold crossings of the Somme from Picquigny to Pont Remy inclusive. This task was to be regarded as most urgent and was to be undertaken as soon as one armoured regiment, one field squadron, one Field Park troop and one Light Anti-Aircraft and Anti-Tank Regiment were available.

(*b*) to concentrate the remainder of the leading brigade in rear of the Somme;

(*c*) when this had been done, to be prepared to move either eastwards or northwards according to circumstances in order to operate in the area of the British Expeditionary Force.

A few hours later Lieutenant-Colonel R. Briggs arrived by aeroplane bringing a confirmation of these instructions. But at General Beauman's headquarters in Rouen, where General Evans and Colonel Briggs conferred with him, local intelligence was that the enemy already held the crossings of the Somme and was feeling his way towards the Seine crossings near Rouen. Accordingly it was agreed to make sure of the latter at once so as to ensure that an advance to the Somme could be made when the armoured regiments arrived. The 101st Light Anti-Aircraft and Anti-Tank Regiment and a field squadron of Royal Engineers from the 1st Armoured Division Support Group were accordingly disposed for the purpose.

Tanks and rail parties, headquarters of the 2nd Armoured Brigade and one armoured regiment (the Queen's Bays) detrained south of the Seine in the early morning of the 22nd and were moved forward with all speed to the Forêt de Lyons area east of Rouen. There they would be in a position to prevent enemy armoured units from penetrating the line of the lower Andelle towards Rouen, or from interfering with the detrainment and assembly of further regiments due to arrive next day.

On the following morning, that is on May the 23rd, General Evans ordered the Bays to move forward to the line of the Bresle from Aumale to Blangy, and while this move was taking place he again met Colonel Briggs in Rouen. Colonel Briggs's information was that the enemy was acting defensively on the southern flank 'as far west as Péronne and possibly further still'; that only 'the mangled remains of six panzer divisions' appeared to have come through the gap between Cambrai and Péronne, to have carried out reconnaissances south of the Somme, found nothing and withdrawn to the river. The main German tank attack then taking place appeared to be on St Omer and on Arras. Moreover, his information concerning the French was that mobile troops of the Seventh Army had gained contact with the enemy on the River Somme the night before (22nd/23rd) between Péronne and Amiens and that the Seventh Army had been ordered to cross the Somme that day (23rd). In the light of this information, and believing that the British and French counter-attacks at Arras on the 21st/22nd were the beginning of a combined effort to close the gap, General Headquarters had sent an operation instruction which stated that 'it is vital to safeguard the right flank of the B.E.F. during its southern advance to cut German communications between Cambrai and Péronne'. Accordingly the 1st Armoured Division was to be employed as already directed by General Headquarters: 'Immediate advance of whatever elements of your division are ready is essential. Action at once may be decisive; tomorrow may be too late.'

It will be realised by the reader of earlier chapters that it was already too late. 'The mangled remains of six panzer divisions' hardly described the ten armoured divisions which were operating in the gap between the British Expeditionary Force and the Somme. Moreover by May the 23rd the Germans had brought up motorised infantry divisions and had a firm hold on the Somme crossings and bridgeheads south of Amiens and Abbeville. To General Headquarters cut off in the north it appeared 'imperative to force the crossings of the River Somme on the left of the French Seventh Army as soon as possible in order to allow for your immediate advance towards St Pol, so that you may cut the rear of the enemy who are about St Omer and relieve the threat to the right of the B.E.F.', but by now this task was quite beyond the power of the 1st Armoured Division—especially as it was not yet concentrated, as the infantry of its support group and a regiment of tanks had already been taken away from it to be sent to Calais, as it had no artillery and as the French Seventh Army were not yet ready to attack.

To General Evans it was clear that 'an operation to secure a crossing over an unreconnoitred water obstacle, attempted without artillery and infantry of my support group and carried out by armoured units arriving piecemeal direct from detrainment, was hazardous and unpromising of success'. Yet the order he had received left him no option, and he issued orders for the move forward.

Meanwhile, the position was not made easier by the fact that General Georges had a different conception of what the 1st Armoured Division should do. He informed the Swayne Mission at his headquarters that: 'While the Seventh Army advance to the north across the Somme' the task of the 1st Armoured Division was to mop up enemy elements in the area south of Abbeville. On this being reported to General Headquarters by the Swayne Mission, Lord Gort (who had no information about the position on the Somme) replied: 'Consider it essential that Armoured Division . . . should carry out its proper role and not be used to chase small packets of enemy tanks. The division should carry out the task already set it and "make itself felt in the battle".'

Yet a third view of what the division should do was intruded at this point. The left wing of the French Seventh Army was commanded by General Robert Altmayer, and an order was received from him stating that the 1st Armoured Division was under his command and giving it the task of covering his left flank in an attack on Amiens. However, the Swayne Mission at General Georges' Headquarters confirmed the fact that the division was not under General Altmayer's orders and would carry out the task already given. Accordingly, as has been told, General Evans ordered the 2nd Armoured Brigade to push on to the Somme that night.

The 2nd Armoured Brigade of the 1st Armoured Division, which was all that was available as yet, consisted of headquarters and three armoured regiments—The Queen's Bays, the 9th Queen's Royal Lancers and the 10th Royal Hussars. Of these, headquarters and the Bays, who had landed at Cherbourg on May the 20th were now on the Bresle between Aumale and Blangy. The 9th Lancers and 10th Hussars disembarked at Cherbourg on the 22nd/23rd, detrained south of the Seine on the 23rd and were moving up with all speed to join their brigade. They arrived early in the morning of the 24th at Hornoy and Aumont, on the road between Aumale on the Bresle and Picquigny on the Somme. They had had to cover sixty-five miles and prepare for battle in the twenty-four hours since they had detrained.

The brigade commander had also under command the 1st Field Squadron Royal Engineers and the 101st Light Anti-Aircraft and Anti-Tank Regiment (though the anti-aircraft unit was without Bofors guns). Three companies of infantry of the 4th Border Regiment from Beauforce were also put under his command and joined the brigade at half past four on the morning of the 24th.

By then an advance party of the 2nd Armoured Brigade (from the Bays) which had been sent forward during the night had reached Airaines (four miles south-west of the Somme at Longpré) at about one o'clock in the morning, and after losing two tanks on mines in an effort to seize the bridge near Longpré, had found that all bridges in the sector were mined, blocked and guarded, while the road along the western bank was also blocked.

Nevertheless an attack was ordered on the crossings at Dreuil, Ailly and Picquigny, one company of the Border Regiment and one troop of the Bays being employed in each case. An attack by such small and dispersed forces was foredoomed to failure. At Ailly the Border Regiment succeeded in getting two platoons across the river though the bridge was blown, but they could not be given adequate support, for the tanks could not cross the river and they were eventually withdrawn. Neither of the other two parties succeeded in reaching the river, owing to the strength in which the Germans were holding bridgeheads on the southern bank. A number of tanks had been destroyed or disabled, and the 4th Border Regiment had suffered considerable casualties when the attack was abandoned. Nothing effective had been achieved. That night the 4th Border Regiment occupied a wood eight miles south of Ferrières, while the Bays remained in observation of the country between Ferrières and Cavillon.

Late that night (24th/25th) a message was sent to General Evans from General Headquarters modifying the role of the 1st Armoured Division, warning him that he would be required to co-operate with the French, and ordering him meanwhile to hold on to his present position. On the same day General Georges had notified the Swayne Mission that the 51st Division was being transferred from the Saar and on arrival would form a group with the 1st Armoured Division, whose first task would be to take up a covering position from Longpré (on the Somme) to the sea coast. He also notified the commander of the Third Group of Armies (the left flank of the French forces south of the Somme–Aisne line) that the 1st Armoured Division was given the task of holding that line till the 51st Division arrived and was to be directed 'to establish small bridgeheads and prepare all bridges for demolition'. This, once more, was a quite impracticable order, for, as already told, the line of the Somme was firmly held by the enemy, whose bridgeheads extended five or six miles south of the

S

Somme in this sector. Moreover, a message from General Head-quarters stated that the enemy was not only reliably reported to be entrenching himself in this position but had strong patrols, including light armoured cars between this line and the Bresle.

However on May the 25th General Georges issued orders addressed to the French Third Group of Armies and 'la division Evans' repeating the above instructions and adding that enemy bridgeheads already established were to be eliminated. General Evans was required to put himself under the orders of the French Seventh Army —a step which had now been approved by the War Office. The telegram confirming this arrangement concluded 'Consider defensive attitude south Somme quite unsuitable role this juncture. Suggest employ both [1st Armoured and 51st Divisions] offensively and go all out.'

When this suggestion was made it was not yet known at the War Office that on this day Lord Gort would be forced by the turn of events to send the two divisions, with which he had been preparing for the projected attack southwards (the Weygand Plan) to fill the widening breach between the British Expeditionary Force and the Belgian Army; and the French inability to stage an effective attack from either the north or the south of the gap was not yet realised. Nor was it known that the enemy, now preparing for Operation Red, regarded his hold on the Somme and on the bridgeheads which he had established as of prime importance—that day by day he had been strengthening his forces on and south of the river and that on this 25th of May he had already two divisions there, facing south from Amiens to the sea, and others moving up.

CHAPTER XVIII

THE FIGHT FOR THE SOMME CROSSINGS

26th May to 4th June, 1940

As soon as it was known that the 1st Armoured Division (and the 51st when it arrived from the Saar) was to come under French orders, General Evans, accompanied by Colonel Briggs, went to see General Altmayer at his headquarters. There he was given verbal instructions. On the following day (the 26th) the 2nd Armoured Brigade was to concentrate in the Biencourt area, six miles east of Gamaches, and be prepared to support the French 2nd Cavalry Division in a further attack on the German positions; the 3rd Armoured Brigade which had now arrived was to concentrate in the Buigny area, three miles east of Beauchamps, and be ready similarly to support the French 5th Mechanised Cavalry Division.

The 3rd Armoured Brigade consisted of the 2nd and 5th Battalions of the Royal Tank Regiment, the 3rd Battalion having been diverted to Calais, as will be remembered.

Orders for an attack on the Abbeville bridgehead were issued at nine o'clock on the morning of the 26th. (See map facing page 270.)

The 2nd Armoured Brigade were placed under the orders of Colonel Berniquet, commanding the French 2nd Light Cavalry Division, and in conjunction with the French division were to capture high ground south of the Somme from Bray to Les Planches inclusive—that is the ground overlooking the Somme immediately south-east of Abbeville. The French were to supply artillery and infantry support for the armour. The 3rd Armoured Brigade was to come under command of General Chenoine, commanding the French 5th Light Cavalry Division, and had as its objective the high ground covering the northern sector of the Somme from Rouvroy to St Valery sur Somme. There also the French were to supply artillery and infantry to support their attack. The enemy were reported to be holding a bridgehead extending as far west as Grébault Mesnil, to have armoured patrols between there and Eu on the Bresle, and to have anti-tank weapons in position. General Evans and Colonel Briggs explained to General Besson (commanding the French Third Group of Armies) and General Frère (commanding the French Seventh Army) that the British tanks were not slow, heavily-armoured tanks designed to fight with infantry but light tanks (about

5 tons) and cruisers (12–14 tons) designed to exploit open warfare and not to support infantry in breaking through prepared positions; they should be compared with those of a French light mechanised division and not with those of a French armoured division.

On May the 27th the attack was launched. It was to have started at five in the morning, but was put back for an hour as the French gunners were not ready. The 2nd Armoured Brigade and the French 2nd Light Cavalry Division were on the right and their advance started from the area Hocquincourt–Frucourt–St Maxent to the east of the Blangy–Abbeville road. The 3rd Armoured Brigade and the French 5th Light Cavalry Division were on the left and started from the line of the Bresle to the north of Gamaches. There had been no time for careful reconnaissance and only vague information about the German strength and positions was available. The country between the Bresle and the Somme is an undulating plateau from which a number of small rivers wind their way down to the Somme and the Bresle through wooded valleys. It is well studded with villages; all of them are half-hidden in trees and stand, wooded oases, in the open cultivated fields through which they must be approached. The outposts of the German bridgehead covering Abbeville were in fact as far out from the river as Moyenneville, Huppy, Caumont and Bailleul, and in each they had anti-tank guns hidden in the woods and well dug-in. Against such prepared positions tanks could do little without the close support of artillery and infantry, but this was not forthcoming in anything like adequate measure. Co-operation with the French divisions was ineffective, and close mutual support almost non-existent.

On the right wing the tanks could make but little progress, and in trying to get forward suffered severely from anti-tank guns in Caumont and Huppy which caught them at close quarters as they crossed ridges of open ground. On the left wing the 3rd Armoured Brigade found less opposition outside the enemy's Abbeville bridgehead and reached the high ground overlooking the Somme near Cambron and Saigneville and the outskirts of St Valery sur Somme at the river mouth. But no supporting troops to occupy the ground were up with them and when it was learned in the afternoon that the French were taking up defensive positions behind them at Behen, Quesnoy, and Brutelles the tanks were withdrawn. Nothing effective had been achieved. The German hold on the Somme and on their bridgeheads had not been disturbed, but in using cruiser tanks unsupported by artillery and infantry to attack prepared defences we had had heavy losses. Sixty-five had been put out of action by the enemy, though some were recovered; fifty-five had mechanical breakdowns for there had been little opportunity for maintenance since they landed and hurried forward into battle. Light repairs could be effected in brigade areas but for serious repairs divisional workshops were south-west of Rouen and there shortage of spare parts slowed down the work.

Next day, May the 28th, the French divisions attacked again, and though some elements reached the Somme on the flanks of the German bridgehead and recovered some of their more advanced positions, they could not loosen the enemy's hold on Abbeville and St Valery. The 1st Armoured Division was not involved in this day's fighting, being busy reorganising its remaining forces. Only one armoured regiment, the 9th Lancers, was placed in reserve and they were not used. The few remaining tanks of the Bays and the 10th Hussars were now formed by the 2nd Armoured Brigade into a Composite Regiment.

General de Gaulle's 4th Armoured Division then arrived—a much more powerful formation than the French partially-horsed cavalry divisions which had so far been employed, though it had suffered heavily in earlier actions. On the 29th the division attacked astride the Blangy–Abbeville road, but was stopped by well-placed anti-tank defences in the woods and on the ridge running north-west from Villers sur Mareuil. He had little artillery support and there were no infantry to consolidate ground won. Nevertheless he attacked again on the 30th, supported by the elements of the other two French divisions on the ground (the 2nd and 5th Light Cavalry Divisions) with the British troops held in reserve. But again the attack failed to dislodge the enemy and for the same reasons. Against prepared positions, now strongly held, armour alone could achieve little. At the end of four days' fighting the enemy's bridgeheads remained untaken and the Somme and its crossings were still his.

The fact that the French had made little use of the 1st Armoured Division after the first day's fighting was doubtless the result of an instruction issued by General Georges on 28th May, following representations made to him by General Evans and by Colonel Briggs and General Swayne. General Georges' instruction No. 1809 drew the attention of the French commanders to the characteristics and proper employment of the British division, and pointed out that:

> The British division therefore bears a closer resemblance to a light mechanised division than to an armoured division It is, in short, composed of light tanks, very lightly armoured and therefore vulnerable against enemy anti-tank guns.
>
> It is possible that during the recent period of crisis material may have had to be used in unfavourable conditions; it is none the less true that the employment of this division should not be contemplated except within the limits allowed by the nature of its equipment unless battle conditions make other arrangements vitally necessary.
>
> Further, we should be ready to use, as soon as possible, the Evans Division within the framework of a tactical group comprising

in particular the 51st Division and the British Armoured Division—a group whose role on our left flank will be determined according to its capabilities.[1]

For while these abortive attempts were being made to recover the Somme crossings, and while the British Expeditionary Force in the north was being withdrawn into the bridgehead at Dunkirk and evacuated to England, the 51st Division had been arriving in the Bresle area from the Saar front. They had moved under French orders and more than one change of plan had increased difficulties which were in any case inevitable when the situation changed almost hourly, when enemy bombing disrupted communications and delayed trains, and when the French armies south of the Somme–Aisne line were regrouping and moving up towards the southern flank of the German break-through. However, their journey was at last completed and divisional headquarters opened at St Léger, seven miles south of Blangy, on May the 28th. There it came under the command of the French IX Corps.

That simple statement, is, however, insufficient to explain the position in regard to command of the British troops in the area south of the Somme. The French Seventh Army, under General Frère, was part of the Third Group of Armies and formed the left wing of the forces in General Georges' command, which were now deployed south of the Somme–Aisne line. The Seventh Army, in turn, included a group of divisions (Group A) commanded by General Altmayer, and the 51st Division, like the 1st Armoured Division, was included in the IX Corps of this group. Thus the chain of command in this area was as follows:

General Weygand
(Supreme Commander)

General Georges
(Commander North-East Front)

General Besson
(Third Group of Armies)

General Frère
(Seventh Army)

General Altmayer
(Group A later to become the Tenth Army)

General Ihler
(IX Corps)

General Evans
(1st Armoured Division)

General Fortune
(51st Division)

The British generals were, however, also liable to receive instructions from the War Office, either direct or through the Swayne

---

[1] See Appendix II, p. 392.

Mission. For supplies they were dependent on the British lines of communication which, with all other troops in the area, were now under command of Lieutenant-General Sir Henry Karslake. These troops included the improvised forces collected by General Beauman —Beauforce, Vicforce and 'Digforce'. The latter had been formed from reservists serving in the Auxiliary Military Pioneer Corps. On 31st May these forces were formed into an improvised Beauman Division.

There were thus in this small area two British forces: the 51st and 1st Armoured Divisions under French command, and Beauman Division and other lines of communication troops under the command of General Karslake. The former force was taking over a position on and in front of the Bresle for yet another attack on the Somme bridgehead, to be launched in conjunction with French divisions; the latter was holding a defensive line behind the Bresle, on the Andelle and Béthune rivers covering Rouen, Dieppe, and Havre. From the latter places, meanwhile, the evacuation of non-fighting troops and surplus stores and equipment had begun.

For while the Government intended to rebuild the British Expeditionary Force as quickly as possible after Dunkirk, it was obvious that this would require time. Only a small fighting force could be sent out in the near future; it must at first be regarded as evidence of British intentions rather than a substantial contribution to the battle. Meanwhile it was desirable to withdraw as many as possible of the surplus non-fighting troops from lines of communication, base depots, and other establishments which had been formed to sustain a far larger army than we could send to France immediately.

The evacuation from Dunkirk was making a deep impression on the mind and heart of the nation, and when it was concluded a great sigh of relief went up; but with it was joined the knowledge that the enemy was now in sight of the cliffs of Dover and that he might attempt at any moment to invade England. Thankfulness merged with tense anxiety, and the nation turned with new fervour and concentration to preparation for defence. So it came about that comparatively little public attention was paid to what was happening in France after Dunkirk. Yet 140,000 British troops were still there.

Further naval operations, designed to cover the evacuation of all but the small fighting forces which remained in France and the services to maintain them, were now beginning. They involved the evacuation of surplus men and material from Dieppe, Havre, Cherbourg, Brest, St Nazaire, and La Pallice. Eventually, when France fell, all remaining British forces were included and evacuations were extended to ports as far south as the Spanish border and to the Mediterranean. But this is looking ahead.

The Navy's complicated task was to be rendered more difficult by the fact that losses at Dunkirk and in operations in Norway and else-where—not directly related to the campaign in France and Flanders and therefore not recorded in this volume—had temporarily weakened the Home Fleet, though its fighting strength was not seriously impaired. In particular the number of flotilla vessels neces-sary to provide escorts for all the shipping which would be needed to evacuate men and material from several widely separated harbours did not at this time exist. On the other hand, as already noted, losses which the Navy had inflicted on the German fleet left the enemy with insufficient strength in surface ships to dispute control of sea com-munications between France and England. For unexplained reasons, though some seven German submarines were stationed off the west coast of France while these evacuations were in progress, they made no effort to intervene; as had been the case in the operations off Holland, only the German Air Force tried to make evacuation impossible. It will be seen later how completely the *Luftwaffe* again failed.

By the end of May all medical stores had been cleared from Dieppe and a demolition party had been landed to destroy the port installa-tion should that become necessary. The progress of naval operations will be followed in due relation to the subsequent events of the campaign.

The big supply depot at Havre had been reduced to small dimensions by the expedient of using it to feed troops in the area and by not replenishing it. All the ordnance stores had been cleared except those needed for immediate use. The assortment of reserve motor transport vehicles at Rouen had been drawn on to equip the improvised fighting forces. Certain special types of ammunition in short supply had been removed from the great ammunition reserves in the Buchy area, but to move the thousands of tons which remained there was beyond our available resources of transport and manpower.

Although by the end of May General Weygand had been forced to abandon the intention to attack northwards from the Somme–Aisne line, he still regarded the recapture of the enemy's bridgeheads south of the Somme as an essential measure of defence against the German attack towards Paris which was now expected daily. So General Georges decided that, after a few days' pause for reorganisa-tion and regrouping, the attack on the Abbeville–St Valery bridge-head should be renewed early on the morning of June the 4th.

Certain changes were taking place in both French and British forces in the area. General Altmayer's Group in the French Seventh Army now became a separate Tenth Army, still under his command and still including the French IX Corps with our 1st Armoured Division and the 51st Division. General de Gaulle's division was however withdrawn (except for the divisional artillery) and in its place two new French divisions, the 31st (Alpine) and the 2nd Armoured were brought in to the Tenth Army.

As already stated the improvised forces under General Beauman had been reorganised as Beauman Division, with headquarters, three infantry brigades, a regiment of anti-tank guns, a battery of field artillery, and other divisional services. There had been a point at which the British Government had informed General Karslake that all improvised forces should be disbanded and evacuated to England, and only sufficient lines of communication troops kept to maintain in France a British force of one armoured and four infantry divisions and an Advanced Air Striking Force—which was all that we could hope to provide in the immediate future. But General Georges represented the importance of retaining Beauman Division on the Andelle–Béthune line. Their withdrawal would, he said, have 'an unfortunate effect on the French Army and the French people'. The War Office accordingly agreed to their remaining.

In the first days of June, therefore, the disposition of British troops in this area was as follows.

The 51st Division, with the Composite Regiment and what remained of the Support Group of the 1st Armoured Division under command, and itself under the command of the IX Corps of General Altmayer's French Tenth Army, was relieving two French divisions in the forward positions facing the Germans' Abbeville–St Valery bridgehead in preparation for the projected renewal of the attempt to recapture them. Of the 51st Division the 152nd and 154th Brigades were forward; the 153rd in reserve on the Bresle between Senarpont and Blangy. The nine-mile stretch of the Bresle on their right was held by an anti-tank battery and a company of the Kensington's machine guns, with the Composite Regiment from the 1st Armoured Division behind them. In the sixteen-mile stretch on the 153rd Brigade's left was the 6th Royal Scots Fusiliers (Pioneers). The Support Group of the 1st Armoured Division held a flanking position between Aumale and Forges. Beauman Division, not yet under French command, was disposed in the fifty-five-mile stretch between Pont St Pierre (eleven miles south-east of Rouen near the junction of the rivers Andelle and Seine) and the coast at Dieppe. Thus we had one Territorial division (the 51st), one improvised division (Beauman) and a fragment of the 1st Armoured Division; and these were distributed over an eighteen-mile-wide front, forty-five miles of the Bresle and fifty-five miles of the Andelle–Béthune line. That was our situation on the morning of June the 4th when for the last time we tried to recover the Abbeville bridgehead. On our right flank were other formations of the French IX Corps.

Abbeville is overlooked from the west by the long Mont de Caubert spur which runs northward from Mareuil-Caubert and by a ridge of high ground west of Rouvroy. These twin ridges, dominating the roads which lead into the town, were to be captured by two French divisions (31st Infantry Division and 2nd Armoured Division). On the right of the 2nd Armoured Division, infantry of the 51st Division (152nd Brigade) were to capture Caubert and the woods which border the road from there to Bray, while the 153rd Brigade on the left of the 31st Infantry Division took the high ground south of Gouy. The 154th Brigade was not to advance but engage enemy troops in the area of St Valery sur Somme by fire, so as to prevent them from reinforcing the Abbeville bridgehead. Finally the Composite Regiment of the 1st Armoured Division was to be held in reserve near St Léger. Thus the result of the operation would depend mainly on whether the French divisions could succeed in their attempt to capture the Mont de Caubert spur and the ridge in the centre. The flank attacks were designed to protect and make good this central position; unless the central position were in our hands, ground won in the flank attacks could not be maintained.

Both the French divisions were put under command of General Fortune's 51st Division. They had just moved into the area; indeed, some units of the 31st Division only arrived there an hour and a half before the attack was timed to begin. Reconnaissance on the previous afternoon was consequently sketchy. Few and inadequate air photographs were available and there was but little opportunity to explain to the troops the tasks they were immediately to undertake. Few of the positions held by the enemy's troops and artillery had been identified, and as no aircraft were there to report enemy movement to the artillery our gunners could only shoot at what seemed to be likely positions for German guns, or for the massing of German troops. The attack was to start at three o'clock in the morning.

On that 4th of June a low summer mist overhung the valley of the lower Somme, shrouding the tanks and troops from distant observation without hampering their movements. Ten minutes before zero hour the quiet of the morning was broken. A barrage, planned to cover the French tank attack in the right centre, came down on the woods round Bienfay and Villers where there were known to be enemy posts. After ten minutes the barrage lifted, and though the heavy French tanks did not appear, the 2nd Seaforth set about their task of clearing enemy posts in the forward edge of the woods. In this they succeeded, but when the tanks arrived they had missed the cover of the barrage and as they advanced between the Blangy–Abbeville road and the woods near Villers they came, first, upon an undetected minefield and, shortly after, under heavy fire from field and anti-tank guns well sited and dug in. A number of tanks were blown up or set on fire in the minefield and subsequent casualties from gunfire were severe, but some reached the base of the Mont de

Caubert ridge and some Mesnil Trois Foetus, from which they drove the enemy.

The 4th Seaforth Highlanders, meanwhile, who were to follow up the attack supported by light tanks, waited till three of the latter arrived and then went forward on the south-eastern side of the Villers woods. They soon came under withering machine-gun fire from Mont de Caubert, but in spite of mounting casualties strove vainly to reach the heavy tanks. Both they and the tanks they sought to reach had shot their bolt. The latter had suffered crippling losses, and when they were ordered to retire to the position held in the morning six out of thirty heavy tanks reported, and only 60 out of 120 of the light tanks.

The 4th Camerons also failed to capture their objective south of Caubert. The whole position was too well covered by dug-in German machine guns. At one point advancing German infantry were encountered and there was hard fighting in the standing corn. Two platoons under Second Lieutenant Ross did indeed succeed in fighting their way into Caubert but they could not be supported and were cut off. (Two days later Ross succeeded in leading his party, most of whom were wounded, back through the enemy's lines to rejoin at Martainneville le Bus.) The 152nd Brigade had lost 20 officers and 543 other ranks.

Things had gone no better in the left centre. The only regiment of the French 31st Division to be employed could make but little progress, being held almost from the start by enemy dug-in in the woods west of Mesnil Trois Foetus.

Only the 153rd Brigade's attack on the left flank was more successful. There the 1st Black Watch, who were holding the line of the Cahon valley when the attack opened, pushed forward and established themselves in the Petit Bois to cover the flank of the 1st Gordons. The latter meanwhile issued from Gouy, drove the enemy out of the Grand Bois, and by noon reached the high ground at the eastern side. This was their objective, and having done all that they were ordered to do they were yet anxious to go on. But while the high ground overlooking the Somme north-west of Caubert remained in enemy hands, it was impracticable to hold the ground won by the Gordons' attack, much less to extend it. To their great disappointment they were ordered to give up their gains and return to their starting point.

The bridgehead which we had sought to wrest from the enemy in this attack was a strong one. The Germans had been holding it for the past fortnight and their troops had had ample time to site their defences and dig themselves in. The Allied troops had had no opportunity for adequate preparation. The Gordons and their supporting artillery had arranged a system of signals by Very lights which worked admirably and was a potent factor in the reduction of German machine-gun positions. But in the rest of the battle no similarly successful co-operation was achieved, and its absence had much to do with the failure of tanks and infantry to overcome the enemy defence in the centre and on the right flank. For the rest, insufficient preparation and consequent faults in the co-ordination of forces largely account for the failure of the action. But chiefly it was due to the fact that, notwithstanding all that had gone before, the strength of the German bridgeheads was still underestimated. Nor was it realised that behind the bridgeheads a reconstituted Army Group B was disposed for attack southwards.

The positions we held when, in the early morning of the 5th, Operation 'Red' began and the German divisions assembled on the north of the Somme went over from the defensive to the attack, lay back from the river on a line running from Caumont south of Abbeville to Sallenelle near the sea.

Nothing has been said so far about the part played by the Air Force in the operations south of the Somme which have been described. Inevitably, as will be seen, it was a small part, for until the final evacuation of the British Expeditionary Force in the north was completed almost all our available air strength was engaged in the battle over Dunkirk and the bridgehead.

Air Marshal Barratt and the small air forces left under his command in France when the Air Component was withdrawn to England were effectively separated from the northern battle. He could only communicate with Lord Gort by way of the Air Ministry and War Office, and in any case the diminished Advanced Air Striking Force, now stationed near Troyes in Champagne, could not intervene at Dunkirk. For the remaining six squadrons of bombers were unsuitable for day bombing without strong fighter protection, and the three fighter squadrons (even if they could have been spared) could not operate so far from their bases. The bombers were therefore employed during this period on night attacks against German communications, while the fighters provided what patrols they could over the fighting south of the Somme. On May the 28th the daily situation report of the German Air Ministry states that 'German battle reconnaissance over the area south of Amiens was thwarted by stiff enemy fighter defence'.[2] But patrols by a small force could be neither strong nor frequent. Anything from one flight (four aircraft) to one squadron (sixteen at full strength) went out at intervals and remained in the air as long as possible: but even this slender cover could only be maintained for periods which added up to about three hours out of the twenty-four. It is not wholly surprising therefore

---

[2] See Appendix II, p. 392.

that they only encountered the enemy on five days in the twelve-day period which ended on June the 4th.

In the days when the battle in which the British Expeditionary Force was engaged drew nearer and nearer to the northern coast, the decision to operate from England both the Air Component and the additional fighter squadrons which the Government supplied on French representations was reasonable. But the Air Ministry realised that if fighting moved further away from the airfields in Kent the fighters would have to use airfields in France to refuel and rearm. Arrangements were accordingly made with the French for the use of three airfields north-west of Paris and two south of the Seine. Air Marshal Barratt's headquarters collected an improvised ground staff, with servicing sections, armourers, defence units and transport; and in the last week of May these airfields were brought into use by the fighter squadrons of the Advanced Air Striking Force based in Champagne. The England-based squadrons were at that time busy over Dunkirk and for the moment had no need to use the French airfields.

This small fighter force became known as South Component. Operational control was at first retained in England. Air Marshal Barratt—surely with good reason—questioned the practicability of such remote control, but the plan was adhered to till the German offensive southwards started on June the 5th. Only then, under the pressure of events, was operational control of South Component transferred to the commander on the spot.

In the situation which existed other inescapable difficulties were sufficiently great in any case. One may be mentioned. Fighters based in Champagne and in England were to operate from South Component airfields near Rouen. Weather must therefore be favourable simultaneously in these widely separated areas and over the battlefield, if all available forces were to be brought to the battle in the due order planned. There were days when unfavourable weather at one point or another prevented this.

So long as the Dunkirk battle in the north absorbed almost all our available air strength, stronger forces could not be supplied for the fighting south of the Somme. But it is clear that the small size of the forces employed, their geographical disposition, and the arrangements for their operational control combine to explain the limited measure of achievement. Of that the most that can be said with certainty is that our bombing of columns and communications and our patrols over the fighting did some damage to the enemy, but not enough to stop him bringing forward the forces he needed or to prevent his air attacks on Allied troops and positions. They did something to hinder movement and to weaken or interrupt *Luftwaffe* assaults, but they could not stop either.

In the two days which preceded the opening of the enemy's new offensive the German air force again designed their bombing attacks to weaken the French defence. Their report records attacks on sixteen French airfields, five depots, on air parks and several aircraft works near Paris.

At nine o'clock in the morning of June the 4th the remnants of the French northern armies who had not been evacuated surrendered at Dunkirk. All depended now on the troops who barred the enemy's progress southwards.

As early as May the 25th General Weygand had seen little hope of a successful defence of the Somme–Aisne line and had then advised his Government that the desirability of asking for an armistice should be discussed with the British Government. He had also told them that he did not consider possible a retreat from the Somme–Aisne line, though a breach of that long, thinly-held front would make it impossible to continue useful military operations. It was thus with inadequate forces and in a mood of inevitable defeat that the French High Command waited for the opening of the final battle.

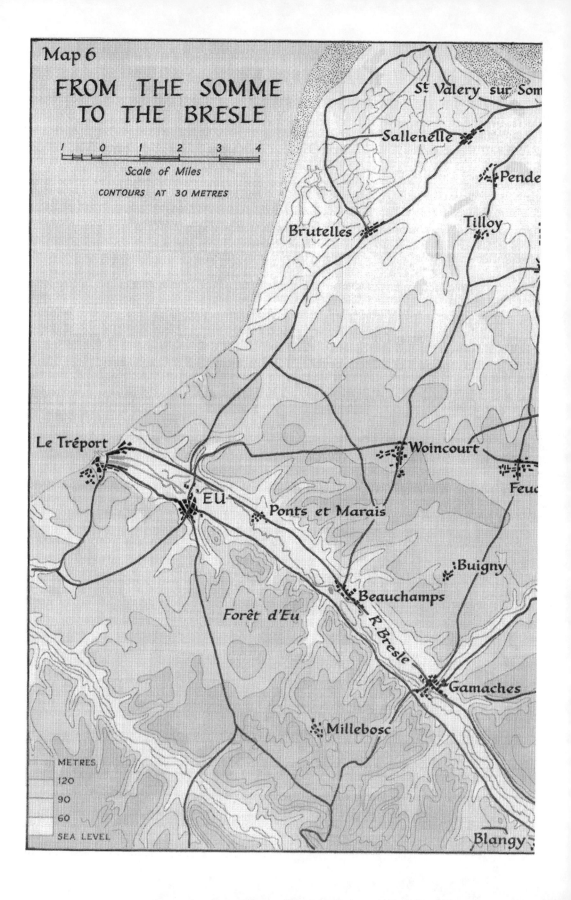

Map 6

FROM THE SOMME
TO THE BRESLE

Scale of Miles

CONTOURS AT 30 METRES

St Valery sur Som

Sallenelle

Pende

Tilloy

Brutelles

Le Tréport

Woincourt

Feuc

EU

Ponts et Marais

Buigny

Beauchamps

Forêt d'Eu

R Bresle

Gamaches

Millebosc

METRES
120
90
60
SEA LEVEL

Blangy

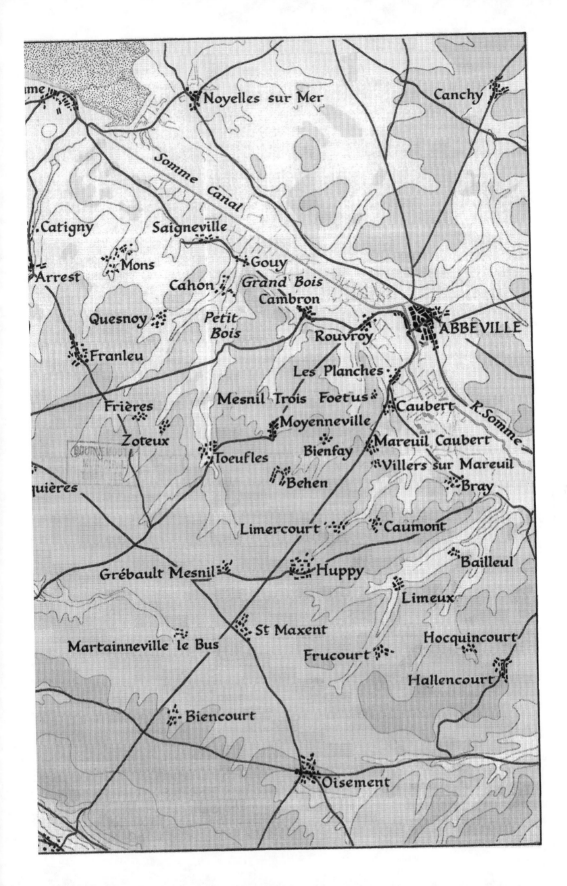

CHAPTER XIX

THE NEW GERMAN OFFENSIVE

5th June to 8th June, 1940

THE night of June the 4th passed quietly except for some desultory artillery fire, but there had been many indications that the enemy were massing for a new offensive, and about four o'clock in the morning of June the 5th the Germans attacked all along the 51st Division's front. Their first thrust came from the bridgehead at St Valery sur Somme where the 154th Brigade held the left sector. The villages of Saigneville, Mons, Catigny, Pende, Tilloy, and Sallenelle—occupied by companies of the 7th and 8th Battalions of the Argyll and Sutherland Highlanders — were all heavily attacked by infantry with artillery and mortar support, while more of the enemy's troops pressed forward through the open country between them. The Highlanders' villages were too widely separated for the companies to give each other effective support, and though they fought with dogged tenacity they were forced back or gradually overwhelmed. Mounting casualties and dwindling ammunition, and the superior numbers of the enemy, were too much for the village garrisons. Saigneville was lost in the late afternoon, and Mons, Catigny, Pende and Tilloy. Back at Franleu the battalion head-quarters of the 7th Argyll and Sutherland Highlanders were sur-rounded by forces which had advanced between Mons and Arrest while those places were being attacked. The only reserve battalion in the division—the 4th Black Watch—were ordered to relieve Franleu, but the enemy continued to advance and they were already approaching Feuquières when the Black Watch arrived and held them up. Another company of the Argyll and Sutherland Highlanders also went to the rescue of battalion headquarters at Franleu, but they were themselves cut off and surrounded in the outskirts of the village. In the evening Lieutenant-Colonel Buchanan sent away three or four crowded truckloads of his men, including many wounded, but he, Captain MacInnes, the padre, and the wounded who remained were later overwhelmed. Something of what lies behind such simple statements is revealed in a few sentences of this battalion's War Diary account of what they knew that night.

The last man to leave at 1800 hrs states that the enemy mortars were still landing around Bn. H.Q. and all the buildings and trucks around there were on fire. Capt. Robertson, Major Younger, Capt. Handley, who had borne great pain since the very beginning, with M.

Ricard the liaison officer and about 30 wounded men remained in the cellar with Capt. MacInnes and presumably Col. Buchanan. Other wounded and many dead had had to be left out in the posts where they had been hit and there may have been isolated parties of men who were unable or unwilling to leave.

Surrounded in the outskirts of the village, the company which had tried vainly to rescue this hard-fighting headquarters held out for over twenty-four hours, and the tide of battle had left them far behind when they were overcome. What remained of the 154th Brigade—and they were very few—were back that night on a front that lay between Woincourt and Eu.

On their right the 153rd Brigade had been fighting hard all day. The enemy used low-flying dive-bombers and much mortar and artillery fire in support of their infantry attacks, and the Scotsmen were gradually driven back till they held a front which ran from Toeufles through Zoteux to Frières and from there was in touch with the 4th Black Watch at Feuquières. Here the attack was held with the help of our artillery and machine-guns. In the evening, when the German infantry had drawn off, the 153rd Brigade positions were again shelled and mortared.

The French 31st Division astride of the Blangy–Abbeville road fought doggedly, but by the evening they were forced back to the Limeux–Limercourt–Behen line, continuing thus the line held by the 153rd Brigade on the left and by the 152nd on their right. For the 152nd had been forced back between Oisemont and the Blangy–Abbeville road. Finally the 1st Lothians, doing flank guard to the division, met the full weight of the enemy's opening attack at Bray early in the morning, and after fighting all day fell back in conformity with the 152nd Brigade to the country east of Oisemont. The Composite Regiment of the 1st Armoured Division had a number of minor engagements at threatened points and had several tanks knocked out. In the evening they assembled at Beauchamps on the Bresle.

Various adjustments were made during the night and when the second day of the German offensive opened the 51st Division and the French 31st Division held a line which ran from Oisemont to Woincourt and from there to the Bresle south-east of Eu.

To write such a 'broad survey' of operations that their shape and significance is disclosed and at the same time to convey even a glimpse of what such a day's fighting involved for the men who took part in it, is difficult if not impossible. The men of the 51st Division had themselves been the attackers throughout the 4th of June. They had had severe casualties and a gruelling and unsuccessful experience. They needed above all things a good night's sleep. But June the 5th had hardly dawned when new and yet more gruelling fighting began. It was high summer, and the days were long and blazing hot. After all their exertions the soldiery had had but little rest, and they were to get none that day. Mostly they were too busy even to eat. Dive-bombers roared down on their positions and they were shelled, mortared and machine-gunned. They were attacked by infantry who outnumbered them, and while they held off their immediate attackers they saw other enemy columns by-pass their strongholds and penetrate their front.

Often it was impossible to get their wounded away. Sometimes it was impossible to get away themselves when retirement was ordered and the troops on their flanks had fallen back. The villages they defended were peopled now only by disconsolate dogs whose owners had forsaken them and by cattle bellowing to be milked.

The Highlanders fought as Highlanders do—and as their casualties bear witness. The 7th Argyll and Sutherland lost that day twenty-three officers and nearly 500 other ranks, killed, wounded, and missing; and the whole division was cruelly mauled. The task laid on them was beyond their powers, beyond the powers of any single division. They and the French 31st Division were made responsible for the defence of a forty-mile front. What this meant can be illustrated by one example. The 1st Black Watch had to defend a $2\frac{1}{2}$-mile frontage of broken country—an impossible task for any battalion when the enemy had the numbers and equipment of this so-far victorious German Army. They did their best. Throughout this scorching day battalions, companies, even platoons, held on till they were overwhelmed or, sadly depleted, fell back to fight on in another position. And all day long the divisional artillery worked their guns unceasingly to give the infantry protection and to stop the enemy's advance. Some batteries maintained forward positions so long that they too were nearly engulfed, and when orders to withdraw reached them they needed all their skill to get the guns away.

On this first day of the new German offensive our air forces could give but little help to the Allied troops engaged. The 51st Division sent to South Component headquarters, now at Boos, to ask for protection against the enemy's bombers, but the Advanced Air Striking Force's three squadrons of fighters, though they were to be made up to strength, were on this day reduced to a total of eighteen serviceable aircraft. They had lost four in battle that morning. Information suggested that the enemy planned a big air attack on targets in and near Rouen itself, which was not only important industrially and as a focal point in road and rail communications, but was also a centre of military and air activity for both the French and the British. No. 1 Squadron was therefore on early patrol and, together with French fighters, engaged a very large formation of German bombers strongly protected by Messerschmitts. In the bitter fight which ensued some of the enemy were shot down or driven off, but enough got through

T

to bomb Boos airfield and a military camp. And again in the evening, when No. 501 Squadron intercepted a second formation sent to renew the attack, enough got through to bomb the camp and airfield, the main bridge, power station, railway, and the factories of Sotteville.

The bald account of these two episodes explains the fact that, while our small fighter forces were exhausting themselves in unequal combat, troops on the ground who suffered the enemy's attacks still complained of inadequate protection.

The close-support bombing undertaken that day by the Advanced Air Striking Force was done in a more easterly sector of the French battlefront, while twenty-four Blenheims of Bomber Command attacked enemy transport immediately behind the new battlefront, with two squadrons of Fighter Command to give cover. By night the enemy concentrations behind the front, his communications in France, and oil targets and marshalling yards in Germany were attacked by 103 bombers, of whom three failed to return.

The German plan for Operation Red had been set out in an order issued by O.K.H. on May the 31st over the signature of the Commander-in-Chief (Brauchitsch). 'The purpose of the Supreme Command is to annihilate the allied forces still remaining in France by means of an operation following the battle in Artois and Flanders as rapidly as possible. Operational enemy reserves in considerable numbers need no longer be expected. It will therefore be possible first to break down under heavy assault the hastily constructed enemy front south of the Somme and the Aisne and then, by rapid, deep penetration, to prevent the enemy from carrying out an ordered retreat or from forming a defence line in rear.'[1]

It is unnecessary in this account of British operations to describe the whole of the German plan. It provided for the employment of three Army Groups (A, B and C) and a reserve, in all nine armies and 140 divisions, of which 137 actually took part. At a conference on June the 2nd Hitler expressed his belief that 'the French and English have at most sixty to sixty-five divisions left for employment against us' which was not far wrong. He was less accurate when he added: 'Doubtless General Weygand will withhold an operational assault group which is to be sought in the area of Paris and eastwards. It must also be expected that the enemy will settle down and prepare resistance further south.'[2] In reality the remaining French Army consisted of forty-three infantry divisions (some only in course of formation), three armoured and three cavalry divisions all greatly reduced in strength by fighting; and the equivalent of thirteen fortress divisions in the Maginot line and on the Swiss frontier.[3]

---

[1] See Appendix II, p. 392.
[2] Ibid.
[3] Lyet, p. 117.

The attack of the German right flank, where the French Tenth Army was and where, alone, British forces would be involved, was to be made by the Fourth Army, now part of the reconstituted Army Group B. Their orders read: 'Fourth Army (two armoured divisions, six infantry divisions, one motorised division, 11th Motorised Brigade and 1st Cavalry Division) will attack from the Abbeville–Amiens area and defending their Paris flank will advance towards the lower Seine. The army will take early possession of Havre and the bridge-heads at Rouen, Les Andelys and Vernon.'[4] Further advance across the lower Seine in a southerly or south-westerly direction was to wait for special orders.

During the night of June the 5th/6th General Fortune wrote a strongly worded letter to Lieutenant-General J. H. Marshall-Cornwall, who had been appointed by the War Office to co-ordinate the actions of the British divisions and was at the headquarters of the French Tenth Army. Pointing out the condition of his men and the length of his front, he asked 'that half my front be taken over at once by someone—that I be authorised with my neighbour [the French 31st Division] to retire on the River Bresle'. But there was no one who could take over additional ground on this front. All that General Marshall-Cornwall could do was to secure from the commander of the Tenth Army authority to retire to the Bresle (which was then 'to be held at all costs') and to arrange that when this move took place the French 31st Division should hold from Senarpont to Gamaches and the 51st from Gamaches to the sea. This would reduce the front of the 51st Division to about $12\frac{1}{2}$ miles.

The 6th of June meanwhile passed fairly quietly on much of the corps front. The enemy tried hard but unsuccessfully to capture Oisemont with the help of repeated air and artillery bombardments, and the 1st Lothians and troops of the French 2nd Light Cavalry Division suffered considerably in beating off these attacks. Elsewhere German attempts to advance broke down under our artillery, machine-gun and rifle fire, and with one or two minor adjustments the line held. Only on the left was the position more threatening, where frontal pressure towards Beauchamps and infiltration at Eu and Ponts et Marais were resisted with difficulty. The Composite Regiment of the 1st Armoured Division was ordered to this danger area early in the morning, and after clearing up enemy posts in front of the Bresle—and capturing an officer and forty-three other prisoners in the process—was then moved back across the river to stop further penetration through Eu.

In the afternoon the French 40th Division moved into position in front of the Bresle between Senarpont and Aumale, where detach-

---

[4] See Appendix II, p. 393. (Les Andelys and Vernon are on the Seine above Rouen.)

ments of Royal Engineers and an anti-tank battery from the 51st Division had a number of flank guard posts.

Throughout the day there were reports that the German armour had broken through on the right flank. Many of these were false or exaggerated, but in fact the German 5th and 7th Armoured Divisions had begun their thrust towards Rouen and their leading elements were already some miles south of the road between Poix and Rouen; their 2nd Motorised Division was to follow close behind; the 6th Infantry Division was coming up on their left and the 32nd Division on their right was only ten miles away. The German XV Corps Diary records: . . . 'Avoiding woods, roads and adjoining villages and favoured by the gently undulating country practically free from ditches, the Corps advanced southwards across country, deployed with tanks in front and infantry in vehicles in rear.'[5]

It was clear to our commanders on the spot and no less clear to the War Office that further enemy success on this flank must compel the retirement of the 51st Division; that unless prompt and effective action were taken there might well be a repetition of events in the north. The 51st Division and the French divisions now fighting alongside would be cut off in the Havre peninsula with their backs to the sea. The British Government intended to send out fresh forces as quickly as possible. Lord Gort was to command a new British Expeditionary Force as soon as it was ready and meanwhile a first corps was already forming. The Swayne Mission was notified that General A. F. Brooke, who would command the corps, would proceed to France within the next week, and a brigade group of the 52nd Division would sail next day (June the 7th). With these plans in view the War Office urged the importance of securing a line of retreat for the 51st Division, not towards the dead end of Havre but towards the main French forces and our own base south of the Seine. This was again a situation where only foresight and prompt action could avert calamity. But General Weygand's orders at this time forbade retirement; the Bresle was to be held 'at all costs'. So nothing came of the War Office representations, and when two days later the German break-through in the south was completed and retirement was ordered, the decision came too late and the full costs of procrastination were duly paid.

During the morning twelve Blenheims flying from England with fighter cover had attacked enemy columns moving towards the Somme crossings, losing five aircraft in the action. In the afternoon twenty-four bombed bridges and roads in the Somme area between Abbeville and St Valery sur Somme, and all returned safely. Fighters of the Advanced Air Striking Force were mainly engaged on protec-

---

[5] See Appendix II, p. 393.

tion patrols in the Rouen area, in giving protection to our bombers, and, in the evening, on a patrol over the area in which the 51st Division and the French IX Corps were fighting. The former had again appealed for fighter cover, and in the afternoon two squadrons flew from England and refuelled at Boos before patrolling over the battle area. Except for one minor clash they met no enemy aircraft, though that afternoon the 51st Division again asked for defence against the enemy's bombing which they had endured for two days. The fighters must have just missed heavy attacks on the 1st Lothians at Oisemont and on Millebosc which, fortunately, 154th Brigade headquarters had left shortly before.

General Weygand also pressed for more fighters to be sent to France and, pending a decision by the Cabinet, the Air Ministry warned a number of squadrons to be ready to move at once.

On this night eighty-four aircraft were employed in attacks on German communications and oil targets, including seventeen from the Advanced Air Striking Force.

The 51st Division was by now only a fraction of its full strength, and 'A' Brigade from 'Beauman Division' (about 900 strong) was sent up to reinforce it. This brigade consisted of the 4th Buffs, 1st/5th Foresters and the 4th Border Regiment. They took over the left or northern sector of the divisional front and the 152nd Brigade, or what remained of it, moved back into reserve at the south-eastern edge of the Haute Forêt d'Eu. By early morning of June the 7th the 51st Division was in its new position on the Bresle with the French 31st Division on its right from Gamaches to Senarpont. At his own request General Fortune was now relieved of responsibility for the command of this French division.

The Bresle makes a good defensive line, with the river, especially in its lower reaches where some flooding had been contrived, as an effective tank obstacle. The only serious weakness was the enemy's penetration at Eu and Ponts et Marais. Throughout the 7th, the 4th Border Regiment and a company of the 1st/5th Foresters made strenuous efforts to eliminate this enemy pocket on the western bank, but they only succeeded in confining German troops to the north-western part of the Eu Forest, and the 1st Lothians and the Composite Regiment of the 1st Armoured Division were both moved up to this northern danger-point as an additional precaution. On the rest of the 51st Division front some enemy detachments made contact and their artillery was active, but it was a day of comparative quiet for most of the troops. Moreover the 900 reinforcements of A Brigade from Beauman Division arrived to make good the 51st Division's losses.

While the situation on General Fortune's immediate front was thus for the time being improved, the situation further south rapidly worsened. Moreover he was now separated by the French

31st Division from the units of the Support Group of the 1st Armoured Division which he had posted as a flank guard between Aumale and Serqueux. He therefore wrote to the commander of the 31st Division explaining the role of the Support Group and its weakness, and suggesting that Brigadier F. E. Morgan, commanding the group, should confer with him as to the best use that could be made of it in co-operation with the infantry of the French 31st Division. On 6th June the 1st Armoured Division was placed under the orders of General Altmayer and on the following day General Evans went to the French Tenth Army Headquarters and there conferred with General Marshall-Cornwall and General Pownall, who had arrived on a visit from England. The latest intelligence was that the German armour was breaking through the French defence between Grandvilliers and Formerie, and this was indeed true, for leading elements of the German 5th Armoured Division had overrun a troop of antitank guns and a company of the 2nd/6th East Surrey in position south of Aumale. Other elements of the Support Group on this Aumale–Serqueux line had repulsed an attack, but the German armour had then turned south-west and had attacked and roughly handled other posts near Forges. What remained of the Support Group was withdrawn that night into Basse Forêt d'Eu.

The German 5th and 7th Armoured Divisions were thus already outflanking the Bresle line. To relieve this position it was decided that what was available of the 1st Armoured Division should move up to Gournay and from there should strike at the flank of the German advance. The force at hand was forty-one cruisers and thirty-one light tanks of the 3rd Armoured Brigade, and six light tanks of the Bays and lorry-borne personnel of the 10th Hussars from the 2nd Armoured Brigade, returned from workshops where the tanks had been for repair and refit since the fighting for the Somme bridgeheads.

That evening, when these moves were well under way, General Weygand arrived at Tenth Army Headquarters and saw General Marshall-Cornwall and General Evans in the presence of the French Tenth Army commander (General Altmayer) and his Chief of Staff. General Weygand described the Tenth Army's fight as 'the decisive battle of the war' and said that, as no French reserves were available, all depended on the 1st Armoured Division. It was to hold 'to the last' ten miles of the Andelle river line from Nolleval to Serqueux; French formations would counter-attack from the south. General Evans explained the state of his division, from which all his artillery, anti-tank weapons and infantry had by now been taken for use elsewhere, and urged that his tanks were quite unsuited for a static, defensive role; moreover they were already on their way to counterattack the enemy flank. General Weygand would not vary his decision. All he would concede was that if it became necessary to retire from the Andelle, the 1st Armoured Division should withdraw across the Seine where it would still be available for counter-attack. So General Evans had to issue fresh orders and recall the units moving up to attack the German flank, some of whom were already in contact with German advanced patrols five miles north-west of Gournay.

Thus dawn came on June the 8th with the German armour nearing Rouen and the French IX Corps, still on the Bresle, being rapidly cut off.

It was to prove another comparatively quiet day for the 51st Division, for the enemy were content to hold our troops forward on the Bresle while their armoured divisions further south drove on round the southern flank. The attempts of the 4th Border Regiment and the 1st/5th Foresters to oust German troops from their position in the Haute Forêt d'Eu went on all day, and though they still failed to clear the woods they stopped further penetration. Near Beauchamps too, there was some outpost fighting, but no serious attack was made on our positions.

The situation further south was very different. At daybreak the enemy's armoured divisions renewed their advance on Rouen. Before describing what happened it may be well to get a clear picture of the state and situation of the British forces at this date. The position of the 51st Division in the north is clear enough. Reinforced and strengthened by a brigade from Beauman division, it was holding the Bresle line from Gamaches to Eu. The division was thus fighting as a division under the immediate control of its own commander. By contrast the 1st Armoured Division had never been allowed the chance to concentrate or to fight as a division. It will be recalled that one armoured regiment and the infantry of the Support Group had been deflected to Calais in the last week of May and had never joined the division or been available for the fighting south of the Somme. For the latter General Evans had under his command the 2nd Armoured Brigade, the 3rd Armoured Brigade less the regiment sent to Calais, and the remainder of the Support Group which had no artillery. Since the fighting to recover the Somme bridgeheads, a Composite Regiment from the 2nd Armoured Brigade had remained to support the 51st Division and was now screening Haute Forêt d'Eu: the remainder of the 2nd and 3rd Armoured Brigades had suffered heavy casualties and could find no more than the improvised formations which were now, by General Weygand's orders, on the Andelle line between Nolleval and Serqueux. What was left of the Support Group was in the Basse Forêt d'Eu under the command of the 51st Division. Finally there was Beauman Division. A Brigade was now with 51st Division, B and C Brigades were on the Béthune–Andelle line between the Seine and Dieppe. Certain additional units had joined the division on June the 6th, namely 'Syme's' Battalion formed of troops from the reinforcement depot at the base; and the 2nd/4th King's Own Yorkshire Light Infantry and 2nd/6th Duke of Wellington's, two battalions of the 46th Division which had been involved in the fighting at Abbeville on May the 20th and had since been reorganising at the base. These three battalions were now occupying defensive positions near Rouen, Syme's Battalion with four 2-pounder guns and a platoon of machine guns in the neighbourhood of Isneauville, the King's Own Yorkshire Light Infantry on a bridge over the Seine and the Duke of Wellington's on the railway south of Boos.

There was scarcely any artillery support for these emergency forces of imperfectly equipped infantry. And there could be no really effective control of units, for they were widely scattered over the fifty-odd miles of country between the Seine south-east of Rouen and St Vaast on the Béthune, and in isolated positions round Rouen. To speak of them as a division is almost inevitably to give a false impression of their operational value. In places they were mixed up with units of the 1st Armoured Division and at some points French troops, of whose plans and positions they had no knowledge, fought in front of them or retired through their lines. Streams of refugees added greatly to the danger and difficulty of their task, making it impossible to close road blocks or prevent espionage. It was doubtless the difficulty of maintaining communications and control which led General Beauman to issue instructions that troops would hold on 'as long as any hope of successful resistance remained' and that 'Brigade commanders will use their discretion as regards withdrawal' which was to be 'to and across the Seine'. Such conditional orders place a heavy responsibility on local commanders who can have little knowledge of the general course of a battle and so can hardly judge what is required of them. In this case there was the further complication that the armoured division's tanks now shared with Beauman's infantry responsibility for defending the Andelle line, but were under a different command.

The position in regard to command was indeed highly complicated at this time. Three small British formations, all acting in the same small area, were under three separate commands. The 51st Division was under the orders of General Ihler, commanding the French IX Corps of the Tenth Army. The 1st Armoured Division was under the orders of the Tenth Army commander, General Altmayer, though at this time it was acting on direct orders of Weygand. Beauman Division was under the orders of General Karslake who, as commander of our lines-of-communication troops, was under General Georges, commanding the French Armies of the North-East. General Evans had had orders direct from General Weygand that retreat if necessary should be across the Seine and not towards Havre.

General Beauman had received from General Karslake, and had passed on to his brigade commanders, orders to a similar effect. But although they were holding the same ground there was no one with an overall knowledge of the battle and of what the French IX Corps were doing to decide when the necessity for withdrawal had arisen and to co-ordinate their actions. Each commander would have to decide this for himself, knowing only the position on his own front.

The first attacks of the German armoured divisions were at Forges and in the neighbourhood of Sigy on the Andelle. A stream of French refugees, stragglers, and vehicles had been passing through Forges throughout the night and early morning, making it impossible for Beauman's infantry to close the road blocks they had built. French tanks were known to be operating in the neighbourhood, and when some arrived they were allowed to go through. They were indeed French tanks, but they had been captured by the enemy and were being used as the leading tanks of a larger German formation. Once past the defences they turned on our posts from the rear while the main forces attacked frontally over a wide area. Serqueux was lost, recovered by counter-attack, but lost again and finally. Sigy was heavily attacked after the defending troops had been subjected to dive-bombing, artillery, mortar and machine-gun fire. Neither the tanks of the 1st Armoured Division, armed only with machine guns, or at best with 2-pounders, nor Beauman Division, armed only with rifles, could for long hold up such an attack. Gradually they were overcome and forced back, and their position was pierced in many places. Meanwhile, further north, Neufchatel was in flames and the enemy's armoured patrols had reached Mathonville and were pushing on towards the road from Neufchatel, which runs through L'Epinay to Rouen.

Early in the morning the Composite Regiment at Haute Forêt d'Eu was ordered to rejoin the 1st Armoured Division to act on the left flank of the formations holding the Andelle line. They reached L'Epinay at about two-thirty in the afternoon. Before squadrons could deploy or any effort could be made to get into touch with the rest of the armoured division, German tanks followed by lorry-borne troops came up the road from Serqueux which by now they had left twelve miles behind. The fight that followed lasted for three hours and, though a number of our tanks were put out of action, damage was also done to the enemy. Only when German dismounted troops threatened complete encirclement was the engagement broken off.

Other units from the German 5th Armoured Division had meanwhile pushed on towards Rouen, and at about four o'clock in the afternoon they ran into Syme's Battalion at Isneauville. The battalion had been dive-bombed during the morning, but they had been very

active in building road blocks and had made the most of dannert wire
and road mines. They were attacked by tanks, after artillery preparation, and by infantry. But they held out for three hours and claim to
have accounted for twelve German tanks, six parachutists, one aircraft and a field gun, besides inflicting considerable casualties on the
German infantry. The battalion had been formed from reinforcements and had been in existence less than a week, but their stand
prevented the enemy from reaching Rouen that night. Eventually
the battalion withdrew, fighting, to the Seine.

In the afternoon and during the night all that remained of the 1st
Armoured Division and Beauman Division also withdrew across the
Seine. Of the British troops only the 51st Division (still on the Bresle)
and a fragment of the Armoured Support Group under their command were now left north of the river.

Now, when it was too late, the retirement of the French IX Corps
was at last ordered. General Weygand sent through the Howard-
Vyse Mission a personal message to the C.I.G.S., saying 'Orders
were given this morning to Commander IX French Corps who
commands 51 British and 31 French Divisions to withdraw these
divisions to area Les Andelys–Rouen'. Thus there was exhibited the
same initial refusal to face facts, and the same subsequent attempt to
mask the consequences of delay by the issue of orders that could not
be carried out, as had been displayed in connection with the
Weygand Plan. The wisdom of early withdrawal from the Bresle,
while it was still possible to retire behind the Seine, was not recognised; and when withdrawal could no longer be avoided the IX
Corps was ordered to retire through an area which had been open to
them earlier but was now occupied by the enemy.

General Ihler received these orders direct, as the French Tenth
Army Headquarters had moved nearer to Paris, and was not at this
time in communication with its IX Corps. He met his divisional
commanders in conference during the afternoon and told them that
by order of French General Headquarters the Corps would withdraw
to Rouen. His plan was to move first behind the Béthune and then,
having pivoted on Torcy, to reach Rouen on the 12th, that is in four
days' time.

This altogether too leisurely programme ignored the fact that the
German armoured divisions were already within a few miles of
Rouen—a distance they could easily cover in four hours—but it was
some gain that retirement from the Bresle was authorised, and while
the conference was still in progress General Fortune sent a staff
officer back to his headquarters to set in motion preparations for a
move during the coming night.

Later in the night the formal order for withdrawal was received
from General Altmayer.

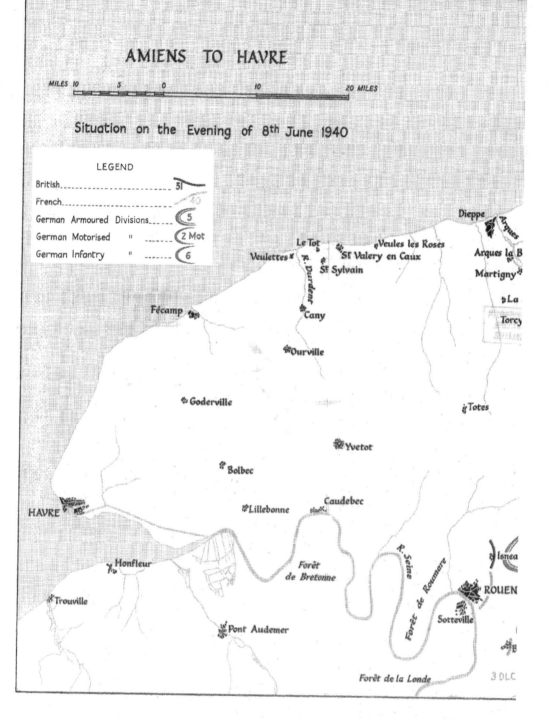

AMIENS TO HAVRE

MILES 10   5   0   10   20 MILES

Situation on the Evening of 8ᵗʰ June 1940

LEGEND

British............................ 51
French............................ 40
German Armoured Divisions....... 5
German Motorised   "   .... 2 Mot
German Infantry   "   6

Dieppe

Arques

Le Tot   Veules les Roses
Veulettes   St Valery en Caux   Arques la B
R. Durdent   St Sylvain   Martigny

La

Torcy

Fécamp

Cany

Ourville   Totes

Goderville

Yvetot

Bolbec

Caudebec

HAVRE   Lillebonne   Isnea

R. Seine   ROUEN

Honfleur   Forêt   Forêt de Roumare
de Bretonne

Trouville   Sotteville

Pont Audemer   B

Forêt de la Londe   3 DLC

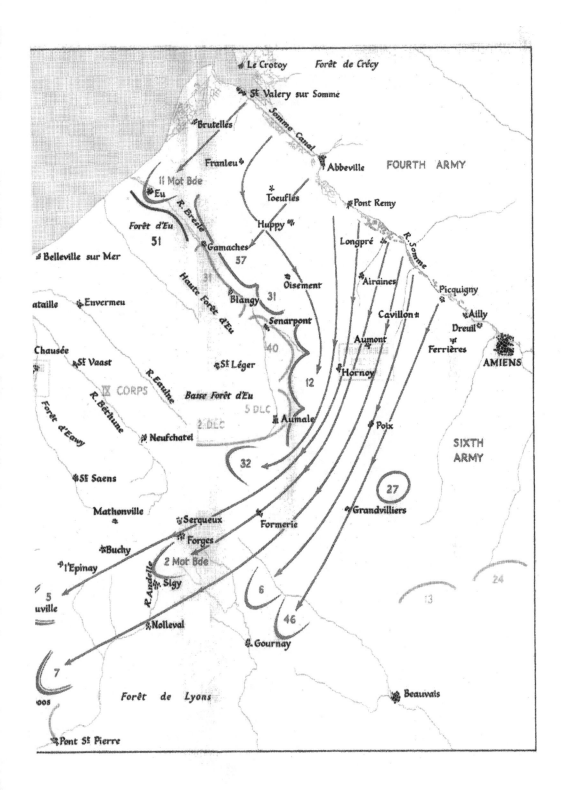

CHAPTER XX

FROM THE BRESLE TO ST VALERY

9th June to 12th June, 1940

ON the morning of June the 9th German armoured troops entered Rouen unopposed. The bridges over the Seine had been destroyed and French and British troops had left the city; the 51st Division (with the French IX Corps) was now finally severed from the main Allied forces for there were no bridges over the Seine below Rouen. Opposite the position they had held on the Bresle and sweeping round the right flank, where there was now no one to stop them, were ten German divisions.

Two movements started that day. The French IX Corps began to retire and the German armoured divisions turned north to intercept them. It will be best to follow these movements to their tragic conclusion before tracing what happened on the Seine and beyond it.

In planning the withdrawal of the 51st Division in conformity with the movements of the French on his right, General Fortune divided his forces into two more or less equal parts; these were to leapfrog over each other as the move progressed. For the first move, 153rd and A Brigades were to retire to a line between Envermeu and Belleville sur Mer, while the 154th and 152nd Brigades occupied the Béthune behind them. Withdrawal began during the night and, although greatly hampered and considerably delayed by congestion of refugee and other traffic on the roads, was duly completed. All available Royal Army Service Corps vehicles made double trips to carry the troops, but even so some units did not reach their new positions till well into the morning of June the 9th.

Fortunately the enemy were slow to follow up the withdrawal— perhaps because they were delayed at two of the Bresle crossings, which were held by D Company of the 4th Border Regiment and A Company of the 1st/5th Sherwood Foresters. Orders for the withdrawal failed to reach these two companies and in default of orders to move they stood fast. For six days they held on, denying for that week the passage of the river which they had been ordered to guard. Not only did they beat off all the enemy's attacks and withstand his efforts to dislodge them, but they made prisoner some of their attackers. Only on June the 13th when the Germans had brought up artillery and mortars to reduce their position and when they learnt that all other fighting north of the Seine had ceased, did they at last yield. It was a soldierly performance in the best tradition.

The remnant of the Support Group in the Basse Forêt d'Eu joined the French 2nd and 5th Light Cavalry Divisions (both very weak in numbers but still strong in fighting spirit) in the Forêt d'Eawy. The French Tenth Army Headquarters had moved south and all communication with their IX Corps had been broken. General Fortune too was 'out of touch with everyone' for reasons which will appear. Only rumours of the German progress had reached him when a dispatch rider arrived during the morning of the 9th with a message from Colonel R. B. Butler who commanded a small British garrison at Havre; he had been told by the French Admiral of the port that the enemy were already in Rouen. On this General Fortune saw the IX Corps commander who agreed that the objective of their withdrawal must now be changed from Rouen to Havre.

The circumstances which had forced this change of plan were not yet known to the War Office. During the morning they received a message from General Marshall-Cornwall (now chiefly concerned with what was happening on the Seine, since the IX Corps was divorced from all control by the French Tenth Army) urging that independent action be taken to extricate the 51st Division, 'possible Havre if Germans too busy elsewhere'. Later he sent another report that the division appeared to have withdrawn successfully to the Béthune and 'its withdrawal via Havre now seems the only chance'.

The War Office then informed the Howard-Vyse Mission at General Weygand's headquarters of a report that 'Admiral commanding Havre had given orders to 51st Division to withdraw to that place. He has also asked for ships to evacuate approximately 60,000 French and 25,000 British from Havre to Trouville, Caen and Cherbourg. Is this in conformity with General Weygand's plan?' The C.I.G.S. had understood that the intention was to direct withdrawal on lower Seine on either side of Rouen and he still considered this to be the right policy. About the time this message was dispatched and before there could be any reply, a report from General Fortune was received that the IX Corps was withdrawing on Havre. It had been sent by dispatch rider to Havre and telephoned from there, for General Fortune wrote 'I am now out of touch with everyone owing to the fact that I am not in possession of the recent code. All communications to me should be in clear or French code.' This report was confirmed by a further message which read:

> . . . Ninth Corps including 31 and 40 French Divisions and two weak cavalry divisions moving west to Le Havre 51 Division on sea. Sending rearguard to reinforce French on line Fécamp–Lillebonne.
>
> My speed depends on French movement about 20 kilos a day. To-morrow morning line should be Dieppe. Essential that air delay enemy movement mostly A.F.V. to south on Saint Saens–Bolbec road also his infantry advance from east. Air support requested to prevent un-

restrained bombing. Naval support along coast also of great moral support. If enemy break through French or cut me off from Le Havre will attempt pivot on one of northern ports or in hope of evacuating a few men from behind bridgehead. My rearguard assisting French Fécamp–Lillebonne has orders to drive on Le Havre to attempt embarkation of as many men as possible.

Thus on the night of the 9th the War Office knew that the 51st was withdrawing to Havre and the French Admiral there was asking for ships to be sent for evacuation. Only General Weygand still clung to the belief that the IX Corps could cross the Seine. For on the following day he issued an order and sent it via the Admiralty and the War Office, with a request that it might be passed to the 51st Division, for delivery to the commander of the IX Corps! This read: 'Orders of General Weygand dated 10th June. Fall back on the Seine below Caudebec inclusive. Protect your front in the direction Gournay–Rouen by occupying defensive position behind anti-tank obstacles. In co-operation with Admiral le Havre reinforce bridge-head Fécamp–Lillebonne. Higher authority will prepare means of crossing'. [i.e. crossing the Seine]

It would have been quite impossible for the depleted IX Corps to carry out all these tasks while north of the Seine ten German divisions were thrusting westwards even if the order had been issued on June the 9th. By the 10th it had no relevance to the facts of the situation, as will be seen when the events of that day are described.

But first the story of the 9th must be completed. Colonel Butler's message had urged the need of stronger forces to protect Havre and General Fortune ordered two brigades of infantry—the 154th and A Brigade, with artillery, engineers and supply units to proceed at once to organise a line covering Havre from Fécamp to Lillebonne. Brigadier A. C. L. Stanley Clarke was to command this force which, as it was formed at Arques la Bataille, was known as 'Arkforce'. He was to take under his command two French battalions and some 75-mm. guns already on the position. General Fortune's orders added: 'Should it be apparent that enemy attack from the south or east on the IX Corps has made any organised evacuation from Havre impossible you will withdraw and evacuate at Havre as many of your force as you can, destroying all material and taking off such material as can be carried'.

With characteristic promptitude Arkforce started for Havre within a few hours, moving off in the night of the 9th/10th while the rest of the 51st Division continued its withdrawal to the Béthune after blowing bridges on the Arques and the Eaulne. This time the enemy followed up quickly. At Arques la Bataille and at Martigny the 4th Seaforth and the 1st Black Watch had to fight hard throughout the 10th to retain the river crossings. In doing so they were greatly assisted by the guns of the 1st Royal Horse Artillery and elsewhere the artillery drove off a number of German attacks.

But, while the two brigades retained in 51st Division thus maintained the integrity of their front throughout June the 10th, a threat to their right rear was developing which General Fortune had no means to combat. As already indicated, the German armoured divisions, having driven the remainder of the French Tenth Army across the Seine and having taken Rouen, had turned north towards Dieppe and the coast. Arkforce, having started early, moved unmolested to its destination, but a wireless lorry, dispatched to follow and form a link between Arkforce and the division, ran into tanks of the 7th Armoured Division near Cany about eleven o'clock in the morning. The operator was only able to send a short message telling of this before the enemy closed in and the lorry was captured.

Cany is on the Durdent, to which river the 51st Division planned to retire in the coming night—the night, that is, of the 10th/11th June. On receipt of this wireless message the 1st Lothians, who had been doing flank-guard duty, with four anti-tank guns and four machine-guns, were ordered to make a reconnaissance to the west. They found that the Durdent crossings not only at Cany but also at Veulettes near the sea coast were already held by the enemy. Meanwhile, too, other reports indicated that the enemy were advancing northwards from the neighbourhood of Rouen towards the coast. The presence of their tanks only six miles from 51st Division's headquarters was reported in the afternoon, and rear formations of the division, which had begun to move westwards in preparation for the night's withdrawal, ran into the enemy at various places near Cany and Veulettes.

More serious news followed. Destroyers which had for some days been operating off the coast in support of the 51st Division found themselves under fire from guns which the enemy had already installed on the cliffs near St Valery. The *Ambuscade* was hit at about five-thirty in the evening and a little later the *Boadicea* was heavily engaged while taking some soldiers off the beach. The 51st Division was now cut off from Havre.

A naval operation 'Cycle' for the evacuation of the northern base troops had already started and shipping began assembling off the coast early in the morning. The Commander-in-Chief Portsmouth (Admiral Sir William James), arrived at Havre during the afternoon. From what he learnt there it seemed to him unlikely that the 51st Division and the rest of the French IX Corps could ever get to Havre, and he sent a message to the Admiralty and the War Office:

> . . . from reports received of enemy mechanised forces and position of our line it appears highly possible that a large number of troops might have to be evacuated from coast in neighbourhood of St Valery. I have moved small craft flotillas to St Valery so as to be in a good central

position if evacuation takes place from this coast and also transports to be assembled off this coast. I can control transport and small craft flotillas through the S.N.O. on the coast and they can be moved as required or withdrawn if not required.

If General 51st Division will keep me informed of his intentions I will direct the evacuation forces to meet his requirements. Understand present intention is to fight back but if this proves impossible flotillas and transports will be ready on the coast.

By now General Fortune had also come to the conclusion that the main body of the IX Corps would not be able to reach Havre. With General Ihler's consent he now issued orders for a withdrawal of the 51st Division to St Valery en Caux. Movement began at nightfall, though the line of the Béthune was not abandoned till eleven o'clock that night when the last troops left it without enemy interference.

Two hours earlier General Fortune had sent a message to the War Office: 'Can I be assured that if I cannot bring my division to Havre I can count on your being able to embark personnel from north coast? Have only two days' rations . . .'. Later he reported again that 'in this rapidly changing situation' he might ask them to embark as much personnel as possible of his division between St Valery and the mouth of the river Durdent. The French corps commander had joined his headquarters to that of 51st Division. Only a part of one day's rations remained and no further supplies could be expected from Havre.

When the move towards St Valery with a view to evacuation began, units were ordered to jettison all non-fighting equipment, such as, for example, blankets, in order to free as much transport as possible for troop carrying, and artillery ammunition was reduced to 100 rounds per gun. By these means all men of the division could be carried by the Royal Army Service Corps. The move proved to be a harassing operation. It was very dark; the allotment of roads which had been made was not adhered to; French transport, much of it horsed, broke from every side road into the route intended to be reserved for the 51st Division and it became choked with a solid mass of slow-moving vehicles. Alarmist rumours that the enemy were approaching added to the anxieties of the night.

There would be little purpose in a detailed description of the moves that took place that night and during the morning of the 11th as the 51st Division and the French divisions drew together a perimeter round St Valery from which it was now hoped to embark. Owing to the confusion on the roads it was broad daylight when the British troops who were to occupy the perimeter reached their positions. Even then French transport continued to come through, so that when contact with the enemy was resumed our men had difficulty at times in distinguishing friend from foe and their fire was sometimes masked. General Fortune, who was joined later by the French corps commander, stationed himself at the road-junction south-east of Veules les Roses, and from this point staff officers directed the incoming troops to their positions. The situation map shows the position on the night of June the 10th.

Early next morning the War Office sent a message to General Fortune referring to General Weygand's order of the previous day and reminding him of 'the importance of acting in strict conformity with any orders IX Corps commander may issue'. To this Fortune answered pointing out the 'physical impossibility corps commander approach Seine. In same boat as me'. He then assembled his brigade and battalion commanders and gave them orders for evacuation arrangements. His directive was as follows:

> The Navy will probably make an effort to take us off by boat, perhaps tonight, perhaps in two nights. I wish all ranks to realise that this can only be achieved by the full co-operation of everyone. Men may have to walk 5 or 6 miles. The utmost discipline must prevail.
>
> Men will board the boats with equipment and carrying arms. Vehicles will be rendered useless without giving away that this is being done. Carriers should be retained as the final rearguard. Routes back to the nearest highway should be reconnoitred and officers detailed as guides.
>
> Finally, if the enemy should attack before the whole force is evacuated all ranks must realise that it is up to them to defeat them. He may attack with tanks and we have quite a number of anti-tank guns behind. If the infantry can stop the enemy's infantry that is all that is required, whilst A/Tk guns and rifles inflict casualties on AFVs. [Armoured Fighting Vehicles].

In order to cover the actual evacuation an inner perimeter was chosen, to include the cliffs overlooking St Valery harbour from both east and west. As divisional headquarters moved into the town the enemy started to bombard it. The Mairie was ablaze and the Post Office selected for divisional headquarters was soon made untenable. The station square was heavily shelled.

The bombardment heralded the enemy's opening attack on the western face of the perimeter at about two o'clock in the afternoon. The 2nd Seaforth in St Sylvain and Le Tot areas were attacked by a large force of German tanks. Much of the artillery and many of the anti-tank guns detailed to support them were still held up on the traffic-jammed roads where riderless French cavalry horses galloping aimlessly about added to the confusion. The rifles and 2-inch mortars of the Seaforth were no match for the infantry guns and heavy mortars of the enemy, and anti-tank rifles alone could not stop the weight of armour brought against them. The German tanks broke through near Le Tot and gained the cliffs overlooking St Valery from the west. A French regiment ordered by General Ihler to hold a sector of the west face of the perimeter had similarly been delayed by traffic congestion and only advanced elements were arriving when the enemy outpaced them for possession of the cliffs. The 201st Anti-Tank Battery joined actively in the battle of the west flank till one by one their guns were all put out of action. Such guns of the 1st Royal Horse Artillery as were able to get into position south of St Valery could not open fire till it was too late to render effective assistance.

A number of small but courageous parties tried to oust the enemy from houses near St Sylvain and Le Tot, but in spite of all efforts the infiltration of St Valery from this quarter was hard to prevent, as the German artillery and machine-guns on the cliff tops maintained a continuous fire on the town and beaches. Small parties of the 1st Kensington and 7th Royal Northumberland Fusiliers (both machine-gun battalions) and of the 7th Royal Norfolk (Pioneers) succeeded at last in pushing the enemy back to the wooded outskirts of the town, but the position of St Valery was now very grave. The enemy's capture of the western cliffs threatened the whole embarkation plan, for the cliffs were within the inner perimeter on which the final stand was intended and some of the planned embarkation points were now under close-range enemy artillery and machine-gun fire—so much so that Commander R. F. Elkins, R.N., a naval liaison officer, was captured by the enemy on the western pier of the harbour while he was setting up communication with the ships off shore. (He escaped on the line of march through France and reached England safely a fortnight later.)

When the enemy broke through to the cliffs they left a number of tanks to mask the 2nd Seaforth at St Sylvain and Le Tot. Five of these were put out of action by the fire of anti-tank rifles, but casualties in the battalion were heavy. When darkness came the two companies about Le Tot tried to work their way down to the shore, but the Germans had by now a series of posts to prevent coastwise movement and but few of the Highlanders got through. The rest of the battalion remained pinned down at St Sylvain.

On the southern face of the perimeter the 1st Gordons were also attacked by tanks early in the afternoon. They too held their ground with great stubbornness and considerable loss, and a company of the 7th Royal Norfolk, who also refused to budge, suffered heavily when the tanks drove through their posts. Other units on the southern face of the perimeter were unmolested.

Enemy air reconnaissance, followed by dive-bombing, preceded the enemy's assault on the eastern perimeter in the later afternoon. The 2nd/7th Duke of Wellington's and 1st Black Watch met the heaviest attacks, but held on grimly though some posts were surrounded. Other battalions were shelled, mortared, and machine-gunned, but were not directly attacked. By now it was clear that the perimeter could not be held against the numbers and strength of the surrounding forces.

At half past five in the afternoon the War Office sent to the Commander at Havre a report of the 51st Division's situation as it had been notified earlier in the day, and added: 'C.-in-C. Portsmouth has prepared evacuation but authority for evacuation must be French Admiral Havre . . .'.

While this message was being sent the Senior Naval Officer at Havre was in fact notifying the Commander-in-Chief Portsmouth that the French Admiral had authorised evacuation that night. Shortly after receipt of this message the Commander-in-Chief Portsmouth signalled to the destroyer *Codrington* that 'evacuation from St Valery is to commence this evening. All available transports are being sent'.

About this time 51st Division sent the Commander-in-Chief Portsmouth the following message:

> Intend to embark whole force tonight Tuesday provided sufficient ships and boat transport are available. If embarkation cannot be completed tonight propose continuing A.M. tomorrow Wednesday. Estimated numbers British [corrupt group]. French at present 5,000 but may reach 10,000. Consider air superiority is essential to neutralise shore batteries. Jumping-ladders and nets are required to assist embarkation. Time of commencement and beaches to be used will be signalled. Embarkation tonight considered essential owing to probability of attack and shortage of rations petrol and ammunition.

Later that evening General Fortune informed the Commander-in-Chief Portsmouth and the War Office that he considered that night (June the 11th) would offer their last chance of evacuation.

General Fortune had made repeated but unsuccessful efforts to communicate with naval ships off the coast, and General Ihler assumed from this failure that the necessary ships would not arrive; he therefore saw no point in discussing plans for embarkation. General Fortune, on the other hand, believed that after the messages he had sent via Havre the ships *would* arrive and his troops must be ready to embark at once when they did. At about nine-thirty in the evening he issued the necessary verbal orders. Shortly before he did so, a Frenchman arrived at 51st Division headquarters; he had been captured by the Germans and was sent to demand surrender by ten o'clock under threat of a further attack. He was sent back to say that the division had no intention to surrender. The War Diary of the German XV Corps notes: 'The capitulation of units in St Valery which was already in progress was interrupted by the interference of British officers.'[1]

---

[1] See Appendix II, p. 393.

ST VALERY EN CAUX

(*above*) Cliffs to the east, commanding the harbour
(*below*) The narrow entrance with cliffs to the west just visible

All the artillerymen and all the infantry who were not surrounded made their way during darkness to the harbour and the beaches. Enemy machine-guns swept over the quays at intervals and the town was subjected to desultory bombardment. Near the sea front, blazing buildings threw a fitful light over the tense scene. A drizzling rain had begun to fall and fog came down over the sea.

So the night passed. The surrounded parties back on the perimeter still held on. The rest of the soldiery waited in St Valery for the ships to take them off.

But no ships came. And by three o'clock in the morning General Fortune realised that with dawn nearing he could not leave his men on exposed beaches or crowded in the centre of the town. Orders were therefore issued for all commanders to rendezvous in the station square so that the defence of a small bridgehead could be organised. This would require the recapture of the western cliffs. His intention was to hold the town and cliffs on either side of it in the hope that his force would be taken off next night. He explained his plan to General Ihler, as the only alternative to surrender. General Ihler thought further resistance impracticable and produced a telegram, already drafted, to be sent to General Weygand's headquarters. This stated that it was proposed to surrender, and General Fortune was asked to dispatch it as the French corps commander had no other means of communication with his chief. General Fortune took the telegram, but said he should not forward it till he saw how the final action developed; he should only send it if and when he was satisfied that there was no alternative to surrender.

The strength of the 51st Division was by now greatly reduced. The 154th Brigade with some artillery and engineers and with A Brigade from Beauman Division had been dispatched, it will be remembered, to cover Havre. Of the remainder, three battalions (2nd Seaforth, the majority of the 1st Gordons and about half of the 1st Black Watch) were surrounded in the positions they held on the perimeter and had not been able to fall back to St Valery. All guns, anti-tank guns, tanks and carriers had been rendered useless in preparation for the expected embarkation on the previous night. The only infantry available for the final action were the 4th Camerons and 5th Gordons, the 4th Seaforth and one company of the 1st Black Watch. These were now preparing for an attempt to recapture the cliffs overlooking the harbour and to hold the town for another day. The situation of the French divisions in the perimeter was not clearly known, but it was realised that the enemy was in many places well inside the originally planned line of defence and indeed in some places his tanks could be seen lying ready for orders to close in.

About seven-thirty in the morning (the 12th) General Fortune sent a message to the Commander-in-Chief Portsmouth: '51 Division

H.Q. waited all night on beach . . . Request co-operating ships be instructed to bombard cliffs west of harbour and machine-gun posts east of harbour. Faint possibility of withdrawal on this being accomplished but position very critical'.

Meanwhile the final action had begun. As the 5th Gordons approached the cliffs east of St Valery German tanks were moving in, but French troops carrying white flags marched across the Highlanders' front masking their fire. The enemy was quick to seize the chance thus created and the Highlanders' forward companies were quickly surrounded. On the west there was similar difficulty, for the 1st Black Watch and the 4th Camerons found their movements hampered by French troops who had capitulated or were about to to so.

At eight-fifteen a white flag fluttered from a steeple near the 51st Division's headquarters. Orders were given that it should be cut down at once and whoever had hoisted it should be arrested. But the offender proved to be a French officer who said that General Ihler had indeed surrendered. A dispatch rider then arrived with an open message informing all concerned that IX Corps would cease fire at eight o'clock. Then came a personal note for General Fortune:

12.6.40

Le feu cessera à huit heures.

IHLER.

51 Div.

With the message came a request that the surrender telegram be sent to French Headquarters.

There was now no possibility of holding the enemy off till nightfall. Moreover, General Fortune was serving under French orders. Yet at half-past ten he notified the War Office: 'I have informed corps commander that I cannot comply with his orders until I am satisfied that there is no possibility of evacuating by boat any of my division later.' But all French troops had ceased fire and white flags were being hung out, and in the end, before sending his message, he added a further note: 'I have now ordered cease fire.' Half an hour later he received a message from the Commander-in-Chief at Portsmouth: 'Regret fog prevented naval forces arriving earlier off St Valery last night. S.N.O. afloat will make every endeavour to get you off and additional ships are being sent to arrive tonight.' When this message was received the cease fire had already been ordered.

It is, of course, impossible to know how many of the 51st Division would have succeeded in getting away if fog had not prevented the ships from closing the shore on that fateful night. But it is very doubtful if any considerable number could have been taken off. Appalling damage to ships and men might have been done by the enemy artillery and machine-guns, which had been posted on the cliffs flanking the narrow estuary since the early afternoon. The evacuation of several thousand men would in any case have been difficult and dangerous: in fog it was impossible. The Navy had assembled 67 merchant ships off Havre and 140 small vessels and these were standing by, ready for all eventualities. But only 16 out of the 207 vessels were equipped with wireless, and only on a clear night could orders be communicated by visual signals. Fog denied the only method of control. By day the ships had at first lain off the shore, but the enemy's guns and dive-bombing from the air had made it necessary to move them further out to sea. On a clear night they might have risked a return inshore but on a clear night the effectiveness of the enemy artillery-cover of the harbour and its approaches would have been correspondingly greater. As it was the assembled shipping could not even pass orders to move. A few small parties were taken off the coast but only at Veules les Roses, four miles away at the eastern extremity of the perimeter, did enough ships get in to embark 2,137 British and 1,184 French troops and 34 seamen and civilians before air bombing sank some of the boats, and the installation by the enemy of guns covering the beaches there made further evacuation impossible. It was indeed only by a brave enterprise that so many were saved.

Arkforce reached its destination, and by half past three on the morning of June the 13th the evacuation of Havre was completed except for a small party of sappers who were taken off during the following night. The Navy had borne 2,222 British troops to England and had carried 8,837 more round the coast to Cherbourg to continue the fight. The operation had again been led by destroyers, and though the *Bulldog, Boadicea* and *Ambuscade* had been damaged, no ships had been lost. Meanwhile over 41,000 tons of stores had been moved south by rail to Nantes and St Nazaire.

While these events were reaching their tragic climax fighters of the Advanced Air Striking Force and of Fighter Command made a great effort to cover the movement of the 51st Division and the projected evacuations from Havre. On the 10th of June patrols flown over the 51st Division met no enemy aircraft, but some were fought over Havre where the smoke of burning oil made operations difficult. One vessel, the troop-carrier *Bruges*, was sunk, but thereafter our fighters prevented enemy interference.

On the 11th, patrols of Fighter Command covered the St Valery area for about seven hours. On three occasions they met and fought the enemy, bringing down a number; and on the 12th they made an even greater effort, patrolling the area for eight hours between five o'clock in the morning and half past nine at night, not realising that St Valery had fallen in the morning and that fighting in the area had ceased.

Meanwhile Battles of the Advanced Air Striking Force and Blenheims of Bomber Command were all employed to attack the enemy in the Seine area. Advancing columns, concentrations, bridges and their approaches were heavily bombed by day in agreement with the French Command, and at night both the Battles and the heavy bombers of Bomber Command attacked widely distributed key points in the enemy's communications, again at the request of the French Command. Among these on the 11th were Laon, La Fère, Soissons, and the Meuse crossings. On the 12th this programme was continued, roads, railways and river crossings again forming the principal targets. By day, bombing attacks were delivered on the enemy's concentrations and columns and on damaged bridges which were being repaired; new bridges which were being built in the Seine area were also repeatedly attacked, some of these operations being covered by fighters of the Advanced Air Striking Force.

During this final phase our air forces in France had operated under great difficulties. South Component were compelled to abandon in turn three groups of airfields, north of the Seine, south of the Seine, and near Caen. Finally they covered the Cherbourg evacuation from airfields in Jersey. The Advanced Air Striking Force in the same period was compelled to move in turn to airfields in the areas of Le Mans, Saumur, and Nantes. To continue bombing action by night and fighting by day under such conditions imposed great strain on all concerned.

Meanwhile on June the 10th Italy had declared war on the Allies. On May the 31st the Supreme War Council had decided that, if Italy declared war, industrial targets and oil plants in northern Italy should then be attacked at the earliest possible moment. With this possibility in view representatives of the Allied Naval and Air Staffs had met and made plans on June the 3rd and the French Air Command put two airfields, conveniently placed to the north of Marseilles, at the disposal of the bombers we were to employ. A special force—oddly named 'Haddock Force'—was assembled there.

On the night of the 11th, bombers of Bomber Command, flying from England, attacked targets in Turin and Genoa in accordance with the agreed plan. Bombers of Haddock Force were to have joined them, but when the time came General Vuillemin asked that the planned operation should be cancelled. On the 13th General Vuillemin removed his embargo, and in spite of bad weather Haddock Force struck a first blow against Genoa on the night of the 15th and a second against Milan and Genoa on the following evening. By then, as will be seen later, France was seeking an armistice and Haddock Force was ordered to England.

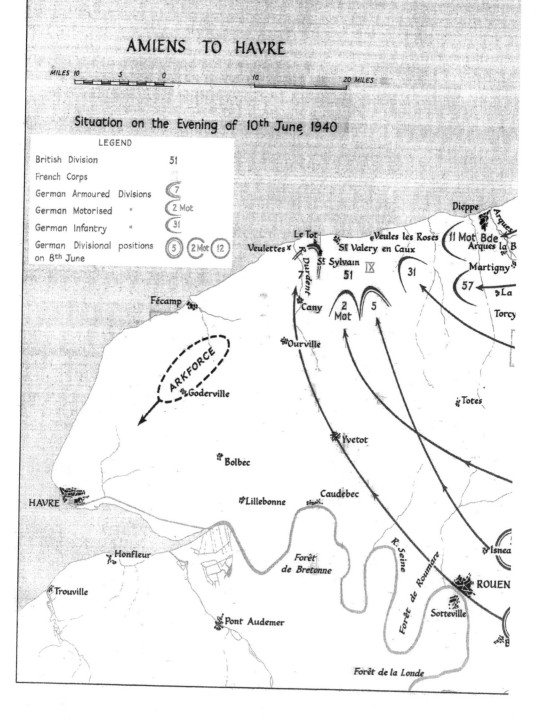

AMIENS TO HAVRE

MILES 10 — 5 — 0 — 10 — 20 MILES

Situation on the Evening of 10th June, 1940

LEGEND

British Division — 51
French Corps
German Armoured Divisions — ⑦
German Motorised " — ② Mot
German Infantry " — ㉛
German Divisional positions on 8th June — ⑤ ② Mot ⑫

Dieppe

Arques

Le Tot · Veules les Roses · 11 Mot Bde

Veulettes · St Valery en Caux · Arques la B

St Sylvain · Martigny

51 · IX

7 · 31 · 57 · La

Cany · Torcy

Veulettes

2 Mot · 5

Fécamp

Ourville

ARKFORCE

Goderville · Totes

Yvetot

Bolbec

Caudebec

Lillebonne · Isnea

HAVRE · R. Seine

Honfleur · ROUEN

Forêt de Bretonne · Forêt de Roumare · Sotteville

Trouville

Pont Audemer

Forêt de la Londe

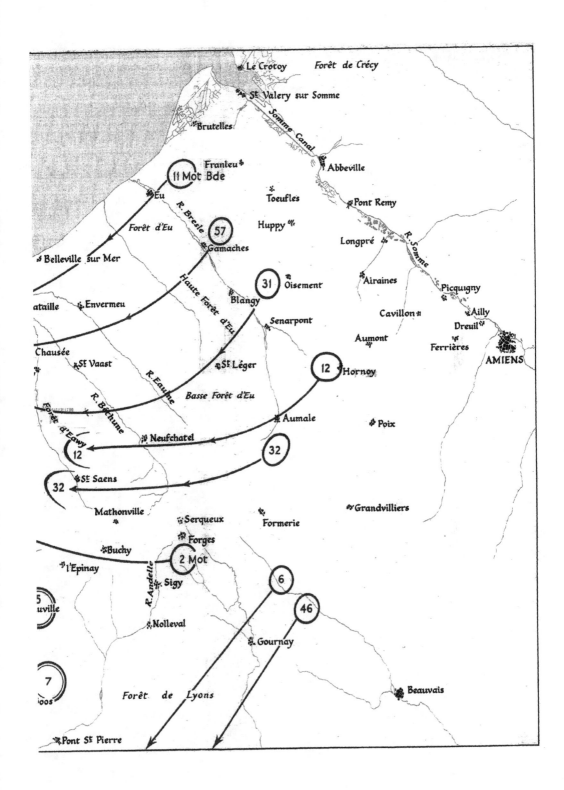

CHAPTER XXI

THE FINAL PHASE

12th June to 18th June, 1940

On June the 13th the Royal Air Force made a great effort to assist the hard-pressed French armies. In the east their defence had been broken through at a number of points; the enemy had crossed the Marne and was threatening to turn the Maginot Line. In the west the Seine had been crossed, the French forces defending Paris were falling back, and a widening breach was opening between them and the French Tenth Army on the extreme left. If the German movement here was continued southwards, the airfields in use by the Advanced Air Striking Force would be exposed. Air Marshal Barratt reported this to the Chief of the Air Staff and asked for a directive should his squadrons be compelled to move. He was told to withdraw, if need be, towards Nantes or Bordeaux: subsequent action must be dictated by the course of events, 'but so long as the French Army is fighting you should endeavour to continue to render support'.

While the inevitable move back was being agreed with the French Air Commander of the Northern Zone—General d'Astier—a heavy day's programme was carried out. Armed reconnaissance of the Seine area began at dawn; thereafter enemy columns were attacked in turn by ten Battles, fifteen and, later, a further fifteen Blenheims. Meanwhile, in the Marne area, at the urgent request of the French, twelve Battles attacked a large concentration of enemy troops and armour. Heavy anti-aircraft fire showed the target's importance, so a further attack was made by twenty-six Battles of which six were lost. Fifteen Blenheims of Bomber Command then attacked a third time, four being shot down. The damage done to the enemy on the ground could not be measured but he was stung to violent reaction.

Our bombing attacks were continued during the night; one hundred and sixty-four heavy bombers of Bomber Command were employed—forty-four in the Seine area, twenty north of Paris, forty-one on the Marne and fifty-nine against road, rail communications and woods in which the French reported that the enemy were concentrated. Fighter operations were restricted by bad flying conditions and were chiefly devoted to patrols over the coastal area.

On the 14th bombing attacks were renewed at daybreak against the German penetration across the Seine, but then and throughout the day bad flying weather seriously limited their effect. The most successful was an escorted attack by twenty-four Blenheims on

Merville airfield which our fighters had reported to be 'covered with enemy aircraft'. The night programme this time included marshalling yards in Germany, parts of the Black Forest in use by the German Army and the dropping of drifting mines in the Rhine (page 52). Seventy-two heavy bombers were engaged in these night operations of which two were lost against seven in the daylight attacks.

By day ten squadrons of fighters from Fighter Command each flew two sorties either in patrols of squadron strength or as escorts to bombers. It was their biggest effort since Dunkirk, but this time they encountered few enemy aircraft. Fighters of the Advanced Air Striking Force operated mainly over the area south of the Seine, where there were still some British troops.

In addition to a considerable number of lines-of-communication troops at various bases and ports, the remaining British forces included the remnant of the 1st Armoured Division, two brigades of Beauman Division and, later, the 157th Brigade of the 52nd Division and leading elements of the 1st Canadian Division which were being sent out from England as a start in the re-building of a British Expeditionary Force. None of these formations except the 157th Brigade were in fact engaged in serious fighting. They occupied successive and often very uncomfortable positions, acting at first under one or other of the French commanders in the retiring French Tenth Army but under General Brooke's command in the final stage.

The situation of the French armies during these days went rapidly from bad to worse. It had been proved, as General Weygand had expected, that the long, thinly held defence line could not withstand the enemy's assaults. It had broken at a number of points, and German forces were dividing the French armies and were pressing southwards through the widening breaches between them. The front was everywhere fluid, so that a report received was likely to be out of date before action could be based on it. General Weygand says that by June the 12th 'it was apparent that our last line of defence was breaking up',[1] and at the French Council of Ministers that evening 'I felt it my duty to ask the Government to start negotiations for an armistice'.[2] At a meeting of the Supreme Council on the following day he asked for instructions concerning the Breton redoubt and he says that 'from such replies as were forthcoming I gathered that the work there was to be continued'.[3] Reference to the 'Breton redoubt' must be explained.

The French Prime Minister had written to General Weygand on the 31st of May: 'I would be glad if you would give some thought to the possibility of forming a national redoubt in the neighbourhood

---

[1] Weygand, p. 126.

[2] Ibid., pp. 128–129.

[3] Ibid., p. 132.

of a naval base, which would enable us to benefit from the freedom of the seas, and likewise to remain in close touch with our Allies. The work should be laid out and provisioned, especially in munitions. It might be situated in the Breton peninsula'.[4] General Weygand has since made it clear that he did not regard this as a practical proposition at this date, but 'bound by the very definite orders I had received, I gave instructions for work to be started'.[5]

At a meeting of the Supreme War Council on 11th June General Weygand records: 'Mr. Churchill then brought up once more the question of a bridgehead on the Atlantic, a variation of the theme of a Breton redoubt. I explained why I did not think it reasonable to base any hopes upon devices of that sort'.[6] There, so far as Mr Churchill knew, the matter was left. And there it might be left now, were it not for what happened after General Brooke arrived in France, late on the evening of June the 12th and assumed command of all the British forces on which the Government still hoped to build up a new Expeditionary Force.

The orders he had received were similar to those which had been given to Lord Gort when he was appointed to command the British Expeditionary Force:

. . .

2. The role of the force under your command is to co-operate in the defeat of the common enemy under the Supreme Command of the French Commandant-en-Chef de l'Ensemble des Théâtres d'Operations. His Majesty's Government have agreed that the latter may delegate the immediate command of your force to a subordinate French commander, of rank not below the commander of a group of armies, as he considers necessary. You will, however, at all times have the right of direct access to the French Commandant-en-Chef.

3. In the pursuit of the common object, the defeat of the enemy, you will carry out loyally any instructions issued by the French commander under whose command you may be serving. At the same time if any order given by him appears to imperil the British Expeditionary Force, it is agreed between the British and French Governments that you are to be at liberty to appeal to the British Government before executing that order.

4. It is the desire of His Majesty's Government to keep the British Forces under your command as far as possible together. If at any time the French High Command finds it essential to transfer any British troops outside the area of operation of your main force, it should be distinctly understood that this is only a temporary arrangement.

. . .

There was nothing at all about a Breton redoubt. But on the day after General Brooke's arrival in France he received the following message from the War Office:

---

[4] Weygand, p. 186.
[5] Ibid., p. 89.
[6] Ibid., p. 121.

At a meeting of Ministers 11 June C.I.G.S. was informed that study was being made for organising bridgehead to secure Brittany in event of co-ordinated defence of France becoming impossible due to present French line breaking . . .

The message went on to suggest that General Marshall-Cornwall might be associated in this 'study', though it was to meet an eventuality which the C.I.G.S. hoped would never occur.

When however General Brooke met General Weygand by appointment on the morning of June the 14th General Weygand told him that organised resistance of the French armies as a whole had come to an end. The Germans were entering Paris and the French Government had moved to Bordeaux, but a 'decision had been taken by the British and French Governments to organise a redoubt in Brittany'. Together they then went to see General Georges to discuss this project. It was news to General Brooke that any such *decision* had been taken by the Allied Governments, and he did not think the plan feasible: it would need at least fifteen divisions to hold the 150-kilometre line proposed. Neither of the French generals seemed to have any better liking for the plan; General Weygand indeed described it to General Brooke as a 'romantic' plan, arrived at without military advice. But he also described it as having been decided by the Allied Governments, and General Brooke, assuming this to be so, acknowledged the role allotted to him by signing the following 'note' (No. 2033) which had been drawn up by the French Chief of Staff:

General Brooke, commanding the British Expeditionary Force, got into touch on the morning of June the 14th with General Weygand, commanding all the theatres of operations, and General Georges, commanding the N.E. Front, to determine how the British troops in France should be employed.

Under the arrangements agreed to by the French and British Governments to organise a redoubt in Brittany, the following decisions were taken:

1. That the British troops now disembarking (the Brooke Corps, the last of the 52nd Division, and the Canadian Division) should be concentrated at Rennes.

2. That the British troops engaged with the Tenth Army (Evans Division, Beauman Division, and the 52nd Division less those elements not yet disembarked) should continue in their present task under the orders of the General commanding the Tenth Army.

Their employment in the overall operations of this army should bring them as far as possible into action in the Le Mans area, so as to facilitate their eventual regrouping with General Brooke's forces.

Signed: BROOKE
WEYGAND
GEORGES.[7]

---

[7] See Appendix II, p. 393.

On leaving the French Generals and before returning to his own headquarters, General Brooke sent the following message to the War Office through the Howard-Vyse Mission:

> Weygand stated organised resistance has come to an end. French Army disintegrating disconnected groups. He told me of decision taken by Governments yesterday to attempt to hold Brittany. He, Georges and I are in complete agreement as to military impossibility of this with troops which can be made available. Strongly recommend decision should be reconsidered as it can only lead to further losses of British troops without hope of result. Present plan is to hold back drafts and corps troops at Rennes and that the others should reassemble in that area after falling back fighting with 10th Army on Le Mans. Recommend Nos. 1 and 2 Mission should be withdrawn as Weygand and Georges will have no effective control.

General Weygand has since expressed surprise that General Brooke took this step in view of the note which had been signed jointly so shortly before. But there was really no cause for surprise. Not only was General Brooke under French orders, but he was told by General Weygand that the decision to hold the Breton redoubt had been taken by the Allied Governments. As such he accepted it—but he was clearly justified in trying without loss of time to get his Government to reverse their decision in view of all he had learnt from General Weygand and General Georges about the position of the French armies. The orders given him on his appointment had specifically provided for such a position: '. . . if any order given by him [the French commander] appears to imperil the British Expeditionary Force it is agreed between the British and French Governments that you are to be at liberty to appeal to the British Government before executing that order. . .'. He took the only proper course open to him of accepting the order of his superior commander and at once raising the matter with the Government to whom he was responsible.

General Brooke did more than merely send the message quoted. He rang up General Dill, now C.I.G.S., and learned that General Weygand was mistaken in thinking that either he or the Prime Minister had done more than acquiesce in a 'study' of the Breton proposal. Certainly no 'decision' had been taken at any meeting of the Supreme War Council. There was therefore no need for the British Government to 'reconsider' the matter. But the other and graver issues raised by General Brooke were less easy to resolve. The suggested withdrawal of the British Missions at the headquarters of General Weygand and General Georges implied that General Brooke and the British forces in France would thereafter be no longer under the French command. The decision to evacuate all personnel and stores not immediately required to sustain our small remaining fighting force had already been taken. But the question now to be decided was whether we should continue our efforts to increase the fighting force—in particular whether the rest of the 52nd Division which had now landed should be sent forward to join the brigade already committed and holding part of the French Tenth Army front. General Brooke was strongly opposed to the addition of two further brigades to the rapidly disintegrating French forces. The Prime Minister, who joined in telephone conversations which went on all the evening, was on the other hand insistent that we must support our Allies to the full extent of our power. Only when General Brooke at last convinced him that such support as the newly arrived 52nd Division might give could not possibly save the position of the Tenth Army and would almost certainly result in the loss of the division, did he agree that they should be held back.

Late that night (the 14th of June) the Secretary of State for War sent General Brooke a message which read:

> You are no longer under French Command but will co-operate with any French forces which may be fighting in your vicinity. In view of your report stating that organised resistance has come to an end you must now prepare for the withdrawal of your force to the U.K. . . . .

The Government's decision was also notified to the French Prime Minister and the C.I.G.S. informed General Weygand.

But General Brooke's determination to save the 52nd Division had not yet succeeded, for the 157th Brigade was till now under French orders. He therefore ordered General Marshall-Cornwall to take over command of all the troops that had been under the command of the French Tenth Army, adding 'While co-operating in the withdrawal of the French forces direct your axis of withdrawal on Cherbourg in order to embark U.K.' He then ordered the 52nd Division (less the brigade already with General Marshall-Cornwall in what was now to be called 'Normanforce') to fall back to a definite line near Cherbourg in order to cover evacuation, orders for which were issued on the 15th.

While General Brooke was thus securing the decision to withdraw British forces, Air Marshal Barratt had been taking similar action. He had informed the Air Ministry on June the 14th that, in view of the situation of the French forces and the danger to which the air-fields used by his few remaining squadrons were exposed, these should now be withdrawn to England. On the 15th he received information that General Brooke was no longer to serve under French Command but was to prepare for the withdrawal; and he was informed that he should now concert operations to that end with General Brooke. When the message reached Air Marshal Barratt his squadrons were moving to the Rennes, Saumur, Angers, Nantes, area. Fresh orders were now issued. The remaining bomber squadrons flew to England. The four fighter squadrons which were to cover withdrawal operations were moved to Nantes. Air operations that day were on a small scale.

After pausing to construct bridges over the Seine the enemy renewed his advance on the 14th, and the 157th Brigade, in positions covering Conches, had to fight to maintain their line unbroken. On that night the French Tenth Army was ordered to withdraw to the line Verneuil–Argentan–river Dives where the 157th Brigade held an eight-mile front astride the Mortagne–Verneuil road. The Germans followed up quickly and on the 16th, under renewed enemy pressure, General Altmayer ordered withdrawal *to Brittany*.

Now that the French armies, falling back everywhere, were broken up into separate groups, there was no longer any possibility of unified command and there could be no rebuilding of a stable front. The Tenth Army's decision to move into Brittany would separate it more widely from other armies (the gap was already fifty miles wide), and General Brooke agreed with General Marshall-Cornwall's decision that the time had come when he must detach the remaining British forces and withdraw them to Cherbourg for embarkation to England. General Altmayer was informed and agreed, and though the move was a difficult one it was successfully carried out. The tanks of the 1st Armoured Division's 2nd Brigade, which were in rearward areas for reconditioning, were entrained for the port, and it was not the division's fault that nothing more was ever heard of the train! The 26 tanks, 11 scout cars and 49 troop-carrying lorries of the 3rd Brigade covered the 200 miles by road and duly reached Cherbourg. The 157th Brigade, in motor transport, arrived there on the 17th and were embarked that evening. Beauman's remaining infantry had left a few hours before. The enemy were entering the outskirts of the town as the last troops sailed.

Soon after midday on the 17th General Brooke received a message from the C.I.G.S. saying that the French had asked for an armistice. There was in any case nothing more that he could do. All the arrangements for evacuation, made under his orders by General de Fonblanque, were working well. Almost all of the 52nd Division had gone, and all that had landed of the 1st Canadian Division; over 40,000 troops had been carried to England in the past two days. General Marshall-Cornwall's remaining troops were coming in. Half an hour before midnight General Brooke boarded the armed trawler *Cambridgeshire*. Early on the 18th she sailed as escort to a slow convoy, so that he did not reach Southampton till six o'clock in the evening of the 19th. Twenty-four hours before his arrival the last ship had left Cherbourg.

So ended the campaign on land; but in base areas farther south there were still large numbers of British and Allied troops to be evacuated. The epilogue belongs to the Royal Navy, covered to the limit of its strength by the Royal Air Force.

The campaign had started with the Navy's successful transportation of the British Expeditionary Force to France; it ended only when they had brought home safely the vast majority of those who had survived the fighting.

The final operation, 'Aerial', which began on June the 14th was commanded by Admiral James, Commander-in-Chief Portsmouth. He could not organise a convoy system for he had not the necessary flotilla vessels (as explained on page 264). He therefore arranged that a continuous flow of troopships, storeships, and motor transport ships would sail between Southampton and the French ports while coasters sailed from Poole Harbour and Dutch schuyts from Weymouth. The few warships available would meanwhile patrol the shipping routes. The customary demolition parties were to be landed, but this time it was hoped that military stores and equipment could be brought home; for after the loss of so much material in the northern campaign there was urgent need of all that could be saved.

The tragic miscarriage of plans to bring away the 51st Division from St Valery has already been explained, and the bare fact has been told that this was followed by the successful evacuation of all the troops from Havre and Cherbourg. It remains only to add that 30,630 men were brought home from Cherbourg and 21,474 from St Malo without the loss of a single life or damage to a single ship. Of these all but 789 were British. The enemy's air force tried to interfere on occasion but was kept in check with the help of the Royal Air Force.

Simultaneous naval operations to clear the more southerly ports on the Bay of Biscay were under Admiral Sir Martin Dunbar-Nasmith, Commander-in-Chief Western Approaches, at Plymouth. His difficulties were increased by the fact that from the base areas (Brest, St Nazaire, and Nantes) information was scanty and inexact. The urgency of the situation was not at first realised there, but after Cabinet orders for immediate evacuation were received embarkation started at once and proceeded rapidly—so rapidly, indeed, that there was some confusion and lack of control in the matter of stores and equipment, and considerable quantities of precious guns and vehicles which could have been brought away were destroyed or abandoned. It is difficult to apportion blame, for in those days no one knew what was happening or where the enemy would appear. It was certain that the Germans were in Paris, and that the French Government had gone to Bordeaux. The British Expeditionary Force had been withdrawn to England and it was said that the French Army was cut in pieces. The German Army was advancing southwards, but only rumour said how near it was. In such circumstances it is understandable, though deplorable, that the chief concern was to avoid capture by the enemy, that some evacuations were concluded prematurely and that much equipment was abandoned which should have been saved.

Fighters from the squadrons which were still in France and others of Fighter Command patrolled the area actively, and the enemy's aircraft mainly confined their efforts at first to minelaying. Although this delayed movement, while minesweepers cleared the channels, it had no other effect on operations. This was fortunate, for the shipping used included large troopships—for example, the *Arandora Star*, the *Strathaird*, and the *Otranto*—which would have been vulnerable to strong attack by the enemy's heavy bombers.

From Brest 32,584 British and Allies were brought to England; evacuation was successfully concluded and the demolitions were carried out by the French with the British demolition party's help. The French warships sailed and by the 19th the great naval base was clear of shipping and the demolition party was brought away by the destroyer *Broke*.

Operations had been proceeding concurrently at St Nazaire and Nantes, where there were greater difficulties to overcome. The former lies at the mouth of the river Loire where there are strong tides and other navigational hazards; the latter is some fifty miles up the river. As pointed out above, the Navy's information was vague and often contradictory. Between 40,000 and 60,000 British and Allied troops were thought to be converging on Nantes, but neither exact numbers nor the times of arrival were known.

In preparation for the lifting of so large a number, Admiral Dunbar-Nasmith ordered the assembly of a considerable concentration of ships, including the destroyers *Havelock*, *Wolverine*, and *Beagle*, the liners *Georgic*, *Franconia*, *Duchess of York*, and *Lancastria*, the Polish ships *Batory* and *Sobieski*, and a number of cargo ships. For the most part these had to lie offshore in Quiberon Bay, twenty miles northwest of the Loire estuary, where there was good anchorage for large ships but no anti-submarine or other defences. It was a risk which had to be taken, for no safer anchorage was available. Movement began on the 16th and over 12,000 troops were embarked that day on the *Georgic*, the *Duchess of York*, and the two Polish ships, and sailed for home. The enemy's bombers attacked the ships in Quiberon Bay, but only the *Franconia* was damaged. The loading of stores went on all night and additional ships arrived from England—and some from Brest. The destroyers *Highlander* and *Vanoc* also joined the flotilla.

The day that followed, June the 17th, was memorable for the only tragedy that marred the success of these difficult and dangerous operations. At Nantes the sun rose on a scene of great activity, large bodies of troops were assembling in the port to be taken home, and in and out of the river entrance destroyers and smaller craft were busy ferrying parties to the ships which were waiting for them in the roads. Overhead, fighters of the Royal Air Force patrolled at frequent intervals to keep the sky clear of the enemy's bombers. And more ships arrived to increase the speed of evacuation.

The morning's achievements raised high hopes that again the Navy's task would be completed without loss, but at a quarter to four in the afternoon, when the fighter patrol which had been maintained throughout the day along a thirty-mile stretch of coast was not over the port, enemy bombers made a heavy attack on the ships assembled in the roadstead and the mouth of the river. While destroyers and all the smaller craft with anti-aircraft weapons defended themselves vigorously, the *Lancastria*, with 5,800 troops—including many of the Royal Air Force—already on board, was heavily hit and set on fire, and within fifteen minutes sank with great loss of life. Nearly 3,000 perished, though why so many lives were lost is something of a mystery. It is true that there were not enough lifebelts on board for the quite exceptional number that had been embarked, and that a film of the ship's oil-fuel spread over the surrounding waters. But the master, who was saved, testified that there was no panic aboard, and the ship sank slowly where small craft were present in considerable numbers. Doubtless many of these were so busy defending themselves from the air attack (which continued for forty-five minutes) that they failed to realise the urgent plight of the *Lancastria's* men, yet this does not fully explain why there was so great a loss of life.

Notwithstanding this sad interruption, embarkation continued throughout the night, and soon after daybreak on the 18th ten ships sailed for Plymouth with some 23,000 men aboard. Only another 4,000 or so remained ashore, but alarmist and (as it was proved later) exaggerated reports of the enemy's near approach led again to a needlessly hurried conclusion of the operation. Twelve ships bearing away the last of the assembled troops sailed at eleven o'clock that morning—and again much equipment which was badly needed in England was left behind. In the afternoon Admiral Dunbar-Nasmith heard that a further 8,000 Polish troops were nearing St Nazaire, and six destroyers and seven transports were sent to bring them home. Again the news was inaccurate, and much shipping had been needlessly risked to save the 2,000 men who were there and were brought away.

Farther south at La Pallice (which with the nearby ports of Rochefort and La Rochelle is an important naval base) the movement of troops had begun on June the 17th. A senior naval officer for the port had arrived by destroyer the day before and, finding some 10,000 men but no transports, he requisitioned some cargo ships in harbour and embarked the troops, though again their vehicles were left behind. The convoy sailed safely on the 18th. Twice after this the Commander-in-Chief Western Approaches was told that further troops were reaching the port and twice he ordered ships to fetch them away. On the 19th 4,000 Polish troops were embarked, but on the 20th very few men were found and the ships which were not required sailed southwards to the ports of the river Gironde. There were now practically no British troops left in France, but there were Embassy and Consular staffs to be brought away; a considerable number, still, of the Polish and Czech troops who had been preparing to fight with the Allied armies; and British and foreign civilians who sought to leave France before the German conquest became effective.

The *Arethusa* had been stationed off Bordeaux on June the 16th to act as wireless link, and next day all British and some Allied shipping in the port was cleared for England, while the embarkation of Czech and Polish troops and civilians started. Similar traffic continued through the next two days, many thousands being got away. On the 19th the destroyer *Berkeley* brought off from Bordeaux the Embassy and Consular staffs and transferred them to the *Arethusa*. The *Berkeley* was then relieved by the cruiser *Galatea* and sailed for Plymouth with the President of Poland and many of his ministers and a number of other important people on board. Embarkation of Allied troops and civilians continued meanwhile from Le Verdon (at the river mouth) and Bayonne. The Polish ships *Batory* and *Sobieski* and the liners *Ettrick* and *Arandora Star* went to Bayonne on the 19th, and, having taken on board the men who were there, moved on to St Jean de Luz on the following day. In the end a large number of Polish and some other Allied troops were brought home from Bayonne and St Jean de Luz.

On June the 24th the French Government announced that evacuation must cease on the following day on account of the armistice terms, and just before two o'clock on June the 25th what was officially the last troopship sailed.

But there were still a number of Allied troops who desired to get to England and evacuation continued from French Mediterranean ports until 14th August by which date the Royal Navy had brought away from the area south of the Somme:

144,171	British
18,246	French
24,352	Polish
4,938	Czech
163	Belgian

These 191,870 have to be added to the 366,162 who had been brought away by the conclusion of Operation Dynamo. A grand total of 558,032 had thus eluded the enemy's attempts to capture or destroy them; 368,491 of these were British troops.

With the fall of France and the withdrawal of our troops and air forces the British campaign in France and Flanders was ended.

W

CHAPTER XXII

REVIEW OF AIR OPERATIONS

BEFORE trying to form an appreciation of the part played by British forces in this campaign it may be well to look back over the accounts of air operations and to bring these together in a brief summary, for it is less easy to trace their course and their effect in the day-to-day story than it is to follow the actions and outcome of land fighting. Moreover the operations of the Royal Air Force involved not only air forces stationed in France—the Air Component of the British Expeditionary Force and the Advanced Air Striking Force—but also home-based squadrons of Bomber, Fighter and Coastal Commands. The air campaign was fought both in France and from England: in that regard it differed widely from the land campaign.

The course of air operations may be divided conveniently into four phases.

In the first phase, extending from May the 10th to the 15th, the Air Component, enlarged progressively by the equivalent of ten additional fighter squadrons, fought successfully to aid and protect the British Expeditionary Force during its move forward to the Dyle. At the same time the Advanced Air Striking Force engaged in intensive attacks on the enemy's advancing armies, and suffered grievous loss in doing so. In these attempts to delay the German advance, squadrons of Bomber Command based in England joined both by day and by night. Air reconnaissance also played an important part in the operations in these opening days.

In the second phase, lasting from May the 16th to the 22nd, the Air Component was further strengthened by six fighter squadrons operating from English bases. It was chiefly engaged in checking the enemy's air attacks where a final break-through to the coast threatened. When that threat became a reality and our northern airfields were endangered or overrun, the Air Component was brought home to continue the fight from England.

During the opening days of this phase the airfields of the Advanced Air Striking Force were also endangered and its squadrons were compelled to move further south. Thereafter they continued the bombing of enemy columns moving up to the battle, but by night only, for their losses by day were too heavy. But the squadrons of Bomber Command, which were equipped with more suitable aircraft, continued similar attacks both by day and by night and in addition engaged in strategic bombing of targets in Germany.

Fighters of the Advanced Air Striking Force were at this time primarily occupied in defence of our airfields, in offensive patrols over the French front on the Aisne and in the protection of reconnaissance sorties.

The third phase of air operations extended from May the 23rd to June the 4th. Although what remained of the fighters of the Air Component had moved to England, the contribution of Fighter Command was greater than ever. It was in these days that the squadrons of No. 11 Group fought their great battle with the *Luftwaffe* above the army withdrawing to the coast and to England—the battle which spoiled Goering's plan to prevent evacuation.

Fighters of the Advanced Air Striking Force, during these days, also flew offensive patrols over the southern portion of the battlefield to counter German dive-bombing, particularly on the positions of the French Army. They had also to give cover for day bombing and to protect the airfields in use by our air forces in France. The bomber squadrons of Air Striking Force continued by night their attacks on enemy reinforcements and supplies, while by day squadrons of Bomber Command based in England gave support to the withdrawing armies by attacking the enemy's columns, transport and communications.

In the final phase, from June the 5th, when the enemy's southward offensive opened, till the French armistice brought the campaign to an end, the Royal Air Force concentrated on attempts to help our few remaining divisions in France and the hardly pressed French armies. For the latter task all the medium bombers of Bomber Command (No. 2 Group) were placed at the disposal of Air Marshal Barratt, who worked throughout in close concert with the French High Command. They attacked the enemy's troop concentrations, forward supply dumps, river crossings and communications while fighters gave them cover and flew offensive patrols. Two additional fighter squadrons were sent out, but as the French Army's resistance was broken it became progressively impossible to co-ordinate air attacks and land defence. When the end approached, what remained of the Advanced Air Striking Force was brought home, only the five fighter squadrons (two of them based on Jersey airfields) remaining till the very last to cover evacuations from southerly harbours.

With this outline of operations in mind and with a knowledge of the course taken by land operations it is possible to appraise more clearly the parts played by the Royal Air Force—to realise the nature and extent of their operations and the measure of their achievement.

Britain could not have employed larger land forces in this campaign, for in the time available we sent to France practically all we had; the undertaking given in 1939 was more than fulfilled. How far is it true that, similarly, we employed all that was available of our air strength? Obviously it was right to keep some for the air defence of Great Britain. The question is therefore one of proportion. What proportion of our air strength was kept in hand for the latter purpose? That question is easy to answer for it is a plain question of fact.

On May the 10th the total number of first-line aircraft in the Royal Air Force was 1,873. Of these 416 were stationed in France. When the fighting began the number in France was at once increased. Subsequently force of circumstances compelled some to move to England, but the number of squadrons *stationed in France* bore no significant relation to the *total air strength employed*. The first was dictated by events, the second by British air policy.

When war was declared the Air Staff and the Government knew that the Royal Air Force must face great odds. Their initial air policy was framed accordingly, but as operations progressed they were beset by British, French and Belgian demands for additional help, on all sides and in every sort of task. If an attempt had been made to meet all demands without regard to a general air policy, the Royal Air Force, as then organised, must have been virtually destroyed.

Two major questions of policy exercised the judgement of the Air Staff and the War Cabinet throughout the campaign. How could our bombers be used to inflict the greatest damage on the enemy? How many of our fighters could be used without undue damage to our home defence? Considerations which shaped the decisions taken on these two questions of grand strategy belong to other volumes of this history but their result is traceable in air operations and especially in the operations of our bombers and fighters.

Bombers are essentially offensive weapons and, whether or not they were used in the best way, *all that we had* were used. None of our striking power was held back. In addition to the squadrons of the Advanced Air Striking Force, the whole strength of Bomber Command was continuously employed.

From the summary of operations outlined above, it is clear that bombers were engaged in five sorts of operations, namely:

(1) daylight attacks by medium bombers of the Advanced Air Striking Force stationed in France, and of Bomber Command's No. 2 Group stationed in England, against enemy columns, concentrations and communications;

(2) night attacks by bombers of the Advanced Air Striking Force against enemy concentrations and communications west of the Rhine;

(3) night attacks by heavy bombers of Bomber Command's Nos. 3, 4 and 5 Groups against enemy concentrations and communications west of the Rhine;

(4) night attacks by bombers of Nos. 3, 4 and 5 Groups against enemy concentrations and communications east of the Rhine;

(5) night attacks by Nos. 3, 4 and 5 Groups against oil plants in Germany.

There were, in addition, subsidiary bombing attacks on enemy airfields, headquarters, and battery positions, and operation 'Royal Marine' in which the Rhine was sown with drifting mines.

Later in the war we could use as many as 1,000 far heavier bombers than any we had in 1940 to attack a single target on a single night. In May, 1940, the Royal Air Force had only 544 bombers of all types for all the operations listed above. To estimate the damage they did by the standards of later years would be meaningless. It is better to measure their strength against the tasks which they were set.

For daylight tactical attacks in the opening phase the Advanced Air Striking Force had but ten squadrons of medium bombers—eight of these being the ill-suited Battles. Their task was to hinder the German armies advancing through country which reached from the North Sea to the Meuse and soon extended from Germany to the English Channel. The points they were to attack by day were those of most importance to the enemy and therefore those most strongly defended: by night they were to bomb bridges and other targets which were hard to distinguish and harder still to hit. Seen thus against the background of German operations, the gallantry of their effort stands vividly displayed, but it is clear that the damage they inflicted could be little more than temporary. The medium bombers of Bomber Command were better suited to daylight bombing, but their effective use in collaboration with ground forces was handicapped by the exercise of control from England, at a time when communications were roundabout and slow.

Division of opinion as to how our heavy bombers should be used—whether, that is, they should be confined to the strategic bombing for which they were designed, or whether they, too, should be used to assist the Allied armies in their fight to stem the German advance—resulted in compromise. They were used for both tasks and so were unable to concentrate on either.

Strategic bombing of military targets in Germany was not authorised by the War Cabinet until May the 15th. As a matter of Allied policy, therefore, Germany enjoyed immunity from air attack not only while she defeated Poland and throughout winter and spring, but for the first five critical days of her western offensive. Once the bombing of German targets was authorised our heavies began night attacks on oil plants and marshalling yards east of the Rhine. But after three nights part of the heavy bomber force was taken off these tasks and, in order to assist the Allied armies, was directed to attack enemy concentrations and communications behind the battlefront, that is, west of the Rhine. From then on until the Dunkirk evacuation was completed the main strength of our heavy bomber force was devoted to this behind-the-battle bombing; only on six nights was a small proportion devoted to attacks on oil plants and railway marshalling yards. After Dunkirk the heavy bombers were again concentrated on oil—but only for one night. With the opening of Germany's new offensive all were again devoted to attacks on enemy concentrations and communications behind the battlefront.

The object of bombing strategic targets in Germany was a four-fold one, namely:

(1) to reduce the enemy's total resources of oil;

(2) to disorganise his lines of communication, especially railways on which he must rely for long-distance supply of his armies;

(3) to compel him to hold back from the battle fighters for home defence;

(4) to divert his bombers from France by inducing retaliation on England.

None of these results was obtained. The attack on oil plants was not heavy enough to inflict seriously damaging loss, and in any case it is now known that German oil resources were under-estimated. The attack on the enemy's lines of communication was not sufficiently sustained to prevent the comparatively quick repair of damage done. The German air force was not diverted from its task of collaboration in the land campaign; only after the French armistice did the *Luftwaffe* turn from France to make serious attacks on England. In fact it is clear that our bomber force was not nearly strong enough in 1940 to affect for long the course of large-scale land fighting. Three hundred and thirty-four bombers were lost in the attempt to do so. How far they delayed the final decision cannot be assessed.

It is equally clear that the fighter forces were not strong enough to perform all the tasks that were asked of them. The fighter is a defensive weapon only in the sense that attack is the best method of defence—its aggressive name well describes its character. It is designed to protect from air attack by fighting the enemy's aircraft wherever they are found—'to cleanse the sky'. In 1939 the Air Staff calculated that sixty squadrons were needed to defend Great Britain, but when the German offensive began we had only fifty-three and of these six were in France, four more were to be sent there as soon as fighting started, and two were earmarked for Norway. Only forty-one squadrons remained then for home defence—two-thirds of what were needed. Nevertheless the original six squadrons in France were increased to the equivalent of sixteen by the end of the first week's fighting. On May the 20th what remained of the Air Component fighters in northern France had to be transferred to fight from English airfields, but this did not reduce the number we employed, for there they were augmented by the squadrons of No. 11 Group. As the battle in France neared the coast, and throughout the nine days of evacuations, squadrons were almost continuously engaged. After Dunkirk, when the new German offensive began, the three squadrons with the Advanced Air Striking Force were increased to five, while squadrons in England again joined in the fighting which was within their range after refuelling near Rouen. During the course of the campaign forty-three fighter squadrons were engaged—only ten of the fifty-three squadrons which we had when fighting started were, in the end, not used in the campaign, and of those two were based in Norway, three were night-fighters and two were re-equipping and non-operational.

The tasks which fighters were asked to perform were exacting:

(1) to protect our own troops and our Allies from enemy air attack;

(2) to defend their own airfields and other bases and key positions from enemy bombers;

(3) to protect our own aircraft in their bombing attacks and reconnaissance;

(4) to protect troops and shipping during evacuation.

The squadrons employed could not possibly do all these things everywhere and at all times. Neither the Army, nor the Navy, nor our Allies had the measure of protection for which they looked (though they had more than they always realised), for the fighter forces employed were not numerically strong enough to keep the *Luftwaffe* at bay. But, again, what was done should be measured not against some theoretical or desirable standard but against the magnitude of the tasks set.

In the first ten days they gave effective cover to the British Expeditionary Force as it advanced to the Dyle and withdrew, fighting, to the Escaut, but out of 261 Hurricanes employed in these operations only sixty-six remained when the Air Component was transferred to England. In addition, fighters of the Advanced Air Striking Force did all they could to protect the medium bombers in their daylight attacks. In the fighting to cover evacuation from Dunkirk, the squadrons of Fighter Command played a splendid part, setting out day by day to find and fight an enemy in greater strength. Had the *Luftwaffe* been allowed to circle unhampered over Dunkirk, as it had done over Warsaw and Rotterdam, evacuation might well have been stopped. Instead German reports constantly record our fighters' interference and only in two days out of nine could the *Luftwaffe* seriously hinder the Navy's work. If our fighters could not do all that the Army and Navy wished, they helped substantially to make evacuation possible. As mentioned above, all but ten of our total fighter squadrons were engaged. They lost 474 aircraft—more than half the total number of fighters with which we had started operations on May the 10th.

Unlike some of the bombers that were unsuited to the operations which they had to undertake, the Hurricane and Spitfire fighters proved their excellence. They enabled our pilots to fight with success enemy formations of greater numerical strength and in individual combat (which the *Luftwaffe* sought to avoid) to obtain a confident mastery.

Nearly half of the total aircraft available to Coastal Command were also employed in the campaign. The first task of Coastal Command was to patrol the seas which surround Great Britain in order to give early notice of enemy surface ships, U-boats and E-boats using these waters or approaching our shores and to protect our shipping convoys in home waters. The responsibility for this coastal protection (which included torpedo or bombing attacks on enemy ships) was divided between three groups of which No. 16 Group (covering the coastal area from, roughly, Flamborough Head to Weymouth) was chiefly concerned. Throughout the campaign an arduous series of patrols over the English Channel and the North Sea was maintained and when evacuation was in progress the five squadrons of the Group were strengthened by the attachment of squadrons from No. 18 Group and from the Fleet Air Arm. Coastal reconnaissance, the protection of ships engaged on evacuating troops, and collaboration with Fighter Command in covering, first, the Dunkirk bridgehead and, later, other evacuation ports on the west coast were then their principal tasks; but minelaying operations and attacks on the enemy's coastal batteries and other land targets were also undertaken in response to specific requests by the Admiralty.

Coastal Command's No. 16 Group, with additional squadrons under its command, had an average daily total of seventy-three aircraft available in May, 1940, rising to ninety in June. During the campaign forty-six were lost or irreparably damaged.

To complete the overall picture of the part which the Royal Air Force played in this campaign it is necessary not only to show the magnitude of the task which it attempted but also to realise the difficult circumstances in which it fought.

The Government's pre-war conception of what would be the role of our air forces in a war with Germany required the Royal Air Force to plan accordingly. When war was declared and an army was sent to France, it was still believed that the Allies could remain on the defensive till their forces were built up. In such a war their primary tasks would have been the maintenance of increasingly heavy and sustained attack on strategic targets in Germany, the provision of air protection for troops who held the front, and the air defence of Great Britain. For these tasks they prepared—not for a war of rapid movement. When the French front was broken and a war of movement was forced on the Allies, the Royal Air Force was required to devote a major part of its strength to the assistance of Allied land forces, a task for which it had not been primarily designed, equipped or organised.

Much less had it been cast to play such a role in a long, fighting withdrawal, when it was necessary to adjust plans frequently and to change bases in conformity with a rapidly changing situation on the ground; when it was difficult to maintain the quick communications which alone make possible effective collaboration with land forces; when transport was short, airfields inadequate, and the means to lay down temporary air strips had not yet been devised; and when the enemy's advance had cut the Allied armies in two and the command of air operations had in consequence to be divided.

These were the circumstances in which the Royal Air Force had to fight in this campaign. And though it did much damage to the enemy and contributed notably to the salvation of the British Expeditionary Force, it could not otherwise greatly affect the course or outcome of the battle in France. It took a good toll of German aircraft and pilots and to that extent weakened the blow which the enemy delivered subsequently in the Battle of Britain. That it did not accomplish more was due to the fact that preparation for a possible war with Germany had been based on a strategic conception which was radically at fault.

Fighting under this great initial handicap, the Royal Air Force showed again the courage and skill of its pilots and the excellence of their latest type of fighter aircraft. And it gained experience which proved to be of great value in later and more successful campaigns.

CHAPTER XXIII

CONDUCT AND CONSEQUENCES
OF THE CAMPAIGN

FROM a military point of view we could hardly have been in worse circumstance to make war on Germany than we were in 1939. We had neither the trained manpower nor the equipment to wage such a war successfully. A last-minute change of policy and hurried preparations could not recover years which had been lost while the British Government hoped that 'by guileful fair words peace may be obtained'—and Germany organised for war. A study of military operations leads back at every point to the conclusion that military failure in 1940 was directly due to the governmental policy of pre-war years.

Up to the last minute it had been the purpose of the British Government to fight Germany (if the need arose) on sea and in the air, though two British divisions would serve with the French armies as a token of our co-operation in the land fighting. As a direct consequence of this policy the early programme of rearmament provided for the armament and equipment of only a small army, while the Royal Air Force was neither trained nor equipped for large-scale collaboration with land forces. When this policy was changed in the spring of 1939, both Services had to embark on tasks for which, under the Government's previous policy, they had not been prepared. Nine months of inactive 'warfare' enabled them to reduce their handicap but could not alter the fact that numerical weakness was but one aspect of inadequate preparation and equipment for the Government's new policy. Even for its size the British Expeditionary Force was weak in armour and anti-tank guns and the Royal Air Force was short of aircraft designed for close co-operation with land forces.

The numerical weakness of the Allies was in some measure hidden by arithmetic, for a true estimate of strength is not obtained by adding together the divisions of allied armies. Divisions may be worth much or little and in any case their total value depends not only on their number but on the efficacy of arrangements for their command. This campaign proved, as many others have done in the past, that allied armies are not welded into a whole by the mere designation of a supreme commander. Here nothing effective was done to counterbalance the advantage which Germany possessed in an army which was organised and staffed at every level by men trained on a common doctrine, speaking the same language, following a single tradition and owing allegiance to a single-minded command. The weakness of the Allies which derived from pre-war policies was thus accentuated by inadequate arrangements for control of the forces which they had available.

This weakness of the overall control was due first to the Belgian adherence to neutrality, for until hostilities had begun there could be no planning of a Supreme Command which would include the Belgian Army. It was due, secondly, to the fact that arrangements to co-ordinate the actions of the French First and Seventh Armies and the British Expeditionary·Force stationed between them were also neglected. The goodwill and mutual understanding which had developed between General Georges and Lord Gort during eight months of preparation had to be sacrificed at the moment when it was most needed by the appointment, after battle was joined, of a 'co-ordinator' without defined authority or any integrated staff. This step was largely ineffective. Control, in so far as it was exercised at all, was tentative and slow when speed and decision were essential. The weakness of overall control was due, thirdly, to the weakness of the Supreme Command itself.

It is not the purpose of this history to discuss the part which the French Army played in a campaign that affords many examples of its fighting qualities. But inasmuch as the British Expeditionary Force served in turn under General Gamelin, General Weygand and General Georges, it is impossible to review British operations without taking into account the influence of the French commanders under whom these were fought.

Three decisions of General Gamelin affected the British operations, two indirectly and a third directly. The first two were his decisions that the French Seventh Army on the British left should adventure unsupported into Holland and that the comparatively weak Ninth Army should form the hinge of the Allied advance into Belgium. The third was his order to move forward to the Dyle. The Seventh Army's excursion served no useful end and wasted what would have been a valuable reserve; the use of the Ninth Army as a pivot for the Allied advance facilitated the fatal break-through of Rundstedt's armies. The unwisdom of these two measures was proved by events. Whether or not it was wise to order the advance to the Dyle is open to argument.

At first sight it may seem to have served German plans to have the Allies as far forward as possible, so that once their line was breached on the Meuse Rundstedt's armies would have room to sweep round their exposed flank. Some critics have indeed been quick to suggest that the Allies 'fell into a German trap'. There is, however, nothing in contemporary German documents to suggest that any trap was set. The German High Command did indeed assume that the Allies would fulfil their promises to Belgium and move to her assistance when she was attacked. They took that prospect into account in their planning, but it would possibly have served them better had we stayed on the French frontier. The position of Holland would hardly have been affected, for the French Seventh Army did little to delay her conquest in five days. But the position of Belgium would have been very different. Had she known that we were not coming to her aid, her resistance would have seemed hopeless. Had the Allies not been stationed on the Dyle, Bock's armies, after breaking through near Maastricht, could have driven straight to Brussels and could have reached the French frontier in a few days. As it was it took them eighteen days to break the Belgian resistance and so uncover the British left, and they did not reach the coastal sector of the French frontier till May the 29th. By then the British Expeditionary Force had begun withdrawing to England.

It is equally difficult to see that the Allies would have been better off had they remained on the French frontier. Certainly they would have been saved some losses and much fatigue. But Bock's armies would also have reached the frontier with less loss and less fatigue. At the coast his troops would have been within eight miles of Dunkirk and it is impossible to say how long the French Seventh Army (assuming also that it had been put in on the British flank) could have held the frontier between Halluin and the sea. It is fair to assume that Rundstedt's armour could still have broken through the French Ninth Army had it remained on the frontier. Unless the French had then shown far greater ability to launch effective counter-attacks promptly, he too might have reached the Channel coast at least as quickly as he did. The French First Army and the British Expeditionary Force would still have been cut off from the armies south of the Somme–Aisne line, and if so, the French First Army and the British Expeditionary Force would still have been contained and there could have been no evacuation from Dunkirk.

Leaving out of account the promises given to Belgium (which General Gamelin certainly felt to be binding) it still seems probable that his decision to advance to the Dyle was a wise one, though its value was discounted by his unwise use of the French Seventh and Ninth Armies.

In this connection there is in the British war archives a report, written early in October 1939, by General Sir Edmund Ironside, then Chief of the Imperial General Staff, which makes it hard to understand General Gamelin's mind. Sir Edmund had just returned from a visit to French General Headquarters, where General Gamelin had explained to him the form which he expected German action to take. General Gamelin 'expected a pinning down attack on the Maginot Line ... He expected this to be accompanied by an attack across the western frontier of Luxembourg into the Ardennes, sweeping south of the Meuse ... against the whole length of the Belgian frontier, south of the Meuse to Namur, then across the Meuse and south of the Sambre to Charleroi. The German right would extend out perhaps to Valenciennes'. Sir Edmund added 'General Gamelin spoke with great clarity'. It will be realised that this was almost an exact forecast of the place and direction for the main weight of attack which the German Command finally adopted and of the course which the battle actually took. No other record of this conversation seems to have been made and no one at the time seems to have recognised its significance, and in his final conclusions on probable enemy action General Gamelin is reported to have held the opposite view—that an attack with large forces through the Ardennes was impracticable. It was indeed only on the latter theory that the use of the French Ninth Army opposite the Ardennes 'south of the Meuse to Namur' could be justified.

After having ordered the advance to the Dyle, General Gamelin took no further part in the northern campaign till the day of his departure, holding that the conduct of the battle was solely the concern of General Georges (page 114). In the first ten days, when disaster threatened, he thus showed an unwillingness to accept responsibility which was markedly at variance with the action of Marshal Foch in the First World War; he regarded the functions of a Supreme Commander, when battle was joined, as purely advisory.

During those first and most fateful ten days General Georges was in fact in sole command of the northern armies. He acted quietly and firmly but the situation was soon largely beyond his control. It is impossible to read without emotion of the fearful experience through which the French Army moved in those ten days, or to ignore the anguish and strain which they involved for General Georges. 'The greatest confusion reigned in the quadrilateral Landrecies–Solre-le-Château–Hirson–Guise. The fighting units and services sweeping back from the Meuse, the civilian population streaming out from the Ardennes and reinforcements coming from the north and west ... all crossed each other's paths. On the initiative of officers on the spot, resistance formed, held, or vanished. Orders of the Command no longer reached those who were to carry them out.'[1] It is difficult to imagine what it meant to be in General Georges' place when three German armies, well equipped, skilfully organised and firmly controlled, drove into the French confusion with a leading phalanx of six armoured divisions and a great weight of

---

[1] Lyet, p. 65. See Appendix II, p. 394.

following troops, and 'orders of the Command no longer reached those who were to carry them out'.

Though General Georges could not stem the flood, he worked unceasingly to fill the breach till General Weygand was appointed, on the 20th of May, to succeed General Gamelin. From then on it was General Weygand who tried to order the shape of Allied operations.

General Weygand's courage and ability were proved in a long and distinguished career of public service, but time was against him in his last campaign. His physical energy in those days of crisis impressed all who met him, but he was seventy-four when he was recalled to command the Allied armies. Even as he arrived the German break-through to the Channel was completed and the Allied forces cut in half. North of the breach the French First Army, the British Expeditionary Force and the Belgian Army were contained; to the south the French Ninth Army was virtually destroyed, the Second badly cut up, the remaining armies stretched between Switzerland and the English Channel, and there was no substantial reserve behind their tenuous defence. The situation which General Weygand faced was indeed appalling.

Five days after his appointment he decided that his available forces on the Somme–Aisne front were 'insufficient for a tactical retreat'. 'We shall not have the required reserves,' he said, 'to operate a retreat in good order from the Somme–Aisne line to the Lower Seine–Marne line. No organised retreat is possible with such numerical inferiority.'[2] It is an unusual military theory that insufficiency of forces makes it impossible to withdraw from a line which is obviously too long for them to hold successfully.

By May the 25th General Weygand seems indeed to have reached the sad conclusion that nothing could be done which might avert defeat. For while he continued to issue orders enjoining resistance 'on the spot' and 'to the end' he warned his Government that a 'definite break in the defensive position on which the French armies have been ordered to fight without thought of retreat' would mean that 'France would find it impossible to carry on usefully a military struggle to protect her soil'.[3] When he said this, the front was so thinly held in places that the enemy could effect a breach whenever he chose to employ sufficient force.

It would have needed a very great soldier indeed, arriving in the theatre of war only on May the 20th, to realise the condition of the Allied armies and the capabilities of their commanders and staffs; to size up the strategic and tactical situation and match it with a practical plan; so to inspire commanders that his plan was translated into action—and to do all at a speed which outpaced the rapid

[2] Lyet, p. 117. See Appendix II, p. 394.
[3] Ibid., p. 118. See Appendix II, p. 394.

movement of adverse events. Perhaps the time had already passed, by May the 20th, when the situation could be retrieved. Perhaps in all the circumstances it never had been possible. For it would certainly have involved a radical shortening of the French front and, with this, the abandonment of some French soil; and such measures would have needed not only far-sighted, firm and most courageous leadership from the military commander but also the political backing of a strong and single-minded government, such as France did not then possess. Neither on the military nor on the political side was the requisite leadership forthcoming.

Whether General Weygand was right or wrong in deciding that the armies south of the Somme and the Aisne had no power to withdraw and could but fight where they stood, till the long line was breached and it became 'impossible to carry on usefully a military struggle', the very fact that the Supreme Commander held this view meant that defeat was certain. A leader who believes that the impossible can be done is on the way to its achievement, but a leader who does not believe that what is needed can be done makes sure of failure. When in due course the French armies had to retreat, it was done piecemeal and on compulsion by the enemy. It was too late then to regroup them more effectively or indeed to use all the forces which had been kept so long, stretched out so far, that when pressure was applied the strained line broke. The fact that French troops obeyed his orders to fight on the spot and to the end, with no thought of retreat, and suffered grievously in doing so, only underlines the tragedy of his position.

It has been said of General Weygand that time was against him, and certainly his chief failure was a failure to realise the supreme importance of timing in this campaign. He went to Ypres to arrange the north and south counter-attack—the Weygand Plan—on May the 21st, but left without seeing Lord Gort and with nothing definite settled. General Billotte, the man on whom action depended, was mortally injured that night, but General Weygand did not appoint his successor till four days later. The northern arm of the double counter-attack which General Georges was planning on May the 18th, which General Gamelin had 'suggested' on the 19th and General Weygand discussed on the 21st, was eventually planned for the 26th. But by the 25th no co-ordinating arrangements had yet been made with forces which were supposed to attack simultaneously from north and south. In any case it was by then too late to cut through the path of the German Army Group A; the counter-attacking divisions of the Allies would themselves have been open to attack on both flanks by stronger enemy forces. The Weygand Plan failed to materialise, not because Arras was evacuated and not because the 5th and 50th Divisions were sent north to the Ypres front, but because General Weygand was not able to launch it while it might still have been effective. Even so it could not have succeeded. As a strategic conception it was the copybook answer, but in the light of what is now known of the strength, situation and condition of Allied and enemy forces, it is clear that it was not a practical plan.

Two other examples of dilatory decision which affected British operations may be quoted. General Weygand was informed on the 26th that the British Government had ordered the evacuation of the British Expeditionary Force and he sent for Admiral Darlan on the same day to discuss French evacuation. But British evacuation had been in full swing for three days before he decided to evacuate French troops. Again, in the subsequent fighting south of the Somme the French IX Corps, and with it the 51st Division, was lost at St Valery simply by delay, for General Weygand only ordered the French IX Corps to move south of the Seine when it was too late to do so. Indeed, General Weygand consistently allowed himself to be overtaken by events, so that his orders were impracticable by the time they were issued. Moreover, inability to act promptly or to move quickly often rendered orders abortive. The French High Command was beaten not only by superiority of numbers and equipment but by the pace of enemy operations, by inability to think ahead, and by unwillingness to relinquish quickly territory which could no longer be defended successfully.

The smaller British operations, on the other hand, were characterised by foresight and by the speed with which orders were carried out. The Arras garrison got away because they moved immediately on receipt of orders. The transfer of the 5th and 50th Divisions to the Ypres front fulfilled its purpose because they moved at once and speedily when the move was ordered. The withdrawal to the coast was achieved because, when it was ordered, the divisions moved each night more quickly than the enemy could follow. The troops got away from Dunkirk because Lord Gort's Staff planned in time for such a possibility, and the War Office and the Admiralty, forewarned of a need which might arise, started at once to prepare for the contingency.

Lord Gort's task was of course far smaller and more limited than that of the French Supreme Commander or of General Georges. There can be no comparison with men who bore such incomparably greater burdens. If any comparison were to be made, it should be with the French army commanders. But that too would be a false comparison, for Lord Gort's responsibility was of a different order. He should be judged by what he did, not by any comparison with others.

To appraise fairly Lord Gort's command of the British Expeditionary Force it is necessary to recognise that he exercised it under

x

most unusual conditions. He commanded the largest army this country had ever sent abroad before hostilities began, for there were nearly half a million men in France by the beginning of May. More-over, a considerable increase of the fighting force was intended, and all plans were framed with this expansion in view. General Head-quarters for such an army must be a large and complex organisation. It is concerned not only with matters of high policy and the general conduct of operations, but also with such matters as supply, equip-ment, training, reinforcements, billets, bases and communications, medical services and hygiene, pay, discipline, and many other highly specialised departments required to administer and maintain an army overseas. The Commander-in-Chief cannot, of course, con-cern himself with any but major decisions, but there are enough of these to occupy much of his attention. Moreover, General Head-quarters is the instrument through which he not only exercises his command but at the same time maintains relations with his own Government and with our Allies—matters which also need much of his time and thought. These multiple duties impose a heavy responsi-bility on him and his staff, and in a force of any considerable size it is usual to group the corps in armies, each under an army com-mander with his own Staff, responsible for the day-to-day conduct of operations under the direction of the Commander-in-Chief. It was planned to appoint two army commanders as soon as the strength of the British Expeditionary Force rose to four corps, but this stage had not been reached when hostilities began, and throughout the campaign Lord Gort played the double role of Commander-in-Chief and army commander. In so far as he was occupied by the duties of one office he could give less time and attention to the duties of the other. In consequence both suffered.

But he had a third role to play which increased still further the difficulties of his position. While he was directly responsible to his own Government for the safety and employment of the British force, he was at the same time responsible to the French High Command. In the one position he was supreme; in the other he was subordinated, three-deep, under French commanders and had to shape his actions to French orders. In these circumstances it is hardly surprising that he left many important decisions to his corps commanders (two of whom were senior to him in service) and that, in consequence, they missed the close grip of their affairs which could have been exercised by an army commander unencumbered by the rival duties of a commander-in-chief. Moreover, this looseness of control was accen-tuated by a faulty organisation of his headquarters; when he separated his Command Post from General Headquarters the distri-bution of responsibilities and staff was not well planned and led to loss of efficiency in both.

Yet this criticism hardly diminishes Lord Gort's achievement. In the fearful position in which his army was placed, with Allies on either flank whose support was crumbling hour by hour, he quickly perceived the probable outcome; he chose the course which alone offered any practical way to avoid disaster and allowed nothing to deflect him from it. All his major decisions were both wise and well-timed. His judgement, not only of what was needed at the time but of what would be needed in the days ahead, was never at fault. He foresaw that, *if* the French could not quickly close the breach in their front, the Allied armies in the north would be contained by the enemy and would be forced to fall back to the coast and attempt evacuation. He saw when Arras must be held and when it must be given up. He realised the importance of the Canal Line in his rear, days before it was attacked, and by the show of opposition which he improvised there he bluffed the enemy into a pause which gave him time to build a more solid defence. He saw the danger of a break in the Ypres front in time to avert it. He initiated the organisation of the Dunkirk bridgehead and the planning of partial evacuation before ever the policy of general evacuation was accepted by his own Government or by the French. Indeed, his sense of timing is apparent throughout the campaign and neither Cabinet suggestion nor French exhortation could persuade him to attempt operations which he considered ill-timed or impracticable. It may be argued that he owed a great deal to the advice and skill of his Chief of the General Staff and of his corps commanders, and especially to General Brooke. That is true. It may be said that Rundstedt's pause on the Canal Line probably helped to save him. That also is true. But it is the business of a Commander-in-Chief to make full use of the wisdom of his Staff and the skill of his Commanders and to take full advantage of his enemy's mistakes. It is to Lord Gort's credit that he did both. And if his conduct of operations made big demands on his corps commanders, his judgement in trusting them was abundantly vindicated.

Lord Gort, though well versed in military history, was not an intellectual man nor had he the mind of an administrator; by temperament and training he was a fighting soldier—probably happiest when he was a regimental officer. He had an insatiable appetite for information on anything that concerned a soldier, and his mind was stored with exact and often peculiar knowledge. No detail was too small to excite his interest, for soldiering was not only his profession but his hobby. He had, moreover, a Guardsman's respect for precision, and any incorrectness distressed him. Before the fighting began he would come to a conference with his corps commanders armed with a list of small things which he had observed as needing to be put right, when matters which seemed to them to be of greater moment required his attention. Moreover, his boyish nature and somewhat impish sense of humour sometimes obscured the underlying seriousness of his purpose. He had had no previous experience of a high command and assumed command of the British Expeditionary Force with the liveliest anticipation; the fact that all his army's fighting was in withdrawal was a cruel disappointment of his hopes. Yet he bore it with fortitude, and when dire catastrophe threatened he stood unmoved and undismayed, a dauntless example to those who stood with him.

The history of the British Expeditionary Force is in reality a multiple biography, for the formations it comprised were but groups of men, of all arms and of every rank. Together they did what has been told. The history is their history; the honour belongs to them all; deliverance was earned by their skill and valour. And yet it is also true that they owe their deliverance largely to Lord Gort's leadership. His good judgement and strong courage averted the disaster which must have come upon them had the enemy been allowed to pierce their defence or to cut them off from the sea. He thus made it possible to deny the enemy something of the fruits of victory.

Circumstances denied Air Marshal Barratt any similar opportunity to lay his mark on the air operations of this campaign. Appointed Commander-in-Chief of British Air Forces in France and instructed to support both British and French Armies, he was soon separated from the former and was insufficiently equipped to meet all the needs of the latter; and after the battle had lasted for little more than a week, his command was progressively drained away till most of our air forces fighting over France were stationed on English airfields and controlled from England. Moreover, the size and composition of air forces employed in the campaign were determined from time to time by the Government and were subject to Cabinet decisions which changed as the overall war situation changed. Demands from France had to be weighed with requirements for the air defence of Britain and other commitments of the Royal Air Force, and an examination of British air policy would involve the discussion of matters which lie outside the scope of this volume. For though they radically affected Air Marshal Barratt's command, such matters lay outside the sphere of his control.

It must already be clear from the account of the campaign that the squadrons of the Royal Air Force which were employed did all, and more than all, that could be expected in the circumstances in which they fought. Throughout the campaign they gave of their best to the British Expeditionary Force and to our Allies. To do more was beyond their power.

It must always be difficult to maintain considerable air forces in effective operation during a long withdrawal which involves frequent moves and the successive use of airfields limited in number and in part indifferently equipped. In this case it was only made possible by the conduct and control of much of the air fighting from England. Air Marshal Barratt, in personal association with the French High Command, saw at close quarters the tragedy which was overtaking France and felt keenly the inability to give all the help which the French required. But if he had had command of every aircraft which Britain then possessed, the result of the campaign could not have been changed, since the battle was not won for Germany by their air force, which played an important but only secondary role. Subsequent events have proved that British air policy was abundantly justified, for it is now clear that, had home defence been still further weakened by the expenditure of larger air forces in support of France, not only would the Battle of France still have been lost but a few months later we must also have lost the Battle of Britain.

The casualties of the Royal Air Force were 1,526 killed in action, died of wounds or injury, lost at sea, wounded, injured or made prisoners of war. Of these a very high proportion were pilots and aircrews. Nine hundred and thirty-one aircraft of the Royal Air Force failed to return from operations, were destroyed on the ground, or were irreparably damaged.

The extent to which the Royal Air Force was adequately equipped for the tasks which were laid upon it has already been discussed in the previous chapter. The Army was on the whole well equipped. There was some shortage of mortars and anti-tank rifles, and of mortar, anti-aircraft and anti-tank ammunition and, inevitably, improvised units which helped to hold the western flanks were but ill armed. Apart from this the most serious handicaps to the operations of our fighting force were the absence of even a single armoured division north of the Somme, the inadequacy of wireless equipment and insufficient provision for air reconnaissance and observation. In a swiftly moving battle rapid communication is essential. In this campaign means for this were inadequate.

So small an army as the British Expeditionary Force could not, however, have done more than it did had it been perfectly equipped. Its front was never broken. It fulfilled the task laid on it by the French High Command. It stood between the French First Army and the Belgian Army in the path of Bock's advance. So long as it was fully engaged in doing this it could not also do something else; the closing of the breach in the French front to the south had to be done, mostly, if at all, by the French. It was only when it had become clear that the French could take no effective steps to close the breach and the Belgian defence was on the point of collapse that the British Government ordered withdrawal to the coast for evacuation. By that time no better course was open.

Withdrawal is a valid operation of war; ability to withdraw when occasion warrants is often a necessary prelude to eventual victory. But a long fighting withdrawal is also one of the most difficult operations of war, for it taxes severely the moral and physical strength of the troops and the skill and steady courage of their commanders. The withdrawal from the Dyle to the Escaut was done well, but both flanks were then covered by the French and Belgian Armies. In the final withdrawal the enemy were attacking both in front and in rear with far stronger forces than those whom they contained. The British withdrawal to the coast will rank high in military annals by any test of planning, discipline or performance, notwithstanding some local confusion. If anyone questions this let him look again at the German map for May the 24th and the situation maps for May the 26th and the days which followed.

In August, 1940, German divisions training for the invasion of England were provided with a report prepared by the German IV Corps, which, in Bock's Sixth Army, had fought the British Expeditionary Force from the Dyle to the coast. It deals mostly with technical details of British fighting methods, but this is the general verdict which it pronounces on its own experience; the underlining (by use of italics) follows the German original:

> *The English soldier* was in excellent physical condition. He bore his own wounds with stoical calm. The losses of his own troops he discussed with complete equanimity. He did not complain of hardships. *In battle he was tough and dogged.* His conviction that England would conquer in the end was unshakable. . . .
>
> The English soldier has always shown himself to be a *fighter of high value.* Certainly the Territorial divisions are inferior to the Regular troops in training, but where morale is concerned they are their equal.
>
> In defence the Englishman *took any punishment that came his way.* During the fighting IV Corps took relatively fewer English prisoners than in engagements with the French or the Belgians. On the other hand, casualties on both sides were high.[4]

British Army casualties were, in fact, 68,111—killed in action, died of wounds, missing, wounded and prisoners of war; a further 599 died as a result of injury or disease. In the casualties of the Royal Navy during this period it has not proved practicable to distinguish those which were attributable to the campaign. The casualties of the Royal Air Force have already been quoted.

The Army's material losses were very heavy. Large quantities of ammunition and supplies were of course consumed or expended in battle. By the time fighting ended, most of the armoured fighting vehicles—tanks, armoured cars and carriers—and considerable quan-

---

[4] See Appendix II, p. 394.

tities of transport, arms and equipment had been destroyed in action or damaged in conditions which made their repair impossible. But all artillery, vehicles, equipment and stores that reached the coast with the main British Expeditionary Force had to be destroyed or left behind and, although a large number of the fighting troops who were evacuated brought home their personal weapons, many who came from the beaches were unable to do so. In subsequent evacuations from ports south of the Somme some stores and equipment were brought away, but much was left behind. The cost of the campaign in material is indicated by the following figures:

	Shipped to France (September 1939– May 1940)	Consumed and expended in action or destroyed or left behind	Brought back to England
Guns . . .	2,794	2,472	322
Vehicles . .	68,618	63,879	4,739
Motor Cycles .	21,081	20,548	533
Ammunition (tons).	109,000	76,697	32,303
Supplies and Stores (tons) . .	449,000	415,940	33,060
Petrol (tons) . .	166,000	164,929	1,071

Only thirteen light tanks and nine cruiser tanks were brought back to England.

To the material cost of the campaign must be added the losses of aircraft, naval vessels and shipping which have already been indicated in the course of this and the previous chapters.

The loss to the Allied cause implied by the conquest of France, Belgium and Holland cannot be measured exactly. Nor can the partial loss of our maritime control of the narrow seas, which resulted from the enemy's occupation of the French, Belgian and Dutch coasts. The adjoining sketch maps show graphically the growth of Germany's hold on the continent of Europe during this first year of the war.

Yet our grievous losses do not give the whole picture. More important in the long run than the losses which the Services had sustained were their gains in experience and in confidence. The men of the British Expeditionary Force came back with a conviction that on reasonably equal terms they could defeat the enemy. The Royal Air Force knew that man for man they could defeat the much-advertised *Luftwaffe*. The Royal Navy had triumphantly proved their ability to control the use of home waters. The Allied armies had indeed suffered a serious defeat. They had been neither well enough prepared, well enough equipped, nor well enough commanded to meet an enemy who was better placed in all three respects. Yet so far as Britain was concerned the three fighting Services had together defeated the enemy's intention to destroy the British Expeditionary Force, and the Services and the Nation behind them faced the future with unshaken courage and a will to fight on which had been toughened and tempered in the fires of adversity. Though Britain and the Commonwealth countries now stood virtually alone they were undismayed, for they were confident that Hitler could neither subject nor destroy the spirit of the British peoples. For them the immediate effect of the campaign was to strengthen their sense of unity and purpose—to consolidate foundations on which were built the forces of final victory.

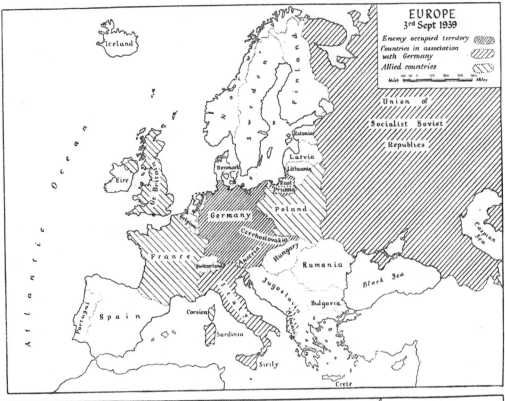

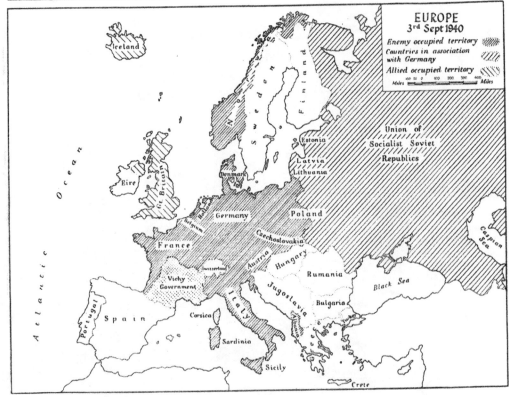

The Planning and Conduct of
the German Campaign

THE PLANNING AND CONDUCT
OF THE GERMAN CAMPAIGN

THE military operations by which Germany conquered Holland in five days, Belgium in eighteen and France, supported by Great Britain, in forty-six, fell short of complete success in that they failed to prevent the withdrawal of over half a million men to fight another day. German military apologists, meditating in captivity after their conspicuous victories of 1940 had been eclipsed by their still more notable defeats of later years, have attributed the success of 1940 to professional skill and its partial failure to the amateur interference of Adolf Hitler. Contemporary German documents do not confirm this simple explanation of events, and as they provide more certain evidence of where responsibility lay than memories likely to be weakened by subsequent strain, the conclusions reached in these notes are drawn wholly from contemporary records now in the Allies' possession. These show that part of the credit for success belongs to the amateur, though most of it to the professionals; and that responsibility for the element of failure rests mainly on professional soldiers, in so far as it was not due to the fighting qualities and skill of the Allies.

By concentrating for the offensive larger and better furnished forces than France and Great Britain could muster at that time, Germany ensured some initial success, but the spectacular pace at which three countries were conquered, while due partly to this preponderance of German forces, owed much to good planning and to the skill with which their operations were conducted. On these two matters the following notes supplement what has been described in the course of the preceding chapters.

The chief German protagonists and the positions they filled in the chain of command are shown in Appendix III.

Brauchitsch, the Commander-in-Chief of the German Army, was an ambitious regular soldier who had played a leading part in the rebuilding of the army. He owed his position to Hitler, and his sense of duty and obligation made him accept his master's orders; but his professional integrity impelled him to advocate firmly any military course which he deemed to be right and he resented the Führer's interference in matters which he regarded as his own responsibility. There were times during this campaign when his temper was sorely tried, for Hitler was apt on occasion to pay less attention to his advice than to that of his subordinate commander, Rundstedt.

There is not much evidence by which to measure the importance óf the part played by his Chief of Staff, Halder. He was a hard-working and efficient staff officer but entries in his personal diary are coloured not only by dislike and distrust of Hitler, but by cynical and sneering references to Brauchitsch, to whom as Chief of Staff he owed complete loyalty. Some of the opinions expressed display poor judgement and after the war his contradictory statements show him to be an unreliable witness. But notes which he made at the time are likely to be accurate if not unbiased.

Rundstedt, the commander of Army Group A, was one of the ablest soldiers in the German Army. He too had played an important part in the army's reconstruction and although he had little sympathy with Nazi leaders he gave them support and he was more successful than Brauchitsch in his personal relations with Hitler. In this he was helped by having done well in Poland, and, as will be seen, by holding independent views on the plan and conduct of the campaign in France and Flanders to which Hitler was sympathetic while Brauchitsch was not.

Bock, the second army group commander principally concerned in the northern campaign, was a less distinguished soldier than either Brauchitsch or Rundstedt. Like them he was a Prussian and a regular soldier, but his rise had been due to zeal and industry rather than to natural talent, and there is nothing very striking in his handling of Army Group B. The British Expeditionary Force was not concerned in the operations of Army Group C.

And over them all was Hitler with, as his instrument, the High Command of the Armed Forces (O.K.W.) under Keitel. Hitler needs no description here. Of his military talent this campaign shows little beyond a natural aptitude to appreciate strategy and to realise the importance of timing. He initiated little and when he interfered with the conduct of the campaign it was only to support Rundstedt rather than Brauchitsch. He was anxious to appear to the German people and to the world as a great military leader, architect of the victory of German arms, and his only rival for such military honour could be the Commander-in-Chief of the Army; he had no similar reason to be jealous of Rundstedt.

In military matters the head of O.K.W. was little more than a secretary to Hitler. Keitel was a regular soldier who had served through the First World War without distinction. But afterwards, when the professional soldiers of the Army offered a hard core of resistance to Nazi Party domination, Keitel had proved a welcome soft spot, applauding Nazi leaders and openly adoring the Führer. He was given appointments of some political importance in the High Command and throughout his subsequent career he was completely subservient to Hitler, who found him a useful tool. He was a competent pianist and politically shrewd, but he had no claim to be

COLONEL-GENERAL VON BRAUCHITSCH

COLONEL-GENERAL VON BOCK

COLONEL-GENERAL VON RUNDSTEDT

taken seriously as a soldier. The Army nicknamed him 'Lakeitel'
—'the little lackey'.

Jodl, Chief of the Operations Staff at O.K.W., also a Hitler's man,
was a better soldier than Keitel but in the operations of this campaign O.K.W. played no significant part. Their orders were merely
O.K.H. decisions dressed up so as to appear as 'the Führer's orders',
except when they similarly endorsed the orders or followed the
advice of Rundstedt.

The Planning of the Campaign

The decision, taken on completion of the war against Poland, to
attack the Allies (with whom Germany was at war) and Holland and
Belgium (whose neutrality Germany was pledged to respect) was
unquestionably Hitler's; the German Army General Staff and the
leading generals were opposed at that date to the opening of a
German offensive against the Allies. They argued that it would in
the end pay better to wait till the Allies took the offensive. From a
purely military point of view, however, the German offensive when it
opened proved to be well timed; in this case the amateur appreciated
the military situation rightly while the professional soldiers misread it.

On September the 27th, 1939, Warsaw having fallen, Hitler announced his decision to attack in the west, and a directive ordering
preparations for the new offensive was issued on October the 9th.
The plan of attack—Plan Yellow—was prepared by the Army
General Staff and was issued on October the 19th. There is no contemporary evidence to suggest that Hitler was concerned in its preparation. This first version of Plan Yellow stated that the attack
would be made on the northern wing of the western front through
Holland, Belgium and Luxembourg. Its aim would be 'to defeat as
strong a portion as possible of the French and Allied Armies' and 'to
win as much as possible of Holland, Belgium and Northern France as
a base offering great possibilities for air and sea warfare against
England and also as a wide protective area in front of the Ruhr'.[1]
After this statement of the general intention, however, the order dealt
only with operations against Holland, Belgium and Luxembourg by
which the northern frontier of France would be reached; the shape of
subsequent operations was not indicated.

The sketch maps (page 342) reproduce, first, a plan of the projected
operations issued with this order. It will be seen that the main
objective of the initial attack was to secure central Belgium. There
the forces of three armies composing Army Group B were to be
concentrated north and south of Brussels so that the Army Group

---

[1] Army Group A War Diary appendices. See Appendix II, p. 395.

would be in position to continue the attack westwards without delay. In the second phase of the attack the armoured and motorised divisions were to be massed on the northern flank for a thrust directed on Ghent and Bruges.

But on October the 25th the Commander-in-Chief of the Army (Brauchitsch) and his Chief of Staff (Halder) were summoned by Hitler to discuss the coming operations. Jodl noted at the time that in the course of the discussion Halder 'wanted to concentrate all armoured formations in the direction of Ghent in order to have a strong flank to carry out encirclement'; but that Hitler said he had 'originally wanted to use all forces south of Liége'[2] with the idea of a break-through in the direction of Reims and Amiens. After a second meeting Hitler said he would think the matter over and give his decision on October the 28th. He is reported by Jodl as having said on the 26th that, while an attack north of Liége should aim at 'the Belgian fortress,' a concentration south of Liége should break through in a western direction and destroy the Anglo-French Armies. On the 28th Brauchitsch and Halder were given his decision. The most important task, they were told, was to defeat great parts of the Anglo-French Armies and as a secondary consequence to seize the Belgian-French coast; there should therefore be forces disposed to break through both to the north and south of Liége, with a group of armoured divisions in each attacking force.

On the following day a revised plan was accordingly issued giving effect to Hitler's instructions. In this second version of Plan Yellow the intention was '*to engage and defeat as strong a portion of the French and Allied Armies as possible in Northern France and Belgium,* thereby creating favourable conditions for the continuation of the war against England and France on land and in the air'.[3] This was the plan of offensive which the Allies anticipated (page 44). The main attack was to be made by Bock's Army Group B whose Sixth Army would strike westwards through Belgium, north of Liége, while his Fourth Army also attacked westwards but to the south of Liége. On the left of Army Group B, Rundstedt's Army Group A was to defend the exposed southern flank of Bock's advancing armies and farther south a third, Army Group C, under Leeb, would make feint attacks on the Maginot Line to pin down the French divisions there. One hundred and two German divisions were to be used. For Bock's frontal attack forty-three divisions were allotted, including nine armoured and four motorised; for flank defence Rundstedt was given twenty-two infantry divisions and no armour; on the frontier to

---

[2] Jodl's Diary, 25th October, 1939. This and the references in notes 4 and 9 are reproduced in Nuremberg Document No. 1811–PS. (unpublished). See Appendix II, p. 395.

[3] Army Group A War Diary appendices. See Appendix II, p. 395.

the south Leeb was to have eighteen infantry divisions; nineteen divisions were to be held in General Reserve. And since the main emphasis of the attack was no longer to be on the extreme north wing, the attack on Holland was omitted, though the 'Maastricht appendix' would be crossed in the advance on Belgium to the north of Liége. The map issued with this second version of Plan Yellow is also reproduced (page 343). It will be seen that the armoured and motorised divisions were no longer to be concentrated in a single thrust in the north, but were to be divided into two forces striking westwards from central Belgium.

Thus by Hitler's direction the original staff plan to aim at encirclement of the Allied northern flank had been changed to one for a frontal attack on either side of Liége. But Hitler had originally wanted to use all forces south of Liége and the compromise embodied in the new Plan Yellow did not wholly satisfy him. For on the day after the revised plan was issued Jodl noted in his diary 'Führer comes with a new idea about having an armoured and a motorised division attack Sedan via Arlon'.[4]

A much more radical 'new idea' was put forward independently by Rundstedt on the following day. He had returned from Poland to take command of Army Group A on the western front just when the plan of October the 29th was issued. He was not only opposed to any attack at this date, but he thought the revised version of Plan Yellow a bad plan. On October the 31st he wrote two letters to Brauchitsch; one was a reasoned argument to show that 'the operation planned cannot have any decisive effect on the war'[5] and that therefore the Allies should be allowed to attack first. The second letter criticised in detail the plan that had been issued. The success of the operation, he wrote, depended on the *annihilation* of all enemy forces north of the Somme. The enemy had to be cut off from the Somme, not merely pushed back there by a frontal attack. Therefore '*the main effort of the whole operation . . . must be on the southern wing.*'[6] 'The danger point on one hand, but on the other the chance of great success . . .' was with Army Group A.[7]

It was hardly likely that Brauchitsch would at once accept this further and still more fundamental alteration of a plan which had already been changed once to meet Hitler's wishes. He discussed the matter with Rundstedt and the latter's Chief of Staff (Manstein) at a meeting on November the 3rd, and after 'initially rejecting' Rundstedt's proposals[8] finally promised to allot an armoured division

---

[4] Jodl's Diary, 30th October, 1939. See Appendix II, p. 395.

[5] Army Group A War Diary appendices. See Appendix II, p. 395.

[6] Ibid.

[7] Ibid., p. 396.

[8] Army Group A War Diary, 3rd November, 1939. See Appendix II, p. 396.

Y

to Army Group A—probably he had learned of Hitler's 'new idea' of an attack through Sedan. On the 5th orders were issued for the offensive to begin but these were cancelled two days later.

There is no evidence that Hitler was told anything of Rundstedt's revolutionary proposals, but on November the 10th Jodl noted in his diary that the Commander-in-Chief, Brauchitsch, proposed to allot to Army Group A one armoured division, one motorised division and one motorised regiment and that the Führer regarded this force as in his opinion 'too weak' for an attack through Sedan.[9] Accordingly next day an order was issued: 'The Führer has now decreed: on the southern wing . . . a third group of mobile troops will be formed and will advance in the direction of Sedan . . .'[10] A third edition of Plan Yellow was accordingly issued on November the 15th. In this Guderian's XIX Corps of two armoured divisions, one motorised division and two motorised regiments was allotted to Army Group A 'to gain by surprise the west bank of the Meuse at and south-east of Sedan, and thus establish favourable conditions for further operations.'[11] There was, however, no fundamental change of the overall plan for a main frontal attack through the Belgian plain. Brauchitsch was unmoved by Rundstedt's arguments and there is no evidence that they had as yet been reported to Hitler. But Hitler had been cogitating on the possibilities which might open from an attack through Sedan and a further directive was issued on November the 20th which said that, while land operations would be on the basis of Plan Yellow, 'all possible preparations will be made to facilitate a quick shift of the main weight of attack from Army Group B to Army Group A in case greater and more rapid successes are scored there . . . which seems likely with the present distribution of enemy forces.'[12]

Rundstedt, however, was not satisfied, and on November the 21st he and his Chief of Staff attended a conference of army group and army commanders with the Commander-in-Chief. Manstein had prepared a memorandum on the probable course of operations of Army Group A showing that if Bock's forces were drawn northwards in their advance, as seemed likely, Army Group A could not both defend the southern flank against the expected French counter-attack from the south and continue the advance westwards unless its forces were strengthened by the addition of another army. But Brauchitsch remained unconvinced and Plan Yellow was not changed.

---

[9] Jodl's Diary, 10th November, 1939. See Appendix II, p. 396.

[10] *Trial of the Major War Criminals*, Nuremberg, 1947–8. Vol. XXX, Document No. 2329–PS. See Appendix II, p. 396.

[11] Sixth Army War Diary appendices. See Appendix II, p. 396.

[12] *Trial of the Major War Criminals*, Nuremberg, 1947–8, Vol. XXVI, Document No. 440–PS. See Appendix II, p. 396.

On November the 27th Rundstedt and two of his subordinate commanders attended a conference with Hitler at which Rundstedt emphasised the need for a strong southern wing, but there is no evidence that his view received particular attention, though Jodl noted afterwards that Hitler wanted two divisions from O.K.H. reserve to be added to the reserve of Army Group A, their place in O.K.H. reserve being taken by two divisions from the reserve of Army Group B. On the 30th Rundstedt wrote another vigorous letter to Brauchitsch, renewing his request for an additional army. He argued that the armoured corps which he had now been allotted only increased his need for further forces, since it would create an opening which, without an additional army, he would be unable to exploit. In reply he was told that Brauchitsch agreed in the main, but the weight of attack must be focused after the initial assault had shown where it could be placed most effectively.

Manstein then wrote to Halder, again arguing that the main weight of German operations must be on the southern wing, and six days later he was told that Brauchitsch proposed shortly to discuss the question again with Rundstedt. As a basis for the discussion Manstein prepared a revised plan for the conduct of the western offensive, providing in Army Group A not only the armoured corps which had been allotted but the additional army for which Rundstedt was asking. The meeting was held on December the 22nd, but apparently nothing resulted.

On December the 28th a directive was issued ordering the opening of the offensive in the middle of January, subject to weather. The Führer would decide where the weight of the attack was to be concentrated when it was seen where initial success was greatest: nothing was to be done which would compromise his freedom to decide where the main emphasis should then be placed. On this, Rundstedt sent a long memorandum to the Commander-in-Chief for submission to Hitler. In it he argued most ably his concept of the forthcoming campaign which required emphasis to be placed on the left from the outset.

The overall aim, he said, should be 'to bring about a decision in land warfare, to annihilate the Allied forces on land and in the air, to eliminate the continental sword of the English and then, as a second step, to attack England herself by air and sea'.[13] He rejected the 'partial' aim, to defeat the Allies in Belgium and northern France and to occupy the Belgian coastline, as disproportionate to the political strain of an assault on three neutral states and to the military risks taken by the army and air force. It would be equivalent to a renunciation of the attempt to bring the war to a speedy end,

---

[13] Army Group A War Diary appendices. See Appendix II, p. 396.

for this could only be expected if there were a possibility of attacking England decisively after land and air victory in France. The decisive blow against England—i.e. the assault of her Atlantic supply line— would be facilitated only by occupation of the whole French coast- line. From these contentions he went on to argue that the strategy of Plan Yellow would lead to a frontal deadlock on the Somme if not before. However, Brauchitsch refused to submit the memorandum to Hitler; a final decision about the focal point of the attack rested, he said, with the Führer and would be made in accordance with his [Brauchitsch's] suggestions.

Hitler now ordered that the offensive should start on January the 17th. It was realised that the forced landing of a German aeroplane in Belgium on January the 10th (page 32) had given the Allies valuable information on Plan Yellow, but although this created much ado and had various reactions, the plan as previously issued was not changed. Subsequently, however, the offensive was again postponed on account of the weather. A fourth edition of Plan Yellow was issued on January the 30th, and notwithstanding the aeroplane incident it did not differ in material respects from the previous version.

Rundstedt and Manstein continued to press their views and Brauchitsch to refuse their requests, though they secured some additional artillery for Army Group A.

On February the 13th Jodl noted in his diary that after studying a detailed survey of troop dispositions Hitler reopened the question of where the main weight of attack should be placed. 'He says', wrote Jodl, 'most of the gun-armed tanks have been expended on places which are not decisive. The armoured divisions with the Fourth Army can do little in areas where there are obstructions and fortifications. They will come to a standstill at the Meuse, if not before, and will have to be withdrawn. Their absence will then be felt by Sixteenth or Twelfth Army. They should be concentrated in the direction of Sedan, where the enemy does not expect our main thrust. The documents carried by the aircraft which made the [forced] landing have still further confirmed their opinion (the enemy's) that our only concern is to occupy the Channel coastline of Holland and Belgium.'[14]

Jodl then handed over to the Führer 'a summarised report' showing the practicability of placing the main emphasis of attack south of the Liége–Namur line and pointing to the Sedan route as 'a tactical secret path' where surprise might be effected.[15] That after-

---

[14] Jodl's Diary, 13th February, 1940. The portion of the diary which contains this entry and the entries quoted in notes 22, 24 and 25 is reproduced in *Trial of the Major War Criminals*, Nuremberg, 1947–8, Vol. XXVIII, Document No. 1809–PS. See Appendix II, p. 397.

[15] Ibid.

noon Jodl discussed the question with Brauchitsch's staff and 'communicated the Führer's ideas to them'.

On February the 7th and again on the 14th war games were played at which Halder was present. Both pointed to the probability that additional forces would be needed to sustain and follow up an attack in the Sedan area. Whether news of the war game on the 7th had reached Hitler before he made the statement attributed to him by Jodl on the 13th is not known.

About this time Manstein was appointed to command an infantry corps and on February the 17th, before taking up his new command, he and others dined with Hitler. Manstein used the opportunity after dinner to expound the views of Army Group A on the conduct of the projected offensive and he recorded shortly afterwards that Hitler agreed with the views he had expressed. It seems possible that this was the first occasion on which Hitler had an opportunity to get a really full exposition of Rundstedt's proposal to alter the whole plan of campaign by placing the main striking power on the left wing, for Brauchitsch had consistently refused to adopt it or to report Rundstedt's views to the Führer. Whether Brauchitsch learned of what had occurred after the dinner is not known, but on the following day (18th) he and Halder reported to Hitler their intention to shift the boundary between Army Group B and Army Group A and to employ stronger armoured forces in front of the latter, and Hitler approved the proposed change. On the 22nd Halder held conferences at O.K.H. to discuss the fifth and final version of Plan Yellow; it was then issued on the 24th. In it Rundstedt got all, and more than all, that he had asked for. The whole weight of the attack was transferred to the left wing. Hitler, too, was at last satisfied. The plan is shown on page 343.

Credit for the final version of Plan Yellow was subsequently claimed by Hitler, by the General Staff, and by Manstein. To the writer it seems that the chief credit should go to Rundstedt, though how much he owed to his Chief of Staff (Manstein) cannot be known. Hitler sensed from the first the importance of striking south of Liége and felt rather fumblingly that an attack through the Ardennes by Sedan might have results which would necessitate a change of the main centre of effort in subsequent operations; but contemporary evidence shows that Hitler did not see, as Rundstedt did, that from the outset the main weight of attack should be delivered there. It was his dissatisfaction with the earlier plans which led to their amendment and it is to his credit that he was not content till the final and more imaginative version was produced.

Brauchitsch, having produced the original plan and having had it amended by Hitler, obstructed every proposal for its further and more radical alteration; but it seems probable that the arguments of

EVOLUTION OF PLAN YELLOW

AS SHOWN ON MAPS ISSUED BY THE GERMAN HIGH COMMAND WITH THE FIRST,
SECOND, AND FINAL VERSIONS, TO INDICATE THE PLANNED LINES OF
ADVANCE. THE POSITION OF THE ARMOURED AND MOTORISED
FORCES IS NOTEWORTHY.

— Legend —

Letters denote Army Groups

Figures denote Armies

Armoured and Motorised Forces shown thus ◄━━━━━

Army Group Boundaries shown thus ────────

Army Boundaries shown thus ──○──○──○──

Defensive Positions shown thus ┬┬┬┬┬┬┬┬┬

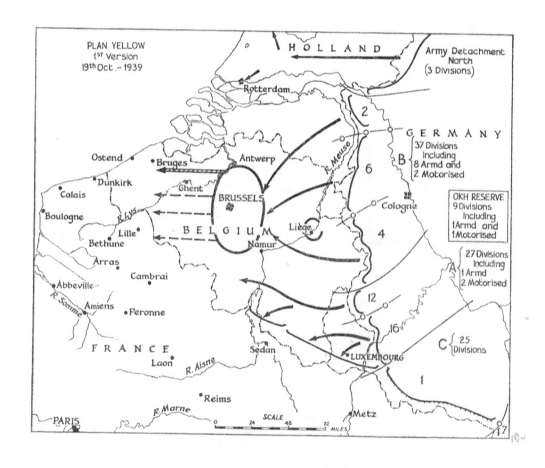

PLAN YELLOW
1ST Version
19th Oct. – 1939

HOLLAND

Army Detachment
North
(3 Divisions)

Rotterdam

GERMANY

B — 37 Divisions
Including
8 Armd and
2 Motorised

OKH RESERVE
9 Divisions
Including
1 Armd and
1 Motorised

A — 27 Divisions
Including
1 Armd and
2 Motorised

C — 25 Divisions

Ostend — Bruges — Antwerp — Dunkirk — Ghent — Calais — Boulogne — BRUSSELS — Cologne — Lille — Bethune — BELGIUM — Liège — Namur — Arras — Cambrai — Abbeville — Amiens — Peronne — FRANCE — Sedan — LUXEMBOURG — Laon — R. Aisne — Reims — R. Marne — Metz — PARIS

R. Meuse — R. Lys — R. Somme

2 — 6 — 4 — 12 — 16 — 1 — 17

SCALE
0   24   48   72
MILES

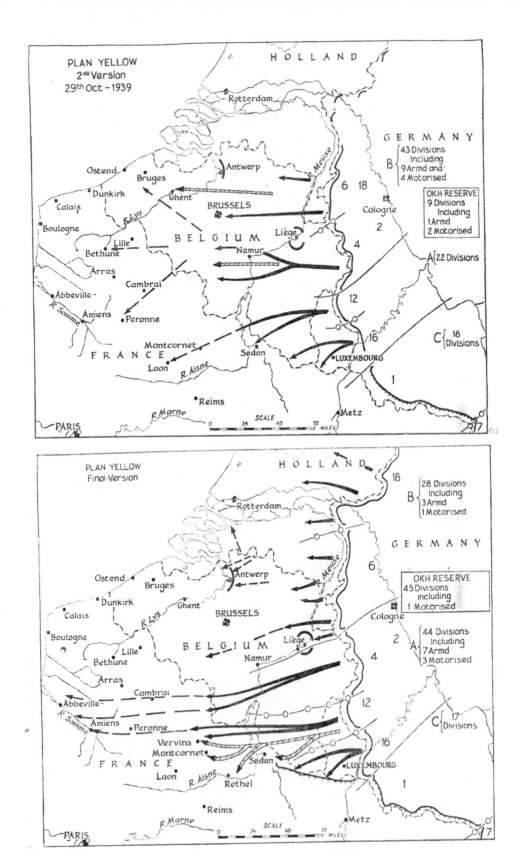

PLAN YELLOW
2ND Version
29th Oct - 1939

HOLLAND

Rotterdam

GERMANY

B { 43 Divisions
Including
9 Armd and
4 Motorised

Ostend
Bruges
Dunkirk
Ghent
Antwerp
Calais
BRUSSELS
R. Lys
Boulogne
Lille
Bethune
Liège
BELGIUM
Arras
Cambrai
Namur
Abbeville
Amiens
Peronne
R. Somme
Montcornet
FRANCE
Laon
Sedan
R. Aisne
LUXEMBOURG
Reims
R. Marne
Metz
PARIS

R. Meuse
6 18
Cologne
2
4
A { 22 Divisions
12
16
C { 18 Divisions
1

OKH RESERVE
9 Divisions
Including
1 Armd
2 Motorised

SCALE
0   24   48   72
MILES

PLAN YELLOW
Final-Version

HOLLAND

Rotterdam

B { 28 Divisions
Including
3 Armd
1 Motorised

GERMANY

18

6

Ostend
Bruges
Dunkirk
Ghent
Antwerp
Calais
BRUSSELS
R. Lys
Boulogne
Lille
Bethune
Liège
BELGIUM
Arras
Namur
Cambrai
Abbeville
Amiens
Peronne
R. Somme
Vervins
Montcornet
FRANCE
Laon
Sedan
Rethel
R. Aisne
LUXEMBOURG
Reims
R. Marne
Metz
PARIS

R. Meuse
Cologne
2
4
A { 44 Divisions
Including
7 Armd
3 Motorised
12
16
C { 17 Divisions
1

OKH RESERVE
45 Divisions
Including
1 Motorised

SCALE
0   24   48   72
MILES

Rundstedt and Manstein and the results of the war games in February had convinced him that it would probably have to be changed once operations started, for he had admitted that the main centre of effort might then have to be switched to the left. When he learnt that Hitler had reopened the question and had expressed dissatisfaction with existing dispositions, he decided to amend the plan so as to put the main weight of the attack in the south from the outset. It is significant that when he reached that position and knew that a redisposition of forces with that aim would have Hitler's approval, he went further than Rundstedt had been bold enough to propose and much further than was provided for in the detailed plan put forward by Manstein in November. As told in Chapter III (page 44) the plan of campaign was radically altered. Two armies (the Fourth and the Second) and most (and eventually all) of the armour were taken from Bock and given to Rundstedt. The main attack was now to be made by Army Group A and the Allied armies in the north were to be cut off and surrounded, not merely pushed back. Thus, while the strategic concept was that which had first been advocated by Rundstedt, the plan in which it was expressed was drawn up by the O.K.H. General Staff. The final dispositions are shown on the adjoining sketch map.

The Conduct of Operations

Notable features of the German campaign were the initial use of airborne troops to get behind an enemy's defence; the use of air forces to assist an army in attack; and the use of armoured divisions in strength to exploit a breach in the enemy's front. The potentialities of all these measures had been recognised in British Service circles, but divergences of opinion on their merits and application had not been resolved, for financial stringency had denied the means for their development. German usage was well ahead of British (or French) practice at this date.

In the German conduct of operations the first point to note is the measure of surprise that was achieved when their offensive, which had long been expected by the Allies, opened on May the 10th. In both November and January when the attack was ordered the Allies were promptly 'alerted' some days before it was timed to begin: in May they were not. Why was this? In the original version of Plan Yellow six days were allowed for the approach-march and final concentration of attacking formations; the offensive was to open on the seventh day. In both November and January the Allies had been warned by the preparatory movement forward of the enemy's troops that an attack was impending. The final version of Plan Yellow

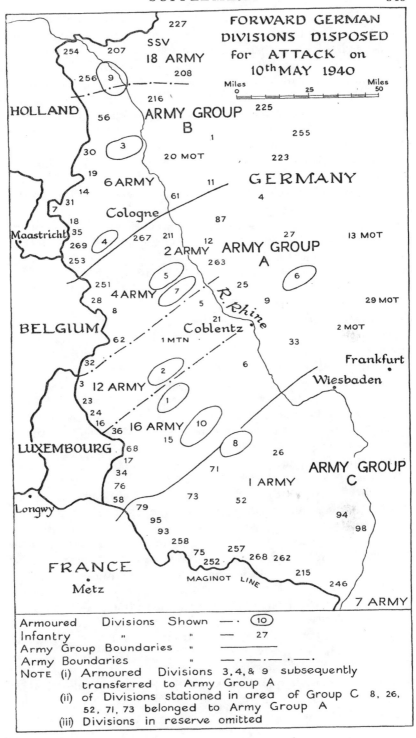

FORWARD GERMAN DIVISIONS DISPOSED for ATTACK on 10th MAY 1940

Armoured   Divisions   Shown   —· (10)
Infantry   "   "   —   27
Army Group Boundaries   "   ⸻
Army Boundaries   "   —·—·—·—·—
NOTE (i) Armoured   Divisions 3, 4, & 9 subsequently
          transferred to Army Group A
      (ii) of Divisions stationed in area of Group C 8, 26,
           52, 71, 73 belonged to Army Group A
      (iii) Divisions in reserve omitted

allowed for no such preliminary moves. They had indeed become unnecessary, for on each of the previous occasions formations had begun moving forward before the order for the offensive was cancelled, and when it was cancelled the troops remained in the positions they had already reached. Thus of the six days' movement originally planned three had taken place. Moreover the fact that the Allies had ordered the 'alert' in November and again in January became known to the German Command and showed them that better disguise of their intentions and greater security were imperative if the Allies were not to be forewarned of an impending attack. In adjusting dispositions to the final plan, therefore, any necessary closing up was effected gradually, so that well before the offensive was ordered the attacking troops were already within easy striking distance of the frontier, as is shown on the adjacent map. When the code word 'Yellow' was issued about midday on May the 9th they could attack at daybreak on the 10th, without further large-scale movements to forewarn the Allies. This time the Allies' 'alert' was only ordered after the enemy attack had begun.

There is nothing particularly significant in the thoroughness of the German organisation: it was more than matched by the Allies in later and larger campaigns. The chief technical innovation was a new reliance on air transport, not only for airborne troops in the opening days but for other purposes throughout the campaign. Advanced armoured formations were regularly supplied with fuel by air and as early as May the 16th a diary notes that the establishment of a forward 'repair shop base' had been initiated and 'two thousand skilled workers are being brought in by plane'.[16] The Allies were not thinking in such terms in May 1940.

In the opening phase of the campaign, German operations went according to plan and little need be added to what has already been told. There were at times delays in road movements caused by Allied bombing and resulting congestion. There were delays in bridge-building from the same cause and with a similar result. And there was controversy about orders to anti-aircraft formations under Luftwaffe control which got in the army's way. But these were all minor affairs which had little or no effect on operations.

Three decisions taken in the course of the campaign in the north had a marked influence on subsequent operations. The first was Bock's decision to attack the right of the Belgian front where it joined up with the left of the British front. As told on page 101, his decision was at variance with orders he had received to put the main weight of his attack in the south. The resulting action was described sourly by Halder as a 'private battle in the area of Audenarde, which

---

[16] Halder's Diary, 16th May, 1940. See Appendix II, p. 397.

will probably cause losses without a return of operational advantage'.[17] In fact it broke the Belgian front and ultimately resulted in the Belgian surrender.

The second significant decision was Rundstedt's decision on May the 23rd to close up his armour on the Canal front before continuing the attack. The third was the closely related order that tanks should not be used to attack Dunkirk.

The significance of these decisions has been magnified by German generals since the war, for they have seen in them a plausible explanation of why the British Expeditionary Force and a part of the French First Army were 'allowed' to escape. Then, by asserting that the decisions were solely Hitler's, they excuse themselves from failure to stop evacuation and lay all blame on him. Whether the amateur Hitler or the professional soldiers were responsible does not much matter to anyone but the German generals who survive. What is important is whether the orders in question did in fact 'allow' the evacuation from Dunkirk, and if so whether a course which would have prevented it was open to the German Army. To understand the German conduct of operations it is necessary to put our after-knowledge out of mind and to see how the situation appeared at the time to the various German commanders.

The German leaders not unreasonably believed that if the Anglo-French forces in the north could be finally contained, their surrender or destruction must inevitably follow. They knew that while encirclement was being achieved some evacuation was going on from Ostend and Dunkirk, but in view of what the Luftwaffe had done at Warsaw and Rotterdam it was assumed that the Luftwaffe could also make these two evacuation ports unusable. That would put an end to evacuation—for the German leaders no more thought that large-scale evacuation could be effected from the beaches than did our own Admiralty and War Office at that time. The important task which remained to the German Army was, therefore, to complete the close encirclement of the Allies with their backs, not to a wall, but to the sea which would serve as well. There were differences of opinion as to how this should be done.

Rundstedt did not consider, on the night of the 23rd, that there was any longer great urgency. The Allies were caught. The Army Group Diary records his opinion that in the north the end was now only a matter of days. What seemed to him to be important was to consolidate his own positions, for he had now five armies extended over a huge area with widely separated fronts to safeguard. French divisions were reported to be moving up against his long southern flank, to the defence of which some twenty-four of his own divisions were already

---

[17] Halder's Diary, 23rd May, 1940. See Appendix II, p. 397.

committed. On his northern flank three divisions were engaged against the French First Army and five against the Arras salient. The high ground north of Arras (the Lorette Heights and the Vimy Ridge), which had been so long fought for in the First World War and to which such importance was attached, was still in enemy hands. In the west the British were landing fresh troops at Boulogne and Calais and two of his divisions were committed at these places. Three of his divisions were approaching the Canal Line and their advanced formations had reached it at Aire that evening, but the line appeared to be defended and it might well prove a difficult obstacle to cross in force. Moreover British columns were reported moving towards it which might be intending a counter-attack on this flank. His armoured divisions were widely dispersed—the 9th near the Somme, the 2nd and 10th at Boulogne and Calais, the 1st fronting Gravelines, the 6th and 8th opposite Aire and the 3rd, 4th, 5th and 7th near Arras. They had already suffered heavily (page 151) and moreover would soon be needed for the coming offensive southwards. O.K.H. had ordered Army Group A to 'wheel with the mobile forces across the line Béthune–St Omer–Calais', but it seemed to Rundstedt that, while clearing up the situation at Arras, Calais and Boulogne and making the defence of the Somme flank secure, it would be wise to close up to the Canal Line but not at present to cross it.[18] Bock's armies on the eastern front—at one point they were only forty miles away—should drive the Allies back till they were caught between two fires. In Halder's phrase Rundstedt's troops were to provide the anvil and Bock's the hammer.

Rundstedt's views were crystallised in a talk (on May the 23rd) with Kluge, the commander of the Fourth Army, who said that 'the troops would be glad if they could close up tomorrow'.[19] He proposed to allow this and Rundstedt agreed. The Fourth Army War Diary subsequently records that Fourth Army 'will, in the main, halt to-morrow in accordance with Colonel-General von Rundstedt's order'. *This entry is timed 6.10 p.m. on May the 23rd.*[20]

Meanwhile, *Bock's* main interest was centred on Belgium and the chance to make a breach between the Belgian and British Armies. He reckoned that he would get better results from that than from an attempt to fight the British in their position on the fortified French frontier. If he could effect and exploit a breach through Belgium and turn the British flank the British would be forced to withdraw from the frontier defences and he could separate them from Ostend— which the Germans regarded as offering the best facilities for evacua-

---

[18] Army Group A War Diary, 23rd May, 1940. See Appendix II, p. 397.
[19] Fourth Army War Diary, 23rd May, 1940. See Appendix II, p. 398.
[20] Ibid.

tion. Thus while Rundstedt was ready to provide the anvil Bock was not at this time in any hurry to play the part of hammer.

The position as *Brauchitsch* saw it is shown on the reproduction of the O.K.H. situation map for May the 24th which is enclosed at the end of this volume, though it must be remembered that the positions of the Allied troops (which have been added) were not marked on the original. Comparison with German formation maps and diaries proves that the O.K.H. map was inaccurate in some respects but that is unimportant—it shows what Brauchitsch believed to be the true position. It was in that belief that he took two decisions. The first was that the encircling attacks should proceed without pause; the second was that they should all be directed by a single commander. He ordered that at 8 p.m. on the 24th Rundstedt's Fourth Army, which contained all the armour and was attacking the British and French forces from the south and west, should come under the command of Army Group B, which was already attacking British, French and Belgian forces from the east. Bock would then command all the forces encircling the Allied armies in northern France and Belgium.

Halder, Brauchitsch's Chief of Staff, thought this order would lead to trouble. His diary shows that he rated his own reputation for sagacity more than his duty of loyalty to his chief, for he noted 'operation order . . . goes out without my signature, to signify my disapproval of the order and its timing'.[21] Rundstedt, too, thought the transfer a mistake but he dutifully issued the necessary orders for its implementation.

At this point *Hitler* comes into the picture. Visiting Rundstedt on the 24th he learned of the 'halt and close up' order which Rundstedt had given eighteen hours before and of Brauchitsch's order for the transfer of command. After listening to the army group commanders' views and without waiting to ascertain the views of the Commander-in-Chief, Hitler endorsed Rundstedt's order and countermanded the order of Brauchitsch.

Jodl, who accompanied Hitler and was present at the meeting with Rundstedt, entered in his notes: 'He [Hitler] is very happy about the measures of the Army Group, which fit in entirely with his ideas. He learns to his surprise that O.K.H. without informing the Führer and the High Command of the Armed Forces [O.K.W.] has subordinated the Fourth Army and a number of divisions to its rear, to Army Group B. Führer is very much displeased and thinks this arrangement is a mistake not only from a military but also from a psychological point of view. Commander-in-Chief [Brauchitsch] is ordered to report and the order shifting the dividing line is rescinded. . .'[22]

Brauchitsch's meeting with Hitler was, according to Halder, 'again

---

[21] Halder's Diary, 23rd May, 1940. See Appendix II, p. 398.
[22] Jodl's Diary, 24th May 1940. See Appendix II, p. 398.

a very unpleasant interview'—which is hardly surprising. Halder (who was *not* present at Hitler's meeting with Rundstedt) says of the halt, ordered by Rundstedt on the 23rd: 'The left wing, consisting of armoured and motorised forces, which has no enemy before it, will thus be stopped dead in its tracks by the direct orders of the Führer!'[23]

Thus the four military leaders, namely the Commander-in-Chief of the Army, his Chief of Staff and the two army group commanders concerned had each a different opinion as to how operations should be continued. Hitler backed Rundstedt and the outcome is known. What would have happened if Rundstedt had advocated a different policy or if Hitler had supported his Commander-in-Chief can only be matters for speculation, but the more carefully the position is studied the less certain it appears that whatever the Germans had done the result would have been very different. For the action taken on this and the next two days does not of itself explain the German failure to prevent evacuation.

Very early on the 25th O.K.H. issued an order authorising the armour to cross the Canal Line but Rundstedt ignored it (pages 150–151). Later in the morning Brauchitsch saw Hitler. Jodl's note of the meeting is: 'In the morning Commander-in-Chief arrives and asks permission for a thrust by the armoured and motorised divisions from the high ground Vimy–St Omer–Gravelines to the flat terrain to the west [clearly he meant the east]. The Führer is opposed to this but leaves the decision to Army Group A. The latter decline, for the time being, since the tanks are to rest to be ready for tasks in the south.'[24] So the halt continued on the 25th and 26th by Rundstedt's decision.

It was Hitler who intervened on the 26th to order a resumption of the attack. Halder recorded that following a telephone message to the effect that Hitler authorised an advance by the left wing Brauchitsch was summoned to Hitler's headquarters. Of this meeting Jodl noted 'In the morning the Führer sends for the Commander-in-Chief, Army. 18th and 6th Armies are making only slow progress and II Corps in the south is meeting very stiff resistance. The Führer therefore agrees to a forward thrust from the west by armoured groups and infantry divisions in the direction Tournai–Cassel–Dunkirk. . . .'[25]

Hitler's responsibility in connection with the halt has been completely misrepresented. He did not initiate it on the 24th, for Rundstedt had ordered it on the 23rd: Hitler merely endorsed it. He did not maintain it on the 25th and 26th for he had specifically left Rundstedt to decide on the next move. But he *was* personally respon-

---

[23] Halder's Diary, 24th May, 1940. See Appendix II, p. 398.

[24] Jodl's Diary, 25th May, 1940. See Appendix II, p. 398.

[25] Jodl's Diary, 26th May, 1940. See Appendix II, p. 399.

sible for terminating the halt and for the order to resume the attack on the 27th.

There is in the War Diaries much more evidence than can be quoted here of the considerations which determined Rundstedt's action. In view of the vulnerability of his own flanks on May the 23rd, he was seriously worried by information which he read as indicating that the Allies were preparing to counter-attack from north and south. On the morning of the 24th he told Hitler, in effect, that he was strengthening his north-western flank by closing his divisions up to the canal and holding them there, where they would be in 'favourable defensive positions' to meet any Allied attack; at the same time infantry divisions were being brought forward with all speed to take over the defence of the lower Somme. The Second Army was being moved up as a tactical reserve but he would not be able to feel that his southern flank was secure before the 26th. When the 26th came he was not only satisfied with his own dispositions but convinced that an Allied counter-attack need no longer be expected. He therefore went forward to discuss with Kluge the resumption of the advance: he was with Kluge when he learnt by telephone that Hitler had already authorised the crossing of the Canal Line. There is nowhere in any of the diaries even the faintest suggestion that Rundstedt was dissatisfied with this or with Hitler's previous action. Indeed it is impossible to imagine that he could be, since his own policy had been so fully endorsed and his armoured divisions had secured time for maintenance.

In regard to the further order that the armour should not be used in close fighting for Dunkirk, it only followed the general instructions for the use of armoured divisions laid down with great firmness by Hitler before the campaign opened. 'The tank arm must be used for operations for which it is best suited. Under no circumstances must the tanks be permitted to become entangled in the endless confusion of rows of houses in Belgian towns.'[26] There is no good reason to suppose that tanks could have been used with much advantage at Dunkirk. The exposed nature of the surrounding country, the congestion of buildings at each approach, its protection by water ways, flooding and organised defence made it a very unsuitable place for attack by tanks. It is noteworthy that at the time neither Guderian nor Kleist *when they saw the position at close quarters* thought that tanks should be used to attack Dunkirk. (Page 208.)

In any case the orders under discussion did not alone account for the German failure to stop evacuation; the true explanation is much more complicated. In the first place it was due to the fighting qualities

---

[26] *Memorandum on the Conduct of the War in the West,* dated 9th October, 1939, reproduced in *Trial of the Major War Criminals,* Nuremberg, 1947–8, Vol. XXXVII, Document No. 052–L, p. 480. See Appendix II, p. 399.

of the Allied armies and the skill of British leadership and organisation. On the German side it was due to a number of factors, namely:

(1) The inability of the German armies, after the break-through on the Meuse, to pierce anywhere the Allies' defence north of the breach, or to attack in such strength as to prevent them from carrying out their planned withdrawals.

(2) Rundstedt's failure to take the Arras salient until it was evacuated on the 24th, to secure the high ground between Arras and the La Bassée Canal till the 25th, to break the Canal Line there before withdrawal to the coast was ordered on the 26th, to exploit the Aire bridgehead during that time or thereafter seriously to interfere with our planned movements.

(3) Bock's inability to exploit the gap on the British left when the Belgian front was broken.

(4) The mistake of the High Command in thinking that Ostend was our most important evacuation port, so that it was bombed more heavily than Dunkirk till after the Belgian surrender.

(5) Failure of the Luftwaffe, in face of Royal Air Force opposition, to prevent the Royal Navy from using Dunkirk and the beaches for large-scale evacuation.

(6) And finally the German Army's failure to reduce the Dunkirk bridgehead before the whole of the British forces there and most of the French forces had been evacuated.

All these combined to explain the German failure to prevent 'Dunkirk', though they leave Germany a large balance of success as the general result of the campaign. Neither the orders of Hitler nor those of anyone else 'allowed' the British Expeditionary Force and much of the French First Army to escape. The plain truth is that the German Army and Air Force did their utmost to prevent it but failed. It was a failure of the professional soldiers and the Army High Command, but it was as much a failure of the fighting troops as it was of the generals. It was not due to any orders initiated by Hitler. The only significance of his small part in the northern phase of operations was his support of Rundstedt as against Brauchitsch. How far that was due to military and how far to political considerations cannot be determined.

In this history of British operations little need be added to what has already been told of the subsequent German offensive southwards, which opened on June the 5th and ended with the surrender of the French Army on June the 25th. What is chiefly noteworthy is the speed with which the German divisions were regrouped and reconditioned, the ability with which a second large and complicated operation was planned and carried through, and the fact that full advantage was taken of their superiority of numbers in order to overwhelm quickly their weaker opponents.

Germany won her land victories primarily by the skilful use of armoured and motorised divisions. The campaign demonstrated vividly the change which armour and mechanised transport had effected in modern warfare. These two, supported by aircraft, completely altered the pace of operations. More than that, they made anything like the long-continued static warfare of 1914–18 practically impossible. No widely extended front can be made so strong that it cannot be breached somewhere, but so long as the exploitation of a breach depended on infantry advancing at foot pace, with the supporting artillery horse-drawn, it was possible for the defence to re-form behind the breach before penetration had gone too far. There is no similar possibility when a large armoured force can advance through a breach and in one day penetrate for a depth of 50 miles, with motor-borne infantry keeping pace with it. All then must depend on the strength of reserves available for prompt counter-attack.

The Germans massed their armour in order to exploit a breach, to penetrate and overrun rearward areas, and to seize places of tactical importance for motorised infantry to hold till slower-moving infantry divisions could occupy them. The tank is essentially a weapon of attack or counter-attack and, in either case, to be fully effective must be concentrated in appropriate weight and accompanied by sufficient infantry. Too many of the Allied tanks were misused in support of static defences or were expended on counter-attack in 'penny packets', and too often infantry support was inadequate.

A notable characteristic of German operations was the effective co-operation between land and air forces. The material damage done by their dive-bombers was not great and was chiefly sustained by troops whose discipline was not of a high order; but the ease with which aircraft were called into co-operation, the speed with which they could give rapidly advancing land forces a useful substitute for artillery support, and the fact that, even if they killed few, they shook the nerve of many, made the German Air Force a valuable partner in land operations.

In the whole campaign the German casualties were 156,556 and they lost much material. Against these losses must be set the great amount of Allied material captured. In the countries they conquered for the time being, they gained resources of manpower, material and territory which helped them to continue and extend the war till the forces against them so grew in strength that the German Army, in its turn, was not only beaten but destroyed.

z

Appendices

APPENDIX I

British Forces Engaged

THE ROYAL NAVY

The following were the principal commands concerned with naval operations in this campaign.

THE NORE
Commander-in-Chief
Admiral The Hon. Sir Reginald A. R. Plunkett-Ernle-Erle-Drax

PORTSMOUTH
Commander-in-Chief
Admiral Sir William M. James

WESTERN APPROACHES
Commander-in-Chief
Admiral Sir Martin E. Dunbar-Nasmith

DOVER
Flag Officer Commanding
Vice-Admiral Sir Bertram H. Ramsay

A full account of the naval ships employed to guard and to carry the British Expeditionary Force to France; to carry out operations off Holland and Belgium; and finally to evacuate our forces from Dunkirk and other French ports belongs to the history of the War at Sea, where the story of naval operations is told in greater detail.

THE ARMY

The lists which follow are not a complete 'Order of Battle'. They give the main composition of the principal fighting formations and Lines of Communication troops, but omit, for considerations of space, details of the administrative and specialist services. It may therefore be well to emphasise the fact that, both in the listed formations and in the rearward organisation which sustained them, the administrative and specialist services played an essential part. Three examples will show this.

The story of this campaign illustrates very clearly the fundamental importance of communications. The responsibilities of the Royal Corps of Signals at every level were very heavy for they were indeed the nerve system of the British Expeditionary Force. They had to provide normal communications within the Expeditionary Force on which the control of operations was entirely dependent and to maintain long-distance communications between General Headquarters, the French High Command

357

and the War Office and Air Ministry in England. Frequent moves greatly increased their difficulties and they were handicapped by inadequacy of wireless equipment.

Though infantry often had to march long distances, it is broadly true that in this campaign the Army moved on wheels and, except for the railways and unit transport, the wheels were provided by the Royal Army Service Corps. They carried troops and their equipment, they carried and distributed ammunition, stores, rations, petrol and mail; they provided transport alike in back areas and at the front for almost every purpose, driving often under most difficult conditions and at times in danger. The Army could not have existed without them.

War diaries and personal accounts of fighting, too detailed for quotation in this history, are liberally sprinkled with praise for the courage and devotion of the medical officers of units at the front, but have less occasion to notice the constructive work of the Royal Army Medical Corps in maintaining the health and hygiene of the troops and all that was involved in the care of the sick and wounded. In fact the Corps provided a complete medical service for half a million men, which included medical officers and trained personnel for units, field ambulances, casualty clearing stations, base hospitals, convalescent depots, ambulances, ambulance trains and hospital ships. It was typical of their spirit and tradition that when the British Expeditionary Force was evacuated and hospitals which could not be cleared in time fell into enemy hands, medical officers and staffs who could have saved themselves remained voluntarily to serve their patients in captivity.

In the Army, specialist and administrative services are performed by the following: the Corps of Royal Engineers, Royal Corps of Signals, Royal Army Chaplains Department, Royal Army Service Corps, Royal Army Medical Corps, Royal Army Ordnance Corps, Corps of Military Police, Royal Army Pay Corps, Military Provost Staff Corps, Royal Army Dental Corps, the Auxiliary Military Pioneer Corps, and the Intelligence Corps.

BRITISH EXPEDITIONARY FORCE
(as organised on 10th May, 1940)

Commander-in-Chief
General The Viscount Gort

Chief of the General Staff   Lieutenant-General H. R. Pownall

Adjutant-General   Lieutenant-General Sir W. D. S. Brownrigg

Quarter-Master-General   Lieutenant-General W. G. Lindsell

G.H.Q. Troops

Royal Armoured Corps
1st Light Armoured Reconnaissance Brigade—Brigadier C. W. Norman
    1st Fife and Forfar Yeomanry
    1st East Riding Yeomanry

2nd Light Armoured Reconnaissance Brigade—Brigadier A. J. Clifton
    5th Royal Inniskilling Dragoon Guards
    15th/19th The King's Royal Hussars

1st Army Tank Brigade—Brigadier D. H. Pratt
    4th and 7th Battalions Royal Tank Regiment

Not brigaded

    4th/7th Royal Dragoon Guards; 12th Royal Lancers; 13th/18th
    Royal Hussars; 1st Lothians and Border Yeomanry

Royal Artillery
    1st and 2nd Regiments Royal Horse Artillery; 32nd, 98th, 115th,
    139th Army Field Regiments; 1st, 2nd, 4th, 58th, 61st, 63rd, 65th,
    69th Medium Regiments; 1st, 51st, 52nd Heavy Regiments; 1st,
    2nd, 3rd Super Heavy Regiments

1st Anti-Aircraft Brigade—Brigadier E. D. Milligan
    1st, 6th, 85th Anti-Aircraft Regiments

2nd Anti-Aircraft Brigade—Brigadier E. W. Chadwick
    60th Anti-Aircraft Regiment
    51st, 58th Light Anti-Aircraft Regiments

4th Anti-Aircraft Brigade—Brigadier J. N. Slater
    4th Anti-Aircraft Regiment
    1st Light Anti-Aircraft Battery

5th Searchlight Brigade—Brigadier E. Rait-Kerr
    1st, 2nd, 3rd Searchlight Regiments

Royal Engineers
    100th, 101st, 216th Army Field Companies; 228th, 242nd Field
    Companies; 223rd Field Park, 19th Army Field Survey, and 58th,
    61st, 62nd Chemical Warfare Companies. In addition there were
    thirty-eight General Construction companies; two Road Construc-
    tion, one Excavator, four Tunnelling companies and one Work-
    shop and Park company; one Field Survey depot; and two Water-
    Boring sections

Infantry
    1st Battalion Welsh Guards

      —Machine Gun
    7th Battalion The Cheshire Regiment; 1st/8th Battalion The Middle-
    sex Regiment; 4th Battalion The Gordon Highlanders; 6th Battalion
    The Argyll and Sutherland Highlanders

      —Pioneer
    6th, 7th, 8th, and 9th Battalions The King's Own Royal Regiment;
    7th Battalion The Royal Norfolk Regiment; 6th Battalion The Royal
    Scots Fusiliers; 1st/6th Battalion The South Staffordshire Regiment

      —Garrison
    9th Battalion The West Yorkshire Regiment

I CORPS

Lieutenant-General M. G. H. Barker

1st Division
2nd Division
48th Division

Corps Troops

Royal Artillery

27th, 140th Army Field Regiments; 3rd, 5th Medium Regiments; 52nd Light Anti-Aircraft Regiment; 2nd Light Anti-Aircraft Battery and 1st Survey Regiment

Royal Engineers

102nd, 107th, 221st Army Field Companies; 105th Corps Field Park and 13th Corps Field Survey Companies

Infantry—Machine Gun

2nd and 4th Battalions The Cheshire Regiment; 2nd Battalion The Manchester Regiment

II CORPS

Lieutenant-General A. F. Brooke

3rd Division
4th Division
5th Division*
50th Division

*(in G.H.Q. reserve on 10th May)

Corps Troops

Royal Artillery

60th, 88th Army Field Regiments; 53rd, 59th Medium Regiments; 53rd Light Anti-Aircraft Regiment and 2nd Survey Regiment

Royal Engineers

222nd, 234th, 240th Army Field Companies; 108th Corps Field Park and 14th Corps Field Survey Companies

Infantry—Machine Gun

2nd Battalion The Royal Northumberland Fusiliers; 2nd and 1st/7th Battalions The Middlesex Regiment

III CORPS

Lieutenant-General Sir R. F. Adam, Bt.

42nd Division
44th Division

Corps Troops

Royal Artillery

5th Regiment Royal Horse Artillery; 97th Army Field Regiment, 51st, 56th Medium Regiments; 54th Light Anti-Aircraft Regiment and 3rd Survey Regiment

Royal Engineers
213th, 214th, 217th Army Field Companies; 293rd Corps Field Park and 514th Corps Field Survey Companies

Infantry—Machine Gun
7th Battalion The Royal Northumberland Fusiliers; 1st/9th Battalion The Manchester Regiment; 1st Battalion Princess Louise's Kensington Regiment, The Middlesex Regiment

1st Division

Major-General The Hon. H. R. L. G. Alexander

1st Guards Brigade—Brigadier M. B. Beckwith-Smith
3rd Battalion Grenadier Guards
2nd Battalion Coldstream Guards
2nd Battalion The Hampshire Regiment

2nd Brigade—Brigadier C. E. Hudson
1st Battalion The Loyal Regiment
2nd Battalion The North Staffordshire Regiment
6th Battalion The Gordon Highlanders

3rd Brigade—Brigadier T. N. F. Wilson
1st Battalion The Duke of Wellington's Regiment
2nd Battalion The Sherwood Foresters
1st Battalion The King's Shropshire Light Infantry

Divisional Troops

Royal Artillery
2nd, 19th, 67th Field Regiments; 21st Anti-Tank Regiment

Royal Engineers
23rd, 238th, 248th Field Companies; 6th Field Park Company

2nd Division

Major-General H. C. Loyd   (to 16th May)
Brigadier F. H. N. Davidson   (acting from 16th–20th May)
Major-General N. M. S. Irwin (from 20th May)

4th Brigade—Brigadier E. G. Warren
1st Battalion The Royal Scots
2nd Battalion The Royal Norfolk Regiment
1st/8th Battalion The Lancashire Fusiliers

5th Brigade—Brigadier G. I. Gartlan
2nd Battalion The Dorsetshire Regiment
1st Battalion The Queen's Own Cameron Highlanders
7th Battalion The Worcestershire Regiment

6th Brigade—Brigadier N. M. S. Irwin (to 20th May)
Brigadier D. W. Furlong (from 20th May)
1st Battalion The Royal Welch Fusiliers
1st Battalion The Royal Berkshire Regiment
2nd Battalion The Durham Light Infantry

Divisional Troops

Royal Artillery
    10th, 16th, 99th Field Regiments; 13th Anti-Tank Regiment
Royal Engineers
    5th, 209th, 506th Field Companies; 21st Field Park Company

3RD DIVISION
Major-General B. L. Montgomery

7th Guards Brigade—Brigadier J. A. C. Whitaker
    1st and 2nd Battalions Grenadier Guards
    1st Battalion Coldstream Guards

8th Brigade—Brigadier C. G. Woolner
    1st Battalion The Suffolk Regiment
    2nd Battalion The East Yorkshire Regiment
    4th Battalion The Royal Berkshire Regiment

9th Brigade—Brigadier W. Robb
    2nd Battalion The Lincolnshire Regiment
    1st Battalion The King's Own Scottish Borderers
    2nd Battalion The Royal Ulster Rifles

Divisional Troops

Royal Artillery
    7th, 33rd, 76th Field Regiments; 20th Anti-Tank Regiment
Royal Engineers
    17th, 246th, 253rd Field Companies; 15th Field Park Company

4TH DIVISION
Major-General D. G. Johnson

10th Brigade—Brigadier E. H. Barker
    2nd Battalion The Bedfordshire and Hertfordshire Regiment
    2nd Battalion The Duke of Cornwall's Light Infantry
    1st/6th Battalion The East Surrey Regiment

11th Brigade—Brigadier K. A. N. Anderson
    2nd Battalion The Lancashire Fusiliers
    1st Battalion The East Surrey Regiment
    5th Battalion The Northamptonshire Regiment

12th Brigade—Brigadier J. L. I. Hawkesworth
    2nd Battalion The Royal Fusiliers
    1st Battalion The South Lancashire Regiment
    6th Battalion The Black Watch

Divisional Troops

Royal Artillery
    22nd, 30th, 77th Field Regiments; 14th Anti-Tank Regiment
Royal Engineers
    7th, 59th, 225th Field Companies; 18th Field Park Company

5TH DIVISION
Major-General H. E. Franklyn

13th Brigade—Brigadier M. C. Dempsey
    2nd Battalion The Cameronians
    2nd Battalion The Royal Inniskilling Fusiliers
    2nd Battalion The Wiltshire Regiment
17th Brigade—Brigadier M. G. N. Stopford
    2nd Battalion The Royal Scots Fusiliers
    2nd Battalion The Northamptonshire Regiment
    6th Battalion The Seaforth Highlanders

Divisional Troops

Royal Artillery
    9th, 91st, 92nd Field Regiments; 52nd Anti-Tank Regiment
Royal Engineers
    38th, 245th, 252nd Field Companies; 254th Field Park Company

12TH (EASTERN) DIVISION
Major-General R. L. Petre

35th Brigade—Lieutenant-Colonel A. F. F. Young (acting 10th–12th May)
          Brigadier V. L. de Cordova (from 13th May)
    2nd/5th, 2nd/6th and 2nd/7th Battalions The Queen's Royal Regiment
36th Brigade—Brigadier G. R. P. Roupell
    5th Battalion The Buffs
    6th and 7th Battalions The Queen's Own Royal West Kent Regiment
37th Brigade—Brigadier R. J. P. Wyatt
    2nd/6th Battalion The East Surrey Regiment
    6th and 7th Battalions The Royal Sussex Regiment

Divisional Troops

Royal Engineers
    262nd, 263rd, 264th Field Companies; 265th Field Park Company

23RD (NORTHUMBRIAN) DIVISION
Major-General A. E. Herbert

69th Brigade—Brigadier The Viscount Downe
    5th Battalion The East Yorkshire Regiment
    6th and 7th Battalions The Green Howards
70th Brigade—Brigadier P. Kirkup
    10th and 11th Battalions The Durham Light Infantry
    1st Battalion The Tyneside Scottish, The Black Watch

Divisional Troops

Royal Engineers
    233rd, 507th Field Companies; 508th Field Park Company
Infantry
    8th Battalion The Royal Northumberland Fusiliers (motor-cycle);
    9th Battalion The Royal Northumberland Fusiliers (machine gun)

42ND (EAST LANCASHIRE) DIVISION
Major-General W. G. Holmes

125th Brigade—Brigadier G. W. Sutton
    1st Battalion The Border Regiment
    1st/5th and 1st/6th Battalions The Lancashire Fusiliers

126th Brigade—Brigadier E. G. Miles
    1st Battalion The East Lancashire Regiment
    5th Battalion The King's Own Royal Regiment
    5th Battalion The Border Regiment

127th Brigade—Brigadier J. G. Smyth
    1st Battalion The Highland Light Infantry
    4th Battalion The East Lancashire Regiment
    5th Battalion The Manchester Regiment

Divisional Troops
Royal Artillery
    52nd, 53rd Field Regiments; 56th Anti-Tank Regiment
Royal Engineers
    200th, 201st, 250th Field Companies; 208th Field Park Company

44TH (HOME COUNTIES) DIVISION
Major-General E. A. Osborne

131st Brigade—Brigadier J. E. Utterson-Kelso
    2nd Battalion The Buffs
    1st/5th and 1st/6th Battalions The Queen's Royal Regiment

132nd Brigade—Brigadier J. S. Steele
    1st, 4th and 5th Battalions The Queen's Own Royal West Kent Regiment

133rd Brigade—Brigadier N. I. Whitty
    2nd, 4th, and 5th Battalions The Royal Sussex Regiment

Divisional Troops
Royal Artillery
    57th, 58th, 65th Field Regiments; 57th Anti-Tank Regiment
Royal Engineers
    11th, 208th, 210th Field Companies; 211th Field Park Company

46TH (NORTH MIDLAND AND WEST RIDING) DIVISION
Major-General H. O. Curtis

137th Brigade—Brigadier J. B. Gawthorpe
    2nd/5th Battalion The West Yorkshire Regiment
    2nd/6th and 2nd/7th Battalions The Duke of Wellington's Regiment

138th Brigade—Brigadier E. J. Grinling
    6th Battalion The Lincolnshire Regiment
    2nd/4th Battalion The King's Own Yorkshire Light Infantry
    6th Battalion The York and Lancaster Regiment

139th Brigade—Brigadier H. A. F. Crewdson (to 22nd May)
    Brigadier R. C. Chichester-Constable (from 22nd May)
 2nd/5th Battalion The Leicestershire Regiment
 2nd/5th and 9th Battalions The Sherwood Foresters

Divisional Troops

Royal Engineers
 270th, 271st, 272nd Field Companies; 273rd Field Park Company

48TH (SOUTH MIDLAND) DIVISION
Major-General A. F. A. N. Thorne

143rd Brigade—Brigadier J. Muirhead
 1st Battalion The Oxfordshire and Buckinghamshire Light Infantry
 1st/7th and 8th Battalions The Royal Warwickshire Regiment
144th Brigade—Brigadier J. M. Hamilton
 2nd Battalion The Royal Warwickshire Regiment
 5th Battalion The Gloucestershire Regiment
 8th Battalion The Worcestershire Regiment
145th Brigade—Brigadier A. C. Hughes (to 15th May)
    Brigadier The Hon. N. F. Somerset (from 15th May)
 2nd Battalion The Gloucestershire Regiment
 4th Battalion The Oxfordshire and Buckinghamshire Light Infantry
 1st Buckinghamshire Battalion, The Oxfordshire and Buckinghamshire Light Infantry

Divisional Troops

Royal Artillery
 18th, 24th, 68th Field Regiments; 53rd Anti-Tank Regiment
Royal Engineers
 9th, 224th, 226th Field Companies; 227th Field Park Company

50TH (NORTHUMBRIAN) DIVISION
Major-General G. le Q. Martel

150th Brigade—Brigadier C. W. Haydon
 4th Battalion The East Yorkshire Regiment
 4th and 5th Battalions The Green Howards
151st Brigade—Brigadier J. A. Churchill
 6th, 8th and 9th Battalions The Durham Light Infantry
25th Brigade—Brigadier W. H. C. Ramsden
 2nd Battalion The Essex Regiment
 1st Battalion The Royal Irish Fusiliers
 1st/7th Battalion The Queen's Royal Regiment

Divisional Troops

Royal Artillery
 72nd, 74th Field Regiments; 65th Anti-Tank Regiment
Royal Engineers
 232nd, 505th Field Companies; 235th Field Park Company

Infantry
    4th Battalion The Royal Northumberland Fusiliers (motor-cycle)

51st (Highland) Division
Major-General V. M. Fortune

152nd Brigade—Brigadier H. W. V. Stewart
    2nd and 4th Battalions The Seaforth Highlanders
    4th Battalion The Queen's Own Cameron Highlanders

153rd Brigade—Brigadier G. T. Burney
    4th Battalion The Black Watch
    1st and 5th Battalions The Gordon Highlanders

154th Brigade—Brigadier A. C. L. Stanley-Clarke
    1st Battalion The Black Watch
    7th and 8th Battalions The Argyll and Sutherland Highlanders

Divisional Troops

Royal Artillery
    17th, 23rd, 75th Field Regiments; 51st Anti-Tank Regiment
Royal Engineers
    26th, 236th, 237th Field Companies; 239th Field Park Company

When the 51st Division moved to the Saar in April, 1940, the following troops were attached to the division:

Royal Armoured Corps
    1st Lothians and Border Yeomanry*
Royal Artillery
    1st Regiment, Royal Horse Artillery (less one battery)*
    97th Field Regiment (one battery)†
    51st Medium Regiment*
Royal Engineers
    213th Army Field Company†
Infantry—Machine Gun
    7th Battalion The Royal Northumberland Fusiliers†
    1st Battalion Princess Louise's Kensington Regiment, The Middlesex Regiment†
    —Pioneer
    7th Battalion The Royal Norfolk Regiment*
    6th Battalion The Royal Scots Fusiliers*

*From G.H.Q. Troops
†From III Corps

Lines of Communication Troops
Major-General P. de Fonblanque

Royal Artillery
3rd Anti-Aircraft Brigade—Brigadier W. R. Shilstone
    2nd, 8th, 79th Anti-Aircraft Regiments
    4th Light Anti-Aircraft Battery

Royal Engineers
104th, 106th, 110th, 212th, 218th Army Troops Companies
In addition there were four Road Construction companies, twelve Artisan Works companies, three General Construction companies, one Map depot, two Engineer Stores (Base) Depots, Engineer Base Workshop, one section Forestry company, and lines of communication depot.

Infantry
4th Battalion The Buffs, 14th Battalion The Royal Fusiliers, 12th Battalion The Royal Warwickshire Regiment, 4th Battalion The Border Regiment, 1st/5th Battalion The Sherwood Foresters
In addition there were two infantry and two general base depots.

With the Advanced Air Striking Force

THE WAR IN FRANCE AND FLANDERS

1939-1940

Erratum

Page 367 : Under the head of " 52nd Lowland Division" *for* 6th and 7th Battalions The Queen's Own Cameron Highlanders *read* 6th and 7th Battalions The Cameronians.

v)

LONDON : H.M. STATIONERY OFFICE 1954

elow)

·/

Royal Engineers
1st Field and 1st Field Park Squadrons

52ND (LOWLAND) DIVISION
Major-General J. S. Drew

155th Brigade—Brigadier T. Grainger-Stewart
7th/9th Battalion The Royal Scots
4th and 5th Battalions The King's Own Scottish Borderers

156th Brigade—Brigadier J. S. N. Fitzgerald
4th/5th Battalion The Royal Scots Fusiliers
6th and 7th Battalions The Queen's Own Cameron Highlanders

157th Brigade—Brigadier Sir J. E. Laurie, Bt.
5th and 6th Battalions The Highland Light Infantry
1st Battalion The Glasgow Highlanders, The Highland Light Infantry

Divisional Troops

Royal Artillery
70th, 71st, 78th Field Regiments; 54th Anti-Tank Regiment

Royal Engineers
      202nd, 241st, 554th Field Companies and 243rd Field Park Company

Defence of Boulogne

20th Guards Brigade—Brigadier W. A. F. L. Fox-Pitt
      2nd Battalion Irish Guards
      2nd Battalion Welsh Guards

Royal Artillery
      275th Anti-Tank Battery, less one troop, 69th Anti-Tank Regiment

Defence of Calais

30th Brigade—Brigadier C. N. Nicholson
      2nd Battalion The King's Royal Rifle Corps
      1st Battalion The Rifle Brigade

      3rd Battalion Royal Tank Regiment
      (all the above from 1st Armoured Division)
      1st Battalion Queen Victoria's Rifles, The King's Royal Rifle Corps
      (motor-cycle)

Royal Artillery
      229th Anti-Tank Battery, less one troop, 58th Anti-Tank Regiment

NOTES ON ORGANISATION AND EQUIPMENT

Since 1940 there have been radical changes in the British Army. It may
be well therefore to add a general indication of its organisation and equipment at the time of this campaign, while emphasising the fact that the
notes have no relevance to the position at any subsequent date. It should
also be recognised that, owing to shortages in 1940, units of the British
Expeditionary Force were not all up to strength or fully equipped in every
respect.

(1) FORMATIONS

G.H.Q. Troops: The troops listed under this heading did not constitute a
      'formation', but were a pool of troops at the disposal of General Head-
      quarters. They were allocated, temporarily or permanently, to corps or
      other formations, or were used for special purposes. The light armoured
      reconnaissance brigades were usually employed in the role of divisional
      cavalry, and most of the artillery shown in G.H.Q. troops was per-
      manently allocated to corps and disposed to cover the corps fronts.
      Thus an infantry brigade in the line was supported not only by the field
      artillery of the division to which it belonged and by the field and
      medium artillery of the corps, but also by the field, medium and heavy
      artillery allocated to corps from G.H.Q. troops.
Corps: Consisted of a headquarters, corps troops and two or more infantry
      divisions. Thus its strength varied from time to time according to the
      number of its divisions.

Infantry Division: Consisted of a headquarters, divisional troops, and three infantry brigades. Its strength was approximately 13,600 of all ranks.

Infantry Brigade: Comprised a headquarters and three infantry battalions and a brigade anti-tank company with nine 25-mm. guns. Its strength was approximately 2,500 of all ranks.

Armoured Division: The establishment of an armoured division in April 1940 provided for a headquarters, divisional troops, two armoured brigades, and a support group which consisted of artillery and two motorised infantry battalions. The 1st Armoured Division, the only one ready for dispatch to France in May 1940, never fought as a complete division.

Armoured Brigade: Consisted of three armoured regiments or three battalions of the Royal Tank Regiment.

Light Armoured Reconnaissance Brigade: Comprised two divisional cavalry regiments.

Army Tank Brigade: Comprised two army tank battalions.

(2) Units

Armoured Regiments

Armoured units of the British Expeditionary Force consisted of mechanised cavalry regiments and battalions of the Royal Tank Regiment. Cavalry were either organised as 'armoured car regiments', 'divisional cavalry regiments', or 'cavalry light tank regiments'. Battalions of the Royal Tank Regiment were either organised as 'armoured regiments' or as 'army tank battalions'.

Armoured Car Regiment: Organised as headquarters and three squadrons, and equipped with 38 armoured cars, each with a light machine gun[1] and an anti-tank rifle.[2] The total strength was about 380.

The 12th Lancers was the only armoured car regiment used in the campaign.

Divisional Cavalry Regiment: Consisted of headquarters and three squadrons equipped with twenty-eight light tanks[3] and forty-four carriers[4]. Each

---

[1] *Light Machine Gun.* (Bren.) Gas operated and air cooled. Fired either from the shoulder and bipod, or from a tripod mounting. Capable of maintaining a high rate of fire—120 rounds a minute—with accuracy. Fed from magazines holding 30 rounds of ·303 ammunition. Weight with bipod 23 pounds. Overall length 45½ inches. Effective range up to 1,000 yards.

[2] *Anti-Tank Rifle.* (Boys.) Calibre ·55 inches, weight 36 pounds, length 5 feet 4 inches. Bullet capable of penetrating light armour up to 500 yards. It had similar firing mechanism to that of the service rifle and was not regarded as a specialist weapon.

[3] The following general characteristics of the tanks referred to may be noted: they varied in detail according to whether they were earlier or later versions.

	Weight	Speed per hour	Armour	Crew
Light Tank	4–5 tons	30 miles	12–14 mm.	3
Cruiser Tank	12–14 tons	18–23 miles	14–30 mm.	4–5
Infantry Tank I	11 tons	8 miles	60 mm.	2
Infantry Tank II	25 tons	15 miles	78 mm.	4

The infantry tank was the 'Matilda'.

[4] *Carrier.* A lightly armoured, open, tracked vehicle designed to carry a light machine gun with a crew of two men and a driver. Having a good cross-country performance carriers provided highly mobile fire-power and they were incorporated in both armoured and infantry units. As they proved to be a valuable means of cross-country transport they were also used for many other purposes.

light tank had two Vickers machine guns and each carrier one light machine gun. The strength was about 480 officers and men and for personal weapons they had 240 pistols, 296 rifles, ten light machine guns and ten anti-tank rifles. The cavalry regiments shown in the list as G.H.Q. troops and those shown in the two light armoured reconnaissance brigades were organised on this basis.

Cavalry Light Tank Regiment: Headquarters, a headquarters squadron and three squadrons equipped with fifty-eight light tanks, five armoured scout carriers and personal weapons. Cavalry regiments listed in the 1st Armoured Division were organised in this way.

Armoured Regiment: Headquarters, headquarters squadron and three squadrons. Equipped with fifty-two cruiser tanks, ten armoured scout cars, and personal weapons. The cruiser tank carried a 2-pounder gun. The total strength was about 575 of all ranks. The battalions of the Royal Tank Regiment shown in the list under the 1st Armoured Division were organised on this basis.

Army Tank Battalion: Organised as headquarters and three squadrons and equipped with 50 'I' tanks, seven light tanks and eight carriers. The infantry or 'I' tank was armed with a machine gun or a 2-pounder gun. Light tanks had machine guns (see above). The strength was about 590; personal weapons were pistols, nine light machine guns and nine anti-tank rifles. Battalions of the Royal Tank Regiment shown in the 1st Army Tank Brigade were organised on this basis.

Artillery
Note: All artillery was tractor-drawn

Field Regiment: Organised as headquarters and two batteries each of twelve guns. Their armament varied. The 18-pounder gun and the 4·5 howitzer were to be superseded by a new 25-pounder gun-howitzer and until this was available 18-pounders were being converted to 25-pounders. At this time field regiments were armed either with 18-pounders and 4·5 howitzers or with converted 18/25-pounders. The strength of a field regiment was approximately 580 officers and men, and for personal weapons they had seventy-five pistols, 113 rifles, fourteen light machine guns and thirteen anti-tank rifles. It was with these personal weapons that many fought as infantry in the last few days of the withdrawal to Dunkirk.

Medium Regiment: Consisted of headquarters and two batteries, each of either eight 6-inch howitzers or eight 60-pounder guns. The new 4·5/60-pounders were just coming into production. The strength was about 650 of all ranks, armed with sixty-eight pistols, 117 rifles, ten light machine guns and nine anti-tank rifles.

Heavy Regiment: Headquarters and four batteries. Each regiment had four 6-inch guns and either twelve 8-inch or twelve 9·2-inch howitzers. The strength of a heavy regiment was about 700 of all ranks, with fifty-three pistols, 205 rifles, ten light machine guns and seventeen anti-tank rifles.

Anti-Tank Regiment: Headquarters and four batteries, each of twelve 2-pounder anti-tank guns or in some cases of 25-mm. guns. The strength was about 540 and their personal weapons were seventy-seven pistols, 182 rifles, sixty-six light machine guns, thirteen anti-tank rifles.

Anti-Aircraft Regiment: Headquarters and three or four batteries, each of eight 3·7 anti-aircraft guns. Personal weapons were pistols, rifles, light machine guns and anti-tank rifles.

Light Anti-Aircraft Regiment: Headquarters and three or four batteries, each of twelve (Bofors) 40-mm. light anti-aircraft guns. Personal weapons were similar to those of an anti-aircraft regiment. The Bofors gun could be set for automatic fire and was capable of firing 120 2-pound shells a minute, for a normal range of up to 1,500 yards.

Light Anti-Aircraft and Anti-Tank Regiment: Planned to consist of headquarters and four batteries, i.e. two batteries each of twelve 40-mm. light anti-aircraft guns and two batteries each of twelve 2-pounder anti-tank guns. The only regiment which went to France (with the 1st Armoured Division), was, however, short of its twenty-four anti-aircraft guns.
The strength of a regiment was about 740, with ninety-six pistols, 168 rifles, sixteen anti-tank rifles and thirty-eight light machine guns as personal weapons.

Infantry

Infantry Battalion: An infantry battalion had a total strength of approximately 780 organised in battalion headquarters, headquarters company and four rifle companies. Its main armament was 734 rifles[5], fifty light machine guns, two 3-inch mortars[6], twelve 2-inch mortars[7] and twenty two anti-tank rifles. It had ten carriers.

Machine-Gun Battalion: Headquarters, headquarters company and four machine-gun companies, each armed with twelve machine guns. These were the Vickers ·303, firing belt ammunition. In addition to these forty-eight machine guns the battalion had, as personal weapons, 175 pistols, 559 rifles and eighteen light machine guns. The full strength was about 740.

Motor-Cycle Battalion: Organised as headquarters, a headquarters company and three motor-cycle companies, and equipped with eleven scout cars, ninety-nine motor-cycle combinations (side-car) and forty-three motor-cycles. The battalion, about 550 strong, was armed with forty-three light machine guns, seventeen anti-tank rifles and nine 2-inch mortars, and had as personal weapons 227 pistols and 335 rifles.

---

[5] *Rifle.* The rifle used by the army at this time was the short magazine Lee-Enfield rifle, Mark III. It fired ·303 ammunition and had a bayonet with a 17-inch blade.

[6] *3-inch Mortar.* Weight, with mounting, 125 pounds. Range 275–1,000 yards. Weight of bomb 10 pounds.

[7] *2-inch Mortar.* Weight 23½ pounds. Capable of firing high-explosive bomb weighing 2½ pounds. or smoke bomb weighing 2 pounds. at a high trajectory. Ranges from 100 to 500 yards.

APPENDIX I

THE ROYAL AIR FORCE

In the Royal Air Force specialised services are not organised in distinct corps. It must therefore be made clear that in addition to the fighting formations shown in the following list, there were also in the British Air Force in France signals, balloon, maintenance and servicing units and medical and other services.

(I) BRITISH AIR FORCES IN FRANCE

Air Officer Commanding in Chief
Air Marshal A. S. Barratt

Senior Air Staff Officer
Air Vice-Marshal D. C. S. Evill

Headquarters—North: Group Captain S. C. Strafford
East: Squadron Leader R. Cleland

AIR COMPONENT
Air Vice-Marshal C. H. B. Blount

No. 14 Group—Group Captain P. F. Fullard

No. 60 (Fighter) Wing—Wing Commander J. A. Boret
Nos. 85 and 87 Squadrons

No. 61 (Fighter) Wing—Wing Commander R. Y. Eccles
Nos. 607 and 615 Squadrons

No. 70 (Bomber Reconnaissance) Wing—Wing Commander W. A. Opie
Nos. 18 and 57 Squadrons

No. 52 (Bomber) Wing—Wing Commander A. F. Hutton
Nos. 53 and 59 Squadrons

No. 50 (Army Co-operation) Wing—Group Captain A. R. Churchman
Nos. 4, 13, and 16 Squadrons

No. 51 (Army Co-operation) Wing—Wing Commander A. H. Flower
Nos. 2 and 26 Squadrons
No. 81 (Communication) Squadron

ADVANCED AIR STRIKING FORCE
Air Vice-Marshal P. H. L. Playfair

No. 71 (Bomber) Wing—Air Commodore R. M. Field
Nos. 105, 114, 139 and 150 Squadrons

No. 75 (Bomber) Wing—Group Captain A. H. Wann
Nos. 88, 103 and 218 Squadrons

No. 76 (Bomber) Wing—Group Captain H. S. Kerby
Nos. 12, 142 and 226 Squadrons

No. 67 (Fighter) Wing—Wing Commander C. Walter
Nos. 1 and 73 Squadrons
No. 212 (Photographic Reconnaissance) Squadron

(II) HOME COMMANDS

Groups principally concerned in Air Fighting in France and Belgium

FIGHTER COMMAND

Air Chief Marshal Sir Hugh Dowding

No. 11 Group—Air Vice-Marshal K. R. Park
Nos. 3, 25, 32, 54, 56, 64, 65, 74, 79, 92, 111, 145, 151, 253, 501, 600, 601, 604, 609, and 610 Squadrons

The following squadrons were also temporarily under operational command of No. 11 Group:

(from No. 12 Group)—Nos. 17, 19, 66, 213, 222, 229, 264, 266, 504, and 611 Squadrons
(from No. 13 Group)—Nos. 41, 43, 72, 242, 245, 605, and 616 Squadrons

Note.—Nos. 3 and 79 Squadrons were sent to the Air Component and No. 501 Squadron to the Advanced Air Striking Force as reinforcements on May the 10th; No. 504 Squadron reinforced the Air Component on May the 12th; Nos. 17 and 242 Squadrons joined the Advanced Air Striking Force as reinforcements on June the 8th, 1940.

BOMBER COMMAND

Air Marshal C. F. A. Portal

No. 2 Group—Air Vice-Marshal J. M. Robb
Nos. 15, 21, 40, 52, 82, 107, 110 Squadrons

No. 3 Group—Air Vice-Marshal J. E. A. Baldwin
Nos. 9, 31, 37, 38, 75, 99, 115, and 149 Squadrons

No. 4 Group—Air Vice-Marshal A. Coningham
Nos. 10, 51, 58, 71, 77, and 102 Squadrons

No. 5 Group—Air Vice-Marshal A. T. Harris
Nos. 44, 49, 50, 61, 83, and 144 Squadrons

COASTAL COMMAND

Air Chief Marshal Sir Frederick Bowhill

No. 16 Group—Air Vice-Marshal J. H. S. Tyssen
Nos. 22, 48, 206, 220, 235, 236, and 500 Squadrons

With the following temporarily under operational control:
(from No. 17 Group)—No. 248 Squadron
(from No. 18 Group)—No. 254 Squadron

The following squadrons of the Fleet Air Arm were also temporarily under operational control of No. 16 Group:

Nos. 801, 812, 815, 816, 818, 819, 825, 826 Squadrons

NOTES ON ORGANISATION AND EQUIPMENT

The following notes refer only to the position during the campaign in France and Flanders in 1939–40. They have no relevance to any later campaign.

FORMATIONS

Group: A formation comprising any number of units, grouped for administrative, training or operational purposes.

Wing: Two or more squadrons grouped for operational purposes.

Squadron: The number of aircraft in a squadron varied according to function—from six in the case of flying boat squadrons of Coastal Command to sixteen in the squadrons of Fighter Command.

EQUIPMENT

Bombers: The aircraft used in this campaign consisted of the following: Battle, Blenheim, Hampden, Wellington, and Whitley. Their normal flying speed was about 200 miles an hour for a round flight of from 1,000 to 1,500 miles. The average bomb load carried was 1,000 pounds though the heavy bombers could carry up to 5,000 pounds for shorter distances. All were armed with ·303 Browning machine guns for their own protection, the number varying from two in Battles to six in Wellingtons. They carried a normal crew of four though Battles had only two.

Fighters: The aircraft used consisted of Blenheim, Defiant, Gladiator, Hurricane and Spitfire. Their speeds varied up to 350 miles an hour, with 'service ceilings' of 27,000 to 37,000 feet and a climbing rate of 20,000 feet in about eight and a half minutes. They were armed with from four to eight ·303 machine guns. Normally fighters were single-seated.

Coastal Command Aircraft: The bomber aircraft used were Anson, Blenheim, Hudson, Wellington and Whitley; torpedo bombers Beaufort and Vildebeeste; flying boats London, Stranraer and Sunderland. The flying boats were able to cruise for up to twelve hours, according to the type of aircraft, at speeds from 86 to 150 knots. They were armed with three to seven ·303 machine guns and carried crews of similar numbers, according not only to the type of aircraft but also to the task on which they were engaged.

In addition the Lysander was used for Army Co-operation.

French and German Texts
quoted in translation

CHAPTER III

Note

(1) *Page* 36

Diese [7 holländische Soldaten] werden als Gefangene zum Schutz gegen feindl. Feuer vor und seitlich der Abteilung mitgeführt.

(2) *Page* 38

. . . la presque totalité des moyens de transport automobiles des groupes de D.C.A. des régiments d'artillerie tractés, et des bataillons de chars modernes. Devant elles opèrent les trois divisions légères mécaniques dont les blindés représentent ce que l'armée française a de plus puissant dans le domaine des unités rapides.

(3) *Page* 38

. . . les IXe et IIe Armées comprennent principalement des divisions de série A et B. Les renforcements en unités des réserves générales sont moins largement calculés et ces unités sont équipées en matériels moins modernes. . . .

. . . les moyens de combat dont disposent les deux divisions de série B qui vont subir le choc sont faibles. Leur encadrement actif est pratiquement inexistant. Elle n'ont pas été aguerries par un séjour au contact de l'ennemi sur le front de Lorraine.

(4) *Page* 39

. . . Il faut remarquer également que le centre de gravité de ces réserves se trouve au G.A.2. alors que ce groupe d'armées n'est pas intéressé dans la pénétration en Belgique.

(6) *Page* 41

Sur la position de résistance où la bataille défensive doit être acceptée, la densité réalisée le 13 mai ainsi que l'organisation générale des moyens sont loin d'avoir atteint le degré désirable si l'on considère que l'attaque est imminente.

(7) *Page* 42

. . . impraticable aux chars et peu propice au déploiement de forces blindées importantes . . .

(8) *Page* 43

A l'aile gauche de la IXe Armée, plusieurs fois en deux jours l'occupation de la position a été modifiée par suite de l'arrivée échelonnée des divisions et de la juxtaposition à l'infanterie de la cavalerie repliée des Ardennes. Il en résulte une mauvaise réalisation des liaisons, un état embryonnaire de l'organisation du terrain, une subordination défectueuse du commandement.

Note

(9) *Page* 43

Malheureusement l'exécution des mouvements de mise en place se poursuit et la bataille se déclenchera alors qu'états majors et troupes ne sont pas encore familiarisés avec leurs nouvelles missions.

(10) *Page* 43

. . . l'effet moral diminue chez certaines (des troupes) les réflexes indispensables au combat.

(11) *Page* 44

La position de la Meuse est forcée sur un front d'une vingtaine de kilomètres. Pour rétablir la situation on s'emploie toute la journée à monter une contre-attaque en direction de Dinant. Mais . . . cette action ne peut se déclencher.

(12) *Page* 45

La situation est *très grave,* car la désorganisation totale des unités bousculées ne permet pas d'escompter leur rétablissement. Face à la brèche, dans laquelle s'engouffrent environ 500 de chars allemands, les réserves immédiates sont minimes . . . Quant aux réserves que le général Georges oriente vers ce point névralgique *elles ne seront pas à même d'intervenir avant plusieurs jours.*

(13) *Page* 46

Ce front de colmatage ne présente le 14 au matin aucune cohésion. Les unités de deux armées sont enchevêtrées, les liaisons mal assurées. *Aucun chef ne coordonne l'ensemble.* . . .

. . . Sur les rives sud de la Meuse, les bataillons de l'extrême aile droite de la IXe Armée sont successivement 'enroulés' par leur droite.

(14) *Page* 46

. . . die feindl. Stellung zwischen Löwen und Namur zu durchstossen, um ein Festsetzen belg./franz. Kräfte in dieser Stellung zu verhindern.

(16) *Page* 54

20.00 Uhr. . . . Die Maastrichtbrücken und Marschkolonnen der 4. Pz. Div. werden vereinzelt von feindl. Bombenflugzeugen angegriffen. Hierdurch entstehen erhebliche Verzögerungen.

(17) *Page* 55

Die feindliche Jagdtätigkeit ist ausserordentlich stark, der Gegner führt in den Abendstunden wiederholt Luftangriffe gegen die Übersetzstellen und hat dabei starke Verluste. Wiederholte Anforderungen von verstärktem eigenen Jagdschutz bleiben bis zu den Abendstunden ohne spürbaren Erfolg.

(18) *Page* 56

bis 20.00 Uhr. . . . Fertigstellung der Kriegsbrücke bei Donchery war infolge starken flankierenden Artl.-Feuers und dauernder Bombenangriffe auf die Brückenstelle noch nicht durchgeführt. . . . Alle drei Divisionen haben während des ganzen Tages unter ständigen Luftangriffen, insbesondere auf die Übergangs- und

Note

Brückenstellen zu leiden. Der eigene Jagdschutz ist unzureichend. Anforderungen bleiben ohne Erfolg.

(19) *Page* 56
  Luftwaffe. (14.5.40). . . . Starke feindl. Jagdtätigkeit, durch die insbesondere die eigene Nahaufklärung stark behindert wird.

(20) *Page* 56
  Luftwaffe. . . . Das Gen. Kdo. verfügt nicht mehr über eine eigene Fernaufklärung; die Pz. Staffeln und die Aufkl. Staffel 3/(H) 14 des Korps sind wegen Ausfall von mehr als die Hälfte ihrer Flugzeuge nicht mehr in der Lage, eine nachdrückliche, weitreichende Aufklärung durchzuführen.

CHAPTER IV

(2) *Page* 60
  La IXe armée est dans une situation critique: tout son front reflue
  . . .

(3) *Page* 60
  . . . Il est absolument nécessaire de ranimer cette armée défaillante. Le général Giraud, dont l'énergie est connue, me paraît désigné pour assurer cette lourde tâche . . .

(4) *Page* 61
  23.30 Uhr. Zum ersten Mal wird dabei die Frage erwogen, dass es notwendig werden kann, die mot. Kräfte an der Oise vorübergehend anzuhalten. Besonders der O.B. betont dabei [sic], dass der Gegner unter keinen Umständen zu einem, auch nur örtlichen Erfolg an der Aisne, oder—später—im Raum um Laon kommen darf. Er würde sich für die Gesamtoperation schädlicher auswirken, als dies durch vorübergehendes 'Abfangen' des Tempos unserer mot. Kräfte der Fall sein werde.

(5) *Page* 62
  Es besteht beim Heeresgruppenkommando kein Zweifel darüber, dass die mot. Verbände bei weiterem Zufassen vor 12. Armee auf die Oise zwischen Guise und La Fère wahrscheinlich mühelos über-schreiten können. Das ist auch Überzeugung und Wunsch der führenden Kommandeure, insbesondere der Generale Guderian und von Kleist. Das damit verbundene Risiko ercheint aber, vom Gesichtspunkt der Gesamtoperation gesehen, nicht tragbar. Die langgestreckte Südflanke zwischen La Fère und Rethel ist—besonders im Raum um Laon—zu empfindlich. Der Angriff gegen sie bietet sich dem Gegner geradezu an . . . Ein vorübergehendes Anhalten der Angriffstèten . . . führt schon innerhalb 24 Stunden zu einer gewissen Absteifung der gefährdeten Flanke.

(6) *Page* 63
  So liege im Augenblick die Entscheidung nicht so sehr im schnellen Vorstoss an die Kanalküste, als vielmehr—unter Freimachung der hier eingesetzten mot. Kräfte für diesen Vorstoss—in schnellster Herstellung unbedingt verlässlicher *Verteidigungs*bereitschaft an der

Note

Aisne, im Raum um Laon und, später, an der Somme. Hierauf seien alle Massnahmen, gegebenenfalls auch unter vorübergehendem Zeitverlust hinsichtlich des Vorstosses nach Westen, abzustellen.

CHAPTER V

(1) *Page 76*

Surpris par une attaque audacieuse au centre . . . alors qu'il s'attendait à une manœuvre par l'aile extérieure renouvelée de 1914, notre haut commandement a, de plus, à faire face à des méthodes nouvelles dont il a sous-estimé l'efficacité sur notre front et dont il ne peut en conséquence prévoir le résultat. Le rythme excessivement rapide imposé par l'ennemi à la bataille lui échappe. Toutes les manœuvres conçues à échéance trop rapprochée, sont déjà dépassées par les événements au moment même de leur transcription en ordres.

. . . En huit jours le commandement n'a pas pu ou n'a pas su modifier suffisamment ses conceptions.

(2) *Page 80*

. . . Div. Kdr. versucht, gesichert durch 1 Panzer und 1 Panzerspähwagen, die abgerissene Verbindung herzustellen, stösst jedoch in Vis en Artois auf schwere feindliche Panzer, die die eigenen Panzer ausser Gefecht setzen, und ist hier mit seiner Funkstaffel mehrere Stunden eingeschlossen.

(3) *Page 80*

Die Verfolgung wurde während des ganzen Tages planmässig fortgesetzt. Während die rechte Marschkolonne auf einen Feind stiess, der nur in der bisherigen schwachen Form Widerstand leistete, traf die linke Marschkolonne erstmalig bei Mondicourt und weiterhin bei Doullens auf eine zäh kämpfende englische Truppe (Bataillon Buffs), welche angeblich—in Le Havre ausgeschifft—seit 3 Tagen in dieser Gegend eingesetzt waren. Der Kampf um Doullens hat die Truppe voll beansprucht. Der Widerstand konnte trotz Einsatz zahlreicher Panzer erst nach etwa $2\frac{1}{2}$ Stunden gebrochen werden.

(4) *Page 80*

ab 13.30 Uhr. . . . Nordwestlich Albert, bei Hédauville, wird von der 2. Pz. Div. eine englische Batterie ohne Munition während einer Felddienstübung gefangen.

(5) *Page 81*

20.V. Die 8. Pz. Div. tritt planmäsig, die 6. Pz. Div. mit einer Verzögerung von annähernd 2 Stunden an . . . Zunächst haben beide Divisionen keine Feindberührung, von etwa 13.00 Uhr ab können sie dagegen nur langsam und in ständigem Kampf mit einem hartnäckig sich wehrenden Gegner Boden gewinnen.

(6) *Page 85*

Beurteilung der Lage: Mit Erreichen der Küste bei Abbeville ist ein erster Abschluss der Operation erreicht . . . Die Möglichkeit einer Einkesselung der Nordgruppe der verbündeten Heere beginnt sich abzuzeichnen.

CHAPTER VI

Note

(1) *Page* 95

Während Panzer-Rgt. 25 den Angriff westlich und ostw. an Warlus vorbei auf Agnez durchführt, wird die Masse der Division überraschend von sehr starken Panzerkräften, denen Infantrie folgt, aus Linie Dainville Süd-u. Südostrand von Arras heraus in der Flanke angegriffen.

Es kommt zwischen 15.30 Uhr und 19.00 Uhr in dem Raum Achicourt–le Bac du Nord–Berneville–Brétencourt–Ficheux–Mercatel–Tilloy zu sehr schwerem Kampf gegen Hunderte feindl. Panzer und ihnen folgende Infantrie. Hierbei erleiden besonders starke Verluste I./S.R.6. unter Major v. Paris und die Pz.—Jäg. Abtlg. 42 unter Oberst Mickl. Gegen die schweren Panzer der Engländer sind die eigenen Paks auch auf nahe Entfernungen nicht wirkungsvoll genug. Die durch sie gebildeten Abwehrfronten werden vom Feind durchbrochen, die Geschütze zusammengeschossen oder überfahren, die Bedienungen grösstenteils niedergemacht.

Schliesslich gelingt es, den sehr schweren Angriff des Feindes durch Abwehrfeuer, vor allem sämtlicher Batterien der A.R. 78, der le. Flak-Abtlg. 86 unter Major Schrader, der 3./Fla. 59 unter Hauptmann v. Hirschfeld, einer 8,8. cm. Battr., Flak 23 u. Teilen der Pz. Jäg. 42 zum Scheitern zu bringen.

(2) *Page* 96

19.45 Uhr. . . . Nachricht . . . vom Durchbruch einer feindl. Pz. Abteilung bei Arras . . .

Folgen . . . Es müssen starke Teile der Divisionen des XIX. A.K. beim Abmarsch des Korps nach Norden in den Brückenköpfen belassen werden, die später beim Angriff auf Boulogne sehr fehlen.

(3) *Page* 97

Ein Angriff der Hgr. A. in nördl. Richtung kommt erst nach Besitznahme des Höhengeländes nordwestl. Arras durch Inf. Div. in Frage.

(4) *Page* 101

Da die Heeresgruppe weiter der Ansicht ist, dass sie ihren Auftrag, den Feind festzuhalten, eher durch einen Durchbruch in Richtung Courtrai als im Festlaufen gegen den Liller Festungsblock erfüllen kann, wird die beabsichtigte Verlegung des Schwerpunkts der 6. Armee um 20.30 Uhr befohlen.

CHAPTER VII

(1) *Page* 107

Il a été indispensable de suspendre la retraite, parce que les unités commençaient à se désagréger par la succession des replis effectués de nuit, néfastes à la discipline.

(2) *Page* 110

Le Roi considérait la situation des armées en Flandre comme

Note

laissant peu ou point d'espoir . . . A la question posée par les ministres:

'Le généralissime français n'a-t-il donc pas le droit d'ordonner cette contre-attaque?', le Roi fit une réponse négative, soulignant qu'en realité l'unité de commandement n'existait pas.

(5) *Page* 112

I. Le groupement de forces dont le Général commandant le Ier Groupe d'Armées assure la coordination au nom du Général Commandant en Chef sur le Front du Nord-Est (Armée belge, Armée britannique, I° Armée française) a pour mission impérative de barrer à l'attaque allemande le chemin de la mer, en vue de maintenir la liaison entre ses Armées, de rétablir la liaison avec le gros des Forces françaises et de recouvrer la disposition de la ligne de communications britannique par AMIENS.

II. L'Armée allemande ne sera contenue, puis battue que par des contre-attaques.

III. Les forces nécessaires à ces contre-attaques existent dans ce groupement, dont le dispositif linéaire est d'ailleurs beaucoup trop dense, savoir:

—certaines divisions de la I° Armée et le Corps de Cavalerie français;

—l'Armée britannique, qu'il y a lieu de porter tout entière à la droite du dispositif en accentuant les mouvements déjà commencés et en étendant le front de l'Armée belge.

Enfin, il faut s'efforcer d'obtenir du Haut Commandement belge la disposition du Corps de Cavalerie belge.

Ces contre-attaques seront soutenues par la totalité de l'aviation britannique basée sur la Métropole.

IV. Cette manœuvre offensive en direction générale du Sud doit être couverte face à l'Est par les forces de l'Armée belge, qui se replient par bonds successifs sur la ligne de l'YSER.

V. Cette couverture doit être complétée par l'occupation et, si nécessaire, par la reprise des passages de la SOMME et le renforcement de la défense des ports de la frontière à la basse SEINE.

Les éléments légers ennemis qui, appuyés par le bombardement des aérodromes et des ports, cherchent à semer le trouble et la panique dans nos arrières entre la frontière et la SOMME sont aventurés et doivent y trouver leur fin.

La plus grande faute d'ensemble commise actuellement est de laisser le réseau routier entier et intact à la disposition de l'ennemi. Tout Commandant de Grande Unité doit donc se saisir dans sa zone de toutes les communications par l'établissement d'un quadrillage complet de points d'appui, sans hésiter à donner à cette zone une profondeur même exagérée.

Les Panzer divisionen allemandes doivent être enfermées dans le champ clos où elles se sont audacieusement lancées.

Elles ne doivent plus en sortir.

Signé: WEYGAND

Note

(6) *Page* 113

III. La mission des Armées reste sans changement. La mission offensive de la VIIe Armée en particulier.

En prévision d'une action allemande par la vallée de l'Oise le Général Commandant en Chef attache le plus grand prix à la constitution aussi rapide que possible de notre couverture sur la Somme de Péronne et d'Amiens. . . .

(7) *Page* 114

Sans vouloir intervenir dans la conduite de la bataille en cours, qui relève de l'autorité du commandant en chef sur le front du nord-est, et approuvant toutes les dispositions qu'il a prises, j'estime qu'actuellement:

1. Il y a lieu, comme il est procedé, de continuer à prolonger vers l'ouest le front de nos armées de l'est et la couverture de Paris et de maintenir la soudure avec le G.A.1.

2. Que, en ce qui concerne le G.A.1. plutôt que de le laisser encercler, il faudra jouer d'extrême audace: d'une part en s'ouvrant s'il le faut, la route de la Somme; d'autre part en jetant des forces spécialement mobiles sur les arrières des Panzer divisionen allemandes et des divisions d'infanterie motorisées qui les suivent. Il semble qu'il y ait actuellement, derrière ce premier échelon, un vide:

3. Préparer avec tous les moyens disponibles, une offensive en direction des ponts de Mezières:

4. Toute l'aviation française et britannique doit actuellement avoir pour but de participer à la bataille; . . .

5. Le tout est une question d'heures.

(8) *Page* 115

. Feind . . . hat am 22.5. seine Stellung am Kanal der Gand und südostw. Gent verstärkt. Vor 6. Armee leistet Gegner, unterstützt von starker Artl., hartnäckigen Widerstand.

(10) *Page* 119

1.30 Uhr Anruf durch Oberst i.G. Schmundt, Adjutant der Wehrmacht beim Führer.

Der Führer will über die Lage bei Arras unterrichtet werden. Dort hat starker Feind versucht, über Arras nach Süden durchzubrechen. Es ist ihm am 21.5 abends gelungen, die 7. Pz.-Div. an wenigen Stellen zurückzudrücken, dann wurde der Stoss aufgefangen. Ein schwächerer Durchbruchsversuch des Gegners zwischen Douai und Arras wurde abgewiesen.

Der Führer fordert, dass alle irgendwie verfügbaren schnellen Truppen in Gegend beiderseits Arras und *westlich* davon bis zum Meer, die *Inf.*-Div. aber *ostw.* Arras eingesetzt werden, um Lage zwischen Maubeuge und Valenciennes zu bereinigen.

Im übrigen sollen alle anderen Inf. Div. der 12. 2., und 16. Armee scharf nach Westen herangeführt werden.

Diese Forderung entspricht den vom Heeresgruppenkommando bereits getroffenen Anordnungen.

Note

(11) *Page* 120

Um 15.00 Uhr trifft Ob.d.H. ein . . .

Ob.d.H. entwickelt alsdann seine Gedankengänge über die Fortsetzung der Operationen im Grossen. Ihre Darlegung unterbleibt hier aus Geheimhaltungsgründen. Jedenfalls wird auf die Bedeutung erweiterter Brückenköpfe bei Abbeville, Amiens, Peronne und in Richtung auf Noyen hingewiesen.

CHAPTER VIII

(3) *Page* 126

Il a été préscrit:

1. de continuer la manœuvre de jonction en cours entre la droite du G.A.1 et le G.A.3 afin de barrer la route de retour aux Divisions blindées allemandes aventurées vers l'Ouest.

2. d'encager l'ennemi en poursuivant la constitution simultanée de barrages sur la Somme d'Amiens à la mer, sur la côte (Marine) et sur le flanc Sud du G.A.1.

II. La manœuvre de jonction pour le G.A.3 consiste à venir border la Somme de Péronne à Amiens inclus de se rebattre vers le N.E. en direction générale d'Albert–Bapaume.

III. En attendant la constitution en cours du Groupement de Cavalerie Altmayer à la gauche de la VIIème Armée, il importe que la Division blindée Evans prenne dès maintenant à son compte avec la fraction actuellement disponible, une action de nettoyage à mener rapidement en direction d'Abbeville. Ultérieurement cette action est à pousser en direction générale de Saint Pol en vue de couvrir la droite du Corps Britannique agissant de la région d'Arras vers le Sud.

Le Général d'Armée Commandant-en-Chef sur le Front Nord-Est
GEORGES.

(4) *Page* 127

I. Les Panzer divisionen se sont aventurées vers la mer en arrière de nos lignes. Il est à prévoir qu'elles vont chercher à reouvrir leur route vers l'Est en attaquant sur le flanc droit du G.A.1. en même temps que celui-ci se bat sur sa gauche.

II. Il importe avant tout de continuer la manœuvre en cours, de faire la jonction du G.A.1 et du G.A.3 et de former le barrage solide qui empêchera le retour en arrière des Panzer divisionen.

III. En même temps que se produit cette jonction de nos forces face à l'Est, il faut donc par tous les moyens de barrages paralyser l'action des Panzer divisionen sur les flancs et sur les arrières.

Organiser immédiatement l'action simultanée du barrage sur la Somme (Détachement Altmayer), sur le flanc droit du G.A.1 (région de Boulogne, Béthune, et au Sud), sur la côte (action de la Marine).

IV. Les Panzer divisionen ainsi aventurées doivent y trouver leur fin.

Signé: WEYGAND.

Note
(5) *Page* 127
    Le Général Aurore fixe comme suit la mission impérative d'Alouette :
    Barrer à l'attaque allemande le chemin de la mer. Rétablir la liaison avec le Gros des forces françaises en vue de recouvrer la disposition des lignes de communication brittanique par Amiens. Contenir puis battre l'Armée allemande par des contre-attaques. Dans ce but, récupérer sur Angelus les moyens nécessaires et sur l'Armée brittanique à porter à droite après extension belge vers le Sud. Argonaute a mission de reprendre les passages de la Somme.
                                        Signé: Georges.

(7) *Page* 132
    . . . O.B. Heeresgruppe entscheidet, *erst* die Lage bei Arras zu bereinigen und *dann* erst mit Gruppe von Kleist auf Calais–Boulogne vorzustossen.

CHAPTER IX

(1) *Page* 138
    (*4th Army War Diary—Entry for 23rd May, 1940*)
    22.55 Uhr orientiert der O.B. persönlich den Chef der Gruppe v. Kleist:
    . . . Im Grossen soll Gruppe Hoth morgen halten, Gruppe v. Kleist auch halten, dabei die Lage klären und aufschliessen.

(2) *Page* 139
    (*Army Group A War Diary—Entry for 24th May, 1940*)
    Um 11.30 Uhr trifft der Führer ein und lässt sich durch O.B. der Heeresgruppe über die Lage unterrichten. Der Auffassung, dass ostw. Arras von der *Infanterie* angegriffen werden müsse, die *schnellen Truppen* dagegen an der erreichten Linie Lens–Bethune–Aire–St Omer–Gravelines angehalten werden können, um den von Heeresgruppe B gedrängten Feind 'aufzufangen' stimmt er voll und ganz zu. Er unterstreicht sie durch die *Betonung*, dass es überhaupt notwendig sei, die Panzerkräfte fur die kommanden [sic] Operationen zu schonen, und dass eine weitere Einengung des Einschliessungsraumes nur eine höchst unerwünschte Einschränkung der Tätigkeit der Luftwaffe zur Folge haben würde.

(3) *Page* 139
    (*Army Group A War Diary—Appendix No. 32 dated 24th May, 1940*)
    Auf Befehl des Führers . . . ist nordwestlich Arras die allgemeine Linie Lens–Bethune–Aire–St Omer–Gravelines (Kanallinie) *nicht zu* überschreiten. . . .

(5) *Page* 143
    Le G.A.1. a dû se replier vers le nord et l'ennemi se renforce devant nous. L'opération offensive n'est donc plus à envisager pour le moment. . .

(6) *Page* 143
    . . . le général Blanchard a envoyé à Paris un officier de liaison

Note

chargé d'exposer les *difficultés* de la manœuvre projetée, le général Weygand a envisagé *l'impossibilité* de la tenter, et le général Besson a donné des ordres pour *l'abandonner.*

(7) *Page* 143

Vous demeurez seul juge des décisions à prendre pour sauver ce qui peut être sauvé et avant tout l'honneur des drapeaux dont vous êtes le gardien.

(8) *Page* 143

Si le repli (sur le canal Haute-Deule) rend impossible la manœuvre ordonnée, efforcez-vous de constituer tête de pont aussi étendue que possible couvrant Dunkerque.

(13) *Page* 150

(*Army Group A War Diary Appendices. No. 37*)

Auf Befehl des Herrn O.B. u. Chefs. *nicht* an A.O.K.4 weitergegeben, da der Führer die Befehlsführung dem O.B. der Heeresgruppe überlassen hat. [Initialed] Bl.

(14) *Page* 150

(*Army Group A War Diary—Entry for 25th May, 1940*)

. . . Der O.B., dem der Führer ausdrücklich die Art der Durchführung der Kämpfe der 4. Armee überlassen hat, hält es für dringend geboten, die mot. Gruppen erst einmal in sich aufschliessen zu lassen, wenn man sie überhaupt weiter vorgehen lassen will. . . .

(15) *Page* 150

Auf Befehl des Führers hat . . . der Nordwestflügel (Gruppen Hoth und Kleist) dagegen die günstige Abwehr Linie Lens–Bethune–Aire–St Omer–Gravelines zu halten und den Feind anrennen zu lassen. Ein Überschreiben [sic] dieser Linie darf nur auf ausdrücklichen Befehl der Heeresgruppe erfolgen. Es kommt jetzt darauf an, die Panzerverbände für spätere grössere Aufgaben zu schonen . . .

(16) *Page* 150

Im Laufe des Nachmittags meldet A.O.K.4, dass der Angriff des rechten Flügels (VIII. A.K.) gegen sehr zähen Feindwiderstand kein Gelände gewonnen hat . . .

(17) *Page* 151

Gegen Abend hat sich die Lage wie folgt entwickelt: Der Angriff der 4. Armee, der mit dem Ostflügel immer noch vor Valenciennes, Denain und der Wasserlinie südwestl. davon hängt, ist in der Mitte bis zur Linie Henin–Liétard–Lens vorgetragen. Die mot. Gruppen stehen—wie befohlen—am Kanal und haben in sich aufgeschlossen . . .

(18) *Page* 151

. . . Der Auftrag der Heeresgruppe A kann im Grossen als erfüllt angesehen werden.

(19) *Page* 151

. . . Zustand der unterstellten Truppen:

Verluste je Pz. Div. etwa 50 tote und verwundete Offz., 1500 tote und verwundete Uffz. und Mannschaften, 30% des Panzermaterials.

Note

Der Verlust an Waffen, besonders an M.G. bei den Schützen-Rgt., ist durch den häufigen Zusammenstoss mit Feind-Panzern hoch . . .

CHAPTER X

(1) *Page* 153

L'artillerie: 2 canons de 75 récupérés. Les moyens anti-chars: 2 canons de 25. Les engins blindés: 2 chars dont un en panne, ne pouvant être utilisé que sur place.

(2) *Page* 154

. . . quelques fractions sans homogéneité d'infanterie et d'artillerie . . . officiers, gradés et hommes refoulés dans Boulogne à la suite de la rapide avance de l'ennemi: divers détachements isolés en cours de déplacement, permissionnaires, militaires sortis des hôpitaux.

(3) *Page* 155

12.40 Uhr . . . Es werden befehlsgemäss angesetzt: 2. *Pz. Div.* über Linie Bainethun–Samer auf Boulogne unmittelbar, 1. Pz. Div. über Desvres auf Marquise, um in dieser Linie die Flanke der 2. Pz. Div. gegen Calais abzudecken.

(4) *Page* 155

Zusammenfassung.

Am 22.5 ist es ohne besondere Schwierigkeit gelungen, die Divisionen nach Norden abzudrehen. Ein schneller Vorstoss kann nach Auffassung des Gen. Kdos. den Feind noch im Aufbau seiner Abwehr treffen. Im Gegensatz dazu legen die Befehle der Gruppe, deren Gründe nicht bekannt sind, das Korps bis auf Abruf fest.

In *Erkenntnis dieser Lage* hat Kdr. General daher die 2. Pz. Div. mittags—ohne auf den Befehl der Gruppe zu warten—au Boulogne angesetzt. Daher glückt es der Division, noch am Abend in die Stadt einzudringen . . .

(5) *Page* 157

14.45 Uhr. Etwa um diese Zeit hat das Gen. Kdo. folgenden *Eindruck*:

Gegner kämpft in und um Boulogne zähe um jede Handbreite Bodens, um den wichtigen Hafen nicht in deutsche Hand fallen zu lassen.

Die *Unterstützung der Luftwaffe* auf die vor Boulogne liegenden Kriegs- und Transportschiffe, bei denen man jedoch nicht erkennt, ob es sich hier um Ein- oder Ausladungen handelt, ist ungenügend. Der Angriff der 2. Pz. Div. schreitet daher nur langsam vorwärts.

(6) *Page* 157

19.30 Uhr. Der seit langem erwartete Luftangriff auf Seeraum um Boulogne bringt der 2. *Pz. Div.* vorübergehend Entlastung . . .

(7) *Page* 158

1400 Uhr. Da Boulogne—insbesondere auch nach der Eroberung —von See her durch engl. Streitkräfte bedroht sein wird, geht 1400

Note

Uhr Befehl an *2 Pz. Div.*, Vorbereitungen für Instandsetzungen und Inbetriebnahme der Befestigungen von Boulogne unter Einsatz von Kriegsgefangenen vorzunehmen . . .

(8) *Page* 158

Zusammenfassung [23.5.]

. . . Wesentlich erscheint dem Gen. Kdo. jetzt der Stoss auf *Dünkirchen*, dem letzten grösseren Hafen, mit dessen Fall die Einkesselung vollständig wäre. Dieser Angriff ist jedoch durch den Befehl der Gruppe zunächst unterbunden.

. . . Wenn man den *Ursachen* nachgeht, weshalb die Angriffe in der Nordwestecke Frankreichs verhältnismässig langsam vorwärtsgehen, so kann man vielleicht auf folgende Gründe stossen:

(1) Aus dem Gen. Kdo. unbekannten Gründen wurde am 22.5. der Angriff auf Boulogne von der Gruppe erst 12.40 Uhr freigegeben. Fast 5 Stunden lang standen 1. und 2. Pz. Div. untätig am Canche-Abschnitt.

(2) Für den schweren Angriff auf die 2 stark verteidigten Seehäfen Boulogne und Calais wurde das Korps um eine ganze Division *geschwächt*, während ausserdem starke Teile (u.a. 1 Btl. Schützen Rgt. 2 und Pz. ALA) an der Somme belassen werden mussten.

. . . Nach Auffassung des Gen. Kdos. wäre es möglich und zweckmässig gewesen, die *drei Aufgaben* des Korps—Aa-Kanal, Calais, Boulogne—schnell und durchschlagend zu lösen, wenn man am 22.5. mit der *gesamten Kraft* des Korps—also mit allen 3 Divisionen—schlagartig einheitlich und damit überraschend aus dem Raum an der Somme heraus nach Norden angetreten wäre.

(9) *Page* 160

D'autre part, les intentions des Britanniques, restées nébuleuses . . . se précisent de façon favorable.

(11) *Page* 161

. . . petites fractions d'unités rabattues par l'avance allemande . . .

(12) *Page* 165

16.00 Uhr. . . . Der Widerstand des Feindes aus kaum erkennbaren Stellungen sei aber derart stark, dass nur ganz geringe örtl. Erfolge erzielt werden konnten . . .

19.00 Uhr. . . . Die Division legt dem Korps den eingeforderten Zustandsbericht vor: 'Truppe ermüdet, bedarf einiger Tage Erholung. Ausfälle an Material, Kraftfahrzeugen und Personal 1/3, an Panzern stark die Hälfte.'

(13) *Page* 167

21.00 Uhr. Kdr. Schtz. Brig. hält unter diesen Umständen nochmaliges Antreten für aussichtslos, da der Gegner noch nicht zermürbt und die Zeit bis zur Dunkelheit zu kurz ist.

(14) *Page* 168

09.00 Uhr. Zwischen 9.00 und 10.00 Uhr erfolgt der vereinbarter Bombenangriff und Artl. Feuerschlag auf Zitadelle Calais und

Note

Vorstadt Les Baraques. Ein sichtbarer Erfolg tritt nicht ein, der Kampf geht weiter, die Engländer verteidigen sich zäh.

(15) *Page* 169

. . . 'Queen Viktoria Brigade', einer in der engl. Kriegs- und Kolonialgeschichte bekannten Truppe . . .

CHAPTER XI

(1) *Page* 172

I. L'ennemi a franchi la Lys de part et d'autre de Courtrai et atteint Menin, Iseghem, Ingelmunster.

Les G.U. britanniques destinées à attaquer en direction Marchiennes–Péronne céssent d'être disponibles à cet effet.

II. En conséquence, l'attaque prévue en direction Marchiennes–Péronne n'aura pas lieu.

La Ière Armée, la B.E.F. et l'Armée Belge se regrouperont progressivement derrière la ligne d'eau marquée par le Canal de l'Aa, La Lys, et le Canal de dérivation de façon à former une tête de pont couvrant largement Dunkerque.

Cette tête de pont sera défendue sans esprit de recul.

III. La Ière Armée entamera ses opérations de repli dès le 26 mai en reportant ses réserves au Nord de la Scarpe.

Le repli de la ligne Sensée–Escaut aura lieu en principe dans la nuit du 26 au 27.

La Ière Armée portera une D.L.M. dans la région Est d'Ypres, en mesure d'agir en direction de Courtrai (ordre particulier).

IV. L'Armée Belge fera tous ses efforts pour réduire la poche réalisée par l'ennemi au nord de la Lys de Courtrai.

La D.L.M. portée dans la région Est d'Ypres pourra agir à son profit sur ordre du Commandant du G.A.

V. Les forces à la disposition de l'Amiral Nord rejetteront à l'Ouest de l'Aa les forces ennemies ayant franchi cette rivière, dont elles assureront ensuite la défense.

Signé: BLANCHARD.

CHAPTER XII

(1) *Page* 191

Am Nachmittag verstärkt sich der feindl. Widerstand vor der ganzen Front, es entstehen an allen Stellen, vor allem um jede Ortschaft, ja jedes Haus, schwere Kämpfe, die es dem Korps nicht ermöglichen, in nennenswertem Umfange nach Osten bzw. Nordosten Boden zu gewinnen. Die Ausfälle an Personal und Gerät sind empfindlich. Der Feind kämpft zähe und hält sich in seinen Stellungen bis zum Letzten; wird er an einer Stelle herausgeschossen, so erscheint er kurze Zeit später an anderer Stelle und nimmt das Gefecht wieder auf. Die feindl. Artl. schiesst mit anscheinend sehr guter Beobachtung aus Gegend nordostw. Merville und nordostw. Cassel auf die Anmarschwege und die vordere Linie (insgesamt etwa 2 bzw. 4 Battr. erkannt).

Note

(2) *Page* 192

Aus den Kämpfen dieses Tages, die, wie schon oben betont, starke Verluste an Personal und Gerät gekostet haben, lässt sich die klare und kurze Folgerung ziehen, dass zum Kampf gegen einen sich hartnäckig verteidigenden Feind in zum Teil. befestigter Feldstellung, besonders in verbarrikadierten Ortschaften, die Pz. Div. weniger geeignet ist, weil sie über zu wenig infanteristische Kraft verfügt und die Panzer den zehlreichen eingebauten Pz.-Abwehrwaffen zu gute Ziele bieten.

(3) *Page* 192

Am 27.5 wirkte sich—wie vorausgesehen—das erzwungene zweitägige Stehenbleiben des Korps auf dem Südufer des Kanals wie folgt aus:

1. die Truppe erlitt beim Angriff über den nunmehr vom Gegner hartnäckig verteidigten La Bassée–Kanal beträchtliche Verluste,

2. der Strom der aus dem Raum von Lille nach Westen in Richtung Kanal flüchtenden englisch—französischen Truppen konnte nicht mehr rechtzeitig und wirksam genug abgefangen werden.

(4) *Page* 198

Général Weygand fait personnellement appel au Général Gort. L'Armée britannique doit participer vigoureusement aux contre-attaques d'ensemble nécessaires. Situation exige qu'on cogne dur.

CHAPTER XIII

(1) *Page* 202

La 60e D.I. a été submergée dans la boucle de l'Yser . . . a été recueillie par la 2e D.L.M. . . . et par les Britanniques qui tiennent le canal de Furnes à Nieuport . . .

(2) *Page* 206

Kdr. General verspricht sich von dem Angriff keinen Erfolg und ist der Ansicht, dass weitere nutzlose Opfer vermieden werden müssen, nachdem Pz. Rgt. 3 beim Gegenangriff starke Verluste erlitten hat.

(3) *Page* 208

1505 Uhr . . . *Allgemeine Auffassung* des Kdr. Generals:
Angriff in dem Polderland mit Panzern wird für falsch gehalten. Nutzloses Opfern unserer besten Soldaten . . . Es erscheint zweckmässiger, die erreichte Stellung zu halten und den Angriff der 18. Armee von Osten her sich auswirken zu lassen.

(4) *Page* 208

20.30 Uhr gibt *Kdr. General* an Chef Gruppe nach seiner Rückkehr von der Frontfahrt folgende Orientierung (Akte VIII, Buch 3, S.33, 34):

(1) Nach der Kapitulation der Belgier ist eine Fortführung der

Note

Operationen hier unerwünscht, weil die Fortführung des Kampfes unnötige Opfer kostet. Die Panzer-Divisionen haben nur noch 50% ihres Panzerbestandes. Dieser Bestand ist dringend reparaturbedürftig, wenn das Korps in kurzer Zeit für andere Operationen wieder verwendungsbereit sein soll.

(2) Ein Angriff mit Panzern in dem durch den Regen völlig aufgeweichten Polderland ist zwecklos. Die Truppe ist im Besitz des Höhengeländes südl. Dünkirchen, sie ist im Besitz der wichtigen Strasse Cassel, Dünkirchen und hat in dem Höhengelände von Crochte und Pitgam günstige Artillerie-Stellungen, aus denen sie Dünkirchen unter Feuer nehmen kann.

Ausserdem kommt der Gruppe die 18 Armee von Osten entgegen, die mit ihren infanteristischen Kräften zum Kampf im Polderland geeigneter ist als Panzer, und der das Schliessen der Lücke an der Küste deshalb überlassen werden kann.

(6) *Page 212*
(*German Air Ministry Situation Report—28th May, 1940*)
Die Masse der Angriffskräfte richtete sich gegen den weichenden Gegner.

(7) *Page 214*
(*4th Army War Diary—Entry for 27th May*)
13.48 Uhr meldet der Chef der Gruppe Kleist, dass sich der Feind in Cassel hartnäckig hält. . . . Die Engländer schiffen sich an der Küste noch immer ein, die Schiffe fahren in grosser Zahl an Gravelines und Calais vorbei nach Westen, 'es ist für unsere Leute sehr bitter, das zu sehen.'

(8) *Page 214*
(*4th Army War Diary*)
Oberst Blumentritt teilt mit, Dünkirchen wird auf Befehl des Generalfeldmarschalls Göring so angegriffen, dass dort ein Einladen angeblich nicht mehr möglich ist.

Darauf erklärt der Chef: Das Bild in den Kanalhäfen ist Folgendes: Grosse Schiffe fahren an die Quais heran, Bretter werden angelegt und Menschen stürmen auf die Schiffe. Jegliches Material bleibt zurück.—Wir haben aber kein Interesse, diese Menschen später wieder neuausgerüstet vor uns zu finden.

CHAPTER XIV

(1) *Page 218*
Da es im Gesamtinteresse der weiteren Operationen, im besonderen auch des Aufmarsches an der Südfront liegt, die Kräfte der 18., 6 und 4 Armee so bald wie möglich freizumachen, soll der Angriff zur Vernichtung der noch im Raume südl. und südostw. Dünkirchen eingeschlossenen Feindkräfte mit allem Nachdruck fortgesetzt werden. Hierzu erlässt die Hgr. noch einmal einen Befehl an die Armeen (Hgr. B, Ia Nr. 2754/40 g.K.) mit entsprechenden Weisungen.

Note

(2) *Page* 220

(*German Air Ministry Situation Report—29th May, 1940*)

Ihn hieran zu hindern und seine Niederlage zur Vernichtung zu gestalten, war das Ziel der Masse der Angriffskräfte.

. . . dann aber auch mit voller Wucht gegen die zahlreichen Transportschiffe im vorgelagerten Seegebiet sowie gegen die sie deckenden Kriegsschiffe richtete.

CHAPTER XV

(1) *Page* 225

(*German Air Ministry Situation Report—30th May, 1940*)

. . . Die aus britischen Truppen bestehende Brückenkopf besátzung kämpft sehr zäh.

(2) *Page* 226

13.40 Uhr spricht der Ia mit dem Chef der Gruppe Kleist: Die Gruppe Kleist müsse so nahe an Dünkirchen heran sein, dass auch 10 cm. Kan. die Stadt erreichen könnten. Es besteht der Eindruck, dass heute nichts geschieht, sich niemand mehr für Dünkirchen interessiert. Stadt und Hafen müssen beschossen, Einschiffungen verhindert, Panik erzwungen werden.

(3) *Page* 226

15.00 Uhr. . . . Oberst Wuthmann übermittelt ihm [Chef der Gruppe Kleist] darauf folgenden Befehl: Die Gruppe Kleist greift beiderseits Dünkirchen an, stösst bis an die Küste durch und setzt anschliessend die Verfolgung nach Osten fort. Die Gruppe Kleist gibt zu bedenken, dass die eigene Gliederung für diesen Angriff nicht geeignet sei, Panzer seien dort nicht verwendbar.

(4) *Page* 226

Oberst Wuthmann entgegnet, das sei bekannt. 'Es muss aber, auch auf Befehl höherer Stellen, mit den Einladungen in Dünkirchen endlich Schluss gemacht werden'. Deshalb solle an Dünkirchen vorbei bis an die Küste vorgestossen werden. Der O.B. bekräftigt den Befehl noch persönlich: 'Die Situation bei Abbeville ist unhaltbar. Sofort mit allen Kräften an die Küste ostwärts Dünkirchen heran, dazu angreifen. Dem Div. Kdeur. ist zu sagen, dass er unbedingt heute noch an der Küste steht!'

(5) *Page* 227

(*German 4th Army War Diary—Entry for 30th May, 1940*)

Die Gruppe Kleist meldet, dass die 20.I.D. (mot.) nunmehr auf Bray Dunes vorgehe, um die Rückzugslinie des Feindes von Furnes abzuschneiden. Der linke Flügel liegt vor Bergues und in Gravelines am Kanal und kann nicht vorwärts, er hat den befestigten Brückenkopf Dünkirchen vor sich.

(6) *Page* 228

Am Anfang steht wohl die Tatsache, dass die Überraschung des Feindes trotz monatelanger Wartezeit voll glückte und in Verbindung mit der Schnelligkeit des Handelns auf der Gegenseite Massnahmen auslöste, die nur verständlich erscheinen, wenn man unterstellt, dass der—bei Heeresgruppe A liegende—Schwerpunkt der deutschen Operation nicht, oder zu spät erkannt wurde.

. . . Man darf hier wohl—ohne zu übertreiben—von einer vorbildlichen Zusammenarbeit beider Wehrmachtsteile sprechen. . . .

Die Tatsache, dass der Raumgewinn nur auf der Erde gesichert und die Vernichtung der Kampfkraft des Feindes letztlich nur dort vollendet werden kann, sichert dem Heer den Ruhmesanteil, der ihm neben der Leistung der Luftwaffe gebührt.

Es bleibt hier nur noch festzustellen, dass das rücksichtslose Draufgängertum der Panzerwaffe und mot. Divisionen und die unerhörten Marschleistungen der Infanterie, die sie vielfach nur wenige Stunden nach den schnellen Verbänden in die Kampfhandlungen eingreifen liessen, den Gegner in einem Tempo überranten [*sic*], dem weder seine Führung, noch die Ausbildung seiner Truppe gewachsen waren.

(7) *Page* 229

Der Oberbefehlshaber des Heeres würde gerne von sich aus einige Anregungen für das Niederringen des Raumes um Dünkirchen geben.

Es sind z.B. folgende Erwägungen dort gepflogen worden:

(a) Abteilungen auf dem Wasserwege in den Rücken der Engländer zu werfen,

(b) vorderste Teile der Infanterie vom Kanalufer abzusetzen, um ungehindert aus der Luft wirksam unterstützen zu können.

(c) Beim Kampf in den Dünen wegen der verringerten Artl. Wirkung Flak mit Brennzündern einzusetzen (eine Anregung des Führers und Obersten Befehlshabers).

(8) *Page* 230

Constituer avec toutes les forces disponibles une tête de pont au sud de Dunkerque–Nieuport . . . pour permettre évacuation progressive par mer.

(9) *Page* 235

. . . die aus Südosten in starker Überhöhung kommend . . .

CHAPTER XVI

(2) *Page* 243

Rollende Angriffe richteten sich während des ganzen Tages gegen zur Verschiffung bereitgestellte Truppen, gegen den Hafen von Dünkirchen sowie gegen Kriegs und Handelsschiffe in Küstennähe und im Seegebiet zwischen Dünkirchen und Grossbritannien.

(6) *Page* 247

. . . le G.Q.G. télégraphie au G.A.1 d'embarquer par bateaux de ravitaillement les organes de commandement en excédent . . .

CHAPTER XVIII

Note

(1) *Page* 262

La Division Britannique ressemble donc plus à une D.L.M. qu'à une D.C.R.: elle est en somme composée 'd'automitrailleuses' très légèrement blindées et par conséquent vulnérables aux coups des canons anti-chars ennemis.

Il est possible que dans la récente période de crise le matériel ait dû être employé dans des conditions peu favorables; il n'est pas moins vrai qu'il faut n'envisager l'emploi de cette Unité que dans les limites permises par les caractéristiques de son matériel, toutes les fois que les conditions du combat n'imposeront pas impérieuse-ment de prendre d'autres dispositions.

En outre, il y aura lieu de s'orienter dès que possible vers l'utilisa-tion de la Division Evans dans le cadre d'un groupement tactique comprenant en particulier la 51ème Division et la Division Blindée Britannique, Groupement dont la mission sera fixée à l'aile gauche de notre dispositif en fonction de ses possibilités.

Le Général d'Armée
Commandant-en-Chef sur le Front Nord-Est
Signé: GEORGES

(2) *Page* 268

Eigene Gefechtsluftaufklärung in Gegend südwärts Amiens wurde durch starken feindl. Jagdschutz unterbunden.

CHAPTER XIX

(1) *Page* 274

(Army Group B War Diary Appendices)

Absicht der Obersten Führung ist es, die den Allierten in Frankreich noch verbliebenen Kräfte durch eine an die Kämpfe im Artois und in Flandern möglichst schnell anschliessende Operation zu vernichten. Mit operativen Reserven des Gegners wird in grösserer Zahl nicht mehr zu rechnen sein. Es wird daher möglich sein, die eilig aufgebaute feindliche Front südl. Somme und Aisne in wuchtigem Angriff zu Fall zu bringen und durch schnellen Durch-stoss in die Tiefe dem Gegner die Möglichkeit eines geordneten Rückzuges oder des Aufbaues einer rückwärtigen Verteidigungs-front zu nehmen.

(2) *Page* 274

(Army Group A War Diary)

Der Führer entwickelte kurz seine Auffassung über die Lage: Es bleiben dem Franzosen-Engländer höchstens 60–65 Divisionen zum Einsatz gegen uns. Zweifellos wird sich General Weygand eine operative Stossgruppe zurückhalten, die in Raum Paris und ostw. zu suchen ist. Man muss auch damit rechnen, dass der Feind sich absetzt und den Widerstand weiter südlich vorbereitet.

Note

(4) *Page 275*
(*Army Group B War Diary Appendices*)

4. Armee (6 J.D., 2 Pz. Div., 1 J.D. (mot), 11. Schtz. Brig. (mot), 1. K.D.) greift aus Gegend Abbeville–Amiens an und geht unter Sicherung gegen Paris gegen die untere Seine vor. Sie setzt sich frühzeitig in den Besitz von Le Havre und von Brückenköpfen bei Rouen, Les Andelys und Vernon. Weiteres Vorgehen über die untere Seine in südl. oder südwestl. Richtung erst auf besonderen Befehl.

(5) *Page 276*

Am 6.6 ging das Korps . . . unter Vermeidung der Wälder und Wege und den an diesen liegenden Ortschaften, begünstigt durch das kaum von Gräben durchzogene flachgewölbte Gelände, querfeldein, Panzer voraus, Schützen auf Fahrzeugen dahinter, entfaltet nach Süden vor.

CHAPTER XX

(1) *Page 290*

Die bereits im Gange befindliche Kapitulation der in St Valery befindlichen Teile wurde durch das Eingreifen engl. Offiziere unterbrochen.

CHAPTER XXI

(7) *Page 298*

Le Général Brooke Cdt. le Corps Expéditionnaire Britannique a pris contact le 14 Juin matin avec le Général Weygand Cdt. l'ensemble des Théâtres d'Opérations et le Général Georges Cdt. le Front N.E. pour prendre des directives en ce qui concerne l'emploi des troupes britanniques en France.

Dans le cadre de la décision prise par les gouvernements britannique et français, d'organiser un réduit en Bretagne, il a été décidé:

1. Que les troupes britanniques en cours de débarquement (E.O.C.A. Brooke, fin de la 52e division et D.I. canadienne) seront concentrées à Rennes

2. Que les troupes britanniques engagées à la X° Armée (D.I. Evans, D.I. Beauman et 52e D.I. non compris ses éléments non encore debarqués) continueront leur mission actuelle sous les ordres du Général Cdt. la Xe Armée.

Leur emploi dans la manœuvre d'ensemble de cette Armée devra les amener autant que possible à agir dans la région du Mans pour faciliter leur regroupement ultérieur avec les forces du Général Brooke.

Signé: BROOKE
WEYGAND ET GEORGES

CHAPTER XXIII

Note

(1) *Page* 318

La plus grande confusion règne dans le quadrilatère Landrecies–Solre-le-Chateau–Hirson–Guise, où se croisent les unités combattantes et les services refluant de la Meuse, les populations civiles déferlant de toute la région des Ardennes, les unités venant du nord et de l'ouest pour renforcer la position frontière sur laquelle le commandement espère rétablir la situation. C'est à l'initiative des chefs locaux que des résistances s'ébauchent, subsistent, s'évanouissent. Les ordres du commandement ne parviennent plus aux exécutants.

(2) *Page* 319

. . . nos forces ne sont pas suffisantes pour envisager une manœuvre en retraite . . . Nous n'aurons pas les réserves voulues pour opérer en bon ordre . . . une retraite de la ligne Somme–Aisne vers la ligne Basse Seine–Marne. Il n'y a pas de retraite méthodique possible avec une pareille infériorité numérique.

(3) *Page* 319

. . . une résistance acharnée sur la position actuelle . . . Il pourrait venir un moment à partir duquel la France se trouverait . . . dans l'impossibilité de continuer une lutte militaire éfficace pour protéger son sol. Ce moment serait marqué par la rupture définitive des positions de défense sur lesquelles les armées françaises ont reçu l'ordre de se battre sans esprit de recul.

(4) *Page* 326

Der englische Soldat

war körperlich in hervorragender Verfassung. Eigene Verwundungen ertrug er mit stoischer Ruhe. Er sprach über Verluste der eigenen Truppe mit voller Gleichgültigkeit, er klagte nicht über Strapazen. *Sein Verhalten im Kampfe war zäh und verbissen.* Seine Überzeugung dass England zuletzt doch siegen würde, war unerschütterlich.

. . .

Zusammenfassung.

Der englische Soldat hat sich stets als *hochwertiger Kämpfer* gezeigt. Die Territorial-Divisionen sind wohl in ihrem Ausbildungsstande den aktiven Truppen unterlegen, aber in ihren moralischen Einstellungen als Soldaten diesen gleichzustellen.

In der Verteidigung liess sich der Engländer '*totschlagen*'. In den Kämpfen sind durch das IV. A.K. auch nur verhältnismässig wenige Engländer gefangen genommen worden, im Vergleich zu den Kämpfen mit Franzosen oder Belgiern. Hingegen waren die blutigen Verluste stets beiderseitig hoch.

SUPPLEMENT ON THE PLANNING AND CONDUCT
OF THE GERMAN CAMPAIGN

Note

(1) *Page* 335

1) *Allgemeine Absicht.*

Die Haltung der Westmächte kann es erforderlich machen, dass das deutsche Heer im Westen zur Offensive übergeht. Der Angriff wird dann unter Einsatz aller zu Gebote stehenden Kräfte geführt werden.

Zweck dieses am Nordflügel der Westfront durch den holländisch-belgischen und luxemburgischen Raum zu führenden Angriffs wird es sein, möglichst starke Teile des französischen Heeres und seiner Verbündeten zu schlagen und gleichzeitig möglichst viel holländischen, belgischen und nordfranzösischen Raum als Basis für eine aussichtsreiche Luft- und Seekriegführung gegen England und als weites Vorfeld des Ruhrgebiets zu gewinnen.

(2) *Page* 336

1) Bei Aussprache über Operation sagt Führer er wollte überhaupt ursprünglich alles sdl. Lüttich einsetzen.

2) Halder verwahrt sich gegen Vorwurf dass er mit Abdrehen der 4. Armee nach Nordwesten östl. Namür eine kleine Umfassung beabsichtigte. Er wollte alle pz. Verb. in Richtung Gent zusammenziehen u. dann einen starken Aussenumfassungsflügel zu haben.

(3) *Page* 336

1) *Allgemeine Absicht:*

Die Haltung der Westmächte kann es erforderlich machen, dass das deutsche Heer im Westen zur Offensive übergeht. Für den Angriff werden dann alle zu Gebote stehenden Kräfte eingesetzt mit dem Zweck, *möglichst starke Teile des französischen Heeres und seiner Verbündeten auf nordfranzösischem und belgischem Boden zur Schlacht zu stellen und zu schlagen* und damit günstige Bedingungen für die Weiterführung des Krieges zu Lande und in der Luft gegen England und Frankreich zu schaffen.

(4) *Page* 337

Führer kommt mit neuem Gedanken eine pz. div. u. 1 mot. div. über Arlon auf Sedan ansetzen.

(5) *Page* 337

1) Die geplante Operation kann eine kriegsentscheidende Wirkung nicht haben.

(6) *Page* 337

Der erstrebte erste Erfolg über Belgien und vorgeworfene franz.-engl. Kräfte ist denkbar. Das Gelingen der Gesamtoperation hängt aber nicht von diesem Anfangserfolg ab, sondern davon, dass es gelingt, die in Belgien bzw. nördlich der Somme kämpfenden Feindkräfte *insgesamt* zu schlagen und zu *vernichten*, nicht nur sie frontal zu werfen. Zugleich muss der mit Sicherheit aus südlicher bzw. südwestl. Richtung, wenn auch erst später, zu erwartende franz. Gegenangriff abgefangen werden.

Diese Überlegungen führen nach Ansicht der H.Gr. zwingend dazu, den *Schwerpunkt der Gesamtoperation*, von der der erstrebte Anfangserfolg der schnellen Kräfte in Belgien doch nur die Einleitung ist, auf den *Südflügel* zu legen. Er muss, südlich Lüttich vorbei, über die Maas aufwärts Namur Richtung Arras–Boulogne vorgetrieben werden, um alles, was der Feind nach Belgien hinein-wirft, nicht frontal auf die Somme zu werfen, sondern an der Somme abzuschneiden.

(7) *Page 337*

Die Gefahr, aber auch andererseits die Chance des grossen Erfolgs, umsomehr wenn der Gegner seinen Nordflügel stark machen sollte, liegt bei der *H.Gr.A.*

(8) *Page 337*

[3.11.39] *Ob.d.H. spricht zunächst bei A.O.K. 12 den O.B. und Chef der H.Gr., anschliessend den O.B. und die Kdr. Generale der 12. Armee.*

Chef des Gen. St. H.Gr. trägt erneut die Gedankengänge des Schreibens vom 31.10. vor.

O.K.H. sagt nach anfänglicher Ablehnung schliesslich die 2. Pz. Div., SS Standarte Adolf Hitler und Regt. Grossdeutschland zu.

(9) *Page 338*

Führer ist [*sic*] Korps Guderian noch zu schwach, noch einmal 2. pz. d. ausser 10. pz. u. 1 mot. SS Leibstandarte u. Rgt. Gross-deutschland nehmen.

(10) *Page 338*

Der Führer hat nunmehr angeordnet:

"Am Südflügel der 12. oder im Streifen der 16. Armee ist eine 3. Gruppe schneller Truppen zu bilden und unter Ausnutzung des waldfreien Streifens beiderseits Arlon, Tintigny, Florenville in Richtung auf Sedan und ostwärts anzusetzen. . . ."

(11) *Page 338*

. . . Ihre Aufgabe ist, nach Südbelgien hinein vorgeworfene bewegliche Feindkräfte zu schlagen, bei und südostwärts Sedan überraschend das Westufer der Maas zu gewinnen und dadurch günstige Voraussetzungen für die Weiterführung der Operation zu schaffen.

(12) *Page 338*

Es sind alle Vorkehrungen zu treffen, um den Schwerpunkt der Operationen rasch von der H.Gr.B. zur H.Gr.A. zu verlegen, falls dort, wie es die augenblickliche Kräfteverteilung des Gegners vermuten lassen könnte, raschere und grössere Erfolge eintreten sollten als bei der H.Gr.B.

(13) *Page 339*

Entscheidend für die Gesamtführung wie für die Führung der Heeresgruppen ist das der Offensive gesteckte Ziel.

Note

Nach Ansicht der Heeresgruppe muss es die *Herbeiführung der Entscheidung im Landkrieg, die Zerschlagung der alliierten Wehrkraft zu Lande und in der Luft*, die Beseitigung des englischen Festlandsdegens sein, der dann als zweiter Schritt der Angriff zur Luft und See auf England selbst folgen kann.

(14) *Page 340*

13.2: Die vom Heer angeforderte Übersicht über die Stärke der Armeen und Res. getrennt nach Btn. Btlen u. Kampfwagen, veranlasst den Führer erneut die Schwerpunktfrage aufzurollen.

Er sagt:

Masse der Geschützkampfwagen ist verausgabt an nicht entscheidenden Stellen.

Pz. Div. bei 4. Armee können in gesperrtem und befestigtem Gebiet wenig ausrichten.

Spätestens an der Maas liegen sie fest und müssen zurückgezogen werden. Bei der 16. oder 12. Armee fehlen sie dann. Man sollte sie Richtung Sedan zusammenführen. Dort erwartet der Feind unseren Hpt. Stoss nicht. Die Dokumente der gelandeten Flieger haben ihn (den Feind) noch mehr in der Auffassung bestärkt, dass es uns nur auf den Besitz der holl. und belgischen Kanalküste ankommt.

(15) *Page 340*

Ich übergebe dem Führer eine Zusammenstellung aus der man ersehen kann, in welch hohem Masse eine Schwerpunktbildung südlich der Linie Lüttich–Namur möglich ist (mindestens die 5fache Stärke der nördlich dieser Linie angesetzten Kräfte). Ich mache darauf aufmerksam, dass der Stoss auf Sedan ein operativer Schleichweg ist, auf dem man durch den Kriegsgott erwischt werden kann.

(16) *Page 346*

20.30 *Gespräch mit Müller und Wagner* über Nachschublage: . . . Aufbau einer Werkstattbasis Namur–Charleville: ist eingeleitet. Zweitausend Facharbeiter kommen mit Flugzeug vor.

(17) *Page 347*

Statt dessen schlägt von Reichenau seine Privatschlacht in Gegend Audenarde, die wahrscheinlich Verluste kostet und kein operatives Ergebnis bringt.

(18) *Page 348*

Eine neue Weisung des O.K.H. (s. Anlage) gibt Anordnungen für die Vollendung der Einschliessung des Feindes in Nordbelgien und -Frankreich. Der Heeresgruppe A fällt dabei die Aufgabe zu, die Einkesselung von Süden her (Valenciennes–Arras) zu verengen, mit den schnellen Kräften über die Linie Béthune–St. Omer–Calais gegen die Linie Armentières–Ypern–Ostende einzuschwenken und die Höhenstufe Lens–St Omer möglichst bald mit infanteristischen Kräften in die Hand zu nehmen.

Note

(19) *Page 348*

16.40 Uhr: meldet der O.B. dem O.B. der Heeresgruppe über die Lage: Südlich Calais und bei Boulogne wird noch gekämpft, südlich St Omer ist es vorwärts gegangen, die Loretto-Höhe ist fest in deutscher Hand, beim II.A.K. ist ostwärts Arras die Bildung eines Brückenkopfes im Gange. Für morgen ist zu entscheiden, ob es nördlich Arras weitergehen soll oder ostwärts Arras. Die Truppe würde es begrüssen, wenn morgen mehr aufgeschlossen würde, sodass er, der O.B., für morgen also vorschlage, Arras zu bereinigen, die mot. Verbände aufschliessen zu lassen und die 2.I.D. (mot). möglichst freizumachen. Vielleicht könnte die Luftlandedivision dafür eingesetzt werden. Mit diesem Vorschlag erklärt sich General-oberst v. Rundstedt einverstanden. Es soll also der rechte Flügel und die Mitte vorgetrieben, im Übrigen aufgeschlossen, Inf. Divisionen vorgeschoben werden . . .

(20) *Page 348*

18.10 Uhr: teilt der O.B. persönlich dem Chef der Gruppe Hoth mit, dass die Armee morgen im Wesentlichen stehen bleiben wird, auch nach Weisung des Generaloberst v. Rundstedt. Es muss morgen aufgeschlossen und Ordnung geschaffen, die gegenwärtige Linie unbedingt gehalten werden . . .

(21) *Page 349*

Der Befehl Op. 5852/40 G K ist von mir nicht signiert, um darzutun, dass ich mit dem Befehl und dem Zeitpunkt seiner Ausgabe nicht einverstanden bin.

(22) *Page 349*

Führer fliegt mit mir und Schmundt z. H.Gr.A nach Charleville. Ist sehr erfreut über die Massnahmen der H.Gr., die sich ganz mit seinen Gedanken decken. Er erfährt zu seiner Überraschung, dass OKH ohne dem Führer u.d.OKW Kenntnis zu geben, die 4. Armee und eine Reihe ruckwärts folgender Divisionen der H.Gr.B unterstellt. Führer ist sehr unwillig und hält diese Regelung nicht nur militärisch sondern auch psychologisch für falsch. Ob.d.H. wird bestellt und Verlegung der Trennungslinie rückgängig gemacht.

(23) *Page 350*

20.00 ObdH kommt von OKW. Anscheinend wieder recht unerfreuliche Aussprache mit Führer. 20.20 Befehl, welcher den gestrigen Befehl aufhebt und Einkreisung im Raum Dünkirchen–Estaires–Lille–Roubaix–Ostende anordnet. Der schnelle linke Flügel, der keinen Feind vor sich hat, wird dabei auf ausdrücklichen Wunsch des Führers angehalten!

(24) *Page 350*

Vorm. kommt Ob.d.H. und will Genehmigung, dass Panzer und mot. Divisionen vom Höhengelände Vimi–St Omer–Graveline in das Niederungsgelände nach Westen vorstossen. Führer ist dagegen,

Note

überlässt Entscheidung d. Heeresgruppe A. Diese lehnt es vorerst
ab, da Panzer sich erholen sollen, um für Aufgaben im Süden bereit
zu sein.

(25) *Page* 350

Vorm. Führer lässt sich Ob.d.H. kommen und genehmigt
nunmehr, da 18. und 6. Armee nur langsam vorwärtskommen und
auch der Widerstand im Süden vor II.A.K. sehr zäh, dass Panzer-
gruppen und Inf. Div. von Westen her in Richtung Tournai, Cassel
und Dünkirchen vorstossen, zumal der Feind auch seinerseits nicht
gegen die Höhenstellung anläuft, sondern sich in Verteid.-Stellungen
festkrallt und sie organisiert.

(26) *Page* 351

Die Panzerwaffe muss dabei jenen Einsatz finden, der unter
Berücksichtigung ihrer Wesensart den grössten Erfolg verspricht.
Sie darf unter keinen Umstände in dem Gewirr der endlosen
Häuserzeilen belgischer Städte verloren gehen.

APPENDIX III

German Forces Engaged

THE following diagrams and notes show how the Command of the German Army was organised for the 1939–40 Campaign in France and Flanders.

The Supreme Command of the Armed Forces (Army, Navy and Air Force) was exercised by Adolf Hitler with, as his instrument for that purpose,

THE HIGH COMMAND OF THE ARMED FORCES
(Oberkommando der Wehrmacht—or O.K.W.)

Chief of O.K.W.
Colonel-General Keitel

Chief of Operations Staff
Major-General Jodl

The Commander-in-Chief of the German Navy was Grand-Admiral Raeder; the head of the Air Force was Field Marshal Goering; the command of the Army was organised as follows:

ARMY HIGH COMMAND
(Oberkommando des Heeres—or O.K.H.)

Commander-in-Chief
Colonel-General von Brauchitsch

Chief of the Army General Staff
General Halder

| Army Group B | Army Group A | Army Group C |

On the next page is shown the composition of Army Group A and Army Group B down to corps level, the corps being shown in Roman numbers. An infantry corps controlled from two to four divisions; an armoured corps normally consisted of two armoured and one motorised division. But the grouping of forces underwent continual changes. The diagram shows their grouping on May the 24th, 1940, according to available evidence.

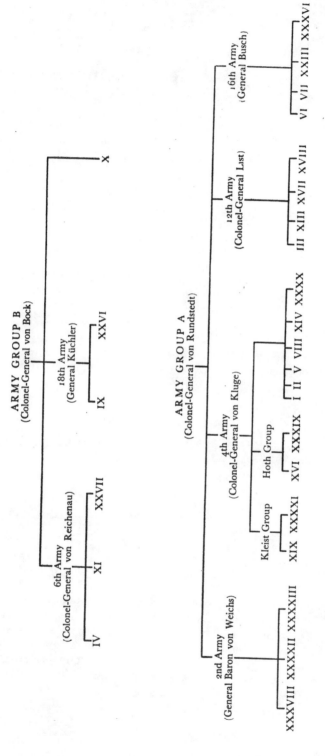

ARMY GROUP B
(Colonel-General von Bock)

6th Army
(Colonel-General von Reichenau)

IV   XI   XXVII

18th Army
(General Küchler)

IX   XXVI

X

ARMY GROUP A
(Colonel-General von Rundstedt)

2nd Army
(General Baron von Weichs)

XXXVIII XXXXII XXXXIII

4th Army
(Colonel-General von Kluge)

Kleist Group

XIX XXXXI

Hoth Group

XVI XXXXIX

I II V VIII XIV XXXX

12th Army
(Colonel-General List)

III XIII XVII XVIII

16th Army
(General Busch)

VI VII XXIII XXXVI

NOTE: Roman numerals denote Corps; those shown in Kleist and Hoth Groups were armoured corps.

NOTES

ARMY GROUP A

I. *Armoured formations*

The corps grouped under General von Kleist and General Hoth were all armoured corps. On May the 24th, 1940, their composition was as follows:

XIX Corps, General Guderian: 1st, 2nd and 10th Armoured Divisions and smaller motorised units.

XXXXI Corps, Lieutenant-General Reinhardt: 6th and 8th Armoured Divisions and the Motorised S.S. *Verfügungs* Division.

XVI Corps, General Hoepner: 3rd and 4th Armoured Divisions and the Motorised S.S. *Totenkopf* Division.

XXXIX Corps, General Schmidt: 5th and 7th Armoured Divisions and the 20th Motorised Division.

The 9th Armoured Division was on this day in reserve.

II. *S.S. Divisions*

These were part of the armed section [*Waffen* S.S.] of the *Schutz Staffel* or protective guard of the Nazi party. They were wholly militarised formations of long-term volunteers, recruited, trained, supplied and administered by the S.S. but, when employed in the field, they were under the orders of the Army High Command.

All the other corps shown were infantry corps.

ARMY GROUP B

All the corps shown were infantry corps. There were no armoured divisions in Army Group B at this time.

ARMY GROUP C

This Army Group was not involved in the fighting in which the British Expeditionary Force was concerned.

Index

INDEX

Ruhr, The : air operations over, 30, 57

Rundstedt, Colonel-General von : 44; orders, 62–3, 95; Hitler's instructions to (22nd May), 119; anxiety *re* southern flank, 120; concern for Operation 'Red', 120, 150, 227; use of armour, 124, 150–1; influence of Arras counter-attack, 132, 347–8; armour halted (23rd May), 138; visited by Hitler (24th May), 138–9, 349; O.K.H. Orders 25th May) ignored, 150–1, 350; 'success' qualified, 227–9; qualities, 334; influence on German plan of campaign, 337–44

Russia : pacts with Germany, 13; invasion and occupation of Poland by, 31; occupation of Estonia, Lithuania and Latvia by, 32; attack on Finland by, 32

Saar Front : British Brigades and 51st Division on, 20, 366; fighting on, 249–52

Saigneville : 271

St Amand : 64, 147

Ste Catherine : 131

St Floris : 137

St Jean de Luz : evacuation from, 305

St Léger : 262, 266

St Malo : 16; numbers evacuated from, 302

St Martin Boulogne : 155

St Momelin : 118, 123; fighting at, 129, 136, 140

St Nazaire : Southern Base of B.E.F. at, 9, 15; evacuations from, 263, 302–4

St Omer : 118, 121; fighting at, 128, 130, 136, 137, 147; air operations over, 138, 193

St Pierre Brouck : 140

St Pol : 88, 111, 118, 177

St Quentin : 63

St Saens : 252

St Sylvain : 288–9

St Valery en Caux : fight of 51st Div., 286–93

St Valery sur Somme : 271

St Venant : 121; fighting at, 137, 140, 146, 175, 189

Sallenelle : 271

Sambre (River) : 62, 63

Samer : 154, 155

Sangatte : 161, 164

Saulty : fighting at, 78, 80

Scarpe (River) : troops holding, 79, 87–9; fighting on, 96, 115, 130, 131

Scheldt : *see* Escaut

Schmidt, General : 403

Schmundt, Colonel : 119

Seclin : 65

Sedan : 37; German break-through, 41, 43; air operations at, 55–7

Seine (River) : German advance ordered, 275; withdrawal across, 282; destruction of bridges, 283; air operations, 295

Senarpont : 265, 275, 277

Senne (River) : 49; definition of line, 59; fighting on, 63, 66

Serqueux : 284

Sigy : 281

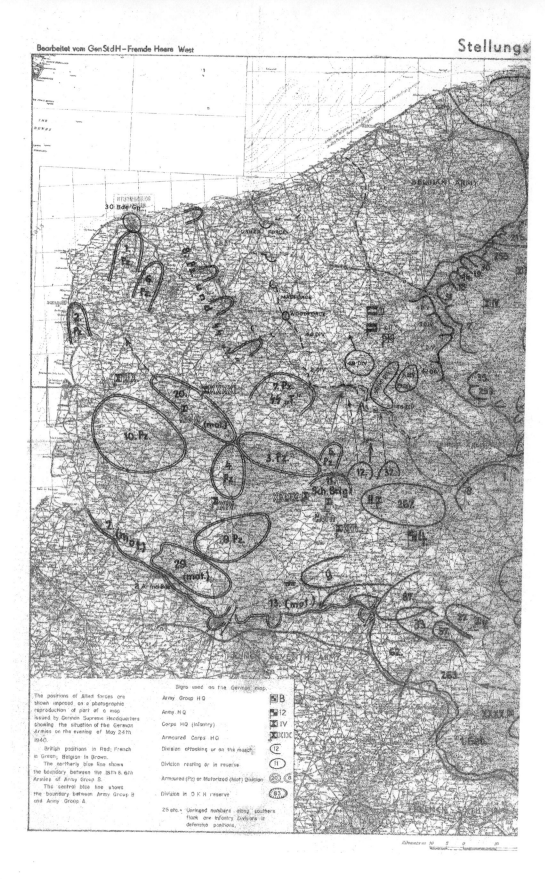

Lage West am 24.5.40 abds.

Erläuterung:

~~~ mot u. Pz.-Verbände

OKH-Reserven

rückw. Grenze Op.Geb.

Brücken:

Zeichen	A	B	E	H
Tragfähigkeit für normale Einzellast	2 t	B = 10 t	16 t	über 16 t: H = Herbert-Brücke = 30 t, S.S. = LZ - Brücke, S.S. = Schwerlastbrücke

H = Brücke aus Kriegsbrückengerät, B = Behelfsbrücke, E = eingeengte Eisb. Brücke

Weitere OKH-Reserven:

Einheit	Unterkunft	Geführt	Zug. Reg.	Unterwegs	Ausladegeb.	z.b.
73. I.I.	Morphaus	26.5	6pp	27.5 23p	Suisburg	OKH
167. I.I.	Schonenberg	28.5	14pp	28.5	3pp	Trier	OKH
178. I.I.	Flensburg	27.5	9pp	30.5. 15pp	nördl Aachen	OKH
296. I.I.	Gräfenwöhr	28.5	13pp	19.5. 2pp	Stadt Kyll	OKH
297. I.I.	Bresl/Schlente	26.5	14pp	30.5. 2pp	Vossen	OKH
H.Inf.XXXII	Rattin	28.5	10pp	3.6 20pp	Rachen	OKH
331. L.F.Div.	Krakau	28.5.	10pp		2.6 6pp	südl. Rachen	OKH
339. L.S.Div.	Neuhaus			2.6 6pp	südl. Rachen	OKH
384. L.S.Div.	Soala	28.5	10pp		2.6 6pp	Südt.-Flora	OKH

Einheit	Unterkunft	Einheit	Unterkunft	Einheit	Unterkunft
164.I.(ostd.)I.	Raugersluh	213.I.D.	Posen	Radf.Pat.102	Holzkirchen
169.I.I.	Pagusdorf	218.I.D.	Altengramme	- 402	Laaber
197.I.D	Schneidemühl	221.I.D.	Deidersheim	378.I.D.	Mundfer(lager)
208.I.I	Ostrolenka	239.I.D.	Brdy-Wald	221.I.D	Dindleuf

Gen.St.d.H. Op.Abt. Prüf.-Nr. 5024

HISTORY OF
THE SECOND WORLD WAR

UNITED KINGDOM MILITARY SERIES

Reprinted by the Naval & Military Press in twenty two volumes with the permission of the Controller of HMSO and Queen's Printer for Scotland.

THE DEFENCE OF THE UNITED KINGDOM

Basil Collier

Official history of Britain's home front in the Second World War, from the Phoney War, through the Battle of Britain and the Blitz to victory in Europe.
ISBN: 1845740556
Price £22.00

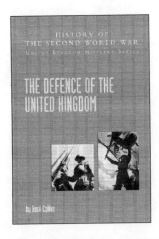

THE CAMPAIGN IN NORWAY

T. H. Derry

The catastrophic 1940 campaign which caused the downfall of Neville Chamberlain and brought Winston Churchill to power.
ISBN: 1845740572
Price: £22.00

THE WAR IN FRANCE AND FLANDERS 1939-1940

Major L. F. Ellis

The role of the BEF in the fall of France and the retreat to Dunkirk.
ISBN: 1845740564
Price £22.00

VICTORY IN THE WEST
Volume I: The Battle of Normandy

Major L. F. Ellis

The build-up, execution and consequences of D-Day in 1944.
ISBN: 1845740580
Price: £22.00

Volume II: The Defeat of Germany

Major L. F. Ellis

The final stages of the liberation of western Europe in 1944-45.
ISBN: 1845740599
Price £22.00

www.naval-military-press.com

THE MEDITERRANEAN AND MIDDLE EAST

Volume I: The Early Successes against Italy (to May 1941)

Major-General I. S. O. Playfair

Britain defeats Italy on land and sea in Africa and the Mediterranean in 1940.
ISBN: 1845740653
Price: £22.00

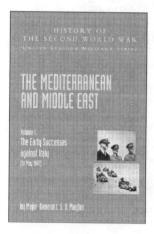

Volume II: The Germans Come to the Help of their Ally (1941)

Major-General I. S. O. Playfair

Rommel rides to Italy's rescue, Malta is bombarded, Yugoslavia, Greece and Crete are lost, and Iraq and Syria are secured for the Allies.
ISBN: 1845740661
Price: £22.00

Volume III: (September 1941 to September 1942) British Fortunes reach their Lowest Ebb

Major-General I. S. O. Playfair

Britain's darkest hour in North Africa and the Mediterranean, 1941–42.
ISBN: 184574067X
Price: £22.00

Volume IV: The Destruction of the Axis Forces in Africa

Major-General I. S. O. Playfair

The battle of El Alamein and 'Operation Torch' bring the Allies victory in North Africa, 1942-43.
ISBN: 1845740688
Price: £22.00

Volume V: The Campaign in Sicily 1943 and the Campaign in Italy — 3rd Sepember 1943 to 31st March 1944

Major-General I. S. O. Playfair

The Allies invade Sicily and Italy, but encounter determined German defence in 1943-44.
ISBN: 1845740696
Price: £22.00

Volume VI: Victory in the Mediterranean Part I: 1st April to 4th June 1944

Brigadier C. J. C. Molony

The Allies breach the Gustav, Hitler and Caesar Lines and occupy Rome.
ISBN: 184574070X
Price: £22.00

Volume VI: Victory in the Mediterranean Part II: June to October 1944

General Sir William Jackson

The 1944 Italian summer campaign breaches the Gothic Line but then bogs down again.
ISBN: 1845740718
Price: £22.00

Volume VI: Victory in the Mediterranean Part III: November 1944 to May 1945

General Sir William Jackson

The messy end of the war in Italy, Greece, and Yugoslavia.
ISBN: 1845740726
Price: £22.00

THE WAR AGAINST JAPAN

Volume I: The Loss of Singapore

Major-General S. Woodburn Kirby

The fall of Hong Kong, Malaya and Singapore in 1941–42.
ISBN: 1845740602
Price: £22.00

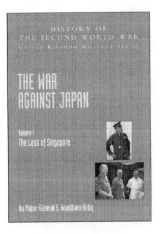

Volume II: India's Most Dangerous Hour

Major-General S. Woodburn Kirby

The loss of Burma and Japan's threat to India in 1941–42.
ISBN: 1845740610
Price: £22.00

Volume III: The Decisive Battles

Major-General S. Woodburn Kirby

Turning the tide in the war against Japan at the battles of Kohima, Imphal and the Chindit campaigns.
ISBN: 1845740629
Price: £22.00

Volume IV: The Reconquest of Burma

Major-General S. Woodburn Kirby

The reconquest of Burma by Bill Slim's 'forgotten' 14th Army.
ISBN: 1845740637
Price: £22.00

Volume V: The Surrender of Japan

Major-General S. Woodburn Kirby

Victory in South-East Asia in 1945 – from Rangoon to Nagasaki.
ISBN: 1845740645
Price: £22.00

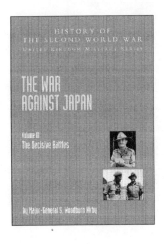
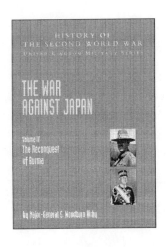
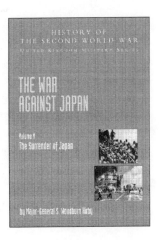

THE WAR AT SEA - 1939—1945

Captain Roskill has long been recognised as the
leading authority on The Royal Navy's part in the
Second World War. His official History is unlikely
ever to be superceded. His narrative is highly
readable and the analysis is clear. Roskill describes
sea battles, convoy actions and the contribution
made by technology in the shape of Asdic &
Radar.

Volume I: The Defensive

Captain S. W. Roskill, D.S.C., R.N.

2004 N&MP reprint (original pub 1954).
SB. xxii + 664pp with 43 maps and numerous
contemporary photos.
ISBN: 1843428032
Price: £32.00

Volume II: The Period of Balance

Captain S. W. Roskill, D.S.C., R.N.

2004 N&MP reprint (original pub 1956).
SB. xvi + 523pp with 42 maps and numerous
contemporary photos.
ISBN: 1843428040
Price: £32.00

Volume III: Part I The Offensive
1st June 1943-31 May 1944

Captain S. W. Roskill, D.S.C., R.N.

2004 N&MP reprint (original pub 1960).
SB. xv + 413pp with 21 maps and numerous
contemporary photos.
ISBN: 1843428059
Price: £32.00

Volume III: Part 2 The Offensive
1st June 1944-14th August 1945

Captain S. W. Roskill, D.S.C., R.N.

2004 N&MP reprint (original pub 1961).
SB. xvi + 502pp with 46 maps and numerous
contemporary photos.
ISBN: 1843428067
Price: £32.00

Made in the USA
Lexington, KY
17 August 2014